Kierkegaard, Søren 1813–1855
Leibniz, Gottfried 1646–1716
Leucippus ca. 490–430 B.C.
Locke, John 1632–1704
Lucretius ca. 96–55 B.C.
Marx, Karl 1818–1883
Mill, John Stuart 1806–1873
Montaigne, Michel de 1533–1592
Newton, Sir Isaac 1642–1727
Nietzsche, Friedrich 1844–1900
Pascal, Blaise 1623–1662
Peirce, Charles S. 1839–1914
Plato ca. 428–ca. 348 B.C.
Protagoras ca. 490–421 B.C.
Pyrrho ca. 361–ca. 270 B.C.
Pythagoras active ca. 525–500 B.C.
Quine, W. V. O. 1908–
Rawls, John 1921–
Rousseau, J. J. 1712–1778
Russell, Bertrand 1872–1970
Ryle, Gilbert 1900–1976
Sartre, Jean-Paul 1905–1980
Schopenhauer, Arthur 1788–1860
Sextus Empiricus ca. 200
Socrates ca. 470–399 B.C.
Spinoza, Baruch 1632–1677
Thales 624–546 B.C.
Whitehead, Alfred North 1861–1947
Wittgenstein, Ludwig 1889–1951
Zeno b. ca. 489 B.C.

ELEMENTS OF PHILOSOPHY

ELEMENTS OF PHILOSOPHY

AN INTRODUCTION

Second Edition

Samuel E. Stumpf
Vanderbilt University

McGraw-Hill Book Company

New York St. Louis San Francisco Auckland Bogotá Hamburg
London Madrid Mexico Montreal New Delhi Panama Paris São Paulo
Singapore Sydney Tokyo Toronto

ELEMENTS OF PHILOSOPHY: AN INTRODUCTION

4567890   DOCDOC   89

ISBN 0-07-062309-0

This book was set in Caledonia and Optima by University Graphics, Inc. (ECU).
The editors were Emily G. Barrosse and James R. Belser;
the designer was Jo Jones;
the production supervisor was Marietta Breitwieser.
The cover was designed by Fern Logan;
Cover photograph: The Human Condition I, *René Magritte (1933).*
© *Georgette Magritte 1985*
R. R. Donnelley & Sons Company was printer and binder.

Library of Congress Cataloging-in-Publication Data

Strumpf, Samuel Enoch, 1918–
  Elements of philosophy.

  Includes bibliographies and index.
  1. Philosophy–Introductions.   I. Title.
BD21.S825   1986   100   85–16813
ISBN 0–07–062309–0

To
the next generation of philosophers
NICHOLAS, ANNA, LAWRENCE, and GILLIAN
*who wonder why they can
catch a ball but
can't catch the dark*

CONTENTS

POLITICS

Why Should I Obey?

RELIGION

What Can I Beleive?

KNOWLEDGE

What Can I Know?

METAPHYSICS

What Is There?

PREFACE

This book is intended for the student just beginning the study of philosophy. The approach to this subject is from the vantage point of some major problems or areas of philosophical concern. Accordingly, the book focuses on the problems of ethics, politics, religion, knowledge, and metaphysics. The book begins with a general introduction entitled What Is Philosophy? This introduction describes the nature and concerns of philosophy and provides a preliminary view of the five problems as exemplified by five selected philosophers repectively. The materials for each problem are organized to include the following: (1) an introduction which focuses on some of the elements of the particular subject under discussion, (2) a listing of the philosophers to be discussed, (3) a brief biographical sketch of each philosopher in order to locate him in time and place, (4) an analysis of each philosopher's ideas in a manner designed to make his thought relatively easy to understand without excessive oversimplification, (5) a selection of a passage from an appropriate original work of the philosopher under discussion in order to provide a brief sample of his mode of thought and style of writing, (6) a list of questions at the end of each part designed primarily for class discussion, and (7) a brief bibliography for further reading limited to readily available books most appropriate to an introductory level.

Some readers of my *Socrates to Sartre* have suggested that I prepare a new introduction to philosophy using material from the earlier book arranged according to selected problems or areas of philosophy while preserving the historical treatment of these problems. This book is in response to that expressed preference. The selected readings have the limited objective of providing the student primarily with a sample of each philosopher's style of writing without intending in every case to use these readings to deal with a philosopher's ideas in depth. Although some teachers begin the study of philosophy with the subject of ethics, others prefer to begin with the theory of knowledge. This book is arranged so that the topics can be followed in whatever sequence the instructor prefers. All the material in quotation marks or set in extract format is from the philosophers' original works, to which references, in most cases, are made in the text. To preserve the simplicity of this book's format, footnotes have been omitted.

Samuel E. Stumpf

ELEMENTS OF PHILOSOPHY

WHAT IS PHILOSOPHY?

Philosophy is for everyone. In fact, we all engage in philosophy every day. Even when we do not know how to define philosophy, we will make such statements as "My philosophy about eating is . . . " or "Let me tell you my philosophy about taxes."

Philosophy begins with our ordinary everyday experiences. We not only *do* things, we *think* about them. Such a simple experience as eating is capable of leading to some major philosophical questions. How much should we eat? Animals do not ask this question. We ask it because it makes a difference in our daily life. The amount we eat can affect the pleasure we get out of life, especially if we eat too much. But eating is in itself a pleasure. We begin to philosophize when we try to decide which pleasures are most important to us, for example, looking slim and trim on the one hand or enjoying bountiful meals on the other. We even ask whether pleasure is the proper standard for making our decisions in life. Before long, we no longer talk about eating but about the more general question that the experience of eating makes us think about, namely, What values are most important to us? How, in short, do we achieve the good life?

La Serpentine, Matisse *(Hirshhorn Museum and Sculpture Garden, Smithsonian Institution)*

Similarly, the person who says "Let me tell you my philosophy about taxes" starts to think about this matter because of the experience of paying taxes. Paying taxes is not always pleasant. We want to know more about this part of our experience. Who should pay and how much? Once again, the discussion soon becomes philosophical. From being only about the inconvenience of paying taxes, the discussion moves to such questions as "What is the purpose of the tax?" or "What is a fair tax?" Before long, this line of thought leads to the philosophical question "What is justice?"

From these examples of eating and paying taxes we learn at least one thing about philosophy—that it is a quest for knowledge. That, after all, is what the Greek roots of the word "philosophy" mean, namely, *philo* (love) and *sophia* (knowledge or wisdom)— hence the love of knowledge. To say that philosophy is the love of knowledge still leaves the question "What kind of knowledge does philosophy involve?"

There was a time when philosophy included almost every kind of knowledge of which human beings were capable. There was no sharp distinction between science and philosophy. Indeed, the term "natural philosophy" was until relatively recently used to describe various sciences, especially physics. Among early philosophers, then, we find thinkers concerned with explaining the structure of nature, including the realm of physical things, the world, and the whole universe. In time, this subject matter was separated from philosophy and became the various sciences, such as physics, astronomy, and astrophysics. Similarly, the philosophical concern regarding human nature in its various aspects represented an attempt to understand the functioning of the body and mind, the elements of health and disease, the causes of pain and pleasure, and the requirements for orderly and peaceful communities and societies. Here too over the years new disciplines arose, as biology, medicine, psychology, sociology, political science, and economics become independent sciences. To some extent, therefore, it appears that the scope of knowledge which philosophy pursues has been reduced to the extent that the special sciences have achieved a certain independence from philosophy.

It is usually said that philosophy deals with those problems which have not as yet been solved by science. To put the matter another way, as soon as science has solved certain problems, there is no further need for the philosopher. This may be true to the extent that the various sciences generate facts and solutions through their unique methods of investigation. But in virtually every area of science there remains the need to understand, interpret, and above all evaluate the body of facts. Facts do not assess themselves. Nor does the body of facts clearly reveal what should or should not be done. That the mind can be altered by drugs, that behavior can be controlled, that genetic engineering or eugenics can modify the course of human reproduction—in all these cases the question remains whether from the simple fact that we can do all these things it follows that we should. There is, then, another kind of knowledge which the philosopher pursues, a knowledge that assimilates and understands these facts and seeks to put them into a larger and more general context, which includes humanity's quest for a rational and fulfilling destiny. But this activity of the philosopher does not necessarily provide a new set of facts, nor does it provide precise answers to all the questions raised by these facts. We are concerned not so much with specific issues as with fundamental principles or modes of thinking which enable us to deal most effectively with the problem areas of philosophy.

Why do we engage in philosophy? What is there about human beings that leads us to engage in reflective thought, thinking about questions which do not appear to produce practical results? It could be argued that in the long run philosophical thought does produce widespread practical consequences. In the political realm, for example, the writings of John Locke significantly influenced the development of American democracy, while the theories of Karl Marx have brought into being a radically new form of government. It could also be said that what separates us from the animal world and from uncivilized human beings is just this intellectual endeavor, which could be justified as valuable even if only for its own sake. But there is a deeper reason for engaging in philosophy, and that is that we simply cannot turn away from certain questions which constantly confront us. Our human constitution or our human condition predisposes us to want to know. It was Ludwig Wittgenstein (1889–1951) of Cambridge University who compared our situation to that of a fly in a bottle. The fly is trying to get out of the bottle but does not know how. The function and aim of philosophy is to show the fly how to get out of the bottle. For us this means that, like the fly, we feel trapped and have difficulty finding our way out. In our case, this fly bottle represents certain levels of ignorance or problems and questions that are difficult to solve and we look to philosophy for help in finding our way out.

Again, to emphasize the many functions of philosophy, Wittgenstein said that philosophy is like a toolbox. We use words and ideas for different purposes, just as we use different tools to do different jobs. Pounding nails calls for a hammer, screws require a screwdriver, and to cut wood we need a saw. All these jobs are different, but in each case they are done with a tool taken from the toolbox.

Philosophy is in a similar way called on to do many jobs. These jobs reflect the richness of our daily experience. First of all, there is the job of helping us to decide how to behave. We want to know how to distinguish right and wrong, good and bad, morality and immorality, and between what we ought to do and ought not to do. In our private moments we wonder how we can achieve the happiest and best life for ourselves. This is the job for ethics. Second, because we cannot avoid constant contact with other persons or groups, the quality of our life is affected by the behavior of others and we realize the need for public rules or laws in order to provide a peaceful and cooperative community based on an appropriate form of government. Working out the principles and design for laws and government is the job of political philosophy. Third, as we extend our thinking beyond ourselves and beyond our communities, we wonder how we fit into the larger setting of the universe and beyond. To deal with questions of our destiny is the job of religion. Fourth, we all have the experience of discovering new insights which affect our ways of thinking. Sometimes we are sure of what we know, while at other times we are not so sure. To help us understand how our minds work in our quest to know is a special job for philosophy. The tool for this job is the theory of knowledge (epistemology). And fifth, we all have the common experience of seeing things appear and disappear, come into being and pass out of being, trees growing, dying, and disintegrating, indeed everything constantly changing. All this fluctuation in things raises the question of whether there is anything that is permanent. What, in short, are things made of, and what does it mean for anything to *be?* There are other jobs for philosophy, but these five problem areas will serve as our introduction to the fundamental elements of philosophy.

It is time now to sample some typical philosophical activity. The leading philosophers rarely ever formulated specific definitions of philosophy, and it would not be fruitful for us to do so either. We discover what philosophy is not from definitions but rather from the way these philosophers *do* philosophy. Having in mind our five problem areas, I have chosen representative philosophers whose thinking even in this brief preliminary form will serve as a further introduction to each of these areas of philosophy.

I

ETHICS

"THE UNEXAMINED LIFE"
Socrates

Socrates (470–399 B.C.), the brilliant teacher in Athens whose most renowned pupil was Plato (428–348 B.C.), said that "the unexamined life is not worth living" (Plato's *Apology*). Nothing is more important, he said, than to develop one's personality or character. Although he was not the first thinker to ask the question "What should I do?" he was among the first to focus on the moral life as a central concern of philosophy. Earlier philosophers had been concerned with what we today call science. Socrates did not criticize the scientists, although he did say in the *Apology* that "the simple truth is . . . that I have nothing to do with physical speculations." More important to him than speculations about physical things were the urgent questions about human nature, about truth and goodness.

In Athens, Socrates engaged in vigorous debate with a group of teachers called "Sophists" or "intellectuals." Some of them were teachers of the art of persuasion who could make an unjust cause appear just or make a bad case look good. The Sophists had said that there is no reliable truth and therefore there are no universally true moral principles. They pointed to the different customs among different peoples. They also referred to the disagreements among those who tried to describe the world of nature. One of the early Sophists, Protagoras (490–421 B.C.), concluded that "man is the measure of all things," meaning that whatever knowledge man could achieve about anything would be limited by his human capacities. And because each person's perceptions will differ from another person's, there cannot be one single absolute truth. There can be no knowledge of the "true" nature of anything. For similar reasons, Protagoras maintained that moral ideas are also relative,

Socrates (*New York Public Library Picture Collection*)

that is, different in each culture and at different times. Another Sophist, Thrasymachus, taught that there is no absolute standard for justice; actually, he said, "might makes right." For this reason, he urged individuals to pursue their own interests aggressively in a virtually unlimited form of self-assertion. He said finally that "the sound conclusion is that what is 'right' is the same everywhere: the interest of the stronger party."

Socrates disagreed with the Sophists. He was convinced that there could be a solid basis for truth and that there are some moral principles to guide human beings when they ask "What should I do?" He rejected the Sophists' skepticism regarding knowledge and their relativism concerning morality. Regarding our knowledge, Socrates was fascinated by the fact, for example, that we can say about something that it is beautiful or about a human action that it is good. How is it that we can recognize something as beautiful or an action as good? No particular thing, he said, is perfectly beautiful, but insofar as it is beautiful it is because it partakes of Beauty. Moreover, when a beautiful thing passes away, the Idea of Beauty remains. Socrates was struck by the ability of the mind to think about general ideas (Beauty, Goodness) and not only about particular things (this beautiful flower, that good mother). Although various beautiful things differ from one another, whether they be flowers or persons, they are each called beautiful because despite their differences they share in common that element by which they are called beautiful.

True knowledge, said Socrates, is more than simply looking at specific things. Knowledge has to do with the power of the mind to discover in facts the permanent elements that remain after the particular facts disappear. To the mind, an imperfect triangle suggests *the* triangle. All triangles are different. If our knowledge consisted only of our impressions of these particular triangles, as well as all other particular things, we would conclude that everything is different. Similarly, if we based our definition of good on the behavior we observed in each of several cultures, we would have as many definitions of good as there are cultures. What Socrates searched for was a definition of the good which makes it possible to say about *any* person that he is good. He thought he discovered a solid basis for the concept of "good"; an action is good, said Socrates, if it is appropriate to man's nature. If man is a rational being, to act rationally is the behavior appropriate to human nature. The good person is the rational person. From this insight it was only a short step for Socrates to say that a person *ought* to act rationally. This is a view that Plato and Aristotle elaborated in considerable detail as they developed their theories of ethics.

II

POLITICAL PHILOSOPHY

"THE WAR OF ALL AGAINST ALL"
Hobbes

Thomas Hobbes (1588–1679) described what would be the condition among human beings if there was no organized society, calling it "a war of every man against every man." He called this condition "the state of nature," where "the life of man is solitary, poor, nasty, brutish and short." How did he know that this would be the condition in a state of nature in the absence of civil government? Obviously, he had no evidence to prove it. Instead, as an example, he pointed to the fact that the nations of the world are even today in virtually such a state of nature. Because these nations are sovereign, that is, recognize no other authority than themselves in deciding their own affairs, so must individuals in a state of nature possess unlimited personal discretion and independence in deciding how to treat others. Among nations there is always the threat of war because of "continual jealousies and [therefore] nations are in the state and posture of gladiators; that is, their forts, garrisons and guns upon the frontiers of their kingdoms; and continual spies upon their neighbors; which is the posture of war." If we want to answer the question "Why should I obey?" Hobbes would point to his vivid description of the treacherous conditions of life in the state of nature. What makes life so hazardous is the unpredictable behavior of each person. Because each person in the state of nature can decide for himself what is right, there is virtually no limit to what people will do to one another. To avoid this situation, that is, because of fear for one's safety, people in the state of nature decide to give up some of their independence. They agree among themselves that instead of everyone deciding what is right, each person will hand over to a "sovereign" (either an individual or a group) the sole right to establish the rules for social and political behavior. Hobbes called this agreement a "Social Contract." Civil society with a system of laws and legal rights begins with this contract. One reason to obey the laws, says Hobbes, is that if everyone reserved the privilege of not obeying, there would be a return to the war of all against all.

III

RELIGION

"THAN WHICH NOTHING IS GREATER"
Anselm

Saint Anselm (1033–1109) defined God as "that than which nothing is greater" (*Proslogium, or Faith Seeking Understanding*). This is obviously a philosophical rather than a religious expression of God's nature, but that is just what Anselm wished to achieve. After all, he had been educated in a Benedictine monastery in France and at the height of his career was named the Archbishop of Canterbury in England. Personally he had no doubts about the existence of God. What he was groping for was an adequate reply to someone who would ask "What can I believe?" As he says on the first page of his *Proslogium,* "I began to ask myself whether there might be found a single argument which would require no other for its proof than itself alone; and alone would suffice to demonstrate that God truly exists, and that there is a supreme good requiring nothing else, which all other things required for their existence and well-being. ... " His purpose, then, was to construct a proof for the existence of God, that is, to provide an intellectual support for belief. His proof appeared to be designed for both the unbeliever who might be persuaded by it and for the believer who, as he says, "seeks to understand what he believes." His "proof" is known as "the ontological argument." The word "ontological" is the key to his argument, since it is composed of the two Greek words *ontos* (being) and *logos* (knowledge)—hence the knowledge of being.

We will elaborate Anselm's line of reasoning in our discussion entitled Religion. For the present, we can state the short version of his argument as follows: Whenever we utter the word "God," we know that we are thinking of a supreme being or that than which no greater can be conceived. But there is something greater than what we can merely *conceive* (which is, after all, only an idea in our heads); that greater is the actual existence of a being than which there is no greater. Again we can see why this is called the onto-logical argument, since it is based on a distinction between different levels of being. The "being" of a human being is very short; a person's being depends on another person's being (parents). By contrast, says Anselm, God's being is perfect, depends on no other being, and is the being upon which everything else depends. Although Anselm was excited by the simplicity and the logical power of his argument, his successors, especially Saint Thomas Aquinas (1225–1274), thought it would be far more impressive to base an argument not simply on our "ideas," but rather on evidence derived from obvious human experiences. Since then, a rich literature has been produced by philosophers providing quite different answers to the question "What can I believe?"

IV

THEORY OF KNOWLEDGE

"I THINK, THEREFORE I AM"

Descartes

We have already seen that people disagree on many important issues, about the ethical rules of conduct, about the meaning of justice, and about whether God exists. It is no wonder that under these circumstances we ask the question "What can I know?" It is not surprising either that because of the uncertainties of our knowledge, many people become "skeptics." What is surprising is to discover how the word "skeptic" has changed over the course of time. Today we think of the skeptic as a person whose basic attitude is one of doubt. But the original Greek word *skepticoi*, from which skeptic is derived, meant something rather different, namely, "seekers" or "inquirers." In the fourth century B.C., a man by the name of Pyrrho (361–270 B.C.) founded a school of philosophy whose members were called "Skeptics." Their original purpose was to achieve a way of thought that could lead to mental peace and calmness. One of their later writers, Sextus Empiricus (ca. A.D. 200), pointed out that people were disturbed by the contradictions in things and plagued by doubt as to which alternatives they should believe. The Skeptics thought that if they could by investigation determine truth from falsehood, they could attain tranquillity of mind. They were struck, however, by the alternative conceptions of truth different philosophers proposed. They also noticed that people who searched for truth could be placed into three groups: (1) those who think they have discovered the truth (and these the Skeptics called "dogmatists," (2) those who confess they have not found it and also assert that it cannot be found (the Skeptics also considered this a dogmatic position), and finally (3) those who continue to search for truth. Unlike the first two, said Sextus in his *Pyrrhonic Sketches*, "the Skeptics keep on searching. . . . We end by ceasing to dogmatize." The Skeptics had no doubt that they lived in a real world. They only wondered whether this world had been accurately described. While they continued to search for truth, they organized their daily life around four items, which Sextus calls (1) the guidance of nature, (2) the constraints of feelings, (3) the tradition of laws and customs, and (4) instruction in the arts of work. Each one of these contributes, he says, to successful and peaceful living, and not one of them requires any dogmatic interpretation or evaluation, only acceptance.

Centuries later, Michel de Montaigne (1533–1592) adopted for his own the formula developed by Pyrrho and Sextus, saying (in his *Essays*), "Pyrrho did not want to make himself into a stone; he wanted to make of himself a living man, discoursing and reasoning, enjoying all pleasures and natural commodities, using all of his bodily and spiritual parts regularly and properly." Montaigne thought that a good place to begin the search for truth is one's own personal experiences, because he believed that "every man carries within himself the whole condition of humanity." Human experiences, he thought, could be described clearly and accurately and did not have to be obscured by technical language. "My page," he writes, "makes love and knows what he is doing. But read to him Leo Hebraeus or Ficino where they speak of the actions and thought of love, and he can't make head or tail of it." However attractive Montaigne's creative skepticism was, the urge to discover a solid basis for intellectual certainty persisted. In a fascinating manner, René Descartes (1596–1650) used the method of doubt to establish that solid base. There is, he said, a limit to what we can doubt; we cannot doubt our own existence. Whether my thinking is right or wrong, occurs while I am asleep or awake, it is nevertheless *I* who think. For this reason, there can be no doubt that I exist; the fact is that "I think, therefore I am." Throughout our discussion of various answers to the question "What can I know?" we will observe an intriguing alternation between the mood of skepticism and the desire for certainty.

V

METAPHYSICS

"THE 'ATOM' AND THE 'CHERRY'"
Democritus and Berkeley

We have already noticed that Socrates was not interested in the general question "What is there?" He was aware that earlier philosophers spent considerable intellectual energy trying to discover the basic stuff underlying the things that make up the inventory of nature. His own major interest was ethics, because nothing is more important, he said, than learning how to develop one's character. But the earlier question about what things are really like could not be avoided. It was a combination of sheer curiosity and practical considerations that pushed this inquiry. On the practical side, there was the question about what happens to a person when he dies? Does any aspect or part of him remain or become transformed? From the point of view of intellectual curiosity, what happens to a tree when it burns or disintegrates? Far more sophisticated questions were raised, for example, "How is motion caused?" and "How did things come to be in the first place?"

The predecessors of Socrates gave some unusual answers to the question "What is there?" These answers are summarized in Aristotle's (384–322 B.C.) *Metaphysics, Book I.* Here we will mention only a few. Thales (624–546 B.C.) thought that everything is made of water probably, says Aristotle, because "the nutriment of all things is moist . . . and that animal life is sustained by it. . . ." (Today we know that the most complex organ in the human body, the brain, is 80 percent water.) Empedocles (490–430 B.C.) thought that there was not just one but four basic kinds of stuff out of which things were made, namely, earth, water, fire, and air. Pythagoras (ca. 580–500 B.C.) thought that the clue to everything was numbers, because everything can be analyzed according to its form. Later, Anaxagoras (500–428 B.C.) suggested that the nature of reality is best understood as a combination of *mind* and *matter.*

But the most fascinating theory about the nature of things was suggested by Democritus (460–360 B.C.). His thought was that everything is made up of *atoms.* Today we speak of these as "elementary particles." Democritus described them as tiny, solid, unbreakable, invisible, and eternal. Everything in the universe consists of these atoms. Their size varies, and therefore, bodies consist of larger atoms, whereas mind is explained by the motion of smaller, smoother, and swifter atoms (or those particles or brain waves which make an impact on an electroencephalograph). There is, then, only one kind of stuff, namely, matter. Nothing is ever lost because although everything eventually comes apart, the atoms thus released find their way into other things. There were some practical consequences to this theory, as Lucretius (98–55 B.C.) pointed out later. There was no place in this theory for a "creator," since atoms had come together, it was supposed, basically by accident. This meant there was no special purpose in human existence

Locke (*New York Public Library Picture Collection*)

and certainly no need to fear future punishment. What makes Democritus's theory fascinating is that in revised form it provided the basic scientific understanding of nature well into the twentieth century. Only recently have atomic scientists succeeded in breaking up the nucleus of the atom.

At the other extreme, Bishop Berkeley (1685–1753) denied the existence of matter. How could he make such a startling claim? Our first reaction is to ridicule him. Dr. Samuel Johnson had great sport when he kicked a stone and said about Berkeley, "I refute him thus." But Berkeley was aware of the radicalism of his thought, as we shall see in our discussion of Metaphysics. Nevertheless, he asks us to consider whether we really have any knowledge of *matter*. Earlier, John Locke (1632–1704) had said that common sense tells us that when we see, for example, the qualities red, round, and soft, there must be *something* that *has* these qualities. That something he called "substance" or matter. He could not specifically

13

define substance but said that "if any one will examine himself concerning his notion of pure substance in general, he will find he has no idea of it at all, but only a supposition of he knows not what support of such qualities. . . . " Although substance, according to Locke, is "I know not what," he nevertheless was convinced that there is solid substance—matter—under the various qualities we perceive through our senses. Berkeley challenged this idea of substance.

In his *Third Dialogue between Hylas and Philonus,* Berkeley develops the proposition that it is thought, that is, mind, and not matter that is the basic reality. His central point is that "to be is to be perceived." If you eliminate perceptions, you eliminate what is perceived. He asks us to think about a cherry:

> I see this *cherry,* I feel it, I taste it: and I am sure *nothing* cannot be seen, or felt, or tasted: it is therefore *real.* Take away the sensations of softness, moisture, redness, tartness, and you take away the *cherry.* Since it is not a being distinct from sensations; a *cherry,* I say, is nothing but a congeries of sensible impressions, or ideas perceived by various senses: which ideas are united into one thing (or have one name given them) by the mind; because they are observed to attend each other. Thus, when the palate is affected with such a particular taste, the sight is affected with a red color, the touch with roundness, softness, etc. Hence, when I see, and feel, and taste . . . I am sure the *cherry* exists, or is real; its reality being in my opinion nothing abstracted from those sensations. But if, by the word *cherry,* you mean an unknown nature, distinct from all those sensible qualities, and by its *existence* something distinct from its being perceived; then, indeed, I own, neither you or I, nor any one else, can be sure it exists.

We are left with an interesting question, namely, "What is there?" Is it matter, or is it mind, or is it a combination of the two? We will ask later on "What difference does it make?"

As we pursue in greater depth these five major problems of ethics, politics, religion, knowledge, and metaphysics, we will consider the ideas of over thirty philosophers. Some of them are alive, while most of them lived ten, fifty, five hundred, or over a thousand years ago. Why should we study voices from the past? There are several reasons for doing so. For one thing, these philosophers were concerned with the same questions and problems which bother us today. These questions will not go away. Second, in some cases, no one else has discovered a better way of understanding or a clearer way of formulating answers to these questions. Third, human nature has not changed all that much over the centuries, even though our cultural surroundings have been altered by technology. That is why Greek literature, Shakespeare's plays, and the works of the great philosophers continue to have some relevance for us today. Fourth, by comparing the ideas of different historic periods, we can discover how philosophers reacted to, disagreed with, or modified the ideas of their predecessors. And fifth, by being aware of various unsuccessful attempts to solve some problems, we will be less likely to make the same mistakes as we face new challenges and opportunities to shape philosophy.

Control and balance, the classical formula for ethics. *Dancer*, Degas

ETHICS

WHAT SHOULD I DO? AND WHY SHOULD I DO IT?

Imagine that you are forced by circumstances to borrow
money. You know that you will not be able to repay it.
Nevertheless, you know that no one will lend you
money unless you promise to repay it at a
definite time. You are about to make such a
promise to repay but you ask yourself
whether you should try to get
yourself out of a difficulty in
this way. To make such a
false promise will no
doubt solve your
immediate
problem,
but you ask yourself, Is it right?

Kant

Fundamental Principles of the Metaphysics of Ethics (1785)

17

INTRODUCTION

Why can't we just do what we want to do? What difference does it make to anyone how we behave? Why does the question of ethics arise in the first place? These questions bother us especially because we resent any limitation on our behavior. We also have the suspicion that nobody knows what is right or good. After all, we see very nice people behaving in opposite ways and each one thinks he is right. Why should we think that one way of behaving is better than another, that telling the truth is better than trying to get ourselves out of trouble by telling a falsehood? And who has the authority to tell us what to do?

We study ethics in order to find answers to the questions "What should I do?" and "Why should I do it?" But before we try to answer these questions, we need to consider what ethics is all about. If we examine the person who is considering making a false promise, we will find in that example some elements which help us to understand what ethics is about.

The Elements of Ethics

FACING ALTERNATIVES

Ethics begins with our being aware that we face alternative possibilities in our behavior. We can either tell the truth or tell a falsehood. These two possibilities are presented to us as options. We are capable of doing either one. We can control our action. A stone does not face this kind of alternative because it cannot distinguish between different courses of action. A stone can behave only in the way an outside force makes it behave. Unlike a stone, a person can start an action by himself. The difference, then, is that a stone is not aware of options, is not conscious of possibilities, whereas human beings are conscious that they face genuine alternatives.

Sometimes we do not want to admit that our behavior is under our control. After all, there are some things about us which are fixed even before we have anything to say about them. The color of our eyes, the general shape of our body, and even the sound of our voice may be the result of our family inheritance. In this respect, we could resemble a stone in that within a certain range we do not face any alternatives. But while a stone faces no alternatives at all, we as human beings do. What is more, we *know* that we face alternative ways of behaving.

DELIBERATING

When a person wonders whether to tell the truth or tell a falsehood in order to get out of trouble, he is engaged in the process of weighing the pros and cons of each alternative action. In short, he is "deliberating." Deliberation always has to do with future actions that are within our power. We do not deliberate about the past. Nor do we deliberate about those actions about which we have no choice. Deliberation means that we are considering what we should do. Sartre speaks of the young woman who deliberates over whether to remove her hand or leave it resting in her companion's. She also deliberates about whether she wants to be involved in the actions that leaving her hand there would make possible. Deliberation means asking the question "Should I do it?" or "What ought I to do?" To a certain extent, we know in general what we want to achieve through our actions—we want to achieve a sense of well-being, of happiness. What we deliberate over is how we shall achieve that end, or as Aristotle says, it is "the mark of a man of practical wisdom to be able to deliberate well about what is good and expedient . . . about what sort of things conduce to the good life in general." Certainly, deliberation has to do with action, and that is why Aristotle calls deliberation "practical wisdom." That is what we mean when we say a person made a conscious, deliberate choice.

CHOICE

Our ability to make choices is what makes ethics possible. If we were machines, the question of ethics would never arise. The keys on the typewriter do not wake up in the morning, look out the window at the bright sunshine, and decide not to make words indoors on such a nice day. The keys have no choice. Although no one would describe a human being in such a thoroughly mechanical way, there are those who say that human behavior resembles the way machines work, that to think that we are free to make choices is an illusion. As we shall see, Nietzsche compares our behavior to that of a waterfall which exhibits beautiful movements of splashing and breaking of waves with subtle turnings and twisting of the water. We imagine, says Nietzsche, that there is "freedom of the will" in those twistings and turnings. But, he says, "everything is compulsory, every movement can be mathematically calculated." and "so it is with human actions." We labor under "the illusion of voluntariness." The only reason we suffer the "supposition of a free will" is that we have not yet fully calculated with mathematical exactitude the causes of each of our actions. In an equally strong denial that we are free to make our own choice, Baron d'Holbach argues that we as human beings are as much a part of nature as any other material things and therefore just as much governed by the "immutable laws that [nature] imposes on all the beings she contains" without our "ever being able to swerve from [these laws], even for an instant." But against this strict determinism which denies the freedom of the will, which would mean that we are never capable of making genuine choices, we find several philosophers taking the opposite point of view. The Stoics believed that our life is to a large extent determined and that "we must not try to anticipate or direct events, but merely accept them with intelligence." Nevertheless, the Stoics assumed that a person does have some choice, namely, either to accept or refuse to accept what life has assigned to him. To this extent, the Stoics would place in our hands the very power to determine whether we will be happy and contented by "accepting" our situation or whether we will become frustrated and unhappy by trying to change things that cannot be changed. Saint Augustine also balances man's freedom with the fact that God is the creator of all things, who controls the destiny of the universe. In his account of human evil, Augustine says that evil is the product of free will, whereby human beings make the wrong choices. Although everything in the world is good because everything comes from God who is goodness itself, it is possible to love some things improperly, that is, to love them more than their position on a scale of valuable objects, ranging from things, to oneself, to other persons, and ultimately, to God, would warrant. In short, human beings are free to "turn away from God" and attach their affections unduly on lesser objects of love. Augustine says "this turning away and this turning to are not forced but voluntary acts."

His conclusion on this matter is therefore that evil is not the result
of compulsion or ignorance but is the product of will. At this point,
Sartre's views are interesting, because while he rejects the religious
view of human nature, he argues as Augustine did that human
beings are essentially free and responsible for their actions. Not
only are we free, but any attempt on our part to say that our actions
were caused by some force other than ourselves renders us unauth-
entic. We are what we make of ourselves. A coward is not a coward
because he has a coward liver but because he chooses to do cowardly things. When Sartre says that "we are condemned to be free,"
he means that there is no way for us to escape the presence of alternatives, between which we need to make a choice. It is William
James who seeks more methodically to confront the point of view
of the determinist by showing that if determinism gives a true
account of human behavior, then many of our experiences would
make no sense. What sense would it make to say that we "regret"
having done something if that something was what we had to do
along with every other action of ours? For William James, human
experience is best understood as exhibiting genuine "possibilities"
between which we must choose.

   As we consider this matter of freedom and determinism, it may
be that we do not have to reject one or the other point of view.
What we are looking for is a coherent account of our experience
and our scientific knowledge which suggests that there are indeed
aspects of our behavior which spring from causes independent of
our will while at the same time other dimensions of our consciousness indicate that we are free, such as when Immanuel Kant says
that "because I must, I can."

BEING RESPONSIBLE

In ethics, being responsible for our behavior means that we understand what we are doing, that we are aware of a moral rule which
tells us to behave in a certain way, and that we have chosen to obey
or disobey that moral rule. If we deliberate over whether to tell the
truth and then choose instead to make a false promise, we are
responsible for that action because it is the product of our choice.
Being responsible means also that it is appropriate that we should
be blamed for our actions. But being responsible is not limited to
"bad" behavior only. We can also be responsible for "good"

actions. In this case, being responsible means that it is appropriate that we should be praised for our behavior. It would not be appropriate, nor would it make any sense, to blame or punish or to praise anyone for those actions for which he is not responsible, that is, for actions which are not the result of his choice. There are many other ways to use the word "responsible," but our concern is with its ethical meaning. In ethics, being responsible focuses on our capacity to deliberate and to choose and therefore on our capacity to originate our actions. It is because these actions are *our* actions that we are said to be responsible for them.

BEING AWARE OF OTHERS

As in most ethical situations, making a true or false promise involves other people. Almost every time we ask "What should I do?" we are aware that other people are involved in our behavior. Why should someone ask himself before making a false promise, "Is it right?" It may be that he is afraid of being found out. He may, however, wonder whether it is fair to the other person. How we relate ourselves to others or how our behavior affects others makes up most of the subject matter of ethics. Being aware of others is more than wondering how our actions will affect them; we are also concerned about how the behavior of others will affect us. There is no satisfactory way for us to avoid the presence of other people. The most we can do is try to arrange the rules of behavior, of ethics, in order to reduce the amount of friction and conflict and thereby achieve the greatest amount of harmony. Whether our actions are right and good will depend to a great extent on the effect they will have on others. Actions such as telling a falsehood, stealing, injuring, and killing are considered wrong most of the time because they result in varying degrees of harm to someone. They also produce reactions from the victims, who in effect say, "If it is right for you to do that to me, then I will not hesitate to do the same thing to you."

BEING CONCERNED WITH ONESELF

When we ask such questions as "Is it right?" or "Why should I do it?" we are concerned not only about how our behavior will affect other people, but also about how it will affect ourselves. For one thing, we want to know whether our behavior will make us liable for punishment. We are also concerned about what people will think about us. Sometimes we decide that it is more important to behave in a certain way than to worry about other people's opinions. We also want to know whether our behavior will make us happy or unhappy. In a broader sense, we are concerned with what kind of a person we want to be or at least how our behavior will affect our character. This personal element in ethics focuses our attention on our individual selves and how we view the purpose of our lives. Our ideas about ethics will reflect our ideas about ourselves.

Defining "Good"

The purpose of moral rules is to guide human behavior toward actions which may be considered good. In most cases, these moral rules grow out of a particular insight into human nature. Theories of ethics will vary, since they reflect different views of human capacities and human possibilities. In some cases, however, a description of human nature and the cultural setting in which human beings find themselves can produce theories of ethics in which moral rules have a very restricted scope and relevance. This is true in such theories as, for example, "psychological egoism" and "cultural relativism."

Suppose that we say that the only motive at work in human behavior is our own self-interest or what is usually called self-love or psychological egoism. From this assumption, it would be possible to fashion a basis for ethics, but it would be the ethics of egoism, from which no moral rules of altruism or concern for others could be drawn. For the psychological egoist, everything turns on the love of self. This is not so much a theory as a description of what human beings in fact do. For example, Helvetius says that "self-love makes us totally what we are. . . . Why are we so coveteous of honors and dignity? Because we love ourselves. . . . The love of power, and the means of preventing it, is therefore, necessarily connected in man with the love of himself. . . . Power is the only object of man's pursuit."

Similarly, the ethical relativist calls good whatever a given culture considers good. Accordingly, William Graham Sumner says in his *Folkways*, "Morals can never be intuitive. They are historical. . . . The notion of right is in the folkways. . . . whatever is, is right." This could mean that what is good and right in our culture could be thought of as bad in another. It may be true, as shown by anthropology and sociology, that different cultures define good and bad in different ways. But moral philosophy goes beyond anthropology by asking whether there are standards of behavior or conceptions of good applicable to all human beings regardless of their unique cultural history.

There is another complication which involves the notion that the word "good" cannot be defined, a view expressed by G. E. Moore in his *Principia Ethica*. Defining good, says Moore, is as difficult as defining the color yellow. What makes it difficult if not impossible is that yellow is a basic and unique quality unlike anything else. But even though we cannot define it, we can confidently use the term "yellow" without difficulty by identifying any object that possesses this quality. One reason it is difficult to define the color yellow is that in the process we shift from what we are trying to define to something else. To say, for example, that the color yellow is present when certain light vibrations strike the normal eye may be an accurate scientific description of the mechanics of perceiving a color. But the word "yellow" is the name of a property we *see* and not the information which results from scientific measurement. In a similar way, when we try to define the word "good," we tend to identify it with something else, as when we say that good can be defined as pleasure. But the problem of defining good in terms of pleasure is that it leaves the question we started with unanswered, namely, "Why is it that we say of pleasure that it is good?" In short, what do we mean by "good"?

Moore said that there are two fallacies involved in this exercise. First, there is the fallacy of thinking that the word could be defined at all. He says,

> If I am asked "what is good?" my answer is that good is good and that is the end of the matter. Or if I am asked "How is good to be defined?" my answer is that it cannot be defined, and that is all I have to say about it.

The other fallacy is what Moore calls the "naturalistic fallacy," which consists of trying to define a nonnatural object (*good*) in

terms of a natural object (*pleasure* or *self-realization*). What is
unsatisfactory or fallacious here is that this definition is not conclusive because it is still significant to ask why pleasure or self-realization are good. To define good, for example, as pleasure begs the
question, because this definition assumes what it is trying to prove
namely, not only that pleasure is good, but that good is pleasure.
Moore's conclusion is therefore that although the concept of good
(in general) cannot be defined, it is nevertheless possible to identify
good things and indeed to define *the* good. *The* good, according to
Moore, is that which is valuable for its own sake, that is, what is
intrinsically good, which he defines as follows: "By far the most
valuable things which we know or can imagine, are certain states of
consciousness, which may be roughly described as the pleasures of
human intercourse and the enjoyment of beautiful objects." He
continues, "No one . . . has ever doubted that personal affection
and appreciation of what is beautiful in Art or nature are good in
themselves; nor, if we consider strictly what things are worth having *purely for their own sake*, does it appear probable that anyone
will think that anything else has nearly so great a value as the things
which are included under these two heads." Therefore, just
because he found no adequate way of defining good, Moore did not
give up the attempt to provide a basis for the moral life. By contrast, A. J. Ayer, looking on ethics from his philosophical orientation of positivism, which holds that only those propositions which
can be verified physically by sense experience have true meaning,
dismissed ethical propositions as nonsense inasmuch as they could
not be appropriately verified.

However difficult it may be to define the word "good," and
whatever fallacies may be involved in the attempt, the theories of
ethics described in the following chapters represent some of the
most influential attempts by philosophers to understand what is
meant by morally good behavior. These philosophers are not so
concerned with listing good actions as they are with providing reasons why an action can be called good.

Summary:
Types of Ethical Theories

Here, then, are the thinkers and their theories that we will study:

1. An early group of philosophers called *"Stoics"* said that few events in our lives can be controlled by us. The script of the drama of life is already written. The only thing in our power is to choose how we will react to what we must do.

2. In a different way, *Aristotle* emphasized that since everything in nature has a purpose, then man too must have a purpose, and therefore, ethics should consist of guiding our behavior in accordance with our purpose. Just as a hammer, or anything else, is called "good" because it does well what it is supposed to do, so also a person is good if his or her behavior is in accordance with what human nature was designed for.

3. When philosophers added religious thought to their theories, as *Saint Augustine* did, it meant that ethics would cover a wider range than just the natural world. It is our nature, says Augustine, to love, that is, to fasten our affections on various objects or subjects, things or persons. We are good when we love the proper things properly. Thus things and other persons cannot be loved properly even though they possess value if they are loved as though they possess more value than God.

4. One of the most impressive philosophers, *Immanuel Kant*, singles out our faculties of will and reason as the key to ethics. Our conduct is right if it is consistent with human reason; that is, if on *principle* we would be willing for everyone to behave the way we do.

5. *Jeremy Bentham* and *John Stuart Mill* place more emphasis on our feelings, especially the feelings of pleasure and pain, as the guide for ethics. Whatever gives us the greatest pleasure and the least amount of pain is the standard for morally good behavior.

6. Seeking a way to account for our deepest yearnings to express our energy and power, *Friedrich Nietzsche* developed his famous and novel statements about the will to power. The highest morality, he said, is to express all our vital energies, saying

"yes" to life and its urgings, expressing our will, using reason primarily to direct, not to deny, our powerful life forces.

7. *Baron d'Holbach* and *William James* take opposite views on the question of whether the human will is free or determined. D'Holbach argues that our nature is very much like a machine, so that all our actions are strictly determined by various causes. William James, by contrast, says that as human beings we face genuine options and are able to make free choices.

8. *Jean-Paul Sartre* asks us to avoid self-deception and bad faith by making excuses for our behavior. Instead, we should seek an authentic life by recognizing that we are responsible for what we become by the decisions we make.

CHAPTER 1

WHAT CAN WE CONTROL?

The Stoics

The Stoics were members of a school founded in Athens by Zeno (334–262 B.C.). They held their meetings on the *stoa* (the Greek word for porch, hence the term "stoic"). Their ideas spread to Rome, where such famous people as Cicero, Seneca, and the Emperor Marcus Aurelius became followers. One of the outstanding Roman Stoics was Epictetus (A.D. 60–117). He overcame major hurdles in his life: He was lame either by birth or through accident, and early in life he was not a free man. He tried to develop an intensely practical guide for how life is to be carried out with satisfaction.

Epictetus based his moral philosophy on this simple teaching: "Two rules," he said, "we must ever bear in mind—that apart from the will there is nothing either good or bad, and that we must not try to anticipate or direct events, but merely accept them with intelligence."

As human beings, we should think of ourselves as being actors

Stoa of Attalos (*Agora Excavations, American School of Classical Studies at Athens*)

in a drama. It would be a mistake to think of this drama as being limited to our family, community, or even country. The drama Epictetus has in mind involves the whole universe, and people everywhere are members of the cast. As actors, we do not choose our role. The author and director of the drama is God or universal reason, who determines what each person will be and how and where each person will be situated in the course of his or her life. If everything is "set" for each person, if the "script" of our lives is already written, what, if anything, can we do about it? Do we have any choice at all?

There is something we can do, says Epictetus. We can recognize and accept what our part or role in this drama is and then perform that part well. Some people have "bit" parts, while others are cast into leading roles. "If it be [God's] will that you should act a poor man, see that you act it well; or a cripple or a ruler, or a private citizen. For this is your business." says Epictetus, "to act well the given part."

Epictetus (*New York Public Library Picture Collection*)

The actor develops a great indifference to those things over which he has no control, for example, the shape and form of the scenery or who the other players will be. He especially has no control over the story or its plot. But there is one thing that the actor can control, and that is his attitude and emotions. He can sulk because he has only a bit part, or he can be consumed with jealousy because someone else was chosen to be the hero, or he can be terribly insulted because the makeup artist put a particularly ugly nose on his face. But neither sulking, nor jealousy, nor feeling insulted can in any way alter the fact that he has a bit part, is not a hero, and must wear an ugly nose. The only thing these feelings and attitudes can do is rob him of his happiness. Therefore, the wise person will choose to control his feelings.

Here is how Epictetus states his point:

> The Gods put in our hands the one blessing that is best of all and master of all, that and nothing else, the power to deal rightly with our impressions, but everything else they did not put in our hands. . . . "Epictetus [says Zeus], if it were possible I would have made your body and your possessions (those trifles that you prize) free and untrammeled. But as things are—and never forget this—the body is not yours, it is but a clever mixture of clay. But since I could not make it free, I gave you a portion of our divinity, this faculty of impulse to act, of will to get and will to avoid, in a word the faculty that can turn impressions to right use. . . . " [A person] must ask himself, "What is mine, and what is not mine? What may I do, and what may I not do? I must die. But must I die groaning? I must be imprisoned. But must I whine as well? I must suffer exile. Can anyone then hinder me from going with a smile, and a good courage, and at peace?" . . . Here you see the results of training as training should be, of the will to get and will to avoid, so disciplined that nothing can hinder or frustrate them. . . . Remember that you are an actor in a play, and the Playwright chooses the manner of it: if he wants it short, it is short; if long, it is long. If he wants you to act a poor man you must act the part with all your powers; and so if your part be a cripple or a magistrate or a plain man. For your business is to act the character that is given you and act it well; the choice of the cast is Another's.[1]

---

[1]From *The Stoic and Epicurean Philosophers*, ed. Whitney J. Oates, Random House, New York, 1940.

CHAPTER 2

FULFILLING HUMAN PURPOSE

Aristotle

Aristotle (382–322 B.C.) was born in Stagira, a small town northeast of Athens. His father was physician to the King of Macedonia. As a boy, Aristotle was introduced to Greek medicine by his father, and this stimulated his lifelong interest in science. At age fifteen he was sent to Athens, where for the next twenty years he studied with Plato at Plato's Athenean Academy. Here he was known as "the mind of the school." Later Aristotle traveled widely, married a king's adopted daughter, and became the tutor of the future Alexander the Great for three years. In 355 B.C. he opened his own school, called the Lyceum, a rival of Plato's Academy. For twelve or thirteen years Aristotle remained as head of the Lyceum, where he lectured, taught classes, but most important of all, formulated his ideas about the classification of the sciences, invented logic, and wrote books in every major area of philosophy and science. The forty-seven books of his that remain cover the whole range of universal knowledge.

Aristotle (*Scala/Editorial Photocolor Archives*)

Aristotle's theory of ethics centers around his belief that man, as everything else in nature, has a special "end" to achieve or a function or purpose to fulfill. For this reason, his theory is called "teleological" (from the Greek word *telos*, meaning end or purpose). He begins his book *Ethics* by saying that "every art and every inquiry, and similarly every action and pursuit, is thought to aim at some good. . . ." If this is so, the question for ethics is "What is the *good* at which human behavior aims?"

For Aristotle, the principle of good and right was embedded within each man; moreover, this principle could be discovered by studying the essential nature of man and could be attained through his actual behavior in daily life. Aristotle warns his reader, however, not to expect more precision in a discussion of ethics than "the subject matter will admit." Still, just because this subject is susceptible of "variation and error" does not mean, said Aristotle, that ideas of right and wrong "exist conventionally only [that is, by local agreement], and not in the nature of things." With this in mind, Aristotle set out to discover the basis of morality in the structure of human nature.

Types of "Ends"

Aristotle sets the framework for his ethical theory with a preliminary illustration. Having said that all action aims toward an end, he now wants to distinguish between two major kinds of ends, which can be called "instrumental" ends (acts that are done as *means* for other ends) and "intrinsic" ends (acts that are done *for their own sake*). These two types of ends are illustrated, for example, in "every action connected with war."

When we consider step by step what is involved in the total activity of a war, we find, says Aristotle, that there is a series of special kinds of acts. These acts have their own ends, but when they are completed, they are only means by which still other ends are to be achieved. There is, for one thing, the art of the bridle maker. But the bridle is a means for the horseman to guide his horse in battle. Also, a carpenter builds a barrack, and when it is completed, he has fulfilled his function as a carpenter. The barracks also fulfill their function when they provide safe shelter for soldiers. But the ends here achieved by the carpenter and the building are not ends in themselves but are merely instrumental in housing soldiers until they move on to their next stage of action. Similarly, the builder of ships fulfills his function when the ship is successfully launched, but again this end is in turn a means for transporting the soldiers to the field of battle. The doctor fulfills his function to the extent that he keeps the soldiers in good health. But the "end" of health in this case becomes a "means" for effective fighting. The officer aims at victory in battle, but victory is the means to peace. Peace itself, though sometimes taken mistakenly as the final end of war, is the means for creating the conditions under which men, *as men*, could fulfill their function as men. When we discover what men aim at, not as carpenters, doctors, or generals, but as *men*, we will then arrive at action *for its own sake*, and for which all other activity is only a means, and this, says Aristotle, "must be the Good of Man."

How shall the word "good" be understood? As Plato before
him, Aristotle tied the word "good" to the special function of a
thing. A hammer is good if it does what hammers are expected to
do. A carpenter is good if he fulfills his function as a builder. This
would be true for all the crafts and professions. But here Aristotle
distinguishes between a man's craft or profession and his activity as
a man. To be a good doctor, for example, did not for Aristotle mean
the same thing as being a good man. One could be a good doctor
without being a good man, and vice versa. There are two different
functions here, the function of doctoring and the function of acting
as a man. To discover the good at which a man should aim, Aristotle
said we must discover the distinctive function of human nature. The
good man, according to Aristotle, is the man who is fulfilling his
function as a man.

The Function of Man

Aristotle asks, "Are we then to suppose that while carpenter and
cobbler have certain works and courses of action, Man as Man has
none, but is left by Nature without a work?" Or if "the eye, hand,
foot and in general each of the parts evidently has a function, may
one lay it down that man similarly has a function apart from all
these?" Surely man too has a distinctive mode of activity, but what
is it? Here Aristotle analyzes man's nature in order to discover his
unique activity, saying, first of all, that man's end "is not mere life,"
because that plainly is shared with him even by vegetables, and,
says Aristotle, "we want what is peculiar to him." Next there is the
life of sensation, "but this again manifestly is common to horses,
oxen and every animal." There remains then "an active life of the
element that has a rational principle. . . . if the function of man is
an activity of soul which follows or implies a rational principle . . .
then the human good turns out to be activity of soul in accordance
with virtue. . . ."
      Since man's function as a man means the proper functioning of
his soul, Aristotle sought to describe the nature of the soul. The
soul is the form of the body. That is, the soul is what provides the
body with its unique life and operation and makes it the kind of
body which is human. As such, the soul refers to the total person.

Accordingly, Aristotle said that the soul has two parts, the irrational and the rational. The irrational part, in turn, is composed of two subparts, the vegetative and the desiring or "appetitive" parts. For the most part, these are "something contrary to the rational principle, resisting and opposing it." The conflict between the rational and irrational elements in man is what raises the problems and subject matter of morality.

Morality involves action, for nothing is called good unless it is functioning. Thus Aristotle says that "as at the Olympic games it is not the finest and strongest men who are crowned, but they who enter the lists, for out of these the prize-men are selected; so too in life, of the honorable and good, it is they who act who rightly win the prizes." The particular kind of action implied here, if we have in mind Aristotle's analysis of the soul, is rational control and guidance of the irrational parts of the soul. Moreover, the good man is not the one who does a good deed here and there, now and then, but whose whole life is good, "for as it is not one swallow or one fine day that makes a spring, so it is not one day or a short time that makes a man blessed and happy."

Happiness as the End

Human action should aim at its proper end. Everywhere men aim at pleasure, wealth, and honor. But none of these ends, although they have value, can occupy the place of the chief good for which man should aim. To be an ultimate end, an act must be *self-sufficient* and *final*, "that which is always desirable in itself and never for the sake of something else," and it must be *attainable* by man. Aristotle seems certain that all men will agree that *happiness* is the end that alone meets all the requirements for the ultimate end of human action. Indeed, we choose pleasure, wealth, and honor only because we think that "through their instrumentality we shall be happy." Happiness, it turns out, is another word or name for good, for like good, happiness is the fulfillment of our distinctive function, or as Aristotle says, "Happiness . . . is a working of the soul in the way of excellence or virtue. . . ."

How does the soul work to attain happiness? The general rule of morality is "to act in accordance with Right Reason." What this means is that the rational part of the soul should control the irrational part. That the irrational part of the soul requires guidance is obvious when we consider what it consists of and what its mechanism is. Referring now only to the appetites or the appetitive part of the soul, we discover first that it is affected or influenced by things outside of the self, such as objects and persons. Also, there are two basic ways in which the appetitive part of the soul reacts to these external factors, these ways being *love* and *hate* or through the *concupiscent* and *irascible* "passions." The concupiscent passion leads one to desire things and persons, whereas the irascible passion leads one to avoid or destroy them. It becomes quickly apparent that these passions or capacities for love and hate, attraction or repulsion, creation or destruction, taken by themselves, could easily "go wild." In themselves they do not contain any principle of measure or selection. What should a person desire? How much? Under what circumstances? How should he relate himself to things, wealth, honor, and other persons?

We do not automatically act the right way in these matters; as Aristotle says, "none of the moral virtues arises in us by nature; for nothing that exists by nature can form a habit contrary to its nature." Morality has to do with developing habits, the habits of right thinking, right choice, and right behavior.

Virtue as the "Golden Mean"

Since the passions are capable of producing a wide range of action, all the way from too little to too much, a person must discover the proper meaning of excess and defect and thereby discover the appropriate *mean*. Virtue is concerned with our various feelings and actions, for it is in them that there can be excess and defect. For example, it is possible, says Aristotle, to feel the emotion of fear, confidence, lust, anger, compassion, pleasure, and pain too much or too little and in either case wrongly. To feel these when we ought to, on appropriate occasions, toward whom, and as we should, is the mean; that is the best state for man to be in, and this is *virtue*. Vice, again, is either extreme, excess or defect, and virtue is the mean. It is through the rational power of the soul that the passions are controlled and action is guided. The virtue of *courage*, for example, is the mean between two vices, namely, fear (defect) and foolhardiness (excess). Virtue, then, is a state of being, "a state apt to exercise deliberate choice, being in the relative mean, determined by reason, and as the man of practical wisdom would determine."

The mean is not the same for every person, nor is there a mean for every act. Each mean is relative to each person inasmuch as the circumstances will vary. In the case of eating, the mean will obviously be different for an adult athlete and a little girl. But for each person, there is nevertheless a proportionate or relative mean, for example, *temperance*, clearly indicating what extremes—namely, gluttony (excess) and starvation (defect)—would constitute vices for them. Similarly, when one gives money, *liberality*, as the mean between prodigality and stinginess, is not an absolute figure but is relative to one's assets. Moreover, for some acts there is no mean at all; their very nature already implies badness, such as spite, envy, adultery, theft, and murder. These are bad in themselves and not in their excesses or deficiencies. One is always wrong in doing them.

Deliberation and Choice

There are in the rational soul two kinds of reasoning. The first is theoretical, giving us knowledge of fixed principles or philosophical wisdom. The other is practical, giving us a rational guide to our action under the particular circumstances in which we find ourselves, and this is practical wisdom. What is important about the role of reason is that without this rational element, man would not have any moral capacity.

Again, Aristotle stressed that although man has a natural capacity for *right* behavior, he does not act rightly *by nature.* A man's life consists of an indeterminate number of possibilities. Goodness is in man *potentially,* but unlike the acorn out of which the oak will grow with almost mechanical certitude, man must move from what is potential in him to its actuality by knowing what he must do, deliberating about it, and then choosing in fact to do it. Unlike Plato and Socrates, who thought that to know the good was sufficient to do the good, Aristotle saw that there must be deliberate choice in addition to knowledge. Thus Aristotle said that "the origin of moral action—its efficient, not its final cause—is choice, and [the origin] of choice is desire and reasoning with a view to an end." There cannot be *choice* without reason: "intellect itself . . . moves nothing, but only the intellect which aims at an end and is practical."

Morality and moral choice imply human responsibility. If some ways of behaving are right and others wrong, it is necessary to discover why a person acts in a wrong instead of a right way. If we are to praise or blame—praise virtue and blame vice—a person must be truly capable of making a choice. Aristotle assumed that an act for which a person could be held responsible must be a voluntary act. A genuine choice is a voluntary action. But not all our actions are voluntary. Thus Aristotle said that "praise and blame arise upon such acts as are voluntary, while for the involuntary allowance is made, and sometimes compassion is excited." The distinction, as he saw it, between voluntary and involuntary acts was in general this: *Involuntary* acts are those for which a person is not responsible because they are (1) done out of ignorance of particular circumstances, (2) done as a result of external compulsion, or (3) done to avoid a greater evil. *Voluntary* acts are those for which a person is responsible because none of these three extenuating circumstances obtain.

The Virtues

In a general way we have already defined virtue as the fulfillment of man's distinctive function and as the mean between extremes. Another way to describe Aristotle's concept of virtue is to consider each virtue as the product of rational control of the passions. In this way we can combine all aspects of human behavior. Human nature consists for Aristotle not simply of rationality but of the full range covered by the vegetative, sensitive or appetitive, and the rational souls. Virtue does not imply the negation or rejection of any of these natural capacities. The moral man employs all his capacities, *physical* and *mental*. Corresponding to these two broad divisions in man there are two functions of reason, the intellectual and the moral, and each has its own virtues. There are accordingly *intellectual virtues* and *moral virtues*.

The intellectual virtues are philosophical wisdom and understanding, and they owe their birth and growth to teaching and
learning. Moral virtue comes about as a result of habit, whence
comes the name "ethics" (*ethike*), "formed by a slight variation
from the word *ethos* (habit)." All the moral virtues have to be
learned and practiced, and they become virtues only through
action, for "we become just by doing just acts, temperate by doing
temperate acts, brave by doing brave acts." The "cardinal" moral
virtues are courage, temperance, justice, and wisdom. In addition
to these, Aristotle considered also the virtues of magnificence, liberality, friendship, and self-respect. And although he acknowledged the central role of reason as a guide to practical and moral
action, he nevertheless concluded that philosophical wisdom is
superior to practical wisdom, that *contemplation* is most likely to
lead to happiness.

Contemplation

Aristotle concludes that if happiness is the product of our acting
according to our distinctive nature, it is reasonable to assume that
it is acting according to our highest nature; "that this activity is contemplative we have already said." This activity is the best, says
Aristotle, "since not only is reason the best thing in us, but the
objects of reason are the best of knowable objects." Moreover, contemplation "is most continuous, since we can contemplate truth
more continuously than we can *do* anything." Finally, "we think
happiness has pleasure mingled with it, but the activity of philosophical wisdom is admittedly the pleasantest of virtuous
activities."

READING

BASING ETHICS ON HUMAN NATURE
Aristotle

Every art and every inquiry, and similarly every action and pursuit, is thought to aim at some good; and for this reason the good has rightly been declared to be that at which all things aim. Now, as there are many actions, arts and sciences, their ends also are many; the end of the medical art is health, that of shipbuilding a vessel, that of strategy victory, that of economics wealth.

If, then, there is some end of the things we do, which we desire for its own sake (everything being desired for the sake of this), and if we do not choose everything for the sake of something else (for at that rate the process would go on to infinity, so that our desire would be empty and vain), clearly this must be the good and the chief good. Will not the knowledge of it, then, have a great influence on life? Shall we not, like archers who have a mark to aim at, be more likely to hit upon what is right? If so, we must try, in outline at least, to determine what it is. . . .

Our discussion will be adequate if it has as much clearness as the subject-matter admits of, for precision is not to be sought for alike in all discussions, any more than in all the products of the crafts. . . .

Let us resume our inquiry and state, in view of the fact that all knowledge and every pursuit aims at some good, . . . what is the highest of all goods achievable by action? Verbally there is very general agreement; for both the general run of men and people of superior refinement say that it is happiness, and identify living well and doing well with being happy; but with regard to what happiness is they differ, and the many do not give the same account as the wise. For the former think it is some plain and obvious thing, like pleasure, wealth, or honour; they differ, however, from one another—and often even the same man identifies it with different things, with health when he is ill, with wealth when he is poor; but, conscious of their ignorance, they admire those who proclaim some great ideal that is above their comprehension. Now some thought that apart from these many

From Aristotle, *Nichomachean Ethics*, vol. V, *The Student's Oxford Aristotle*, trans. W. D. Ross, by permission of the Oxford University Press, New York, 1946.

goods there is another which is self-subsistent and causes the goodness of all these as well. . . .

Let us again return to the good we are seeking, and ask what it can be. It seems different in different actions and arts; it is different in medicine, in strategy, and in the other arts likewise. What then is the good of each? Surely that for whose sake everything else is done. In medicine this is health, in strategy victory, in architecture a house, in any other sphere something else, and in every action and pursuit the end; for it is for the sake of this that all men do whatever else they do. Therefore, if there is an end for all that we do, this will be the good achievable by action, and if there are more than one, these will be the goods achievable by action.

So the argument has by a different course reached the same point; but we must try to state this even more clearly. Since there are evidently more than one end, and we choose some of these (e.g., wealth, flutes, and, in general, instruments) for the sake of something else, clearly not all ends are final ends; but the chief good is evidently something final. Therefore, if there is only one final end, this will be what we are seeking, and if there are more than one, the most final of these will be what we are seeking. Now we call that which is in itself worthy of pursuit more final than that which is worthy of pursuit for the sake of something else, and that which is never desirable for the sake of something else more final than the things that are desirable both in themselves and for the sake of that other thing, and therefore we call final without qualification that which is always desirable in itself and never for the sake of something else.

Now such a thing happiness, above all else, is held to be; for this we choose always for itself and never for the sake of something else, but honour, pleasure, reason, and every virtue we choose indeed for themselves (for if nothing resulted from them we should still choose each of them), but we choose them also for the sake of happiness, judging that by means of them we shall be happy. Happiness, on the other hand, no one chooses for the sake of these, nor, in general, for anything other than itself. . . .

Presumably, however, to say that happiness is the chief good seems a platitude, and a clearer account of what it is is still desired. This might perhaps be given, if we could first ascertain the function of man. For just as for a flute-player, a sculptor, or any artist, and, in general, for all things that have a function or activity, the good and the "well" is thought to reside in the function, so would it seem to be for man, if he has a function. Have the carpenter, then, and the tanner certain functions or activities, and has man none? Is he born without a function? Or as eye, hand, foot, and in general each of the parts evidently has a function, may one lay it down that man similarly has a function apart from all these? What then can this be? Life seems to be common even to plants, but we are seeking what is peculiar to man. Let us exclude, therefore, the life of nutrition and growth. Next there would be a life of perception, but *it* also seems to be common even to the horse, the ox, and every animal. There remains, then, an active life of the element that has a rational principle; of this, one part has such a principle in the sense of being obedient to one, the other in the sense of possessing one and exercising thought. And, as "life of the rational element" also has two meanings, we must state that life in the sense of activity is what we mean; for this seems to be the more proper sense of the term. Now if the function of man is an activity of soul which follows or implies a rational principle, and if we say "a so-and-so" and "a good so-and-so" have a function which is the same in kind, e.g., a lyre-player and a good lyre-player, and so without qualification in all cases, eminence in respect of goodness being added to the name of the function (for the function of a lyre-player is to play the lyre, and that of a good lyre-player is to do so well): if this is the case, (and we state the function of man to be a certain kind of life, and this to be an activity or actions of the soul implying a rational principle, and the function of a good man to be the good and noble performance of these, and if any action is well performed when it is performed in accordance with the appropriate excellence: if this is the case,) human good turns out to be activity of soul in accordance with virtue, and if there are more than one virtue, in accordance with the best and most complete.

But we must add "in a complete life." For one swallow does not make a summer, nor does one day; and so too one day, or a short time, does not make a man blessed and happy. . . .

Since happiness is an activity of soul in accordance with perfect virtue, we must consider the nature of virtue; for perhaps we shall thus see better the nature of happiness. . . . But clearly the virtue we must study is human virtue; for the good we were seeking was human good and the happiness human happiness. By human virtue we mean not that of the body but that of the soul; and happiness also we call an activity of soul. . . .

Some things are said about it [the soul], adequately enough, even in the discussions outside our school, and we must use these; e.g., that one element in the soul is irrational and one has a rational principle. . . .

Of the irrational element one division seems to be widely distributed, and vegetative in its nature, I mean that which causes nutrition and growth; for it is this kind of power of the soul that one must assign to all nurslings and embryos, and this same power to full-grown creatures; this is more reasonable than to assign some different power to them. Now the excellence of this seems to be common to all species and not specifically human; for this part or faculty seems to function most in sleep, while goodness and badness are least manifest in sleep (whence comes the saying that the happy are no better off than the wretched for half their lives; and this happens naturally enough, since sleep is an inactivity of the soul in that respect in which it is called good or bad), unless perhaps to a small extent some of the movements actually penetrate to the soul, and in this respect the dreams of good men are better than those of ordinary people. Enough of this subject, however; let us leave the nutritive faculty alone, since it has by its nature no share in human excellence.

There seems to be also another irrational element in the soul—one which in a sense, however, shares in a rational principle. For we praise the rational principle of the continent man and of the incontinent, and the part of their soul that has such a principle, since it urges them aright and towards the best objects; but there is found in them also another element naturally opposed to the rational principle, which fights against and resists that principle. For exactly as paralysed limbs when we intend to move them to the right turn on the contrary to the left, so is it with the soul; the impulses of incontinent people move in contrary directions. But while in the body we see that which moves astray, in the soul we do not. No doubt, however, we must none the less suppose that in the soul too there is something contrary to the rational principle, resisting and opposing it. In what sense it is distinct from the other elements does not concern us. Now even this seems to have a share in a rational principle, as we said; at any rate in the continent man it obeys the rational principle—and presumably in the temperate and brave man it is still more obedient; for in him it speaks, on all matters, with the same voice as the rational principle. . . .

Virtue, then, being of two kinds, intellectual and moral, intellectual virtue in the main owes both its birth and its growth to teaching (for which reason it requires experience and time), while moral virtue comes about as a result of habit; for nothing that exists by nature can form a habit contrary to its nature. For instance the stone which by nature moves downwards cannot be habituated to move upwards, not even if one tries to train it by throwing it up ten thousand times; nor can fire be habituated to move downwards, nor can anything else that by nature behaves in one way be trained to behave in another. Neither by nature, then, nor contrary to nature do the virtues arise in us; rather we are adapted by nature to receive them, and are made perfect by habit.

If happiness is activity in accordance with virtue, it is reasonable that it should be in accordance with the highest virtue; and this will be that of the best thing in us. Whether it be reason or something else that is this element which is thought to be our natural ruler and guide and to take thought of things noble and divine, whether it be itself also divine or only the most divine element in us, the activity of this in accordance with its proper virtue will be perfect happiness. That this activity is contemplative we have already said.

Now this would seem to be in agreement both with what we said before and with the truth. For, firstly, this activity is the best (since not only is reason the best thing in us, but the objects of reason are the best of knowable objects); and, secondly, it is the most continuous, since we can contemplate truth more continuously than we can *do* anything. And we think happiness has pleasure mingled with it, but the activity of philosophic wisdom is admittedly the pleasantest of virtuous activities; at all events the pursuit of it is thought to offer pleasures marvellous for their purity and their enduringness, and it is to be expected that those who know will pass their time more pleasantly than those who inquire. And the self-sufficiency that is spoken of must belong to the contemplative activity. For while a philosopher, as well as a just man or one possessing any other virtue, needs the necessaries of life, when they are sufficiently equipped with things of that sort the just man needs people towards whom and with whom he shall act justly, and the temperate man, the brave man, and each of the others is in the same case, but the philosopher, even when by himself, can contemplate truth, and the better the wiser he is; he can perhaps do so better if he has fellow-workers, but still he is the most self-sufficient. And this activity alone would seem to be loved for its own sake; for nothing arises from it apart from the contemplating, while from practical activities we gain more or less apart from the action. And happiness is thought to depend on leisure; for we are busy that we may have leisure, and make war that we may live in peace. . . .

But such a life would be too high for man; for it is not in so far as he is man that he will live so, but in so far as something divine is present in him; and by so much as this is superior to our composite nature is its activity superior to that which is the exercise of the other kind of virtue. If reason is divine, then, in comparison with man, the life according to it is divine in comparison with human life. But we must not follow those who advise us, being men, to think of human beings, and, being mortal, of mortal things, but must, so far as we can, make ourselves immortal, and strain every nerve to live in accordance with the best thing in us; for even if it be small in bulk, much more does it in power and worth surpass everything. This would seem, too, to be each man himself, since it is the authoritative and better part of him. It would be strange, then, if he were to choose not the life of his self but that of something else. And what we said before will apply now; that which is proper to each thing is by nature best and most pleasant for each thing; for man, therefore, the life according to reason is best and pleasantest, since reason more than anything else *is* man. This life therefore is also the happiest.

CHAPTER 3

THE MODES
OF LOVE

Augustine

Saint Augustine was born in northern Africa in A.D. 354. His father was a pagan, but his mother, Monica, was a devout Christian. During his student days in the bawdy port town of Carthage, while he vigorously pursued his studies, he abandoned his religious faith and took a mistress. He could never overcome his intense concern about his personal morality and destiny. He read widely in philosophy and moved to Milan to study rhetoric. While there, he was influenced by Ambrose, the Bishop of Milan. He finally discovered a version of Platonic thought which helped overcome his intellectual difficulties with Christianity. Eventually he became the author of an astonishing number of books whose influence can be felt even today. His life was emotionally tempestuous, and his deepest concerns focused on the problem of moral evil. With his massive learning, he brought together philosophy and theology to form a unique way of looking at morality. He concluded his career in North Africa, where he was Bishop of Hippo, dying in the posture of prayer at the age of seventy-five.

Augustine (*Scala/Editorial Photocolor Archives*)

As a student, Augustine found Christianity unsatisfactory, especially because he could not understand why there should be so much moral evil among people if there is a good God. How can one explain the existence of evil in human experience? The Christians had said that God is the Creator of all things and that God is good. How, then, is it possible for evil to arise out of a world that a perfectly good God had created? Because Augustine could find no satisfactory answer in the Christianity he learned as a youth, he turned to a group called Manichaeans who were sympathetic to much of Christianity but who, boasting of their intellectual superiority, rejected the idea of the Old Testament that there is only one God who is both the Creator and Redeemer of man. Instead, the Manichaeans taught the doctrine of "dualism," according to which there were two basic principles or powers in the universe, the principle of light or goodness on the one hand and the principle of darkness or evil on the other. These two principles or powers were said to be equally eternal and were seen as eternally in conflict with each other. This conflict was reflected in human life as the conflict between the soul, composed of light, and the body, composed of darkness. This seemed to make sense to Augustine. He could now blame his sensual desires on the external power of darkness. But this did not solve his personal problem. The presence of fierce passion was just as bothersome even when he shifted the blame for it to something outside himself. He gave up his interest in the Manichees, became a skeptic for awhile, and was attracted to the notion that everything is material in nature, that there are no nonmaterial substances, such as, for example, the soul. Augustine eventually found the best solution to his intellectual problems, especially the problem of evil, in some new forms of Plato's philosophy. He now understood that evil is not a positive thing but rather the absence of good, just as darkness is the absence of light. Through Platonic thought Augustine was able to make Christianity intellectually reasonable.

In describing man's moral situation, Augustine put together his insights about human nature, the nature of God, and the idea of creation. Man's condition, says Augustine, is that he is made in such a way that he always seeks happiness. Although the ancient Greeks had also considered happiness the goal of life, Augustine went farther because to the natural ends or purposes of man he added the supernatural element. He expressed this key idea in both religious and philosophical language. In his *Confessions* he wrote, "Oh God Thou hast created us for Thyself so that our hearts are restless until they find their rest in Thee." In more philosophical language he makes this same point by saying that human nature is so made that "it cannot itself be the good by which it is made happy." There is, in short, no purely "natural" man. The reason there is no purely natural man, says Augustine, is that nature did not produce man. God did. Consequently, man always bears the marks of his creation, which means, among other things, that there are some permanent relations, actual and possible, between man and God. It is not by accident that man *seeks* happiness. That he seeks it is a consequence of his incompleteness, his finitude. That he can find happiness only in God is also no accident, since he was made by God to find happiness only in God. Augustine elaborates this aspect of man's nature through his doctrine of love.

The Role of Love

Man inevitably loves. To love is to go beyond oneself and to fasten one's affection on an object of love. What makes it inevitable that man will love is, again, his incompleteness. There is a wide range of objects that man can choose to love, reflecting the variety of ways in which man is incomplete. A person can love (1) physical objects, (2) other persons, or even (3) himself. From these he can derive satisfaction for some of his desires and passions. Augustine stressed that all things in the world are good because all things come from God, who is goodness itself. Consequently, all things are legitimate objects of love. Everything that man loves will provide him with some measure of satisfaction and happiness. Nothing is evil in itself; evil is not a positive thing but the absence of something. Man's moral problem consists not so much in loving or even in the objects he loves. What causes man's moral problem is the *manner* in which he attaches himself to his objects of love and his *expectations* regarding the outcome of his love. Everyone expects to achieve happiness and fulfillment from love, yet men are miserable, unhappy, restless. Why? Augustine lays the blame on man's "disordered" love.

Evil and Disordered Love

Each object of love is different, and for this reason the consequences of loving them will be different. Similarly, the human needs which prompt the act of love are also different. Augustine thought that there is some sort of correlation between various human needs and the objects that can satisfy them. Love is the act that harmonizes these needs and their objects. What constitutes the chief fact about man is that the range of his needs includes not only (1) objects, (2) other persons, and (3) himself, but also, and most of all, (4) God. There is no way to unmake this fact about man. Augustine formulates this point in virtually quantitative terms. Each object of love can give only so much satisfaction and no more. Each of man's needs likewise has a measurable quantity. Clearly, satisfaction and happiness require that an object of love contain a sufficient amount of whatever it takes to fulfill or satisfy the particular need. Thus we love food and we consume a quantity commensurate with our hunger. But our needs are not all physical in that primary sense. We love objects of art, too, for the aesthetic satisfaction they give. At a higher level we have the need for love between persons. Indeed, this level of affection provides quantitatively and qualitatively more in the way of pleasure and happiness than mere physical things, such as the various forms of property, can.

From this it becomes clear that certain human needs cannot be met by an interchange of objects; the deep human need for human companionship cannot be met any other way than by a relationship with another person. Things cannot be a substitute for a person, because things do not contain within themselves the unique ingredients of a human personality. Therefore, although each thing is a legitimate object of love, one must not expect more from it than its unique nature can provide. The basic need for human affection cannot be satisfied by things. But this is particularly the case with man's spiritual need. Man was made, said Augustine, to love God. God is infinite. In some way, then, man's nature was made so that only God, the infinite, can give him ultimate satisfaction or happiness. "When," says Augustine, "the will which is the intermediate good, cleaves to the immutable good . . . man finds therein the blessed life," for "to live well is nothing else but to love God. . . ." To love God is, then, the indispensable requirement for happiness, because only God, who is infinite, can satisfy that peculiar need in man that is precisely the need for the infinite.

If objects are not interchangeable, if things cannot substitute for a person, neither can any finite thing or person substitute for God. Yet all men confidently expect that they can achieve true happiness by loving objects, other persons, and themselves. While these are all legitimate objects of love, man's love of them is disordered when these are loved for the sake of ultimate happiness. "Disordered love" consists in expecting more from an object of love than it is capable of providing. Disordered love produces all forms of pathology in human behavior. Normal self-love becomes pride, and pride is the cardinal sin that affects all aspects of man's conduct. The essence of pride is the assumption of self-sufficiency. Yet the permanent fact about man is precisely that he is not self-sufficient, neither physically, nor emotionally, nor spiritually.

Man's pride, which turns him away from God, leads him to many forms of overindulgence, since he tries to satisfy an infinite need with finite entities. He therefore loves things more than he should in relation to what they can do for him. His love for another person can become virtually destructive of the other person, since he tries again to derive from that relationship more than it can possibly give. Appetite flourishes, passion multiplies, and there is a desperate attempt to achieve peace by satisfying all desires. The soul becomes seriously disfigured and is now implicated in envy, greed, jealousy, trickery, panic, and a pervading restlessness. It does not take long for disordered love to produce a disordered person, and disordered persons produce a disordered community. No attempt to reconstruct an orderly or peaceful community or household is possible without reconstructing each human being. The rigorous and persistent fact is that personal reconstruction, salvation, is possible only by reordering love, by loving the proper things properly. Indeed, Augustine argued that we can love a person properly only if we love God first, for then we will not expect to derive from human love what can be derived only from our love of God. Similarly, we can love ourselves properly only as we subordinate ourselves to God, for there is no other way to overcome the destructive consequences of pride than by eliminating pride itself.

Free Will as the Cause of Evil

Augustine did not agree with Plato that the cause of evil is simply ignorance. To be sure, there can be some circumstances under which a person does not know the ultimate good, is not aware of God. Still, Augustine says that "even the ungodly" have the capacity to "blame and rightly praise many things in the conduct of men." The overriding fact is that in daily conduct men understand praise and blame only because they already understand that they have an obligation to do what is praiseworthy and to abstain from what is blameworthy. Under these circumstances, man's predicament is not that he is ignorant but that he stands in the presence of alternatives. He must choose to turn toward God or away from God. He is, in short, free. Whichever way man chooses, he does so with the hope of finding happiness. He is capable of directing his affections exclusively toward finite things, persons, or himself and away from God. Augustine says that "this turning away and this turning to are not forced but voluntary acts." Evil, or sin, is a product of the will. It is not, as Plato said, ignorance, nor, as the Manichaeans said, the work of the principle of darkness permeating the body. In spite of the fact of original sin, all men still possess the freedom of their will. This freedom (*liberum*) of the will is not, however, the same as spiritual freedom (*libertas*), for true spiritual liberty is no longer possible in its fullness in this life. Man now uses his free will to choose wrongly, but even when man chooses rightly, he does not, says Augustine, possess the spiritual power to do the good he has chosen. He must have the help of God's grace.

READING

LOVE OF GOD THE HIGHEST GOOD

St. Augustine

How then, according to reason, ought man to live? We all certainly desire to live happily, and there is no human being but assents to this statement almost before it is made. But the title happy cannot, in my opinion, belong either to him who has now what he loves, whatever it may be, or to him who has what he loves if it is hurtful, or to him who does not love what he has, although it is good in perfection. For one who seeks what he cannot obtain suffers torture, and one who has got what is not desirable is cheated, and one who does not seek for what is worth seeking for is diseased. Now in all these cases the mind cannot be but unhappy, and happiness and unhappiness cannot reside at the same time in one man: so in none of these cases can the man be happy. I find, then, a fourth case, where the happy life exists—when that which is man's chief good is both loved and possessed. For what do we call enjoyment but having at hand the objects of love? And no one can be happy who does not enjoy what is man's chief good, nor is there any one who enjoys this who is not happy. We must then have at hand our chief good, if we think of living happily.

From Augustine, "City of God," *The Writings against the Manichaeans and against the Donatists (a Select Library of the Nicene and post-Nicene Fathers)*, First Series, ed., Philip Schaff, vol. IV, The Christian Literature Publishing Co., New York, 1886–1890.

We must now inquire what is man's chief good, which of course cannot be anything inferior to man himself. For whoever follows after what is inferior to himself, becomes himself inferior. But every man is bound to follow what is best. Wherefore man's chief good is not inferior to man. Is it then something similar to man himself? It must be so, if there is nothing above man which he is capable of enjoying. But if we find something which is both superior to man, and can be possessed by the man who loves it, who can doubt that in seeking for happiness man should endeavor to reach that which is more excellent than the being who makes the endeavor. For if happiness consists in the enjoyment of a good than which there is nothing better, which we call the chief good, how can a man be properly called happy who has not yet attained to his chief good? or how can that be the chief good beyond which something better remains for us to arrive at? Such, then, being the chief good, it must be something which cannot be lost against the will. For no one can feel confident regarding a good which he knows can be taken from him, although he wishes to keep and cherish it. But if a man feels no confidence regarding the good which he enjoys, how can he be happy while in such fear of losing it?

Let us then see what is better than man. This must necessarily be hard to find, unless we first ask and examine what man is. I am not now called upon to give a definition of man. The question here seems to me to be—since almost all agree, or at least, which is enough, those I have now to do with are of the same opinion with me, that we are made up of soul and body—What is man? Is he both of these? or is he the body only, or the soul only?

Now if we ask what is the chief good of the body, reason obliges us to admit that it is that by means of which the body comes to be in its best state. But of all the things which invigorate the body, there is nothing better or greater than the soul. The chief good of the body, then, is not bodily pleasure, not absence of pain, not strength, not beauty, not swiftness, or whatever else is usually reckoned among the goods of the body, but simply the soul. For all the things mentioned the soul supplies to the body by its presence, and, what is above them all, life. Hence I conclude that the soul is the chief good of man, whether we give the name of man to soul and body together, or to the soul alone.

If, again, the body is man, it must be admitted that the end is the chief good of man. But clearly, when we treat of morals—when we inquire what manner of life must be held in order to obtain happiness—it is not the body to which the precepts are addressed, it is not bodily discipline which we discuss. In short, the observance of good *customs* belongs to that part of us which inquires and learns, which are the prerogatives of the soul. . . . So the question seems to me to be not, whether soul and body is man, or the soul only, or the body only, but what gives perfection to the soul. . . .

EVERYTHING IN NATURE IS GOOD

EVIL IS A PRODUCT OF THE WILL

All natures, then, inasmuch as they are, and have therefore a rank and species of their own, and a kind of internal harmony, are certainly good. And when they are in the places assigned to them by the order of their nature, they preserve such being as they have received. And those things which have not received everlasting being, are altered for better or for worse, so as to suit the wants and notions of those things to which the Creator's law has made them subservient; and thus they tend in the divine providence to that end which is embraced in the general scheme of the government of the universe. So that, though the corruption of transitory and perishable things brings to utter destruction, it does not prevent their producing that which was designed to be their result. And this being so, God, who supremely is, and who therefore created every being which has not supreme existence (for that which was made of nothing could not be equal to Him, and indeed could not be at all had He not made it), is not to be found fault with on account of the creature's faults, but is to be praised in view of the natures He has made. . . .

Let no one, therefore, look for an efficient cause of the evil will; for it is not efficient, but deficient, as the will itself is not an effecting of something, but a defect. For defection from that which supremely is, to that which has less of being—this is to begin to have an evil will.

This I do know, that the nature of God can never, nowhere, nowise be defective, and that natures made of nothing can. These latter, however, the more being they have, and the more good they do (for then they do something positive), the more they have efficient causes; but in so far as they are defective in being, and consequently do evil (for then what is their work but vanity?) they have deficient causes. And I know likewise, that the will could not become evil, were it unwilling to become so; and therefore its failings are justly punished, being not necessary, but voluntary. For its defections are not to evil things, but are themselves evil; that is to say, are not towards things that are naturally and in themselves evil, but the defection of the will is evil, because it is contrary to the order of nature, and an abandonment of that which has supreme being for that which has less. For avarice is not a fault inherent in gold, but in the man who inordinately loves gold, to the detriment of justice, which ought to be held in incomparably higher regard than gold. Neither is luxury the fault of lovely and charming objects, but of the heart that inordinately loves sensual pleasures, to the neglect of temperance, which attaches us to objects more lovely in their spirituality, and more delectable by their incorruptibility. Nor yet is boasting the fault of human praise, but of the soul that is inordinately fond of the applause of men, and that makes light of the voice of conscience. Pride, too, is not the fault of him who delegates power, nor of power itself, but of the soul that is inordinately enamored of its own power, and despises the more just dominion of a higher authority. Consequently he who inordinately loves the good which any nature possesses, even though he obtains it, himself becomes evil in the good, and wretched because deprived of a greater good. . . .

And therefore there is a nature in which evil does not or even cannot exist; but there cannot be a nature in which there is no good. Hence not even the nature of the devil himself is evil, in so far as it is nature, but it was made evil by being perverted. . . .

THE LOVE OF GOD

Let us see how the Lord Himself in the gospel has taught us to live, focusing on the chief end after which we are told to strive with supreme affection. "Thou shalt love," He says, "the Lord thy God." Tell me also, I pray Thee, what must be the measure of love; for I fear lest the desire enkindled in my heart should either exceed or come short in fervor. "With all thy heart," He says. Nor is that enough. "With all thy soul." Nor is it enough yet. "With all thy mind." What do you wish more? I might, perhaps, wish more if I could see the possibility of more. What does Paul say on this? "We know," he says, "that all things issue in good to them that love God." Let him, too, say what is the measure of love. "Who then," he says, "shall separate us from the love of Christ? Shall tribulation, or distress, or persecution, or famine, or nakedness, or peril, or the sword?" We have heard, then, what and how much we must love; this we must strive after, and to this we must refer all our plans. The perfection of all our good things and our perfect good is God. We must neither come short of this nor go beyond it: the one is dangerous, the other impossible.

Following after God is the desire of happiness; to reach God is happiness itself. We follow after God by loving Him; we reach Him, not by becoming entirely what He is, but in nearness to Him, and in wonderful and immaterial contact with Him, and in being inwardly illuminated and occupied by His truth and holiness. He is light itself; we get enlightenment from Him. The greatest commandment, therefore, which leads to happy life, and the first, is this: "Thou shalt love the Lord thy God with all thy heart, and soul, and mind." For to those who love the Lord all things issue in good, and if, as no one doubts, the chief or perfect good is not only to be loved, but to be loved so that nothing shall be loved better, as is expressed in the words, "With all thy soul, with all thy heart, and with all thy mind," who, I ask, will not at once conclude, when these things are all settled and most surely believed, that our chief good which we must hasten to arrive at in preference to all other things is nothing else than God? And then, if nothing can separate us from His love, must not this be surer as well as better than any other good?

The farther the mind departs from God, not in space, but in affection

and lust after things below Him, the more it is filled with folly and wretchedness. So by love it returns to God—a love which places it not along with
God, but under Him. And the more ardor and eagerness there is in this, the
happier and more elevated will the mind be, and with God as sole governor
it will be in perfect liberty. Hence it must know that it is a creature. It must
believe what is the truth—that its Creator remains ever possessed of the
inviolable and immutable nature of truth and wisdom, and must confess,
even in view of the errors from which it desires deliverance, that it is liable
to folly and falsehood. But then again, it must take care that it be not separated by the love of the other creature, that is, of this visible world, from
the love of God Himself, which sanctifies it in order to lasting happiness.
No other creature, then—for we are ourselves a creature—separates us
from the love of God which is in Christ Jesus our Lord.

THE CONVERSION OF THE GREEK VIRTUES

As to virtue leading us to a happy life, I hold virtue to be nothing else than
perfect love of God. For the fourfold division of virtue I regard as taken from
four forms of love. For these four virtues (would that all felt their influence
in their minds as they have their names in their mouths!), I should have no
hesitation in defining them: that *temperance* is love giving itself entirely to
that which is loved; *fortitude* is love readily bearing all things for the sake
of the loved object; *justice* is love serving only the loved object, and therefore ruling rightly; *prudence* is love distinguishing with sagacity between
what hinders it and what helps it. The object of this love is not anything,
but only God, the chief good, the highest wisdom, the perfect harmony. So
we may express the definition thus: that temperance is love keeping itself
entire and incorrupt for God; fortitude is love bearing everything readily for
the sake of God; justice is love serving God only, and therefore ruling well
all else, as subject to man; prudence is love making a right distinction
between what helps it towards God and what might hinder it. [italics mine]

CHAPTER 4

A SENSE OF DUTY

Kant

Immanuel Kant lived all his eighty years (1724–1804) in the small town of Konigsburg in East Prussia. At the university he studied classics, physics, and philosophy. The strongest influences shaping his early thinking were Sir Isaac Newton's physics, the tradition of philosophy which emphasized the power of human reason, and the pietistic religious nurture in his family. A bachelor all his life, he worked with incredible discipline—the story is told that neighbors could set their watches when he stepped out of the house each day at half past four to walk up and down the street eight times. His books revolutionized philosophy. Philosophers who came after might disagree with what he wrote, but no one could ever ignore him.

"Two things fill the mind with ever new and increasing admiration and awe," says Kant, "the starry heavens above and the moral law within." To him the starry heavens were a reminder that the world, as pictured by Sir Isaac Newton, is a system of physical bodies in motion, where every event has a specific cause. At the same time, all men experience the sense of moral duty which implies that human beings, unlike physical objects, possess freedom of choice in their behavior. Because human beings have this freedom of choice, we can ask ourselves "What shall I do?" But this was not the question of greatest importance for Kant. That question merely asks "Which of the various alternative ways of behaving do I want to choose?—as if I were asking myself which street I should take on my way home today. The key question in ethics according to Kant is this: "Given the fact that I face alternatives, which choice *ought* I to make?" That is, "What *must* I do?"

The task of moral philosophy, said Kant, is to discover how we can arrive at principles of behavior that apply to all persons. To include all persons is a way of testing whether my own personal behavior is right, just as we test if a scientific theory works for every scientist. That is, if I am not willing for others to act according to my rule of behavior, there could be something wrong with my ethical idea. He was sure that we cannot find these principles simply by studying the actual behavior of people. Such a study would give us interesting anthropological information about how people *do* behave. What impressed Kant was that we do make moral judgments when we say, for example, that we ought to tell the truth. How do we know that we should tell the truth? Kant's answer is that our knowledge of moral principles resembles our knowledge of scientific principles in an important way. For Kant, the moral judgment that "we ought to tell the truth" is on principle the same kind of mental activity as the scientific judgment that "every change must have a cause." How do we know that every change must have a cause? We have not observed every change. Our mind, our rational power, enables us to think of every change even though we see or experience only one or a few changes. This represents our capacity for theoretical thinking. We know that two and two equals four no matter two of what. This knowledge does not come from simply looking at two apples or two dollars. Similarly, the conclusion that we must tell the truth does not come from observing Mary and John. Our reason *brings* to the objects or events in our experience certain ways of thinking about them, as though we were looking at them through intellectual glasses or lenses. Our knowledge begins with our experience but is not limited to it.

Both in science and in moral philosophy we use concepts that go beyond any particular facts we experience at any one time. In both science and morality, experience is the occasion for triggering

Kant (*Culver Pictures*)

the mind to think in broader, universal terms. When we experience
a given example of change, our minds bring to this event the idea
of causality, which makes it possible to explain the relation of cause
and effect not only in this case but in all cases of change. Similarly,
in our human relations, our practical reason is able to determine
how we should behave, not only at this moment, but at all times.
Our practical reason can make judgments about "ought" just as our
theoretical reason can make judgments about "cause." In both
cases, our reason is dealing with a *principle* which applies to all
cases. Just as there are laws of physics, so there are "laws" of moral
behavior. Ethics, then, is for Kant the study of principles that apply
to all rational beings and that lead to behavior that we call "good."

Good Defined as the Good Will

According to Kant, "Nothing can possibly be conceived in the world, or even out of it, which can be called good, without qualification, except a good will." He would admit, of course, that other things can be considered good, such as, for example, the control of the passions, "and yet," he says, "one can hardly call this unreservedly good . . . for without the principles of a good will this may become evil indeed. The cold-bloodedness of a villain not only makes him far more dangerous, but also makes him seem more despicable to us than he would have seemed without it." Kant's chief point is that the essence of the morally good act is the principle that a person acts on when he behaves. "The good will is good not because of what it accomplishes, not because of its usefulness in the attainment of some set purpose, but alone because of the willing, that is to say, it is good of itself."

Good Will and the Motive of Duty

The will is good in the moral sense when it acts out of the proper motive. Kant distinguishes between three motives behind our actions, namely, (1) inclination, (2) self-interest, and (3) duty. It makes a difference in judging the morality of our behavior whether we act out of inclination (which means that we will do a particular act if we happen to feel like doing it at that moment), self-interest (where we calculate the benefit to us in a given action), or out of duty (because we believe it is the right thing to do). The reason Kant makes the startling statement that "the good will is good not because of what it accomplishes" is that he wants to emphasize the dominant role of the will in ethics. It is not enough for the effects or the consequences of our behavior to *agree with* the moral law; the truly moral act is done *for the sake of* the moral law, "for all these effects—even the promotion of the happiness of others— could have also been brought about by other causes, so that there

would have been no need of the will of a rational being. . . . "
Instead of acting out of inclination or self-interest, we must act out
of a sense of duty "so that nothing remains which can determine
the will except objectively the (moral) *law* and subjectively *pure
respect* for this practical law."

Motives and Types
of Imperatives

Our sense of duty implies that we are under some kind of obligation, a moral law. As rational beings, says Kant, we are aware of this
obligation when it comes to us in the form of an *imperative*. Not all
imperatives or commands are connected with morality. To be a
moral imperative, the command must be directed to all men, to all
rational beings. There are three types of imperatives: (1) *Technical
imperatives*—these are rules of skill, and they command us to do
certain things *if* we want to achieve certain ends. Thus *if* we want
to build a bridge, we *must* use materials of a certain strength. But
we do not absolutely have to build a bridge. We can either build a
tunnel or use surface craft to get to the other side. (2) *Prudential
imperatives*—which say, for example, that *if* I want to be popular
with certain people, I *must* do and say certain things. But again, it
is not absolutely necessary that I should achieve this popularity. (3)
Moral imperatives—these moral commands are directed to us as
rational human beings, requiring of us in each case "an action necessary of itself without reference to another end, that is, as objectively necessary." So the moral imperative requires that we tell the
truth not to achieve this or that purpose but because, as we will see
later, our rationality, our being human, requires it.

Hypothetical and Categorical
Imperatives

We have just seen that the technical and prudential imperatives are
connected with the condition "if "; if I want to build a bridge—if

I want to be popular. For this reason, these two imperatives are *hypothetical*, that is, they command our behavior only if we want to achieve bridges or popularity or other ends. By contrast, the moral imperative contains nothing hypothetical—moral commands always require necessarily that we should behave in certain ways. For this reason, the moral imperative is categorical, meaning that there are no "ifs" about what we must do.

Having discussed motives and types of imperatives and having indicated which are hypothectical and which are categorical, we can arrange and relate these ideas in the following way:

Motives	Imperatives	
1. Inclination	1. Technical }	A. Hypothetical: "if"
2. Self-interest	2. Prudential	
3. Duty	3. Moral }	B. Categorical: no "ifs"

The Categorical Imperative

We have emphasized the difference between the behavior of physical objects and the behavior of rational human beings. Kant has a striking way of stating this difference: "Everything in nature works according to laws. Rational beings alone have the faculty of acting according to the conception of laws. . . ." And what is our *conception* of the moral law? The moral law does not give us a list of dos and don'ts. Instead, Kant defined the categorical imperative in terms of basic principles. His point is that once we understand these principles, we will be prepared to know what we ought to do in any given set of circumstances.

The categorical imperative can be formulated in three ways as follows:

1. "Act only on that maxim [principle] whereby you can at the same time will that this maxim should become a universal law."
2. "So act as to treat humanity, whether in your own person or in that of any other, in every case as an end withal, never as a means only."
3. "Always so act that the will could regard itself at the same time as making universal law through its own maxim."

Again, it is clear that the categorical imperative does not give us specific rules of conduct, for it appears to be simply an abstract formula. Still this was what Kant thought moral philosophy should provide us in order to guide our moral behavior, for once we understand the fundamental principle of the moral law, we can then apply it to specific cases. To illustrate how the categorical imperative enables us to discover our moral duties, Kant gives the following example.

> [A man] finds himself forced by necessity to borrow money. He knows that he will not be able to repay it, but sees also that nothing will be lent to him unless he promises stoutly to repay it in a definite time. He desires to make this promise, but he has still so much conscience as to ask himself: Is it not unlawful and inconsistent with duty to get out of a difficulty in this way? Suppose, however, that he resolves to do so, then the maxim of his action would be expressed thus: When I think myself in want of money, I will borrow money and promise to repay it, although I know that I never can do so. Now this principle of self-love or of one's own advantage may perhaps be consistent with my whole future welfare; but the question now is, Is it right? I change then the suggestion of self-love into a universal law, and state the question thus: How would it be if my maxim were a universal law? Then I see at once that it could never hold as a universal law of nature, but would necessarily contradict itself. For supposing it to be a universal law that everyone when he thinks himself in a difficulty should be able to promise whatever he pleases, with the purpose of not keeping his promise, the promise itself would become impossible, as well as the end that one might have in view in it, since no one would consider that anything was promised to him but would ridicule all such statements as vain pretenses.

If one were still to ask why he must tell the truth or why he should avoid the contradiction involved in a false promise, Kant answers that there is something about a human being that makes him resist and resent being treated as a *thing* instead of a *person.* What makes us persons is our rationality, and to be a person, or a rational being, is therefore an end in itself. We become a thing when someone uses us as a means for some other end, such as when one tells us a lie. But however necessary such use of us may be at times, we nevertheless consider ourselves as being of absolute intrinsic worth as persons. The individual human being as possessing absolute worth becomes the basis for the supreme principle of morality: "the foundation of this principle is: *rational nature exists as an end in itself.* All men everywhere want to be considered persons instead of things for the same reason that I do, and this affirmation of the absolute worth of the individual leads to a second formulation of the categorical imperative which says: *So act as to treat humanity, whether in thine own person or in that of any other, in every case as an end withal, never as a means only."*

There is a third formulation of the categorical imperative, which is already implied in the first two, but which Kant wants to make explicit by saying that we should "always so act that the *will could regard itself at the same time as making universal law through its own maxim."* Here Kant speaks of the *autonomy* of the will, that each person through his own act of will legislates the moral law. He distinguishes autonomy from *heteronomy,* the determination (of a law or action) by someone or something other than the self. Thus an heteronomous will is influenced or even determined by desires or inclination. An autonomous will, however, is free and independent, and as such is the "supreme principle of morality." Central to the concept of the autonomy of the will is the idea of *freedom,* the crucial regulative idea, which Kant employed to distinguish between the worlds of science and morality, the phenomenal and noumenal worlds. Kant says that "the *will* is a kind of causality belonging to living beings in so far as they are rational, and *freedom* would be this property of such causality that it can be efficient, independently of foreign causes determining it; just as *physical* necessity is the property that the causality of all irrational being has of being determined to activity by the influence of foreign causes." And again, " . . . I affirm that we must attribute to every rational being which has a will that it has also the idea of freedom and acts entirely under this idea. For in such a being we conceive a reason that is practical, that is, has causality in reference to its objects." The categorical imperative, therefore, speaks of the universality of the moral law, affirms the supreme worth of each rational person, and assigns freedom or autonomy to the will.

Postulate of Freedom

Our experience of the moral law suggested to Kant some further insights concerning the postulate of, or assumptions about, our freedom of the will. Kant did not think it possible to prove or demonstrate that the human will is free. Freedom is an idea that it is necessary to assume because of our experience of moral obligation; that is, "because I must, I can." Although we cannot demonstrate that our wills are free, we are intellectually compelled to assume such freedom, for freedom and morality "are so inseparably united that one might define practical freedom as independence of the will of anything but the moral law alone." How can a person be responsible or have a duty if he is not able or free to fulfill his duty or respond to the moral command? Freedom must be assumed, and as such, it is a major postulate of morality.

READING

THE CATEGORICAL IMPERATIVE
Kant

THE CHIEF GOOD IS A GOOD WILL

Nothing can possibly be conceived in the world, or even out of it, which can be called good without qualification, except a *good will*. Intelligence, wit, judgment, and other *talents* of the mind, however they may be named, or courage, resolution, perseverance, as qualities of temperament, are undoubtedly good and desirable in many respects; but these gifts of nature may also become extremely bad and mischievous if the will which is to make use of them, and which, therefore, constitutes what is called *character,* is not good. It is the same with the *gifts of fortune*. Power, riches, honor, even health, and the general well-being and contentment with one's condition which is called *happiness,* inspire pride, and often presumption, if there is not a good will to correct the influence of these on the mind, and with this also to rectify the whole principle of acting, and adapt it to its end. The sight of a being who is not adorned with a single feature of a pure and good will, enjoying unbroken prosperity, can never give pleasure to an impartial rational spectator. Thus a good will appears to constitute the indispensable condition even of being worthy of happiness.

There are even some qualities which are of service to this good will

---

From Immanuel Kant, "Fundamental Principles of the Metaphysics of Morals," in *Kant's Critique of Practical Reason and Other Works on the Theory of Ethics*, trans. T. K. Abbott, Longmans, London, 1909.

itself, and may facilitate its action, yet which have no intrinsic unconditional value, but always presuppose a good will, and this qualifies the esteem that we justly have for them, and does not permit us to regard them as absolutely good. Moderation in the affections and passions, self-control, and calm deliberation are not only good in many respects, but even seem to constitute part of the intrinsic worth of the person; but they are far from deserving to be called good without qualification, although they have been so unconditionally praised by the ancients. For without the principles of a good will, they may become extremely bad; and the coolness of a villain not only makes him far more dangerous, but also directly makes him more abominable in our eyes than he would have been without it.

THE GOODNESS OF THE WILL INDEPENDENT OF CONSEQUENCES

A good will is good not because of what it performs or effects, not by its aptness for the attainment of some proposed end, but simply by virtue of the volition—that is, it is good in itself, and considered by itself is to be esteemed much higher than all that can be brought about by it in favor of any inclination, nay, even of the sum-total of all inclination. Even if it should happen that, owing to special disfavor or fortune, or the niggardly provision of a stepmotherly nature, this will should wholly lack power to accomplish its purpose, if with its greatest efforts it should yet achieve nothing, and there should remain only the good will (not, to be sure, a mere wish, but the summoning of all means in our power), then, like a jewel, it would still shine by its own light, as a thing which has its whole value in itself. Its usefulness or fruitlessness can neither add to nor take away anything from this value. . . .

FIRST PROPOSITION: TO HAVE MORAL WORTH, AN ACTION MUST BE DONE FROM DUTY

We have then to develop the notion of a will which deserves to be highly esteemed for itself, and is good without a view to anything further, a notion which exists already in the sound natural understanding, requiring rather to be cleared up than to be taught, and which in estimating the value of our actions always takes the first place and constitutes the condition of all the rest. In order to do this, we will take the notion of duty, which includes that of a good will, although implying certain subjective restrictions and hindrances. These, however, far from concealing it or rendering it unrecognizable, rather bring it out by contrast and make it shine forth so much the brighter. . . .

We can readily distinguish whether the action which agrees with duty is done *from duty* or from a selfish view. It is much harder to make this distinction when the action accords with duty, and the subject has besides a *direct* inclination to it. For example, it is always a matter of duty that a dealer should not overcharge an inexperienced purchaser; and wherever there is much commerce the prudent tradesman does not overcharge, but keeps a fixed price for everyone, so that a child buys of him as well as any other. Men are thus *honestly* served; but this is not enough to make us believe that the tradesman has acted from duty and from principles of honesty; his own advantage required it; it is out of the question in this case to suppose that he might besides have a direct inclination in favor of the buyers, so that, as it were, from love he should give no advantage to one over another. Accordingly the action was done neither from duty nor from direct inclination, but merely with a selfish view.

On the other hand, it is a duty to maintain one's life; and, in addition, everyone has also a direct inclination to do so. But on this account the often anxious care which most men take for it has no intrinsic worth, and their maxim has no moral import. They preserve their life *as duty requires,* no doubt, but not *because duty requires.* On the other hand, if adversity and hopeless sorrow have completely taken away the relish for life, if the unfortunate one, strong in mind, indignant at his fate rather than desponding or dejected, wishes for death, and yet preserves his life without loving it—not from inclination or fear, but from duty—then his maxim has a moral worth.

EXAMPLE OF THE PHILANTHROPIST

To be beneficent when we can is a duty; and besides this, there are many minds so sympathetically constituted that, without any other motive of vanity or self-interest, they find a pleasure in spreading joy around them, and can take delight in the satisfaction of others so far as it is their own work. But I maintain that in such a case an action of this kind, however proper, however amiable it may be, has nevertheless no true moral worth, but is on a level with other inclinations, for example, the inclination to honor, which, if it is happily directed to that which is in fact of public utility and accordant with duty, and consequently honorable, deserves praise and encouragement, but not esteem. For the maxim lacks the moral import, namely, that such actions be done *from duty,* not from inclination. Put the case that the mind of that philanthropist was clouded by sorrow of his own, extinguishing all sympathy with the lot of others, and that while he still has the power to benefit others in distress, he is not touched by their trouble because he is absorbed with his own; and now suppose that he tears himself out of this dead insensibility and performs the action without any inclination to it, but simply from duty, then first has his action its genuine moral worth. . . .

SECOND PROPOSITION: MORAL WORTH OF AN ACTION DERIVES NOT FROM RESULTS BUT BECAUSE IT WAS BASED ON PRINCIPLE

The second proposition is: That an action done from duty derives its moral worth, *not from the purpose* which is to be attained by it, but from the maxim by which it is determined, and therefore does not depend on the realization of the object of the action, but merely on the principle of volition by which the action has taken place, without regard to any object of desire. The purposes which we may have in view in our actions, or their effects regarded as ends and springs of the will, cannot give to actions any unconditional or moral worth. In what, then, can their worth lie if it is not to consist in the will and in reference to its expected effect? It cannot lie anywhere but in the *principle of the will* without regard to the ends which can be attained by the action. For the will stands between two roads, and as it must be determined by something, it follows that it must be determined by the formal principle of volition when an action is done from duty, in which case every material principle has been withdrawn from it.

THIRD PROPOSITION: DUTY IS THE NECESSITY OF ACTING FROM RESPECT OF THE (MORAL) LAW

The third proposition, which is a consequence of the two preceding, I would express thus: *Duty is the necessity of acting from respect for the law.* I may have *inclination* for an object as the effect of my proposed action, but I cannot have respect for it just for this reason that it is an effect and not an energy of will. Similarly, I cannot have respect for inclination, whether my own or another's; I can at most, if my own, approve it; of another's, sometimes even love it, that is, look on it as favorable to my own interest. It is only what is connected with my will as a principle, by no means as an effect—what does not subserve my inclination, but overpowers it, or at least in case of choice excludes it from its calculation—in other words, simply the law of itself, which can be an object of respect, and hence a command. Now an action done from duty must wholly exclude the influence of inclination, and with it every object of the will, so that nothing remains which can determine the will except objectively the *law,* and subjectively *pure respect* for this practical law, and consequently the maxim that I should follow this law even to the thwarting of all my inclinations.

Thus the moral worth of an action does not lie in the effect expected from it, nor in any principle of action which requires to borrow its motive from this expected effect. For all these effects—agreeableness of one's condition, and even the promotion of the happiness of others—could have been also brought about by other causes, so that for this there would have been no need of the will of a rational being; whereas it is in this alone that the supreme and unconditional good can be found. The pre-eminent good which we call moral can therefore consist in nothing else than *the conception of law* in itself, *which certainly is only possible in a rational being,* in so far as this conception, and not the expected effect, determines the will.

PROMISE—AN EXAMPLE OF MORAL LAW

But what sort of law can that be the conception of which must determine the will, even without paying any regard to the effect expected from it, in order that this will may be called good absolutely and without qualification?

As I have deprived the will of every impulse which could arise to it from obedience to any law, there remains nothing but the universal conformity of its actions to law in general, which alone is to serve the will as a principle, that is, I am never to act otherwise than *so that I could also will that my maxim should become a universal law* Here, now, it is the simple conformity to law in general, without assuming any particular law applicable to certain actions, that serves the will as its principle, and must so serve it if duty is not to be a vain delusion and a chimerical notion. The common reason of men in its practical judgments perfectly coincides with this, and always has in view the principle here suggested. Let the question be, for example: May I when in distress make a promise with the intention not to keep it? I readily distinguish here between the two significations which the question may have: whether it is prudent or whether it is right to make a false promise? The former may undoubtedly often be the case. I see clearly indeed that it is not enough to extricate myself from a present difficulty by means of this subterfuge, but it must be well considered whether there may not hereafter spring from this lie much greater inconvenience than that from which I now free myself, and as, with all my supposed *cunning,* the consequences cannot be so easily foreseen but that credit once lost may be much more injurious to me than any mischief which I seek to avoid at present, it should be considered whether it would not be more *prudent* to act herein according to a universal maxim, and to make it a habit to promise nothing except with the intention of keeping it. But it is soon clear to me that such a maxim will still only be based on the fear of consequences. Now it is a wholly different thing to be truthful from duty, and to be so from apprehension of injurious consequences. In the first case, the very notion of the action already implies a law for me; in the second case, I must first look about elsewhere to see what results may be combined with it which would affect myself. For to deviate from the principle of duty is beyond all doubt wicked; but to be unfaithful to my maxim of prudence may often be very advantageous to me, although to abide by it is certainly safer. The shortest way, however, and an unerring one, to discover the answer to this question whether a lying promise is consistent with duty, is to ask myself, Should I be content that my maxim (to extricate myself from difficulty by a false promise) should hold good as a universal law, for myself as well as for others; and should I be able to say to myself, "Every one may make a deceitful promise when he finds himself in a difficulty from which he cannot otherwise extricate himself"? Then I presently become aware that, while I can will the lie, I can by no means will that lying should be a universal law. For with such a law there would be no promises at all, since it would be in vain to allege my intention in regard to my future actions to those who would not believe this allegation, or if they over-hastily did so, would pay me back in my own coin. Hence my maxim, as soon as it should be made a universal law, would necessarily destroy itself.

IMPERATIVES: HYPOTHETICAL AND CATEGORICAL

Everything in nature works according to laws. Rational beings alone have
the faculty of acting according to *the conception* of laws—that is, according
to principles, that is, have a *will.*

Now all imperatives command either *hypothetically* or *categorically.*
The former represent the practical necessity of a possible action as means
to something else that is willed (or at least which one might possibly will).
The categorical imperative would be that which represented an action as
necessary of itself without reference to another end, that is, as objectively
necessary. . . .

If [an] action is good only as a means to *something else,* then the imperative is *hypothetical;* if it is conceived as good *in itself* and conforms to reason, then it is *categorical.* . . .

There is therefore but one categorical imperative, namely, this: *Act only
on that maxim whereby you can at the same time will that it should become
a universal law.* . . .

SOME EXAMPLES

A [man] finds in himself a talent which with the help of some culture might
make him a useful man in many respects. But he finds himself in comfort-
able circumstances and prefers to indulge in pleasure rather than to take
pains in enlarging and improving his happy natural capacities. He asks,
however, whether his maxim of neglect of his natural gifts, besides agreeing
with his inclination to indulgence, agrees also with what is called duty. He
sees then that a system of nature could indeed subsist with such a universal
law, although men (like the South Sea islanders) should let their talents rest
and resolve to devote their lives merely to idleness, amusement, and propagation of their species—in a word, to enjoyment; but he cannot possibly
will that this should be a universal law of nature, or be implanted in us as
such by a natural instinct. For, as a rational being, he necessarily wills that
his faculties be developed, since they serve him, and have been given him,
for all sorts of possible purposes.

[Another] who is in prosperity, while he sees that others have to contend with great wretchedness and that he could help them, thinks: What
concern is it of mine? Let everyone be as happy as Heaven pleases, or as
he can make himself; I will take nothing from him nor even envy him, only
I do not wish to contribute anything to his welfare or to his assistance in
distress! Now no doubt, if such a mode of thinking were a universal law,
the human race might very well subsist, and doubtless even better than in
a state in which everyone talks of sympathy and good-will, or even takes
care occasionally to put it into practice, but, on the other side, also cheats
when he can, betrays the rights of men, or otherwise violates them. But
although it is possible that a universal law of nature might exist in accor-

dance with that maxim, it is impossible to *will* that such a principle should have the universal validity of a law of nature. For a will which resolved this would contradict itself, inasmuch as many cases might occur in which one would have need of the love and sympathy of others, and in which, by such a law of nature, sprung from his own will, he would deprive himself of all hopes of the aid he desires.

THE SUPREME PRACTICAL PRINCIPLE OF ETHICS

Let us suppose that there were something *whose existence* has *in itself* an absolute worth, something which, being *an end in itself,* could be a source of definite laws, then in this and this alone would lie the source of a possible categorical imperative, that is, a practical law.

Now I say: man and generally any rational being *exists* as an end in himself, *not merely as a means* to be arbitrarily used by this or that will, but in all his actions, whether they concern himself or other rational beings, must be always regarded at the same time as an end. All objects of the inclinations have only a conditional worth; for if the inclinations and the wants founded on them did not exist, then their object would be without value. But the inclinations themselves, being sources of want, are so far from having an absolute worth for which they should be desired that, on the contrary, it must be the universal wish of every rational being to be wholly free from them. Thus the worth of any object which is *to be acquired* by our action is always conditional. Beings whose existence depends not on our will but on nature's, have nevertheless, if they are not rational beings, only a relative value as means, and are therefore called *things;* rational beings, on the contrary, are called *persons,* because their very nature points them out as ends in themselves, that is, as something which must not be used merely as means, and so far therefore restricts freedom of action (and is an object of respect). These, therefore, are not merely subjective ends whose existence has a worth *for us* as an effect of our action, but *objective ends,* that is, things whose existence is an end in itself—an end, moreover, for which no other can be substituted, which they should subserve *merely* as means, for otherwise nothing whatever would possess *absolute worth;* but if all worth were conditioned and therefore contingent, then there would be no supreme practical principle of reason whatever.

If then there is a supreme practical principle or, in respect of the human will, a categorical imperative, it must be one which, being drawn from the conception of that which is necessarily an end for everyone because it is *an end in itself,* constitutes an *objective* principle of will, and can therefore serve as a universal practical law. The foundation of this principle is: rational nature exists as an end in itself. Man necessarily conceives his own existence as being so; so far then this is a *subjective* principle of human actions. But every other rational being regards its existence similarly, just on the same rational principle that holds for me; so that it is at the same time an objective principle from which as a supreme practical law all laws of the will must be capable of being deduced. Accordingly the practical imperative will be as follows: *So act as to treat humanity, whether in thine own person or in that of any other, in every case as an end withal, never as a means only.*

CHAPTER 5

PLEASURE VERSUS PAIN

Bentham and Mill

Jeremy Bentham was born in London in 1748. A brilliant youngster, he entered Oxford when he was twelve years old. He was not happy at Oxford, because he disapproved of the vice and laziness of his fellow students. Nevertheless, at the age of fifteen he took his B.A. and then entered Lincoln's Inn in London to study law in accordance with his father's wishes. He returned to Oxford to hear the lectures of the University's first professor of jurisprudence, Sir William Blackstone, who was expounding his theory of "natural rights." Bentham rejected Blackstone's theory of natural rights, calling it "rhetorical nonsense, nonsense on stilts." After taking an M.A. degree, he returned once again to London but decided against the practice of law. Instead, he entered on a literary career in which he sought to bring some order out of the deplorable condition both of the law and of the social realities which that law made possible. He became an effective reformer. His first book, *Fragment on Government,* an attack on Blackstone, appeared in 1776, the same year as the Declaration of Independence, which Bentham thought was a confused and absurd jumble of words in which the authors had all along assumed the natural rights of man, which was what they wanted to demonstrate. His most famous book is his *Introduction to the Principles of Morals and Legislation*. He remained a powerful public figure until his death in 1832 at the age of eighty-four.

___

For more than a hundred years, the moral and political philosophy of Jeremy Bentham and John Stuart Mill influenced the thinking and political action of Englishmen. Rarely has a way of thinking captured the imagination of generations of men so completely as did this philosophy called "utilitarianism." What attracted people to it was its simplicity and its way of confirming what most men already believed, for it set forth the general thesis that pleasure and happiness are what everyone desires. From this simple fact that everyone desires pleasure and happiness, the utilitarians inferred that the whole moral idea of what is "good" can be best understood in terms of the principle of happiness, which they spoke of as "the greatest happiness of the greatest number," and by which they meant that "good" is achieved when the aggregate of pleasure is greater than the aggregate of pain. An act is good, therefore, if it is useful in achieving pleasure and diminishing pain.

Such a swift account of what is good had not only the merit of simplicity but had, according to Bentham and Mill, the additional virtue of scientific accuracy. Whereas earlier theories of ethics, which defined the good as the commands of God or the dictates of reason or the fulfillment of the purposes of human nature or the duty to obey the Categorical Imperative, raised vexing questions as to just what these commands, dictates, purposes, and imperatives consist of, the principle of utility seemed to measure every act by a standard everyone knows, namely, pleasure. To bypass the moral teachings of theology and the classical theories of Plato and Aristotle as well as the recently formulated ethics of Kant, the utilitarians followed in the philosophical footsteps of their own countrymen, the British empiricists.

In moral philosophy, Bentham and Mill were not innovators, for the principle of utilitarianism had already been stated in its general form by their predecessors Hobbes and Hume. What makes Bentham and Mill stand out as the most famous of the utilitarians is that they, more than the others, succeeded in connecting the prin-

ciple of utility with the many problems of their age, thereby providing nineteenth-century England with a philosophical basis not
only for moral thought but also for practical reform.

Principle of Utility

Bentham begins his *Introduction to the Principle of Morals and Legislation* with the classic sentence: "Nature has placed mankind
under the governance of two sovereign masters, *pain* and *pleasure.*
It is for them alone to point out what we ought to do, as well as
determine what we shall do." To be subject to pleasure and pain is
a fact we all recognize, and that we desire pleasure and want to
avoid pain is also a fact. But in a few sentences, without indicating
just how he does it, Bentham moves from the *fact* that we *do* desire
pleasure to the *judgment* that we *ought* to pursue pleasure. He
moves from a psychological fact to the moral principle of utility. By
the *principle of utility* he means "that principle which approves or
disapproves of every action whatsoever, according to the tendency
which it appears to have to augment or diminish . . . happiness. . . ." In Bentham's language, to *approve* or *disapprove* is the
same as saying about an act that it is *good* or *bad,* or *right* or *wrong.*
Between saying that men desire pleasure and saying that they *ought*
to or that it is *right* that they should, there is a gap that Bentham
does not fill with any careful argument. Still he says that it is only
about an action "that is conformable to the principle of utility" that
one can always say either that it "ought to be done" or that "it is a
right action. . . ." Tying "ought" to "pleasure," says Bentham, is
the only way "the words *ought,* and *right* and *wrong,* and others of
that stamp have a meaning: when, otherwise, they have none."
Bentham was aware that he had not proved that happiness is the
basis of "good" and "right," but this was not an oversight. It is
rather the very nature of the principle of utility, he says, that one
cannot demonstrate its validity: "Is it susceptible to any proof? It
should seem not: for that which is used to prove every thing else,
cannot itself be proved: a chain of proofs must have their commencement somewhere. To give such proof is as impossible as it is
needless."

But if Bentham could not *prove* the validity of the principle of

Bentham (*The Bettmann Archive*)

utility, he felt that he could at least demonstrate that so-called higher theories of morality were either reducible to the principle of utility or else were inferior to this principle because they had no clear meaning or could not be consistently followed. For example, Bentham takes the Social Contract theory as an explanation for our obligation to obey the law. Apart from the difficulty of determining whether there ever was such a contract or agreement, Bentham argues that the obligation to obey, even in the Social Contract theory itself, rests on the principle of utility, for it really says that the greatest happiness of the greatest number can be achieved only if we obey the law. This being the case, why develop an involved and scientifically dubious theory when the whole problem can be swiftly solved by saying simply that obedience is better because disobedience does more harm than good? The case is the same when others say that goodness and right in an act are determined by our *moral sense* or *understanding* or *right reason* or the *theological principle* of the will of God. All these, says Bentham, are similar to each other and are reducible to the principle of utility. For example, "The principle of theology refers everything to God's pleasure. But what is God's pleasure? God does not, he confessedly does not now, either speak or write to us. How then are we to know what is his pleasure? By observing what is our own pleasure and pronouncing it to be his." Only pains and pleasures, therefore, give us the real value of actions, and in private and public life we are in the last analysis all concerned with maximizing happiness.

Sanctions

Just as pleasure and pain give the real values to acts, so do they also constitute the efficient causes of our behavior. Bentham distinguishes four sources from which pleasure and pain can come and identifies these as causes of our behavior, calling them *sanctions*. A "sanction" is what gives binding force to a rule of conduct or to a law, and these four sanctions are termed the *physical*, the *political*, the *moral*, and the *religious* sanctions. Bentham indicates the special character of each sanction by an example, where "a man's goods, or his person, are consumed by fire." He explains:

> If this happened to him by what is called accident, it was a calamity: if by reason of his own imprudence (for instance, from his neglecting to put his candle out), it may be styled a punishment of the *physical* sanction: if it happened to him by the sentence of the political magistrate, a punishment belonging to the *political* sanction; that is, what is commonly called a punishment: if for want of any assistance which his *neighbor* withheld from him out of some dislike to his moral character, a punishment of the *moral* sanction: if by an immediate act of *God's* displeasure, manifested on account of some *sin* committed by

him . . . a punishment of the *religious* sanction.

In all these areas, then, the sanction, or the efficient cause of behavior, is the threat of pain. In public life, the legislator understands that men feel bound to do certain acts only when such acts have some clear sanction connected with them, and this sanction consists of some form of pain if the mode of conduct prescribed by the legislator is violated by the citizen. The legislator's chief concern is, therefore, to decide what forms of behavior will tend to increase the happiness of society and what sanctions will be most likely to bring about such increased happiness. The word "obligation" was given concrete meaning by Bentham's concept of sanction, for obligation now meant not some undefined duty, but the prospect of pain if one did not obey the moral or legal rule. Unlike Kant, who argued that the morality of an act depends on having the right motive and not on the consequences of the act, the utilitarians took the opposite position, saying that morality depends directly on the consequences. Bentham admits that some motives are more likely than others to lead to more useful conduct, that is, conduct which increases happiness, but it is still pleasure and not the motive that confers the quality of morality on the act. Moreover, Bentham took the position that, especially in the social arena, where the law is at work, the law can punish only those who have actually inflicted pain, whatever their motive may be, although some exceptions were admitted. While it may be true that the legislator cannot always take account of motives, this whole question of motives does loom large in morality. Bentham, however, seemed to regard both the moral and legal obligations as being similar in that in both cases the external consequences of the action were considered more important than the motives behind them.

Pleasure-Pain Calculus

Each individual and each legislator is concerned with avoiding pain and achieving pleasure. But pleasures and pains differ from each other and therefore have different values. With an attempt at mathematical precision, Bentham speaks of units, or what he calls "lots," of pleasure or pain, suggesting that before we act, we should, and really do, calculate the values of these lots. Their value, taken by themselves, will be greater or less depending, says Bentham, on a pleasure's *intensity, duration, certainty,* and *propinquity* or nearness. When we consider not only the pleasure by itself but what consequences it can lead to, other circumstances must be calculated, such as a pleasure's *fecundity,* or its chances of being followed by more of the same sensations, that is, by more pleasure, and its *purity,* or the chances that pleasure will not be followed by pleasure but by pain. The seventh circumstance is a pleasure's *extent,* that is, the number of persons to whom it extends or who are affected by it.

As this calculus indicates, Bentham was interested chiefly in the quantitative aspects of pleasure, so that all actions are equally good if they produce the same amount of pleasure. Therefore, we "sum up all the values of all the *pleasures* on the one side, and those of all the *pains* on the other. The balance, if it be on the side of pleasure, will give the *good* tendency of the act . . . if on the side of pain, the *bad* tendency. . . ."

Whether we actually do engage in this kind of calculation was a question Bentham anticipated, and he replies that "there are some, perhaps, who . . . may look upon the nicety employed in the adjustment of such rules as so much labor lost: for gross ignorance, they will say, never troubles itself about laws, and passion does not calculate. But the evil of ignorance admits of cure: and . . . when matters of such importance as pain and pleasure are at stake, and these in the highest degree . . . who is there that does not calculate? Men calculate, some with less exactness, indeed, and some with more: but all men calculate."

Mill

Born in 1806 in London, John Stuart Mill was put through a rigorous "educational experiment" by his father. So intense was his tutoring between the ages of three and fourteen that later he could say, "Through the training bestowed on me by my father, I started, I may fairly say, with an advantage of a quarter of a century over my contemporaries." But the heavy emphasis on memorizing and analytical thinking caused young Mill to fall into "a dull state of nerves." He said later that the overemphasis on analysis, without at the same time developing adequately his emotions and feelings, led to his breakdown. "I was, I said to myself, left stranded at the beginning of my voyage, with a well equipped ship and rudder, but no sail. . . . " He therefore turned to such authors as Coleridge, Carlyle, and Wordsworth, who spoke to his feelings. "The cultivation of the feelings," he said, "became one of the cardinal points in my ethical and philosophical creed." Besides his book on ethics entitled *Utilitarianism,* he published his *System of Logic, Principles of Political Economy,* an *Essay on Liberty,* and other books. He died in 1873 at the age of sixty-seven.

John Stuart Mill said that all ethical philosophies could be reduced, in the last analysis, to the simple principle of *utility.* What is good or bad, right or wrong can be tested by the principle of utility in this way: An action is good if it is useful (has utility) in producing pleasure or happiness. This way of thinking became known as "utilitarianism," which taught that the "good" is achieved when the amount of pleasure is greater than the amount of pain. When people act according to the principle of utility, they will achieve "the greatest happiness for the greatest number."

As we have seen, this principle of utility had been developed earlier by John Stuart Mill's fellow Englishman Jeremy Bentham (1748–1832). Mill had known Bentham well, "owing," he says "to the close intimacy which existed between Mr. Bentham and my father." In his *Autobiography* he describes how influential his father was in making Bentham's ideas of utility well known: "It was my father's opinions which gave the distinguishing character to Benthamic or Utilitarian propagandism . . . [since] my father was the earliest Englishman of any mark, who thoroughly understood and in the main adopted, Bentham's general views of ethics. . . . "

John Stuart Mill (*The Bettmann Archive*)

Mill's Version
of Utilitarianism

Mill's purpose in writing his famous essay *Utilitarianism* was to
defend the principle of utility that he learned from his father and
Bentham against their critics. In the course of his defense, however,
he made such important changes in this theory that his version of
utilitarianism turned out to be different from Bentham's in several
ways. His definition of the doctrine of utility was perfectly consistent with what Bentham had taught. Mill writes, "The creed which
accepts as the foundation of morals Utility, or the greatest Happiness Principle, holds that actions are right in proportion as they
tend to promote happiness, wrong as they tend to produce the

83

reverse of happiness. By happiness is intended pleasure, and the absence of pain; by unhappiness, pain, and the privation of pleasure." But even though he started with the same general ideas as Bentham did, especially relating *happiness* with *pleasure*, Mill soon took a different tack by his novel treatment of the role of pleasure in morality.

Qualitative versus Quantitative Approach

Bentham had said that pleasures differ only in their amount, that is, that different ways of behaving produce different *quantities* of pleasure. He had also said that "pushpin is as good as poetry," by which he meant that the only test for goodness is the amount of pleasure an act can produce. It would have to follow in this calculation that all kinds of behavior that produce the same amount of pleasure would be equally good, whether such behavior be the game of pushpin or the writing or enjoyment of poetry. Bentham was so convinced that the simple quantitative measurement of pleasure is the chief test of the morality of an act that he even suggested that "there ought to be a moral thermometer." Just as a thermometer measures the different degrees of heat or temperature, so also a "moral thermometer" could measure the degrees of happiness or unhappiness. This analogy with a thermometer reveals Bentham's exclusive emphasis on quantity in his treatment of goodness and pleasure. To him, just as it is possible to achieve the same degree of heat whether one burns coal, wood, or oil, so also it is possible to achieve equal quantities of pleasure through pushpin, poetry, or other modes of behavior. Goodness, for Bentham, is not connected with any particular *kinds* of behavior, but only with the amounts of pleasure as measured by his "calculus." Inevitably, the utilitarians were accused of being moral relativists who had rejected all moral absolutes in favor of each person's own opinion about what is good. John Stuart Mill sought to defend utilitarianism against these charges, but in the course of his defense he was drawn into the position of altering Bentham's quantitative approach to pleasure by substituting instead a qualitative approach.

Whereas Bentham had said that "pushpin is as good as poetry,"

Mill said that he would "rather be Socrates dissatisfied than a pig satisfied." Pleasures, said Mill, differ from each other in kind and quality, not only in quantity. He took his stand with the ancient Epicureans, who had also been attacked for their "degrading" emphasis on pleasure as the end of all behavior. The Epicureans replied that it was their critics who had a degrading conception of human nature, for in their attacks they assumed that men are capable of only those pleasures of which swine are capable. But this assumption is obviously false, said Mill along with the Epicureans, because "human beings have faculties more elevated than the animal appetites, and when once conscious of them, do not regard anything as happiness which does not include their gratification." The pleasures of the intellect, of feelings and imagination, and of the moral sentiments have a higher value than the pleasures of mere sensation.

Although Mill had referred to these higher pleasures originally in order to answer the critics of utilitarianism, his concern over higher pleasures led him to criticize the very foundation of Bentham's doctrine of utility. Mill said that "it would be absurd that . . . the estimation of pleasures should be supposed to depend on quantity alone." For Mill, the mere quantity of pleasure produced by an act was of secondary importance when a choice had to be made between pleasures. If a person, says Mill, is acquainted with two different kinds of pleasures and places one of these far above the other in his preference, "even though knowing it to be attended with a greater amount of discontent, and would not resign it for any quantity of the other pleasure which [man's] nature is capable of, we are justified in ascribing to the preferred enjoyment a superiority in quality, so far outweighing quantity as to render it, in comparison, of small account."

The qualitative aspect of pleasure, Mill thought, was as much an observable fact as was the quantitative element on which Bentham placed his entire emphasis. Mill departed even further from Bentham by grounding the qualitative difference between pleasures in the structure of human nature, thereby focusing on certain human faculties whose full use, instead of pleasure only, were to be the test of true happiness and, therefore, of goodness. For this reason, says Mill, "few human creatures would consent to be changed into any of the lower animals, for a promise of the fullest allowance of a beast's pleasures; no intelligent human being would consent to be a fool, no instructed person would be an ignoramus, no person of feeling and conscience would be selfish and base, even though they should be persuaded that the fool, the dunce, or the rascal is better satisfied with his lot than they are with theirs." Pleasures, according to Mill, have to be graded not for their quantity, but for their quality. But if pleasures must be graded for their quality, pleasure is no longer the standard of morality; if, that is, only the full use of our higher faculties can lead us to true happiness, the standard of goodness in behavior has to do not with pleasure directly, but with the fulfillment of our human faculties.

Bentham had simply assumed that we *ought* to choose those acts which produce for us the greatest quantity of pleasure. He also assumed that we should naturally help other people achieve happiness because in that way we should secure our own, and this was his *greatest happiness principle.* Mill accepted this point but added the quality of *altruism* to this principle, saying that "the happiness which forms the utilitarian standard of what is right in conduct, is not the agent's own happiness, but that of all concerned." Mill modified Bentham's egoistic pleasure seeking by indicating "as between his own happiness and that of others, utilitarianism requires [each of us] to be as strictly impartial as a disinterested and benevolent spectator." Mill thus gives the impression that the true utilitarian interprets the greatest happiness principle to mean not *my* greatest happiness but the greatest happiness of the greatest number. He could say, therefore, that "in the golden rule of Jesus of Nazareth, we read the complete spirit of the ethics of utility. To do as one would be done by, and to love one's neighbor as oneself, constitute the ideal of utilitarian perfection." Mill is here trying to defend utilitarian ethics from the charge of egoism, and to emphasize further the "golden rule" character of utilitarianism, he adds that

> Utility would enjoin, first, that laws and social arrangements should place the happiness, . . . or the interest of every individual, as nearly as possible in harmony with the interest of the whole; and secondly, that education and opinion, which have so vast a power over human character, should so use that power as to establish in the mind of every individual an indissolvable association between his own happiness and the good of the whole . . . so that a direct impulse to promote the general good may be in every individual one of the habitual motives of action. . . .

READING

OF THE PRINCIPLE OF UTILITY
Bentham

I. Nature has placed mankind under the governance of two sovereign masters, *pain* and *pleasure*. It is for them alone to point out what we ought to do, as well as to determine what we shall do. On the one hand the standard of right and wrong, on the other the chain of causes and effects, are fastened to their throne. They govern us in all we do, in all we say, in all we think: every effort we can make to throw off our subjection, will serve but to demonstrate and confirm it. In words a man may pretend to abjure their empire: but in reality he will remain subject to it all the while. The *principle of utility* recognises this subjection, and assumes it for the foundation of that system, the object of which is to rear the fabric of felicity by the hands of reason and of law. Systems which attempt to queston it, deal in sounds instead of sense, in caprice instead of reason, in darkness instead of light. By the principle of utility is meant that principle which approves or disapproves of every action whatsoever, according to the tendency which it appears to have augment or diminish the happiness of the party whose interest is in question: or, what is the same thing in other words, to promote or to oppose that happiness. I say of every action whatsoever; and therefore not only of every action of a private individual, but of every measure of government. . . .

III. By utility is meant that property in any object, whereby it tends to produce benefit, advantage, pleasure, good, or happiness, (all this in the present case comes to the same thing) or (what comes again to the same thing) to prevent the happening of mischief, pain, evil, or unhappiness to the party whose interest is considered: if that party be the community in general, then the happiness of the community: if a particular individual, then the happiness of that individual.

IV. The interest of the community is one of the most general expressions that can occur in the phraseology of morals: no wonder that the meaning of it is often lost. When it has a meaning, it is this. The community is a fictitious *body*, composed of the individual persons who are considered as constituting as it were its *members*. The interest of the community then

---

From Jeremy Bentham, *An Introduction to The Principles of Morals and Legislation,* 1789.

is, what?—the sum of the interests of the several members who compose it.

V. It is in vain to talk of the interest of the community, without understanding what is the interest of the individual. A thing is said to promote the interest, or to be *for* the interest, of an individual, when it tends to add to the sum total of his pleasures: or, what comes to the same thing, to diminish the sum total of his pains.

VI. An action then may be said to be conformable to the principle of utility, or, for shortness sake, to utility, (meaning with respect to the community at large) when the tendency it has to augment the happiness of the community is greater than any it has to diminish it. . . .

X. Of an action that is conformable to the principle of utility one may always say either that it is one that ought to be done, or at least that it is not one that ought not to be done. One may say also, that it is right it should be done; at least that it is not wrong it should be done: that it is a right action; at least that it is not a wrong action. When thus interpreted, the words *ought,* and *right* and *wrong,* and others of that stamp, have a meaning: when otherwise, they have none.

XI. Has the rectitude of this principle been ever formally contested? It should seem that it had, by those who have not known what they have been meaning. Is it susceptible of any direct proof? It should seem not: for that which is used to prove everything else, cannot itself be proved: a chain of proofs must have their commencement somewhere. To give such proof is as impossible as it is needless. . . .

VALUE OF A LOT OF PLEASURE OR PAIN, HOW TO BE MEASURED

I. Pleasures then, and the avoidance of pains, are the *ends* which the legislator has in view: it behoves him therefore to understand their *value.* Pleasures and pains are the *instruments* he has to work with: it behoves him therefore to understand their force, which is again, in other words, their value.

II. To a person considered *by himself,* the value of a pleasure or pain considered *by itself,* will be greater or less, according to the four following circumstances:

1 Its *intensity.*
2 Its *duration.*
3 Its *certainty* or *uncertainty.*
4 Its *propinquity* or *remoteness.*

III. These are the circumstances which are to be considered in estimating a pleasure or a pain considered each of them by itself. But when the value of any pleasure or pain is considered for the purpose of estimating the tendency of any *act* by which it is produced, there are two other circumstances to be taken into the account; these are,

1 Its *fecundity,* or the chance it has of being followed by sensations of the *same* kind: that is, pleasures, if it be a pleasure: pains, if it be a pain.

2 Its *purity,* or the chance it has of *not* being followed by sensations of the *opposite* kind: that is, pains, if it be a pleasure: pleasures, if it be a pain.

3 These two last, however, are in strictness scarcely to be deemed properties of the pleasure or the pain itself; they are not, therefore, in strictness to be taken into the account of the value of that pleasure or that pain. They are in strictness to be deemed properties only of the act, or other event, by which such pleasure or pain has been produced; and accordingly are only to be taken into the account of the tendency of such act or such event.

IV. To a *number* of persons, with reference to each of whom the value of a pleasure or a pain is considered, it will be greater or less, according to seven circumstances: to wit, the six preceding ones; *viz.*

1 Its *intensity.*

2 Its *duration.*

3 Its *certainty* or *uncertainty.*

4 Its *propinquity* or *remoteness.*

5 Its *fecundity.*

6 Its *purity.*

7 And one other; to wit:

8 Its *extent;* that is, the number of persons to whom it *extends;* or (in other words) who are affected by it.

V. To take an exact account then of the general tendency of any act, by which the interests of a community are affected, proceed as follows. Begin with any one person of those whose interests seem most immediately to be affected by it: and take an account,

1 Of the value of each distinguishable *pleasure* which appears to be produced by it in the *first* instance.

2 Of the value of each *pain* which appears to be produced by it in the *first* instance.

3 Of the value of each pleasure which appears to be produced by it *after* the first. This constitutes the *fecundity* of the first *pleasure* and the *impurity* of the first *pain.*

4 Of the value of each *pain* which appears to be produced by it after the first. This constitutes the *fecundity* of the first *pain,* and the *impurity* of the first pleasure.

5 Sum up all the values of all the *pleasures* on the one side, and those of all the pains on the other. The balance, if it be on the side of pleasure, will give the *good* tendency of the act upon the whole, with respect to the interests of that *individual* person; if on the side of pain, the *bad* tendency of it upon the whole.

6 Take an account of the *number* of persons whose interests appear to be concerned; and repeat the above process with respect to each. *Sum*

up the numbers expressive of the degrees of *good* tendency, which the act has, with respect to each individual, in regard to whom the tendency of it is *good* upon the whole: do this again with respect to each individual, in regard to whom the tendency of it is *bad* upon the whole. Take the *balance;* which, if on the side of *pleasure,* will give the general the total number or community of individuals concerned; if on the side of pain, the general *evil-tendency,* with respect to the same community.

VI. It is not to be expected that this process should be strictly pursued previously to every moral judgment, or to every legislative or judicial operation. It may, however, be always kept in view: and as near as the process actually pursued on these occasions approaches to it, so near will such process approach to the character of an exact one

VII. The same process is alike applicable to pleasure and pain, in whatever shape they appear: and by whatever denomination they are distinguished: to pleasure, whether it be called *good* (which is properly the cause or instrument of pleasure) or *profit* (which is distant pleasure, or the cause or instrument of distant pleasure,) or *convenience,* or *advantage, benefit, emolument, happiness,* and so forth: to pain, whether it be called *evil,* (which corresponds to *good*) or *mischief,* or *inconvenience,* or *disadvantage,* or *loss,* or *unhappiness,* and so forth.

VIII. Nor is this a novel and unwarranted, any more than it is a useless theory. In all this there is nothing but what the practice of mankind, wheresoever they have a clear view of their own interest, is perfectly conformable to. An article of property, an estate in land, for instance, is valuable, on what account? On account of the pleasures of all kinds which it enables a man to produce, and what comes to the same thing the pains of all kinds which it enables him to avert. But the value of such an article of property is universally understood to rise or fall according to the length or shortness of the time which a man has in it: the certainty or uncertainty of its coming into possession: and the nearness or remoteness of the time at which, if at all, it is to come into possession. As to the *intensity* of the pleasures which a man may derive from it, this is never thought of, because it depends upon the use which each particular person may come to make of it; which cannot be estimated till the particular pleasures he may come to derive from it, or the particular pains he may come to exclude by means of it, are brought to view. For the same reason, neither does he think of the *fecundity or purity* of those pleasures. . . .

READING

THE CALCULUS OF PAIN AND PLEASURE
Mill

PLEASURE—THE "GREATEST HAPPINESS" PRINCIPLE

The creed which accepts as the foundation of morals "utility" or the "greatest happiness principle" holds that actions are right in proportion as they tend to promote happiness, wrong as they tend to produce the reverse of happiness. By happiness is intended pleasure, and the absence of pain; by unhappiness, pain, and the privation of pleasure. To give a clear view of the moral standard set up by the theory, much more requires to be said; in particular, what things it includes in the ideas of pain and pleasure; and to what extent this is left an open question. But these supplementary explanations do not affect the theory of life on which this theory of morality is grounded—namely, that pleasure and freedom from pain are the only things desirable as ends; and that all desirable things (which are as numerous in the utilitarian as in any other scheme) are desirable either for the pleasure inherent in themselves, or as means to the promotion of pleasure and the prevention of pain.

Now such a theory of life excites in many minds, and among them in some of the most estimable in feeling and purpose, inveterate dislike. To suppose that life has (as they express it) no higher end than pleasure—no better and nobler object of desire and pursuit—they designate as utterly mean and groveling; as a doctrine worthy only of swine, to whom the followers of Epicurus were, at a very early period, contemptuously likened; and modern holders of the doctrine are occasionally made the subject of equally polite comparsions by its German, French, and English assailants.

From John Stuart Mill, *Utilitarianism*, chap. 2, "What Utilitarianism Is," London, 1863.

When thus attacked, the Epicureans have always answered that it is not they, but their accusers, who represent human nature in a degrading light, since the accusation supposes human beings to be capable of no pleasures except those of which swine are capable. If this supposition were true, the charge could not be gainsaid, but would then be no longer an imputation; for if the sources of pleasure were precisely the same to human beings and to swine, the rule of life which is good enough for the one would be good enough for the other. The comparison of the Epicurean life to that of beasts is felt as degrading, precisely because a beast's pleasures do not satisfy a human being's conceptions of happiness. Human beings have faculties more elevated than the animal appetites and, when once made conscious of them, do not regard anything as happiness which does not include their gratification. I do not, indeed, consider the Epicureans to have been by any means faultless in drawing out their scheme of consequences from the utilitarian principle. To do this in any sufficient manner, many Stoic, as well as Christian, elements require to be included. But there is no known Epicurean theory of life which does not assign to the pleasures of the intellect, of the feelings and imagination, and of the moral sentiments, a much higher value of pleasures than to those of mere sensation. It must be admitted, however, that utilitarian writers in general have placed the superiority of mental over bodily pleasures chiefly in the greater permanency, safety, uncostliness, etc., of the former—that is, in their circumstantial advantages rather than in their intrinsic nature. And on all these points utilitarians have fully proved their case; but they might have taken the other and, as it may be called, higher ground with entire consistency. It is quite compatible with the principle of utility to recognize the fact that some kinds of pleasure are more desirable and more valuable than others. It would be absurd that, while, in estimating all other things, quality is considered as well as quantity, the estimation of pleasures should be supposed to depend on quantity alone.

SOME PLEASURES BETTER THAN OTHERS

If I am asked what I mean by difference of quality in pleasures, or what makes one pleasure more valuable than another, merely as a pleasure, except its being greater in amount, there is but one possible answer. Of two pleasures, if there be one to which all or almost all who have experience of both give a decided preference, irrespective of a feeling of moral obligation to prefer it, that is the more desirable pleasure. If one of the two, is, by those who are competently acquainted with both, placed so far above the other that they prefer it, even though knowing it to be attended with a greater amount of discontent, and would not resign it for any quantity of the other pleasure which their nature is capable of, we are justified in ascribing to the preferred enjoyment a superiority in quality so far outweighing quantity as to render it, in comparison, of small account.

Now it is an unquestionable fact that those who are equally acquainted with and equally capable of appreciating and enjoying both, do give a most marked preference to the manner of existence which employs their higher faculties. Few human creatures would consent to be changed into any of the lower animals for a promise of the fullest allowance of a beast's pleasures; no intelligent human being would consent to be a fool, no instructed person would be an ignoramus, no person of feeling and conscience would be selfish and base, even though they should be persuaded that the fool, the dunce, or the rascal is better satisfied with his lot than they are with theirs. They would not resign what they possess more than he for the most complete satisfaction of all the desires which they have in common with him. If they ever fancy they would, it is only in cases of unhappiness so extreme that to escape from it they would exchange their lot for almost any other, however undesirable in their own eyes. A being of higher faculties requires more to make him happy, is capable probably of more acute suffering, and certainly accessible to it at more points, than one of an inferior type; but in spite of these liabilities, he can never really wish to sink into what he feels to be a lower grade of existence. We may give what explanation we please of this unwillingness; we may attribute it to pride, a name which is given indiscriminately to some of the most and to some of the least estimable feelings of which mankind are capable: we may refer it to the love of liberty and personal independence, an appeal to which was with the Stoics one of the most effective means for the inculcation of it; to the love of power or to the love of excitement, both of which do really enter into and contribute to it; but its most appropriate appellation is a sense of dignity, which all human beings possess in one form or other, and in some, though by no means in exact, proportion to their higher faculties, and which is so essential a part of the happiness of those in whom it is strong that nothing which conflicts with it could be otherwise than momentarily an object of desire to them. Whoever supposes that this preference takes place at a sacrifice of happiness—that the superior being, in anything like equal circumstances, is not happier than the inferior—confounds the two very different ideas of happiness and content. It is indisputable that the being whose capacities of enjoyment are low has the greatest chance of having them fully satisfied; and a highly endowed being will always feel that any happiness which he can look for, as the world is constituted, is imperfect. But he can learn to bear its imperfections, if they are at all bearable; and they will not make him envy the being who is indeed unconscious of the imperfections, but only because he feels not at all the good which those imperfections qualify. It is better to be a human being dissatisfied than a pig satisfied; better to be Socrates dissatisfied than a fool satisfied. And if the fool, or the pig, are of a different opinion, it is because they only know their own side of the question. The other party to the comparison knows both sides.

WHO IS THE BEST JUDGE OF PLEASURES?

It may be objected that many who are capable of the higher pleasures occa-sionally, under the influence of temptation, postpone them to the lower. But this is quite compatible with a full appreciation of the intrinsic superi-ority of the higher. Men often, from infirmity of character, make their elec-tion of the nearer good, though they know it to be the less valuable; and this no less when the choice is between two bodily pleasures than when it is between bodily and mental. They pursue sensual indulgences to the injury of health, though perfectly aware that health is the greater good. It may be further objected that many who begin with youthful enthusiasm for everything noble, as they advance in years, sink into indolence and selfish-ness. But I do not believe that those who undergo this very common change voluntarily choose the lower description of pleasures in preference to the higher. I believe that, before they devote themselves exclusively to the one, they have already become incapable of the other. Capacity for the nobler feelings is in most natures a very tender plant, easily killed, not only by hostile influences, but by mere want of sustenance; and in the majority of young persons it speedily dies away if the occupations to which their position in life had devoted them, and the society into which it has thrown them, are not favorable to keeping that higher capacity in exercise. Men lose their high aspirations as they lose their intellectual tastes, because they have not time or opportunity for indulging them; and they addict them-selves to inferior pleasures, not because they deliberately prefer them, but because they are either the only ones to which they have access, or the only ones which they are any longer capable of enjoying. It may be ques-tioned whether any one who has remained equally susceptible to both classes of pleasures, ever knowingly and calmly preferred the lower, though many, in all ages, have broken down in an ineffectual attempt to combine both.

From this verdict of the only competent judges, I apprehend there can be no appeal. On a question which is the best worth having of two plea-sures, or which of two modes of existence is the most grateful to the feel-ings, apart from its moral attributes and from its consequences, the judg-ment of those who are qualified by knowledge of both, or, if they differ, that of the majority of them, must be admitted as final. And there needs be the less hesitation to accept this judgment respecting the quality of plea-sures, since there is no other tribunal to be referred to even on the question of quantity. What means are there of determining which is the acutest of two pains, or the intensest of two pleasurable sensations, except the gen-eral suffrage of those who are familiar with both? Neither pains nor plea-sures are homogeneous, and pain is always heterogeneous with pleasure. What is there to decide whether a particular pleasure is worth purchasing at the cost of a particular pain, except the feelings and judgment declare the pleasures derived from the higher faculties to be preferable *in kind,* apart from the question of intensity, to those of which the animal nature, disjoined from the higher faculties, is susceptible, they are entitled on this subject to the same regard.

QUALITY VERSUS THE QUANTITY OF PLEASURES

According to the greatest happiness principle, the ultimate end, with reference to and for the sake of which all other things are desirable—whether we are considering our own good or that of other people—is an existence exempt as far as possible from pain, and as rich as possible in enjoyments, both in point of quantity and quality; the test of quality and the rule for measuring it against quantity being the preference felt by those who, in their opportunities of experience, to which must be added their habits of self-consciousness and self-observation, are best furnished with the means of comparison. This, being according to the utilitarian opinion, the end of human action, is necessarily also the standard of morality, which may accordingly be defined "the rules and precepts for human conduct," by the observance of which an existence such as has been described might be, to the greatest extent possible, secured to all mankind; and not to them only, but so far as the nature of things admits, to the whole sentient creation.

Against this doctrine, however, arises another class of objectors who say that happiness, in any form, cannot be the rational purpose of human life and action; because, in the first place, it is unattainable; and they contemptuously ask, What right hast thou to be happy?—a question which Mr. Carlyle clinches by the addition, What right, a short time ago, hadst thou even to *be*? Next they say that men can do *without* happiness; that all noble human beings have felt this, and could not have become noble but by learning the lesson of renunciation; which lesson, thoroughly learnt and submitted to, they affirm to be the beginning and necessary condition of all virtue.

PLEASURE AND SELF-SACRIFICE

The utilitarian morality does recognize in human beings the power of sacrificing their own greatest good for the good of others. It only refuses to admit that the sacrifice is itself a good. A sacrifice which does not increase or tend to increase the sum total of happiness, it considers as wasted. The only self-renunciation which it applauds is devotion to the happiness, or to some of the means of happiness, of others, either of mankind collectively or of individuals within the limits imposed by the collective interests of mankind.

I must again repeat what the assailants of utilitarianism seldom have the justice to acknowledge, that the happiness which forms the utilitarian standard of what is right in conduct is not the agent's own happiness but that of all concerned. As between his own happiness and that of others, utilitarianism requires him to be as strictly impartial as a disinterested and benevolent spectator. In the golden rule of Jesus of Nazareth, we read the complete spirit of the ethics of utility. "To do as you would be done by," and "to love your neighbor as yourself," constitute the ideal perfection of utilitarian morality.

IS THERE ENOUGH TIME TO CALCULATE PAINS AND PLEASURES?

Again, defenders of utility often find themselves called upon to reply to such objections as this—that there is not time, previous to action, for calculating and weighing the effects of any line of conduct on the general happiness. This is exactly as if any one were to say that it is impossible to guide our conduct by Christianity because there is not time, on every occasion on which anything has to be done, to read through the Old and New Testaments. The answer to the objection is that there has been ample time, namely, the whole past duration of the human species. During all that time, mankind have been learning by experience the tendencies of actions; on which experience all the prudence, as well as all the morality, of life are dependent. People talk as if the commencement of this course of experience had hitherto been put off, and as if, at the moment when some man feels tempted to meddle with the property or life of another, he had to begin considering for the first time whether murder and theft are injurious to human happiness.

ARE WE BORN WITH THE FEELING OF MORAL DUTY?

It is not necessary, for the present purpose, to decide whether the feeling of duty is innate or implanted. Assuming it to be innate, it is an open question to what objects it naturally attaches itself; for the philosophic supporters of that theory are now agreed that the intuitive perception is of principles of morality and not of the details. If there be anything innate in the matter, I see no reason why the feeling which is innate should not be that of regard to the pleasures and pains of others. If there is any principle of morals which is intuitively obligatory, I should say it must be that. If so, the intuitive ethics would coincide with the utilitarian, and there would be no further quarrel between them. Even as it is, the intuitive moralists, though they believe that there are other intuitive moral obligations, do already believe this to be one; for they unanimously hold that a large *portion* of morality turns upon the consideration due to the interests of our fellow creatures. Therefore, if the belief in the transcendental origin of moral obligation gives any additional efficacy to the internal sanction, it appears to me that the utilitarian principle has already the benefit of it.

On the other hand, if, as is my own belief, the moral feelings are not innate but acquired, they are not for that reason the less natural. It is natural to man to speak, to reason, to build cities, to cultivate the ground, though these are acquired faculties. The moral feelings are not indeed a part of our nature, in the sense of being in any perceptible degree present in all of us;

but this, unhappily, is a fact admitted by those who believe the most stren-
uously in their transcendental origin. Like the other acquired capacities
above referred to, the moral faculty, if not a part of our nature, is a natural
outgrowth from it; capable, like them, in a certain, small degree, of spring-
ing up spontaneously; and susceptible of being brought by cultivation to a
high degree of development. Unhappily it is also susceptible, by a sufficient
use of the external sanctions and of the force of early impressions, of being
cultivated in almost any direction, so that there is hardly anything so absurd
or so mischievous that it may not, by means of these influences, be made
to act on the human mind with all the authority of conscience. To doubt
that the same potency might be given by the same means to the principle
of utility, even if it had no foundation in human nature, would be flying in
the face of all experience.

CHAPTER 6

TURNING VALUES UPSIDE DOWN

Nietzsche

Friedrich Nietzsche was fifty-five years old when he died in August of 1900. Although he was the son and grandson of Lutheran ministers, he expressed the judgment that "God is dead." He grew up in a German household dominated by females, and yet he advocated the most masculine ethic of the "superman." He urged people to express their fullest human vitality in the name of the "Will to Power." At the same time, he believed that to be truly human requires that we should sublimate and control our passions through reason. He was a brilliant student, was appointed professor at the University of Basel even before he completed his doctor's degree, and produced a steady stream of influential books, including *Beyond Good and Evil* and *A Genealogy of Morals*. As a student, he came under the spell of Wagner's music. "I could not have stood my youth without Wagner's music," he once said. "When one wants to rid oneself of an intolerable pressure, one needs hashish. Well, I needed Wagner." He was also influenced by the atheism of the German philosopher Schopenhauer. As a student of Greek literature, his own thought was significantly shaped by the contrast between Dionysus (the symbol of the dynamic stream of life) and Apollo (the symbol of order and restraint). For the last eleven years of his life, Nietzsche was hopelessly insane as a result of an infection that affected his brain. He was therefore unable to complete his major work, *Revaluation of Values.*

Master Morality versus Slave Morality and the Will to Power

Nietzsche rejected the notion that there is a universal and absolute system of morality that everyone must equally obey. People are different, he thought, and to conceive of morality in universal terms is to disregard basic differences among individuals. It is unrealistic to assume that there is only one kind of human nature whose direction can be prescribed by one set of rules. There is, however, one thing that does characterize all human beings, says Nietzsche, and that is the drive to dominate the environment. This drive, so central to human nature, is the *will to power.* This will to power is more than simply the will to survive. It is, rather, an inner drive to express a vigorous affirmation of all of man's powers. As Nietzsche says, "the strongest and highest Will to Life does not find expression in a miserable struggle for existence, but in a Will to War. A Will to Power, a Will to Overpower!" Whenever someone proposes a universal moral rule, he invariably seeks really to deny the fullest expression of man's elemental vital energies. In this respect, Christianity along with Judaism is the worst offender, for the Judeo-Christian ethic is so contrary to man's basic nature that its antinatural morality debilitates man and produces only "botched and bungled" lives.

How did human beings ever produce such unnatural systems of morality? There is, says Nietzsche, a "twofold early history of good and evil," which shows the development of two primary types of morality, namely, the *master morality* and the *slave morality.* In the master morality, "good" has always meant "noble" in the sense of "with a soul of high calibre" and "evil" meant "vulgar" or "plebeian." The noble type of man regards himself as the creator and

Nietzsche (*The Bettmann Archive*)

determiner of values. He does not look outside of himself for any approval of his acts. He passes judgment on himself. His morality is one of self-glorification. This noble individual acts out of a feeling of power, which seeks to overflow. He may help the unfortunate, but not out of pity, rather from an impulse generated by an abundance of power. He honors power in all its forms and takes pleasure in subjecting himself to rigor and toughness and has reverence for all that is severe and hard.

By contrast, the slave morality originates with the lowest elements of society, the abused, the oppressed, the slaves, and those who are uncertain of themselves. For the slave, "good" is the symbol for all those qualities which serve to alleviate the existence of sufferers, such as "sympathy, the kind helping hand, the warm heart, patience, diligence, humility and friendliness. . . . " This slave morality, says Nietzsche, is essentially the morality of utility, where goodness refers to whatever is beneficial to those who are weak and powerless. Whereas for the slave morality the man who arouses fear is "evil," according to the master morality it is precisely the "good" man who is able to arouse fear.

The challenge to the master morality resulted from a deep-seated *resentment* on the part of the "slaves," a resentment, says Nietzsche, "experienced by creatures who, deprived as they are of the proper outlet of action, are forced to find their compensation in an imaginary revenge." This revenge took the form of translating the virtues of the noble aristocrat into evils. Nietzsche's great protest against the dominant Western morality was that it exalted the mediocre values of the "herd," which "knows nothing o the fine impulses of great accumulations of strength, as something high, or possibly as the standard of all things." Incredibly, the "herd mentality" in time overcame the master morality by succeeding in making all the noble qualities appear to be vices and all the weak qualities appear to be virtues. The positive affirmation of life in the master morality was made to seem "bad" and something for which one should have a sense of "guilt." The fact is, says Nietzsche, that

> men with a still natural nature, barbarians in every terrible sense of the word, men of prey, still in possession of unbroken strength of will and desire for power, threw themselves upon weaker, more moral, more peaceful races. . . . At the commencement, the noble caste was always the barbarian caste: their superiority did not consist first of all in their physical, but in their psychical power—they were *complete* men. . . .

But the power of the master race was broken by the undermining of its psychic strength. Against the natural impulse to exert aggressive strength, the weak races had erected elaborate psychic defenses. New values, new ideals, such as peace and equality, were put forward under the guise of "the fundamental principle of society." This, said Nietzsche, was a not-so-subtle desire on the part of the weak to undermine the power of the strong. The weak have created a negative psychic attitude toward the most natural drives of man. This slave morality is, says Nietzsche, "a Will to the *denial of life, a principle of dissolution and decay*." But a skillful psychological analysis of the herd's resentment and its desire to exact revenge against the strong will show, says Nietzsche, what must be done; namely, one must "resist all sentimental weakness: life is essentially appropriation, injury, conquest of the strange and weak, suppression, severity, obtrusion of peculiar forms . . . and at the least, putting it mildest, exploitation. . . . " Nietzsche wanted particularly to emphasize that "exploitation" is not some depraved act, that it does not belong to an imperfect or primitive society. It belongs, he said, "to the nature of the living being as a primary function." Exploitation is, he said, "a consequence of the intrinsic Will to Power, which is precisely the Will to Life—a *fundamental fact* of all history. . . . " Come now, he said, "let us be so far honest toward ourselves!"

European morality, by denying the primacy of the Will to Power, was basically dishonest, in Nietzsche's view. He assigned primary responsibility for this dishonest morality to Judaism and Christianity. With utter directness he said that "I regard Christianity as the most fatal and seductive lie that has ever existed—as the greatest and most *impious lie*. . . . " He was appalled that Europe should be subjected to the morality of that small group of wretched outcasts who clustered around Jesus. Imagine, he said, "the *morality of paltry people* as the measure of all things. . . . " This he considered "the most repugnant kind of degeneracy that civilization has ever brought into existence." Worse yet was the fact that New Testament ethics is still hanging, under the name of "God," over men's heads. To Nietzsche it was incredible that in the New Testament "the least qualified people . . . have their say in its pages in regard to the greatest problems of existence." With what impudent levity "the most unwieldy problems are spoken of here (life, the world, God, the purpose of life) as if they were not problems at all, but the most simple things which these little bigots know all about!!!"

Christianity contradicts nature when it requires us to love our enemies, for Nature's injunction is to *hate* your enemy. Moreover, the natural origin of morality is denied by requiring that before man can love anything, he must first love God. To inject God into men's affections, said Nietzsche, is to subvert the immediate, natural moral standard of utility. All the vital energies of the strong are diluted by routing men's thinking toward God. Again, this is the revenge that the resentment of the weak has engendered. Among men there is always a surplus of "defective, diseased, degenerating, infirm, and necessarily suffering individuals." These are the "failures," which the Judeo-Christian religions seek to keep alive and preserve.

Nietzsche was willing to admit that the "spiritual men" of Christianity had rendered invaluable services to Europe by offering comfort and courage to the suffering. But at what price was Christian charity achieved? The price, Nietzsche said, was "the deterioration of the European race." It was necessary "to *reverse* all esti-

mates of value—*that* is what they had to do! And to shatter the
strong, to spoil great hopes, to cast suspicion on the delight in
beauty, to break down everything autonomous, manly, conquering,
and imperious." In addition, all instincts that are natural to the full
"man" had to be transmuted into "uncertainty, distress of conscience, and self-destruction." Christianity succeeded in inverting
"all love of the earthly and of supremacy over the earth into hatred
of the earth and earthly things. . . . "

Nietzsche was willing for the weak and the herd to have their
own morality, provided that they did not impose it on the higher
ranks of men. Why should men of great creative powers be reduced
to the common level of mediocrity characteristic of the herd?
When Nietzsche spoke of rising "beyond good and evil," he had in
mind simply rising above the dominant herd morality of his day. He
envisioned a new day, when once again the truly complete man
would achieve new levels of creative activity and thereby become
a higher type of man. This new man will not reject morality; he will
reject only the negative morality of the herd. Again, Nietzsche
argued that morality based on the will to power is only an honest
version of what the slave morality has carefully disguised. If the
"superman" is "cruel," said Nietzsche, one must recognize that,
actually, almost everything that we now call "higher culture" is
simply a spiritualized intensification of cruelty. "This is my thesis,"
he said, that "the 'wild beast' has not been slain at all, it lives, it
flourishes, it has only been—transfigured." He refers to the
Romans' pleasures in the arena, the Christian ecstasy of the cross,
the Spaniard's delight at the gory sight of the bullfight, the Parisian
workman's homesickness for a bloody revolution, and the Wagner-
ian who "with unhinged will" *undergoes* a performance of *Tristan
and Isolde.* "What all these enjoy and strive with mysterious ardour
to drink in," said Nietzsche, "is the philtre of the great Circe 'cruelty.' . . . " Looked at from the vantage point of the master morality, the word "cruelty" refers simply to the basic will to power,
which is a natural expression of strength. Men are differentiated
into ranks, and it is, he says, "quanta of power, and nothing else,
which determine and distinguish ranks." For this reason, such
ideals as equality among men are nonsensical. There can be no
equality where there are in fact different quanta of power. Equality
can only mean the leveling downward of everyone to the mediocrity of the herd. Nietzsche wanted to preserve the natural distinction between the two ranks or types of men, namely, between that

"type which represents ascending life and a type which represents decadence, decomposition, weakness." To be sure, a higher culture will always require as its basis a strongly consolidated mediocre herd, but only to make possible the development and emergence of the higher type of man, the "superman" (*Übermensch*). If the superman is to emerge, he must go beyond good and evil as conceived by the lower ranks of men.

Revaluation of All Morals

What would Nietzsche want to put in the place of the traditional morality, which he believed was clearly dying? His positive prescriptions are not so clear as his critical analyses. Much of the content of his new values can, however, be inferred from his rejection of the slave morality. If the slave morality originated in resentment and revenge, there must again occur a *revaluation* of all values. By revaluation, Nietzsche did not intend the creation of a new table of moral values. He meant rather to declare war on the presently accepted values, like Socrates, to apply "the knife vivisectionally to the very virtues of the time. . . . " Since traditional morality is a perversion of original natural morality, revaluation must consist of rejecting traditional morality in the name of honesty and accuracy. Revaluation implies, said Nietzsche, that all the "stronger motives are still extant, but that now they appear under false names and false valuations, and have not yet become conscious of themselves." It is not necessary to legislate new values, but only to reverse values once again. Just as "Christianity was a revaluation of all the values of antiquity," so today the dominant morality must be rejected in favor of man's original and deepest nature. Thus Nietzsche's program of revaluation was essentially a critical analysis of modern man's ideals. He showed that what modern man called "good" was not at all virtuous, that his so-called truth was disguised selfishness and weakness and that his religion was a skillful creation of psychological weapons with which moral pygmies domesticated natural giants. Once the disguise is removed from modern morality, he thought, the true values will emerge.

Moral values must in the last analysis be built on the true nature of man and his environment. Unlike Darwin, who laid great stress on external circumstances when describing the evolution of the species, Nietzsche focused on the internal power within man, which is capable of shaping and creating events, "a power which *uses* and *exploits* the environment." Nietzsche's grand hypothesis was that everywhere and in everything the Will to Power is seeking to express itself. "This world," he says, "is the Will to Power—and nothing else." Life itself is a plurality of forces, "a lasting form of processes of assertions of force. . . . " Man's psychological makeup shows that his preoccupation with pleasure and pain reflects a striving after an increase of power. Pain can be the spur for exerting power to overcome an obstacle, whereas pleasure can represent a feeling of increased power.

The Superman (Übermensch)

The will to power has its greatest relevance for Nietzsche's philosophy in his notion of the "superman" (*Übermensch*)—again, the "superior" man, sometimes referred to as the "overman." We have already seen that Nietzsche rejected the concept of equality. He also indicated that morality must suit each rank of man. Even after the revaluation of all values, the "common herd" will not be intellectually capable of reaching the heights of the "free spirits." There can, in short, be no "common good." Great things, says Nietzsche, remain for the great, "everything rare for the rare." The superman will be rare, but he is the next stage in human evolution. History is moving not toward some abstract developed "humanity" but toward the emergence of some exceptional men: "Superman is the goal," says Nietzsche. But the superman will not be the product of an automatic process of evolution. Only when superior individuals have the courage to revalue all values and respond with freedom to their internal will to power can the next stage be reached. "Man is something to be surpassed," and it is the superman who represents the highest level of development and expression of physical, intellectual, and emotional strength. The superman will be the truly free man for whom nothing is forbidden except what obstructs the will to power. He will be the very embodiment of the spontaneous affirmation of life.

Nietzsche did not contemplate that his superman would be a tyrant. To be sure, there would be much of the Dionysian element in him. But his passions would be controlled and his animal nature harmonized with his intellect, giving style to his behavior. Such a superman is not to be confused with a totalitarian bully. Nietzsche had in mind as a model for the superman his hero Goethe, suggesting also as an ideal "the Roman Caesar with Christ's soul." As Nietzsche's thought matured, he realized that his superior man would have to possess a balanced unity of the passionate (Dionysian) and rational (Apollonian) elements. Earlier, when his thought was influenced by Wagner and Schopenhauer, Nietzsche had criticized Socrates for having caused Western man to take a wrong turn in history, the turn toward rationality. Even at the end, Nietzsche believed that knowledge and rationality must be used in the service of life and that life must not be sacrificed for knowledge. Still Socrates was important historically precisely because he saved men from self-destruction, which would have occurred if, says Nietzsche, "this whole incalculable sum of energy [in human striving was] *not* employed in the service of knowledge. . . . " The lust for life, he says, would otherwise have led to wars of annihilation. The Dionysian element by itself could lead to pessimism and destruction. That it was necessary to harness man's vital energies already suggested a basic decadent tendency in man, which could be halted only by the kind of influence Socrates represented. But while the rational, or Apollonian, element could stifle the vital streams of life, Nietzsche did not see how, in the end, life could be lived without its form-giving guidance. Socrates became important for Nietzsche precisely because this ancient philosopher was the first to see the proper relation between thought and life. Socrates recognized, said Nietzsche, that thought serves life, while for previous philosophers, life served thought and knowledge. Here, then, was Nietzsche's ideal, the passionate man who has his passions under control.

Apollonian versus Dionysian

Nietzsche found in Homer's account of Apollo and Dionysus a striking symbolism of the two powerful elements in human nature, the

Dionysus (*Hirmer Fotoarchiv, Munich*)

power of passion and the power of reason. Dionysus was for
Nietzsche the symbol of the dynamic stream of life, which knows
no restraints or barriers and defies all limitations. In the worship of
Dionysus, the individual would lapse into intoxication and thereby
lose his own identity in the larger ocean of life. In the photo of
Dionysus, we see a devotee in the presence of Dionysus who
exhibits the stirrings of her deep feelings produced by the drinking
of wine and the hearing of appropriate music. Apollo, however, was
the symbol of order, restraint, and form, the power to create beauty
through art. If the Dionysian mood was best expressed in the feeling of abandonment in some types of music, the Apollonian form-
giving force found its highest expression, according to Nietzsche,
in Greek sculpture. Thus Dionysus symbolized man's unity with
life, where his own individuality is absorbed in the larger reality of

Apollo (*Courtesy Museum of Fine Arts, Boston*)

the life force, whereas Apollo was the symbol of that power which controls and restrains the dynamic processes of life in order to create a formed work of art or a controlled personal character. Looked at from another point of view, the Dionysian represents the negative and destructive dark powers of the soul, which culminate, when unchecked, as Nietzsche says, in "that disgusting mixture of voluptuousness and cruelty" typical of "the most savage beasts of nature." Again, the Apollonian represents the power to deal with the powerful surge of vital energy, to harness destructive powers and to transmute these into a creative act, just as the charioteer (Apollo), by holding the reins, prevents the powerful horses from running wild (see photo of Apollo).

Greek tragedy, according to Nietzsche, is a great work of art. It represents the conquest of Dionysus by Apollo. But from this account Nietzsche drew the conclusion that man is not faced with a choice between the Dionysian and the Apollonian. To assume that one has such a choice to make is to misunderstand the true nature of the human condition. The fact is that human life inevitably includes the dark and surging forces of passion, and the awareness of these driving forces becomes the occasion for producing a work of art in literature or in the plastic arts through the imposition of form on a resisting material or in one's own character through moderation. Nietzsche saw the birth of tragedy or the creation of art as a response of the basically healthy element in man, the Apollonian, to the challenge of the energy and frenzy of the Dionysian.

The Dionysian element in human beings is not necessarily or intrinsically "diseased"—only when it is uncontrolled is it unhealthful. In this view, art could not occur without the stimulus

109

of the Dionysian; at the same time, if the Dionysian were considered either the only element in human nature or the dominant element, one might very well despair and come finally to a negative attitude toward life. But for Nietzsche the supreme achievement of human nature occurred in Greek culture, where the Dionysian and Apollonian elements were brought together. To deny that the Dionysian element had a rightful place in life was to postpone, as Nietzsche saw, to some later date the inevitable explosion of vital forces which cannot be permanently denied expression. To ask whether life should dominate knowledge or knowledge dominate life is to raise the question of which of these two is the higher and more decisive power. There is no doubt, said Nietzsche, that life is the higher and dominating power, but raw vital power is finally life-defeating. For this reason, Nietzsche looked to the Greek formula, the fusion of the Dionysian and Apollonian elements, by which human life is transformed into an aesthetic phenomenon, a work of art.

READING

BEYOND GOOD AND EVIL
Nietzsche

In a tour through the many finer and coarser moralities which have hitherto prevailed or still prevail on the earth, I found certain traits recurring regularly together and connected with one another, until finally two primary types revealed themselves to me, and a radical distinction was brought to light. There is *master*-morality and *slave*-morality;—I would at once add, however, that in all higher and mixed civilizations, there are also attempts at the reconciliation of the two moralities; but one finds still oftener the confusion and mutual misunderstanding of them, indeed, sometimes their close juxtaposition—even in the same man, within one soul. The distinc-

From Friedrich Nietzsche, *Beyond Good and Evil*, trans. Helen Zimmern, in *The Complete Works of Friedrich Nietzsche*, translated under Oscar Levy (1909–1911).

tions of moral values have either originated in a ruling caste, pleasantly conscious of being different from the ruled—or among the ruled class, the slaves and dependents of all sorts. In the first case, when it is the rulers who determine the conception "good," it is the exalted, proud disposition which is regarded as the distinguishing feature, and that which determines the order of rank. The noble type of man separates from himself the beings in whom the opposite of this exalted, proud disposition displays itself: he despises them. Let it at once be noted that in this first kind of morality the antithesis "good" and "bad" means practically the same as "noble" and "despicable";—the antithesis "good" and "evil" is of a different origin. The cowardly, the timid, the insignificant, and those thinking merely of narrow utility are despised; moreover, also, the distrustful, with their constrained glances, the self-abasing, the dog-like kind of men who let themselves be abused, the mendicant flatterers, and above all the liars:—it is a fundamental belief of all aristocrats that the common people are untruthful. "We truthful ones"—the nobility in ancient Greece called themselves. It is obvious that everywhere the designations of moral value were at first applied to *men,* and were only derivatively and at a later period applied to *actions*; it is a gross mistake, therefore, when historians of morals start with questions like, "Why have sympathetic actions been praised?" The noble type of man regards himself as a determiner of values; he does not require to be approved of; he passes the judgment: "What is injurious to me is injurious in itself." He knows that it is he himself only who confers honour on things; he is a creator of values. He honours whatever he recognises in himself: such morality is self-glorification. In the foreground there is the feeling of plenitude, of power, which seeks to overflow, the happiness of high tension, the consciousness of a wealth which would fain give and bestow:—the noble man also helps the unfortunate, but not—or scarcely—out of pity, but rather from an impulse generated by the superabundance of power. The noble man honours in himself the powerful one, him also who has power over himself, who knows how to speak and how to keep silence, who takes pleasure in subjecting himself to severity and hardness, and has reverence for all that is severe and hard. "Wotan placed a hard heart in my breast," says an old Scandinavian Saga: it is thus rightly expressed from the soul of a proud Viking. Such a type of man is even proud of *not* being made for sympathy; the hero of the Saga therefore adds warningly: "He who has not a hard heart when young, will never have one." The noble and brave who think thus are the furthest removed from the morality which sees precisely in sympathy, or in acting for the good of others, or in *désinteressement,* the characteristic of the moral; faith in oneself, pride in oneself, a radical enmity and irony towards "selflessness," belong as definitely to noble morality, as do a careless scorn and precaution in the presence of sympathy and the "warm heart."—It is the powerful who *know* how to honour, it is their art, their domain for invention. The profound reverence for age and for tradition—all law rests on this double reverence,—the belief and prejudice in favour of ancestors and unfavourable to newcomers, is typical in the morality of the powerful; and if, reversely, men of "modern ideas" believe almost instinctively in "progress" and the "future," and are more and more lacking in respect for old age, the ignoble origin of these "ideas" has complacently betrayed itself thereby. A morality of the ruling class, however, is more especially foreign and irritating to present-day taste in the sternness of its principle that one has duties only to one's equals; that one may act towards beings of a lower rank, towards all that is foreign, just as seems good to one, or "as the heart desires," and in any case "beyond good and evil": it is here that sympathy and similar sentiments can have a place. The ability and obligation to exercise prolonged gratitude and prolonged revenge—both only within the circle of equals,—artfulness in retaliation, *raffinement* of the idea in friendship, a certain necessity to have enemies (as outlets for the emotions of envy, quarrelsomeness, arrognace—in fact, in order to be a good *friend*): all these are typical characteristics of the noble morality, which, as has been pointed out, is not the morality of "modern ideas," and is therefore at present difficult to realise, and also to unearth and disclose.—It is otherwise with the second type of morality, *slave-morality*. Supposing that the abused, the oppressed, the suffering, the unemancipated, the weary, and those uncertain of themselves, should moralise, what will be the common element in their moral estimates? Probably a pessimistic suspicion with regard to the entire situation of man will find expression, perhaps a condemnation of man, together with his situation. The slave has an unfavourable eye for the virtues of the powerful; he has a scepticism and distrust, a *refinement* of distrust of everything "good" that is there honoured—he would fain persuade himself that the very happiness there is not genuine. On the other hand, *those* qualities which serve to alleviate the existence of sufferers are brought into prominence and flooded with light; it is here that sympathy, the kind, helping hand, the warm heart, patience, diligence, humility, and friendliness attain to honour; for there these are the most useful qualities, and almost the only means of supporting the burden of existence. Slave-morality is essentially the morality of utility. Here is the seat of the origin of the famous antithesis "good" and "evil":—power and dangerousness are assumed to reside in the evil, a certain dreadfulness, subtlety, and strength, which do not admit of being despised. According to slave-morality, it is precisely the "good" man who arouses fear and seeks to arouse it, while the bad man is regarded as the despicable being. The contrast attains its maximum when, in accordance with the logical consequences of slave-morality, a shade of depreciation—it may be slight and well-intentioned—at least attaches itself even to the "good" man of this morality; because, according to the servile mode of thought, the good man must in any case be the *safe* man: he is good-natured, easily deceived, perhaps a little stupid, *un bon-*

homme. Everywhere that slave-morality gains the ascendency, language shows a tendency to approximate the significations of the words "good" and "stupid."—A last fundamental difference: the desire for *freedom,* the instinct for happiness and the refinements of the feeling of liberty belong as necessarily to slave-morals and morality, as artifice and enthusiasm in reverence and devotion are the regular symptoms of an aristocratic mode of thinking and estimating.—Hence we can understand without further detail why love as a *passion*—it is our European speciality—must absolutely be of noble origin; as is well known, its invention is due to the Provencal poet-cavaliers, those brilliant ingenious men of the "gai saber," to whom Europe owes so much, and almost owes itself.

READING

THE TWILIGHT OF IDOLS
Nietzsche

What then, alone, can our teaching be?—That no one gives man his qualities, neither God, society, his parents, his ancestors, nor himself. . . . No one is responsible for the fact that he exists at all, that he is constituted as he is, and that he happens to be in certain circumstances and in a particular environment. The fatality of his being cannot be divorced from the fatality of all that which has been and will be. This is not the result of an individual attention, of a will, of an aim, there is no attempt at attaining to any "ideal man," or "ideal happiness" or "ideal morality" with him—it is absurd to wish him to be careering towards some sort of purpose. *We* invented the concept "purpose"; in reality purpose is altogether lacking. One is necessary, one is a piece of fate, one belongs to the whole, one is in the whole— there is nothing that could judge, measure, compare, and condemn our existence, for that would mean judging, measuring, comparing and condemning the whole. *But there is nothing outside the whole!* The fact that no one shall any longer be made responsible, that the nature of existence may

From Friedrich Nietzsche, *The Twilight of Idols,* trans. A. M. Ludovici, in *The Complete Works of Friedrich Nietzsche,* translated under Oscar Levy (1909–1911).

not be traced to a *causa prima,* that the world is an entity neither as a spirit—*this alone is the great deliverance*—thus alone is the innocence of Becoming restored. . . .

READING

THE WILL TO POWER
Nietzsche

I regard Christianity as the most fatal and seductive lie that has ever yet existed—as the greatest and most *impious* lie: I can discern the last sprouts and branches of its ideal beneath every form of disguise, I decline to enter into any compromise or false position in reference to it—I urge people to declare open war with it.

The morality of paltry people as the measure of all things: this is the most repugnant kind of degeneracy that civilisation has ever yet brought into existence. And this *kind of ideal* is hanging still, under the name of "God," over men's heads!!

However modest one's demands may be concerning intellectual cleanliness, when one touches the New Testament one cannot help experiencing a sort of inexpressible feeling of discomfort; for the unbounded cheek with which the least qualified people will have their say in its pages, in regard to the greatest problems of existence, and claim to sit in judgment on such matters, exceeds all limits. The impudent levity with which the most unwieldy problems are spoken of here (life, the world, God, the purpose of life), as if they were not problems at all, but the most simple things which these little bigots *know all about!!!*

This was the most fatal form of insanity that has ever yet existed on earth:—when these little lying abortions of bigotry begin laying claim to the words "God," "last judgment," "truth," "love," "wisdom," "Holy Spirit," and thereby distinguishing themselves from the rest of the world; when such men begin to transvalue values to suit themselves, as though they

From Friedrich Nietzsche, trans. Helen Zimmern, *Human, All Too Human,* in *The Complete Works of Friedrich Nietzsche,* trans. under Oscar Levy, (1909–1911).

were the sense, the salt, the standard, and the measure of all things; then all that one should do is this: build lunatic asylums for their incarceration. To *persecute* them was an egregious act of antique folly: this was taking them too seriously; it was making them serious.

The whole fatality was made possible by the fact that a similar form of megalomania was already *in existence,* the *Jewish* form (once the gulf separating the Jews from the Christian-Jews was bridged, the Christian-Jews *were compelled* to employ those self-preservative measures afresh which were discovered by the Jewish instinct, for their own self-preservation, after having accentuated them); and again through the fact that Greek moral philosophy had done everything that could be done to prepare the way for moral-fanaticism, even among Greeks and Romans, and to render it palatable. . . . Plato, the great importer of corruption, who was the first who refused to see Nature in morality, and who had already deprived the Greek gods of all their worth by his notion *"good,"* was already tainted with *Jewish bigotry* (in Egypt?). . . .

The *law,* which is the fundamentally realistic formula of certain self-preservative measures of a community, forbids certain actions that have a definite tendency to jeopardise the welfare of that community: it does *not* forbid the attitude of mind which gives rise to these actions—for in the pursuit of other ends the community requires these forbidden actions, namely, when it is a matter of opposing its *enemies.* The moral idealist now steps forward and says: "God sees into men's hearts: the action itself counts for nothing; the reprehensible attitude of mind from which it proceeds must be extirpated. . . . " In normal conditions men laugh at such things; it is only in exceptional cases, when a community lives *quite* beyond the need of waging war in order to maintain itself, that an ear is lent to such things. Any attitude of mind is abandoned, the utility of which cannot be conceived.

This was the case, for example, when Buddha appeared among a people that was both peaceable and afflicted with great intellectual weariness.

This was also the case in regard to the first Christian community (as also the Jewish), the primary condition of which was the absolutely *unpolitical* Jewish society. Christianity could grow only upon the soil of Judaism—that is to say, among a people that had already renounced the political life, and which led a sort of parasitic existence within the Roman sphere of government. Christianity goes a step *farther:* it allows men to "emasculate" themselves even more; the circumstances actually favour their doing so.— *Nature* is *expelled* from morality when it is said, "Love ye your enemies": for *Nature's* injunction, "Ye shall *love* your neighbour and *hate* your enemy," has now become senseless in the law (in instinct); now, even *the love a man feels for his neighbour* must first be based upon something (a *sort of love of God*). *God* is introduced everywhere, and *utility* is withdrawn; the natural *origin* or morality is denied everywhere: the *veneration of*

Nature, which lies in *acknowledging a natural morality,* is *destroyed* to the roots. . . .

Whence comes the *seductive charm* of this emasculate ideal of man? Why are we not *disgusted* by it, just as we are disgusted at the thought of a eunuch? . . . The answer is obvious: it is not the voice of the eunuch that revolts us, despite the cruel mutilation of which it is the result; for, as a matter of fact, it has grown sweeter. . . . And owing to the very fact that the "male organ" has been amputated from virtue, its voice now has a feminine ring, which, formerly, was not to be discerned.

On the other hand, we have only to think of the terrible hardness, dangers, and accidents to which a life of manly virtues leads—the life of a Corsican, even at the present day, or that of a heathen Arab (which resembles the Corsican's life even to the smallest detail: the Arab's songs might have been written by Corsicans)—in order to perceive how the most robust type of man was fascinated and moved by the voluptuous ring of this "goodness" and "purity." . . . A pastoral melody . . . an idyll . . . the "good man": such things have most effect in ages when tragedy is abroad.

The *Astuteness of moral castration.*—How is war waged against the virile passions and valuations? No violent physical means are available; the war must therefore be one of ruses, spells, and lies—in short, a "spiritual war."

First recipe: One appropriates virtue in general, and makes it the main feature of one's ideal; the older ideal is denied and declared to be *the reverse of all ideals.* Slander has to be carried to a fine art for this purpose.

Second recipe: One's own type is set up as a general *standard;* and this is projected into all things, behind all things, and behind the destiny of all things—as God.

Third recipe: The opponents of one's ideal are declared to be the opponents of God; one arrogates to oneself a *right* to great pathos, to power, and a right to curse and to bless.

Fourth recipe: All suffering, all gruesome, terrible, and fatal things are declared to be the results of opposition to *one's* ideal—all suffering is *punishment* even in the case of one's adherents (except it be a trial, etc.).

Fifth recipe: One goes so far as to regard Nature as the reverse of one's ideal, and the lengthy sojourn amid natural conditions is considered a great trial of patience—a sort of martyrdom; one studies contempt, both in one's attitudes and one's looks towards all "natural things."

Sixth recipe: The triumph of anti-naturalism and ideal castration, the triumph of the world of the pure, good, sinless, and blessed, is projected into the future as the consummation, the finale, the great hope, and the "Coming of the Kingdom of God."

I hope that one may still be allowed to laugh at this artificial hoisting up of a small species of man to the position of an absolute standard of all things?

To what extent psychologists have been corrupted by the moral idio-syncrasy!—Not one of the ancient philosophers had the courage to advance the theory of the non-free will (that is to say, the theory that denies morality);—not one had the courage to identify the typical feature of hap-piness, of every kind of happiness ("pleasure"), with the will to power: for the pleasure of power was considered immoral;—not one had the courage to regard virtue as a *result of immorality* (as a result of a will to power) in the service of a species (or of a race, or of a *polis*); for the will to power was considered immoral. . . .

At the waterfall. In looking at a waterfall we imagine that there is free-dom of will and fancy in the countless turnings, twistings, and breakings of the waves; but everything is compulsory, every movement can be mathe-matically calculated. So it is also with human actions; one would have to be able to calculate every single action beforehand if one were all-knowing; equally so all progress of knowledge, every error, all malice. The one who acts certainly labors under the illusion of voluntariness; if the world's wheel were to stand still for a moment and an all-knowing, calculating reason were there to make use of this pause, it could foretell the future of every creature to the remotest times, and mark out every track upon which that wheel would continue to roll. The delusion of the acting agent about himself, the supposition of a free will, belongs to this mechanism which still remains to be calculated.

Irresponsibility and innocence. The complete irresponsibility of man for his actions and his nature is the bitterest drop which he who under-stands must swallow if he was accustomed to see the patent of nobility of his humanity in responsibility and duty. All his valuations, distinctions, dis-inclinations, are thereby deprived of value and become false—his deepest feeling for the sufferer and the hero was based on an error; he may no longer either praise or blame, for it is absurd to praise and blame nature and necessity. In the same way as he loves a fine work of art, but does not praise it, because it can do nothing for itself; in the same way as he regards plants, so must he regard his own actions and those of mankind. He can admire strength, beauty, abundance in themselves; but must find no merit therein—the chemical progress and the strife of the elements, the torments of the sick person who thirsts after recovery, are all equally as little merits as those struggles of the soul and states of distress in which we are torn hither and thither by different impulses until we finally decide for the strongest—as we say (but in reality it is the strongest motive which decides for us). All these motives, however, whatever fine names we may give them, have all grown out of the same root, in which we believe the evil poisons to be situated; between good and evil actions there is no difference of species, but at most of degree. Good actions are sublimated evil ones; evil actions are vulgarized and stupefied good ones. The single longing of the individual for self-gratification (together with the fear of losing it) satisfies itself in all circumstances: man may act as he can, that is as he must, be it in deeds of vanity, revenge, pleasure, usefulness, malice, cunning; be it in deeds of sacrifice, of pity, of knowledge. The degrees of the power of judgment determine whether anyone lets himself be drawn through this longing; to every society, to every individual, a scale of possessions is continually present, according to which he determines his actions and judges those of others. But this standard changes constantly; many actions are called evil and are only stupid, because the degree of intelligence which decided for them was very low. In a certain sense, even, *all* actions are still stupid; for the highest degree of human intelligence which can now be attained will assuredly be yet surpassed, and then, in a retrospect, all our actions and judgments will appear as limited and hasty as the actions and judgments of primitive wild peoples now appear limited and hasty to us. To recognize all this may be deeply painful, but consolation comes after: such pains are the pangs of birth. The butterfly wants to break through its chrysalis: it rends and tears it, and is then blinded and confused by the unaccustomed light, the kingdom of liberty. In such people as are *capable* of such sadness—and how few are!—the first experiment made is to see whether *mankind can change itself* from a *moral* into a *wise* mankind. The sun of a new gospel throws its rays upon the highest point in the soul of each single individual, then the mists gather thicker than ever, and the brightest light and the dreariest shadow lie side by side. Everything is necessity—so says the new knowledge, and this knowledge itself is necessity. Everything is innocence, and knowledge is the road to insight into this innocence. Are pleasure, egoism, vanity *necessary* for the production of the moral phenomena and their highest result, the sense for truth and justice in knowledge; were error and the confusion of the imagination the only means through which mankind could raise itself gradually to this degree of self-enlightenment and self-liberation—who would dare to undervalue these means? Who would dare to be sad if he perceived the goal to which those roads led? Everything in the domain of morality has evolved, is changeable, unstable, everything is dissolved, it is true; but *everything is also streaming toward one goal.* Even if the inherited habit of erroneous valuation, love and hatred, continue to reign in us, yet under the influence of growing knowledge it will become weaker; a new habit, that of comprehension, of not loving, not hating, of overlooking, is gradually implanting itself in us upon the same ground, and in thousands of years will perhaps be powerful enough to give humanity the strength to produce wise, innocent (consciously innocent) men, as it now produces unwise, guilty, conscious men—*that is the necessary preliminary step, not its opposite.*

CHAPTER 7

IS THE WILL FREE?

Holbach and James

Baron d'Holbach was born in 1723 and died in 1789. Although he was born in Edesheim of a German family, he became a naturalized citizen of France. His name was Paul Henri Thiry, to which he added Baron d'Holbach, after his uncle F. A. Holbach, from whom he inherited not only his last name but also a considerable fortune which enabled him to pursue his studies, to engage in leisurely conversation with interesting intellectuals, and to devote his energies to a career of extensive authorship. He studied in Paris and at the University of Leiden. His early interests were directed toward science, especially geology and minerology, and he wrote several articles on various scientific subjects. Most of these articles, which totaled about 376, were submitted to Diderot's *Encyclopedie.* D'Holbach became a celebrated French philosopher who counted among his friends Diderot and J. J. Rousseau. His most influential book was his *System of Nature,* in which he expressed his views on atheism, materialism, and determinisim. His conclusions were that man has no soul, that human nature is a machine, and that all human actions are determined or caused just as some parts of a machine are moved by the other parts. Although such notables as Voltaire disagreed with these conclusions, d'Holbach did find a sympathetic reception from Goethe.

William James was born in New York City in 1843. He was the brother of the renowned novelist Henry James. He received his M.D. from the Harvard Medical School and soon joined that faculty as an instructor in physiology. From medicine he moved to psychology and philosophy, producing in 1890 his famous book *Principles of Psychology*. He became a member of the illustrious Harvard department of philosophy which included George Santayana and Josiah Royce. His published essays were widely influential, and as collections in book form, they were and still are read around the world. By the time he died in 1910 at the age of fifty-eight he had created a new approach to philosophy and had managed to communicate his principles of pragmatism to an unusually wide audience. James did not believe that the human mind can achieve a single, unified concept of the world. Nor did he think it was important to have such a concept. All we can know, he said, is certain parts of the universe. Moreover, these parts look different to different people. These many parts and views provide the basis for a *pluralistic* view of the world. And the main thing about these plural views, he said, is not whether they are consistent with one another but whether they lead to successful action, that is, whether they work or not.

One of the persistent problems of ethics is the question of whether a person is capable of voluntary actions or whether all human behavior is the product of causes which determine how the will itself will act. The question is whether the will is free or whether it is forced. Two opposing views are those of Baron d'Holbach (1723–1789) and William James (1842–1910). Although Holbach's view was formulated in the latter part of the eighteenth century, his argument against the notion of the freedom of the will contains, in essence, what determinists argue even today. For his part, William James, whose approach to philosophy we discuss in more detail in Chapter 24, approaches this difficult question from the point of view of Pragmatism. Holbach, who spent most of his life in Paris, was famous as a philosophical materialist, believing that all nature, including human beings, is best understood as a mechanical system, a machine, all of whose parts move according to strict laws of nature. This view obviously rules out the possibility of the freedom of the will. By contrast, William James raises the question of the practical consequences of accepting the notion of determinism. He concludes that it makes more sense, that is, it fits more obviously with human experience, to assume that human beings face genuine options or possibilities and that the human will is free to choose or reject alternative options.

READING

THE ILLUSION OF FREE WILL
Holbach

Man is a being purely physical; in whatever manner man is considered, he is connected to universal nature, and submitted to the necessary and immutable laws that she imposes on all the beings she contains, according to their peculiar essences or to the respective properties with which, without consulting them, she endows each particular species. Man's life is a line that nature commands him to describe upon the surface of the earth, without his ever being able to swerve from it, even for an instant. He is born without his own consent; his organization does in nowise depend upon himself; his ideas come to him involuntarily; his habits are in the power of those who cause him to contract them; he is unceasingly modified by causes, whether visible or concealed, over which he has no control, which necessarily regulate his mode of existence, give the hue to his way of thinking, and determine his manner of acting. He is good or bad, happy or miserable, wise or foolish, reasonable or irrational, without his will being for anything in these various states. Nevertheless, in spite of the shackles by which he is bound, it is pretended he is a free agent, or that independent of the causes by which he is moved, he determines his own will, and regulates his own condition.

However slender the foundation of this opinion, of which everything ought to point out to him the error, it is current at this day and passes for an incontestable truth with a great number of people, otherwise extremely

From Baron d'Holbach, *System of Nature*, chaps. 11 and 12, trans. by H. D. Robinson, 1770.

enlightened; it is the basis of religion, which, supposing relations between man and the unknown being she has placed above nature, has been incapable of imagining how man could merit reward or deserve punishment from this being, if he was not a free agent. Society has been believed interested in this system; because an idea has gone abroad, that if all the actions of man were to be contemplated as necessary, the right of punishing those who injure their associates would no longer exist. At length human vanity accommodated itself to a hypothesis which, unquestionably, appears to distinguish man from all other physical beings, by assigning to him the special privilege of a total independence of all other causes, but of which a very little reflection would have shown him the impossibility.

As a part subordinate to the great whole, man is obliged to experience its influence. To be a free agent, it were needful that each individual was of greater strength than the entire of nature; or that he was out of this nature, who, always in action herself, obliges all the beings she embraces to act, and to concur to her general motion. . . .

The will . . . is a modification of the brain, by which it is disposed to action, or prepared to give play to the organs. This will is necessarily determined by the qualities, good or bad, agreeable or painful, of the object or the motive that acts upon his senses, or of which the idea remains with him, and is resuscitated by his memory. In consequence, he acts necessarily, his action is the result of the impulse he receives either from the motive, from the object, or from the idea which has modified his brain, or disposed his will. When he does not act according to this impulse, it is because there comes some new cause, some new motive, some new idea, which modifies his brain in a different manner, gives him a new impulse, determines his will in another way, by which the action of the former impulse is suspended: thus, the sight of an agreeable object, or its idea, determines his will to set him in action to procure it; but if a new object or a new idea more powerfully attracts him, it gives a new direction to his will, annihilates the effect of the former, and prevents the action by which it was to be procured. This is the mode in which reflection, experience, reason, necessarily arrests or suspends the action of man's will: without this he would of necessity have followed the anterior impulse which carried him towards a then desirable object. In all this he always acts according to necessary laws from which he has no means of emancipating himself.

If when tormented with violent thirst, he figures to himself in idea, or really perceives a fountain, whose limpid streams might cool his feverish want, is he sufficient master of himself to desire or not to desire the object competent to satisfy so lively a want? It will no doubt be conceded, that it is impossible he should not be desirous to satisfy it; but it will be said—if at this moment it is announced to him that the water he so ardently desires is poisoned, he will, notwithstanding his vehement thirst, abstain from drinking it: and it has, therefore, been falsely concluded that he is a free agent. The fact, however, is, that the motive in either case is exactly the same: his own conservation. The same necessity that determined him to drink before he knew the water was deleterious upon this new discovery equally determined him not to drink; the desire of conserving himself either annihilates or suspends the former impulse; the second motive becomes stronger than the preceding, that is, the fear of death, or the desire of preserving himself, necessarily prevails over the painful sensation caused by his eagerness to drink: but, it will be said, if the thirst is very parching, an inconsiderate man without regarding the danger will risk swallowing the water. Nothing is gained by this remark: in this case, the anterior impulse only regains the ascendency; he is persuaded that life may possibly be longer preserved, or that he shall derive a greater good by drinking the poisoned water than by enduring the torment, which, to his mind, threatens instant dissolution: thus the first becomes the strongest and necessarily urges him on to action. Nevertheless, in either case, whether he partakes of the water, or whether he does not, the two actions will be equally necessary; they will be the effect of that motive which finds itself most puissant; which consequently acts in the most coercive manner upon his will.

This example will serve to explain the whole phenomena of the human will. This will, or rather the brain, finds itself in the same situation as a bowl, which, although it has received an impulse that drives it forward in a straight line, is deranged in its course whenever a force superior to the first obliges it to change its direction. The man who drinks the poisoned water appears a madman; but the actions of fools are as necessary as those of the most prudent individuals. The motives that determine the voluptuary and the debauchee to risk their health, are as powerful, and their actions are as necessary, as those which decide the wise man to manage his. But, it will be insisted, the debauchee may be prevailed on to change his conduct: this does not imply that he is a free agent; but that motives may be found sufficiently powerful to annihilate the effect of those that previously acted upon him; then these new motives determine his will to the new mode of conduct he may adopt as necessarily as the former did to the old mode.

. . .

The *ambitious man* cries out: you will have me resist my passion; but have they not unceasingly repeated to me that rank, honours, power, are the most desirable advantages in life? Have I not seen my fellow citizens envy them, the nobles of my country sacrifice every thing to obtain them? In the society in which I live, am I not obliged to feel, that if I am deprived of these advantages, I must expect to languish in contempt; to cringe under the rod of oppression?

The *miser* says: you forbid me to love money, to seek after the means of acquiring it: alas! does not every thing tell me that, in this world, money is the greatest blessing; that it is amply sufficient to render me happy? In the country I inhabit, do I not see all my fellow citizens covetous of riches? But do I not also witness that they are little scrupulous in the means of obtaining wealth? As soon as they are enriched by the means which you censure, are they not cherished, considered and respected? By what authority, then, do you defend me from amassing treasure? What right have you to prevent my using means, which, although you call them sordid and criminal, I see approved by the sovereign? Will you have me renounce my happiness?

The *voluptuary* argues: you pretend that I should resist my desires; but was I the maker of my own termperament, which unceasingly invites me to pleasure? You call my pleasures disgraceful; but in the country in which I live, do I not witness the most dissipated men enjoying the most distinguished rank? Do I not behold that no one is ashamed of adultery but the husband it has outraged? Do not I see men making trophies of their debaucheries, boasting of the libertinism, rewarded with applause?

The *choleric man* vociferates: you advise me to put a curb on my passions, and to resist the desire of avenging myself: but can I conquer my nature? Can I alter the received opinions of the world? Shall I not be forever disgraced, infallibly dishonoured in society, if I do not wash out in the blood of my fellow creatures the injuries I have received?

The *zealous enthusiast* exclaims: you recommend me mildness; you advise me to be tolerant; to be indulgent to the opinions of my fellow men; but is not my temperament violent? Do I not ardently love my God? Do they not assure me, that zeal is pleasing to him; that sanguinary inhuman persecutors have been his friends? As I wish to render myself acceptable in his sight, I therefore adopt the same means.

In short, the actions of man are never free; they are always the necessary consequence of his temperament, of the received ideas, and of the notions, either true or false, which he has formed to himself of happiness; of his opinions, strengthened by example, by education, and by daily experience. So many crimes are witnessed on the earth only because every thing conspires to render man vicious and criminal; the religion he has adopted, his government, his education, the examples set before him, irresistibly drive him on to evil: under these circumstances, morality preaches virtue to him in vain. In those societies where vice is esteemed, where crime is crowned, where venality is constantly recompensed, where the most dreadful disorders are punished only in those who are too weak to enjoy the privilege of committing them with impunity, the practice of virtue is considered nothing more than a painful sacrifice of happiness. Such societies chastise, in the lower orders, those excesses which they respect in the higher ranks; and frequently have the injustice to condemn those in the penalty of death, whom public prejudices, maintained by constant example, have rendered criminal.

Man, then, is not a free agent in any one instant of his life; he is necessarily guided in each step by those advantages, whether real or fictitious, that he attaches to the objects by which his passions are roused: these passions themselves are necessary in a being who unceasingly tends towards his own happiness; their energy is necessary, since that depends on his temperament; his temperament is necessary, because it depends on the physical elements which enter into his composition; the modification of this temperament is necessary, as it is the infallible and inevitable consequence of the impulse he receives from the incessant action of moral and physical beings. . . .

If he understood the play of his organs, if he were able to recall to himself all the impulsions they have received, all the modifications they have undergone, all the effects they have produced, he would perceive that all his actions are submitted to that fatality, which regulates his own particular system, as it does the entire system of the universe: no one effect in him, any more than in nature, produces itself by chance; this, as has been before proved, is word void of sense. All that passes in him; all that is done by him; as well as all that happens in nature, or that is attributed to her, is derived from necessary causes, which act according to necessary laws, and which produce necessary effects from whence necessarily flow others.

Fatality, is the eternal, the immutable, the necessary order, established in nature; or the indispensable connexion of causes that act, with the effects they operate. Conforming to this order, heavy bodies fall: light bodies rise; that which is analogous in matter reciprocally attracts; that which is heterogeneous mutually repels; man congregates himself in society, modifies each his fellow; becomes either virtuous or wicked; either contributes to his mutual happiness, or reciprocates his misery; either loves his neighbour, or hates his companion necessarily, according to the manner in which the one acts upon the other. From whence it may be seen, that the same necessity which regulates the physical, also regulates the moral world, in which every thing is in consequence submitted to fatality. Man, in running over, frequently without his own knowledge, often in spite of himself, the route which nature has marked out for him, resembles a swimmer who is obliged to follow the current that carries him along: he believes himself a free agent, because he sometimes consents, sometimes does not consent, to glide with the stream, which, notwithstanding, always hurries him forward. . . .

READING

THE DILEMMA OF DETERMINISM
James

What does determinism profess?

It professes that those parts of the universe already laid down absolutely appoint and decree what the other parts shall be. The future has no ambiguous possibilities hidden in its womb: the part we call the present is compatible with only totality. Any other future complement than the one fixed from eternity is impossible. The whole is in each and every part, and welds it with the rest into an absolute unity, an iron block, in which there can be no equivocation or shadow of turning.

> With earth's first clay they did the last man knead,
>
> And there of the last harvest sowed the seed.
>
> And the first morning of creation wrote
>
> What the last dawn of reckoning shall read.

Indeterminism, on the contrary, says that the parts have a certain amount of loose play on one another, so that the laying down of one of them does not necessarily determine what the others shall be. It admits that possibilities may be in excess of actualities, and that things not yet revealed to our knowledge may really in themselves be ambiguous. Of two alternative futures which we conceive, both may now be really possible; and the one becomes impossible only at the very moment when the other excludes it by becoming real itself. Indeterminism thus denies the world to be one unbending unit of fact. It says there is a certain ultimate pluralism in it; and, so saying, it corroborates our ordinary unsophisticated view of things. To that view, actualities seem to float in a wider sea of possibilities from out of which they are chosen; and, *somewhere,* indeterminism says, such possibilities exist, and form a part of truth.

From William James, "Dilemma of Determinism," 1884.

Determinism, on the contrary, says they exist *nowhere,* and that necessity on the one hand and impossibility on the other are the sole categories of the real. Possibilities that fail to get realized are, for determinism, pure illusions: they never were possibilities at all. There is nothing inchoate, it says, about this universe of ours, all that was or is or shall be actual in it having been from eternity virtually there. The cloud of alternatives our minds escort this mass of actuality withal is a cloud of sheer deceptions, to which "impossibilities" is the only name that rightfully belongs.

The issue, it will be seen, is a perfectly sharp one, which no eulogistic terminology can smear over or wipe out. The truth *must* lie with one side or the other, and its lying with one side makes the other false.

The question relates solely to the existence of possibilities, in the strict sense of the term, as things that may, but need not, be. Both sides admit that a volition, for instance, has occurred. The indeterminists say another volition might have occurred in its place: the determinists swear that nothing could possibly have occurred in its place. Now, can science be called in to tell us which of these two point-blank contradicters of each other is right? Science professes to draw no conclusions but such as are based on matters of fact, things that have actually happened; but how can any amount of assurance that something actually happened give us the least grain of information as to whether another thing might or might not have happened in its place? Only facts can be proved by other facts. With things that are possibilities and not facts, facts have no concern. If we have no other evidence than the evidence of existing facts, the possibility-question must remain a mystery never to be cleared up.

And the truth is that facts practically have hardly anything to do with making us either determinists or indeterminists. Sure enough, we make a flourish of quoting facts this way or that; and if we are determinists, we talk about the infallibility with which we can predict one another's conduct; while if we are indeterminists, we lay great stress on the fact that it is just because we cannot foretell one another's conduct, either in war or statecraft or in any of the great and small intrigues and businesses of men, that life is so intensely anxious and hazardous a game. But who does not see the wretched insufficiency of this so-called objective testimony on both sides? What fills up the gaps in our minds is something not objective, not external. What divides us into *possibility* men and *antipossibility* men is different faiths or postulates—postulates of rationality. To this man the world seems more rational with possibilities in it—to that man more rational with possibilities excluded; and talk as we will about having to yield to evidence, what makes us monists or pluralists, determinists or indeterminists, is at bottom always some sentiment like this.

The stronghold of the deterministic sentiment is the antipathy to the idea of chance. As soon as we begin to talk indeterminism to our friends, we find a number of them shaking their heads. This notion of alternative possibility, they say, this admission that any one of several things may come to pass, is, after all, only a round-about name for chance; and chance is something the notion of which no sane mind can for an instant tolerate in the world. What is it, they ask, but barefaced crazy unreason, the negation of intelligibility and law? And if the slightest particle of it exist anywhere, what is to prevent the whole fabric from falling together, the stars from going out, and chaos from recommencing her topsy-turvy reign? . . .

Nevertheless, many persons talk as if the minutest dose of disconnectedness of one part with another, the smallest modicum of independence, the faintest tremor of ambiguity about the future, for example, would ruin everything, and turn this goodly universe into a sort of insane sand-heap or nulliverse—no universe at all. Since future human volitions are as a matter of fact the only ambiguous things we are tempted to believe in, let us stop for a moment to make ourselves sure whether their independent and accidental character need be fraught with such direful consequences to the universe as these. . . .

We have seen what determinism means: we have seen that indeterminism is rightly described as meaning chance; and we have seen that chance, the very name of which we are urged to shrink from as from a metaphysical pestilence, means only the negative fact that no part of the world, however big, can claim to control absolutely the destinies of the whole. . . . I said at the outset, that, from any strict theoretical point of view, the question is insoluble. To deepen our theoretic sense of the *difference* between a world with chances in it and a deterministic world is the most I can hope to do; and this I may now at last begin upon, after all our tedious clearing of the way.

I wish first of all to show you just what the notion that this is a deterministic world implies. The implications I call your attention to are all bound up with the fact that it is a world in which we constantly have to make what I shall, with your permission, call judgments of regret. Hardly an hour passes in which we do not wish that something might be otherwise. . . . Even from the point of view of our own ends, we should probably make a botch of remodelling the universe. How much more then from the point of view of ends we cannot see! Wise men therefore regret as little as they can. But still some regrets are pretty obstinate and hard to stifle—regrets for acts of wanton cruelty or treachery, for example, whether performed by others or by ourselves. Hardly any one can remain *entirely* optimistic after reading the confession of the murderer at Brockton the other day: how, to get rid of the wife whose continued existence bored him, he inveigled her into a desert spot, shot her four times, and then, as she lay on the ground and said to him, "You didn't do it on purpose, did you, dear?" replied, "No, I didn't do it on purpose," as he raised a rock and smashed her skull. Such an occurrence, with the mild sentence and self-satisfaction of the prisoner, is a field for a crop of regrets, which one need not take up in detail. We feel that, although a perfect mechanical fit to the rest of the universe, it is a bad moral fit, and that something else would really have been better in its place.

But for the deterministic philosophy the murder, the sentence, and the prisoner's optimism were all necessary from eternity; and nothing else for a moment had a ghost of a chance of being put into their place. To admit such a chance, the determinists tell us, would be to make a suicide of reason; so we must steel our hearts against the thought. And here our plot thickens, for we see the first of those difficult implications of determinism and monism which it is my purpose to make you feel. If this Brockton murder was called for by the rest of the universe, if it had to come at its preappointed hour, and if nothing else would have been consistent with the sense of the whole, what are we to think of the universe? Are we stubbornly to stick to our judgment of regret, and say, though it *couldn't* be, yet it *would* have been a better universe with something different from this Brockton murder in it? That, of course, seems the natural and spontaneous thing for us to do; and yet it is nothing short of deliberately espousing a kind of pessimism. The judgment of regret calls the murder bad. Calling a thing bad means, if it mean anything at all, that the thing ought not to be, that something else ought to be in its stead. Determinism, in denying that anything else can be in its stead, virtually defines the universe as a place in which what ought to be is impossible—in other words, as an organism whose constitution is afflicted with an incurable taint, an irremediable flaw. The pessimism of a Schopenhauer says no more than this—that the murder is a symptom; and that it is a vicious symptom because it belongs to a vicious whole, which can express its nature no otherwise than by bringing forth just such a symptom as that at this particular spot. Regret for the murder must transform itself, if we are determinists and wise, into a larger regret. It is absurd to regret the murder alone. Other things being what they are, *it* could not be different. What we should regret is that whole frame of things of which the murder is one member. I see no escape whatever from this pessimistic conclusion if, being determinists, our judgment of regret is to be allowed to stand at all.

The only deterministic escape from pessimism is everywhere to abandon the judgment of regret. That this can be done, history shows to be not impossible. The devil, *quoad existentiam,* may be good. That is, although he be a *principle* of evil, yet the universe, with such a principle in it, may practically be a better universe than it could have been without. On every hand, in a small way, we find that a certain amount of evil is a condition by which a higher form of good is brought. There is nothing to prevent anybody from generalizing this view, and trusting that if we could but see things in the largest of all ways, even such matters as this Brockton murder would appear to be paid for by the uses that follow in their train. An optimism *quand même,* a systematic and infatuated optimism like that ridiculed by Voltaire in his *Candide,* is one of the possible ideal ways in which a man may train himself to look on life. Bereft of dogmatic hardness and lit up with the expression of a tender and pathetic hope, such an optimism has been the grace of some of the most religious characters that ever lived. . . .

But does not this immediately bring us into a curious logical predicament? Our determinism leads us to call our judgments of regret wrong, because they are pessimistic in implying that what is impossible yet ought to be. But how then about the judgments of regret themselves? If they are wrong, other judgments, judgments of approval presumably, ought to be in their place. But as they are necessitated, nothing else *can* be in their place; and the universe is just what it was before—namely, a place in which what ought to be appears impossible. We have got one foot out of the pessimistic bog, but the other one sinks all the deeper. We have rescued our actions from the bonds of evil, but our judgments are now held fast. When murders and treacheries cease to be sins, regrets are theoretic absurdities and errors. The theoretic and the active life thus play a kind of see-saw with each other on the ground of evil. The rise of either sends the other down. Murder and treachery cannot be good without regret being bad: regret cannot be good without treachery and murder being bad. Both, however, are supposed to have been foredoomed; so something must be fatally unreasonable, absurd, and wrong in the world. It must be a place of which either sin or error forms a necessary part. From this dilemma there seems at first sight no escape. Are we then so soon to fall back into the pessimism from which we thought we had emerged? And is there no possible way by which we may, with good intellectual consciences, call the cruelties and the treacheries, the reluctances and the regrets, *all* good together? . . .

The only consistent way of representing a pluralism and a world whose parts may affect one another through their conduct being either good or bad is the indeterministic way. What interest, zest, or excitement can there be in achieving the right way, unless we are enabled to feel that the wrong way is also a possible and a natural way—nay, more, a menacing and an imminent way? And what sense can there be in condemning ourselves for taking the wrong way, unless we need have done nothing of the sort, unless the right way was open to us as well? I cannot understand the willingness to act, no matter how we feel, without the belief that acts are really good and bad. I cannot understand the belief that an act is bad, without regret at its happening. I cannot understand regret without the admission of real, genuine possibilities in the world. Only *then* is it other than a mockery to feel, after we have failed to do our best, that an irreparable opportunity is gone from the universe, the loss of which it must forever after mourn.

If you insist that this is all superstition, that possibility is in the eye of science and reason impossibility, and that if I act badly 'tis that the universe was foredoomed to suffer this defect, you fall right back into the dilemma, the labyrinth, of pessimism and subjectivism, from out of whose toils we have just wound our way.

CHAPTER 8

CREATING OURSELVES

Sartre

Born in 1905, Jean-Paul Sartre was educated at the École Normale Supérieure in Paris, exhibiting at an early age his precocious gift for literary expression. He was attracted to philosophy while at the École Normale by Henri Bergson, whose *Essay sur les donnés immédiates de la conscience* left him "bowled over" and with the feeling that "philosophy is absolutely terrific, you can learn the truth through it." He spent the years 1934–1945 at the Institut Français in Berlin, where he studied Husserl's phenomenology. Sartre wrote his *Transcendental Ego* (1936) in Germany while at the Institut, and, as he says, "I wrote it actually under the direct influence of Husserl. . . ." During World War II, Sartre was active in the French Resistance movement and became a German prisoner of war. Afterwards he taught at the lycee at Havre, the lycee Henri IV, and the lycee Condorcet, resigning after this brief teaching career to devote himself exclusively to his writings, which ultimately numbered over thirty volumes. While still a student at the elite École Normale Supérieure, he met a fellow student, Simone de Beauvoir, with whom he enjoyed a lifelong companionship. He lived simply and with few possessions in a small apartment on the Left Bank in Paris. In declining health and virtually blind, Sartre died on April 15, 1980 at the age of seventy-four.

Sartre's name has become identified with existentialism primarily because he took the more technical writings of the contemporary German philosophers, especially Heidegger, who had probed into the meaning of Being through the deep recesses of man's anxious and restless soul and expressed their findings with great lucidity and popular appeal. What had appeared first in the heavy language of philosophy now came forth from Sartre's pen in the open and captivating style of novels and short stories. As a philosopher, Sartre was himself capable of writing about existentialism in the most exacting and complex style, which one finds in his massive major book *Being and Nothingness (Être et le Neant,* 1943). But his best known work is his lecture *Existentialism Is a Humanism (L'Existentialisme est un humanisme),* published in 1946, a work which has become famous because of its brilliance and despite Sartre's later desire to define existentialism in somewhat different terms.

Sartre's version of existentialism is the product of a special mixture of at least three contemporary modes of thought, stemming from Marx, Husserl, and Heidegger. What these three strands of thought had in common for Sartre was their concern about man's active role in forging his own destiny. Marx had expressed his passion for action when he wrote that "hitherto philosophers had merely understood the world; the point, however, is to change it." Husserl also focused his new brand of philosophy, which he called "phenomenology," on the individual, saying that "true philosophy should seek its foundation exclusively in man and, more specifically, in the essence of his concrete worldly existence." And Heidegger, in his great work *Being and Time (Sein und Zeit),* which relies somewhat on Kierkegaard and Husserl, wrote that our basic understanding of the large question of Being is achieved best through the existential analysis of the *person.* Heidegger's analysis strongly shaped Sartre's thought, but whereas Heidegger was concerned chiefly with *Being,* and with the *existence* of the *person* only as a means for understanding Being, Sartre became preoccupied almost solely with the existence of the individual. Accordingly,

Sartre in cafe (*The Bettmann Archive*)

Sartre's classical formulation of the basic principle of existentialism, namely, that *existence precedes essence,* is a reversal not only of Heidegger's intentions, but of traditional metaphysics, which ever since Plato's time has said that essence precedes existence.

What does it mean to say that existence precedes essence, and how does this formula bear on our understanding of human nature? Sartre argues that we cannot explain the nature of man in the same way that we describe an article of manufacture. When we consider, for example, a paper knife, we know that it has been made by someone who had in his mind a conception of it, including what it would be used for and how it would be made. Thus even before it is made, the paper knife is already conceived of as having a definite purpose and as being the product of a definite process. If by the *essence* of the paper knife we mean the procedure by which it was made and the purposes for which it was produced, the paper knife's essence can be said to precede its existence. To look on a paper knife is to understand exactly what its useful purpose is. When we think about man's nature, we tend to describe him also as the product of a maker, of a creator, of God. We think of God most of the time, says Sartre, as a "supernal artisan," implying that when God creates, He knows precisely what He is creating. This would mean that in the mind of God the conception of man is comparable to the conception of the paper knife in the mind of the artisan. Each individual, in this view, is the fulfillment or realization of a definite conception, which resides in God's understanding.

Although it is true that some of the philosophers of the eighteenth century, including Diderot, Voltaire, and Kant, were either atheists or else suppressed the idea of God, they nevertheless retained the notion, distinctive of the theist, that man possesses a "human nature," a nature that is found in every man. Each man, they said, is a particular example of the universal conception of Man. Whatever may be the level of development to which various men have attained, whether they be primitive natives, men in the state of nature, or cultured bourgeois, they all have the same fundamental qualities and are therefore all contained in the same definition or conception of Man. In short, they all possess the same essence, and their essence precedes their concrete or historic existence, which they confront in experience.

Sartre turned all this around by taking atheism seriously. He believed that if there is no God, there is no *given* human nature precisely because there is no God to have a conception of it. Human nature cannot be defined in advance because it is not completely thought out in advance. Man as such merely exists and only later becomes his essential self. To say that existence precedes essence means, says Sartre, that man first of all exists, confronts himself, emerges in the world, and defines himself afterwards. At first, man simply is. Whether it follows that man does not have a basic and given nature simply because there is no God who stands in relation to man the way the artisan stands in relation to the knife is questionable. But what Sartre wants particularly to argue is that man is simply that which he makes of himself.

One's first reaction to this formulation of the first principle of Sartre's existentialism is that it is highly subjective, that each man can presumably set out to make of himself anything he wishes. Sartre's chief point here is that man has a greater dignity than a stone or a table. What gives him dignity is his possession of a sub-jective life, meaning that man is something which moves itself toward a future and is conscious that it is doing so. Sartre wants to call attention to two different modes of being, which he calls *being-in-itself (l'en-soi)* and *being-for-itself (le pour-soi)*. Applying this distinction to man, one can say that man shares both these two modes of being, the *en-soi* indicating that he *is* (the way a stone is) and the *pour-soi* indicating that he is a *conscious subject* (which therefore differentiates him from a stone). To be a conscious sub-ject is to stand constantly before a future. The most important con-sequence of placing existence before essence in human nature is not only that man creates himself, but also that the responsibility for each man's existence rests squarely on each man. A stone cannot be responsible. And if man's essential nature were already given and fixed, he could not be responsible for what he is.

What began in Sartre's analysis as an amoral subjectivism now turns out to be an ethics of strict accountability based on individual responsibility. If, that is, man is what he makes of himself, he has no one to blame for what he is except himself. Moreover, when man *chooses* in the process of making himself, he chooses not only for himself but for all men. He is therefore responsible not only for his own individuality, but, says Sartre, he is responsible for all men. This last point seems to contradict the line of reasoning that Sartre has so far been developing, for to say that before one can choose a way of action one must ask "What would happen if everyone else acted so?" is to assume a general human essence, which makes *my* mode of action relevant to *all* men. Sartre does in fact say that even though we create our own values and thereby create ourselves, we nevertheless create at the same time an image of our human nature as we believe it ought to be. When we choose this or that way of acting, we affirm the value of what we have chosen, and nothing can be better for any one of us unless it is better for all. This all sounds very much like Kant's categorical imperative. But Sartre does not wish to invoke any universal law to guide man's choice. He is calling attention to one of the clearest experiences of human beings, namely, that all men must choose, must make decisions and although they have no authoritative guide, they must still choose and at the same time ask whether they would be willing for others to choose the same action. One cannot escape at times the disturb-ing thought that one would not want others to act as one does. To say that others will not so act is a case of *self-deception*. The act of choice, then, is one that all men must accomplish with a deep sense of *anguish,* for in this act men are responsible not only for themselves but also for each other. Whoever evades his responsibility through *self-deception* will not, says Sartre, be at ease in his conscience.

Although Sartre's moral language sounds at times very much like traditional moral discourse, his intention is to carry out the rigorous implications of atheism. Sartre accepts Nietzsche's announcement that "God is dead" and takes seriously Dostoevsky's notion that "if God did not exist, everything would be permitted." In a Godless world, man's psychological condition is one of *abandonment,* a word Sartre takes from Heidegger. "Abandonment" means for Sartre that with the dismissal of God there also disappears every possibility of finding values in some sort of intelligible heaven. Again, there cannot now be any "good" prior to my choice, since there is no infinite or perfect consciousness to think it. Man's sense of abandonment is a curious consequence of the fact that everything is indeed permitted, and as a consequence, man is forlorn, for he cannot find anything on which he can rely either within or outside himself. Man is without any excuse. His existence precedes his essence. Apart from his existence there is nothingness. There is only the present. In his *Nausea,* Sartre writes that the true nature of the present was revealed as what exists, that what is not present does not exist. Things are entirely what they appear to be, and apart from them, there is nothing. To say there is nothing besides the existing individual means for Sartre that there is no God, no objective system of values, no built-in essence, and most important of all, *no determinism.* Man, says Sartre, is free; man is freedom. In a classic phrase, he says that man is *condemned* to be free. Condemned because he finds himself thrown into the world, yet free because as soon as he is conscious of himself, he is responsible for everything he does. Sartre rejects the notion that human behavior is swept up by a torrent of passion as though such a passion could be regarded as an excuse for certain actions. He rejected the Freudian analysis of human behavior because it appeared to him that it provided an excuse in the form of psychological determinism. Man is responsible even for his passions, because even his feelings are formed by his deeds. Freedom is appalling (Kierkegaard had similarly spoken of the *dizziness* of freedom) precisely because it means that there is nothing forcing me from behind, so to speak, to behave in any given way, nor is there a precise pattern luring me into the future. I am the only thing that exists. We are all free, says Sartre; therefore we must choose, that is, *invent*, because no rule of general morality can show us what we ought to do. There are no guidelines guaranteed to us in this world.

There is an element of despair in human existence, which comes, says Sartre, from the realization that we are limited to what is within the scope of our own wills. We cannot expect more from our existence than the finite probabilities it possesses. Here Sartre believes that he is touching the genuine theme of personal existence by emphasizing man's finitude and his relation to nothingness. "Nothingness," he says, "lies coiled in the heart of being, like a worm." Heidegger located the cause of human anxiety in man's awareness of his finitude when, for example, I confront death—not death in general but *my* death. It is not only man who faces nothingness, says Heidegger, but all Being has this relation to nothingness. Human finitude is therefore not simply a matter of temporary ignorance or some shortcoming or even error. Finitude is the very structure of the human mind, and words such as "guilt," "loneliness," and "despair" describe the consequences of human finitude. The ultimate principle of Being, says Heidegger, is *will*. Sartre concurs by saying that only in action is there any reality. Man is only the sum of his actions and purposes; besides his actual daily life he is nothing. If a person is a coward, he *made* himself one. He is not a coward because of a cowardly heart or lungs or cerebrum, or because of his physiological organism; he is a coward because he made himself into one by his actions.

Although there is no prior essence in all men, no human *nature*, there is nevertheless, says Sartre, a universal human *condition*. He rejects a narrow individual subjectivism as the standard of truth. Rather, to discover oneself in the act of conscious thought is to discover the condition of all men. We are in a world of *intersubjectivity*. This is the kind of world in which an individual must live, choose, and decide. For this reason, no purpose chosen by any individual is ever wholly foreign to another individual. This does not mean that every purpose defines man forever, but only that all men may be striving against the same limitations in the same way. For this reason, Sartre would not agree that it does not matter what we do or how we choose. Man is always obliged to act in a *situation*, that is, in relation to other persons, and consequently, his actions cannot, must not, be capricious, since he must take responsibility for all his actions. Moreover, to say that man must make his essence, invent his values, does not mean that one cannot *judge* human actions. It is still possible to say that one's action was based either on error or self-deception, for any man who hides behind the excuse of his passions or by espousing some doctrine of determinism deceives himself. To invent values, says Sartre, means only that there is no meaning or sense in life prior to acts of will. Life cannot be anything until it is lived, but each individual must make sense of it. The value of life is nothing else but the sense each person fashions into it. To argue that we are the victims of fate, of mysterious forces within us, of some grand passion, of heredity, is to be guilty of bad faith (*mauvaise foi*) or self-deception—of *inauthenticity.* A woman who consents to go out with a particular man knows very well, says Sartre, what the man's cherished intentions are, and she knows that sooner or later she will have to make a decision. She does not want to admit the urgency of the matter, preferring rather to interpret all his actions as discreet and respectful. She is, says Sartre, in self-deception; her actions are inauthentic. All human beings are guilty, on principle, of similar inauthenticity, of bad faith, of playing roles, of trying to disguise their actual personality behind a facade. The conclusion of Sartre's existentialism is, therefore, that if man expresses his genuine humanity in all his behavior, he will never deceive himself, and honesty will then become not his ideal but rather his very being.

The Human Reality

Underlying Sartre's popular formulation of existentialism is his technical analysis of existence. In one respect, human nature is no different from any other kind of existing reality. Man is, just the same way anything else *is*, as simply *being there.* Unlike other things, however, man possesses consciousness. For this reason, he is related to the world of things and people in a variety of ways. At one level, man is conscious of "the world," which is everything that is beyond or other than himself and which therefore transcends him. At this level, the world is experienced simply as a solid, massive, undifferentiated, single something that is not yet separated into individual things.

Sartre describes this mode of consciousness in his *Nausea*

where the character Roquentin is sitting on a park bench. He looks at all the things before him in the park and all at once he *sees* everything differently, everything as a single thing—"Suddenly existence had unveiled itself." Words had vanished and the points of reference which men use to give meaning to things also vanished. What Roquentin saw was existence as "the very paste of things": "The root [of the tree], the park gates, the bench, the sparse grass, all that had vanished: the diversity of things, their individuality, were only an appearance, a veneer. This veneer had melted, leaving soft, monstrous masses, all in disorder—naked." Only later, when man reflects, does the world become our familiar one. But, says Sartre, "The world of explanations and reasons is not the world of existence." At the level of Roquentin's experience, the world is the unity of all the objects of consciousness.

Sartre agrees that all consciousness is consciousness of *something,* which means that there is no consciousness without affirming the existence of an object which exists beyond, that is, transcends, itself. As we have seen, the object of consciousness can be "the world" as simply "being there." But in addition to the world as a single solid mass, we speak of specific objects such as trees, benches, and tables. Whenever we identify a specific object, we do this by saying what it is not—we differentiate a thing from its background. A chair appears as a chair because human beings give it that meaning by blacking out the background. What we call a chair is fashioned or drawn out of the solid context of the world by the activity of consciousness. The world of things appears as an intelligible system of separate and interrelated things only to consciousness. Without consciousness, the world simply is, it is *being-in-itself (l'en soi)* and as such it is without meaning. Consciousness constitutes the meaning of things in the world, although it does not constitute their being.

When he views the world as being-in-itself, as simply being there, Sartre says that "the essential point is contingency. I mean that by definition existence is not necessity. To exist is simply to be there." Contingency means that when something exists, it does so by chance and not because it necessarily follows from something else: "Existences appear . . . but you cannot deduce them." The world we experience is "uncreated, without reason for being, without any relation to another being; being-in-itself is gratuitous for all eternity." The meaning anything will have in the world will depend, says Sartre, on choices men make. Even a table will have alternative meanings depending on what a particular person chooses to use it for, to serve dinner or to write a letter. A mountain valley will mean one thing to a farmer and something else to a camper. Here, consciousness shifts a person from simply being there, being-in-itself, to *being-for-itself (le pour-soi)*, where consciousness dramatically differentiates the objects of the world from the conscious self as subject.

The activity of consciousness is at this point twofold. First, consciousness defines the specific things in the world and invests them with meaning. Second, consciousness transcends, that is, puts a distance between itself and objects and in that way possesses a freedom from those objects. Because the conscious self has this freedom from the things in the world, it is within the power of consciousness to confer different or alternative meanings on things. The activity of consciousness is what is usually called "choice." Man chooses to undertake this project or that project, and the meaning of things in the world will depend to a considerable extent on what project a man chooses. If he chooses to be a farmer, the mountains, the valley, and the impending storm will have special meanings for him, whereas if he chooses to be a camper in that valley, the surroundings and the storm will present different meanings. Man, as man, at first simply *is;* his existence is primary and precedes what he is to become. What he becomes will depend on how his consciousness deals with the world—a world which he views from a distance. From this distance, in this position of freedom from things and persons, man makes a choice regarding how he will relate himself to them. It follows, also, that because man has this freedom from the world, the world does not, cannot, *mechanically and totally* affect man's consciousness and his choices. There is no way for man to alter the fact that he transcends the world, is able to view it, so to speak, from above and must therefore constantly make choices, take sides, undertake projects. In short, man is condemned to be free. By his free choices, man makes himself— not that he creates himself out of nothing, but rather by a series of choices and decisions he converts his existence into the essence of his final self. Man possesses this freedom to create himself within some limitations, such as the conditions of his birth and the circumstances of each particular situation. Nevertheless, Sartre says that any attempt on the part of a person to make excuses for his behavior by attributing his actions to external or underlying causes is self-deception and in bad faith. This strong emphasis on human freedom as worked out in *Being and Nothingness* (1943) was softened by Sartre in the sequel to that book, his *Critique of Dialectical Reason* (1960).

Although Sartre believed that Marxism is the philosophy of our time, he was aware of a striking contradiction between his existentialism and Marxist dialectical materialism. Indeed, one reason why Sartre never became a member of the Communist party is, he says, because "I would have had to turn my back on *Being and Nothingness*," in which he had placed such a strong emphasis on human freedom. By contrast, Marxist dialectical materialism emphasized that all the structures and organizations of society and the behavior and thinking of human beings are determined by antecedent events. In this view, freedom of choice is an illusion and man is simply a vehicle through which the forces of history realize themselves. Whereas Sartre had argued that it is man's consciousness that "makes history" and confers meaning on the world, Marxism holds that history is a process which produces the material foundations of social and economic structures, a process which therefore contains within itself the conditions and the reasons for its own development. Rather than conferring meaning on the world, the mind, says the Marxist, discovers this meaning within the historical context as a matter of scientific knowledge.

In his earlier writings, Sartre focused primarily on the individual and his freedom. For this reason, he never would accept Freud's theory of the unconscious, which Sartre saw as an irrational and mechanical causation of human behavior. Later, as in his *Critique of Dialectical Reason*, he focused more specifically on the historical and social context in which man finds himself and which has an effect on man's behavior. He thought that Marx had succeeded more than anyone else in describing how social and economic structures develop and how they bear on human decisions. Sartre accepted increasingly the limitations on human choice—the limitations of birth, status in society, and family background. Earlier, he sought to describe how an individual is capable of deceiving himself by making excuses for his behavior, as if he were not free to have behaved otherwise, a form of self-deception Sartre labeled as "bad faith." He never did depart from this emphasis on the freedom of the individual. But he did adjust his thinking under the influence of Marxism by facing the fact of man's social existence, his relationship with other persons, especially as a member of a group—such as, for example, a labor union. Acknowledging the influence of group structures on human behavior and consciousness, resulting particularly in labor's sense of alienation, Sartre revised his optimistic view of human freedom to some extent. Recalling that he had written earlier (1945) that "no matter what the situation might be, one is always free" (giving as an example that "a worker is always free to join a union or not, as he is free to choose the kind of battle he wants to join, or not"), Sartre says this "all strikes me as absurd today" (1972). And he admits, "There is no question that there is some basic change in [my] concept of freedom." In his lengthy work on Flaubert, he concludes that although Flaubert was free to become uniquely Flaubert, his family background and his status in society meant that "he did not have all that many possibilities of becoming something else . . . he had the possibility of becoming a mediocre doctor . . . and the possibility of being Flaubert." This means, says Sartre, that social conditioning exists every minute of our lives. Nevertheless, he concludes that "I am still faithful to the notion of freedom." It is true, he says, that "you become what you are in the context of what others have made of you"; nevertheless, within these limitations, man is still free and responsible. This is Sartre's way of reconciling the fact that historical conditions affect human behavior with his intuitive certainty that human beings are also capable of shaping history. In doing this, Sartre sought to overcome with his existentialism what he considered the major flaw of Marxist philosophy, namely, its failure to recognize man as a "real person."

READING

THE LIMITS OF ATHEISTIC FREEDOM

Sartre

Man is nothing else but what he makes of himself. Such is the first principle of existentialism. It is also what is called subjectivity, the name we are

From Jean-Paul Sartre, "The Humanism of Existentialism" *The Philosophy of Existentialism*, ed. Wade Baskin, Philosophical Library, New York, 1965. By permission.

labeled with when charges are brought against us. But what do we mean by this, if not that man has a greater dignity than a stone or table? For we mean that man first exists, that is, that man first of all is the being who hurls himself toward a future and who is conscious of imagining himself as being in the future. Man is at the start a plan which is aware of itself, rather than a patch of moss, a piece of garbage, or a cauliflower; nothing exists prior to this plan; there is nothing in heaven; man will be what he will have planned to be. Not what he will want to be. Because by the word "will" we generally mean a conscious decision, which is subsequent to what we have already made of ourselves. I may want to belong to a political party, write a book, get married; but all that is only a manifestation of an earlier, more spontaneous choice that is called "will." But if existence really does precede essence, man is responsible for what he is. Thus, existentialism's first move is to make every man aware of what he is and to make the full responsibility of his existence rest on him. And when we say that a man is responsible for himself, we do not only mean that he is responsible for his own individuality, but that he is responsible for all men.

The word subjectivism means, on the one hand, that an individual chooses and makes himself; and, on the other, that it is impossible for man to transcend human subjectivity. The second of these is the essential meaning of existentialism. When we say that man chooses his own self, we mean that every one of us does likewise; but we also mean by that that in making this choice he also chooses all men. In fact, in creating the man that we want to be, there is not a single one of our acts which does not at the same time create an image of man as we think he ought to be. To choose to be this or that is to affirm at the same time the value of what we choose, because we can never choose evil. We always choose the good, and nothing can be good for us without being good for all.

If, on the other hand, existence precedes essence, and if we grant that we exist and fashion our image at one and the same time, the image is valid for everybody and for our whole age. Thus, our responsibility is much greater than we might have supposed, because it involves all mankind. If I am a workingman and choose to join a christian trade-union rather than be a communist, and if by being a member I want to show that the best thing for man is resignation, that the kingdom of man is not of this world, I am not only involving my own case—I want to be resigned for everyone. As a result, my action has involved all humanity. To take a more individual matter, if I want to marry, to have children; even if this marriage depends solely on my own circumstances or passion or wish, I am involving all humanity in monogamy and not merely myself. Therefore, I am responsible for myself and for everyone else. I am creating a certain image of man of my own choosing. In choosing myself, I choose man.

This helps us understand what the actual content is of such rather grandiloquent words as anguish, forlornness, despair. As you will see, it's all quite simple.

First, what is meant by anguish? The existentialists say at once that man is anguish. What that means is this: the man who involves himself and who realizes that he is not only the person he chooses to be, but also a lawmaker who is, at the same time, choosing all mankind as well as himself, can not help escape the feeling of his total and deep responsibility. Of course, there are many people who are not anxious; but we claim that they are hiding their anxiety, that they are fleeing from it. Certainly, many people believe that when they do something, they themselves are the only ones involved, and when someone says to them, "What if everyone acted that way?" they shrug their shoulders and answer, "Everyone doesn't act that way." But really, one should always ask himself, "What would happen if everybody looked at things that way?" There is no escaping this disturbing thought except by a kind of double-dealing. A man who lies and makes excuses for himself by saying "Not everybody does that," is someone with an uneasy conscience, because the act of lying implies that a universal value is conferred upon the lie.

Anguish is evident even when it conceals itself. This is the anguish that Kierkegaard called the anguish of Abraham. You know the story: an angel has ordered Abraham to sacrifice his son; if it really were an angel who has come and said, "You are Abraham, you shall sacrifice your son," everything would be all right. But everyone might first wonder, "Is it really an angel, and am I really Abraham? What proof do I have?"

There was a madwoman who had hallucinations; someone used to speak to her on the telephone and give her orders. Her doctor asked her, "Who is it who talks to you?" She answered, "He says it's God." What proof did she really have that it was God? If an angel comes to me, what proof is there that it's an angel? And if I hear voices, what proof is there that they come from heaven and not from hell, or from the subconscious, or a pathological condition? What proves that they are addressed to me? What proof is there that I have been appointed to impose my choice and my conception of man on humanity? I'll never find any proof or sign to convince me of that. If a voice addresses me, it is always for me to decide that this is the angel's voice; if I consider that such an act is a good one, it is I who will choose to say that it is good rather than bad.

Now, I'm not being singled out as an Abraham, and yet at every moment I'm obliged to perform exemplary acts. For every man, everything happens as if all mankind had its eyes fixed on him and were guiding itself by what he does. And every man ought to say to himself, "Am I really the kind of man who has the right to act in such a way that humanity might guide itself by my actions?" And if he does not say that to himself, he is masking his anguish.

There is no question here of the kind of anguish which would lead to quietism, to inaction. It is a matter of a simple sort of anguish that anybody who has had responsibilities is familiar with. For example, when a military officer takes the responsibility for an attack and sends a certain number of men to death, he chooses to do so, and in the main he alone makes the choice. Doubtless, orders come from above, but they are too broad; he interprets them, and on this interpretation depend the lives of ten or fourteen or twenty men. In making a decision he can not help having a certain anguish. All leaders know this anguish. That doesn't keep them from acting; on the contrary, it is the very condition of their action. For it implies that they envisage a number of possibilities, and when they choose one, they realize that it has value only because it is chosen. We shall see that this kind of anguish, which is the kind that existentialism describes, is explained, in addition, by a direct responsibility to the other men whom it involves. It is not a curtain separating us from action, but is part of action itself.

When we speak of forlornness, a term Heidegger was fond of, we mean only that God does not exist and that we have to face all the consequences of this. The existentialist is strongly opposed to a certain kind of secular ethics which would like to abolish God with the least possible expense. About 1880, some French teachers tried to set up a secular ethics which went something like this: God is a useless and costly hypothesis; we are discarding it; but, meanwhile, in order for there to be an ethics, a society, a civilization, it is essential that certain values be taken seriously and that they be considered as having an *a priori* existence. It must be obligatory, *a priori,* to be honest, not to lie, not to beat your wife, to have children, etc., etc. So we're going to try a little device which will make it possible to show that values exist all the same, inscribed in a heaven of ideas, though otherwise God does not exist. In other words—and this, I believe, is the tendency of everything called reformism in France—nothing will be changed if God does not exist. We shall find ourselves with the same norms of honesty, progress, and humanism, and we shall have made of God an outdated hypothesis which will peacefully die off by itself.

The existentialist, on the contrary, thinks it very distressing that God does not exist, because all possibility of finding values in a heaven of ideas disappears along with Him; there can no longer be an *a priori* Good, since there is no infinite and perfect consciousness to think it. Nowhere is it written that the Good exists, that we must be honest, that we must not lie; because the fact is we are on a plane where there are only men. Dostoievsky said, "If God didn't exist, everything would be permitted." That is the very starting point of existentialism. Indeed, everything is permissible if God does not exist, and as a result man is forlorn, because neither within him nor without does he find anything to cling to. He can't start making excuses for himself.

If existence really does precede essence, there is no explaining things away by reference to a fixed and given human nature. In other words, there is no determinism, man is free, man is freedom. On the other hand, if God does not exist, we find no values or commands to turn to which legitimize our conduct. So, in the bright realm of values, we have no excuse behind us, nor justification before us. We are alone, with no excuses.

That is the idea I shall try to convey when I say that man is condemned to be free. Condemned, because he did not create himself, yet, in other respects is free; because, once thrown into the world, he is responsible for everything he does. The existentialist does not believe in the power of passion. He will never agree that a sweeping passion is a ravaging torrent which fatally leads a man to certain acts and is therefore an excuse. He thinks that man is responsible for his passion.

Questions for Discussion:
Ethics

1. The Stoics urged us to "accept" what we could not change and to change whatever is in our power to change. When you consider your daily life, what do you think you could change, if you wanted to, and what can you not change?

2. Aristotle says "The function of man is an activity of the soul which follows or implies a rational principle." Do you agree that this is the function of man? Are there other alternatives?

3. According to Augustine, everything we love is good. How, then, is it that some kinds of love can have such bad consequences? Consider also whether there is anything which is intrinsically evil.

4. If it were discovered that *all* cultures adhered to the same moral principles, would these necessarily be the correct moral principles? What would Kant say about this? Would he be correct? What would Kant say about moral principles which varied from culture to culture?

5. Kant claimed that by invoking the categorical imperative we could see that it is never right to break a promise. How would Mill decide whether to break a promise? Which is the better view, Mill's or Kant's?

6. Compare and contrast Aristotle's golden mean to Nietzsche's discussion of the Apollonian and Dionysian forces in a person's life.

7. In their debate over determinism versus freedom of the will, who, in your judgment, makes the more persuasive argument, Holbach or James?

8. Sartre says that all of us are *condemned* to be free. Why does he use this language? Isn't freedom one of our most cherished values, something that people want desperately?

Suggested Additional Readings: Ethics

1. Barnes, Hazel: *An Existentialist Ethics*, Vintage Books, Random House, New York, 1971. An ethics founded on Sartre's philosophy.

2. Hospers, John: *Human Conduct*, Harcourt, Brace & World, New York, 1972. A comprehensive, but animated, discussion of major moral theories.

3. Huby, Pamela: *Greek Ethics*, Macmillan, New York, 1967. For those intrigued by Epictetus and Aristotle.

4. Kaufmann, Walter: *Nietzsche. Philosopher, Psychologist, Antichrist*, Vintage Books, Random House, New York, 1968. An excellent guide to Nietzsche.

5. Lerner, Max (ed.): *Essential Works of John Stuart Mill*, Bantam, New York, 1961. Includes Mill's *Autobiography* and several important essays.

6. MacIntyre, Alaisdair: *A Short History of Ethics*, Macmillan, New York, 1966. The title aptly describes the contents.

7. Nell, Onora: *Acting on Principle*, Columbia, New York, 1975. A Kantian ethics done by a contemporary philosopher.

8. Ross, W. D.: *Kant's Ethical Theory*, Oxford University Press, New York, 1953. A straightforward account of Kant.

9. Walsh, J. J., and Shapiro, H. L. (eds.) *Aristotle's Ethics*, Wadsworth, Belmont, Calif., 1967. Seven excellent essays on this topic.

10. Wasserstrom, Richard (ed.): *Today's Moral Problems*, Macmillan, New York, 1975. A collection of essays which apply ethical theory to contemporary problems.

Parliament in the 1400s (*New York Public Library Picture Collection*)

POLITICS

WHY SHOULD I OBEY?

The only purpose for which power can be rightfully exercised
over any member of a civilized community, against his
will, is to prevent harm to others. His own good,
either physical or moral, is not a sufficient
warrant. He cannot rightfully be compelled
to do or forbear because it will be
better for him to do so, because it
will make him happier,
because, in the opinions
of others, to do so
would be wise or
even right.
These
are good reasons for remonstrating with him, or reasoning
with him, or persuading him, or entreating him, but not for
compelling him. . . .

John Stuart Mill
On Liberty (1859)

INTRODUCTION

If we did not have any government, would we miss it? If we were completely free, how would we get along? It is difficult to imagine any circumstances where we would not require the power of government to help us achieve many of our human aspirations. Still, the question of what things would be like without government is a useful one to ask, since it is a way of forcing us to explain how government comes into existence and whether government is necessary.

It was in the presence of strong governments that Rousseau wrote that "man is born free: and everywhere he is in chains." He recognized the practical fact that "as long as a people is compelled to obey, and obeys, it does well." At the same time, he said that "as soon as it can shake off the yoke, and shakes it off, it does still better." What Rousseau was driving at was a compromise between his romantic ideal of complete freedom, which he thought was natural to all men, and the fact of governmental control of human behavior, which he considered an artificial creation of selfish men. If, that is, there is going to be government in any case, it should at least be made legitimate by acknowledging the prior rights and values of all citizens.

By contrast, Aristotle thought that the state or government is a perfectly natural institution just as marriage is. When he said that "man is by nature a political animal," he meant that no individual can survive without associating with someone else. This makes the family the basic social unit. But neither is the family self-sufficient. Families must associate with one another in order to achieve more than the recurrent daily needs, and this gives rise to the village. Then, says Aristotle, "when we come to the final and perfect association, formed from a number of villages, we have already reached the *polis*—an association which may be said to reach the height of full self-sufficiency."

As a political animal, man requires the help of government to perfect his nature. That is the purpose of government. For this reason, Aristotle believed that "man, when perfected, is the best of animals, but when separated from law and justice he is the worst of all." Those who consider government an artificial and arbitrary creation and those who see it as a natural institution have contributed quite different points of view to the continuing debate over the elements of political thought.

The Elements of Politics

FREEDOM

In its simplest definition, "freedom" means the absence of external restraints. If we were totally free, if we faced no restraints, in short, if there were no government, it would appear that we could do whatever we wished over a wide range of possibilities. Physically, we could go wherever we wanted to go, since nobody would interfere with our bodily movements. Socially, we would be free to associate with everyone and to join any group. Economically, we would be free to produce, sell, buy, and use whatever we could acquire, and we could enter whatever job or profession we chose. Culturally, we could pursue education at all levels and we could think, believe, say, and publish whatever we wished. Morally, we could engage in any behavior that pleased us.

Who has all these freedoms? There was a time when only one person, the ruler, was free. Later, a small group, the aristocracy, was free. In a democracy it is assumed that everyone is free. But even in a democracy there are several restraints to freedom. Some of these restraints are clearly necessary, such as traffic regulations; others are unavoidable, such as when we lack the ability or talent to enter a profession; still other restraints are debatable, such as when the government seeks to enforce a particular mode of moral behavior. There are other limitations to our freedom which have become the concern of political society, such as the absence of opportunities because of a disadvantaged childhood or the frustration of a free market caused by an economic monopoly. If there were no restraints, if there were total freedom as Hobbes described it in the original state of nature, the result might well be what he called "the war of all against all." If we had too many restraints, the result would be tyranny. What political thought and action seek to achieve in society is an appropriate balance between a wide range of freedom, order, and the satisfaction of human needs.

AUTHORITY

The authority of government can be compared to the authority of an umpire at a baseball game. Both these forms of authority are required for similar reasons. Whenever there is a dispute about a play in the game, each party to the dispute thinks he is right. Not everybody holding opposite views can be right. Nevertheless, a decision has to be made. Only the umpire has the authority to make the official decision. If there were no umpire, there would be no way of resolving the dispute. The argument could become severe and end in violence. Similarly, without some political or legal authority, a multitude of people would become involved in endless arguments about what belongs to whom and who is responsible for injuring someone.

But how do governments acquire their authority to govern the lives of people? Political authority has been accounted for in different ways. Kings once assumed that they governed by divine right. Philosophers developed theories of the Social Contract, saying that sovereigns acquired political authority when individuals handed over some or all of their freedoms in exchange for the benefits of an orderly and secure society. Still others believe that the authority to govern was and even now can be acquired through superior power or the force of conquest. In democratic societies the source of political authority is taken to be the consent of the governed. Most people will agree that in order to have a civil society it is necessary to have a supreme authority. But it makes a difference how civil society will be governed when a people accepts one explanation over another of how the sovereign acquires authority. Some of these differences in sovereign authority become apparent when we consider the nature of law.

LAW

We normally think of law as a set of rules telling us how to behave. But the rules which make up the law are different from any other kind of rules. What makes them different, for example, from the rules governing baseball is that if we do not want to play that game, we do not have to pay any attention to its rules. The rules of law, on the other hand, apply to us whether we like them or not. Chief Justice John Marshall once said that "the Judicial Department comes home in its effects to every man's fireside; it passes on his property, his reputation, his life, his all." What used to be a simple set of rules has become an enormous system of rules and regulations.

What makes our obedience to these laws mandatory is that they come from the source of authority. That is why "law" can be defined as a command of the sovereign. Before there was a sovereign, law as we know it did not exist. Everyone, in a sense, was his or her own lawgiver. That was the problem in the state of nature where everyone had complete freedom. With the establishment of a single authority came the beginning of law in the sense of officially announced rules. A rule is not a law unless it comes officially from the sovereign. But is every command of the sovereign a law? Suppose that the sovereign commands a law which is contrary to morality. Is that command still a law? Here is the point where different theories of authority lead to different theories of law. If, for example, authority is achieved simply through power, then it might be argued that might is right. But from the earliest times, philosophers have tried to distinguish between a law, on the one hand, and an arbitrary command, on the other. What makes a command arbitrary, in their judgment, is that it pays no attention to reason or morality. What makes a rule *law* is not only the fact that it is officially created, but that it fits the requirements of reasoned morality. Aquinas went so far as to say that "a tyrannical law, not being according to reason, is not law at all in the strict sense but is a perversion of law."

To say this, however, is to assume that everybody is in agreement over what reason requires. Because of these questions about what really is the nature of law, the concept of law has been expanded to include not only the body of rules but also the process—the judicial process of the courts—by which the rules are interpreted and applied. The judicial process provides the occasion, especially in the American system, for the judges to test a law to see if it is constitutional, that is, to make sure that a law does not violate the various rights set forth in the Constitution. The judicial process represents a continuing effort to clarify and advance the ends and purposes of law. The underlying purpose of law is to achieve justice.

JUSTICE

"Justice" can be defined simply as fairness. This assumes that everybody has an intuitive sense of what constitutes fairness in any particular case. Other definitions are similar. One of the earliest definitions says that "justice is rendering to each his own." This, of course, raises the question of what is each's own, just as the classic definition that "justice means treating equals equally" leaves open the question of who are equals?

One reason for the difficulty of defining justice is that we tend to identify our own self-interest with what is right and just. One way to overcome this is to think of justice as meaning what the law says it is. Hobbes once said that there can be no unjust law. All he meant by that was that justice is defined as any action which complies with the law as it is. But the law itself does not always measure up to a community's sense of justice. Indeed, Justice Cardozo, a member of the United States Supreme Court, wrote that "what we are seeking is not merely the justice that one receives when his rights and duties are determined by the law as it is; what we are seeking is the justice to which the law in its making should conform."

In making its laws, a community always has to balance the pressures from special groups with the common good. But the final test of the justice of a society is to be found in the way individuals are treated—how much freedom, how much opportunity, and how much of a share in the society's resources each has. Justice does not require mathematical equality in all things. Justice does require that everyone should be free, that nobody should be arbitrarily denied opportunities, and that if the distribution of resources is unequal, it should nevertheless be fair.

Summary

We began by asking whether government is necessary. To find an answer, we wondered what life would be like under a condition of complete freedom. We discovered that (1) if freedom means the absence of external restraints, then everybody would decide individually what was right, that there would be differences that could not be resolved, and that this would lead to chaos. (2) To avoid anarchy, people, just like contestants in a game, need an umpire, that is, an authority to settle disputes and to make the rules for everyone. (3) Law is a set of rules, but only those rules which the sovereign announces. Are these rules law only because the sovereign made them, or must the sovereign, when making laws, consider the dictates of reason and morality? The broader view that sees law not only as a body of official rules but also as a process, the judicial process, underscores the continuing effort of law to achieve (4) justice. Although justice is very difficult to define with exactness, it includes freedom for everyone, equal opportunities, and a fair distribution of resources. These are some of the elements of political thought that we will find discussed by our selected philosophers.

APPROACHES TO THE ELEMENTS OF POLITICAL PHILOSOPHY

(1) Both Plato and Aristotle were aware of the confusion frequently encountered in political discussions. This confusion existed, they thought, because participants in these discussions were simply expressing their opinions. Accordingly, Plato and Aristotle sought to overcome this conflict of opinions by discovering in human nature some objective clue to political and social life. They both made use of the concept of purpose. Plato regarded the state as a large-scale version of the individual. Nature seemed to design the state so that each social class in it represented an extension of the three faculties found in man. Just as each faculty in man has a purpose, so also the corresponding class in society has a special function. For example, the faculty of reason, which governs the individual, finds its counterpart in society in the ruling class. The good or just society exists according to Plato when the social classes are in harmony by fulfilling their special function or purpose.

Aristotle did not visualize the structure of the state in such precise terms. He emphasized chiefly the role of the state as a natural institution whose purpose it is to make men good. Because he approached this subject in a scientific way, he was aware of the different forms a state can take, depending on the number of people and the size of the territory involved. What Plato and Aristotle had in common was their concept of the natural purposefulness of government.

(2) Aquinas composed a classic treatise concerning the nature of law. He is known especially as an advocate of natural law. The central feature of his theory is that law is a product of reason. As a theologian and philosopher, he combined these two disciplines in his theory of law. For him, natural law represents those principles of conduct which human reason shares with God's reason. Aquinas argued, therefore, that laws made by governments are morally valid only if they do not violate the principles of natural law.

(3) Hobbes and Locke described the condition of human life as it might have been before governments existed. Hobbes takes a pessimistic view of man's nature. He accounts for the authority of government by referring to the Social Contract as the solution to anarchy. Men enter into the Social Contract out of fear, not out of love for one another. By contrast, Locke has an optimistic view of human nature. He argues that human beings have natural rights even before there is a government. People leave the state of nature to set up an independent or impartial authority in order to avoid a glaring unfairness in the state of nature by which a person is both a party and a judge in his own cause.

(4) Bentham and Mill were the great exponents of utilitarianism. This was a new philosophy of ethics which had a strong influence on social and political thought. The effect of utilitarianism was to simplify moral and political philosophy by using pleasure and pain as the standard for good and evil, as well as for justice and injustice. Whatever causes pain is evil or unjust; whatever causes or increases pleasure is good and just. Each individual must be his own judge on these matters, and the only justification for the government to compel anyone to obey is to prevent him from doing harm to others. Utilitarianism emphasized individualism and liberty.

(5) Marx thought he had discovered a scientific clue to the dynamic movement of history. What makes history move from one stage to another is the class struggle. This struggle is caused by a

contradiction between the way men produce things and earn a living, on the one hand, and the way the fruits of industry and society are distributed, on the other. Only when there is a classless society will the conflicts and alienation be overcome.

(6) Rawls devised a theory of justice based on a novel concept of the Social Contract. Unlike Hobbes, who had a pessimistic view of human nature, Rawls assumes that rational individuals can agree on the basic principles of justice which take into account both the equalities and inequalities among people. He believes, moreover, that if, in the "original position," individuals could step behind a "veil of ignorance," they would in the end agree on "two principles of justice" which would require freedom for all and a distribution of wealth which, although not mathematically equal, would be fair.

CHAPTER 9

NATURAL BASIS FOR SOCIETY

Plato and Aristotle

Plato (428–348 B.C.) was born in a distinguished family in Athens at a time when culture there was flourishing. Although Plato was aware of the various modes of philosophy circulating in Athens, the most important influence in the formation of his thought was the life and teaching of Socrates (470–399 B.C.). From Socrates he learned that the surest way of going after knowledge is through orderly conversation or dialogue. That is why Plato wrote dialogues, because the dialectic method enabled him to demonstrate how an idea must be constantly subjected to argument and counterargument. Plato wrote about twenty books or dialogues. The first group reflects the influence of Socrates, while the later group shows the development of his new concepts. When he was about forty years old, after writing most of his books, he founded his school, called the Academy of Athens, probably the first university. Aristotle entered this Academy in 367 B.C. at the age of eighteen. The trial and death of Socrates disillusioned Plato about public political life, but he continued to exert great influence through his teaching at the Academy until his death at the age of eighty.

In Plato's thought, political theory is closely connected with moral philosophy. Indeed, Plato considered the state as being "man writ large." But Plato does not simply say that there is an interesting or coincidental connection between the just man and the just society. He argues, rather, that there is a structural and natural as well as logical relation between man and the state.

The State as Man Writ Large

Plato's whole argument is that the state grows out of the nature of the individual, so that logically the individual comes prior to the state. The state, said Plato, is a natural institution, natural because it reflects the structure of human nature. The origin of the state is a reflection of man's economic needs, for, says Plato, "a state comes into existence because no individual is self-sufficing; we all have many needs." Our many needs require many skills, and no one possesses all the skills needed to produce food, shelter, and clothing, to say nothing of the various arts. There must, therefore, be a division of labor, for "more things will be produced and the work more easily and better done, when every man is set free from all other occupations to do, at the right time, the one thing for which he is naturally fitted."

Man's needs are not limited to his physical requirements, for his goal is not simply survival but a life higher than an animal's. Still, the healthy state soon becomes affected by a wide range of desires and becomes "swollen up with a whole multitude of callings not ministering to any bare necessity." Now there will be "hunters and fishermen . . . artists in sculpture, painting and music; poets with their attendant train of professional reciters, actors, dancers, producers; and makers of all sorts of household gear, including everything for women's adornment. And we shall want more servants . . . lady's maids, barbers, cooks and confectioners." This desire for more things will soon exhaust the resources of the community and before long, says Plato, "we shall have to cut off a slice of our neighbor's territory . . . and they will want a slice of ours." At this rate, neighbors will inevitably be at war. Wars have their "origin in desires which are the most fruitful source of evils both to individuals and states." With the inevitability of war, it will now be necessary to have "a whole army to go out to battle with an invader, in defence of all this property and of the citizens. . . ." Thus emerge the guardians of the state, who, at first, represent the vigorous and powerful men who will repel the invader and preserve internal order. Now there are two distinct classes of men: those who fill all the crafts—farmers, artisans, and traders—and those who guard the community. From this latter class are then chosen the most highly trained guardians, who will become the rulers of the state and will represent a third and elite class.

The relation between the individual and the state now becomes plain, for the three classes in the state are an extension of the three parts of the soul. The craftsmen or artisans represent as a class the lowest part of the soul, namely, the appetites. The guardians embody the spirited element of the soul. And the highest class, the rulers, represent the rational element. So far, this analysis seems to have logical rigor, for it does not strain the imagination to see the connection (1) between the individual's appetites and the class of workers who satisfy these appetites, (2) between the spirited element in man and the large-scale version of this dynamic force in the military establishment, and (3) between the rational element and the unique function of leadership in the ruler. But Plato was aware that it would not be simple to convince people to accept this system of classes in the state, particularly if they found themselves in a class that might not be the one they would choose if they had the chance. The assignment of all persons to their respective classes would come only after extensive training, where only those capable of doing so would progress to the higher levels. Although theoretically each person would have the opportunity to reach the highest level, he would in fact stop at the level of his natural aptitudes.

	The Individual (Three Parts of the Soul)	The Virtues	The State (The Three Classes)	
Justice	1. Rational ←	1. Wisdom →	1. Rulers	Justice
	2. Spirited ←	2. Courage →	2. Guardians	
	3. Appetitive ←	3. Temperance →	3. Craftsmen	

To make everyone satisfied with his lot, Plato thought it would be necessary to employ a "convenient fiction . . . a single bold flight of invention." He writes, "I shall try to convince, first the Rulers and the soldiers, and then the whole community, that all that nurture and education which we gave them was only something they seemed to experience as it were in a dream. In reality they were the whole time down inside the earth, being molded . . . and fashioned . . . and at last when they were complete, the earth sent them up from her womb into the light of day."

This "noble lie" would also say that the god who fashioned all men "mixed gold in the composition" of those who were to rule and "put silver in the guardians, and iron and brass in the farmers and craftsmen." This would imply that by nature some would be rulers and others craftsmen and that this would provide the basis for a perfectly stratified society. But whereas later societies in Europe assumed that the children born into such a stratified society would stay at the level at which they were born, Plato recognized that children would not always have the same qualities as their parents. He said, therefore, that among the injunctions laid by heaven on the rulers "there is none that needs to be so carefully watched as the mixture of metals in the souls of children. If a child of their own is born with an alloy of iron or brass, they must, without the smallest pity, assign him the station proper to his nature and thrust him out among the farmers and craftsmen." Similarly, if a child with gold or silver is born to craftsmen, "they will promote him according to his value. . . . " Most important of all, Plato thought that everyone should agree on who is to be the ruler and agree also on the reason why the ruler should be obeyed.

The Philosopher-King

To Plato it seemed natural that competence should be the qualification for authority. The ruler of the state should be the one who has the peculiar abilities to fulfill that function. Disorder in the state is caused by the same circumstances that produce disorder in the individual, namely, the attempt on the part of the lower elements to usurp the role of the higher faculties. In both the individual and the state, the uncontrolled drives of the appetites and spirited action lead to internal anarchy. At both levels, the rational element must be in control. Who should be the captain of a ship— should it be the most "popular" man, or the one who knows the art of navigation? Who should rule the state—should it be someone whose training is in war or commerce? The ruler, said Plato, should be the one who has been fully educated, one who has come to understand the difference between the visible world and the intelligible world, between the realm of opinion and the realm of knowledge, between appearance and reality. The philosopher-king is one whose education, in short, has led him up step by step through ever higher degrees of knowledge until at last he has a knowledge of the Good, that synoptic vision of the interrelation of all truths to each other.

To reach this point, the philosopher-king will have progressed through many stages of education. By the time he is eighteen years old, he will have had training in literature, music, and elementary mathematics. His literature would be censored, for Plato accused certain poets of outright falsehood and of impious accounts of the behavior of the gods. Music also would be prescribed so that seductive music would be replaced by a more wholesome, martial meter. For the next few years there would be extensive physical and military training, and at age twenty, a few would be selected to pursue an advanced course in mathematics. At age thirty, a five-year course in dialectic and moral philosophy would begin. The next fifteen years would be spent gathering practical experience through public service. Finally, at age fifty, the ablest men would reach the highest level of knowledge, the vision of the Good, and would then be ready for the task of governing the state.

The Virtues in the State

Whether justice could ever be achieved in a state would depend, Plato thought, on whether the philosophical element in society could attain dominance. He wrote that "I was forced to say in praise of the correct philosophy that it affords a vantage-point from which we can discern in all cases what is just for communities and for individuals," and he believed that "the human race will not be free of evils until either the stock of those who rightly and truly follow philosophy acquire political authority, or the class who have power in the cities be led by some dispensation of providence to become real philosophers." But justice is a general virtue. It means that all parts are fulfilling their special functions and are achieving their respective virtues. Justice in the state will be attained only when and if the three classes fulfill their functions.

Acropolis (*Royal Ontario Museum, Toronto*)

As the craftsmen embody the element of the appetites, they will also reflect the virtue of temperance. Temperance is not limited to the craftsmen but applies to all the classes, for it indicates, when it is achieved, the willingness of the lower to be ruled by the higher. Still, temperance applies in a special way to the craftsmen insofar as they are the lowest and must subordinate to the two higher levels.

The guardians, who defend the state, manifest the virtue of courage. To assure the state that these guardians will always fulfill their function, special training and provision are made for them. Unlike the craftsmen, who marry and own property, the guardians will have both property and wives in common. Plato considered these arrangements essential if the guardians were to attain true courage, for courage means knowing what to fear and what not to fear. The only real object of fear for the guardian should be fear of moral evil. He must never fear poverty or privation, and for this reason, his mode of life should be isolated from possessions. Although wives will be held in common, this was by no means to suggest any form of promiscuity. On the contrary, Plato believed that men and women were equal in respect to certain things, saying, for example, that "a man and a woman have the same nature if both have a talent for medicine." This being the case, they should both be assigned to the same task whenever they possess the appropriate talent. For this reason, Plato believed that women could be guardians as well as men.

In order to preserve the unity of the members of the class of guardians, the permanent individual family would be abolished, and the whole class would become a single family. Plato's reasoning here was that the guardians must be free not only from the temptation to acquire property, but free also from the temptation to prefer the advantages of one's family to those of the state. Moreover, he thought it rather foolish to take such pains in breeding racing dogs and horses and at the same time rely on pure chance in producing the guardians and rulers of the state. For this reason, sexual relations would be strictly controlled and would be limited to the special marriage festivals. These festivals would occur at stated times, and the partners, under the illusion that they had been paired by drawing lots, would, instead, be brought together through the careful manipulation of the rulers to ensure the highest eugenic possibilities. Plato does say that "young men who acquit themselves well in war and other duties, should be given, among other rewards and privileges, more liberal opportunities to sleep with a wife," but only for the utilitarian purpose that "with good excuse, as many as possible of the children may be begotten of such fathers." As soon as children are born to the guardians, they will be taken in charge by officers appointed for that purpose and will be reared in a crechè in the care of nurses living in a special part of the city. Under these circumstances, thought Plato, the guardians would be most likely to fulfill their true function of defending the state without being deflected by other concerns and would thereby achieve their appropriate virtue of courage.

Justice in the state is therefore just the same as justice in the individual (see illustration on page 167). It is the product of everyone's staying in his place and doing his special task. Justice is the harmony of the virtues of temperance, courage, and wisdom. Since the state is made up of individuals, it will also be necessary for each of these virtues to be attained by each person. For example, even the craftsman must have the virtue of wisdom, not only to keep his appetites in check, but also to know that he rightly belongs where he is and that he must obey the rules. Similarly, as we have seen, the guardians must have sufficient wisdom to know what to fear and what not to fear so that they can develop genuine courage. Most important of all, the ruler must come as close as possible to a knowledge of the Good, for the well-being of the state depends on his knowledge and character.

The Decline of the Ideal State

If the state is "man writ large," then, said Plato, a state will reflect the kind of people a community has become. What he had in mind was that although the nature of man is fixed, in that all men possess a tripartite soul, the kind of men people become will depend on the degree of internal harmony they achieve. The state will therefore reflect these variations in human character. For this reason, Plato argued that "constitutions cannot come out of stocks and stones; they must result from the preponderance of certain characters which draw the rest of the community in their wake. So if there are five forms of government, there must be five kinds of mental constitution among individuals." And these five forms of government are *aristocracy, timocracy, plutocracy, democracy,* and *despotism.*

Plato considered the transition from aristocracy to despotism as a step-by-step decline in the quality of the state corresponding to a gradual deterioration of the moral character of the rulers and the citizens. His ideal state was, of course, aristocracy, in which the rational element embodied in the philosopher-king was supreme and where each person's reason controlled his appetites. Plato emphasized that this was only an ideal, although significant, nevertheless, as a target to aim at. He was deeply disenchanted with politics, particularly because of the way Athens had executed Socrates and had failed to produce consistently good leaders. "As I gazed upon the whirlpool of public life," he said, "[I] saw clearly in regard to all States now existing that without exception their system of government is bad." Still, the norm for a state is *aristocracy*, for in that form is found the proper subordination of all classes.

Even if this ideal were achieved, however, there would be a possibility for change, since nothing is permanent, and aristocracy would decline first of all into a *timocracy.* This represents a degeneration, for timocracy represents the love of honor, and insofar as an ambitious member of the ruling class loves his own honor more than the common good, the spirited part of his soul has usurped the role of reason. Although this is only a small break in the structure of the soul, it does begin a process whereby the irrational part assumes a progressively larger role. From love of honor to the desire for wealth is a short step, for it means allowing the appetites to rule.

Even under a timocracy there would be the beginning of a system of private property, and this desire for riches paves the way for a *plutocracy*, where power resides in the hands of men whose main concern is wealth. And, says Plato, "as the rich rise in social esteem, the virtuous sink." What is serious about plutocracy, according to Plato, is that it breaks the unity of the state into two contending classes, the rich and the poor. Moreover, the plutocrat is a consumer of goods, and when he has used up his money, he becomes dangerous because he wants more of what he has become accustomed to. The plutocrat is like the person who seeks constant pleasure. But the very nature of pleasure is that it is momentary and must therefore be repeated. There can never be a time of perfect satisfaction; the seeker of pleasure can never be satisfied any more than a leaky pail can be filled. Still, although the plutocrat is torn between many desires, "his better desires will usually keep the upper hand over the worse," and so the plutocrat, says Plato, "presents a more decent appearance than many."

Democracy is a further degeneration, said Plato, for its principles of equality and freedom reflect the degenerate human characters whose whole range of appetites are all pursued with equal freedom. To be sure, Plato's concept of democracy, and his criticism of it, was based on his firsthand experience with the special form democracy took in the small city-state of Athens. Here democracy was direct in that all citizens had the right to participate in the government. The Athenian Assembly consisted, theoretically at least, of all citizens over eighteen years of age. Thus Plato did not have in mind modern liberal and representative democracy. What he saw in his day was rather a mode of direct popular government that clearly violated his notion that the rulership of a state should be in the hands of those with the special talent and training for it. What produced this spirit of equality was the legitimizing of all the appetites under the plutocracy, where the aim of life was to become as rich as possible, and, said Plato, "this insatiable craving would bring about the transition to democracy," for "a society cannot hold wealth in honour and at the same time establish self-control in its citizens."

Even the dogs in a democracy exhibit equality and independence by refusing to move out of the way in the streets. It is, however, when the rich and poor find themselves in a contest under plutocracy that the turning point is reached, for "when the poor win, the result is a democracy." Then "liberty and free speech are rife everywhere; anyone is allowed to do what he likes." Now "you are not obliged to be in authority . . . or to submit to authority, if you do not like it. . . . " All this political equality and freedom stem from a soul whose order has been shattered. It is a soul whose appetites are now all equal and free and act as a "mob" of passions. The life of liberty and equality declares that "one appetite is as good as another and all must have their equal rights."

But the continuous indulgence of the appetites leads one inevitably to the point where a single master passion will finally enslave the soul. One cannot yield to every craving without finally having to yield to the strongest and most persistent passion. At this point we say that a person is under the tyranny of his master passion. Likewise, in the state, the passion for money and pleasures leads the masses to plunder the rich. Since the rich resist, the masses seek out a strong man who will be their champion. But this man demands and acquires absolute power and makes the people his slaves, and only later do the people realize to what depths of subjugation they have fallen. This is the unjust society, the enlargement of the unjust soul. The natural end of democracy is *despotism*.

Aristotle

In his *Politics*, as in his *Ethics*, Aristotle stresses the element of purpose. The state, as man, is endowed by nature with a distinctive function. Combining these two ideas, Aristotle says that "it is evident that the state is a creation of nature, and that man is by nature a political animal." So closely does he relate man and the state that he concludes, "He who is unable to live in society, or who has no need because he is sufficient for himself, must be either a beast or a god." Not only is man by nature destined to live in a state, but the state, as every other community, "is established with a view to some good," exists for some end. The family exists primarily to preserve life. The state comes into existence in the first instance to preserve life for families and villages, which in the long run are not self-sufficing. But beyond this economic end, the function of the state is to ensure the supreme good of man, namely, his moral and intellectual life.

Unlike Plato, Aristotle did not create a blueprint for an ideal state. Even though Aristotle viewed the state as the agency for enabling men to achieve their ultimate goals as human beings, he nevertheless realized that any practical theory of the state must take note of "what kind of government is adapted to particular states . . . [that] the best is often unattainable . . . " and that the legislator must be acquainted with "which is best relatively to circumstances . . . how a state may be constituted under any given conditions . . . [and] how it may be longest preserved," concluding that "political writers, although they have excellent ideas, are often unpractical." For these reasons, Aristotle had little patience with Plato's most radical ideas. Ridiculing Plato's arrangement for the abolition of the family for the guardian class and providing a public nursery for their children, Aristotle said that "there is no reason why the so-called father should care about the son, or the son about the father, or brothers about one another." The communal ownership of property would likewise destroy certain basic human pleasure as well as engender inefficiency and endless disputes.

Types of States

Aristotle was willing to recognize that under appropriate circumstances a community could organize itself into at least three different kinds of government. The basic difference between them is primarily the number of rulers each has. A government can have as its rulers either *one*, a *few*, or *many*. But each of these forms of government can have a true or a perverted form. When a government is functioning rightly, it governs for the common good of all the people. A government is perverted when its rulers govern for their own private gain or interests. The true forms of each type of government, according to Aristotle, are *monarchy* (one ruler), *aristocracy* (a few rulers), and *polity* (many rulers). The perverted forms are *tyranny* (one), *oligarchy* (few), and *democracy* (many). His own preference was aristocracy, chiefly because even though ideally an individual of exceptional excellence would be desirable, such persons do not exist with sufficient frequency. In an aristocracy, there is the rule of a group of men whose degree of excellence, achievement, and ownership of property makes them responsible, able, and capable of command.

Differences and Inequalities

Because he relied so heavily on his observation of things, it was inevitable that Aristotle would make some mistakes. Nowhere is this more true than in his estimate of slavery. Observing that slaves invariably were strong and large, he concluded that slavery was a product of nature. "It is clear," said Aristotle, "that some men are by nature free, and others slaves, and that for these slavery is both expedient and right." To be sure, Aristotle took great care to distinguish between those who become slaves by nature, a mode he accepted, and those who became slaves by military conquest, a mode he rejected. He rejected slavery by conquest on the highly defensible grounds that to overpower someone does not mean that one is superior to him in nature. Moreover, the use of force may or may not be justified, in which case enslavement could very well be the product and extension of an unjust act. At the same time, speaking of the "proper treatment of slaves," he proposed that "liberty should be always held out to them as the reward of their services." The fact is that in his own last will and testament Aristotle provided for the emancipation of some of his slaves.

Aristotle also believed in the inequality of citizenship. He held that the basic qualification for citizenship was a person's ability to take his share in ruling and being ruled in turn. A citizen had the right and the obligation to participate in the administration of justice. Since a citizen would therefore have to sit in the assembly and in the law courts, he would have to have both ample time as well as an appropriate temperament and character. For this reason, Aristotle did not believe that laborers should be citizens, as they had neither the time nor the appropriate mental development, nor could they benefit from the experience of sharing in the political process.

Good Government
and Revolution

Over and over again Aristotle made the point that the state exists for the sake of man's moral and intellectual fulfillment. "A state," he said, "exists for the sake of a good life, and not for the sake of life only"; also, "the state is the union of families and villages in a perfect and self-sufficing life, by which we mean a happy and honourable life." Finally, he said, "our conclusion . . . is that political society exists for the sake of noble actions, and not mere companionship." Still, whether a state produces the good life depends on how its rulers behave. We have already said that the perverted forms of government are distinguished from the true forms by this, that the good rulers seek to achieve the good of all, whereas the perverted rulers seek their own private gain.

Whatever form a government has, it will rest on some conception of justice and proportionate equality. But these conceptions of justice can bring disagreement and ultimately revolution. Democracy, as Aristotle knew it, arises out of the assumption that those who are equal in any respect are equal in all respects; "because men are equally free, they claim to be absolutely equal." On the other hand, Aristotle said that *oligarchy* is based on the notion that "those who are unequal in one respect are in all respects unequal." Hence "being unequal . . . in property, they suppose themselves to be unequal absolutely." For these reasons, whenever the democrats or oligarchs are in the minority and the philosophy of the incumbent government "does not accord with their preconceived ideas, [they] stir up revolution. . . ."

Aristotle concludes that "the universal and chief cause of this revolutionary feeling [is] the desire of equality, when men think they are equal to others who have more than themselves." He did not overlook other causes, such as "insolence and avarice," as well as fear and contempt. Knowing these causes of revolution, Aristotle said that each form of government could take appropriate precautions against it; for example, a king must avoid despotic acts, an aristocracy should avoid the rule by a few rich men for the benefit of the wealthy class, and a polity should provide more time for its abler members to share in the government. Another precaution is to guard against the beginning of change. Most important of all,

Aristotle urged that "there is nothing which should be more jealously maintained than the spirit of obedience to law." In the end, men will always criticize the state unless their conditions of living within it are such that they can achieve happiness in the form of what they consider the good life.

READING

THE NATURAL BASIS OF SOCIETY
Aristotle

Every state is a community of some kind, and every community is established with a view to some good; for mankind always act in order to obtain that which they think good. But, if all communities aim at some good, the state or political community, which is the highest of all, and which embraces all the rest, aims and in a greater degree than any other, at the highest good.

Now there is an erroneous opinion that a statesman, king, householder, and master are the same, and that they differ, not in kind, but only in the number of their subjects. For example, the ruler over a few is called a master; over more, the manager of a household; over a still larger number, a statesman or king, as if there were no difference between a great household and a small state. The distinction which is made between the king and the statesman is as follows: When the government is personal, the ruler is a king; when, according to the principles of the political science, the citizens rule and are ruled in turn, then he is called a statesman.

But all this is a mistake; for governments differ in kind, as will be evident to any one who considers the matter according to the method which has hitherto guided us. As in other departments of science, so in politics, the compound should always be resolved into the simple elements or least parts of the whole. We must therefore look at the elements of which the state is composed, in order that we may see in what they differ from one another, and whether any scientific distinction can be drawn between the different kinds of rule.

From Aristotle, *Politics*, trans. Benjamin Jowett, ed. H. W. C. Davis, Clarendon Press, Oxford, 1905.

He who thus considers things in their first growth and origin, whether a state or anything else, will obtain the clearest view of them. In the first place (1) there must be a union of those who cannot exist without each other; for example, of male and female, that the race may continue; and this is a union which is formed, not of deliberate purpose, but because, in common with other animals and with plants, mankind have a natural desire to leave behind them an image of themselves. And (2) there must be a union of natural ruler and subject, that both may be preserved. For he who can foresee with his mind is by nature intended to be lord and master, and he who can work with his body is a subject, and by nature a slave; hence master and slave have the same interest. Nature, however, has distinguished between the female and the slave. For she is not niggardly, like the smith who fashions the Delphian knife for many uses; she makes each thing for a single use, and every instrument is best made when intended for one and not for many uses. But among barbarians no distinction is madebetween women and slaves, because there is no natural ruler among them: they are a community of slaves, male and female. Wherefore the poets say,—

It is meet that Hellenes should rule over barbarians;

as if they thought that the barbarian and the slave were by nature one.

Out of these two relationships between man and woman, master and slave, the family first arises, and Hesiod is right when he says,—

First house and wife and an ox for the plough,

for the ox is the poor man's slave. The family is the association by nature for the supply of men's every-day wants, and the members of it are called by Charondas "companions of the cupboard" and by Epimenides the Cretan, "companions of the manger." But when several families are united, and the association aims at something more than the supply of daily needs, then comes into existence the village. And the most natural form of the village appears to be that of a colony from the family, composed of the children and grandchildren, who are said to be "suckled with the same milk." And this is the reason why Hellenic states were originally governed by kings; because the Hellenes were under royal rule before they came together, as the barbarians still are. Every family is ruled by the eldest, and therefore in the colonies of the family the kingly form of government prevailed because they were of the same blood.

When several villages are united in single community, perfect and large enough to be nearly or quite self-sufficing, the state comes into existence, originating in the bare needs of life, and continuing in existence for the sake of a good life. And therefore, if the earlier forms of society are natural, so is the state, for it is the end of them, and the (completed) nature is the end.

For what each thing is when fully developed, we call its nature, whether we are speaking of a man, a horse, or a family. Besides, the final cause and end of a thing is the best, and to be self-suffing is the end and the best.

Hence it is evident that the state is a creation of nature, and that man is by nature a political animal. And he who by nature and not by mere accident is without a state, is either above humanity, or below it; he is the

Tribeless, lawless, hearthless one,

whom Homer denounces—the outcast who is a lover of war; he may be compared to an unprotected piece in the game of draughts.

Now the reason why man is more of a political animal than bees or any other gregarious animals is evident. Nature, as we often say, makes nothing in vain, and man is the only animal she has endowed with the gift of speech. And whereas mere sound is but an indication of pleasure or pain, and is therefore found in other animals (for their nature attains to the perception of pleasure and pain and the intimation of them to one another, and no further), the power of speech is intended to set forth the expedient and inexpedient, and likewise the just and the unjust. And it is a characteristic of man that he alone has any sense of good and evil, of just and unjust, and the association of living beings who have this sense makes a family and a state.

Thus the state is by nature clearly prior to the family and to the individual, since the whole is of necessity prior to the part; for example, if the whole body be destroyed, there will be no foot or hand. . . . The proof that the state is a creation of nature and prior to the individual is that the individual, when isolated, is not self-suffing; and therefore he is like a part in relation to the whole. But he who is unable to live in society, or who has no need because he is sufficient for himself, must be either a beast or a god: he is no part of a state. A social instinct is implanted in all men by nature, and yet he who first founded the state was the greatest of all benefactors. For man, when perfected, is the best of animals, but, when separated from law and justice, he is the worst of all; since armed injustice is the more dangerous, and he is equipped at birth with the arms of intelligence and with moral qualities which he may use for the worst ends. Wherefore, if he have not virtue, he is the most unholy and the most savage of animals, and the most full of lust and gluttony. But justice is the bond of men in states, and the administration of justice, which is the determination of what is just, is the principle of order in political society. . . .

Of forms of democracy first comes that which is said to be based strictly on equality. In such a democracy the law says that it is just for the poor to have no more advantage than the rich; and that neither should be masters, but both equal. For if liberty and equality, as is thought by some, are chiefly to be found in democracy, they will be best attained when all persons alike share in the government to the utmost. And since the people are the majority, and the opinion of the majority is decisive, such a government must necessarily be a democracy. Here then is one sort of democracy. There is another, in which the magistrates are elected according to a certain property qualification, but a low one; he who has the required amount of property has a share in the government, but he who loses his property loses his rights. Another kind is that in which all the citizens who are under no disqualification share in the government, but still the law is supreme. In another, everybody, if he be only a citizen, is admitted to the government, but the law is supreme as before. A fifth form of democracy, in other respects the same, is that in which, not the law, but the multitude, have the supreme power, and supersede the law by their decrees. This is a state of affairs brought about by the demagogues. For in democracies which are subject to the law the best citizens hold the first place, and there are no demagogues; but where the laws are not supreme, there demagogues spring up. For the people becomes a monarch, and is many in one; and the many have the power in their hands, not as individuals, but collectively. Homer says that "it is not good to have a rule of many," but whether he means by this corporate rule, or the rule of many individuals, is uncertain.

At all events this sort of democracy, which is now a monarch, and no longer under the control of law, seeks to exercise monarchical sway, and grows into a despot; the flatterer is held in honour; this sort of democracy being relatively to other democracies what tyranny is to other forms of monarchy. The spirit of both is the same, and they alike exercise a despotic rule over the better citizens. The decrees of the demos correspond to the edicts of the tyrant; and the demagogue is to the one what the flatterer is to the other. Both have great power;—the flatterer with the tyrant, the demagogue with democracies of the kind which we are describing. The demagogues make the decrees of the people override the laws, by referring all things to the popular assembly. And therefore they grow great, because the people have all things in their hands, and they hold in their hands the votes of the people, who are too ready to listen to them. Further, those who have any complaint to bring against the magistrates say, "let the people be judges"; the people are too happy to accept the invitation; and so the authority of every office is undermined. Such a democracy is fairly open to the objection that it is not a constitution at all; for where the laws have no authority, there is no constitution. The law ought to be supreme over all, and the rulers should judge of particulars, and only this should be considered a constitution. . . .

THE FUNCTION OF A STATE

A state exists for the sake of a good life, and not for the sake of life only: if life only were the object, slaves and brute animals might form a state, but they cannot, for they have no share in happiness or in a life of free choice.

Nor does a state exist for the sake of alliance and security from injustice, nor yet for the sake of exchange and mutual intercourse; for then the Tyrrhenians and the Carthaginians, and all who have commercial treaties with one another, would be the citizens of one state. True, they have agreements about imports, and engagements that they will do no wrong to one another, and written articles of alliance. But there are no magistracies common to the contracting parties who will enforce their engagements; different states have each their own magistracies. Nor does one state take care that the citizens of the other are such as they ought to be, nor see that those who come under the terms of the treaty do no wrong or wickedness at all, but only that they do no injustice to one another. Whereas those who care for good government take into consideration virtue and vice in states. Whence it may be further inferred that virtue must be the care of a state which is truly so called, and not merely enjoys the name: for without this end the community becomes a mere alliance which differs only in place from alliances of which the members live apart. . . .

It is clear then that a state is not a mere society, having a common place, established for the prevention of mutual crime and for the sake of exchange. These are conditions without which a state cannot exist; but all of them together do not constitute a state, which is a community of families and aggregations of families in well-being, for the sake of a perfect and self-sufficing life. Such a community can only be established among those who live in the same place and intermarry. Hence arise in cities family connexions, brotherhoods, common sacrifices, amusements which draw men together. But these are created by friendship, for the will to live together is friendship. The end of the state is the good life, and these are the means towards it. And the state is the union of families and villages in a perfect and self-sufficing life, by which we mean a happy and honourable life.

CHAPTER 10

NATURAL LAW

Aquinas

Saint Thomas Aquinas was born near Naples in A.D. 1225. At the age of five he was placed in the Abbey of Monte Cassino, and for the next nine years he pursued his studies in this Benedictine abbey. He then entered the Dominican order and in A.D. 1245 went to the University of Paris. Here he came under the influence of Albert the Great, who was known as the "Universal Teacher" because of his immense learning. The great achievement of Saint Thomas Aquinas was bringing together the insights of classical philosophy and Christian theology. He "Christianized" the philosophy of Aristotle. At the same time he drew on medieval writers, including Arabian and Jewish philosophers, as well as other Christian fathers, including Saint Augustine. Aquinas was primarily a theologian, but he relied heavily on the philosophy of Aristotle in writing his theological works. His view was that philosophy and theology play complementary roles in man's quest for truth.

To understand Aquinas's views about law and the state, we need to consider his interpretation of the moral dimension of human life. Morality, as Aquinas viewed it, is not an arbitrary set of rules for

Aquinas, Botticelli (*New York Public Library Picture Collection*)

behavior. The basis of moral obligation, he thought, is found, first of all, in the very nature of man. Built into man's nature are various inclinations, such as the preservation of his life, the propagation of his species, and, because he is rational, the inclination toward the search for truth. The basic moral truth is simply to "do good and avoid evil." As a rational being, then, man is under a basic natural obligation to protect his life and health, in which case suicide and carelessness are wrong. Second, the natural inclination to propagate the species forms the basis of the union of man and wife, and any other basis for this relation would be wrong. And third, because man seeks for truth, he can do this best by living in peace in society with his fellow men, who are also engaged in this quest. To ensure an ordered society, human laws are fashioned for the direction of the community's behavior. Preserving life, propagating the species, forming an ordered society under human laws, and pursuing the quest for truth—all these activities pertain to man at his natural level. The moral law is founded on human nature, on the natural inclinations toward specific modes of behavior, and on the reason's ability to discern the right course of conduct. Because human nature has certain fixed features, the rules for behavior that correspond to these features are called *natural law*.

Much of this theory of natural law was already developed by Aristotle. In his *Ethics*, Aristotle distinguished between natural justice and conventional justice. Some forms of behavior, he said, are wrong only because, and only after, a law has been made to regulate such behavior. To use a modern example, it is wrong to drive a vehicle at certain speeds only because a speed limit has been set, but there is nothing in nature that requires that vehicles travel at that speed. Such a law is therefore not natural but conventional, because before the law was passed, there was nothing wrong with traveling at speeds exceeding the new limit. However, there are some laws the precepts of which are derived from nature, so that the behavior they regulate has always been wrong, as in the case of murder. But Aquinas did not limit his treatment of natural law to the simple notion that in some way man's reason is able to discover the natural basis for human conduct. Instead, he reasoned that if man's existence and nature can be fully understood only when seen in relation to God, then natural law must be described in metaphysical and theological terms, as the Stoics and St. Augustine had done.

Law, says Aquinas, has to do primarily with reason. The rule and measure of acts is the reason, because it belongs to reason to direct a man's whole activity toward his end. Law consists of these rules and measures of human acts and therefore is based on reason. The natural law is dictated by the reason. But Aquinas argues that since God created all things, human nature and the natural law are best understood as the product of God's wisdom or reason. From this standpoint, Aquinas distinguishes four kinds of law.

Eternal Law

This law refers to the fact that "the whole community of the universe is governed by Divine Reason. Therefore, the very notion of the government of things in God, the Ruler of the universe, has the nature of a law. And since the Divine Reason's conception of things is not subject to time but is eternal . . . therefore it is that this kind of law must be called eternal."

Natural Law

For Aquinas, natural law consists of that portion of the eternal law that pertains particularly to man. His reasoning is that "all things partake in some way of the eternal law . . . from its being imprinted on them," and from this all things "derive their respective inclinations to their proper acts and ends." This is particularly true of man, because his rational capacity "has a share of the Eternal Reason, whereby it has a natural inclination to proper act and end." And, says Aquinas, "this participation of the eternal law in the rational creature is called the natural law," and again, "the natural law is nothing else than the rational creature's participation of the eternal law." We have already indicated the basic precepts of the natural law as being the preservation of life, propagation and education of offspring, and pursuit of truth and a peaceful society. Thus the natural law consists of broad general principles that reflect God's intentions for man in creation.

Human Law

Human law refers to the specific statutes of governments. These statutes or human laws are derived from the general precepts of natural law. Just as "we draw conclusions of the various sciences" from "naturally known indemonstrable principles," so also "from the precepts of the natural law . . . the human reason needs to proceed to the more particular determination of certain matters." And "these particular determinations, devised by human reason, are called human laws. . . ."

What was so far-reaching about this conception of human law was that it repudiated the notion that a law was a law only because it was decreed by a sovereign, by the state. Aquinas argued that what gives a rule the character of law is its moral dimension, its conformity with the precepts of natural law, its agreement with the moral law. Taking Saint Augustine's formula, namely, that "that which is not just seems to be no law at all," Aquinas said that "every human law has just so much of the nature of law, as it is derived from the law of nature." But, he adds, "if in any point it deflects from the law of nature, it is no longer a law but a perversion of law." Such laws no longer bind in conscience, but are sometimes obeyed to prevent an even greater evil. Aquinas went farther than simply denying the character of law to a command of a government that violated the natural moral law; such a command, he said, should not be obeyed. Some laws, he said, "may be unjust through being opposed to the Divine Good: such are the laws of tyrants inducing to idolatry, or to anything else contrary to the Divine Law. ... " He concluded that "laws of this kind must nowise be observed, because ... *we ought to obey God rather than men.*"

Divine Law

The function of law, said Aquinas, is to direct man to his proper end. Since man is ordained to an end of eternal happiness, in addition to his temporal happiness, there must be a kind of law that can direct him to that supernatural end. Here, in particular, Aquinas parted company with Aristotle, for Aristotle knew only about man's natural purpose and end, and for this purpose, the natural law known by man's reason was considered a sufficient guide. But the eternal happiness to which man is ordained, said Aquinas, is "in proportion to man's natural faculty." Therefore, "it was necessary that besides the natural and the human law, man should be directed to his end by a law given by God." The divine law, then, is available to man through revelation and is found in the Scriptures. It is not the product of man's reason but is given to man through God's grace to ensure that men know what they must do to fulfill both their natural and, especially, their supernatural ends. The difference between the natural law and divine law is this: The natural law represents man's rational knowledge of the good, by which the intellect directs the will to control man's appetites and passions, leading men to fulfill their natural end by achieving the cardinal virtues of justice, temperance, courage, and prudence. The divine law, on the other hand, comes directly from God through revelation, a gift of God's grace, whereby men are directed to their supernatural ends, having obtained the higher or theological virtues of faith, hope, and love, not through any of man's natural powers, for these virtues are "infused" into man by God's grace. In this way, Aquinas completed and surpassed the naturalistic ethics of Aristotle, showed how the natural desire of man to know God can be ensured, indicated how revelation becomes the guide for reason, and described the manner in which man's highest nature is perfected through God's grace.

The State

The state, said Aquinas, is a natural institution. It is derived from the nature of man. In this view, Aquinas was following the political theory of Aristotle, from whom he had taken the phrase that "man is by nature a social animal." But insofar as Aquinas had a different view of human nature, he was bound to have a somewhat different political philosophy as well. The difference lay in the two conceptions of the role or task of the state. Aristotle supposed that the state could provide for all the needs of man because he knew only about man's natural needs. Aquinas, on the other hand, believed that in addition to his material or natural needs, man also has a supernatural end. The state is not equipped to deal with this more ultimate end of man. It is the church that directs man to this end. But Aquinas did not simply divide these two realms of human concern, giving one to the state and the other to the church. Instead, he looked on the state, and explained its origin, in terms of God's creation.

The state, in this view, is willed by God and has its God-given function. It was required because of the social nature of man. The state is not, for Aquinas, as it was for Augustine, a product of man's sinfulness. On the contrary, Aquinas says that even "in the state of innocence man would have lived in society." But even then, "a common life could not exist, unless there were someone in control, to attend to the common good." The state's function is to secure the common good by keeping the peace, organizing the activities of the citizens into harmonious pursuits, providing for the resources to sustain life, and preventing, as far as possible, obstacles to the good life. This last item concerning threats to the good life gives to the state not only a function tied to man's ultimate end; it also accounts for the state's position in relation to the church.

The state is subordinate to the church. To say this did not mean that Aquinas considered the church a superstate. Aquinas saw no contradiction in saying that the state has a sphere in which it has a legitimate function and that at the same time it must subordinate itself to the church. Within its own sphere the state is autonomous or independent. But insofar as there are aspects of human life that bear on man's supernatural end, the state must not put arbitrary hindrances in the way to frustrate man's spiritual life. The church does not challenge the independence of the state; it only says that the state is not absolutely independent. Within its own sphere, the state is what Aquinas calls a "perfect society," having its own end and the means for achieving it. But the state is like man; neither the state nor man has only a natural end. Man's spiritual end cannot be achieved, as Aquinas says, "by human power, but by divine power." Still, because man's destiny does include attaining to the enjoyment of God, the state must recognize this aspect of human affairs; in providing for the common good of the citizens, the sovereign must pursue his community's end with a consciousness of man's spiritual end. Under these circumstances, the state does not become the church, but it does mean that the sovereign "should order those things which lead to heavenly beatitude and prohibit, as far as possible, their contraries." In this way, Aquinas affirmed the legitimacy of the state and its autonomy in its own sphere, subordinating it to the church only to ensure that the ultimate spiritual end of man be taken into account.

Since the state rules the behavior of its citizens through the agency of law, the state is in turn limited by the requirements of just laws. Nowhere is Aquinas's rejection of the absolute autonomy or independence of the state so clearly stated as when he describes the standards for the making of human or positive law. We have already analyzed the different types of law—eternal, natural, human, and divine. The state is particularly the source of human law. Each government is faced with the task of fashioning specific laws or statutes to regulate the behavior of its citizens under the particular circumstances of its own time and place. Lawmaking, however, must not be an arbitrary act, but must be done under the influence of the natural law, which is man's participation in God's eternal law. Positive laws must consist of particular rules derived from the general principles of natural law. Any positive human law that violates the natural law loses its character as law, is a "perversion of law," and loses its binding force in the consciences of men. The lawmaker has his authority to legislate from God, the source of all authority, and to God he is responsible. If the sovereign decrees an unjust law by violating God's divine law, such a law, says Aquinas, "must nowise be observed."

The political sovereign has his authority from God, and the purpose of his authority is to provide for the common good. Authority is never to be used as an end in itself or for selfish ends. Nor must the common good be interpreted in such a way that the individual is lost sight of in the collective whole. The common good must be the good of concrete persons. Thus Aquinas says that "the proper effect of law is to lead its subjects to their proper virtue . . . to make those to whom it is given good. . . . " The only "true ground" of the lawgiver is his intention to secure "the common good regulated according to divine justice," and thus it follows that "the effect of the law is to make men good. . . . " This is to say that the phrase "common good" has no meaning for Aquinas except insofar as it results in the good of individuals. At the same time, Aquinas says that "the goodness of any part is considered in comparison with the whole. . . . Since then every man is a part of the state, it is impossible that a man be good unless he be well proportionate to the common good." The entire scheme of society and its laws is characterized by the rational elements in it. Law itself, says Aquinas, is "an ordinance of reason for the common good, made by him who has care of the community, and promulgated." Thus although the sovereign has authority and power, the laws must not reflect this power in a naked sense but as power domesticated by reason and aimed at the common good.

READING

NATURAL LAW
Aquinas

Law is a rule and measure of acts, whereby man is induced to act or is restrained from acting; for *lex* (law) is derived from *ligare* (to bind), because it binds one to act. Now the rule and measure of human acts is the reason, which is the first principle of human acts. . . . For it belongs to the reason to direct to the end, which is the first principle in all matters of action. . . .

Now as reason is a principle of human acts, so in reason itself there is something which is the principle in respect of all the rest. Hence to this principle chiefly and mainly law must needs be referred. Now the first principle in practical matters, which are the object of the practical reason, is the last end: and the last end of human life is happiness or beatitude, as we have stated above. Consequently, law must needs concern itself mainly with the order that is in beatitude. Moreover, since every part is ordained to the whole as the imperfect to the perfect, and since one man is a part of the perfect community, law must needs concern itself properly with the order directed to universal happiness. . . .

Law is nothing else but a dictate of practical reason emanating from the ruler who governs a perfect community. Now it is evident, granted that the world is ruled by divine providence, as was stated in the First Part, that the whole community of the universe is governed by the divine reason. Therefore the very notion of the government of things in God, the ruler of the universe, has the nature of a law. And since the divine reason's conception of things is not subject to time, but is eternal, according to Prov. viii. 23, therefore it is that this kind of law must be called eternal. . . .

Law being a rule and measure, can be in a person in two ways: in one way, as in him that rules and measures; in another way, as in that which is ruled and measured, since a thing is ruled and measured in so far as it partakes of the rule or measure. Therefore, since all things subject to divine providence are ruled and measured by the eternal law, as was stated above, it is evident that all things partake in some way in the eternal law, in so far

From Aquinas, *Treatise on Law* in *Introduction to Saint Thomas Aquinas*, ed. Anton C. Pegis. The Modern Library, Random House, Inc., New York, 1948.

as, namely, from its being imprinted on them, they derive their respective inclinations to their proper acts and ends. Now among all others, the rational creature is subject to divine providence in a more excellent way, in so far as it itself partakes of a share of providence, by being provident both for itself and for others. Therefore it has a share of the eternal reason, whereby it has a natural inclination to its proper act and end; and this participation of the eternal law in the rational creature is called the natural law. . . . The light of natural reason, whereby we discern what is good and what is evil, which is the function of the natural law, is nothing else than an imprint on us of the divine light. It is therefore evident that the natural law is nothing else than the rational creature's participation of the eternal law. . . .

As we have stated above, a law is a dictate of the practical reason. Now it is to be observed that the same procedure takes place in the practical and in the speculative reason, for each proceeds from principles to conclusions, as we stated above. Accordingly, we conclude that, just as in the speculative reason, from naturally known indemonstrable principles we draw the conclusions of the various sciences, the knowledge of which is not imparted to us by nature, but acquired by the efforts of reason, so too it is that from the precepts of the natural law, as from common and indemonstrable principles, the human reason needs to proceed to the more particular determination of certain matters. These particular determinations, devised by human reason, are called human laws, provided that the other essential conditions of law be observed. . . .

Besides the natural and the human law it was necessary for the directing of human conduct to have a divine law. And this for four reasons. First, because it is by law that man is directed how to perform his proper acts in view of his last end. Now if man were ordained to no other end than that which is proportionate to his natural ability, there would be no need for man to have any further direction, on the part of his reason, in addition to the natural law and humanly devised law which is derived from it. But since man is ordained to an end of eternal happiness which exceeds man's natural ability, as we have stated above, therefore it was necessary that, in addition to the natural and the human law, man should be directed to his end by a law given by God.

Secondly, because, by reason of the uncertainty of human judgment, especially on contingent and particular matters, different people form different judgments on human acts; whence also different and contrary laws result. In order, therefore, that man may know without any doubt what he ought to do, and what he ought to avoid, it was necessary for man to be directed in his proper acts by a law given by God, for it is certain that such a law cannot err.

Thirdly, because man can make laws in those matters of which he is competent to judge. But man is not competent to judge of interior movements, that are hidden, but only of exterior acts which are observable; and yet for the perfection of virtue it is necessary for man to conduct himself rightly in both kinds of acts. Consequently, human law could not sufficiently curb and direct interior acts, and it was necessary for this purpose that a divine law should supervene.

Fourthly, because, as Augustine says, human law cannot punish or forbid all evil deeds, since, while aiming at doing away with all evils, it would do away with many good things, and would hinder the advance of the common good, which is necessary for human living. In order, therefore, that no evil might remain unforbidden and unpunished, it was necessary for the divine law to supervene, whereby all sins are forbidden. . . .

As we have stated above, man has a natural aptitude for virtue; but the perfection of virtue must be acquired by man by means of some kind of training. Thus we observe that a man is helped by diligence in his necessities, for instance, in food and clothing. Certain beginnings of these he has from nature, viz., his reason and his hands; but he has not the full complement, as other animals have, to whom nature has given sufficiently of clothing and food. Now it is difficult to see how man could suffice for himself in the matter of this training, since the perfection of virtue consists chiefly in withdrawing man from under undue pleasures, to which above all man is inclined, and especially the young, who are more capable of being trained. Consequently a man needs to receive this training from another, whereby to arrive at the perfection of virtue. And as to those young people who are inclined to acts of virtue by their good natural disposition, or by custom, or rather by the gift of God, paternal training suffices, which is by admonitions. But since some are found to be dissolute and prone to vice, and not easily amenable to words, it was necessary for such to be restrained from evil by force and fear, in order that, at least, they might desist from evil-doing, and leave others in peace, and that they themselves, by being habituated in this way, might be brought to do willingly what hitherto they did from fear, and thus become virtuous. Now this kind of training, which compels through fear of punishment, is the discipline of laws. Therefore, in order that man might have peace and virtue, it was necessary for laws to be framed; for as the Philosopher says, *as man is the most noble of animals if he be perfect in virtue, so he is the lowest of all, if he be severed from law and justice.* For man can use his reason to devise means of satisfying his lusts and evil passions, which other animals are unable to do. . . .

As Augustine says, *that which is not just seems to be no law at all.* Hence the force of a law depends on the extent of its justice. Now in human affairs a thing is said to be just from being right, according to the rule of reason. But the first rule of reason is the law of nature, as is clear from what has been stated above. Consequently, every human law has just so much of the nature of law as it is derived from the law of nature. But if in any point it departs from the law of nature, it is no longer a law but a perversion of law.

But it must be noted that something may be derived from the natural law in two ways: first, as a conclusion from principles; secondly, by way of a determination of certain common notions. The first way is like to that by which, in the sciences, demonstrated conclusions are drawn from the principles; while the second is likened to that whereby, in the arts, common forms are determined to some particular. Thus, the craftsman needs to determine the common form of a house to the shape of this or that particular house. Some things are therefore derived from the common principles of the natural law by way of conclusions: e.g., that *one must not kill* may be derived as a conclusion from the principle that *one should do harm to no man;* while some are derived therefrom by way of determination: e.g., the law of nature has it that the evil-doer should be punished, but that he be punished in this or that way is determination of the human law.

CHAPTER 11

THE SOCIAL CONTRACT

Hobbes and Locke

Thomas Hobbes was born in England in 1588. He graduated from Oxford in 1608 and became the tutor of the Earl of Devonshire, William Cavendish. In this position he traveled with the Cavendish family extensively on the Continent, where he met leading thinkers of the day, including Galileo. Known especially as a great political thinker, he became one of the most famous Englishmen abroad in his day. He designed a natural philosophy based on the law of motion. In a series of books, *Concerning Body (De Corpore)*, *Concerning Man (De Homine)*, and *Concerning the Citizen (De Cive)*, he tried to show that all behavior, including physical movement, thinking, and political arrangements, represents bodies in motion. In England, Hobbes was much admired by Sir Francis Bacon, who enjoyed conversation with him and frequently dictated his thoughts to Hobbes during "delicious walks at Gorambery." Hobbes became best known for his influential book *Leviathan*. He died in Derbyshire in 1679 at the age of ninety-one.

What strikes one first about Hobbes's theory of state is that he approaches the subject not from an historical point of view, but from the vantage point of logic and analysis. He does not ask "*When* did civil societies emerge?" but rather "*How* do you explain the emergence of society?" He is concerned to discover the *cause* of civil society, and in harmony with his general method, he sets out to explain the cause of the state by describing the motion of bodies. His thought about political philosophy resembles the method of geometry in the sense that from axiomlike premises he deduces all the consequences of his political theory. Most of these premises cluster around his conception of human nature.

* ALSO - Refer To Methods of
OrDuction in Notes

The State of Nature

Hobbes describes men, first of all, as they appear in what he calls the *state of nature,* which is the condition of men before there is any state or civil society. In this state of nature, all men are equal and equally have the right to whatever they consider necessary for their survival. "Equality" here means simply that anyone is capable of hurting his neighbor and taking what he judges he needs for his own protection. Differences in strength can in time be overcome, and the weak can destroy the strong. The "right of all to all" that prevails in the state of nature does not mean that one man has a right whereas others have corresponding duties. The word "right" in the bare state of nature is a man's *freedom* "to do what he would, and against whom he thought fit, and to possess, use and enjoy all that he would, or could get." The driving force in man is the will to survive, and the psychological mood pervading all men is fear— the fear of death and particularly the fear of violent death. In the state of nature, all men are relentlessly pursuing whatever acts they think will secure their safety. The picture one gets of this state of nature is of men moving against each other, bodies in motion, or the anarchic condition Hobbes called "the war of all against all."

Why do men behave this way? Hobbes analyzes human motivation by saying that all men possess a twofold *endeavor,* namely *appetite* and *aversion.* These two endeavors account for man's motions to and from persons or objects and have the same meanings as the words "love" and "hate." Men are attracted to what they

Hobbes (*National Portrait Gallery, London*)

think will help them survive, and they hate whatever they judge to be a threat to them. The words "good" and "evil" have whatever meaning each individual will give them, and each person will call good whatever he loves and evil whatever he hates, "there being nothing simply and absolutely so." Men are fundamentally egotistical in that they are concerned chiefly about their own survival and identify goodness with their own appetites. It would appear therefore that in the state of nature there is no obligation for men to respect others or that there is no morality in the traditional sense of goodness and justice. Given this egotistical view of human nature, it would appear also that men do not possess the capacity to create an ordered and peaceful society.

But Hobbes argued that several logical conclusions or consequences can be deduced from man's concern for his survival, among these being what Hobbes called *natural laws*. Even in the state of nature, men *know* these natural laws, which are logically consistent with man's principal concern for his own safety. A natural law, said Hobbes, "is a precept, or general rule, found out by reason," telling what to do and what not to do. If the major premise is that I want to survive, I can logically deduce, even in the state of nature, certain rules of behavior that will help me to survive. The first law of nature is therefore that every man ought to "seek peace and follow it." Now this law that urges me to seek peace is natural because it is a logical extension of my concern for survival. It is obvious that I have a better chance to survive if I help to create the conditions of peace. My desire for survival therefore impels me to seek peace.

From this first and fundamental law of nature is derived the second law, which states that "a man be willing, when others are so too, as farforth as for peace and defense of himself he shall think it necessary, to lay down his right to all things; and be contented with so much liberty against other men, as he would allow other men against himself. . . ."

Obligation in the State of Nature

If men know these and other natural laws even in the state of nature, do they have an obligation to obey them? Hobbes answers that these laws are always binding, in the state of nature as well as in civil society. But he distinguishes between two ways in which these natural laws are applicable in the state of nature, saying that "the laws of nature oblige *in foro interno* [i.e., in the court of conscience]; that is to say, they bind to a desire they should take place: but *in foro externo* [i.e., in actual practice]; that is, to putting them in act, not always." Thus it isn't as if there were no obligation in the state of nature. Rather, the circumstances for living by these laws in the state of nature are not always present. Men have a right to all things in the state of nature not because there is no obligation, but because if a man were modest, tractable, and kept his promises "in such time and place where no man else should do so, [he] should but make himself a prey to others, and procure his own ruin, contrary to the ground of all laws of nature, which tend to nature's preservations." And even when men act to preserve themselves, they are not free from rational natural laws, for even in the state of nature they ought to act in good faith: " . . . if any man *pretend* somewhat to tend necessarily to his preservation, which yet he himself doth not confidently believe so, he may offend against the laws of nature."

Hobbes was aware that the logical outcome of egotistical individuals all deciding how best to survive would be anarchy, where there were "no arts; no letters; no society; and which is worst of all, continual fear, and danger of violent death; and the life of man, solitary, poor, nasty, brutish, and short. . . . " To avoid such a condition of anarchy, the chief cause of which is the conflict of individual and egotistical judgments of right, men, following the dictates of natural law, seeking peace, renounce some of their rights or freedoms and enter into a Social Contract and thereby create an artificial man, that great leviathan, called a commonwealth or state.

The Social Contract

The contract by which men avoid the state of nature and enter civil society is an agreement between individuals, "as if every man should say to every man, *I authorize and give up my right of governing myself, to this man, or to this assembly of men, on this condition, that you give up your right to him, and authorize all his actions in like manner.*" Two things stand out clearly in this contract. First, the parties to the contract are individuals who promise each other to hand over their right to govern themselves to the sovereign; it is not a contract between the sovereign and the citizens. The sovereign has absolute power to govern and is in no way subject to the citizens. Second, Hobbes clearly states that the sovereign can be either "this man" or "this assembly of men," suggesting that, in theory at least, his view of sovereignty was not identified with any particular form of government. It may be that he had a preference for a single ruler with absolute power, but he recognized the possible compatibility of his theory of sovereignty with "democracy." But whatever form the sovereign would take, it is clear that Hobbes saw the transfer of the right to rule from the people to the sovereign as both absolute and irrevocable.

Hobbes was particularly anxious to demonstrate with logical rigor that sovereign power is indivisible. Having shown that in the state of nature anarchy is the logical consequence of independent individual judgments, he concluded that the only way to overcome such anarchy is to make a single body out of the several bodies of the citizens. The only way to transform multiple wills into a single will is to agree that the sovereign's single will and judgment represent the will and judgment of all the citizens. In effect, this is what the contract says when men agree to hand over their right to govern themselves. The sovereign now acts not only on behalf of the citizens but *as if* he embodied the will of the citizens, thereby affirming an identity between the wills of the sovereign and citizens. Resistance against the sovereign by a citizen is therefore illogical on two counts, first because it would amount to resistance to himself, and second, because to resist is to revert to independent judgment, which is to revert to the state of nature or anarchy. The power of the sovereign must therefore be absolute in order to secure the conditions of order, peace, and law.

Civil Law versus Natural Law

Law begins only when there is a sovereign. This is a logical truism, for, in the judicial or *legal* sense, a law is defined as a command of the sovereign. It follows that where there is no sovereign, there is no law. To be sure, Hobbes affirmed that even in the state of nature men have knowledge of the natural law, and in a special sense, the natural law is binding even in the state of nature. But only after there is a sovereign can there be a legal order, because only then is there the apparatus of law in which the power of enforcement is central. Without the power to enforce, said Hobbes, covenants are "mere words." Hobbes identifies law with sovereign command and makes the additional point that "there can be no unjust law."

Nowhere does Hobbes's severe authoritarianism express itself in more startling form than when he argues that there can be no unjust law. It appears that justice and morality begin with the sovereign, that there are no principles of justice and morality that precede and limit the acts of the sovereign. Hobbes affirmed this in a notable passage: "To the care of the sovereign, belongeth the making of good laws. But what is a good law? By good law, I mean not a just law: for no law can be unjust." Hobbes gives two reasons for saying no law can be unjust: first, because justice means obeying the law, and this is why justice comes into being only after a law has been made and cannot itself be the standard for law; second, when a sovereign makes a law, it is as though the people were making the law, and what they agree on cannot be unjust. Indeed, the third natural law Hobbes speaks of is *"that men perform their covenants made,"* and he indicated that this is the "fountain of justice." Hence to keep the contract in which you agreed to obey the sovereign is the essence of Hobbesian justice.

It is evident that Hobbes forces the reader to take each word seriously and "reckon" all the "consequences" that can be deduced from it. If law means the sovereign's command and if justice means obeying the law, there can be no *unjust* law. But there can be a *bad* law, for Hobbes was enough of an Aristotelian to recognize that a sovereign has a definite purpose "for which he was trusted with the sovereign power, namely, the procuration of *the safety of the people;* to which he is obliged by the law of nature, and to render an account thereof to God. . . . " But even in such a case, where the sovereign has commanded a "bad" law, the citizens are not the ones to judge it as such, nor does this justify their disobedience. The sovereign has the sole power to judge what is for the safety of the people; if the people disagreed with him, they would revert to anarchy. If the sovereign engages in iniquitous acts, this is a matter between the sovereign and God, not between the citizens and the sovereign. And because he feared anarchy and disorder so deeply, Hobbes pushed his logic of obedience to the point of making religion and the church subordinate to the state. To the Christian who felt that the sovereign's command violated the law of God, Hobbes gave no comfort but insisted that if such a person could not obey the sovereign, he must "go to Christ in martyrdom. . . . "

READING

THE STATE OF NATURE
Hobbes

CHAPTER 1

The greatest part of those men who have written aught concerning commonwealths, either suppose, or require us, or beg of us to believe, that man is a creature born fit for society. The Greeks call him *political animal;* and on this foundation they so build up the doctrine of civil society, as if for the preservation of peace, and the government of mankind, there were nothing else necessary, than that men should agree to make certain covenants and conditions together, which themselves should then call laws. Which axiom, though received by most, is yet certainly false, and an error proceeding from our too slight contemplation of human nature. For they who shall more narrowly look into the causes for which men come together, and delight in each other's company, shall easily find that this happens not because naturally it could happen no otherwise, but by accident. For if by nature one man should love another (that is) as man, there could no reason be returned why every man should not equally love every man, as being equally man, or why he should rather frequent those whose society affords him honour or profit. We do not therefore by nature seek society for its own sake, but that we may receive some honour or profit from it. ... I hope no body will doubt but that men would much more greedily be carried by nature, if all fear were removed, to obtain dominion, than to gain society. We must therefore resolve, that the original of all great and lasting societies consisted not in the mutual good will men had towards each other, but in the mutual fear they had of each other.

The cause of mutual fear consists partly in the natural equality of men, partly in their mutual will of hurting: whence it comes to pass that we can neither expect from others, nor promise to ourselves the least security. For if we look on men full-grown, and consider how brittle the frame of our human body is, ... and how easy a matter it is, even for the weakest man to kill the strongest, there is no reason why any man trusting to his own strength should conceive himself made by nature above others: they are

From Hobbes, *De Cive,* ed. Sterling P. Lamprecht, Appleton-Century-Crofts, New York, 1949.

equals who can do equal things one against the other; but they who can do the greatest things (namely, kill) can do equal things. All men therefore among themselves are by nature equal; the inequality we now discern, hath its spring from the civil law.

All men in the state of nature have a desire and will to hurt, but not proceeding from the same cause, neither equally to be condemned. For one man, according to that natural equality which is among us, permits as much to others, as he assumes to himself (which is an argument of a temperate man, and one that rightly values his power). Another, supposing himself above others, will have a license to do what he wishes, and challenges respect and honour, as due to him before others (which is an argument of a fiery spirit). This man's will to hurt ariseth from vain glory, and the false esteem he hath of his own strength; the other's, from the necessity of defending himself, his liberty, and his goods, against this man's violence. . . .

But the most frequent reason why men desire to hurt each other, ariseth hence, that many men at the same time have an appetite to the same thing; which yet very often they can neither enjoy in common, nor yet divide it; whence it follows that the strongest must have it, and who is strongest must be decided by the sword.

Among so many dangers therefore, as the natural lusts of men do daily threaten each other withal, to have a care of one's self is not a matter so scornfully to be looked upon, as if so be there had not been a power and will left in one to have done otherwise. For every man is desirous of what is good for him, and shuns what is evil, but chiefly the chiefest of natural evils, which is death; and this he doth, by a certain impulsion of nature, no less than that whereby a stone moves downward. It is therefore neither absurd, nor reprehensible, neither against the dictates of true reason, for a man to use all his endeavours to preserve and defend his body and the members thereof from death and sorrows. . . . Therefore the first foundation of natural right is this, that every man as much as in him lies endeavour to protect his life and members.

But because it is in vain for a man to have a right to the end, if the right to the necessary means be denied him; it follows, that since every man hath a right to preserve himself, he must also be allowed a right to use all the means, and do all the actions, without which he cannot preserve himself.

Now whether the means which he is about to use, and the action he is performing, be necessary to the preservation of his life and members, or not, he himself, by the right of nature, must be judge. . . .

Nature hath given to every one a right to all; that is, it was lawful for every man in the bare state of nature, or before such time as men had engaged themselves by any covenants or bonds, to do what he would, and against whom he thought fit, and to possess, use, and enjoy all what he would, or could get. Now because whatsoever a man would, it therefore seems good to him because he wills it, and either it really doth, or at least seems to him to contribute towards his preservation, it follows, that in the state of nature, to have all, and do all, is lawful for all. And this is that which is meant by that common saying, nature hath given all to all, from whence we understand likewise, that in the state of nature, profit is the measure of right.

But it was the least benefit for men thus to have a common right to all things; for the effects of this right are the same, almost, as if there had been no right at all. For although any man might say of every thing, this is mine, yet could he not enjoy it, by reason of his neighbour, who having equal right, and equal power, would pretend the same thing to be his.

If now to this natural proclivity of men, to hurt each other, which they derive from their passions, but chiefly from a vain esteem of themselves, you add, the right of all to all, wherewith one by right invades, the other by right resists, and whence arise perpetual jealousies and suspicions on all hands, and how hard a thing it is to provide against an enemy invading us, with an intention to oppress, and ruin, though they come with a small number, and no great provision; it cannot be denied but that the natural state of men, before they entered into society, was a mere war, and that not simply, but a war of all men against all men. . . .

But it is easily judged how disagreeable a thing to the preservation either of mankind, or of each single man, a perpetual war is. But it is perpetual in its own nature, because in regard of the equality of those that strive, it cannot be ended by victory; for in this state the conqueror is subject to so much danger, as it were to be accounted a miracle, if any, even the most strong, should close up his life with many years, and old age. . . . Whosoever therefore holds, that it had been best to have continued in that state in which all things were lawful for all men, he contradicts himself. For every man by natural necessity desires that which is good for him: nor is there any that esteems a war of all against all, which necessarily adheres to such a state, to be good for him. And so it happens, that through fear of each other we think it fit to rid ourselves of this condition, and to get some fellows; that if there needs must be war it may not yet be against all men, nor without some helps.

Yet cannot men expect any lasting preservation continuing thus in the state of nature, that is, of war, by reason of that equality of power, and other human faculties they are endued withal. Wherefore to seek peace, where there is any hope of obtaining it, and where there is none, to enquire out for auxiliaries of war, is the dictate of right reason, that is, the law of nature. . . .

CHAPTER II

The first and fundamental law of nature is, that peace is to be sought after, where it may be found; and where not, there to provide ourselves for helps of war. . . .

But one of the natural laws derived from this fundamental one is this: that the right of all men to all things, ought not to be retained, but that some certain rights ought to be transferred, or relinquished. For if every one should retain his right to all things, it must necessarily follow, that some by right might invade, and others, by the same right, might defend themselves against them (for every man, by natural necessity, endeavours to defend his body). Therefore war would follow. He therefore acts against the reason of peace, that is, against the law of nature, whosoever he be, that doth not part with his right to all things. . . .

No man is obliged by any contracts whatsoever not to resist him who shall offer to kill, wound, or any other way hurt his body. For there is in every man a certain high degree of fear, through which he apprehends that evil which is done to him to be the greatest; and therefore by natural necessity he shuns it all he can, and it is supposed he can do no otherwise. When a man is arrived to this degree of fear, we cannot expect but he will provide for himself either by flight or fight. Since therefore no man is tied to impossibilities, they who are threatened either with death (which is the greatest evil to nature) or wounds, or some other bodily hurts, and are not stout enough to bear them, are not obliged to endure them. . . .

Likewise no man is tied by any compacts whatsoever to accuse himself, or any other, by whose damage he is like to procure himself a bitter life. Wherefore neither is a father obliged to bear witness against his son, nor a husband against his wife, nor a son against his father, nor any man against any one by whose means he hath his subsistence; for in vain is that testimony which is presumed to be corrupted from nature. . . .

CHAPTER III

As it was necessary to the conservation of each man, that he should part with some of his rights, so it is no less necessary to the same conservation, that he retain some others, to wit, the right of bodily protection, of free enjoyment of air, water, and all necessaries for life. Since therefore many common rights are retained by those who enter into a peaceable state, and that many peculiar ones are also acquired, hence ariseth this dictate of the natural law, to wit, that what rights soever any man challenges to himself, he also grant the same as due to all the rest. . . .

The laws of nature are immutable and eternal: what they forbid, can never be lawful; what they command, can never be unlawful. For pride, ingratitude, breach of contracts (or injury), inhumanity, contumely, will never be lawful, nor the contrary virtues to these ever unlawful, as we take them for dispositions of the mind, that is, as they are considered in the court of conscience, where only they oblige, and are laws. . . .

CHAPTER V

Since therefore the exercise of the natural law is necessary for the preservation of peace, and that for the exercise of the natural law security is no less necessary, it is worth the considering what that is which affords such a security. For this matter nothing else can be imagined, but that each man provide himself of such meet helps, as the invasion of one on the other may be rendered so dangerous, as either of them may think it better to refrain, than to meddle. But first, it is plain, that the consent of two or three cannot make good such a security; because that the addition but of one, or some few on the other side, is sufficient to make the victory undoubtedly sure, and heartens the enemy to attack us. It is therefore necessary, to the end the security sought for may be obtained, that the number of them who conspire in a mutual assistance be so great, that the accession of some few to the enemy's party may not prove to them a matter of moment sufficient to assure the victory. . . .

Wherefore consent or contracted society, without some common power whereby particular men may be ruled through fear of punishment, doth not suffice to make up that security which is requisite to the exercise of natural justice.

Since therefore the conspiring of many wills to the same end doth not suffice to preserve peace, and to make a lasting defence, it is requisite that, in those necessary matters which concern peace and self-defence, there be but one will of all men. But this cannot be done, unless every man will so subject his will to some other one, to wit, either man or council, that whatsoever his will is in those things which are necessary to the common peace, it be received for the wills of all men in general, and of every one in particular. Now the gathering together of many men who deliberate of what is to be done, or not to be done, for the common good of all men, is that which I call a council.

This submission of the wills of all those men to the will of one man, or one council, is then made, when each one of them obligeth himself by contract to every one of the rest, not to resist the will of that one man, or council, to which he hath submitted himself; that is, that he refuse him not the use of his wealth and strength against any others whatsoever (for he is supposed still to retain a right of defending himself against violence) and this is called union. But we understand that to be the will of the council, which is the will of the major part of those men of whom the council consists. . . .

Now union thus made is called a city, or civil society, and also a civil person; for when there is one will of all men, it is to be esteemed for one person, and by the word one it is to be known, and distinguished from all particular men, as having its own rights and properties. Insomuch as neither any one citizen, nor all of them together (if except him whose will stands for the will of all), is to be accounted the city. A city therefore (that we may define it) is one person, whose will, by the compact of many men, is to be received for the will of them all; so as he may use all the power and faculties of each particular person, to the maintenance of peace, and for common defence.

Locke

John Locke's life resembled Hobbes's in many ways. Also an English-man, Locke was born in 1632 and died in 1704. He lived through the Civil War, the Bloodless Revolution, and the Restoration. At West-minster School he developed an early interest in science which was to stay with him for the rest of his life. At Oxford he was particularly influenced by the philosophy of Descartes, which furthered his bent in science. He studied to become a doctor, later becoming associ-ated with the Earl of Shaftesbury and his family as a friend, physician, and adviser. His most famous writings include his *Essay on Human Understanding,* considered by some to have proposed a theory of knowledge so influential that it provided support for the foundations of modern science. His *Two Treatises of Government* was enormously influential and his "Second Treatise," from which the following read-ing is selected, was especially significant in the development of the American philosophy of democracy. As in the case of Hobbes, Locke drew much of his political philosophy from his interpretation of human nature and from historical events which he witnessed, espe-cially wars. As in the case of Hobbes, Locke also fashioned a theory of the State of Nature and the Social Contract.

READING

NATURAL RIGHTS AND CIVIL SOCIETY
Locke

OF THE STATE OF NATURE

To understand political power aright, and derive it from its original, we must consider what state all men are naturally in, and that is a state of perfect freedom to order their actions and dispose of their possessions and persons as they think fit, within the bounds of the law of nature, without asking leave, or depending upon the will of any other man.

A state also of equality, wherein all the power and jurisdiction is reciprocal, no one having more than another; there being nothing more evident than that creatures of the same species and rank, promiscuously born to all the same advantages of nature, and the use of the same faculties, should also be equal one amongst another without subordination or subjection. . . .

But though this be a state of liberty, yet it is not a state of licence; though man in that state has an uncontrollable liberty to dispose of his person or possessions, yet he has not liberty to destroy himself, or so much as any creature in his possession, but where some nobler use than its bare preservation calls for it. The state of nature has a law of nature to govern it, which obliges every one; and reason, which is that law, teaches all mankind who will but consult it, that, being all equal and independent, no one ought to harm another in his life, health, liberty, or possessions. For men being all the workmanship of one omnipotent and infinitely wise Maker—all the servants of one sovereign Master, sent into the world by His order, and about His business—they are His property, whose workmanship they are, made to last during His, not one another's pleasure; and being furnished with like faculties, sharing all in one community of nature, there cannot be supposed any such subordination among us, that may authorise us to destroy one another, as if we were made for one another's uses, as the inferior ranks of creatures are for ours. Every one, as he is bound to preserve himself, and not to quit his station wilfully, so, by the like reason, when his own preservation comes not in competition, ought he, as much as he can, to preserve the rest of mankind, and not, unless it be to do justice on an offender, take away or impair the life, or what tends to the preservation of the life, the liberty, health, limb, or goods of another.

And that all men may be restrained from invading others' rights, and from doing hurt to one another, and the law of nature be observed, which willeth the peace and preservation of all mankind, the execution of the law on nature is in that state put into every man's hand, whereby every one has a right to punish the transgressors of that law to such a degree as may hinder its violation. For the law of nature would, as all other laws that concern men in this world, be in vain if there were nobody that, in the state of nature, had a power to execute that law, and thereby preserve the innocent and restrain offenders. And if any one in the state of nature may punish another for any evil he has done, every one may do so. For in that state of perfect equality, where naturally there is no superiority or jurisdiction of one over another, what any may do in prosecution of that law, every one must needs have a right to do.

OF POLITICAL OR CIVIL SOCIETY . . .

Man being born, as has been proved, with a title to perfect freedom, and an uncontrolled enjoyment of all the rights and privileges of the law of nature equally with any other man or number of men in the world, hath by nature a power not only to preserve his property—that is, his life, liberty, and estate—against the injuries and attempts of other men, but to judge of and punish the breaches of that law in others as he is persuaded the offence deserves, even with death itself, in crimes where the heinousness of the fact in his opinion requires it. But . . . there, and there only, is political society, where every one of the members hath quitted this natural power, resigned it up into the hands of the community in all cases that exclude him not from appealing for protection to the law established by it; and thus all private judgment of every particular member being excluded, the community comes to be umpire; and . . . decides all the differences that may happen between any members of that society concerning any matter of right, and punishes those offences which any member hath committed against the society with such penalties as the law has established. . . .

Wherever, therefore, any number of men so unite into one society, as to quit every one his executive power of the law of nature, and to resign it to the public, there, and there only, is a political, or civil society. And this is done wherever any number of men, in the state of nature, enter into society to make one people, one body politic, under one supreme government, or else when any one joins himself to, and incorporates with, any government already made. For thereby he authorises the society, or, which is all one, the legislative thereof, to make laws for him, as the public good of the society shall require, to the execution whereof his own assistance . . . is due. And this puts men out of a state of nature into that of a commonwealth, by setting up a judge on earth with authority to determine all the controversies and redress the injuries that may happen to any member of the commonwealth; which judge is the legislative, or magistrates appointed by it. And wherever there are any number of men, however associated, that have no such decisive power to appeal to, there they are still in the state of nature. . . .

The great and *chief End* therefore, of Men's uniting into Commonwealths, and putting themselves under Government, *is the Preservation of their Property*. To which in the State of Nature there are many Things wanting.

First, There wants an establish'd, settled, known Law, received and allow'd by common Consent to be the Standard of Right and Wrong, and the common Measure to decide all Controversies between them. For though the Law of Nature be plain and intelligible to all rational Creatures; yet Men being biassed by their Interest, as well as ignorant for want of Study of it, are not apt to allow of it as a Law binding to them in the Application of it to their particular Cases.

Secondly, In the State of Nature there wants a known and indifferent Judge, with Authority to determine all Differences according to the establish'd Law. For every one in that State, being both Judge and Executioner of the Law of Nature, Men being partial to themselves, Passion and Revenge is very apt to carry them too far, and with too much Heat in their own Cases; as well as Negligence and Unconcernedness, to make them too remiss in other Men's.

Thirdly, In the State of Nature there often wants Power to back and support the Sentence when Right, and to give it due Execution. They who by any Injustice offend, will seldom fail, where they are able, by Force to make good their Injustice; such Resistance many times makes the Punishment dangerous, and frequently destructive to those who attempt it.

Thus Mankind, notwithstanding all the Privileges of the state of Nature, being but in an ill Condition, while they remain in it, are quickly driven into Society. Hence it comes to pass, that we seldom find any Number of Men live any time together in this State. The Inconveniencies that they are therein exposed to, by the irregular, and uncertain Exercise of the Power every Man has of punishing the Transgressions of others, make them take Sanctuary under the establish'd Laws of Government, and therein seek the Preservation of their Property. 'Tis this makes them so willingly give up every one his single Power of punishing, to be exercised by such alone, as shall be appointed to it amongst them; and by such Rules as the Community, or those authorized by them to that Purpose, shall agree on. And in this we have the original Right and Rise of both the legislative and executive Power, as well as of the Governments and Societies themselves.

For in the State of Nature, to omit the Liberty he has of innocent Delights, a Man has two Powers:

The first is to do whatsoever he thinks fit for the Preservation of himself and others, within the Permission of the Law of Nature; by which Law, common to them all, he and all the rest of Mankind are of one Community, make up one Society, distinct from all other Creatures. . . .

The other Power a Man has in the State of Nature, is the Power to punish the Crimes committed against that Law. Both these he gives up, when he joins in a private, if I may so call it, or particular political Society, and incorporates into any Common-wealth, separate from the rest of Mankind.

The first Power, . . . he gives up to be regulated by Laws made by the Society, so far forth as the Preservation of himself, and the rest of that Society shall require; which Laws of the Society in many Things confine the Liberty he had by the Law of Nature.

Secondly, the Power of punishing he wholly gives up, and engages his natural Force (which he might before employ in the Execution of the Law of Nature, by his own single Authority, as he thought fit) to assist the executive Power of the Society, as the Law thereof shall require. For being now in a new State, wherein he is to enjoy many conveniencies, from the Labour, Assistance, and Society of others in the same Community, as well as Protection from its whole Strength; he is to part also with as much of his natural Liberty in providing for himself, as the Good, Prosperity, and Safety of the Society shall require; which is not only necessary, but just; since the other Members of the Society do the like.

But though Men when they enter into Society, give up the Equality, Liberty, and executive Power they had in the State of Nature, into the Hands of the Society, . . . yet it being only with an Intention in every one the better to preserve himself his Liberty and Property; (For no rational Creature can be supposed to change his Condition with an Intention to be worse) the Power of the Society, or Legislative constituted by them, can never be suppos'd to extend farther than the common Good; but is obliged to secure every ones Property, by providing against those three Defects above-mention'd, that made the State of Nature so unsafe and uneasie. And so whoever has the Legislative or supreme Power of any Common-wealth, is bound to govern by establish'd standing Laws, promulgated and known to the People, and not by extemporary Decrees; by indifferent and upright Judges, who are to decide Controversies by those Laws; and to employ the Force of the Community at Home, only in the Execution of such Laws, or Abroad to prevent or redress foreign Injuries, and secure the Community from Inroads and Invasion. And all this to be directed to no other End, but the Peace, Safety, and publick Good of the People.

CHAPTER 12

INDIVIDUALISM AND LIBERTY

Bentham and Mill

Both Bentham and Mill applied the principle of utility to the practical concerns of government. For Bentham, two leading questions were "How can the principle of utility clarify the purpose and objectives of law?" and "What is the justification for punishment?" For Mill, the central concern was the matter of human liberty, or "When is it appropriate or inappropriate for the government to interfere with an individual's freedom?" To all these questions, Bentham and Mill provided answers based squarely on the principle of utility. In this way, the foundation of moral philosophy which guides an individual's conduct became for them also the basis for political philosophy which involves the role of government in directing the behavior of citizens.

Law and Punishment

It was particularly in connection with law and punishment that Bentham made impressive use of the principle of utility. Since it is the

211

function of the legislator to discourage some acts and encourage others, how shall he classify those which should be discouraged as opposed to those which should be encouraged?

OBJECT OF LAW

Bentham's method of legislation was first of all to measure the "mischief of an act." This mischief consisted of the consequences, the pain or evil inflicted by the act. Acts that produce evil must be discouraged. There are, says Bentham, both primary and secondary evils that concern the legislator. A robber inflicts an evil on his victim, who loses his money: this is a case of primary evil. But robbery creates a secondary evil because successful robbery suggests that theft is easy. This suggestion is evil because it weakens respect for property, and property becomes insecure. From the point of view of the legislator, the secondary evils are frequently more important than the primary evils because, taking the example of robbery again, the actual loss to the victim may very well be considerably less than the loss in stability and security to the community as a whole.

The law is concerned with augmenting the total happiness of the community, and it must do this by discouraging those acts which would produce evil consequences. A criminal act or offense is by definition one that is clearly detrimental to the happiness of the community, and the only act that ought to be the concern of the law is one that in some specific way does in fact inflict some sort of pain and thereby diminish the pleasure of some specific individual or group. For the most part, the government accomplishes its business of promoting the happiness of society by punishing men who commit offenses that the principle of utility has clearly measured as evil.

It was Bentham's confirmed belief that if the legislator used only the principle of utility in deciding which acts should be considered "offenses," many acts that the laws of his day controlled would have to be considered a matter of private morals to be subject only to the sanction of opinion. Utilitarianism had the effect, then, of requiring a reclassification of behavior to determine what is and is not appropriate for the government to regulate. In addition, the principle of utility provided Bentham with a new and sim-

Inns of Court (*New York Public Library Picture Collection*)

ple theory of punishment, a theory that he thought could not only be justified more readily than the older theories, but could also achieve the purposes of punishment far more effectively.

PUNISHMENT

"All punishment," said Bentham, "is in itself evil" because it inflicts suffering and pain. At the same time, the "object which all laws have in common is to augment the total happiness of the community." If punishment is to be justified from a utilitarian point of view, it must be shown, said Bentham, that the pain inflicted by

213

punishment in some way prevents or excludes some greater pain. Punishment must therefore be "useful" in achieving a greater aggregate of pleasure and happiness and has no justification if its effect is simply to add still more units or lots of pain to the community. The principle of utility would clearly call for the elimination of pure "retribution," where someone is made to suffer only because his act caused his victim pain, for no useful purpose is served by adding still more pain to the sum total society suffers.

This is not to say that utilitarianism rejects the category of punishment, but only that the principle of utility, particularly in the hands of Bentham, called for a reopening of the question of why society should punish offenders and urged a reclassification of cases that are "meet" and "unmeet" for punishment. Punishment should not be inflicted (1) where it is *groundless*, where, for example, there is an offense that admits of compensation and where there is virtual certainty that compensation is forthcoming, or (2) where it must be *inefficacious* in that it cannot prevent a mischievous act, such as when a law made after the act is retroactive, or *ex post facto*, or where a law has already been made but not been announced. Punishment would be inefficacious also where an infant, an insane person, or a drunkard was involved, although Bentham admitted that neither infancy nor intoxication was sufficient grounds for "absolute impunity." Nor should punishment be inflicted (3) where it is *unprofitable* or too *expensive*, "where the mischief it would produce would be greater than what it prevented," or (4) where it is *needless*, "where the mischief may be prevented, or cease of itself, without it: that is at a cheaper rate," particularly in cases "which consist in disseminating pernicious principles in matters of duty," since in these cases persuasion is more efficacious than force.

Whether a given kind of behavior should be left to *private ethics* instead of becoming the object of *legislation* was a question Bentham answered by simply applying the principle of utility. If to involve the whole legislative process and the apparatus of punishment does more harm than good, the matter should be left to private ethics. He was convinced that attempts to regulate sexual immorality would be particularly unprofitable, since this would require intricate supervision, as would "such offenses as ingratitude or rudeness, where the definition is so vague that the judge could not safely be entrusted with the power to punish." Duties that we owe to ourselves could hardly be the concern of law and punishment, nor must we be "coerced" to be "benevolent," although we can be liable on certain occasions for failing to help. But the main concern of law must be to encourage those acts which would lead to the greatest happiness of the community. There is, then, a justification for punishment, which is that through punishment the greatest good for the greatest number is most effectively secured.

Besides providing a rationale for punishment, the principle of utility also gives us some clue to what punishment should consist of. Bentham describes the desirable properties of each unit or lot of punishment by considering "the proportion between punishments and offenses," and he gives the following rules: The punishment must be great enough to outweigh the profit that the offender might get from the offense; the greater the offense, the greater the punishment. Where two offenses come in competition, the punishment for the greater offense must be sufficient to induce a man to prefer the less. Punishments should be variable and adaptable to fit the particular circumstances, although each offender should get the same punishment for the same offense. The amount of punishment should never be greater then the minimum required to make it effective. The more uncertain that an offender will be caught, the greater should be the punishment, and if an offense is habitual, the punishment must outweigh not only the profit of the immediate offense but of the undiscovered offenses. These rules led Bentham to conclude that punishment should be *variable* to fit the particular case, *equable* so as to inflict equal pain for similar offenses, *commensurable* in order that punishments for different classes of crimes be proportional, *characteristic* so as to impress the imagination of potential offenders, *frugal* so as not to be excessive, *reformatory* in order to correct faulty behavior, *disabling* in order to deter future offenders, *compensatory* to the sufferer, and, in order not to create new problems, have *popular* acceptance and be capable of *remittance* for sufficient cause.

Bentham's Radicalism

It was inevitable that Bentham would discover elements in the law and the general social structure of England that did not fit the requirements set by the principle of utility. Bentham wanted the legislative process to operate on the principle of utility with practically the same rigor with which the stars obey the principle of gravitation. To systematic thought he wanted to add systematic action, so that wherever he found a discrepancy between the actual legal and social order on the one hand and the principle of utility on the other, he wanted to press for reforms. He traced most of the evils of the legal system to the judges who, he charged, "made the common law. Do you know how they make it? Just as a man makes laws for his dog. When your dog does anything you want to break him of, you wait till he does it and then beat him . . . this is the way judges make laws for you and me." Having exposed one monstrous evil after another, Bentham was impelled by his zeal to reform these evils and to become an aggressive philosophical radical.

Bentham laid the cause for the breakdown of the principle of utility to the very structure of the aristocratic society of his day. Why should social evils and evils of the legal system persist even after he had demonstrated that certain new modes of behavior would produce the "greatest happiness of the greatest number?" The answer, he thought, was that those in power did not want the "greatest happiness of the greatest number." The rulers were more concerned with their own interests. Bentham was acutely aware that men seek their own happiness. The object of government, however, is to help achieve the greatest happiness of the greatest number. Whenever those in power represent only a class or a small group, their self-interest will be in conflict with the proper end of government. The way to overcome this conflict or contradiction is to identify the rulers and the ruled, or to put the government into the hands of the people. If there is an identity between the rulers and the ruled, their interests will be the same and the greatest happiness of the greatest number will be assured. This identity of interest cannot, by definition, be achieved under a monarchy, for the monarch acts in his own interests or at best aims at the happiness of a special class grouped around him. It is in a democracy that the greatest happiness of the greatest number is most apt to be realized, for the rulers are the people, and representatives of the people are chosen precisely because they promise to serve the greatest good. The application of the principle of utility clearly required, as Bentham saw it, the rejection of monarchy with all its corollaries, and so he would do away with king, house of peers, and the established church and would prefer to construct a democratic order after the model of the United States. Although Bentham rejected the doctrine of natural rights, he found in the principle of utilitarianism a strong argument for democracy. Each person, he said, can achieve his greatest happiness in an environment of freedom, which democracy makes possible. He believed, moreover, that since "all government is in itself one vast evil," its only justification is to apply evil in order to prevent or exclude some greater evil.

Bentham's radicalism consisted of his desire to press for major social reforms in order to put his philosophical principles into practice, and his reforms were required in order to construct the kind of society and legal process that could most likely contribute the greatest happiness to the greatest number.

Mill

Mill was as much concerned with the problems of society as was Bentham. The principle of the greatest happiness inevitably led all utilitarians to consider how the individual and the government should be related. Bentham had put his faith in democracy as the great cure for social evils inasmuch as in a democracy the interests of the rulers and the ruled are the same because the rulers are the ruled. But Mill did not have the same implicit faith in democracy that Bentham had. Although Mill agreed that democracy is the best form of government, he set forth in his essay *On Liberty* certain dangers inherent in the democratic form of government. Principally, he warned that the will of the people is most often the will of the majority, and it is entirely possible for the majority to oppress the minority. In addition, there is in a democracy the tyranny of opinion, a danger as great as oppression. Even in a democracy, therefore, it is necessary to set up safeguards against the forces that would deny men their free and full self-development. In his concern to eliminate clear social evils, Mill reflected Bentham's desire for reform. But Mill was particularly concerned to preserve liberty by setting limits to the actions of government.

Mill argued that "the sole end for which mankind are warranted, individually or collectively, in interfering with the liberty of action of any of their number, is self-protection. That the only purpose for which power can be rightly exercised over any member

John Stuart Mill (*The Bettmann Archive*)

of a civilized community, against his will, is to prevent harm to others." There is, of course, a legitimate role for government, but, said Mill, no government should interfere with its subjects (1) when the action can be done better by private persons, (2) when, although the government could possibly do the action better than private individuals, it is desirable for the individuals to do it for their development and education, and (3) when there is danger that too much power will unnecessarily accrue to the government. Mill's argument for liberty was, therefore, an argument for individualism. Let each individual pursue his happiness in his own way. Even in the realm of ideas, men must be free to express their thoughts and beliefs, because truth is most quickly discovered when opportunity is given to refute falsehoods. Mill took the position that "there is the greatest difference between presuming an opinion to be true because, with every opportunity for contesting it, it has not been refuted, and assuming its truth for the purpose of not permitting its refutation." He assumed, however, that it is important that the truth be known, and his whole concept of liberty, unlike Bentham's, was conceived as the precondition for developing the full possibilities of human nature.

As he considered the ideal goal of man, Mill asked, "What more or better can be said of any condition of human affairs than that it brings human beings themselves nearer to the best thing they can be?" But is it the function of government to make human beings the best thing they can be? Mill had a deep dislike for the totalitarian state even though he lived too early to see its ugliest manifestations. When he set forth the limits beyond which the government must not go, Mill argued forcefully that a man must not, except to prevent harm, be subject to the power of government, and especially "his own good, either physical or moral, is not a sufficient warrant."

Still, Mill had departed sufficiently from Bentham's version of utilitarianism to set in motion subtle forces that moved Mill from his clear individualism to tepid forms of collectivism. If he was concerned with quality instead of quantity in pleasures, and if this quality is based on human beings' being "the best thing they can be," and, finally, if only those persons who have experienced the higher pleasures can know them, there is the natural urge for those who know these qualitatively higher pleasures to want others to have them also. But what is to be done if those who do not know and appreciate the higher values do not want them? It is not surprising that in this situation Mill advocated, for example, compulsory education, thereby reversing his earlier view that men must not interfere with the liberty of any member of mankind even for "his own good." It is most often in the name of man's good that the state moves into the area of man's freedom.

What Mill said about liberty has particular relevance in the twentieth century, which has witnessed the encroachment of government on the actions and thoughts of men everywhere. But the difficulties of stating utilitarianism as a consistent philosophy are nowhere better seen than in Mill's own attempts to defend its principle. A good example of his thought is found in his essay *On Liberty*, a portion of which is found in the following selected reading.

READING

THE LIMITS OF STATE POWER
Mill

The object of this essay is to assert one very simple principle, as entitled to govern absolutely the dealings of society with the individual in the way of compulsion and control, whether the means used be physical force in the form of legal penalties or the moral coercion of public opinion. The principle is that the sole end for which mankind are warranted, individually or collectively, in interfering with the liberty of action of any of their number is self-protection. That the only purpose for which power can be rightfully exercised over any member of a civilized community, against his will, is to prevent harm to others. His own good, either physical or moral, is not a sufficient warrant. He cannot rightfully be compelled to do or forbear because it will be better for him to do so, because it will make him happier, because, in the opinions of others, to do so would be wise or even right. These are good reasons for remonstrating with him, or reasoning with him, or persuading him, or entertaining him, but not for compelling him or visiting him with any evil in case he do otherwise. To justify that, the conduct from which it is desired to deter him must be calculated to produce evil to someone else. The only part of the conduct of anyone for which he is amenable to society is that which concerns others. In the part which merely concerns himself, his independence is, of right, absolute. Over himself, over his own body and mind, the individual is sovereign. . . .

It is proper to state that I forego any advantage which could be derived to my argument from the idea of abstract right as a thing independent of utility. I regard utility as the ultimate appeal on all ethical questions; but it must be utility in the largest sense, grounded on the permanent interests of man as a progressive being. Those interests, I contend, authorize the subjection of individual spontaneity to external control only in respect to those actions of each which concern the interest of other people. . . .

. . . This, then, is the appropriate region of human liberty. It comprises, first, the inward domain of consciousness, demanding liberty of conscience in the most comprehensive sense, liberty of thought and feeling, absolute freedom of opinion and sentiment on all subjects, practical or speculative,

From John Stuart Mill,*On Liberty*, London, 1859.

scientific, moral, or theological. The liberty of expressing and publishing opinions may seem to fall under a different principle, since it belongs to that part of the conduct of an individual which concerns other people, but, being almost of as much importance as the liberty of thought itself and resting in great part on the same reasons, is practically inseparable from it. Secondly, the principle requires liberty of tastes and pursuits, of framing the plan of our life to suit our own character, of doing as we like, subject to such consequences as may follow, without impediment from our fellow creatures, so long as what we do does not harm them, even though they should think our conduct foolish, perverse, or wrong. Thirdly, from this liberty of each individual follows the liberty, within the same limits, of combination among individuals; freedom to unite for any purpose not involving harm to others; the persons combining being supposed to be of full age and not forced or deceived.

No society in which these liberties are not, on the whole, respected is free, whatever may be its form of government; and none is completely free in which they do not exist absolute and unqualified. The only freedom which deserves the name is that of pursuing our own good in our own way, so long as we do not attempt to deprive others of theirs or impede their efforts to obtain it. Each is the proper guardian of his own health, whether bodily *or* mental and spiritual. Mankind are greater gainers by suffering each other to live as seems good to themselves than by compelling each to live as seems good to the rest. . . .

. . . If all mankind minus one were of one opinion, mankind would be more justified in silencing that one person then he, if he had the power, would be justified in silencing mankind. Were an opinion a personal possession of no value except to the owner, if to be obstructed in the enjoyment of it were simply a private injury, it would make some difference whether the injury was inflicted only on a few persons or on many. But the peculiar evil of silencing the expression of an opinion is that it is robbing the human race, posterity as well as the existing generation—those who dissent from the opinion, still more than those who hold it. If the opinion is right, they are deprived of the opportunity of exchanging error for truth; if wrong, they lose, what is almost as great a benefit, the clearer perception and livelier impression of truth produced by its collision with error. . . .

. . . But it is not the minds of heretics that are deteriorated most by the ban placed on all inquiry which does not end in the orthodox conclusions. The greatest harm done is to those who are not heretics, and whose whole mental development is cramped and their reason cowed by the fear of heresy. Who can compute what the world loses in the multitude of promising intellects combined with timid characters, who dare not follow out any bold, vigorous, independent train of thought, lest it should land them in something which would admit of being considered irreligious or immoral?

We have now recognized the necessity to the mental well-being of mankind (on which all their other well-being depends) of freedom of opinion, and freedom of the expression of opinion, on four distinct grounds, which we will now briefly recapitulate:

First, if any opinion is compelled to silence, that opinion may, for aught we can certainly know, be true. To deny this is to assume our own infallibility.

Secondly, though the silenced opinion be an error, it may, and very commonly does, contain a portion of truth; and since the general or prevailing opinion on any subject is rarely or never the whole truth, it is only by the collision of adverse opinions that the remainder of the truth has any chance of being supplied.

Thirdly, even if the received opinion be not only true, but the whole truth; unless it is suffered to be, and actually is, vigorously and earnestly contested, it will, by most of those who receive it, be held in the manner of a prejudice, with little comprehension or feeling of its rational grounds. And not only this, but, fourthly, the meaning of the doctrine itself will be in danger of being lost or enfeebled, and deprived of its vital effect on the character and conduct; the dogma becoming a mere formal profession, inefficacious for good, but cumbering the ground and preventing the growth of any real and heartfelt conviction from reason or personal experience. . . .

Such being the reasons which make it imperative that human beings should be free to form opinions and to express their opinions without reserve; and such the baneful consequences to the intellectual; and through that to the moral nature of man, unless this liberty is either conceded or asserted in spite of prohibition; let us next examine whether the same reasons do not require that men should be free to act upon their opinions—to carry these out in their lives without hindrance, either physical or moral, from their fellow men, so long as it is at their own risk and peril. This last proviso is of course indispensable. No one pretends that actions should be as free as opinions. On the contrary, even opinions lose their immunity when the circumstances in which they are expressed are such as to constitute their expression a positive instigation to some mischievous act. An opinion that corn dealers are starvers of the poor, or that private property is robbery, ought to be unmolested when simply circulated through the press, but may justly incur punishment when delivered orally to an excited mob assembled before the house of a corn dealer, or when handed about among the same mob in the form of a placard. Acts, of whatever kind, which without justifiable cause do harm to others may be, and in the more important cases absolutely require to be, controlled by the unfavorable sentiments, and, when needful, by the active interference of mankind. The liberty of the individual must be thus far limited; he must not make himself a nuisance to other people. But if he refrains from molesting others in what concerns them, and merely acts according to his own inclination and judgment in things which concern himself, the same reasons which show that opinion should be free prove also that he should be allowed, without molestation, to carry his opinions into practice at his own cost. That mankind are not infallible; that their truths, for the most part, are only half-truths; the unity of opinion, unless resulting from the fullest and freest comparison of opposite opinions, is not desirable, and diversity not an evil, but a good, until mankind are much more capable than at present of recognizing all sides of the truth, are principles applicable to men's modes of action not less than to their opinions. As it is useful that while mankind are imperfect there should be different opinions, so it is that there should be different experiments of living; that free scope should be given to varieties of character, short of injury to others; and that the worth of different modes of life should be proved practically, when anyone thinks fit to try them. It is desirable, in short, that in things which do not primarily concern others, individuality should assert itself. Where not the person's own character but the traditions or customs of other people and the rule of conduct, there is wanting one of the principal ingredients of human happiness, and quite the chief ingredient of individual and social progress. . . .

What, then, is the rightful limit to the sovereignty of the individual over himself? Where does the authority of society begin? How much of human life should be assigned to individuality, and how much to society?

Each will receive its proper share if each has that which more particularly concerns it. To individuality should belong the part of life in which it is chiefly the individual that is interested; to society, the part which chiefly interests society.

Though society is not founded on a contract, and though no good purpose is answered by inventing a contract in order to deduce social obligations from it, everyone who receives the protection of society owes a return for the benefit, and the fact of living in society renders it indispensable that each should be bound to observe a certain line of conduct toward the rest. This conduct consists, first, in not injuring the interests of one another, or rather certain interests which, either by express legal provision or by tacit understanding, ought to be considered as rights; and secondly, in each person's bearing his share (to be fixed on some equitable principle) of the labors and sacrifices incurred for defending the society or its members from injury and molestation. These conditions society is justified in enforcing at all costs to those who endeavor to withhold fulfillment. Nor is this all that society may do. The acts of an individual may be hurtful to others or wanting in due consideration for their welfare, without going to the length of violating any of their constituted rights. The offender may then be justly punished by opinion, though not by law. As soon as any part of a person's conduct affects prejudicially the interests of others, society has jurisdiction over it, and the question whether the general welfare will or will not be promoted by interfering with it becomes open to discussion. But there is no room for entertaining any such question when a person's conduct affects the interests of no person besides himself, or needs not affect them unless they like (all the persons concerned being of full age and the ordinary amount of understanding). In all such cases, there should be perfect freedom, legal and social, to do the action and stand the consequences.

It would be a great misunderstanding of this doctrine to suppose that it is one of selfish indifference which pretends that human beings have no business with each other's conduct of life, and that they should not concern themselves about the well-doing or well-being of one another, unless their own interest is involved. Instead of any diminution, there is need of a great increase of disinterested exertion to promote the good of others. But disinterested benevolence can find other instruments to persuade people to their good than whips and scourges, either of the literal or the metaphorical sort. . . .

. . . But neither one person, nor any number of persons, is warranted in saying to another human creature of ripe years that he shall not do with his life for his own benefit what he chooses to do with it. . . .

CHAPTER 13

CLASS CONFLICT

Marx

Karl Marx was born in Trier, Germany, in 1818. His father was a law-yer and his grandfather a rabbi. After high school, Marx went to the University of Bonn, where in 1835 at the age of seventeen he began the study of law. A year later he transferred to the University of Ber-lin, giving up the study of law and pursuing instead the study of phi-losophy. At the age of twenty-three, he received his doctoral degree from the University of Jena. While at the University of Berlin, he came under the spell of Hegel's philosophy. In time, however, Marx gave up certain aspects of Hegel's thought. Nevertheless, Marx did take from Hegel the notion that there is a process going on in history, a conflict of opposites, or what Hegel called a "dialectic." But whereas Hegel said this dialectic represents ideas in conflict, Marx, under the influence of the philosopher Feuerbach, came to believe that this conflict in history was located in the material conditions of life. That is why Marx developed his central theory of *dialectical materialism* as an explanation of where history is moving. At age twenty-five, Marx went to Paris, then to Brussels, and finally to Lon-don. In London, he met Friedrich Engels, with whom he wrote a statement of principles for the international Communist League which was published in 1848 as *The Manifesto of the Communist Party*. Marx became a prolific writer, submitting articles on European affairs to the *New York Daily Tribune*. His most famous work is *Das Capital*. Karl Marx died in London in 1883 at the age of sixty-five.

In his early writing, namely *The Communist Manifesto*, Marx had formulated his basic doctrine, which he considered in many ways original. "What I did that was new," he said, "was to prove (1) that the *existence of classes* is only bound up with particular historic phases in the development of production; (2) that the class struggle necessarily leads to the dictatorship of the proletariat; (3) that the dictatorship itself only constitutes the transition to the *abolition of all classes* and to a classless society." Later, while in London, he worked out in painstaking detail his argument, which he thought provided scientific support for the more general pronouncements in his *Manifesto*. Accordingly, he stated in the preface to *Das Capital* that "it is the ultimate aim of this work, to lay bare the economic law of motion of modern society." This law of motion became his theory of *dialectical materialism*.

Five Epochs

Marx indicated that the class struggle is bound up with "particular historic phases." He distinguished five such phases, dividing history into five separate epochs. These he called (1) the primitive communal, (2) slave, (3) feudal, (4) capitalist, and, as a prediction of things to come, (5) the socialist and communist phases. For the most part, this was a more or less conventional division of Western social history into its major periods. But what Marx wanted to do was to discover the "law of motion," which could explain not only *that* history had produced these various epochs, but also the *reasons why* these particular epochs unfolded as they did. If he could discover history's law of motion, he could not only explain the past but also predict the future. He had assumed that the behavior of individuals and societies is subject to the same kind of analysis as are the objects of physical and biological science. He considered the commodity and value products of economics as being "of the

Marx at age 42 (*Culver Pictures*)

same order as those [minute elements] dealt with in microscopic anatomy." When he analyzed the structure of each historical epoch, he thought he discovered there the fact of class conflict as the decisive force at work.

Change: Quantitative and Qualitative

What history shows is that social and economic orders are in a process of change. The effect of Marx's dialectical materialism was to show, also, that since the material order is primary, since it is the basis of what is truly real, there are no stable, fixed points in reality because everything is involved in the dialectic process of change. With this view, Marx had rejected the notion that somewhere there are stable, permanent structures of reality or certain "eternal verities." Materialism meant to Marx that the world as we see it is all there is, that the materialist outlook on the world "is simply the conception of nature as it is, without any reservations." Moreover, with Engels he agreed that all of nature, "from the smallest thing to the biggest, from a grain of sand to the sun . . . to man, is in . . . a ceaseless state of movement and change." History is the process of change from one epoch to another in accordance with the rigorous and inexorable laws of historical motion.

For Marxism, change is not the same as mere growth. A society does not simply mature the way a boy becomes a man. Nor does nature simply move in an eternally uniform and constantly repeated circle. It passes through a real history. Change means the emergence of new structures, novel forms. What causes change is simply the *quantitative* alteration of things, which leads to something *qualitatively* new. For example, as one increases the temperature of water, it not only becomes warmer, but it finally reaches the point at which this quantitative change changes water from a liquid into vapor. Reversing the process, by gradually decreasing the temperature of water, one finally changes it from liquid to a solid, to ice. Similarly, a large pane of glass can be made to vibrate, the range of vibrations increasing as the quantity of force applied to it is increased. But finally, a further addition of force will no longer add to the quantity of vibration but will, instead, cause a qualitative change, the shattering of the glass.

Marx thought that history displays this kind of change by which certain quantitative elements in the economic order finally force a qualitative change in the arrangements of society. This is the process that has moved history from the primitive communal to the slave and in turn to the feudal and capitalist epochs. Indeed, Marx's prediction that the capitalist order would fall was based on this notion that changes in the quantitative factors in capitalism would inevitably destroy capitalism. With the low-key expression of one who was describing how water will turn into steam as the heat is increased, Marx wrote in his *Das Capital* that "while there is a progressive diminution in the number of capitalist magnates, there is of course a corresponding increase in the mass of poverty, enslavement, degeneration and exploitation, but at the same time a steady intensification of the role of the working class." Then "the centralization of the means of production and the socialization of labor reach a point where they prove incompatible with their capitalist husk. This bursts asunder. The knell of private property sounds. The expropriators are expropriated." This, on the social level, is what Marx describes as the *qualitative leap*, which is "the leap to a new aggregate state . . . where consequently quantity is transformed into quality."

Determinism or Inexorable Law

There is a basic difference between the transformation of water into steam as a laboratory experiment and the movement of society from feudalism to capitalism and finally from capitalism to socialism. The difference is that one can *choose* to raise or not to raise the temperature of the water. But there are no such hypothetical qualifications surrounding history. Although one can say "*if* the temperature is raised," one cannot say "*if* the social order is thus and so." Marxism holds that there *is* a fundamental "contradiction within the very essence of things" causing the dialectic movement, and although there are ways of delaying or accelerating this inner movement in the nature of things, there is no way to prevent its ultimate unfolding. All things are related to each other *causally;* nothing floats freely. For this reason, there are no isolated events either in physical nature or in human behavior or, therefore, in history. That there is a definite and inexorable process of movement and change at work producing "history" is as certain as the plain fact that nature exists.

End of History

For Marx, history would have an end with the emergence of socialism and finally communism. Here, again, he followed Hegel's theory in an inverted way. For Hegel, the dialectic process comes to an end when the idea of freedom is perfectly realized, for by definition this would mean the end of all conflict and struggle. Marx, however, seeing that the dialectic or struggle of opposites is in the material order and therefore in the struggle between the classes, predicted that when the inner contradictions between the classes were resolved, the principle cause of movement and change would disappear, a classless society would emerge where all the forces and interests would be in perfect balance, and this equilibrium would be perpetual. For this reason, there could be no further development in history, inasmuch as there would no longer be any conflict to impel history on to any future epoch.

Marx's theory of the dialectic development of the five epochs of history rested on the distinction between the order of material reality on the one hand and the order of human thought on the other. He was convinced that the only way to achieve a realistic understanding of history, and therefore to avoid errors in the practical program of revolutionary activity, was to assess properly the roles of the material order and the order of human thought. Accordingly, Marx made a sharp distinction between the substructure (i.e., the infrastructure) and the superstructure of society. The *infrastructure* is the material order, containing the energizing force that moves history, whereas the *superstructure* consists of men's ideas and simply reflects the configurations of the material order.

Infrastructure: The Material Order

To Marx materialism meant the sum total of the natural environment, and this included for him all of inorganic nature, the organic world, social life, and human consciousness. Unlike Democritus, who defined matter in terms of irreducible tiny particles, atoms, Marx defines matter as "objective reality existing outside the human mind. . . . " Again, unlike Democritus, who considered atoms as the "bricks of the universe," Marxist materialism did not take this approach of trying to discover a single form of matter in all things. The chief characteristic of Marxist materialism is that it recognizes a wide diversity in the material world without reducing it to any one form of matter. The material order contains everything in the natural world that exists outside our minds; the notion that any spiritual reality, God, for example, exists outside our minds and as something other than nature is denied. That human beings possess minds means only that organic matter has developed to the point where the cerebral cortex has become an organ capable of the intricate process of reflex action called "human thought."

Moreover, the human mind has been conditioned by the labor activity of man as a social being. For this reason, relying on the Darwinian notion of the evolution of man, Marxism affirms the primacy of the material order and regards mental activity as a secondary by-product of matter. The earliest forms of life were without mental activity until man's ancestors developed the use of their forelimbs, learned to walk erect, and began to use natural objects as tools to procure food and to protect themselves against harm. The big transformation from animal to human being came with the ability to fashion and use tools and to control such forces as fire, which, in turn, made possible a wider variety of food and the further development of the brain. Even now the complex material order is the basic reality, whereas the mental realm is derivative from it. In particular, the material order consists of (1) the *factors* of production and (2) the *relations* of production.

FACTORS OF PRODUCTION

The basic fact of human life is that in order to live, men must secure food, clothing, and shelter, and in order to have these material things, men must produce them. Wherever we find any society of men, there are always at hand those factors of production—the raw materials, instruments, and the experienced labor skill—by which things are produced to sustain life. But these factors or forces of production represent chiefly the way men are related to these material things. Of greater importance is the way men are related to one another in the process of production. What Marx wanted to emphasize was that production always takes place as a social act, where men struggle against and utilize nature not as individuals but as groups, as societies. The static analysis of what goes into production was for Marx, therefore, not as important as the dynamic relations of men to each other as a producing society. To be sure, the factors of production were seen by Marx as affecting the relations of production, inasmuch as such circumstances as the scarcity of raw materials or the ownership by some of the instruments of production could have a considerable effect on the way men would become related to one another in the process of production. In any case, Marx centered his analysis of the material order on the way men engaged in the act of production, on the *relations of production.*

RELATIONS OF PRODUCTION

Marx considered his analysis of the relations of production to be virtually the core of his social analysis. It was here that he thought he had located the energizing force of the dialectic process. The key to the relations of production was the status of property or its ownership; that is, what determined how men were related to one another in the process of production was their relation to property. Under the slave system, for example, the slave owner owned the means of production, even owning the slave, whom he could purchase or sell. The institution of slavery was a necessary product of the dialectic process, since it arose at a time when advanced forms of tools made possible more stable and sustained agricultural activity and a division of labor. But in the slave epoch, as well as in the subsequent historical epochs, the laborer, slave or hired, was "exploited" in that he shared in neither the ownership nor the fruits of production. The basic struggle between the classes is seen already in the slave system, for the ownership of property divides the society between those who have and those who have not. In the feudal system, the feudal lord owned the means of production. The serf rose above the level of the former slaves, had some share in the ownership of tools, but still worked for the feudal lord and, says Marx, felt exploited and struggled against his exploiter. In capitalism, the workers are free as compared with the slaves and the serfs, but they do not own the means of production, and in order to survive, they must sell their labor to the capitalist.

The shift from slave to feudal to capitalist relations of production is not the result of rational design but a product of the inner movement and logic of the material order. Specifically, the impelling force to survive leads to the creation of tools, and, in turn, the kinds of tools created affect the way men become related to each other. Certain tools, such as the bow and arrow, permit independent existence, while the plough logically implies a division of labor. Similarly, whereas a spinning wheel can be used in the home or in small shops, heavier machinery requires large factories and a new concentration of workers in a given locality. Such is the survey

Marx makes of the unfolding of the epochs of history, emphasizing that this process moves in a deterministic way, impelled by basic economic drives whose direction is set by the technological requirements of the moment. The thoughts and behavior of all men are determined by their relations to one another and to the means of production. Although in all periods there is conflict and struggle between the different classes, the class struggle is particularly violent under capitalism.

There are at least three characteristics of the class struggle under capitalism. *First,* the classes have now been reduced basically to two, the owners, or bourgeoisie, and the workers, or proletariat. *Second,* the relation of these classes to each other rests on a fundamental contradiction, namely, that although both classes participate in the act of production, the mode of distribution of the fruits of production does not correspond to the contribution made by each class. The reason for this discrepancy is that the price of labor in the capitalist system is determined by the forces of supply and demand, and the large supply of workers tends to send wages down to a subsistence level. But the products created by labor can be sold for more than it costs to hire the labor force. Marx's analysis assumed the labor theory of value, that the value of the product is created by the amount of labor put into it. From this point of view, since the product of labor could be sold for more than the cost of labor, the capitalist would then reap the difference, which Marx called "surplus value."

The existence of surplus value constituted the contradiction in the capitalistic system for Marx. For this reason, Marx argued that in the capitalistic system exploitation was not merely an isolated occurrence here or there, now or then, but always and everywhere, because of the manner in which the iron law of wages operates. Still, Marx made no moral judgment of this condition, saying that as a matter of fact the worker received what he was worth if determination of the wage through the supply and demand of labor is the norm. "It is true," he said, "that the daily maintenance of labor power costs only half a day's labor, and that nevertheless the labor power can work for an entire working day, with the result that the value which its use creates during a working day is twice the value of a day's labor power. So much the better for the purchaser, but it is nowise an injustice to the seller [worker]."

In a sense, Marx did not "blame" the capitalist for this arrangement any more than he would attribute to him the organization of

the laborers into a self-conscious and powerful group. These are
rather the consequences of the material forces of history, which
have determined the existence of these arrangements. Labor
became a coherent group only because large-scale machinery
required large factories, and suddenly the multitude of workers
who were required to run the machines found themselves living
close together. That history had produced the capitalist system was
one thing, but that the system rested on a contradiction was something else. For this reason, Marx "excused" the capitalist but
argued that for "scientific reasons" he must say that the class conflict caused by this contradiction of surplus value would force the
dialectic movement to the next stage in history, namely, socialism
and finally communism.

The *third* characteristic of this class struggle was the prediction
that the condition of the workers in capitalism would become progressively more wretched, that the poor would become poorer and
more numerous, while the rich would become richer and fewer
until the masses would take over all the means of production. As a
matter of historic fact, Marx could not have been more wrong than
he was on this point, since it is precisely the workers whose condition has improved most dramatically in the highly developed capitalistic economies. Still, Marx argued that as long as the means of
production remained in the hands of a few, the class struggle would
continue inexorably until the contradiction was resolved, ending
the dialectic movement.

With this rigorous view of the nature of the class struggle, Marx
had clearly assigned to the infrastructure, to the material order, the
supreme significance in the dialectic process of history. What, then,
is the status and role of human thought? Do ideas have power and
consequences? For Marx, ideas represented a mere reflection of the
basic material reality, and for this reason, he described the enterprise of human thought as the *superstructure*.

Superstructure: The Origin and Role of Ideas

Each epoch, said Marx, has its dominant ideas. Men formulate ideas
in the areas of religion, morality, and law. Hegel had argued that

men agreed for the most part in their religious, moral, and juristic thought because there was at work in them a universal spirit, the Idea. Marx, on the contrary, said that the ideas of each epoch grow out of and reflect the actual material conditions of the historic period. For this reason, thinking comes *after* the material order has affected men's minds. Thus Marx accounted for the relationship between man's conscious life and his material environment by saying, "It is not the consciousness of men that determines their being, but, on the contrary, their social being that determines their consciousness."

The source of ideas is rooted in the material order. Such ideas as justice and goodness and even religious salvation, says Marx, are only various modes of rationalizing the existing order. Justice, for the most part, represents the will of the economically dominant class and its desire to "freeze" the relations of production as they are. Marx had been impressed during his early years as a law student with the teachings of the jurist Savigny, who had defined law as the "spirit" of each epoch. Savigny argued that law is like language and is therefore different for each society. Like Savigny, but now for different reasons, Marx rejected the notion of a universal and eternal standard of justice. Indeed, he thought it followed with logical rigor that if ideas simply reflect the inner order of the relations of production, each successive epoch will have its own set of ideas, its own dominant philosophy.

The conflict of ideas within a society at a given time is caused by the dynamic nature of the economic order. The dialectic process, which is a struggle of opposites, has its material aspect but also its ideological side. Since members of a society are related to the dialectic process by belonging to different classes, their interests are different, and therefore their ideas are opposed. Moreover, the greatest error, according to Marx, is to fail to realize that ideas that accurately reflected the material order at an earlier time no longer do so because, in the meantime, the substructure of reality has moved on. Those who hold on to old ideas do not realize that there is no longer any reality corresponding to those ideas, and their desire to reverse the order of things to fit these ideas makes them "reactionaries." However, an astute observer can discover the direction in which history is moving and will adjust his thinking and behavior to it. The fact is, says Marx, that the dialectic process involves the disappearance of some things and the birth of new things; that is why one epoch dies and another is born, and there is no way to stop the process. Those who assume the objective reality of "eternal principles" of justice, goodness, and righteousness do not realize that such notions cannot refer to reality since the material order, which is the only reality, is constantly changing. "The sum total of the productive relations," says Marx, "constitutes the economic structure of society—the real foundation on which rise legal and political superstructures . . . [and which] determines the general character of the social, political and spiritual processes of life."

Because he believed that ideas were chiefly a reflection of the material order, Marx attributed a limited role or function to them. Ideas are particularly useless when they bear no relationship to the economic reality. Marx's impatience with reformers, do-gooders, and utopians was intense. He argued that ideas cannot determine the direction of history, that they can only hinder or accelerate the inexorable dialectic. For this reason, Marx thought that his own ideas about capitalism did not constitute a moral condemnation. He did not say that capitalism was either wicked or due to human folly; it was caused by the "law of motion of society." In the end, Marx assumed that he was proceeding in his analysis as a scientist, limiting his thought to objective reality, abstracting from it the laws of motion.

Alienation: Marx's Concept of the Condition of Man

Marx described the condition of man in industrial society with the word "alienation." Man, he said, is alienated. To be alienated means to be separated, to be estranged. It is especially the worker, the laborer, who is alienated. What is he alienated or separated from and why?

The cause of man's alienation, said Marx, is the very organization of the world of work. The existence of private property means that the worker invests his labor in materials and things which are not his. The finished product which results from his labor does not belong to the laborer. The worker is used as a means to produce objects and is paid a wage. But the worker is separated or alienated from the things he produces because they are not the things *he* wants to make. Also, in the process of working on things, the worker cannot use his own ideas but must do what others tell him to do and do it the way others direct or order him. In many respects, the workers begin to take on the characteristics of machines. Even more serious is the reduction of human beings to extensions or even slaves of machines.

All this leads Marx to say that man is alienated from his humanity, from what it truly means to be a human being. The worker's labor is put into the objects he makes. This is what Marx means when he says that labor is "objectified" or when he speaks of the "objectification of labor." His labor, and therefore a part of himself, has been put into the objects of his work. And since the finished objects are not his, that part of himself which is now in the object has been separated, alienated, from himself.

The very process of working represents a special form of alienation. This is so because a person's work is no longer an expression of his own creative powers. Work ceases to express a worker's individual feelings and ideas or even his unique nature. As a result, the worker, as Marx says, "does not fulfill himself in his work but denies himself, has a feeling of misery rather than well-being, does not develop fully his mental and physical energies but is physically exhausted and mentally debased." For this reason, the worker "feels himself at home only during leisure time, whereas at work he feels homeless."

Marx's chief criticism of industrial society is that it transforms human beings into things. In addition to the exploitation of the working class by capitalists, which results in the unfair distribution of wealth, Marx was even more concerned with the gradual degradation of all men by the demands of the industrial system. The ultimate result of the process of alienation, he said, was that the joy of life was destroyed. Men now failed to become what their human nature could under better circumstances lead them to be. Everywhere human beings are reduced, even in their own sight and experience, to a level of life far below their capacity or their hopes. This represents not only a loss of personal power, but also a reduction of personal dignity and a serious absence of the sense of meaning and purpose to life. In the end, the worker sees many objects around him, but they are alien to him, they are not his. So he reflects on himself, he sees that he too is alien to himself. He is alienated from himself in that he can see the difference between

London, Cheapside (*Culver Pictures*)

what his actual daily life consists of as compared with what his life could or even ought to be. The reality is that his life is dominated by objects and people external to and alienated from himself. His internal life—the life of feelings, of spontaneous and creative choices, in short his very personal and individual life directed toward self-fulfillment and higher values—remains virtually undeveloped and unfulfilled.

As Marx points out in the selected reading which follows, the only time men feel that they are acting freely is when they are expressing their animal functions, namely, eating, drinking, and procreating. To be sure, says Marx, these are human as well as animal functions, but under the circumstances of alienation in all the rest of life, they are reduced to animal functions.

238

READING

ALIENATED LABOR
Marx

We proceed from a *present* fact of political economy.

The worker becomes poorer the more wealth he produces, the more his production increases in power and extent. The worker becomes a cheaper commodity the more commodities he produces. The *increase in value* of the world of things is directly proportional to the *decrease in value* of the human world. Labor not only produces commodities. It also produces itself and the worker as a *commodity,* and indeed in the same proportion as it produces commodities in general.

This fact simply indicates that the object which labor produces, its product, stands opposed to it as an *alien thing,* as a *power independent* of the producer. The product of labor is labor embodied and made objective in a thing. It is the *objectification* of labor. The realization of labor is its objectification. In the viewpoint of political economy this realization of labor appears as the *diminution* of the worker, the objectification as the *loss of and subservience to the object,* and the appropriation as *alienation* as externalization.

So much does the realization of labor appear as diminution that the worker is diminished to the point of starvation. So much does objectification appear as loss of the object that the worker is robbed of the most essential objects not only of life but also of work. Indeed, work itself becomes a thing of which he can take possession only with the greatest effort and with the most unpredictable interruptions. So much does the appropriation of the object appear as alienation that the more objects the worker produces, the fewer he can own and the more he falls under the domination of his product, of capital.

All these consequences follow from the fact that the worker is related to the *product of his labor* as to an *alien* object. For it is clear according to this premise: The more the worker exerts himself, the more powerful becomes the alien objective world which he fashions against himself, the poorer he and his inner world become, the less there is that belongs to him. It is the same in religion. The more man attributes to God, the less he retains in himself. The worker puts his life into the object; then it no longer belongs to him but to the object. The greater this activity, the poorer is the worker. What the product of his work is, he is not. The greater this product is, the smaller he is himself. The *externalization* of the worker in his product means not only that his work becomes an object, an *external* existence, but also that it exists *outside him* independently, alien, an autonomous power, opposed to him. The life he has given to the object confronts him as hostile and alien. . . .

Let us now consider more closely the *objectification,* the worker's production and with it the *alienation* and *loss* of the object, his product.

The worker can make nothing without *nature,* without the *sensuous external world.* It is the material wherein his labor realizes itself, wherein it is active, out of which and by means of which it produces.

But as nature furnishes to labor the *means of life* in the sense that labor cannot *live* without objects upon which labor is exercised, nature also furnishes the *means of life* in the narrower sense, namely, the means of physical subsistence of the *worker* himself.

The more the worker *appropriates* the external world and sensuous nature through his labor, the more he deprives himself of the *means of life* in two respects: first, that the sensuous external world gradually ceases to be an object belonging to his labor, a *means of life* of his work; secondly, that it gradually ceases to be a *means of life* in the immediate sense, a means of physical subsistence of the worker.

In these two respects, therefore, the worker becomes a slave to his objects; first, in that he receives an *object of labor,* that is, he receives *labor,* and secondly that he receives the *means of subsistence.* The first enables him to exist as a *worker* and the second as a *physical subject.* The terminus of this slavery is that he can only maintain himself as a *physical subject* so far as he is a *worker* and only as a *physical subject* is he a worker.

(The alienation of the worker in his object is expressed according to the laws of political economy as follows: the more the worker produces, the less he has to consume; the more values he creates the more worthless and unworthy he becomes; the better shaped his product, the more misshapen is he; the more civilized his product, the more barbaric is the worker; the more powerful the work, the more powerless becomes the worker; the more intelligence the work has, the more witless is the worker and the more he becomes a slave of nature.)

Political economy conceals the alienation in the nature of labor by ignoring the direct relationship between the worker (labor) *and production.* To be sure, labor produces marvels for the wealthy but it produces deprivation for the worker. It produces palaces, but hovels for the worker. It produces beauty, but mutilation for the worker. It displaces labor through machines, but it throws some workers back into barbarous labor and turns others into machines. It produces intelligence, but for the worker it produces imbecility and cretinism. . . .

Up to now we have considered the alienation, the externalization of the worker only from one side: his *relationship to the products of his labor.*

But alienation is shown not only in the result but also in the *process of production,* in the *producing activity* itself. How could the worker stand in an alien relationship to the product of his activity if he did not alienate himself from himself in the very act of production? After all, the product is only the résumé of activity, of production. If the product of work is externalization, production itself must be active externalization, externalization of activity, activity of externalization. Only alienation—and externalization in the activity of labor itself—is summarized in the alienation of the object of labor.

What constitutes the externalization of labor?

First is the fact that labor is *external* to the laborer—that is, it is not part of his nature—and that the worker does not affirm himself in his work but denies himself, feels miserable and unhappy, develops no free physical and mental energy but mortifies his flesh and ruins his mind. The worker, therefore feels at ease only outside work, and during work he is outside himself. He is at home when he is not working and when he is working he is not at home. His work, therefore, is not voluntary, but coerced, *forced labor.* It is not the satisfaction of a need but only a *means* to satisfy other needs. Its alien character is obvious from the fact that as soon as no physical or other pressure exists, labor is avoided like the plague. External labor, labor in which man is externalized, is labor of self-sacrifice, of penance. Finally, the external nature of work for the worker appears in the fact that it is not his own but another person's, that in work he does not belong to himself but to someone else. In religion the spontaneity of human imagination, the spontaneity of the human brain and heart, acts independently of the individual as an alien, divine or devilish activity. Similarly, the activity of the worker is not his own spontaneous activity. It belongs to another. It is the loss of his own self.

The result, therefore, is that man (the worker) feels that he is acting freely only in his animal functions—eating, drinking, and procreating, or at most in his shelter and finery—while in his human functions he feels only like an animal. The animalistic becomes the human and the human the animalistic.

To be sure, eating, drinking, and procreation are genuine human functions. In abstraction, however, and separated from the remaining sphere of human activities and turned into final and sole ends, they are animal functions.

We have considered labor, the act of alienation of practical human activity, in two aspects: (1) the relationship of the worker to the *product of labor* as an alien object dominating him. This relationship is at the same time the relationship to the sensuous external world, to natural objects as an alien world hostile to him; (2) the relationship of labor to the *act of production* in *labor.* This relationship is that of the worker to his own activity as alien and not belonging to him, activity as passivity, power as weakness, procreation as emasculation, the worker's *own* physical and spiritual energy, his personal life—for what else is life but activity—as an activity turned against him, independent of him, and not belonging to him. *Self-alienation,* as against the alienation of the *object,* stated above.

We have now to derive a third aspect of *alienated labor* from the two previous ones.

Man is a species-being [*Gattungswesen*] not only in that he practically and theoretically makes his own species as well as that of other things his object, but also—and this is only another expression for the same thing— in that as present and living species he considers himself to be a *universal* and consequently free being.

The life of the species in man as in animals is physical in that man (like the animal) lives by inorganic nature. And as man is more universal than the animal, the realm of inorganic nature by which he lives is more universal. As plants, animals, minerals, air, light, etc., in theory form a part of human consciousness, partly as objects of natural science, partly as objects of art— his spiritual inorganic nature or spiritual means of life which he first must prepare for enjoyment and assimilation—so they also form in practice a part of human life and human activity. Man lives physically only by these products of nature; they may appear in the form of food, heat, clothing, housing, etc. The universality of man appears in practice in the universality which makes the whole of nature his *inorganic* body: (1) as a direct means of life, and (2) as the matter, object, and instrument of his life activity. Nature is the *inorganic body* of man, that is, nature insofar as it is not the human body. Man *lives* by nature. This means that nature is his *body* with which he must remain in perpetual process in order not to die. That the physical and spiritual life of man is tied up with nature is another way of saying that nature is linked to itself, for man is a part of nature.

In alienating (1) nature from man, and (2) man from himself, his own active function, his life activity, alienated labor also alienated the *species* from him; it makes *species-life* the means of individual life. In the first place it alienates species-life and the individual life, and secondly it turns the latter in its abstraction into the purpose of the former, also in its abstract and alienated form.

For labor, *life activity,* and *productive life* appear to man at first only as a *means* to satisfy a need, the need to maintain physical existence. Productive life, however, is species-life. It is life begetting life. In the mode of life activity lies the entire character of a species, its species-character; and free conscious activity is the species-character of man. Life itself appears only as a *means of life.*

The animal is immediately one with its life activity, not distinct from it. The animal is *its life activity.* Man makes his life activity itself into an object of will and consciousness. He has conscious life activity. It is not a determination with which he immediately identifies. Conscious life activity distinguishes man immediately from the life activity of the animal. Only thereby is he a species-being. Or rather, he is only a conscious being—that is, his own life is an object for him—since he is a species-being. Only on that account is his activity free activity. Alienated labor reverses the relationship in that man, since he is a conscious being, makes his life activity, his *essence,* only a means for his *existence.*

The practical creation of an *objective world,* the *treatment* of inorganic nature, is proof that man is a conscious species-being, that is, a being which is related to its species as to its own essence or is related to itself as a species-being. To be sure animals also produce. They build themselves nests, dwelling places, like the bees, beavers, ants, etc. But the animal produces only what is immediately necessary for itself or its young. It produces in a one-sided way while man produces universally. The animal produces under the domination of immediate physical need while man produces free of physical need and only genuinely so in freedom from such need. The animal only produces itself while man reproduces the whole of nature. The animal's product belongs immediately to its physical body while man is free when he confronts his product. The animal builds only according to the standard and need of the species to which it belongs while man knows how to produce according to the standard of any species and at all times knows how to apply an intrinsic standard to the object. Thus man creates also according to the laws of beauty.

In the treatment of the objective world, therefore, man proves himself to be genuinely a *species-being.* This production is his active species-life. Through it nature appears as *his* work and his actuality. The object of labor is thus the *objectification of man's species-life;* he produces himself not only intellectually, as in consciousness, but also actively in a real sense and sees himself in a world he made. In taking from man the object of his production, alienated labor takes from his *species-life,* his actual and objective existence as a species. It changes his superiority to the animal to inferiority, since he is deprived of nature, his inorganic body.

By degrading free spontaneous activity to the level of a means, alienated labor makes the species-life of man a means of his physical existence.

The consciousness which man has from his species is altered through alienation, so that species-life becomes a means for him.

(3) Alienated labor hence turns the *species-existence of man,* and also nature as his mental species-capacity, into an existence *alien* to him, into the *means* of his *individual existence.* It alienates his spiritual nature, his *human essence,* from his own body and likewise from nature outside him.

(4) A direct consequence of man's alienation from the product of his work, from his life activity, and from his species-existence, is the *alienation of man* from *man.* When man confronts himself, he confronts *other* men. What holds true of man's relationship to his work, to the product of his work, and to himself, also holds true of man's relationship to other men, to their labor, and the object of their labor.

In general, the statement that man is alienated from his species-existence means that one man is alienated from another just as each man is alienated from human nature.

The alienation of man, the relation of man to himself, is realized and expressed in the relation between man and other men.

Thus in the relation of alienated labor every man sees the others according to the standard and the relation in which he finds himself as a worker.

We began with an economic fact, the alienation of the worker and his product. We have given expression to the concept of this fact: *alienated, externalized* labor. We have analyzed this concept and have thus analyzed merely a fact of political economy.

Let us now see further how the concept of alienated, externalized labor must express and represent itself in actuality.

If the product of labor is alien to me, confronts me as an alien power, to whom then does it belong?

If my own activity does not belong to me, if it is an alien and forced activity, to whom then does it belong?

To a being *other* than myself?

Who is this being?

Gods? To be sure, in early times the main production, for example, the building of temples in Egypt, India, and Mexico, appears to be in the service of the gods, just as the product belongs to the gods. But gods alone were never workmasters. The same is true of *nature*. And what a contradiction it would be if the more man subjugates nature through his work and the more the miracles of gods are rendered superfluous by the marvels of industry, man should renounce his joy in producing and the enjoyment of his product for love of these powers.

The *alien* being who owns labor and the product of labor, whom labor serves and whom the product of labor satisfies can only be *man* himself.

That the product of labor does not belong to the worker and an alien power confronts him is possible only because this product belongs to *a man other than the worker*. If his activity is torment for him, it must be the *pleasure* and the life-enjoyment for another. Not gods, not nature, but only man himself can be this alien power over man.

Let us consider the statement previously made, that the relationship of man to himself is *objective* and *actual* to him only through his relationship to other men. If man is related to the product of his labor, to his objectified labor, as to an *alien,* hostile, powerful object independent of him, he is so related that another alien, hostile, powerful man independent of him is the lord of this object. If he is unfree in relation to his own activity, he is related to it as bonded activity, activity under the domination, coercion, and yoke of another man.

Every self-alienation of man, from himself and from nature, appears in the relationship which he postulates between other men and himself and nature. Thus religious self-alienation appears necessarily in the relation of laity to priest, or also to a mediator, since we are here now concerned with the spiritual world. In the practical real world self-alienation can appear only in the practical real relationships to other men. The means whereby the alienation proceeds is a *practical* means. Through alienated labor man thus not only produces his relationship to the object and to the act of production as an alien man at enmity with him. He also creates the relation in which other men stand to his production and product, and the relation in which he stands to these other men. Just as he begets his own production as loss of his reality, as his punishment; just as he begets his own product as a loss, a product not belonging to him, so he begets the domination of the nonproducer over production and over product. As he alienates his own activity from himself, he confers upon the stranger an activity which is not his own.

CHAPTER 14

JUSTICE AS FAIRNESS

Rawls

Professor John Rawls (1921–   ), a member of the philosophy department at Harvard, has written a captivating theory of justice. Although he begins with the familiar theory of the Social Contract, he gives this old theory a fresh look. The key idea he develops is that the principles of justice which are to be the foundation of society are the result of an agreement in what he calls "the original position" (what Hobbes called "the state of nature").

Imagine yourself in the original position, a situation where you are about to establish an organized society. You, and everybody else, will have to decide how to create a good society, one in which everyone is treated in a fair way. What should each person's place or situation, job, class position, and social status be? How should questions of this kind be answered? To make sure that the answers, and therefore each person's position and status, are decided on fairly, Rawls asks us to forget what our present situation is. To make sure that the principles of justice we are about to agree to are fair and objective, it is necessary for us, says Rawls, to step behind a "veil of ignorance." This veil of ignorance simply means that none of us knows (that is, we act as though we do not know) what our special circumstances are. We are to suppose that the slate is wiped clean and we are starting all over. No one knows what his or her special talents are. The purpose, then, of the veil of ignorance is to eliminate from our minds any prejudice based on our special circumstances so that we can approach the task of formulating the principles of justice from as objective a point of view as possible. Under these circumstances, how should we go about devising an arrangement among people which would amount to justice?

Rawls assumes that all men have a sense of justice. This does not mean that everybody always agrees with a particular definition of justice. It does mean, however, that all people have a certain rational ability through which they understand what is and what is not fair. Moreover, rational human beings also know which principles will be respected. Rational persons know, for example, that it is not fair to achieve the good life for some at the expense of others.

From his ideas about the "original position" and the "veil of ignorance," Rawls arrives at "two principles of justice." The first principal is based on the special way in which each person is assumed to be equal. Hence Rawls says, "First: each person is to have an equal right to the most extensive basic liberty compatible with a similar liberty for others." This form of liberty is basically political liberty. It includes the right to vote and to be eligible for public office as well as freedom of speech and assembly, freedom of conscience, and freedom to hold property.

The second principle of justice, says Rawls, recognizes certain inequalities among people. People are, after all, different in many ways. These differences are reflected in the distribution of wealth and income. Recognizing these differences, Rawls describes this principle as follows: "Social and economic inequalities are to be arranged so that they are both (a) reasonably expected to be to everyone's advantage, and (b) attached to positions and offices open to all." What Rawls is attempting to accomplish in this second principle is, first, to recognize the facts of inequality and differences among individuals, and second, to make sure that these differences do not lead to injustice. Justice, says Rawls, does not require that wealth and income should be divided equally. However, an unequal division is justified only if everyone is better off, that is, if such an unequal division results in everyone's advantage.

These two principles must be arranged in a special sequence

that Rawls calls "a serial order." The first principle deals with political freedom. The second principle deals with social and economic arrangements. Justice requires that political freedoms should always remain the highest priority and that the social and economic arrangements should be adapted to these political freedoms. Accordingly, it would be a violation of justice if a society sacrificed personal and political freedoms, the basic liberties, in exchange for some additional social and economic benefits.

The following brief selection from Rawls's *A Theory of Justice* will provide a further elaboration of some of these central elements of his political philosophy.

READING

JUSTICE AS FAIRNESS
Rawls

THE MAIN IDEA OF THE THEORY OF JUSTICE

My aim is to present a conception of justice which generalizes and carries to a higher level of abstraction the familiar theory of the social contract. . . . In order to do this we are not to think of the original contract as one to enter a particular society or to set up a particular form of government. Rather, the guiding idea is that the principles of justice for the basic structure of society are the object of the original agreement. They are the principles that free and rational persons concerned to further their own interests would accept in an initial position of equality as defining the fundamental terms of their association. These principles are to regulate all further agree-

From John Rawls, *A Theory of Justice*, The Belknap Press of Harvard Univ. Press, Cambridge, Mass., 1971. Copyright © 1971 by the President and Fellows of Harvard College.

ments; they specify the kinds of social cooperation that can be entered into and the forms of government that can be established. This way of regarding the principles of justice I shall call justice as fairness.

Thus we are to imagine that those who engage in social cooperation choose together, in one joint act, the principles which are to assign basic rights and duties and to determine the division of social benefits. Men are to decide in advance how they are to regulate their claims against one another and what is to be the foundation charter of their society. Just as each person must decide by rational reflection what constitutes his good, that is, the system of ends which it is rational for him to pursue, so a group of persons must decide once and for all what is to count among them as just and unjust. The choice which rational men would make in this hypothetical situation of equal liberty, assuming for the present that this choice problem has a solution, determines the principles of justice.

In justice as fairness the original position of equality corresponds to the state of nature in the traditional theory of the social contract. This original position is not, of course, thought of as an actual historical state of affairs, much less as a primitive condition of culture. It is understood as a purely hypothetical situation characterized so as to lead to a certain conception of justice. Among the essential features of this situation is that no one knows his place in society, his class position or social status, nor does any one know his fortune in the distribution of natural assets and abilities, his intelligence, strength, and the like. I shall even assume that the parties do not know their conceptions of the good or their special psychological propensities. The principles of justice are chosen behind a veil of ignorance. This ensures that no one is advantaged or disadvantaged in the choice of principles by the outcome of natural chance or the contingency of social circumstances. Since all are similarly situated and no one is able to design principles to favor his particular condition, the principles of justice are the result of a fair agreement or bargain. For given the circumstances of the original position, the symmetry of everyone's relations to each other, this initial situation is fair between individuals as moral persons, that is, as rational beings with their own ends and capable, I shall assume, of a sense of justice. The original position is, one might say, the appropriate initial status quo, and thus the fundamental agreements reached in it are fair. This explains the propriety of the name "justice as fairness": it conveys the idea that the principles of justice are agreed to in an initial situation that is fair. The name does not mean that the concepts of justice and fairness are the same, any more than the phrase "poetry as metaphor" means that the concepts of poetry and metaphor are the same. . . .

One feature of justice as fairness is to think of the parties in the initial situation as rational and mutually disinterested. This does not mean that the parties are egoists, that is, individuals with only certain kinds of interests, say in wealth, prestige, and domination. But they are conceived as not taking an interest in one another's interests. They are to presume that even their spiritual aims may be opposed, in the way that the aims of those of different religions may be opposed. Moreover, the concept of rationality must be interpreted as far as possible in the narrow sense, standard in economic theory, of taking the most effective means to given ends. . . .

I maintain instead that the persons in the initial situation would choose two rather different principles: the first requires equality in the assignment of basic rights and duties, while the second holds that social and economic inequalities, for example inequalities of wealth and authority, are just only if they result in compensating benefits for everyone, and in particular for the least advantaged members of society. The principles rule out justifying institutions on the grounds that the hardships of some are offset by a greater good in the aggregate. It may be expedient but it is not just that some should have less in order that others may prosper. But there is no injustice in the greater benefits earned by a few provided that the situation of persons not so fortunate is thereby improved. The intuitive idea is that since everyone's well-being depends upon a scheme of cooperation without which no one could have a satisfactory life, the division of advantages should be such as to draw forth the willing cooperation of everyone taking part in it, including those less well situated. Yet this can be expected only if reasonable terms are proposed. The two principles mentioned seem to be a fair agreement on the basis of which those better endowed, or more fortunate in their social position, neither of which we can be said to deserve, could expect the willing cooperation of others when some workable scheme is a necessary condition of the welfare of all. . . .

THE ORIGINAL POSITION

The veil of ignorance. The idea of the original position is to set up a fair procedure so that any principles agreed to will be just. The aim is to use the notion of pure procedural justice as a basis of theory. Somehow we must nullify the effects of specific contingencies which put men at odds and tempt them to exploit social and natural circumstances to their own advantage. Now in order to do this I assume that the parties are situated behind a veil of ignorance. They do not know how the various alternatives will affect their own particular case and they are obliged to evaluate principles solely on the basis of general considerations.

It is assumed, then, that the parties do not know certain kinds of particular facts. First of all, no one knows his place in society, his class position or social status; nor does he know his fortune in the distribution of natural assets and abilities, his intelligence and strength, and the like. Nor, again, does anyone know his conception of the good, the particulars of his rational plan of life, or even the special features of his psychology such as his aversion to risk or liability to optimism or pessimism. More than this, I assume that the parties do not know the particular circumstances of their own society. That is, they do not know its economic or political situation, or the level of civilization and culture it has been able to achieve. The persons in the original position have no information as to which generation they belong. These broader restrictions on knowledge are appropriate in part because questions of social justice arise between generations as well as within them, for example, the question of the appropriate rate of capital saving and of the conservation of natural resources and the environment of nature. There is also, theoretically anyway, the question of a reasonable genetic policy. In these cases too, in order to carry through the idea of the original position, the parties must not know the contingencies that set them in opposition. They must choose principles the consequences of which they are prepared to live with whatever generation they turn out to belong to.

As far as possible, then, the only particular facts which the parties know is that their society is subject to the circumstances of justice and whatever this implies. It is taken for granted, however, that they know the general facts about human society. They understand political affairs and the principles of economic theory; they know the basis of social organization and the laws of human psychology. Indeed, the parties are presumed to know whatever general facts affect the choice of the principles of justice. . . .

The veil of ignorance makes possible a unanimous choice of a particular conception of justice. Without these limitations on knowledge the bargaining problem of the original position would be hopelessly complicated. . . .

Now the reasons for the veil of ignorance go beyond mere simplicity. We want to define the original position so that we get the desired solution. If a knowledge of particulars is allowed, then the outcome is biased by arbitrary contingencies. As already observed, to each according to his threat advantage is not a principle of justice. If the original position is to yield agreements that are just, the parties must be fairly situated and treated equally as moral persons. The arbitrariness of the world must be corrected for by adjusting the circumstances of the initial contractual situation. . . .

The rationality of the parties. There is one further assumption to guarantee strict compliance. The parties are presumed to be capable of a sense of justice and this fact is public knowledge among them. This condition is to insure the integrity of the agreement made in the original position. . . . In reaching an agreement, then, they know that their undertaking is not in vain: their capacity for a sense of justice insures that the principles chosen will be respected. It is essential to observe, however, that this assumption still permits the consideration of men's capacity to act on the various conceptions of justice. . . . The assumption only says that the parties have a capacity for justice in a purely formal sense: taking everything relevant into account, including the general facts of moral psychology, the parties will adhere to the principles eventually chosen. They are rational in that they will not enter into agreements they know they cannot keep, or can do so only with great difficulty.

The maximin rule.   The term "maximin" means the *maximum minimorum;* and the rule directs our attention to the worst that can happen under any proposed course of action, and to decide in the light of that. . . .

The maximin rule tells us to rank alternatives by their worst possible outcomes: we are to adopt the alternative the worst outcome of which is superior to the worst outcomes of the others. . . .

TWO PRINCIPLES OF JUSTICE

I shall now state in a provisional form the two principles of justice that I believe would be chosen in the original position.

The first statement of the two principles reads as follows.

First: each person is to have an equal right to the most extensive basic liberty compatible with a similar liberty for others.

Second: social and economic inequalities are to be arranged so that they are both (a) reasonably expected to be to everyone's advantage, and (b) attached to positions and offices open to all. There are two ambiguous phrases in the second principle, namely "everyone's advantage" and "open to all."

By way of general comment, these principles primarily apply, as I have said, to the basic structure of society. They are to govern the assignment of rights and duties and to regulate the distribution of social and economic advantages. As their formulation suggests, these principles presuppose that the social structure can be divided into two more or less distinct parts, the first principle applying to the one, the second to the other. They distinguish between those aspects of the social system that define and secure the equal liberties of citizenship and those that specify and establish social and economic inequalities. The basic liberties of citizens are, roughly speaking, political liberty (the right to vote and to be eligible for public office) together with freedom of speech and assembly; liberty of conscience and freedom of thought; freedom of the person along with the right to hold (personal) property; and freedom from arbitrary arrest and seizure as defined by the concept of the rule of law. These liberties are all required to be equal by the first principle, since citizens of a just society are to have the same basic rights.

The second principle applies, in the first approximation, to the distribution of income and wealth and to the design of organizations that make use of differences in authority and responsibility, or chains of command. While the distribution of wealth and income need not be equal, it must be to everyone's advantage, and at the same time, positions of authority and offices of command must be accessible to all. One applies the second principle by holding positions open, and then, subject to this constraint, arranges social and economic inequalities so that everyone benefits.

These principles are to be arranged in a serial order with the first principle prior to the second. This ordering means that a departure from the institutions of equal liberty required by the first principle cannot be justified by, or compensated for, by greater social and economic advantages. The distribution of wealth and income, and the hierarchies of authority, must be consistent with both the liberties of equal citizenship and equality of opportunity.

It is clear that these principles are rather specific in their content, and their acceptance rests on certain assumptions that I must eventually try to explain and justify. A theory of justice depends upon a theory of society in ways that will become evident as we proceed. For the present, it should be observed that the two principles (and this holds for all formulations) are a special case of a more general conception of justice that can be expressed as follows.

All social values—liberty and opportunity, income and wealth, and the bases of self-respect—are to be distributed equally unless an unequal distribution of any, or all, of these values is to everyone's advantage. Injustice, then, is simply inequalities that are not to the benefit of all. Of course, this conception is extremely vague and requires interpretation.

As a first step, suppose that the basic structure of society distributes certain primary goods, that is, things that every rational man is presumed to want. These goods normally have a use whatever a person's rational plan of life. For simplicity, assume that the chief primary goods at the disposition of society are rights and liberties, powers and opportunities, income and wealth. These are the social primary goods. Other primary goods such as health and vigor, intelligence and imagination, are natural goods; although their possession is influenced by the basic structure, they are not so directly under its control. Imagine, then, a hypothetical initial arrangement in which all the social primary goods are equally distributed: everyone has similar rights and duties, and income and wealth are evenly shared. This state of affairs provides a benchmark for judging improvements. If certain inequalities of wealth and organizational powers would make everyone better off than in this hypothetical starting situation, then they accord with the general conception.

Now it is possible, at least theoretically, that by giving up some of their fundamental liberties men are sufficiently compensated by the resulting social and economic gains. The general conception of justice imposes no restrictions on what sort of inequalities are permissible; it only requires that everyone's position be improved. We need not suppose anything so drastic as consenting to a condition of slavery. Imagine instead that men forego certain political rights when the economic returns are significant and their capacity to influence the course of policy by the exercise of these rights would be marginal in any case. It is this kind of exchange which the two principles as stated rule out; being arranged in serial order they do not permit exchanges between basic liberties and economic and social gains. The serial ordering of principles expresses an underlying preference among primary social goods. When this preference is rational so likewise is the choice of these principles in this order.

Questions for Discussion: *Politics*

1. Do you think it is important for government leaders to be highly competent, or is it more important for them to be popular with the people? Why did Plato think that rulers should be philosophers?

2. Aquinas says that a human law (i.e., a law made by a legislature) which is contrary to natural law is "a perversion of law." Can you think of any laws which would be a "perversion of law" in Aquinas's sense?

3. Hobbes said that "no law can be unjust." What did he mean by that?

4. Mill sought to protect individual liberties by arguing that the government has no right to interfere in purely personal activities which do no harm to anyone else. List several activities of this sort. Reflect on your list, asking yourself if there is any way at all in which these activities could be considered harmful to other people.

5. Bentham and Mill seem to see freedom exclusively as something to be protected from government power and control. Marx instead refers to the lack of freedom which results from certain economic relationships. Explain these two views. Which do you think is a greater threat to freedom, a society's economic organization or its political organization? Why?

6. Do you agree with Rawls that we should never sacrifice liberty for economic advantage? Can you think of any situation in

which you would make such a sacrifice? Would any of the think-ers we have looked at in this section agree with Rawls? Disagree?

Suggested Additional Readings: Politics

Berlin, Isaiah: *Karl Marx: His Life and Environment,* 3d ed., Oxford University Press, New York, 1963. A useful introduction to Marx.

Bloom, Allan: *The Republic of Plato,* Basic Books, New York, 1968. A lively literal translation with careful notes and a rich inter-pretative essay.

D'Entrèves, A. P.: *Natural Law,* 2d ed., rev., Humanities Press, New York, 1964. A spirited, modern defense of natural law theory.

Hayek, Friedrich A.: *The Constitution of Liberty,* Gateway Editions, Henry Regnery Company, Chicago, 1972. A discussion of indi-vidualism and liberty by an economist who won the Nobel Prize.

Marx, Karl: *Early Writings,* McGraw-Hill, New York, 1963. For those interested in reading more Marx.

Milgram, Stanley: *Obedience to Authority*, Harper & Row, New York, 1975. A provocative study in psychology which raises many issues closely related to the problems of obedience.

Rawls, John: *A Theory of Justice*, Harvard, Cambridge, Mass., 1971. This book uses present-day language and examples to discuss systematically the concept and practice of justice.

Sabine, G. H.: *A History of Political Theory*, 4th ed., Holt, New York, 1973. A thorough, standard history of political thought.

Skinner, B. F.: *Walden Two*, Macmillan, New York, 1948. A literary utopia which raises concerns about individual liberty.

RELIGION

WHAT CAN I BELIEVE?

Love God and do as you please.

Saint Augustine
Homilies on Saint John's Epistle (A.D. 407)

If God did not exist, then everything would be permitted.

Dostoevski
The Brothers Karamazov (1880)

There is no human nature since there is no God to conceive it. ... [M]an is only what he wills himself to be.

Jean-Paul Sartre
Existentialism and Humanism (1946)

Cathedral of St. Etienne de Bourges, begun in the thirteenth century and completed about 1300 (*Tudor Publishing Co., New York*)

INTRODUCTION

We have often heard the statement that "money is his religion." What makes this an appropriate comment is that it comes very close to an accurate definition of what religion is about. Not that religion has anything to do with money; rather, it is that religion describes a relationship. "Religion" can be defined as the way a person relates himself to what he considers most important, or to what he considers ultimate reality. There is also the statement that in one way or another every person is religious. This is so because everybody has some idea of what is most important or what constitutes ultimate reality. Why is it that everybody is concerned with ultimate reality? The concern with what is most important or ultimately real grows out of three aspects of human experience. First, every human being has a certain sense of physical insecurity. We are vulnerable to accident, disease, hunger, war, and death. How do we protect ourselves against a series of disasters which threaten our physical existence? The threat to our survival raises the second question about the meaning of our existence. Is our life, as Thomas Hobbes said, "solitary, poor, nasty, brutish, and short?" Or is there some deeper meaning to it which makes life important and full of purpose? Third, there is the sense of moral duty. Should we do whatever we please? Are we willing for others to do anything they please? At its highest levels, religion has brought all these concerns together by referring to God as the source of man's existence, the source of man's nature and destiny, and the guide to man's scale of values and daily conduct. Philosophers have developed various points of view about these matters, as we shall see when we consider several elements of religion.

The Elements of Religion

THE NATURE OF RELIGIOUS KNOWLEDGE

Religion is a form of experience which is difficult to put into words. Religious experience is frequently a matter of feeling or emotion rather than intellectual knowledge. In religion one is more apt to ask "What can I believe?" instead of "What can I know?" This implies that to believe something is different from knowing something. All knowledge is not of the same kind. If knowledge is limited to what we can see, touch, and measure, then we can never have knowledge of God, who is not available to the sense of sight and touch. Some religious people claim that their feelings, emotions, and their beliefs provide for them a kind of knowledge, just as when a person who loves another has a special knowledge of that relationship. Besides personal feelings or emotions, religious knowledge is based on the experience of a community of people who are witnesses to religious ideas. Moreover, religious wisdom is preserved in literature and continues to appear valid from one generation to another. Others claim a special source of religious knowledge that they call "revelation." God is said to reveal significant knowledge through special persons, such as prophets and writers of sacred scriptures. For some, nature is a source of revelation: Saint Augustine said that when he looked at flowers they said to him, "God made us." Most of these sources of religious knowledge seem to be either private with individuals or limited to a special community.

Philosophers, however, seek to provide a broader, even universal, rational basis for religious knowledge. They try to discover in nature or human experience some clear grounds for the claims of religion. Some philosophers conclude that there cannot be any exact knowledge either for or against religion; they call themselves "agnostics." Still others are certain that religious knowledge about God is not valid; such persons call themselves "atheists." All these various attitudes toward religious knowledge become apparent especially when we consider the problem of the existence of God.

THE EXISTENCE OF GOD

Most religions are based on ideas about a supreme being. Also, most religious people believe in the existence of this supreme being as the major element in their religious commitment. Religious leaders do not question the existence of God. They assume that God exists, and they build the rest of their teachings on this belief. Philosophers, however, try to find reasons to show that a belief in God can be defended intellectually. Using certain logical procedures, they develop what are called "proofs" for the existence of God. Instead of relying on tradition, custom, literature, or revelation, philosophers have tried to construct their "proofs" by relying solely on the operation of human reason. These so-called proofs are designed not only to provide a rational support for what people already believe. Rather, some philosophers consider the existence of God a necessary part of any complete understanding of the natural world and of human destiny. Without the existence of God, they feel, we cannot fully explain many of our experiences. One experience we all have is the impression that nature seems to work with almost clockwork precision. The seasons come and go on time, the planets move in their regular orbits, the parts of our bodies carry out their specific functions, and the various species reproduce themselves through intricate procedures. Surely, some say, this natural order resembles the inner workings of a clock. And just as a clock has a maker, so also the natural order must be the product of some mind, a supreme designer.

As another example, consider the question raised by a boy who asks his father where that log came from as he throws it into the fireplace. It may be that he simply wants to know whether his father bought it or had cut down one of the trees on their land. But the boy's question could be more philosophical. He may want to know what caused the tree to come into existence. To this question his father may give him a series of answers referring to a series of causes. This is like answering the question about where a child came from by referring to parents, grandparents, and those farther back through a long series of generations. But however far this series of causes can be traced, one must still ask about the earliest cause. How did the series of causes get started? There must be, it is argued, a first cause whose nature is such that it did not itself need to be caused, and this first cause some philosophers call God. Not all philosophers agree with the so-called proofs of this kind, and we will consider the views for and against these arguments.

DAILY LIFE

One of the strongest reasons for pursuing religion is the hope that it will provide a person with a sense of purpose and power to live a rich and satisfying life. Both Dostoevski and Saint Augustine have suggested an interesting link between the existence of God and the range of human behavior that is permissible. Dostoevski said that if God did not exist, then everything would be permitted. What Dostoevski appears to be saying is that God is not only an abstract supreme being but also the source of man's creation, purpose, and value. Each person understands his own nature, purpose, and value only as he understands his relation to God. By definition, then, if there were no God, there would be no standard of value by which a person could measure, or evaluate, his own life and behavior. Everything would be permitted in the sense that there would be no standard to violate. By contrast, Saint Augustine says, "Love God and do as you please." He gives the impression that if a person loves God, he can do whatever he pleases without limit. But what Saint Augustine really means is that if a person truly loves God, his relationship with God will deeply affect what he will find pleasing to do. The philosophical issue raised here is whether the existence or nonexistence of God has any bearing on our daily life.

BODY AND SOUL

Socrates thought that nothing was more important than the care of the soul, the *psyche.* The interior of man, said Socrates, is the place where a unique action takes place, namely, the activity of knowing, which leads to the practical activity of doing. For him, the soul was not a particular faculty, nor a special kind of substance, but was rather the capacity for intelligence and character. Today we think of the soul as being almost synonymous with the concept of mind, and so we speak of the mind-body problem. Nothing seems more obvious to us than the difference between our physical bodies, on the one hand, and our soul, that is, our mental, emotional, and volitional activities, on the other. What is not so obvious is how these two spheres of human nature are to be understood. Are they separate and distinct? If so, how are they related to each other? Are they both material, or is the body material and the mind or soul nonmaterial or spiritual?

The soul has been referred to as the principle of life. Since the body is material, it is not capable of moving itself. The soul is thought to possess various kinds of moving forces, including anger and love, and all the appetites, intellectual powers of choice, and the element of life itself. Plato spoke of the soul as being in the prisonhouse of the body. The soul, he said, has a life both before and after its union with its body. This concept of the soul has played an important role in certain major religions. But philosophers have not been able to describe to anyone's satisfaction either the nature of the soul or how the soul and body are related. Some have tried to solve the problem by saying, as Democritus did, that what we call mind is really no different from body. Both body and mind are composed of the same material, namely, atoms. The atoms which make up the mind, according to this theory, are smaller, smoother, and swifter than those of the body, and they make possible what we call sensation, movement, and thought. In this view there is no body-mind problem because there is only one continuous substance in human nature. We are left with two major views, namely, that the soul and body are different, on the one hand, and that our personal identity does not require the concept of the soul or mind, on the other.

DEATH AND BEYOND

The question of whether there is life after death has occupied human beings for various reasons. One reason is the apparent incompleteness of any particular person's life. Immanuel Kant said that we cannot demonstrate by reason that the soul is immortal. But, he said, we are commanded by the moral law to pursue perfect virtue. We cannot achieve this perfection in our limited lifetime. This ideal requires an indefinite progress. Therefore, says Kant, "this endless progress is possible only on the supposition of the unending duration of the existence and personality of some rational being, which is called the immortality of the soul." Some religions consider life after death a necessary occasion for appropriate rewards and punishments. Still others believe that the capacity of the mind to know eternal truths such as mathematics is already evidence that there is something eternal about the mind itself. The principle of conservation suggests to some that nothing is lost in nature and, especially, that the highest capacity in man, his mind or soul, is never lost. These and other reasons are suggested to support the concept of the continuance of the soul after death. But what philosophical basis can be found for the immortality of the soul?

Summary

A religious person, just like a person deeply in love, does not wish to analyze or dissect what to him is a deep and rich experience. Nevertheless, certain questions are bound to come up, and philosophers pursue these questions with as much rigor as possible. There is the question concerning *the nature of religious knowledge* and whether belief is compatible with or contrary to rational knowledge. For this reason, the religious belief in God is supplemented by attempts at *proofs for the existence of God.* From a practical point of view, one can ask "What is the *relation between the existence of God and daily life?*" A partial answer to this question will depend on how we understand the relation between *soul and body.* Moreover, the way we think about the soul and body will determine what can be said about the *immortality of the soul.* We need to consider these elements of religion more fully from several points of view.

ALTERNATIVE APPROACHES TO THE ELEMENTS OF RELIGION

Our aim in this section is to provide alternative views on the five elements of religion which we have chosen for consideration.

(1) The claim for religious knowledge has its defenders and its critics. Saint Thomas Aquinas combined elements of the Christian faith with Aristotle's philosophy to show how faith and reason participate in religious knowledge. William James approached religious knowledge from a pragmatic point of view, saying that the willingness to believe can under certain circumstances determine what we can know, even in matters of religion. Bertrand Russell insisted that if language is to contain meaningful information, its words and phrases must refer to something with which we are acquainted in our experience. Otherwise language does not increase our knowledge, as is the case, he thought, with the language of religion. For Sigmund Freud, religion appeared to be the product of a deep and primal wish.

(2) Two of the most significant attempts to prove the existence of God were made by Anselm and Aquinas. Anselm employed a purely intellectual argument known as the "ontological argument."

By contrast, Aquinas chose certain aspects of our experience, such as the movement of things or the appearance of order and design, upon which he constructed his five proofs. David Hume, the empiricist, rejected the arguments; in particular, with respect to the argument from design, he said that there is as much evidence of disorder as there is of design to refute the argument. While Kant had reasons for finding the concept of God significant, he did not agree that there is any rational way to prove God's existence.

(3) Søren Kierkegaard, the Christian existentialist, was especially concerned about daily life. Every day each person faces moments of decision, either to do this or to do that, or what Kierkegaard calls an "either/or." Is it possible, he asks, to avoid these decisions by saying that there is really no difference between the "either" and the "or"?

(4) The classic theory that the soul and body represent two distinct substances was formulated by René Descartes. The most important recent reply to Descartes's dualistic theory has come from Oxford's Gilbert Ryle, who argues from the point of view of philosophical or linguistic analysis.

(5) Plato provides a clear statement and argument for the immortality of the soul based on his conviction that mind or the soul is something separate from the body. Hume, however, replies that neither metaphysical, moral, nor physical considerations are sufficient to establish the proof of immortality. Kierkegaard says that we cannot discuss death and immortality objectively; we must discuss these personally, that is, subjectively.

CHAPTER 15

THE NATURE OF RELIGIOUS KNOWLEDGE

Aquinas, James, Russell, and Freud

According to Saint Thomas Aquinas, religious knowledge is possible in two different ways. One way is through faith and the other through reason. Faith is what theology is concerned about, while reason is the way of philosophy. What is the difference between these two? The most notable difference between theology and philosophy is that each begins from a different starting point. Although they both have something to say about God, they do so for different reasons. The philosopher begins with the simplest object of sense experience and through a process of reasoning moves beyond that object to more general principles. By thinking about a tree, it is possible to raise the most profound questions about existence. How does the tree come into existence? What does it mean for anything to be? Is everything that exists the same, on principle, as a tree, namely, that at one time it did not exist, then it exists, and finally it ceases to exist? Must not there be a being which always is? The human mind can know certain truths that seem eternal, as, for example, that 7 and 3 always make 10. The permanence, the etern-

Aquinas (*Culver Pictures*)

ity of these truths, is in sharp contrast to the limited span of existence of a tree.

As we shall see later, Aquinas reasons his way from simple things, as did Aristotle, to the highest forms of being, ending with the idea of God. Theology, however, begins with a faith in God and considers all things we find in nature as being the creatures of God. The theologian's faith comes from the tradition of his religious community. And that tradition is assumed to be the product of God's revelation to man. There is, then, a sharp difference in the starting point and the method of theology and philosophy. The philosopher draws his conclusions from his rational interpretations of the things in nature, whereas the theologian rests the demonstrations of his conclusions on the authority of revealed knowledge.

Aquinas took great pains to point out that philosophy and theology do not necessarily contradict each other. Theology, however, is far more concerned with what is urgent for man's religious life and destiny, while philosophy deals with matters that are not always significant for man's religious end. Some truths available to theology can never be discovered by natural reason, as for example the doctrine of the trinity. Some truths can be discovered by reason, as for example that God exists; these truths are also revealed in order to make sure that they are known. There is, said Aquinas, some overlapping between philosophy and theology. For the most part, however, philosophy and theology are two separate disciplines. Wherever reason is capable of knowing something, faith, strictly speaking, is not necessary. Also, what faith uniquely knows through revelation cannot be known by natural reason alone. Philosophy can only infer that God exists as the first cause of things. But philosophy cannot by studying the objects of experience understand what God is like. Nevertheless, both theology and philosophy are concerned with truth: both affirm the existence of God as the truth about the created world, but they do this in different ways.

James

William James was born in New York City in 1843. He was the brother of the renowned novelist Henry James. He received his M.D. from the Harvard Medical School and soon joined that faculty as an instructor in physiology. From medicine he moved to psychology and philosophy, producing in 1890 his famous book *Principles of Psychology*. He became a member of the illustrious Harvard department of philosophy which included George Santayana and Josiah Royce. His published essays were widely influential, and as collections in book form, they were and still are read around the world. By the time he died in 1910 at the age of fifty-eight he had created a new approach to philosophy and had managed to communicate his principles of *pragmatism* to an unusually wide audience. James did not believe that the human mind can achieve a single, unified concept of the world. Nor did he think it was important to have such a concept. All we can know, he said, is certain parts of the universe. Moreover, these parts look different to different people. These many parts and views provide the basis for a *pluralistic* view of the world. And the main thing about these plural views, he said, is not whether they are consistent with one another but whether they lead to successful action, that is, whether they work or not.

William James raised this question "Can our will either help or hinder our intellect in its perceptions of truth?" In answering this question, James did not intend to propose the fanciful thesis that "wishing will make it true." His intention was to give a defense of "our right" to believe something of which our purely logical intellect may not have been persuaded. Religious questions in particular have a way of running ahead of evidence. But if the evidence for God's existence is lacking, there is, nevertheless, the fact of human behavior. James put great store in the concrete fact that men engage in moral discourse and also religious practice. It is necessary to recognize this fact of religious behavior when considering the issue of religious truth. Moreover, pragmatism recognizes the close relation between thinking and doing and therefore between belief and action. This makes belief an important element in life, and what James wanted to do was to discover just how relevant the will to believe is in relation to truth.

James said that the will to believe is relevant only under highly restricted conditions. One cannot will to believe just anything under any and all circumstances. First of all, there must be a clear *hypothesis* that is proposed for our belief. Such a hypothesis must be *live* rather than *dead;* that is, it must, like an electric wire, make a connection with my life. If an American Protestant is asked to believe in the Mahdi, this makes no connection with him and arouses no credibility at all and could, therefore, be only a dead hypothesis. Further, there must be an *option.* James argued that a genuine option requires that both alternative hypotheses be *live* and not dead; the option must be *forced* and not avoidable; and it must be *momentous* and not trivial. The will to believe, then, is relevant and can operate only when we are confronted with an option that (1) is *forced* upon us, in that it is impossible not to choose one way or the other, (2) is a *living* option because both hypotheses make a genuine appeal, and (3) is a *momentous* option because the opportunity to choose might not present itself again. Moreover, a belief is relevant only where reason alone cannot settle the matter.

Having stated these conditions, James then argues that it is frequently the case that our wills influence our convictions. The clearest example, he thought, was our postulate that there is truth and that our minds can attain it. How do we know there is truth? We don't, says James; our belief that there is truth is but a "passionate affirmation of desire." We want to have truth, and we want to believe that our experiments will unfold more truth, and in this desire we have the support of the community. For these reasons, James says that "our passionate nature not only lawfully may, but must, decide an option between propositions, whenever it is a genuine option that cannot by its nature be decided on intellectual grounds; for to say, under such circumstances, 'Do not decide, but leave the question open,' is itself a passional decision . . . and is attended with the . . . risk of losing the truth."

James argues that certain kinds of truths become possible only when we put ourselves in the position for the truth fully to materialize itself. If we fail to make ourselves "available," we risk losing the truth. Suppose a young man wants to know whether a certain young woman loves him. Let us also suppose that objectively it is a fact that she loves him but he does not *know* it. If he assumes that she does not, if, that is, he does not will to believe that she loves him, his doubt will prevent him from saying or doing what would cause her to reveal her love. In this case, he would "lose the truth." His will to believe would not necessarily create the love; that is already there. Belief has the effect of making what is already there become known. If the young man required evidence before he could know the truth, he would never know it, because the evidence he is looking for can become available only after he wills to believe it is true. In this case, the will to believe would have discovered a fact that already existed. Projecting this method deeper into the realm of religious experience, James did not want to argue that the will to believe would "create" the existence of God as the product of mere wish. He rather thought that the truth of religion and the power of God in human experience is the discovery, through the will to believe, of what is in fact "there." Some truths will forever escape us until we plunge into the stream of experience.

Besides *discovering* facts, the will to believe can *create* facts. An individual, says James, frequently gains a promotion chiefly because he believed he could achieve it and acted resolutely on that belief. Taking his own estimate of his powers as true, such a person *lives* by it, sacrifices for its sake, and takes risks. His faith *creates* its own verification. In a political campaign, the will to believe can provide the psychic energy for creating a majority for a candidate. When one person is impressed by the optimism of another, he is energized to express the same optimism about the outcome of the election, and this *energy* can eventually create the majority vote. James gives the illustration of passengers on a train, all of whom are individually brave, but when held up by robbers, each one is afraid that if he resists he will be shot. If they believe that the others would arise, resistance could begin. The robbers know that they can count on one another. The passengers, however, are paralyzed. Although they possess superior force, they are not *sure* their fellows would support their resistance. But if one passenger actually arose, that evidence of resolve could influence the others, and this will to believe would help to create the fact of total resistance.

In the end, religious experience was for James a fact that is both *discovered* and *created* through the will to believe. His pragmatism led him to distinguish between organized religion and that firsthand religion whose "cash value" could be realized only when a person put himself into a position to be affected by it. Religion grows out of the deep personal experience of the fragmentary or broken character of life, and this awareness leads one to discover a power that can overcome this sense of incompleteness. James thought of God in these terms, as a power able to reconstruct human life. For this reason, James concluded that "the universe is no longer a mere *It* to us, but a *Thou*, if we are religious; any relation that may be possible from person to person might be possible here."

Russell

Born in England in 1872, Bertrand Russell was ninety-eight years old when he died in north Wales in 1970. As an orphan, he was raised by his grandparents; he inherited his title of 3d Earl Russell from his grandfather. His brilliance became apparent at an early age, and at Cambridge University he won a long list of honors. He eventually wrote more than forty books and became one of the most influential philosophers of the twentieth century. As an empiricist, he sought to define the limits of human knowledge. He also sought to give all thinking the rigor of mathematics. In particular, he analyzed language to its most basic elements, namely, its "atomic facts," making sure in this way that language and the world to which it refers are related to each other accurately. Russell wrote on all subjects, including philosophy, politics, mathematics, and religion.

In his late teens, just before he went to Cambridge University, Bertrand Russell wrote down his "beliefs" and "unbeliefs." He wrote, for example, "I may say to begin with that I do believe in God, and that I shall call myself a theist if I had to give my creed a name." In setting forth his reasons for believing in God, Russell said, "I shall take account of scientific arguments." He found in the orderly behavior of nature a strong reason for believing in "a cause which regulates the action of force on nature" and this cause can be attributed, he said, only "to a divine controlling power which I accordingly call God." As his interest in mathematics grew, Russell developed a desire to make philosophical language as clear and accurate as the language of mathematics. Indeed, Russell eventually became known for his attempt to invent a new language which he called "logical atomism." This language of logical atomism would, he thought, have the exactness and rigor of mathematics because it was supposed to correspond exactly to "facts." As we shall see, in order to make language fit the "facts" of experience, only certain kinds of facts could be admitted for consideration. Russell concluded, as did the empiricists, that only that language which refers to things we all experience can be meaningful. Clearly, discussions about God could not pass this test of meaningfulness.

Russell wondered whether he could devise a way to construct a language that could accurately express everything that could be stated clearly. In the beginning, he made a major assumption, namely, that the world could and would correspond to his specially constructed language. The vocabulary of his language would correspond to the particular objects in the world. What kind of "facts" would form the basis of this language? "The things in the world," said Russell, "have various properties, and stand in various relations to each other. That they have these properties and relations are facts. . . . " Language, according to Russell, consists of a unique arrangement of words, and the meaningfulness of language is determined by the accuracy with which the words represent facts.

A fact is either simple or complex. Words match facts. If there is no fact to match a word, then the word is meaningless. Words are arranged in the form of propositions; the words in a proposition must correspond one by one with corresponding facts. Words and propositions must be analyzed to discover what they symbolize. The simplest word or proposition symbolizes the simplest fact, which is called an "atomic fact." When two or more atomic propositions are linked together with such words as "and" and "or," the result is what Russell calls "molecular propositions." But no matter how complex a proposition is, it can be analyzed into its parts, and each part must correspond to a fact. These facts must be contained in our actual experience. Or, as Russell says, "Every proposition which we can understand must be composed wholly of constituents with which we are acquainted."

Once again, this puts Russell squarely in the camp of empiricism, which says that all knowledge is based on experience. Propositions which cannot be traced back to facts with which we are actually acquainted cannot be considered meaningful propositions. For this reason, Russell comes to the conclusion that many of the propositions of traditional religious language could not meet the test of logical atomism. There is no way, for example, to relate the proposition that "God is all-powerful" with any facts with which we are acquainted. Russell was not prepared to say that God does not exist, which is the position of the atheist. Instead, he called himself an *agnostic,* saying that "the agnostic suspends judgment, saying that there are not sufficient grounds either for affirmation or for denial."

Freud

Sigmund Freud was born in Freiberg in Moravia in 1856 and died in London in 1939 at the age of eighty-three. He began his medical studies at the University of Vienna in 1873. In 1882 he studied at the General Hospital of Vienna to qualify for private practice. There he served in the department of internal medicine and later in the psychiatric clinic. He pursued his advanced studies with distinguished medical scientists in the fields of anatomy, neurology, and psychiatry. After further study in Paris, Freud returned to Vienna, where in collaboration with the famous physician Joseph Brewer he published in 1893 a significant article, "The Psychical Mechanism of Hysterical Phenomena." Out of this research, involving the cure of symptoms of hysteria by helping the patient recall under hypnosis the circumstances of the development of these symptoms, there emerged the beginnings of psychoanalysis. His books became widely influential. His first, in 1900, was *The Interpretation of Dreams.* His last book, entitled *Moses and Monotheism,* was published in 1939. His other works include the *General Introduction to Psychoanalysis* (1920), *Civilization and Its Discontents* (1929), and *The Future of an Illusion* (1927).

Freud approached religion from the point of view of a psychoanalyst. He was aware of the strong support for religion found in tradition, in the widespread practice of religion, and in the genuine consolation provided by religion. Nevertheless, Freud concluded that "religious ideas are illusions." These illusions, he said, grow out of deep-rooted wishes. The strength of these wishes provides the power of illusions. The origin of these wishes is traced back to early experiences of childhood. "We know," says Freud, "that the terrifying effect of infantile helplessness aroused the need for protection—protection through love—which the father relieved. . . . " As we grow older, says Freud, we discover that the same helplessness we experienced as a child continues throughout life. Before human beings developed scientific knowledge and abilities, they tried to overcome the sense of helplessness by use of the "illusion" that behind nature there exists a strong father, God, and that God provides protection against life's dangers. God also provides the conditions for a moral world order where justice will finally triumph. Moreover, religion promises the continuation of life beyond the short span on earth. All these ideas, says Freud, are the product of wish-fulfillment, a projection of the father-image on the world scene, and are no more than illusions.

Freud emphasized that an illusion is not necessarily an error. After all, a poor girl may have an illusion that a prince will come

Freud (*Library of Congress*)

after her and take her away with him. Although this may be an illusion, it is not an error and it need not necessarily be false, since this experience is possible and indeed has happened. But certain beliefs are illusions because they have no relationship with reality. As Freud says, "We call a belief an illusion when wish-fulfillment is a prominent factor in its motivation. . . . " There is no scientific proof for the claims of religion, says Freud. He realizes that science does not have an answer for everything. Freud admits moreover that neither can science disprove the ideas of religion. Nevertheless, Freud concludes that religion is based overwhelmingly on the wish for security and that this wish results in the development of illusions. These illusions prevent the development of intelligence because they encourage attempts to solve problems through uncritical emotions instead of through the use of reason. The solution to this problem, according to Freud, is for people to "grow up" so that just as children ultimately learn how to take care of themselves after they leave home, so also mankind can learn how to achieve brotherly love and morality without a cosmic father.

READING

THE WILL TO BELIEVE

James

The thesis I defend is, briefly stated, this: *Our passional nature not only lawfully may, but must, decide an option between propositions, whenever it is a genuine option that cannot by its nature be decided on intellectual grounds; for to say, under such circumstances, "Do not decide, but leave the question open," is itself a passional decision—just like deciding yes or no—and is attended with the same risk of losing the truth.* The thesis thus abstractly expressed will, I trust, soon become quite clear. But I must first indulge in a bit more of preliminary work.

It will be observed that for the purposes of this discussion we are on "dogmatic" ground—ground, I mean, which leaves systematic philosophical scepticism altogether out of account. The postulate that there is truth, and that it is the destiny of our minds to attain it, we are deliberately resolving to make, though the sceptic will not make it. We part company with him, therefore, absolutely, at this point. But the faith that truth exists, and that our minds can find it, may be held in two ways. We may talk of the *empiricist* way and of the *absolutist* way of believing in truth. The absolutists in this matter say that we not only can attain to knowing truth, but we can *know* when we have attained to knowing it; while the empiricists think that although we may attain it, we cannot infallibly know when. To *know* is one thing, and to know for certain *that* we know is another. One may hold to the first being possible without the second; hence the empiricists and the absolutists, although neither of them is a sceptic in the usual philosophic sense of the term, show very different degrees of dogmatism in their lives. . . .

From William James, "The Will to Believe," 1896.

In truths dependent on our personal action, then, faith based on desire is certainly a lawful and possibly an indispensable thing.

But now, it will be said, these are all childish human cases, and have nothing to do with great cosmical matters, like the question of religious faith. Let us then pass on to that. Religions differ so much in their accidents that in discussing the religious question we must make it very generic and broad. What then do we now mean by the religious hypothesis? Science says things are; morality says some things are better than other things; and religion says essentially two things.

First, she says that the best things are the more eternal things, the overlapping things, the things in the universe that throw the last stone, so to speak, and say the final word. "Perfection is eternal"—this phrase of Charles Secrétan seems a good way of putting this first affirmation of religion, an affirmation which obviously cannot yet be verified scientifically at all.

The second affirmation of religion is that we are better off even now if we believe her first affirmation to be true.

Now, let us consider what the logical elements of this situation are *in case the religious hypothesis in both its branches be really true.* (Of course, we must admit that possibility at the outset. If we are to discuss the question at all, it must involve a living option. If for any of you religion be a hypothesis that cannot, by any living possibility, be true, then you need go no farther. I speak to the "saving remnant" alone.) So proceeding, we see, first, that religion offers itself as a *momentous* option. We are supposed to gain, even now, by our belief, and to lose by our non-belief, a certain vital good. Secondly, religion is a *forced* option, so far as that good goes. We cannot escape the issue by remaining sceptical and waiting for more light, because, although we do avoid error in that way *if religion be untrue,* we lose the good, *if it be true,* just as certainly as if we positively chose to disbelieve. It is as if a man should hesitate indefinitely to ask a certain woman to marry him because he was not perfectly sure that she would prove an angel after he brought her home. Would he not cut himself off from that particular angel-possibility as decisively as if he went and married some one else? Scepticism, then, is not avoidance of option; it is option of a certain particular kind of risk. *Better risk loss of truth than chance of error*—that is your faith-vetoer's exact position. He is actively playing his stake as much as the believer is; he is backing the field against the religious hypothesis, just as the believer is backing the religious hypothesis against the field. To preach scepticism to us as a duty until "sufficient evidence" for religion be found, is tantamount therefore to telling us, when in presence of the religious hypothesis, that to yield to our fear of its being error is wiser and better than to yield to our hope that it may be true. It is not intellect against all passions, then; it is only intellect with one passion laying down its law. And by what, forsooth, is the supreme wisdom of this passion warranted? Dupery for dupery, what proof is there that dupery through hope is so much worse than dupery through fear? I, for one, can see no proof; and I simply refuse obedience to the scientist's command to imitate his kind of option, in a case where my own stake is important enough to give me the right to choose my own form of risk. If religion be true and the evidence for it be still insufficient, I do not wish, by putting your extinguisher upon my nature (which feels to me as if it had after all some business in this matter), to forfeit my sole chance in life of getting upon the winning side—that chance depending, of course, on my willingness to run the risk of acting as if my passional need of taking the world religiously might be prophetic and right.

All this is on the supposition that it really may be prophetic and right, and that, even to us who are discussing the matter, religion is a live hypothesis which may be true. Now, to most of us religion comes in a still further way that makes a veto on our active faith even more illogical. The more perfect and more eternal aspect of the universe is represented in our religions as having personal form. The universe is no longer a mere *It* to us, but a *Thou,* if we are religious; and any relation that may be possible from person to person might be possible here. For instance, although in one sense we are passive portions of the universe, in another we show a curious autonomy, as if we were small active centers on our own account. We feel, too, as if the appeal of religion to us were made to our own active goodwill, as if evidence might be forever withheld from us unless we met the hypothesis half-way. To take a trivial illustration: just as a man who in a company of gentlemen made no advances, asked a warrant for every concession, and believed no one's word without proof, would cut himself off by such churlishness from all the social rewards that a more trusting spirit would earn—so here, one who should shut himself up in snarling logicality and try to make the gods extort his recognition willy-nilly, or not get it at all, might cut himself off forever from his only opportunity of making the gods' acquaintance. This feeling, forced on us we know not whence, that by obstinately believing that there are gods (although not to do so would be so easy both for our logic and out life) we are doing the universe the deepest service we can, seems part of the living essence of the religious hypothesis. If the hypothesis *were* true in all its parts, including this one, then pure intellectualism, with its veto on our making willing advances, would be an absurdity; and some participation of our sympathetic nature would be logically required. I, therefore, for one, cannot see my way to accepting the agnostic rules for truth-seeking, or willfully agree to keep my willing nature out of the game. I cannot do so for this plain reason, that *a rule of thinking which would absolutely prevent me from acknowledging certain kinds of truth if those kinds of truth were really there, would be an irrational rule.* That for me is the long and short of the formal logic of the situation, no matter what the kinds of truth might materially be.

READING

WHAT IS AN AGNOSTIC?
Russell

ARE AGNOSTICS ATHEISTS?

No. An atheist, like a Christian, holds that we *can* know whether or not there is a God. The Christian holds that we can know there is a God; the atheist, that we can know there is not. The agnostic suspends judgment, saying that there are not sufficient grounds either for affirmation or for denial. At the same time, an agnostic may hold that the existence of God, though not impossible, is very improbable; he may even hold it so improbable that it is not worth considering in practice. In that case, he is not far removed from atheism. His attitude may be that which a careful philosopher would have toward the gods of ancient Greece. If I were asked to *prove* that Zeus and Poseidon and Hera and the rest of the Olympians do not exist, I should be at a loss to find conclusive arguments. An agnostic may think the Christian God as improbable as the Olympians; in that case, he is, for practical purposes, at one with the atheists.

SINCE YOU DENY "GOD'S LAW," WHAT AUTHORITY DO YOU ACCEPT AS A GUIDE TO CONDUCT?

An agnostic does not accept any "authority" in the sense in which religious people do. He holds that a man should think out questions of conduct for himself. Of course, he will seek to profit by the wisdom of others, but he will have to select for himself the people he is to consider wise, and he will not regard even what they say as unquestionable. He will observe that what passes as "God's law" varies from time to time. The Bible says both that a woman must not marry her deceased husband's brother, and that, in certain circumstances, she must do so. If you have the misfortune to be a childless widow with an unmarried brother-in-law, it is logically impossible for you to avoid disobeying "God's law."

DOES AN AGNOSTIC DO WHATEVER HE PLEASES?

In one sense, no; in another sense, everyone does whatever he pleases. Suppose, for example, you hate some one so much that you would like to

Cambridge (*Culver Pictures*)

murder him. Why do you not do so? You may reply: "Because religion tells me that murder is a sin." But as a statistical fact, agnostics are not more prone to murder than other people, in fact, rather less so. They have the same motives for abstaining from murder as other people have. Far and away the most powerful of these motives is the fear of punishment. In lawless conditions, such as a gold rush, all sorts of people will commit crimes, although in ordinary circumstances they would have been law-abiding. There is not only actual legal punishment; there is the discomfort of dreading discovery, and the loneliness of knowing that, to avoid being hated, you must wear a mask even with your closest intimates. And there is also what may be called "conscience": If you ever contemplated a murder, you would dread the horrible memory of your victim's last moments or lifeless corpse. All this, it is true, depends upon your living in a law-abiding community, but there are abundant secular reasons for creating and preserving such a community.

I said that there is another sense in which every man does as he pleases. No one but a fool indulges every impulse, but what holds a desire in check is always some other desire. A man's anti-social wishes may be restrained by a wish to please God, but they may also be restrained by a wish to please his friends, or to win the respect of his community, or to be

281

able to contemplate himself without disgust. But if he has no such wishes, the mere abstract precepts of morality will not keep him straight.

READING

THE FUTURE OF AN ILLUSION
Freud

If we fix our attention on the psychical origin of religious ideas, we will find [that these ideas] which profess to be dogmas, are not the residue of experience or the final result of reflection; they are illusions, fulfilments of the oldest, strongest and most insistent wishes of mankind; the secret of their strength is the strength of these wishes. We know already that the terrifying effect of infantile helplessness aroused the need for protection—protection through love—which the father relieved, and that the discovery that this helplessness would continue through the whole of life made it necessary to cling to the existence of a father—but this time a more powerful one. Thus the benevolent rule of divine providence allays our anxiety in face of life's dangers, the establishment of a moral world order ensures the fulfilment of the demands of justice, which within human culture have so often remained unfulfilled, and the prolongation of earthly existence by a future life provides in addition the local and temporal setting for these wish-fulfilments. Answers to the questions that tempt human curiosity, such as the origin of the universe and the relation between the body and the soul, are developed in accordance with the underlying assumptions of this system; it betokens a tremendous relief for the individual psyche if it is released from the conflicts of childhood arising out of the father complex, which are never wholly overcome, and if these conflicts are afforded a universally accepted solution.

When I say that they are illusions, I must define the meaning of the word. An illusion is not the same as an error, it is indeed not necessarily an error. Aristotle's belief that vermin are evolved out of dung, to which igno-

From Sigmund Freud, *The Future of an Illusion*, trans. W. D. Robson-Scott, Liveright Publishing Corporation, New York, 1953.

rant people still cling, was an error; so was the belief of a former generation of doctors that *tabes dorsalis* was the result of sexual excess. It would be improper to call these errors illusions. On the other hand, it was an illusion on the part of Columbus that he had discovered a new sea-route to India. The part played by his wish in this error is very clear. One may describe as an illusion the statement of certain nationalists that the Indo-Germanic race is the only one capable of culture, or the belief, which only psycho-analysis destroyed, that the child is a being without sexuality. It is characteristic of the illusion that it is derived from men's wishes; in this respect it approaches the psychiatric delusion, but it is to be distinguished from this, quite apart from the more complicated structure of the latter. In the delusion we emphasize as essential the conflict with reality; the illusion need not be necessarily false, that is to say, unrealizable or incompatible with reality. For instance, a poor girl may have an illusion that a prince will come and fetch her home. It is possible; some such cases have occurred. That the Messiah will come and found a golden age is much less probable; according to one's personal attitude one will classify this belief as an illusion or as analogous to a delusion. Examples of illusions that have come true are not easy to discover, but the illusion of the alchemists that all metals can be turned into gold may prove to be one. The desire to have lots of gold, as much gold as possible, has been considerably damped by our modern insight into the nature of wealth, yet chemistry no longer considers a transmutation of metals into gold as impossible. Thus we call a belief an illusion when wish-fulfilment is a prominent factor in its motivation, while disregarding its relations to reality, just as the illusion itself does.

If after this survey we turn again to religious doctrines, we may reiterate that they are all illusions, they do not admit of proof, and no one can be compelled to consider them as true or to believe in them. Some of them are so improbable, so very incompatible with everything we have laboriously discovered about the reality of the world, that we may compare them—taking adequately into account the psychological differences—to delusions. Of the reality value of most of them we cannot judge; just as they cannot be proved, neither can they be refuted. We still know too little to approach them critically. The riddles of the universe only reveal themselves slowly to our enquiry, to many questions science can as yet give no answer; but scientific work is our only way to the knowledge of external reality. Again, it is merely illusion to expect anything from intuition or trance; they can give us nothing but particulars, which are difficult to interpret, about our own mental life, never information about the questions that are so lightly answered by the doctrines of religion. It would be wanton to let one's own arbitrary action fill the gap, and according to one's personal estimate declare this or that part of the religious system to be more or less acceptable. These questions are too momentous for that; too sacred, one might say.

At this point it may be objected: well, then, if even the crabbed sceptics admit that the statements of religion cannot be confuted by reason, why should not I believe in them, since they have so much on their side—tradition, the concurrence of mankind, and all the consolation they yield? Yes, why not? Just as no one can be forced into belief, so no one can be forced into unbelief. But do not deceive yourself into thinking that with such arguments you are following the path of correct reasoning. If ever there was a case of facile argument, this is one. Ignorance is ignorance; no right to believe anything is derived from it. No reasonable man will behave so frivolously in other matters or rest content with such feeble grounds for his opinions or for the attitude he adopts; it is only in the highest and holiest things that he allows this. In reality these are only attempts to delude oneself or other people into the belief that one still holds fast to religion, when one has long cut oneself loose from it. Where questions of religion are concerned people are guilty of every possible kind of insincerity and intellectual misdemeanour. Philosophers stretch the meaning of words until they retain scarcely anything of their original sense; by calling "God" some vague abstraction which they have created for themselves, they pose as deists, as believers, before the world; they may even pride themselves on having attained a higher and purer idea of God, although their God is nothing but an insubstantial shadow and no longer the mighty personality of religious doctrine. Critics persist in calling "deeply religious" a person who confesses to a sense of man's insignificance and impotence in face of the universe, although it is not this feeling that constitutes the essence of religious emotion, but rather the next step, the reaction to it, which seeks a remedy against this feeling. He who goes no further, he who humbly acquiesces in the insignificant part man plays in the universe, is, on the contrary, irreligious in the truest sense of the word.

CHAPTER 16

PROVING THE EXISTENCE OF GOD

Anselm, Aquinas, Hume, and Kant

Anselm was born in 1033 in Aosta, a town in northwest Italy. His parents came from noble families and had hoped that their son would pursue a political career. He received an excellent classical education and soon showed powers of considerable intellectual ability. He disappointed his parents when he decided to enter the Benedictine monastery at Bec, in Normandy, France. There he studied with the renowned scholar Lanfranc. In time, Anselm succeeded Lanfranc as Abbot at the monastery and later as Archbishop of Canterbury in England. He was one of the most significant thinkers between Augustine (354–430) and Aquinas (1255–1274) and became famous for his "ontological argument" for the existence of God, which he set forth in his book *Proslogium*. He insisted on the need for precise logical philosophy, not as a substitute for faith, but as a means for making faith mature. He died in 1109 at Canterbury at the age of seventy-six.

Anselm's Ontological Argument

For Anselm, there was no clear line between philosophy and theology. As Augustine before him, he was particularly concerned with providing rational support for the doctrines of Christianity, which he already accepted as a matter of faith. He was convinced that faith and reason lead to the same conclusions. Moreover, Anselm believed that human reason can create a natural theology that is rationally coherent and does not depend on any authority other than rationality. This did not mean, however, that Anselm denied any connection between natural theology and faith. On the contrary, his view was that natural theology consists of giving a rational version of what is believed. He was not trying to *discover* the truth about God through reason alone, but wanted rather to employ reason in order to *understand* what he was believing. His method therefore was *faith seeking understanding;* "I do not seek to understand in order that I may believe," he said, "but I believe in order that I may understand." He made it particularly clear that his enterprise of proving God's existence could not even begin unless he had already believed in His existence. The human mind cannot penetrate into the profundity of God, "for I deem my intellect in no way sufficient thereunto. . . . " From the rational proof of God's existence, Anselm had a limited expectation, as he said that "I desire only a little understanding of the truth which my heart believes and loves."

The first thing to notice about this proof is that Anselm's thought proceeds from within his mind, and in that way he is unlike Aquinas, who starts with the assumption that each proof must begin with some empirical evidence from which the mind can then move logically to God. Anselm followed Augustine's doctrine of divine illumination, which gave him direct access to certain truths. Indeed, Anselm asks the reader, before beginning the ontological argument, to "enter the inner chamber of your mind" and to "shut out all things save God and whatever may aid you in seeking God." Clearly, Anselm is assured of the existence of God before he begins, saying, again, that "unless I believe, I shall not understand."

The argument itself moves swiftly. We believe, says Anselm, that God is "something than which nothing greater can be thought." The question then is "Does this something, than which nothing greater can be thought, really exist?'' There are those who would deny God's existence. Anselm quotes Psalm 13:1, where it says, "The fool has said in his heart: There is no God." What is meant by the word "fool" in this context? It means that one who denies God's existence is involved in a flat contradiction. For when the fool hears the phrase "something than which nothing greater can be thought," he understands what he hears, and what he understands can be said to be in his intellect. But it is one thing for something to be in the intellect; it is another to understand that something actually exists. A painter, for example, thinks in advance what he is about to portray. At this point, there is in his intellect an understanding of what he is about to make, although not an understanding that the portrait, which is still to be made, actually exists. But when he has finally painted it, he both has in his understanding and understands as existing the portrait he has finally made. This proves that something can be in the intellect even before the intellect knows it to exist. There is, then, in the fool's intellect an understanding of what is meant by the phrase "something than which nothing greater can be thought."

what?

This brings Anselm to the crux of his argument, which is this: Anyone, even the fool, can think of something greater than a being which is only in the intellect as an *idea*, and this something is the *actual existence* of that than which there is no greater. The contradiction in which the fool finds himself is in understanding what is meant by the word "God," namely, a being than which nothing greater can be thought, realizing that its actual existence is greater than just having an idea of it in the intellect, and still denying that God exists. Therefore, says Anselm, "there exists beyond doubt something than which a greater cannot be thought, both in understanding and in reality." In a concluding prayer, Anselm thanks God "because through your divine illumination I now so understand that which, through your generous gift, I formerly believed. . . ."

GAUNILON'S REBUTTAL

In the Abbey of Marmontier near Tours, another Benedictine monk, Gaunilon, came to the defense of the "fool." Gaunilon did not want to deny God's existence but simply to argue that Anselm had not constructed an adequate proof. For one thing, Gaunilon argued that the first part of the "proof" is impossible to achieve: It requires that there be in the understanding an idea of God, that upon hearing this word the fool is expected to have a conception of that than which there is no greater. But, says Gaunilon, the fool cannot form a concept of such a being since there is nothing among other realities he experiences from which this concept can be formed, in addition to which Anselm has already argued that there is no reality like Him. Actually, if the human mind could form such a concept, no "proof" would be necessary, for one would then already connect existence as an aspect of a perfect being. Gaunilon's other major objection is that we often think of things that in fact do not exist. We can imagine a perfect island, an island than which no greater can exist, but there is no way to prove that such a perfect island exists.

ANSELM'S REPLY TO GAUNILON

Anselm gave two replies. First, he said that we, along with the fool, are able to form a concept of that than which there is no greater. We do this whenever we compare different degrees of perfection in things and move upward to the maximum perfection, than which there is no more perfect. Second, he thought Gaunilon's reference to a perfect island showed that he had missed the point of the argument. Anselm points out that we can move from an idea to its necessary existence in only one case, namely, in the case of that Being whose nonexistence cannot be thought. An island does not *have to be,* it is a *possible* or *contingent* kind of being. This would be similarly true of every finite thing. There is only one something through which everything else has its being but that is itself not derived from anything else but has its existence necessarily from itself, and this is God.

Aquinas's Five Ways

Aquinas formulated five *proofs* or ways of demonstrating the existence of God. His approach was the opposite of Anselm's. Anselm began his proof with the *idea* of a perfect being "than which no greater can be conceived," from which he inferred the existence of that being inasmuch as the actual existence of it is greater than the mere idea of a perfect being. By contrast, Aquinas said that all knowledge must begin with our experience of sense objects. Instead of beginning with innate ideas of perfection, Aquinas rested all five of his proofs on the ideas derived from a rational under-standing of the ordinary objects that we experience with our senses. The chief characteristic of all sense objects is that their exis-tence requires a *cause*. That every event or every object requires a cause is something the human intellect knows as a principle when-ever, but not until, it comes in contact with experience. By the light of natural reason, the intellect knows, by experiencing events, that for every effect there must be a cause, that *ex nihilo nihil fit*, noth-ing comes from nothing. To demonstrate that God exists, Aquinas relied, then, first on his analysis of sense objects and second on his notion that the existence of these objects requires a finite series of causes and ultimately a First Cause, or God.

PROOF FROM MOTION

We are certain, because it is evident to our senses, that in the world some things are in motion. It is equally clear to us that whatever is in motion was moved by something else. If a thing is at rest, it is only potentially in motion. Motion occurs when something poten-tially in motion is moved and is then actually in motion; motion is the transformation of *potentiality* into *actuality*. Imagine a series of dominoes standing next to each other. When they are set up in a row, it can be said that they are all potentially in motion, although actually at rest. Consider a particular domino. Its potentiality is that it will not move until it is knocked over by the one next to it. It will move only if it is moved by something actually moving. From this fact, Aquinas drew the general conclusion that nothing can be transformed from a state of potentiality by something that is also in a mere state of potentiality. A domino cannot be knocked over by another domino that is standing still. "Potentiality" means the absence of something and is therefore, in this case, the absence of motion; for this reason, potential motion in the neighboring domino cannot move the next one because potential motion is nonmotion, and you cannot derive motion from nonmotion. As Aquinas says, "nothing can be reduced from potentiality to actuality except by something in a state of actuality." Moreover, it is not possible for the same thing, for example, a domino, to be *at the same time* in actuality and potentiality regarding motion. What is actually at rest cannot be simultaneously in motion. This means that the particular domino cannot be simultaneously the thing that is moved and also the mover. Something potentially in motion cannot move itself. Whatever is moved must be moved by another. The last domino to fall was potentially in motion, but so was the next to the last. Each domino could become a *mover* only after it had been moved by the one prior to it. Here we come to Aquinas's decisive point: If we are to account for motion, we cannot do so by going back in an infinite regress. If we must say about each mover in this series that it in turn was moved by a prior mover, we would never discover the source of motion, because every mover would then be only potentially in motion. Even if such a series went back infinitely, each one would still be only potential, and from that no actual motion could ever emerge. The fact is, however, that there *is* motion. There must therefore be a mover which is able to move things but which does not itself have to be moved, and this, says Aquinas, "everyone understands to be God."

Two things need to be noticed about this proof. First, Aquinas does not limit his concept of motion to things such as dominoes, that is, to locomotion. He has in mind the broadest meaning of motion so as to include the idea of generation and creation. Second, for Aquinas, the First Mover is not simply the first member of a long series of causes, as though such a mover were just like the others, its only distinction being that it is the first. Clearly, this could not be the case, for then this mover would also be only potentially in motion. The First Mover must therefore be pure actuality without potentiality and is therefore first not in the series but in actuality.

PROOF FROM EFFICIENT CAUSE

We experience various kinds of effects, and in every case we assign an efficient cause to each effect. The efficient cause of the statue is the work of the sculptor. If we took away the activity of the sculptor, we should not have the effect, the statue. But there is an order of efficient causes; the parents of the sculptor are his efficient cause. Workers in the quarry are the efficient cause of this particular piece of marble's availability to the sculptor. There is, in short, an intricate order of efficient causes traceable in a series. Such a series of causes is demanded because no event can be its own cause; the sculptor does not cause himself, and the statue does not cause itself. A cause is prior to an effect. Nothing, then, can be prior to itself; hence events demand a prior cause. Each prior cause must itself have its own cause, as parents must have their own parents. But it is impossible to go backward to infinity, because all the causes in the series depend on a first efficient cause that has made all the other causes to be actual causes. There must then be a first efficient cause "to which everyone gives the name of God."

PROOF FROM NECESSARY VERSUS POSSIBLE BEING

In nature we find that things are possible to be and not to be. Such things are *possible* or *contingent* because they do not always exist; they are *generated* and are *corrupted.* There was a time when a tree did not exist; it exists, and finally it goes out of existence. To say, then, that it is *possible* for the tree to exist must mean that it is also possible for it *not* to exist. The possibility for the tree *not* to exist must be taken two ways; first, it is possible for the tree *never* to come into existence, and second, once the tree is in existence, there is the possibility that it will go out of existence. To say, then, that something is *possible* must mean that at both ends of its being, that is, before it comes into being and after it goes out of being, it does not exist. *Possible* being has this fundamental characteristic, namely, that it can *not-be.* It can not-be not only after having existed but more important *before* it is generated, caused, or moved. For this reason, something that is possible, which can not-be, in fact "at some time is not."

All *possible* beings, therefore, at one time did not exist, will exist for a time, and will finally pass out of existence. Once possible things *do* come into existence, they can cause other similar possible beings to be generated, such as when parents beget children, and so on. But Aquinas is making the argument that possible beings do not have their existence in themselves or from their own essence, and if *all* things in reality were only *possible*, that is, if about *every-thing* one could say that it could not-be *both* before it is and after it is, then at one time there was nothing in existence. But if there was a time when nothing existed, then nothing could start to be and even now there would be nothing in existence, "because that which does not exist begins to exist only through something already existing." But since our experience clearly shows us that things do exist, this must mean that not all beings are *merely possible*. Aquinas concludes from this that "there must exist something the existence of which is necessary." We must therefore admit, he says, "the existence of some being having of itself its own necessity, and not receiving it from another, but rather causing in others this necessity. This all men speak of as God."

PROOF FROM THE DEGREES OF PERFECTION

In our experience we find that some beings are more and some less good, true, and noble. But these and other ways of comparing things are possible only because things resemble in their different ways something that is the maximum. There must be something that is truest, noblest, and best. Similarly, since it can be said about things that they have more or less being, or a lower or higher form of being, such as when we compare a stone with a rational creature, there must also be "something which is most being." Aquinas then argues that the maximum in any genus is the cause of everything in that genus, as fire, which is the maximum of heat, is the cause of all hot things. From this Aquinas concludes that "there must also be something which is to all beings the cause of their being, goodness, and every other perfection; and this we call God."

PROOF FROM THE ORDER OF THE UNIVERSE

We see that things which do not possess intelligence, such as parts of the natural world or parts of the human body, behave in an orderly manner. They act in special and predictable ways to achieve certain ends or functions. Because these things act to achieve ends always, or nearly always, in the same way and to achieve the best results, "it is plain that they achieve their end, not fortuitously, but designedly." But things that lack intelligence, such as an ear or a lung, cannot carry out a function unless they are directed by something that does have intelligence, as the arrow is directed by the archer. Aquinas concludes, therefore, that "some intelligent being exists by whom all natural things are directed to their ends; and this being we call God."

The two major characteristics of these five proofs are (1) their foundation in sense experience and (2) their reliance on the notion of causality. In addition, the first three proofs do not as obviously lead to the idea of what all men call God, a personal being. These are, however, proofs that Aquinas considered philosophical corroborations of the religious notion of God, and they, it must be remembered, were composed in the context of his theological task. Moreover, many of Aquinas's illustrations, such as, for example, that fire is the maximum of heat, and his assumptions, that order, for example, presupposes an intelligence independent of the natural process, raise for the modern mind critical questions. Still, Aquinas was deliberately employing the insights he had derived from Aristotle, Maimonides, and Albert the Great in order, by means of these philosophical arguments, to make the religious claim of God's existence intellectually defensible. His own view was that the argument from motion was the most obvious of all. The third one, comparing possible and necessary being, appears, however, to contain the most philosophical rigor and the basic assumption of all the other proofs, namely, that possible beings must derive their existence from something that has its existence necessarily in itself.

Hume

David Hume was born in Edinburgh in 1711 of Scottish parents. He attended the University of Edinburgh but did not graduate. His parents wanted him to be a lawyer, but he rejected their wishes, regarding, as he said, "every object as contemptible except the improvement of my talents in literature." His first book, *A Treatise of Human Nature* (1739), was not an immediate success, and Hume expressed his disappointment by saying that "never literary attempt was more unfortunate, [for the book] fell deadborn from the press." His next book *Essays Moral and Political* (1741) was an immediate success. Hume then revised his first book and gave it a new title, *An Enquiry concerning Human Understanding*. He wrote several other books, including *Dialogues on Natural Religion*. Hume became very famous. For a while he was secretary to the British Ambassador in France and was for two years Under-Secretary of State. He returned in 1769 to Edinburgh, where his house became the gathering place of distinguished persons. By now he was wealthy and lived his last seven years quietly among his friends and admirers, among whom Adam Smith was included. He died in 1776 at the age of sixty-five. He became the most influential member of the group (which also included Locke and Berkeley) known as the British Empiricists, who said that knowledge is limited to experience ("empiricism": the practice of emphasizing experience or observation rather than intuition or speculation in the pursuit of knowledge).

Hume and the Argument from Design

It was inevitable that Hume's rigorous premise that "our ideas reach no further than our experience" would lead him to raise skeptical questions about the existence of God. Most attempts to demonstrate the existence of God rely on some version of causality. Among these, the argument from *design* has always made a powerful impact on the mind. Hume was aware of the power of this argument, but he quickly sorted out the elements of the problem, leaving the argument with less than its usual force.

The argument from design begins with the observance of a beautiful order in nature. This order resembles the kind of order the human mind is able to impose on unthinking materials. From this preliminary observation, the mind concludes that unthinking materials do not contain the principles of orderliness within themselves: "Throw several pieces of steel together, without shape or form; they will never arrange themselves so as to compose a watch. . . . " Order, it is held, requires the activity of mind, an orderer. Our experience tells us that neither a watch nor a house can come into being without a watchmaker or an architect. From this it is inferred that the natural order bears an analogy to the order fashioned by human effort and that just as the watch requires an ordering cause, so the natural order of the universe requires one. But such an inference, says Hume, "is uncertain, because the subject lies entirely beyond the reach of human experience."

If the whole argument from design rests on the proposition *"that the cause or causes of order in the universe probably bear some remote analogy to human intelligence,"* then, says Hume, the argument cannot prove as much as it claims. Hume's criticism of the idea of causality has particular force here. Since we derive the idea of cause from repeated observations of the contiguity, priority, and constant conjunction of two things, how can we assign a cause to the universe when we have never experienced the universe as related to anything we might consider a cause? The use of analogy does not solve the problem, since the analogy between a watch and the universe is not exact. Why not consider the universe the product of a vegetative process instead of a rational designer? And even if the cause of the universe is something like an intelligence, how can moral characteristics be ascribed to such a being? Moreover, if analogies are to be used, which one should be selected? Houses and ships are frequently designed by a group of designers: Should we say there are many gods? Sometimes experimental models are built with no present knowledge of what the finished form will be like: Is the universe a trial model or the final design? By this line of probing, Hume wished to emphasize that the order of the universe is simply an empirical fact and that we cannot infer from it the existence of God. This does not make Hume an atheist. He is simply testing our idea of God the way he had tested our ideas of the *self* and *substance* by his rigorous principle of empiricism. He ends, to be sure, as a skeptic, but finally makes the telling point that "to whatever length any one may push his speculative principles of scepticism, he must act and live and converse like other men. . . . It is impossible for him to persevere in total scepticism, or make it appear in his conduct for a few hours."

Kant's Criticism of Traditional Proofs

With his critical estimate of the powers and scope of human reason, it was inevitable that Kant would reject the traditional proofs for the existence of God, namely, the *ontological, cosmological,* and *teleological* proofs. His argument against the *ontological* proof is that it is all a verbal exercise, for the essence of this proof is the assertion that since we have the idea of a most perfect being, it would be contradictory to say that such a being does not exist. Such a denial would be contradictory because the concept of a perfect being necessarily includes the predicate of *existence*. That is, a being that does not exist can hardly be considered a perfect being. But Kant argues that this line of reasoning is "taken from judgments, not from things and their existence," that the idea of God is made to have the predicate of existence by simply fashioning the concept in such a way that existence is made to be included in the idea of a perfect being. This argument nowhere indicates why it is necessary to have the subject, *God*. There would be a contradiction if a perfect being did exist and we denied that such a being was omnipotent. But to say that we avoid a contradiction by agreeing that a supreme being is omnipotent does not by itself demonstrate that such a being exists. Moreover, to deny that God exists is not simply to deny a predicate but to abandon the subject and thereby all the predicates that go with it, and "if we reject subject and predicate alike, there is no contradiction; for nothing is then left to be contradicted." Kant concluded, therefore, that "all the trouble and labour bestowed on the famous ontological or cartesian proof of the existence of a supreme being from concepts alone is trouble and labour wasted. A man might as well expect to become richer in knowledge by the aid of mere ideas as a merchant to increase his wealth by adding some noughts to his cash account."

Whereas the ontological proof begins with an idea (of a perfect being), the *cosmological* proof "takes its stand on experience" for it says that "I exist, therefore, an absolutely necessary being exists," on the assumption that if anything exists, an absolutely necessary being must also exist. The error of this argument, according to Kant, is that while it begins with experience, it soon moves beyond experience. Within the realm of sense experience it is legitimate to infer a cause for each event, but "the principle of causality has no meaning and no criterion for its application save only in the sensible world." Here is the direct application of Kant's critical method, for he argues that we cannot employ certain categories of the mind in trying to describe realities beyond sense experience. The cosmological argument cannot, therefore, securely lead us to a first cause of all things, for the most we can infer from our experience of things is a regulative idea of God. Whether there actually is such a being, a ground of all contingent things, raises the same question posed by the ontological argument, namely, whether we

Kant (*New York Public Library Picture Collection*)

can successfully bridge the gap between our idea of a perfect being and demonstrative proof of its existence.

Similarly, the *teleological* argument begins with considerable persuasiveness, for it says that "in the world we everywhere find clear signs of an order in accordance with a determinate purpose.

. . . The diverse things could not of themselves have cooperated, by so great a combination of diverse means, to the fulfillment of determinate final purposes, had they not been chosen and designed for these purposes by an ordering rational principle in conformity with underlying ideas." To this argument Kant replies that it may well be that our experience of order in the universe suggests an orderer, but order in the world does not demonstrate that the material stuff of the world could not exist without an orderer. The most this argument from design can prove, says Kant, "is an *architect* of the world who is always very much hampered by the adaptability of the material in which he works, not a *creator* of the world to whose idea everything is subject." To prove the existence of a creator leads us back to the cosmological argument with its idea of causality, but since we cannot use the category of causality beyond the things in experience, we are left simply with an idea of a first cause or creator, and this takes us back to the ontological argument, with its deficiencies. Kant's conclusion, therefore, is that we cannot use theoretical principles, which have no application beyond the field of sense experience, to demonstrate the existence of God.

It follows from Kant's critical remarks about the "proofs," however, that just as we cannot demonstrate God's existence, neither can we demonstrate that God does not exist. By pure reason alone we can neither prove nor disprove God's existence. If, therefore, the existence of God cannot be effectively dealt with by the theoretical reason, which Kant has gone to such lengths to show has relevance only in the realm of sense experience, some other aspect of reason must be considered as the source of the idea of God. Thus despite the inability of human reason to prove the existence of God, the idea of God has importance in Kant's philosophy.

READING

THAT GOD TRULY EXISTS
Anselm

After I had published, at the pressing entreaties of several of my brethren, a certain short tract [the *Monologium*] as an example of mediation on the meaning of faith from the point of view of one seeking, through silent reasoning within himself, things he knows not—reflecting that this was made up of a connected chain of many arguments, I began to wonder if perhaps it might be possible to find one single argument that for its proof required no other save itself, and that by itself would suffice to prove that God really exists, that He is the supreme good needing no other and is He whom all things have need of for their being and well-being, and also to prove whatever we believe about the Divine Being. . . .

Judging, then, that what had given me such joy to discover would afford pleasure, if it were written down, to anyone who might read it, I have written the following short tract dealing with this question as well as several others, from the point of view of one trying to raise his mind to contemplate God and seeking to understand what he believes. . . .

Well then, Lord, You who give understanding to faith, grant me that I may understand, as much as You see fit, that You exist as we believe You to exist, and that You are what we believe You to be. Now we believe that You are something than which nothing greater can be thought. Or can it be that a thing of such a nature does not exist, since "the Fool has said in his heart, there is no God" [Ps. xiii. i, lii. i]? But surely, when this same Fool hears what I am speaking about, namely, "something-than-which-nothing-greater-can-be-thought," he understands what he hears, and what he understands is in his mind, even if he does not understand that it actually exists. For it is one thing for an object to exist in the mind, and another thing to understand that an object actually exists. Thus, when a painter plans beforehand what he is going to execute, he has [the picture] in his mind, but he does not yet think that it actually exists because he has not yet executed it. However, when he has actually painted it, then he both has it in his mind and understands that it exists because he has now made it. Even the Fool, then, is forced to agree that something-than-which-nothing-

From St. Anselm, *Proslogium*, trans. M. J. Charlesworth, Clarendon Press, Oxford, 1965.

greater-can-be-thought exists in the mind, since he understands this when he hears it, and whatever is understood is in the mind. And surely that-than-which-a-greater-cannot-be-thought cannot exist in the mind alone. For if it exists solely in the mind even, it can be thought to exist in reality also, which is greater. If then that-than-which-a-greater-cannot-be-thought exists in the mind alone, this same that-than-which-a-greater-*cannot*-be-thought is that-than-which-a-greater-*can*-be-thought. But this is obviously impossible. Therefore there is absolutely no doubt that something-than-which-a-greater-cannot-be-thought exists both in the mind and in reality.

READING

THE FIVE WAYS

Aquinas

. . . The existence of God can be proved in five ways.

The first and more manifest way is the argument from motion. It is certain, and evident to our senses, that in the world some things are in motion. Now whatever is moved is moved by another, for nothing can be moved except it is in potentiality to that towards which it is moved; whereas a thing moves inasmuch as it is in act. For motion is nothing else than the reduction of something from potentiality to actuality. But nothing can be reduced from potentiality to actuality, except by something in a state of actuality. Thus that which is actually hot, as fire, makes wood, which is potentially hot, to be actually hot, and thereby moves and changes it. Now it is not possible that the same thing should be at once in actuality and potentiality in the same respect but only in different respects. For what is actually hot cannot simultaneously be potentially hot; but it is simultaneously potentially cold. It is therefore impossible that in the same respect and in the same way a thing should be both mover and moved, i.e., that it should move itself. Therefore, whatever is moved must be moved by another, and that by another. But this cannot go on to infinity, because then there would

From *Introduction to St. Thomas Aquinas*, edited by Anton Pegis. The Modern Library, Random House, Inc., New York, 1965.

be no first mover, and consequently, no other mover, seeing that subsequent movers move only inasmuch as they are moved by the first mover; as the staff moves only because it is moved by the hand. Therefore it is necessary to arrive at a first mover, moved by no other; and this everyone understands to be God.

The second way is from the nature of efficient cause. In the world of sensible things we find there is an order of efficient causes. There is no case known (neither is it, indeed, possible) in which a thing is found to be the efficient cause of itself; for so it would be prior to itself, which is impossible. Now in efficient causes it is not possible to go on to infinity, because in all efficient causes following in order, the first is the cause of the intermediate cause, and the intermediate is the cause of the ultimate cause, whether the intermediate cause be several, or one only. Now to take away the cause is to take away the effect. Therefore, if there be no first cause among efficient causes, there will be no ultimate, nor any intermediate, cause. But if in efficient causes it is possible to go on to infinity, there will be no first efficient cause, neither will there be an ultimate effect, nor any intermediate efficient causes; all of which is plainly false. Therefore it is necessary to admit a first efficient cause, to which everyone gives the name of God.

The third way is taken from possibility and necessity, and runs thus. We find in nature things that are possible to be and not to be, since they are found to be generated, and to be corrupted, and consequently, it is possible for them to be and not to be. But it is impossible for these always to exist, for that which can not-be at some time is not. Therefore, if everything can not-be, then at one time there was nothing in existence. Now if this were true, even now there would be nothing in existence, because that which does not exist begins to exist only through something already existing. Therefore, if at one time nothing was in existence, it would have been impossible for anything to have begun to exist; and thus even now nothing would be in existence—which is absurd. Therefore, not all being are merely possible, but there must exist something the existence of which is necessary. But every necessary thing either has its necessity caused by another, or not. Now it is impossible to go on to infinity in necessary things which have their necessity caused by another, as has been already proved in regard to efficient causes. Therefore we cannot but admit the existence of some being having of itself its own necessity, and not receiving it from another, but rather causing in others their necessity. This all men speak of as God.

The fourth way is taken from the gradation to be found in things. Among beings there are some more and some less good, true, noble, and the like. But *more* and *less* are predicated of different things according as they resemble in their different ways something which is the maximum, as a thing is said to be hotter according as it more nearly resembles that which is hottest; so that there is something which is truest, something best, something noblest, and consequently, something which is most being, for those things that are greatest in truth are greatest in being, as it is written in *Metaph. ii.* Now the maximum in any genus is the cause of all in that genus, as fire, which is the maximum of heat, is the cause of all hot things, as is said in the same book. Therefore there must also be something which is to all beings the cause of their being, goodness, and every other perfection; and this we call God.

The fifth way is taken from the governance of the world. We see that things which lack knowledge, such as natural bodies, act for an end, and this is evident from their acting always, or nearly always, in the same way, so as to obtain the best result. Hence it is plain that they achieve their end, not fortuitously, but designedly. Now whatever lacks knowledge cannot move towards an end, unless it be directed by some being endowed with knowledge and intelligence; as the arrow is directed by the archer. Therefore some intelligent being exists by whom all natural things are directed to their end; and this being we call God.

READING

EVIL AND THE PROOF FROM DESIGN

Hume

If a person whom we shall suppose utterly unacquainted with the universe were assured that it were the production of a very good, wise, and powerful Being, however finite, he would, from his conjectures, form *beforehand* a different notion of it from what we find it to be by experience; nor would he ever imagine, merely from these attributes of the cause of which he is informed, that the effect could be so full of vice and misery and disorder, as it appears in this life. Supposing now that this person were brought into the world, still assured that it was the workmanship of such a sublime and benevolent Being, he might, perhaps, be surprised at the disappointment, but would never retract his former belief if founded on any very solid argument, since such a limited intelligence must be sensible of his own blindness and ignorance, and must allow that there may be many solutions of

From David Hume, *Dialogues concerning Natural Religion*, published 1779.

those phenomena which will forever escape his comprehension. But supposing, which is the real case with regard to man, that this creature is not antecedently convinced of a supreme intelligence, benevolent, and powerful, but is left to gather such a belief from the appearances of things—this entirely alters the case, nor will he ever find any reason for such a conclusion. He may be fully convinced of the narrow limits of his understanding, but this will not help him in forming an inference concerning the goodness of superior powers, since he must form that inference from what he knows, not from what he is ignorant of. The more you exaggerate his weakness and ignorance, the more diffident you render him, and give him the greater suspicion that such subjects are beyond the reach of his faculties. You are obliged, therefore, to reason with him merely from the known phenomena, and to drop every arbitrary supposition or conjecture.

Did I show you a house or palace where there was not one apartment convenient or agreeable, where the windows, doors, fires, passages, stairs, and the whole economy of the building were the source of noise, confusion, fatigue, darkness, and the extremes of heat and cold, you would certainly blame the contrivance, without any further examination. The architect would in vain display his subtilty, and prove to you that, if this door or that window were altered, greater ills would ensue. What he says may be strictly true: the alteration of one particular, while the other parts of the building remain, may only augment the inconveniences. But still you would assert in general that, if the architect had had skill and good intentions, he might have formed such a plan of the whole, and might have adjusted the parts in such a manner as would have remedied all or most of these inconveniences. His ignorance, or even your own ignorance of such a plan, will never convince you of the impossibility of it. If you find any inconveniences and deformities in the building, you will always, without entering into any detail, condemn the architect.

In short, I repeat the question: Is the world, considered in general and as it appears to us in this life, different from what a man or such a limited being would, *beforehand*, expect from a very powerful, wise, and benevolent Deity? It must be strange prejudice to assert the contrary. And from thence I conclude that, however consistent the world may be, allowing certain suppositions and conjectures with the idea of such a Deity, it can never afford us an inference concerning his existence. . . .

Look round this universe. What an immense profusion of beings, animated and organized, sensible and active! You admire this prodigious variety and fecundity. But inspect a little more narrowly these living existences, the only beings worth regarding. How hostile and destructive to each other! How insufficient all of them for their own happiness! How contemptible or odious to the spectator! The whole presents nothing but the idea of a blind nature, impregnated by a great vivifying principle, and pouring forth from her lap, without discernment or parental care, her maimed and abortive children!

READING

CRITIQUE OF PURE REASON
Kant

THE IMPOSSIBILITY OF THE PHYSICO-THEOLOGICAL [TELEOLOGICAL] PROOF

The chief points of the physico-theological proof are as follows: (1) In the world we everywhere find clear signs of an order in accordance with a determinate purpose, carried out with great wisdom; and this in a universe which is indescribably varied in content and unlimited in extent. (2) This purposive order is quite alien to the things of the world, and only belongs to them contingently; that is to say, the diverse things could not of themselves have co-operated, by so great a combination of diverse means, to the fulfilment of determinate final purposes, had they not been chosen and designed for these purposes by an ordering rational principle in conformity with underlying ideas. (3) There exists, therefore, a sublime and wise cause (or more than one), which must be the cause of the world not merely as a blindly working all-powerful nature, by *fecundity,* but as intelligence, through *freedom.* (4) The unity of this cause may be inferred from the unity of the reciprocal relations existing between the parts of the world, as members of an artfully arranged structure—inferred with certainty in so far as our observation suffices for its verification, and beyond these limits with probability, in accordance with the principles of analogy. . . .

The inference, therefore, is that the order and purposiveness everywhere observable throughout the world may be regarded as a completely contingent arrangement, and that we may argue to the existence of a cause *proportioned* to it. But the concept of this cause must enable us to know something quite *determinate* about it, and can therefore be no other than the concept of a being who possesses all might, wisdom, etc. in a word, all the perfection which is proper to an all-sufficient being. For the predicates—"very great," "astounding," "immeasurable" in power and excellence—give no determinate concept at all, and do not really tell us what the thing is in itself. They are only relative representations of the magnitude of the object, which the observer, in contemplating the world, compares

From Immanuel Kant, *Critique of Pure Reason*, trans. Norman Kemp Smith, St. Martin's Press, Macmillan & Co., Ltd., London, 1969.

with himself and with his capacity of comprehension, and which are equally terms of eulogy whether we be magnifying the object or be depreciating the observing subject in relation to that object. Where we are concerned with the magnitude (of the perfection) of a thing, there is no determinate concept except that which comprehends all possible perfection; and in that concept only the allness (*omnitudo*) of the reality is completely determined.

Now no one, I trust, will be so bold as to profess that he comprehends the relation of the magnitude of the world as he has observed it (alike as regards both extent and content) to omnipotence, of the world order to supreme wisdom, of the world unity to the absolute unity of its Author, etc. Physico-theology is therefore unable to give any determinate concept of the supreme cause of the world, and cannot therefore serve as the foundation of a theology which is itself in turn to form the basis of religion.

To advance to absolute totality by the empirical road is utterly impossible. None the less this is what is attempted in the physico-theological proof. What, then, are the means which have been adopted to bridge this wide abyss?

The physico-theological argument can indeed lead us to the point of admiring the greatness, wisdom, power, etc., of the Author of the world, but can take us no further. Accordingly, we then abandon the argument from empirical grounds of proof, and fall back upon the contingency which, in the first steps of the argument, we had inferred from the order and purposiveness of the world. With this contingency as our sole premise, we then advance, by means of transcendental concepts alone, to the existence of an absolutely necessary being, and (as a final step) from the concept of the absolute necessity of the first cause to the completely determinate or determinable concept of that necessary being, namely, to the concept of an all-embracing reality. Thus the physico-theological proof, failing in its undertaking, has in face of this difficulty suddenly fallen back upon the cosmological proof; and since the latter is only a disguised ontological proof, it has really achieved its purpose by pure reason alone—although at the start it disclaimed all kinship with pure reason and professed to establish its conclusions on convincing evidence derived from experience.

Thus the physico-theological proof of the existence of an original or supreme being rests upon the cosmological proof, and the cosmological upon the ontological. And since, besides these three, there is no other path open to speculative reason, the ontological proof from pure concepts of reason is the only possible one, if indeed any proof of a proposition so far exalted above all empirical employment of the understanding is possible at all.

CHAPTER 17

RELIGION AND DAILY LIFE

Kierkegaard

Søren Kierkegaard was born in 1813 in Copenhagen. He went to the university there to study theology but was instead captivated by philosophy. He reacted against the dominant mode of philosophy of his day, namely, against Hegel's system of universal knowledge. He was influenced by Friedrich Schelling (1775–1854), a former classmate of Hegel's, who ultimately rejected Hegel's philosophy. Schelling turned from Hegel's universal system to an emphasis on the individual, calling attention to the irrational and darker aspects of man's deepest nature. George Wilhelm Friedrich Hegel (1770–1831) had been professor of philosophy at the University of Berlin, where he formulated a highly technical philosophy attempting to include all of existence in an objective system. Kierkegaard attacked this approach on the grounds that it overlooked the subjective nature of personal life with all its agonizing requirements for making decisions and commitments. Kierkegaard's father left him a considerable fortune, providing the resources for Søren's brilliant literary career, during which he produced over a dozen major works. His father's strict religious convictions coupled with a brooding melancholy strongly affected Kierkegaard. So did Søren's love affair with Regine Olsen. After breaking off their engagement, Kierkegaard left her and spent six months at the University of Berlin, where he wrote his book *EITHER/OR* (1843), which can be read as an attempt to explain his attitude toward her, but it is at the same time a major treatise on the crucial role of decision and choice in human existence. When he died in 1855 at the age of forty-two, he left his remaining possessions to Regine, who by then was happily married to a governor in the Danish West Indies. Kierkegaard's enormous literary output remained almost unnoticed by the world until the Second World War when translations began to appear, creating a powerful impact on contemporary existentialism.

Daily life is the arena where a person's religion is put into practice. Each person has to contend with his human condition. To be alive, to exist, requires that we make countless decisions every day. Philosophers who are especially concerned with the human condition of the existing individual are known as "existentialists." There are theistic as well as atheistic existentialists. Kierkegaard and Sartre represent these two points of view respectively. Søren Kierkegaard writes from a strong Christian perspective, while Jean-Paul Sartre, as we noticed in Chapter 7, tries to show what it means for daily life if one denies the existence of God.

Many of the themes of contemporary existentialism were first expressed in the writings of Søren Kierkegaard. Born in Copenhagen in 1813, he spent his short life in a brilliant literary career, producing an extraordinary number of books before his death in 1855 at the age of forty-two. Although his books were forgotten soon after his death, they made an enormous impact after being rediscovered by some German scholars in the early decades of the twentieth century.

At the University of Copenhagen Kierkegaard was trained in Hegel's philosophy and was not favorably impressed by it. When he heard Schelling's lectures at Berlin, which were critical of Hegel, Kierkegaard agreed with this attack on Germany's greatest speculative thinker. "If Hegel had written the whole of his *Logic* and then said . . . that it was merely an experiment in thought," wrote Kierkegaard, "then he could certainly have been the greatest thinker who ever lived. As it is, he is merely comic." What made Hegel comic for Kierkegaard was that this great German philosopher had tried to capture all of reality in his system of thought, yet in the process lost the most important element, namely, *existence*. For Kierkegaard, the term "existence" was reserved for the individual human being. To exist, he said, implies being a certain kind of individual, an individual who strives, who considers alternatives, who chooses, who decides, and who, above all, commits himself. Virtually none of these acts were implied in Hegel's philosophy. Kierkegaard's whole career might well be considered as a self-conscious revolt against abstract thought and an attempt on his part to live up to the admonition of one of Hegel's former students, Ludwig Feuerbach: "Do not wish to be a philosopher in contrast to being a man . . . do not think as a thinker . . . think as a living, real being . . . think in Existence."

To "think in Existence" meant for Kierkegaard to recognize that one is faced with personal choices. Men find themselves constantly in an "existential situation." For this reason, their thinking ought to deal with their own personal situation with a view to coming to terms with the problem of alternatives and choices. Hegel's philosophy falsified man's understanding of reality because it shifted attention away from the concrete individual to the concept of universals. It called upon men *to think* instead of *to be*, to think the Absolute Thought instead of being involved in decisions and commitments. Kierkegaard drew the distinction between the *spectator* and the *actor*, arguing that only the actor is involved in existence. To be sure, the spectator can be said to exist, but the term "existence" does not properly belong to inert or inactive things, whether these be spectators or stones.

Kierkegaard illustrated this distinction by comparing two kinds of men in a wagon, one who holds the reins in his hands but is asleep and the other who is fully awake. In the first case, the horse goes along the familiar road without any direction from the sleeping man, whereas in the other case the man is truly a driver. Surely, in one sense it can be said that both men exist, but Kierkegaard insists that existence must refer to a quality in the individual, namely, his conscious participation in an act. Only the conscious driver exists, and so, too, only a person who is engaged in conscious activity of will and choice can be truly said to exist. Thus while both the spectator and the actor exist in a sense, only the actor is involved in existence.

Kierkegaard (*Royal Danish Ministry*)

Kierkegaard's criticism of rational knowledge was severe. He revolted against the rational emphasis in Greek wisdom, which, he charged, had permeated subsequent philosophy and Christian theology. His specific argument was that Greek philosophy had been too greatly influenced by a high regard for mathematics. Although he did not want to reject either mathematics or science in their proper uses, he did reject the assumption that the mode of thought characteristic of science could be successfully employed when trying to understand human nature. Mathematics and science have no place for the human individual, only for the general, the universal. Likewise, Platonic philosophy emphasizes the universal, the Form, the True, the Good. Plato's whole assumption was that if one *knew* the Good, he would do it. Kierkegaard thought that such an approach to ethics was a falsification of man's real predicament.

What Kierkegaard wanted to underscore was that even when a person has knowledge, he is still in the predicament of having to make a decision. The grand formulations of philosophical systems are, in the long run, only prolonged detours, which eventually come to nothing unless they lead attention back once again to the individual. To be sure, there are problems that can be solved by mathematics and science as well as by ethics and metaphysics. But over against such universal or general problems stands life, each person's life, making demands on the individual, and at these critical moments, general and abstract thought do not help.

Kierkegaard saw in the biblical story of Abraham the typical condition of man: "God did tempt Abraham and said unto him, Abraham: and he said, here I am. And he said, take now thy son, thine only son, Isaac, whom thou lovest." What kind of knowledge can help Abraham decide whether to obey God, to sacrifice his son? The most poignant moments in life are personal ones, during which the individual becomes aware of himself as a subject. This subjective element is obscured if not denied by rational thought, which considers only man's objective characteristics, those characteristics which *all* men have in common. But subjectivity is what makes up each person's unique existence. For this reason, objectivity cannot give the whole truth about the individual self. This is why rational, mathematical, and scientific thought is incapable of guiding man to genuine existence.

Truth, said Kierkegaard, is subjectivity. By this strange notion he meant for existing, striving, deciding persons there is not available "out there" a prefabricated truth. Anticipating the pragmatic view of William James, who said that "truth is made" by an act of will, Kierkegaard wrote that what is "out there" is "an objective uncertainty"; he argued that "the highest truth attainable for an Existing individual" is simply "an objective uncertainty held fast in the most passionate personal experience. . . . " Whatever may have been his criticism of Plato, he did nevertheless find in Socrates's claim to ignorance a good example of this notion of truth, saying that "the Socratic ignorance which Socrates held fast with the entire passion of his personal experience, was thus an expression of the principle that the eternal truth is related to the Existing individual." This would suggest that the cultivation of the mind is not the only important or decisive thing in life. Of more consequence is the development and maturity of personality.

In describing man's *existential situation*, Kierkegaard distinguished between man's present estate, that is, what he now *is*, and what he *ought* to be or what he is *essentially*. There is, says Kierkegaard, a movement in the life of man from his *essential* to his *existential* condition, a movement from *essence* to *existence*. The traditional explanation of this movement in theology is made in terms of the doctrine of sin, of the Fall. Kierkegaard translated this doctrine into a profound psychological analysis, in which he isolated man's anxiety over his own finitude as the cause of his estrangement or alienation from his essential being. Sensing his insecurity and finitude, a person tries to "do something" to overcome his finitude, and invariably what he does only aggravates his problem by adding guilt and despair to his anxiety.

Kierkegaard has in mind throughout his analysis the Christian understanding of man. Man's *essential* nature entails his relation to God, the infinite. His *existential* condition is a consequence of his alienation from God. If, then, a person's actions drive him even farther from God, his alienation and despair are compounded. This is why it is not of any help to lose oneself in a crowd. Whatever be the nature of a crowd or collectivity—whether rich or poor or political in makeup or even a congregation in a church—in every case, says Kierkegaard, "a crowd in its very concept is the untruth, by reason of the fact that it renders the individual completely impenitent and irresponsible, or at least weakens his sense of responsibility by reducing it to a fraction." Being in a crowd, in short, unmakes one's nature as an individual by diluting the self. From the point of view of Christian faith, being thus immersed in a crowd appears as an attempt on man's part to derive some meaning for his existence. But this is a wrong attempt, for "to relate oneself to God is a far higher thing than to be related to" any other thing, whether a person, race, or even church. Until man does actualize his essential self in God, says Kierkegaard, his life is full of anxiety. His anxiety is caused by his awareness, however obscure, of a deep alienation of his existential from his essential self. This alienation creates in man a dynamic drive to recover his essential self. In describing this dynamic movement, Kierkegaard speaks of the "stages on life's way."

Three Stages

Kierkegaard's analysis of the "three stages" represents the movement of the self from one level of existence to another through an act of will, an act of choice. The first stage in this process, says Kierkegaard, is the *aesthetic stage.* At this level, a person behaves according to his impulses and emotions. Although he is not simply sensual at this stage, he is for the most part governed by his senses. For this reason, the aesthetic person knows nothing of any universal moral standards. He has no specific religious belief. His chief motivation is a desire to enjoy the widest variety of pleasures of the senses. His life has no principle of limitation except his own taste; he resents anything that would limit his vast freedom of choice. At this stage an individual can exist inasmuch as he deliberately chooses to be an aesthetic man. But even though *existence* can be achieved at this level, Kierkegaard injects the element of *quality* into the matter of existence. Later existentialists were to speak of this quality in terms of authenticity. That is, an individual on the aesthetic level is aware, notwithstanding his variety of sense experiences, that his life consists, or *ought* to consist, of more than his emotive and sense experiences.

Kierkegaard distinguishes between man's capacity to be *spirit* on the one hand and *sensuousness* on the other, calling the first the *building* and the second the *cellar.* Man, he says, "prefers to dwell in the cellar." To be able to make this distinction about someone else is one thing, but for each individual to have an awareness of these two possibilities within himself is what triggers the conflict of opposites in the individual. In experience, this conflict produces anxiety and despair when the individual discovers that he is in fact living in the "cellar" but that life at this level cannot possibly produce his *authentic* self (that is, essential self), cannot result in true *existence.* The individual is now face to face with an *either/or;* either he remains on the aesthetic level with its fatal attractions, whose limitations he knows, or he moves to the next stage. This transition, says Kierkegaard, cannot be made by thinking alone but must be achieved by making a decision, or by an act of will, by a commitment.

The second level is the *ethical stage.* Unlike the aesthetic man, who has no universal standards but only his own taste, the ethical man does recognize and accept rules of conduct that reason formulates. Moral rules give the ethical man's life the elements of form and consistency. Moreover, the ethical man accepts the limitations on his life that moral responsibility imposes. Kierkegaard illustrates the contrast between the aesthetic man and the ethical man in their attitude toward sexual behavior, saying that whereas the former yields to his impulses wherever there is an attraction, the ethical man accepts the obligations of marriage as an expression of reason, the universal reason of man. If Don Juan exemplifies the aesthetic man, it is Socrates who typifies the ethical man or the reign of the universal moral law. The ethical man has the sense of moral self-sufficiency; he takes a firm stand on moral questions and, as Socrates argued, assumes that to know the good is to do the good.

For the most part, the ethical man considers moral evil as being a product either of ignorance or of weakness of will. But the time comes, says Kierkegaard, when the process of choice begins to work in the consciousness of the ethical man. He begins to realize that he is involved in something more profound than an inadequate knowledge of the moral law or insufficient strength of will. He is, in short, doing something more serious than merely making mistakes. The ethical man ultimately comes to realize that he is in fact incapable of fulfilling the moral law, that he deliberately violates that law, and therefore he becomes conscious of his guilt. Guilt, or the sense of sin, says Kierkegaard, is what places before man a new *either/or.* Now he must either remain at the ethical level and try to fulfill the moral law, or he must respond to his new awareness, the awareness of his own finitude and estrangement from God to whom he belongs and from whom he must derive his strength. Again, man's movement from the ethical to the next stage cannot be achieved by thinking alone but by an act of commitment, by a *leap* of faith.

The difference between faith and reason is particularly striking for Kierkegaard when man arrives at the third level, the *religious stage.* Man's movement from the aesthetic to the ethical level required an act of choice and commitment; it ushered man into the presence of reason inasmuch as the moral law is an expression of the universal reason of man. But the movement from the ethical to the religious level is quite different. The leap of faith does not bring one into the presence of a God who can be philosophically or rationally described as the Absolute and Knowable Truth (and therefore objective) but into the presence of a Subject. The secret of religious consciousness, says Kierkegaard, "is in all eternity impossible because God is subject, and therefore exists only for subjectivity in inwardness."

At the ethical level, it is possible for the existing individual to give his life, as Socrates did, for the moral law that he rationally understands. But when it is a question of man's relation to God, there is available no rational or conceptual or objective knowledge about this relationship. The relationship between God and each individual is a unique and subjective experience. There is no way, prior to the actual relationship, to get any knowledge about it. Any attempt to get such objective knowledge about it is, says Kierkegaard, entirely an *approximation process.* Only an act of faith can assure the existing individual of his personal relation to God. That he must find his self-fulfillment in God becomes clear to him as he discovers the inadequacy of his existence at the aesthetic and ethical levels. Through despair and guilt he is brought to the decisive moment in life when he confronts the final *either/or* of faith.

The existence of God is suggested to man in his awareness of his self-alienation, that subjective awareness of the contrast between his existential and his essential self. That God has disclosed Himself in Christ is a further complication, indeed a *paradox.* To say, as Christian faith does, that God, the infinite, is revealed in Christ, the finite, is an extraordinary affront to human reason, "to the Jews a stumbling block and to the Greeks foolishness." But Kierkegaard wanted to maintain that the only way to cross the span between man and God, that "infinite qualitative distinction between time and eternity," is not through speculative reason, not even Hegel's, but through faith. Again, truth for Kierkegaard was a subjective matter, a consequence of commitment. Without risk, said Kierkegaard, there is no faith. And with faith, the existing individual realizes his true self.

Kierkegaard's existentialism can be summed up in his statement that "every human being must be assumed in essential possession of what essentially belongs to being a man." This being the case, "the task of the subjective thinker is to transform himself into an instrument that clearly and definitely expresses in existence whatever is essentially human." This is Kierkegaard's central point, namely, that each person possesses an essential self, which he *ought* to actualize. This essential self is fixed by the very fact that man must inescapably become related to God. To be sure, man can *exist* at any one of the three stages along life's way. But the experience of despair and guilt creates in man an awareness of qualitative differences in various modes of existence. Some modes of human existence are more authentic than others. But arriving at authentic existence is not a matter of the intellect; it is a matter of faith and commitment, a continuous process of choice by the existing individual in the presence of varieties of *either/or.*

READING

THE SERIOUSNESS OF MAKING CHOICES
Kierkegaard

This passage from *EITHER/OR* was written by Kierkegaard in the form of a letter from "Judge William" to his "young friend," giving some autobiographical references to Kierkegaard's character as a young university student.

My friend, *I think of my early youth,* when without clearly comprehending what it is to make a choice I listened with childish trust to the talk of my elders and the instant of choice was solemn and venerable, although in choosing I was only following the instructions of another person. I think of the occasions in my later life when I stood at the crossways, when my soul was matured in the hour of decision. I think of the many occasions in life less important but by no means indifferent to me, when it was a question of making a choice. For although there is only one situation in which either/or has absolute significance, namely, when truth, righteousness and holiness are lined up on one side, and lust and base propensities and obscure passions and perdition on the other; yet, it is always important to choose rightly, even as between things which one may innocently choose, it is important to test oneself, lest some day one might have to beat a retreat to the point from which one started, and might have reason to thank God if one had to reproach oneself for nothing worse than a waste of time. In common parlance I use these words [either/or] as others use them, and it would indeed be foolish to give up using them. And although my life now has to a certain degree its either/or behind it, yet I know well that it may still encounter many a situation where the either/or will have its full significance. I hope, however, that these words may find me in a worthy state of mind when they check me on my path, and I hope that I may be successful in choosing the right course; at all events, I shall endeavor to make the choice with real earnestness, and with that I venture, at least, to hope that I shall the sooner get out of the wrong path.

And now as for you—this phrase is only too often on your lips, it has almost become a byword with you. What significance has it for you? None at all. You, according to your own expression, regard it as a wink of the eye, a snap of the fingers, a *coup de main,* an abracadabra. At every opportunity you know how to introduce it, nor is it without effect; for it affects you as strong drink affects a neurasthenic, you become completely intoxicated by what you call the higher madness. . . . [You are like] that great thinker and true practical philosopher who said to a man who had insulted him by pulling off his hat and throwing it on the floor, "If you pick it up, you'll get a thrashing; if you don't pick it up, you'll also get a thrashing; now you can choose." You take great delight in "comforting" people when they have recourse to you in critical situations. You listen to their exposition of the case and then say, "Yes, I perceive perfectly that there are two possibilities, one can either do this or that. My sincere opinion and my friendly counsel is as follows: Do it / or don't do it—you will regret both." But he who mocks others mocks himself, and your rejoinder is not a mere nothing but a profound mockery of yourself, a sorry proof how limp your soul is, that your whole philosophy of life is concentrated in one single proposition, "I say merely either/or." In case this really were your serious meaning, there would be nothing one could do with you, one must simply put up with you as you are and deplore the fact that melancholy [literally, heavy-mindedness] or light-mindedness had enfeebled your spirit. Now on the contrary, since one knows very well that such is not the case, one is not

Kierkegaard house, between Town Hall and corner house, near Copenhagen
(*Royal Danish Ministry*)

tempted to pity you but rather to wish that some day the circumstances of your life may tighten upon you the screws in its rack and compel you to come out with what really dwells in you, may begin the sharper inquisition of the rack which cannot be beguiled by nonsense and witticisms. Life is a masquerade, you explain, and for you this is inexhaustible material for amusement; and so far, no one has succeeded in knowing you; for every revelation you make is always an illusion. Your occupation consists in preserving your hiding-place, and that you succeed in doing, for your mask is the most enigmatical of all. In fact you are nothing . . . an enigmatic figure on whose brow is inscribed Either/or—"For this," you say, "is my motto. . . ."

Now although nothing you say in that style has the slightest effect upon me, nevertheless, for your own sake I will reply to you. Do you not know that there comes a midnight hour when every one has to throw off his mask? Do you believe that life will always let itself be mocked? Do you think you can slip away a little before midnight in order to avoid this? Or are you not terrified by it? I have seen men in real life who so long deceived others that at last their true nature could not reveal itself; I have seen men who played hide and seek so long that at last madness through them obtruded disgustingly upon others their secret thoughts which hitherto they had proudly concealed. Or can you think of anything more frightful than that you thus would have lost the inmost and holiest thing of all in a man, the unifying power of personality? Truly, you should not jest with that which is not only serious but dreadful. In every man there is something which to a certain degree prevents him from becoming perfectly transparent to himself; and this may be the case in so high a degree, he may be so inexplicably woven into relationships of life which extend far beyond himself that he almost cannot reveal himself. But he who cannot reveal himself cannot love, and he who cannot love is the most unhappy man of all.

CHAPTER 18

SOUL
AND
BODY

Descartes and Ryle

René Descartes was born in France in 1596 and died in Sweden in 1650. He had gone to Sweden at the invitation of Queen Christina, who was impressed by his enormous intellectual achievements and wanted to receive instruction from him. The queen could see him only at five o'clock in the morning, and the unaccustomed exposure to the bitter cold at this early hour made him an easy prey to illness. Within a few months he suffered from fever and died at the age of fifty-four. Earlier he had left France and settled in Holland, where he wrote his celebrated books, including his *Discourse on Method* and *Meditations on First Philosophy*. Descartes was concerned chiefly with the problem of intellectual certainty. He had been educated, as he says, "at one of the most celebrated schools in Europe," and yet, "I found myself embarrassed with . . . many doubts and errors. . . . " The philosophy he learned left him confused and uncertain, for "no single thing is to be found in it which is not subject to dispute, and in consequence which is not dubious. . . . " He was most impressed by the exactness of mathematics and wondered whether it might be possible for the human mind to achieve this same exactness and certainty on all subjects. Descartes is usually called the "father of modern philosophy" because he set out to establish a new way of approaching philosophy. Instead of quoting earlier philosophers or relying on the authority of past traditions, he sought to build the foundation of knowledge simply on the powers of human reason.

In modern philosophy, it was René Descartes who formulated the notion that the soul, or mind, and body are two distinct substances. This theory of dualism has been subjected to a contemporary critical analysis by Oxford's Gilbert Ryle, who has called Descartes's theory the myth of the "Ghost in the Machine."

The whole drift of Descartes's thought is in the direction of dualism, that is, the notion that there are two different kinds of substances in nature. We know a substance by its attribute, and since we clearly and distinctly know two quite different attributes, namely, *thought* and *extension*, there must be two different substances, the spiritual and the corporeal, mind and body. Because Descartes defines a substance as "an existent thing which requires nothing but itself to exist," he considers each substance as thoroughly independent of the other. To know something about the mind, therefore, we need make no reference to the body, and similarly, the body can be thoroughly understood without any reference to mind. One of the consequences of this dualism was that Descartes hereby separated theology and science and assumed that there need be no conflict between them. Science would study physical nature in isolation of any other discipline, since material substance possessed its own sphere of operation and could be understood in terms of its own laws.

If thought and extension are so distinct and separate, how can one account for living things? Descartes reasoned that because living bodies partake of extension, they are part of the material world. Consequently, living bodies operate according to the same

Descartes and Queen Christina of Sweden (*Culver Pictures*)

mechanical and mathematical laws that govern other things in the material order. Speaking, for example, of animals, Descartes considered them to be *automata*, which behave automatically like machines, saying, "The greatest of all prejudices we have retained from infancy is that of believing that brutes think." We assume animals think, says Descartes, only because we see them act as humans do on occasion, as when dogs do acrobatic tricks. Because *men* have two principles of motion, one physical and the other mental, we assume that when animals perform humanlike acts their physical movements are caused by their mental powers. But Descartes saw no reason for attributing mental powers to animals, because all their motions, or actions, can be accounted for by mechanical considerations alone, since it is "nature which acts in them according to the disposition of their organs, just as a clock, which is only composed of wheels and weights. . . . " Thus animals are machines or automata. But what about human beings?

Many activities of the human body, said Descartes, are as mechanical as those of animals. Such physical acts as respiration, circulation of the blood, and digestion are automatic. The workings of the human body could be reduced, he thought, to physics. Every physical event can be adequately accounted for by a consideration of mechanical or efficient causes; there is no need to consider a final cause when describing the physical processes of the body. Moreover, since Descartes believed that the total quantity of motion in the universe is constant, he was led to conclude that the movements of the human body could not *originate* in the human mind or soul; the soul, he said, could only affect or alter the direction of the motion in certain elements and parts of the body. Just how the mind could do this was difficult to explain precisely, because thought and extension, mind and body, were for Descartes such different and separate substances. He said that the soul does not move the various parts of the body directly, but having "its principal seat in the brain," in the pineal gland, it comes first of all in contact with the "vital spirits" and through these interacts with the body. Clearly, Descartes tried to give the human body a mechanical explanation and at the same time preserve the possibility of the soul's influence, through the activity of the will, on human behavior. Man, therefore, unlike an animal, is capable of several kinds of activities; he can engage in pure thought, his mind can be influenced by physical sensations and perceptions, his body can be directed by his mind, and his body is moved by purely mechanical forces.

But Descartes's strict dualism made it difficult for him to describe how the mind and body could interact on each other. If each substance is completely independent, the mind must dwell in the body as a pearl in an oyster, or, to use Descartes's own metaphor, as a pilot in a ship. Scholastic philosophy had described man as a unity, in which mind is the form and body is the matter, and said that without one there could not be the other. Hobbes had reduced mind to bodies in motion and achieved the unity of man in that way.

But Descartes aggravated the separation of mind and body by his novel definition of "thinking." For Descartes included in the act of thinking some experiences that had traditionally been referred to the body, namely, the whole sphere of sense perceptions, for example, "feeling." When Descartes defines "what I am" as "a thing which thinks," he makes no mention of the body, for everything is included in "thinking": a thinking thing "is a thing which doubts, understands, affirms, denies, wills, refuses, and which also imagines and *feels*." Presumably the self could feel heat without a body. But here Descartes cannot, apparently, accept his own dualism, for he admits that "nature also teaches me by these sensations of pain, hunger, thirst, etc., that I am not lodged in my body as a pilot in a vessel, but that I am very closely united to it, and, so to speak, so intermingled with it that I seem to compose with it one whole." He attempted to locate the mind in the pineal gland, although even there the technical problem of interaction remains, for if there is interaction, there would have to be contact, and so mind would have to be extended. Concerning this problem, his rules of method did not lead him to any clear and distinct conclusion.

Ryle

Gilbert Ryle was born in 1900 and died in October of 1976. He spent most of his life at Oxford University. At age twenty-four he became a lecturer, and shortly after World War II he was appointed Oxford's Waynefleet Professor of Metaphysical Philosophy. His writings, including *Philosophical Arguments, Dilemmas,* and his influential article "Systematically Misleading Expression," established him as a significant figure in the world of philosophy. His book *The Concept of Mind,* published in London in 1949, is recognized as a classic. Our discussion of the main argument of this book and our brief selected reading from it will provide not only a provocative analysis of the mind-body problem but also a sample of Ryle's novel style of analytical philosophy.

As early as 1932, Ryle had already established his commitment to a new style in philosophy in his vigorous essay "Systematically Misleading Expressions." In this essay he wrote that to enquire "what it means to say so and so . . . is what philosophical analysis is, and . . . this is the sole and whole function of philosophy." Philosophy, says Ryle in the introduction to *The Concept of Mind*, does not give new information about minds, or for that matter about any other subject. "The philosophical arguments which constitute this book," he writes, "are not intended to increase what we know about minds, but to rectify the logical geography of the knowledge which we already possess."

The Ghost in the Machine

Ryle contends that the "official doctrine" about the nature and the place of minds is unsound and contradicts virtually everything we know about minds. In its simplest form, the official doctrine holds that every human being has both a mind and a body, that these two are coordinated, but that upon the death of the body, the mind may continue both to exist and exert its powers. Not only is this basic theory of mind-body incorrect, says Ryle, but it also leads to many other serious errors as one elaborates the implications of this doctrine.

It must follow from the official doctrine that each person has two collateral histories, one consisting of the events of his body and the other consisting of what transpires in and happens to his mind. Whereas human bodies are in space and are governed by mechanical physical laws, minds do not exist in space and are not subject to mechanical laws. A person's bodily life is publicly observable, while the activities of the mind are not accessible to external observers and are therefore private.

At this point a rather serious difficulty is encountered, because the contrast between the public character of the body and the private status of the mind requires one to say that the workings of the body are external whereas the workings of the mind are internal. It is then a short step to say that the mind is *in* the body. Although this language describing the place of the mind may be "metaphorical," since the mind which occupies no space could hardly be in any particular place, it is Ryle's contention that for the most part the contrast between the outer and inner realms is taken literally. Theorists in various disciplines take this contrast between "inner"

Ryle at Magdalen College, Oxford University (*Stumpf*)

and "outer" for granted. Stimuli are assumed to come from "out-side" and from far distances generating responses inside the skull. Activity of the mind is said to produce external events such as a motion of the hand or eye; smiles suggest activities of the mind. All this suggests, too, some mode of transaction between the mind and body, but there is no method for either observing or reporting just how these transactions between mind and body take place. No laboratory experiment can discover this relationship.

Self-analysis and introspection are special modes of perception requiring no physical eye and are so private as to be a special privilege of the mind itself, to which no one else has direct access. Even though one were to assume that minds similar to one's own are located in other human bodies, there is no way to discover what they do or undergo. And so, says Ryle, "absolute solitude is on this showing the ineluctable destiny of the soul. Only our bodies can meet." Accordingly, our language, which presumes to describe someone's mental activities such as knowing, hoping, dreading, or intending, must be construed as signifying special events in the secret histories of people. No one has direct access to these mental operations, neither biographer, teacher, critic, or friend. But because we know how to use mental-conduct words and to use them with general correctness, earlier philosophers constructed their theories of the nature and place of minds in conformity with the official doctrine. They sought to identify the logical geography of their mental-conduct concepts, and thus arose what Ryle has called the basically incorrect "dogma of the Ghost in the Machine."

The Category-Mistake

What Ryle finds wrong with the official doctrine of the Ghost in the Machine is not that some details here and there are ambiguous, but that the very principle on which the theory rests is false. It is not even a series of particular mistakes. It is, says Ryle, one big mistake of a unique kind; this he calls a *category-mistake*. The big mistake consists in representing the facts of mental life as if they belonged to one and the same logical category, whereas in fact they belong to quite different and separate ones. The official doctrine is therefore a "myth," and it is necessary to "rectify the logic of mental-conduct concepts."

To indicate what is meant by a category-mistake, Ryle describes the imaginary visit of a foreigner to Oxford for the first time. The visitor is shown the playing fields, museums, scientific laboratories, and some of the colleges. Having seen these various places, the visitor asks, "But where is the University?" The question assumes that the University is yet another institution, a counterpart to the colleges and laboratories, another entity that can be seen in the same way as the others. Actually, the University is simply the way all he has already seen is coordinated. Thus the visitor's mistake consists in his assumption that one can correctly speak of the Bodleian Library, the Ashmolean Museum, All Souls College, *and* the University as if the University were the same kind of member in the class to which the others belong. In short, the visitor mistakenly placed the University into the wrong category, a category in which it does not belong. In a similar illustration, Ryle speaks of

Oxford, High Street (*Culver Pictures*)

the mistake made by a child watching a military parade in which a division is marching by. Having been told that he was seeing battalions, batteries, and squadrons, the child wanted to know when the division was going to appear. Again, he assumed that the division is another unit similar to the others, not realizing that in seeing the battalions, batteries, and squadrons, he had already seen the division. His mistake was in thinking it correct to speak of battalions, batteries, squadrons, *and* a division. He placed the division in the wrong category. The category-mistake indicates an inability to use certain elements in the English language correctly. What is more significant, says Ryle, is that people who are perfectly capable of applying concepts are nevertheless liable in their abstract thinking to allocate these concepts to logical categories to which they do not belong.

What Ryle has sought to do through these illustrations is to show, as he says, that "a family of radical category-mistakes is the source of the double-life theory." The notion that a person is a ghost mysteriously ensconced in a machine is a consequence of thinking that because a person's feeling, thinking, and purposive activity cannot be described solely in terms of physics, it must be described as something similar to or having bodily characteristics, even though the mind is not a body. Moreover, because mental conduct differs so from bodily activities, the official theory sought to invest mind with its own status, although made of a different stuff and having a different structure, and possessing its own complex organization. Body and mind were thought to be separate fields of causes and effects, the body's being mechanical and the mind's nonmechanical.

How did this category-mistake originate? Although Ryle designates Descartes as the major culprit of this error, it is obvious that the mind-body dualism has a history extending very much farther back than the seventeenth century. Still, Descartes's special formulation of this official doctrine for modern philosophy, says Ryle, followed Galileo's assertion that his methods of scientific discovery were capable of providing a mechanical theory which would be applicable to every occupant in space. From a strictly scientific point of view, Descartes was impressed with the mechanical description of nature, but as a religious and moral person, he was reluctant to agree with the claim that human nature in its mental aspects differs only in degree of complexity from a machine. Consequently, Descartes and subsequent philosophers wrongly construed mental-conduct words to signify nonmechanical processes and concluded that nonmechanical laws must explain the nonspatial workings of minds. But what this explanation retained was the assumption that mind, although different from body, was nevertheless a member of the categories of "thing," "stuff," "state," "process," "cause," and "effect." Thus, just as the visitor expected the University to be another extra unit, so Descartes and his heirs treated minds as additional, although special, centers of the causal process.

From these conclusions a host of theoretical difficulties arose. How are the mind and body related? How do they cause effects in each other? If the mind is governed by strict laws analogous to the law governing the body, does this not imply a determinism, in which case such notions as responsibility, choice, merit, and freedom make no sense? Worst of all, only negative terms could be used to speak of the mind as compared with the body, since minds are not in space, have no motions, are not aspects of matter, and are not capable of observation. For these and others reasons, Ryle concludes that the entire argument of the Ghost in the Machine is "broken-backed."

In a sustained and careful analysis of several assertions "about the mind," Ryle seeks to clarify the assertions by arguing in each case that mental-conduct words do indeed refer to mental acts but not to minds. The acts of knowing, exercising intelligence, understanding, willing, feeling, imagining, and the like, according to the official theory, were considered as being unconnected with the body and as occurring, when referred to in the present tense, in the mind. Refuting this, Ryle holds that in virtually every assertion about the mind some facts about bodily behavior are relevant. For example, in speaking of human emotions, one does not infer the working of some interior and obscure forces. In favorable circumstances, says Ryle, "I find out your inclinations and your moods more directly than this. I hear and understand your conversational avowals, your interjections and your tones of voice; I see and understand your gestures and facial expressions." Or, if we consider that the act of theorizing is the distinctive act of human intelligence and that this supports the dogma of the Ghost in the Machine, Ryle gives various rejoinders, including the following: "To find that most people have minds . . . is simply to find that they are able and prone to do certain sorts of things, and this we do by witnessing the sorts of things they do." Or, "overt intelligent performances are not clues to the workings of minds; they are those workings." Ryle says, further, that "in opposition to this entire dogma, I am arguing that in describing the workings of a person's mind we are not describing a second set of shadowy operations. We are describing his one career; namely we are describing the ways in which parts of his conduct are managed." And again, in speaking about the act of *understanding*, Ryle says, "It is being maintained throughout this book that when we characterize people by mental predicates, we are not making untestable inferences to, say, ghostly processes occurring in streams of consciousness which we are debarred from visiting; we are describing the ways in which those people conduct parts of their predominantly public behavior." Things we say about the mind are therefore made true or false not by inner private events but by what has happened or will happen publicly. To say of someone that he is intelligent appears to be an assertion about his mind, but Ryle argues that it is rather a statement of our knowledge about him and a description of his public performance.

What Ryle has sought to achieve through his analysis is a new theory of mind. It may appear that he is arguing that only bodies exist, that mental-conduct words are really statements about bodily behavior, and that there is no independent private inner life. It was his intention in his *The Concept of Mind* to "dissipate the contrast between Mind and Matter," not by reducing the one to the other, but by demonstrating that the polar opposition between mind and matter can be solved by rejecting the assumption that they are terms of the same logical type.

READING

ON THE RELATION BETWEEN SOUL AND BODY

Descartes

Simply from knowing that I exist, and that, meantime, I do not observe any other thing as evidently pertaining to my nature, i.e., to my essence, except this only, that I am a thinking thing, I rightly conclude that my essence consists in this alone, that I am a thinking thing (i.e., a substance, the whole nature or essence of which consists in thinking). And although possibly (or rather certainly, as I shall shortly be declaring) I have a body with which I am very closely conjoined, yet since on the one hand I have a clear and distinct idea of myself, in so far as I am only a thinking unextended thing, and on the other hand a distinct idea of the body, in so far as it is only an extended unthinking thing, it is certain that I am truly distinct from my body, and can exist without it.

I am also aware in me of certain faculties, such as the power of changing location, of assuming diverse postures, and the like, which cannot be thought, and cannot therefore exist, any more than can the preceding, apart from some substance in which they reside. But evidently, since the clear and distinct apprehension of these faculties involves the feature of extension, but not any intellection, they must, if they indeed exist, belong to some substance which is corporeal, i.e., extended and unthinking.

Now there is nothing which nature teaches me more expressly, or more sensibly, than that I have a body which is adversely affected when I sense pain, and stands in need of food and drink when I suffer hunger or

From René Descartes, "Meditations" in *DESCARTES: Philosophical Writings*, ed. & trans. Norman Kemp Smith, Modern Library, Random House, Inc., New York, 1958.

thirst, etc.; and consequently I ought not to doubt there being some truth in all this.

Nature also teaches me by these sensings of pain, hunger, thirst, etc., that I am not lodged in my body merely as a pilot in a ship, but so intimately conjoined, and as it were intermingled with it, that with it I form a unitary whole. Were not this the case, I should not sense pain when my body is hurt, being, as I should then be, merely a thinking thing, but should apprehend the wound in a purely cognitive manner, just as a sailor apprehends by sight any damage to his ship; and when my body has need of food and drink I should apprehend this expressly, and not be made aware of it by confused sensings of hunger, thirst, pain, etc. For these sensings of hunger, thirst, pain, etc., are in truth merely confused modes of thinking, arising from and dependent on the union, and, as it were, the intermingling of mind and body.

Besides this, nature teaches me that my body exists as one among other bodies, some of which are to be sought after and others shunned. And certainly on sensing colors, sounds, odors, tastes, heat, hardness, and the like, I rightly conclude that in the bodies from which these various sensory apprehensions proceed, there are variations corresponding to them, though not perhaps resembling them; and since among these sense-apprehensions some are pleasing to me, and others displeasing, there can be no doubt that my body, or rather my entire self, inasmuch as I am composed of body and mind, can be variously affected, beneficially or harmfully, by surrounding bodies. Many things included in that totality of mind and body belong to the mind alone, e.g., the notion I have of the truth that what has once taken place can no longer not have taken place, and all these other truths which are known by the natural light, without the aid of the body, of these latter I am not here speaking. The term nature likewise extends to many things which pertain only to body, such as its having weight, and the like, and with these also I am not here dealing, but only with what God has given me as a being composed of body as well as of mind. Nature, taken in this special [restricted] sense, does indeed teach me to shun whatever causes me to sense pain, or to pursue what causes me to sense pleasure, and other things of that sort; but I do not find that it teaches me, by way of sensory apprehensions, that we should, without previous careful and mature mental examination of them, likewise draw conclusions regarding things located in the world outside us; for, as would seem, it is the task of the mind alone, not of the composite mind-body, to discern truth in questions of this kind.

In this inquiry, what I first note is the great difference between mind and body, in that body, from its very nature, is always divisible, and mind altogether indivisible. For truly, when I consider the mind, that is to say, my self in so far only as I am a thinking thing, I can distinguish in myself no parts; I apprehend myself to be a thing single and entire. Although the whole mind may seem to be united to the whole body, yet if a foot, an arm, or any other part of the body, is cut off, I know that my mind is not thereby diminished. Nor can its faculties of willing, sensing, understanding, etc., be spoken of as being its parts; it is one and the same mind which wills, which senses, which understands. The opposite holds in respect of a corporeal, i.e., of an extended, thing. I cannot think of it save as readily divisible into parts, and therefore recognize it as being divisible. This, of itself, would suffice to convince me that the mind is altogether different from the body, even if I had not already so decided on other grounds.

READING

DESCARTES'S MYTH: A CATEGORY-MISTAKE
Ryle

(1) The official doctrine.   There is a doctrine about the nature and place of minds which is so prevalent among theorists and even among laymen that it deserves to be described as the official theory. Most philosophers, psychologists and religious teachers subscribe, with minor reservations, to its main articles and, although they admit certain theoretical difficulties in it, they tend to assume that these can be overcome without serious modifications being made to the architecture of the theory. It will be argued here that the central principles of the doctrine are unsound and conflict with the whole body of what we know about minds when we are not speculating about them.

The official doctrine, which hails chiefly from Descartes, is something like this. With the doubtful exceptions of idiots and infants in arms every human being has both a body and a mind. Some would prefer to say that every human being is both a body and a mind. His body and his mind are ordinarily harnessed together, but after the death of the body his mind may continue to exist and function.

Human bodies are in space and are subject to the mechanical laws which govern all other bodies in space. . . .

But minds are not in space, nor are their operations subject to mechanical laws. The workings of one mind are not witnessable by other observers; its career is private. Only I can take direct cognisance of the states and processes of my own mind. A person therefore lives through two collateral histories, one consisting of what happens in and to his body, the other consisting of what happens in and to his mind. The first is public, the second private. The events in the first history are events in the physical world, those in the second are events in the mental world. . . .

It is customary to express this bifurcation of his two lives and of his two worlds by saying that the things and events which belong to the physical world, including his own body, are external, while the workings of his own mind are internal. This antithesis of outer and inner is of course meant to be construed as a metaphor, since minds, not being in space, could not be described as being spatially inside anything else, or as having things going on spatially inside themselves. But relapses from this good intention are common and theorists are found speculating how stimuli, the physical sources of which are yards or miles outside a person's skin, can generate mental responses inside his skull, or how decisions framed inside his cranium can set going movements of his extremities.

Even when "inner" and "outer" are construed as metaphors, the problem how a person's mind and body influence one another is notoriously charged with theoretical difficulties. What the mind wills, the legs, arms and the tongue execute; what affects the ear and the eye has something to do with what the mind perceives; grimaces and smiles betray the mind's moods and bodily castigations lead, it is hoped, to moral improvement. But the actual transactions between the episodes of the private history and those of the public history remain mysterious, since by definition they can belong to neither series. . . .

Underlying this partly metaphorical representation of the bifurcation of a person's two lives there is a seemingly more profound and philosophical assumption. It is assumed that there are two different kinds of existence or status. What exists or happens may have the status of physical existence, or it may have the status of mental existence. Somewhat as the faces of coins are either heads or tails, or somewhat as living creatures are either male or female, so, it is supposed, some existing is physical existing, other existing is mental existing. It is a necessary feature of what has physical existence that it is in space and time; it is a necessary feature of what has mental existence that it is in time but not in space. What has physical existence is composed of matter, or else is a function of matter; what has mental existence consists of consciousness, or else is a function of consciousness. . . .

What sort of knowledge can be secured of the workings of a mind? On the one side, according to the official theory, a person has direct knowledge

Magdalen College, Oxford (*Alfred Savage, Ltd.*)

of the best imaginable kind of the workings of his own mind. Mental states and processes are (or are normally) conscious states and processes, and the consciousness which irradiates them can engender no illusions and leaves the door open for no doubts. A person's present thinkings, feelings and willings, his perceivings, rememberings and imaginings are intrinsically "phosphorescent"; their existence and their nature are inevitably betrayed to their owner. The inner life is a stream of consciousness of such a sort that it would be absurd to suggest that the mind whose life is that stream might be unaware of what is passing down it.

True, the evidence adduced recently by Freud seems to show that there exist channels tributary to this stream, which run hidden from their owner. People are actuated by impulses the existence of which they vigorously disavow; some of their thoughts differ from the thoughts which they acknowledge; and some of the actions which they think they will to perform they do not really will. They are thoroughly gulled by some of their own hypocrisies and they successfully ignore facts about their mental lives which on the official theory ought to be patent to them. Holders of the official theory tend, however, to maintain that anyhow in normal circumstances a person must be directly and authentically seized of the present state and workings of his own mind.

On the other side, one person has no direct access of any sort to the events of the inner life of another. He cannot do better than make problematic inferences from the observed behaviour of the other person's body to the states of mind which, by analogy from his own conduct, he supposes to be signalised by that behaviour. Direct access to the workings of a mind is the privilege of that mind itself; in default of such priviledged access, the workings of one mind are inevitably occult to everyone else. For the supposed arguments from bodily movements similar to their own to mental workings similar to their own would lack any possibility of observational corroboration. Not unnaturally, therefore, an adherent of the official theory finds it difficult to resist this consequence of his premises, that he has no good reason to believe that there do exist minds other than his own. Even if he prefers to believe that to other human bodies there are harnessed minds not unlike his own, he cannot claim to be able to discover their individual characteristics, or the particular things that they undergo and do. Absolute solitude is on this showing the ineluctable destiny of the soul. Only our bodies can meet. . . .

(2) The absurdity of the official doctrine.   Such in outline is the official theory. I shall often speak of it, with deliberate abusiveness, as "the dogma of the Ghost in the Machine." I hope to prove that it is entirely false, and false not in detail but in principle. It is not merely an assemblage of particular mistakes. It is one big mistake and a mistake of a special kind. It is, namely, a category-mistake. It represents the facts of mental life as if they belonged to one logical type or category (or range of types or categories), when they actually belong to another. The dogma is therefore a philosopher's myth. In attempting to explode the myth I shall probably be taken to be denying well-known facts about the mental life of human beings, and my plea that I aim at doing nothing more than rectify the logic of mental-conduct concepts will probably be disallowed as mere subterfuge.

[An illustration of category-mistake.] A foreigner watching his first game of cricket learns what are the functions of the bowlers, the batsmen, the fielders, the umpires and the scorers. He then says, "But there is no one left on the field to contribute to the famous element of team-spirit. I see who does the bowling, the batting and the wicket-keeping; but I do not see whose role it is to exercise *esprit de corps*." It would have to be explained that he was looking for the wrong type of thing. Team-spirit is not another cricketing-operation supplementary to all of the other special tasks. It is, roughly, the keenness with which each of the special tasks is performed, and performing a task keenly is not performing two tasks. Certainly exhibiting team-spirit is not the same thing as bowling or catching, but nor is it a third thing such that we can say that the bowler first bowls *and* then exhibits team-spirit or that a fielder is at a given moment *either* catching *or* displaying *esprit de corps.*

Illustrations of category-mistakes have a common feature which must be noticed. The mistakes were made by people who did not know how to wield the concepts *University, division* and *team-spirit.* Their puzzles arose from inability to use certain items in the English vocabulary. . . .

My destructive purpose is to show that a family of radical category-mistakes is the source of the double-life theory. The representation of a person as a ghost mysteriously ensconced in a machine derives from this argument. Because, as is true, a person's thinking, feeling and purposive doing cannot be described solely in the idioms of physics, chemistry and physiology, therefore they must be described in counterpart idioms. As the human body is a complex organised unit, so the human mind must be another complex organised unit, though one made of a different sort of stuff and with a different sort of structure. Or, again, as the human body, like any other parcel of matter, is a field of causes and effects, so the mind must be another field of causes and effects, though not (Heaven be praised) mechanical causes and effects.

CHAPTER 19

DEATH AND BEYOND

Plato, Hume, and Kierkegaard

Three philosophers who were specifically concerned with the question of immortality were Plato, Hume, and Kierkegaard. Each had a different notion of human nature. Consequently, each had a quite different view of life after death.

We have already seen that Plato believed that the body is the prison house of the soul. Moreover, Plato believed that the soul exists even before it enters the body. Bodily existence is an unhappy and discouraging experience because the body tends to drag the soul down from its higher or purer form of life. The pleasures of the body and of wealth are incapable of providing lasting happiness. Also, the senses such as sight, touch, hearing, and taste are deceptive because they are never accurate. Man's pursuit of truth and true pleasure is always frustrated by the body, which is an obstacle to the clear working of the soul or mind. Our best thinking and our longest-lasting pleasures come when the mind is functioning independently of the body. Daily life is complicated by the passions and appetites of the body, against which the soul must constantly struggle. Most important of all, says Plato, is the fact that we cannot achieve through our bodily faculties the objectives we long for most of all, namely, the highest in everything, of beauty, goodness, justice, and truth. Plato asks, "Did you ever reach with bodily senses . . . absolute greatness, health, and strength and the essence or true nature of everything? Has the reality of them ever been perceived by you through the bodily organs?" The body is the "source of endless trouble," says Plato, because "it fills us full of loves and lusts, and fears, and fancies of all kinds, and endless foolery, and in fact, as men say, takes away from us the power of thinking at all."

This whole line of reasoning is not a proof of immortality. It is rather a way of saying that one should not fear death. Life in bodily form is not so great. Death means the liberation of the soul from the body. What makes this analysis possible for Plato is his view that the soul or mind is more real than the body. Ideas and the mind are eternal. The separation of the soul from the body at death represents a purification of the soul.

Hume, however, denied that man has a soul. Nor does man have a *self*. We do not even have an idea of a self. It may be paradoxical that *I* should say that I do not have an idea of myself. But Hume asks, "From what impression could this idea be derived?" Is there any continuous and identical reality which forms our ideas of self? Do we have any one impression that is invariably associated with our ideas of *self*? "When I enter most intimately into what I call *myself*," says Hume, "I always stumble on some particular perception or other, of heat, cold, love, or hatred, pain or pleasure. I never catch *myself* at any time without a perception and never can observe anything but the perception." Hume therefore denies the existence of a continuous self-identity and says about the rest of mankind that "they are nothing but a bundle or collection of different perceptions." How then do we account for what we think is the self? It is, says Hume, our power of memory that gives the impression of our continuous identity. Hume compares the mind to "a kind of theatre where several perceptions successively make their appearance" but adds that "we have not the most distant notion of the place where these scenes are represented. . . ."

If there is no self, then there is nothing that can have immortality. Earlier philosophers, including Plato, described the self, or mind, as a form of *substance*. Hume denied the existence of substance. Substance was supposed to be the reality which *has* certain qualities: the statement "the apple is red" suggests that the color red is one thing while the apple, which has the color, is the reality underneath the color and is therefore a different thing. Similarly, thinking suggests, as Descartes said, that there is a thing that thinks. In this view, mind or soul is a substance. But Hume denied the self for the same reason that he denied substance. He saw no way philosophically to prove that there is any self that could have immortality.

In the reading that concludes this section, Kierkegaard has some provocative things to say about death and immortality. The most important point he wants to drive home is the difference between general subjects, on the one hand, and intensely personal subjects, on the other. It is one thing, for example, to talk about world, or what he calls universal, history. It is even one thing to talk about death or immortality *in general.* It is quite a different thing to talk about death as *my* death or immortality as *my* immortality.

READING

THE IMMORTALITY OF THE SOUL
Plato

I desire to prove to you that the real philosopher has reason to be of good cheer when he is about to die, and that after death he may hope to obtain the greatest good in the other world. And how this may be, Simmias and Cebes, I will endeavour to explain. For I deem that the true votary of philosophy is likely to be misunderstood by other men; they do not perceive that he is always pursuing death and dying; and if this be so, and he has had the desire of death all his life long, why when his time comes should he repine at that which he has been always pursuing and desiring?

Simmias said laughingly: Though not in a laughing humour, you have made me laugh, Socrates; for I cannot help thinking that the many when they hear your words will say how truly you have described philosophers, and our people at home will likewise say that the life which philosophers desire is in reality death, and that they have found them out to be deserving of the death which they desire.

And they are right, Simmias, in thinking so, with the exception of the words "they have found them out"; for they have not found out either what is the nature of that death which the true philosopher deserves, or how he

From Plato, "Phaedo," in *Dialogues of Plato*, trans. Benjamin Jowett, Oxford, 1920.

deserves or desires death. But enough of them:—let us discuss the matter among ourselves. Do we believe that there is such a thing as death?

To be sure, replied Simmias.

Is it not the separation of soul and body? And to be dead is the completion of this; when the soul exists in herself, and is released from the body and the body is released from the soul, what is this but death?

Just so, he replied.

There is another question, which will probably throw light on our present inquiry if you and I can agree about it:—Ought the philosopher to care about the pleasures—if they are to be called pleasures—of eating and drinking?

Certainly not, answered Simmias.

And what about the pleasures of love—should he care for them?

By no means.

And will he think much of the other ways of indulging the body, for example, the acquisition of costly raiment, or sandals, or other adornments of the body? Instead of caring about them, does he not rather despise anything more than nature needs? What do you say?

I should say that the true philosopher would despise them.

Would you not say that he is entirely concerned with the soul and not with the body? He would like, as far as he can, to get away from the body and to turn to the soul.

Quite true.

In matters of this sort philosophers, above all other men, may be observed in every sort of way to dissever the soul from the communion of the body.

Very true.

Whereas, Simmias, the rest of the world are of opinion that to him who has no sense of pleasure and no part in bodily pleasure, life is not worth having; and that he who is indifferent about them is as good as dead.

That is also true.

What again shall we say of the actual acquirement of knowledge?—is the body, if invited to share in the enquiry, a hinderer or a helper? I mean to say, have sight and hearing any truth in them? Are they not, as the poets are always telling us, inaccurate witnesses? and yet, if even they are inaccurate and indistinct, what is to be said of the other senses?—for you will allow that they are the best of them?

Certainly, he replied.

Then when does the soul attain truth?—for in attempting to consider anything in company with the body she is obviously deceived.

True.

Then must not true existence be revealed to her in thought, if at all?

Yes.

And thought is best when the mind is gathered into herself and none of these things trouble her—neither sounds nor sights nor pain nor any pleasure—when she takes leave of the body, and has as little as possible to do with it, when she has no bodily sense or desire, but is aspiring after true being?

Certainly.

And in this the philosopher dishonours the body; his soul runs away from his body and desires to be alone and by herself?

That is true.

Well, but there is another thing, Simmias: Is there or is there not an absolute justice?

Assuredly there is.

And an absolute beauty and absolute good?

Of course.

But did you ever behold any of them with your eyes?

Certainly not.

Or did you ever reach them with any other bodily sense?—and I speak not of these alone, but of absolute greatness, and health, and strength, and of the essence or true nature of everything. Has the reality of them ever been perceived by you through the bodily organs? or rather, is not the nearest approach to the knowledge of their several natures made by him who so orders his intellectual vision as to have the most exact conception of the essence of each thing which he considers?

Certainly.

And he attains to the purest knowledge of them who goes to each with the mind alone, not introducing or intruding in the act of thought sight or any other sense together with reason, but with the very light of the mind in her own clearness searches into the very truth of each; he who has got rid, as far as he can, of eyes and ears and, so to speak, of the whole body, these being in his opinion distracting elements which when they infect the soul hinder her from acquiring truth and knowledge—who, if not he, is likely to attain to the knowledge of true being?

What you say has a wonderful truth in it, Socrates, replied Simmias.

And when real philosophers consider all these things, will they not be led to make a reflection which they will express in words something like the following? "Have we not found," they will say, "a path of thought which seems to bring us and our argument to the conclusion, that while we are in the body, and while the soul is infected with the evils of the body, our desire will not be satisfied? and our desire is of the truth. For the body is a source of endless trouble to us by reason of the mere requirement of food; and is liable also to diseases which overtake and impede us in the search after true being: it fills us full of loves, and lusts, and fears, and fancies of all kinds, and endless foolery, and in fact, as men say, takes away from us the power of thinking at all. Whence come wars, and fightings, and factions? whence but from the body and the lusts of the body? Wars are occasioned by the love of money, and money has to be acquired for the sake and in the service of the body; and by reason of all these impediments we have no time to give to philosophy; and, last and worst of all, even if we are at leisure and betake ourselves to some speculation, the body is always breaking in upon us, causing turmoil and confusion in our enquiries, and so amazing us that we are prevented from seeing the truth. It has been proved to us by experience that if we would have pure knowledge of anything we must be quit of the body—the soul in herself must behold things in themselves: and then we shall attain the wisdom which we desire, and of which we say that we are lovers; not while we live, but after death; for if while in company with the body, the soul cannot have pure knowledge, one of two things follows—either knowledge is not to be attained at all, or, if at all, after death. For then, and not till then, the soul will be parted from the body and exist in herself alone. In this present life, I reckon that we make the nearest approach to knowledge when we have the least possible intercourse or communion with the body, and are not surfeited with the bodily nature, but keep ourselves pure until the hour when God himself is pleased to release us. And thus having got rid of the foolishness of the body we shall be pure and hold converse with the pure, and know of ourselves the clear light everywhere, which is no other than the light of truth." For the impure are not permitted to approach the pure. These are the sort of words, Simmias, which the true lovers of knowledge cannot help saying to one another, and thinking. You would agree; would you not?

Undoubtedly, Socrates.

But, O my friend, if this be true, there is great reason to hope that, going whither I go, when I have come to the end of my journey, I shall attain that which has been the pursuit of my life. And therefore I go on my way rejoicing, and not I only, but every other man who believes that his mind has been made ready and that he is in a manner purified.

Certainly, replied Simmias.

And what is purification but the separation of the soul from the body, as I was saying before; the habit of the soul gathering and collecting herself into herself from all sides out of the body; the dwelling in her own place alone, as in another life, so also in this, as far as she can;—the release of the soul from the chains of the body?

Very true, he said.

And this separation and release of the soul from the body is termed death?

To be sure, he said.

And the true philosophers, and they only, are ever seeking to release the soul. Is not the separation and release of the soul from the body their especial study?

That is true.

And, as I was saying at first, there would be a ridiculous contradiction in men studying to live as nearly as they can in a state of death, and yet repining when it comes upon them.

Clearly.

And the true philosophers, Simmias, are always occupied in the practice of dying, wherefore also to them least of all men is death terrible. Look
at the matter thus:—if they have been in every way the enemies of the
body, and are wanting to be alone with the soul, when this desire of theirs
is granted, how inconsistent would they be if they trembled and repined,
instead of rejoicing at their departure to that place where, when they arrive,
they hope to gain that which in life they desired—and this was wisdom—
and at the same time to be rid of the company of their enemy. Many a man
has been willing to go to the world below animated by the hope of seeing
there an earthly love, or wife, or son, and conversing with them. And will
he who is a true lover of wisdom, and is strongly persuaded in like manner
that only in the world below he can worthily enjoy her, still repine at death?
Will he not depart with joy? Surely he will, O my friend, if he be a true
philosopher. For he will have a firm conviction that there, and there only,
he can find wisdom in her purity. And if this be ture, he would be very
absurd, as I was saying, if he were afraid of death.

READING

CONCERNING THE IMMORTALITY
OF THE SOUL

Hume

The physical arguments from the analogy of nature are strong for the mortality of the soul: and these are really the only philosophical arguments,
which ought to be admitted with regard to this question, or indeed any
question of fact.

Where any two objects are so closely connected, that all alterations,
which we have seen in the one, are attended with proportionable alterations in the other: we ought to conclude, by all rules of analogy, that, when
there are still greater alterations produced in the former, and it is totally
dissolved, there follows a total dissolution of the latter.

From David Hume, "Of the Immortality of the Soul," written 1755.

Hume's lodgings, Edinburgh (*New York Public Library Picture Collection*)

Sleep, a very small effect on the body, is attended with a temporary extinction: at least, a great confusion in the soul.

The weakness of the body and that of the mind in infancy are exactly proportioned; their vigour in manhood, their sympathetic disorder in sickness, their common gradual decay in old age. The step further seems unavoidable; their common dissolution in death.

The last symptoms, which the mind discovers, are disorder, weakness, insensibility, and stupidity; the forerunners of its annihilation. The further progress of the same causes, increasing the same effects, totally extinguish it.

Judging by the usual analogy of nature, no form can continue, when transferred to a condition of life very different from the original one, in which it was placed. Trees perish in the water; fishes in the air; animals in the earth. Even so small a difference as that of climate is often fatal. What reason then to imagine, that an immense alteration, such as is made on the soul by the dissolution of its body, and all its organs of thought and sensation, can be effected without the dissolution of the whole?

Everything is in common betwixt soul and body. The organs of the one are all of them the organs of the other. The existence therefore of the one must be dependent on the other.

The souls of animals are allowed to be mortal: and these bear so near a resemblance to the souls of men, that the analogy from one to the other forms a very strong argument. Their bodies are not more resembling: yet no one rejects the argument drawn from comparative anatomy.

Nothing in this world is perpetual; Everything, however seemingly firm, is in continual flux and change: The world itself gives symptoms of frailty and dissolution: How contrary to analogy, therefore, to imagine, that one single form, seeming the frailest of any, and subject to the greatest disorders is immortal and indissoluble! What a daring theory is that! How lightly, not to say how rashly, entertained!

How to dispose of the infinite number of posthumous existences ought also to embarrass the religious theory. Every planet, in every solar system, we are at liberty to imagine peopled with intelligent, mortal beings: At least we can fix on no other supposition. For these, then, a new universe must, every generation, be created beyond the bounds of the present universe: or one must have been created at first so prodigiously wide as to admit of this continual influx of beings. Ought such bold suppositions to be received by philosophy: and that merely on the pretext of a bare possibility?

When it is asked, whether *Agamemnon, Thersites, Hannibal, Nero,* and every stupid clown, that ever existed in *Italy, Scythia, Bactria,* or *Guinea,* are now alive; can any man think, that a scrutiny of nature will furnish arguments strong enough to answer so strange a question in the affirmative? The want of argument, without revelation, sufficiently establishes the negative. . . .

Were our horrors of annihilation an original passion, not the effect of our general love of happiness, it would rather prove the mortality of the soul: For as nature does nothing in vain, she would never give us a horror against an impossible event. She may give us a horror against an unavoidable event, provided our endeavours, as in the present case, may often remove it to some distance. Death is in the end unavoidable; yet the human species could not be preserved, had not nature inspired us with an aversion towards it. All doctrines are to be suspected which are favoured by our passions. And the hopes and fears which give rise to this doctrine are very obvious.

'Tis an infinite advantage in every controversy, to defend the negative. If the question be out of the common experienced course of nature, this circumstance is almost, if not altogether, decisive. By what arguments or analogies can we prove any state of existence, which no one ever saw, and which no way resembles any that ever was seen? Who will repose such trust in any pretended philosophy, as to admit upon its testimony the reality of so marvelous a scene? Some new species of logic is requisite for that purpose; and some new faculties of the mind, that they may enable us to comprehend that logic.

Nothing could set in a fuller light the infinite obligations which mankind have to Divine revelation; since we find, that no other medium could ascertain this great and important truth.

READING

DEATH AND IMMORTALITY ARE *MY* DEATH AND IMMORTALITY

Kierkegaard

Christianity protests every form of objectivity; it desires that the subject should be infinitely concerned about himself. It is subjectivity that Chris-

---

From Søren Kierkegaard, *Concluding Unscientific Postscript*, trans. David F. Swenson and Walter Lowrie, Copyright 1941 © 1969 by Princeton University Press; Princeton Paperback, 1968. Reprinted by permission of Princeton Univ. Press and the American Scandinavian Foundation.

tianity is concerned with, and it is only in subjectivity that its truth exists, if it exists at all; objectively, Christianity has absolutely no existence. If its truth happens to be in only a single subject, it exists in him alone; and there is greater Christian joy in heaven over this one individual than over universal history and the System, which as objective entities are incommensurable for that which is Christian. . . .

For example, the problem of *What it means to die.* I know that I shall die if I take a dose of sulphuric acid, and also if I drown myself, or go to sleep in an atmosphere of coal gas, and so forth. I know that Napoleon always went about with poison ready to hand, and that Juliet in Shakespeare poisoned herself. I know that the Stoics regarded suicide as a courageous deed, and that others consider it a cowardly act. I know that death may result from so ridiculous and trivial a circumstance that even the most serious-minded of men cannot help laughing at death; I know that it is possible to escape what appears to be certain death, and so forth. I know that the tragic hero dies in the fifth act of the drama, and that death here has an infinite significance in pathos; but that when a bartender dies, death does not have this significance. I know that the poet can interpret death in a diversity of moods, even to the limit of the comical; I pledge myself to produce the same diversity of effects in prose. I know furthermore what the clergy are accustomed to say on this subject, and I am familiar with the general run of themes treated at funerals. If nothing else stands in the way of my passing over to world-history, I am ready; I need only purchase black cloth for a ministerial gown, and I shall engage to preach funeral sermons as well as any ordinary clergyman. I freely admit that those who wear a velvet inset in their gowns do it more elegantly; but this distinction is not essential any more than the difference between five dollars and ten dollars for the hearse.

Nevertheless, in spite of this almost extraordinary knowledge or facility in knowledge, I can by no means regard death as something I have understood. Before I pass over to universal history—of which I must always say: "God knows whether it is any concern of yours"—it seems to me that I had better think about this, lest existence mock me, because I had become so learned and highfalutin that I had forgotten to understand what will some time happen to me as to every human being—sometime, nay, what am I saying: suppose death were so treacherous as to come tomorrow! Merely this one uncertainty, when it is to be understood and held fast by an existing individual, and hence enter into every thought, precisely because it is an uncertainty entering into my beginning upon universal history even, so that I make it clear to myself whether if death comes tomorrow, I am beginning upon something that is worth beginning—merely this one uncertainty generates inconceivable difficulties, difficulties that not even the speaker who treats of death is always aware of, in that he thinks that he apprehends the uncertainty of death, while nevertheless forgetting to think it into what he says about it, so that he speaks movingly and with emotion about the uncertainty of death, and yet ends by encouraging his hearers to make a resolution for the whole of life. This is essentially to forget the uncertainty of death, since otherwise the enthusiastic resolve for the whole of life must be made commensurable with the uncertainty of death. To think about it once for all, or once a year at matins of New Year's morning, is of course nonsense, and is the same as not thinking about it at all.

If, on the other hand, the uncertainty of death is merely something in general, then my own death is itself only something in general. Perhaps this is also the case for systematic philosophers, for absent-minded people. For the late Herr Soldin, his own death is supposed to have been such a something in general: "when he was about to get up in the morning he was not aware that he was dead." But the fact of my own death is not for me by any means such a something in general, although for others, the fact of my death may indeed be something of that sort. Nor am I for myself such a something in general, although perhaps for others I may be a mere generality. But if the task of life is to become subjective, then every subject will for *himself* become the very opposite of such a something in general. And it would seem to be a somewhat embarrassing thing to be so significant for universal history, and then at home, in company with oneself, to be merely a something in general. It is already embarrassing enough for a man who is an extraordinarily important figure in the public assembly to come home to his wife, and then to be for her only such a something in general; or to be a world-historical Diedrich Menschenschreck, and then at home to be— aye, I do not care to say anything more. But it is still more embarrassing to have so low a standing with oneself, and it is most embarrassing of all to remain unaware of the fact that this is so.

The question then arises as to what death is, and especially as to what it is for the living individual. We wish to know how the conception of death will transform a man's entire life, when in order to think its uncertainty he has to think it in every moment, so as to prepare himself for it. We wish to know what it means to prepare for death, since here again one must distinguish between its actual presence and the thought of it. This distinction appears to make all my preparation insignificant, if that which really comes is not that for which I prepared myself; and if it is the same, then my preparation is in its perfection identical with death itself. And I must take into account the fact that death may come in the very moment that I begin my preparation. The question must be raised of the possibility of finding an ethical expression for the significance of death, and a religious expression for the victory over death; one needs a solving word which explains its mystery, and a binding word by which the living individual defends himself against the ever recurrent conception; for surely we dare scarcely recommend mere thoughtlessness and forgetfulness as wisdom.

When death thus becomes something to be related to the entire life of

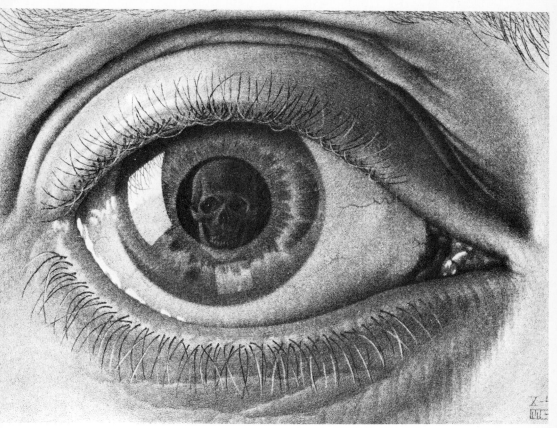

The Eye, Escher (*Gemeentelijke Dienst Voor Schone Kunsten*) Reproduction rights arranged courtesy of the Vorpal Galleries, New York, Chicago, San Francisco, Laguna Beach. Each person must visualize his own death.

the subject, I must confess I am very far indeed from having understood it, even if it were to cost me my life to make this confession. Still less have I realized the task existentially. And yet I have thought about this subject again and again; I have sought for guidance in books—and I have found none.

For example, what does it mean to be immortal? In this respect, I know what people generally know. I know that some hold a belief in immortality, that others say they do not hold it; whether they actually do not hold it I know not; it does not occur to me therefore to want to combat them, for such an undertaking is so dialectically difficult that I should need a year and a day before it could become dialectically clear to me whether there is any reality in such a contest; whether the dialectic of communication, when it is properly understood, would approve of such a proceeding or transform it into a mere beating of the air; whether the consciousness of immortality is a doctrinal topic which is appropriate as a subject for instruction, and how the dialectic of instruction must be determined with relation to the learner's presuppositions; whether these presuppositions are not so essential that the instruction becomes a deception in case one is not at once aware of them, and in that event the instruction is transformed into non-instruction. A book raises the question of the immortality of the soul. The contents of the book constitute the answer. But the contents of the book, as the reader can convince himself by reading it through, are the opinions of the wisest and best men about immortality, all neatly strung on a thread. Oh! thou great Chinese god! Is this immortality? So then the question about immortality is a learned question. All honor to learning! All honor to him who can handle learnedly the learned question of immortality! But the question of immortality is essentially not a learned question, rather it is a question of inwardness, which the subject by becoming subjective must put to himself. Objectively the question cannot be answered, because objectively it cannot be put, since immortality precisely is the potentiation and highest development of the developed subjectivity. Only by really willing to become subjective can the question properly emerge, therefore how could it be answered objectively? The question cannot be answered in social terms, for in social terms it cannot be expressed, inasmuch as only the subject who wills to become subjective can conceive the question and ask rightly, "Do I become immortal, or am I immortal?" Of course, people can combine for many things; thus several families can combine for a box at the theater, and three single gentlemen can combine for a riding horse, so that each of them rides every third day. But it is not so with immortality; the consciousness of my immortality belongs to me alone, precisely at the moment when I am conscious of my immortality I am absolutely subjective, and I cannot become immortal in partnership with three single gentlemen in turn. People who go about with a paper soliciting the endorsement of numerous men and women, who feel a need in general to become immortal, get no reward for their pains, for immortality is not a possession which can be extorted by a list of endorsements. Systematically, immortality cannot be proved at all. The fault does not lie in the proofs, but in the fact that people will not understand that viewed systematically the whole question is nonsense, so that instead of seeking outward proofs, one had better seek to become a little subjective. Immortality is the most passionate interest of subjectivity; precisely in the interest lies the proof. When for the sake of objectivity (quite consistently from the systematic point of view), one systematically ignores the interest, God only knows in this case what immortality is, or even what is the sense of wishing to prove it, or how one could get into one's head the fixed idea of bothering about it.

Quite simply therefore the existing subject asks, not about immortality in general, for such a phantom has no existence, but about his immortality, about what it means to become immortal, whether he is able to contribute anything to the accomplishment of this end, or whether he becomes immortal as a matter of course, or whether he is that and can become it. . . .

The question is raised, how he, while he exists, can hold fast his consciousness of immortality, lest the metaphysical conception of immortality proceed to confuse the ethical and reduce it to an illusion; for ethically, everything culminates in immortality, without which the ethical is merely use and wont, and metaphysically, immortality swallows up existence, yea, the seventy years of existence, as a thing of naught, and yet ethically this naught must be of infinite importance. The question is raised, how immortality practically transforms his life; in what sense he must have the consciousness of it always present to him, or whether perhaps it is enough to think this thought once for all.

And the fact of asking about his immortality is at the same time for the existing subject who raises the question a deed—as it is not, to be sure, for absent-minded people who once in a while ask about the matter of being immortal quite in general, as if immortality were something one has once in a while, and the question were some sort of thing in general. So he asks how he is to behave in order to express in existence his immortality, whether he is really expressing it; and for the time being, he is satisfied with this task, which surely must be enough to last a man a lifetime since it is to last for an eternity. And then? Well, then, when he has completed this task, then comes the turn for world-history. In these days, to be sure, it is just the other way round: now people apply themselves first to world-history, and therefore there comes out of this the ludicrous result (as another author has remarked), that while people are proving and proving immortality quite in general, faith in immortality is more and more diminishing.

Questions for Discussion: *Religion*

1. James claimed that we have a right to believe things of which we have not been rationally persuaded. Do you agree? Or must we believe only those things for which we already have solid evidence?

2. Do you think that a cogent proof for the existence of God is a necessary support for faith? Which arguments for or against the existence of God do you find most persuasive?

3. Kierkegaard said that there are times in life when we face the "either/or"; that is, there are times when if we are honest, we must commit ourselves one way or another. Do you find this disquieting? Comforting? Why?

4. Does it make any difference to you whether your mind and body are two different things? Why or why not?

5. Compare Plato's and Hume's views of the development of the soul prior to death and how death is naturally related to this development. Which do you think is the more plausible account?

Suggested Additional Readings: *Religion*

Agee, James: *A Death in the Family*, Bantam Books, New York, 1971. A profoundly moving account, in which various religious attitudes are illustrated, of the effect of a death on a loving family.

Auden, W. H. (ed.): *The Living Thought of Kierkegaard*, Indiana University Press, Bloomington, 1963. A good collection of Kierkegaard's writings.

Broad, C. D.: *The Mind and Its Place in Nature*, reprinted Humanities Press, New York, 1976. A modern classic on the relation of soul and body.

Copleston, F. C.: *Thomas Aquinas*, Barnes & Noble, New York, 1977. An excellent introduction to the philosophy of Aquinas.

Dean, Sidney (ed.): *Basic Writings of Saint Anselm*, Open Court, La Salle, Ill., 1974. This edition includes Anselm's text, early criticisms, and discussions by later philosophers.

Dostoevski, Feodor: *The Brothers Karamazov*, Critical Editions Series, Norton, New York, 1976. Includes useful discussions of all the topics in our discussion of Religion.

Ducasse, C. J.: *A Philosophical Scrutiny of Religion*, Ronald, New York, 1953. A clear and broad examination of philosophy and religion.

Hume, David: *Dialogues concerning Natural Religion: Text and Critical Essays*, Nelson Pike (ed.) Bobbs-Merrill, Indianapolis, 1970. This work, by David Hume, is one of the most provocative in the philosophy of religion.

James, William: *Human Immortality*, Folcroft, 1977. A clear and careful work on this difficult topic.

Kaufmann, Walter: *Critique of Religion and Philosophy*, Harper & Row, New York, 1958. A wide-ranging and influential book.

In Praise of Dialectic, Magritte (*Reproduced by permission of the National Gallery of Victoria, Melbourne*)

KNOWLEDGE

WHAT CAN I KNOW?

There is the fact that I am here, seated by the fire, attired in a
dressing gown, having this paper in my hands. . . . And
how could I deny that these hands and this body are
mine. [But] how often has it happened to me
that in the night I dreamt that I found
myself in this particular place, that I
was dressed and seated near the
fire, while in reality I was lying
undressed in bed! . . . I
remind myself that on
occasions I have
in sleep
been
deceived by similar illusions and in dwelling carefully on this
reflection I see no certain indications by which we may
clearly distinguish wakefulness from sleep. . . .

Descartes

Meditations (1640)

INTRODUCTION

It may seem strange to ask the question "What can I know?" Common sense tells us that we know a great deal and that what we do not know may be discovered in the future. But the philosophical question "What can I know?" is a way of challenging the common-sense attitude toward knowledge. Our common sense leads us to believe that our knowledge will help us live through the events of each day successfully. We know that the sun will rise in the morning, that the food we eat will nourish our bodies, that the aspirin we swallow will cause our headache to disappear, that gasoline will make our automobiles move, and that our calculations will accurately guide a vehicle to the moon. But even though we seem to have knowledge about these things, it turns out that we do not really have a clear idea of what it means *to know*. When we try to describe *how* we know something, we discover that the process of knowing is full of surprises. How, for example, can we be absolutely sure that we are not dreaming? Descartes said we could never be sure because there are "no certain indications," no clear way to distinguish wakefulness from sleep. We may, moreover, think that seeing a physical object will give us reliable knowledge about it. But when we see a stick in the water which looks bent, we discover when we remove it from the water that it is not bent. If we can be mistaken about the exact shape of the stick in the water, does that not raise doubts in our minds about other experiences we once thought would give us exact knowledge? When, therefore, philosophers ask the question "What can I know?" they are really asking what we can know about which no reasonable person would raise any doubt. In order to deal with these questions, we need to consider a series of problems which cluster around the process of knowing, and we will call these problems the "elements of knowing."

The Elements of Knowing

APPEARANCE AND REALITY

Nothing seems more obvious to us than the presence and existence of a physical object which we see. But when we look, for example, at an apple, what do we see and what do we know about it? We say it is red, has a round shape, and has a certain texture and taste. Is it really red or has an artificial light or plastic bag made it look red? Is it round or is it that my looking at it from an angle makes it appear round? Is it sweet or has its taste been affected by the candy I ate earlier? More important, is the redness in the apple or is that color in my eye or brain? To see an apple, or any other physical object, is to perceive it through my sense of sight. In short, I have a sensation of it. The content of this sensation is, for example, the color red. This sensation is inside of me.

We now have three parts of my experience of seeing the apple: (1) myself, who has the sensation, (2) the content of the sensation, namely, the color and shape, or what are called "sense data," and (3) the apple, upon which my sensation depends. What, then, do we know about the apple? There is no doubt that I have a sensation of color, but can I be sure that the redness is in, or is part of, the apple? Is the apple *really* what it *appears* to be? Similarly, we saw earlier that the stick in the water does appear to be bent; there is no doubt that we have a sensation of a bent stick. But is the stick really bent? Is it *true* that the stick is bent, even though it is true that I perceive the stick to be bent? It is clear that appearance can differ from reality. The information we get from our sensation does not always tell us the truth about the object. We cannot be sure whether other qualities such as hardness or weight belong to things that appear to have them. Even hardness and weight might not be a part of the apple. These qualities might instead depend on other circumstances, such as, for example, altitude and gravity. We discover that we know less about the apple and the stick than we orig-

Duke of Urbino's study, fifteenth century (*The Metropolitan Museum of Art, Roger Fund, 1939*)

inally thought we did. In any case, the information we get directly from our senses does not necessarily tell us the truth about an object, the truth about what an object is really like. In the picture on this page we think we see cupboards, bookshelves, books, other objects, and benches against the wall. Actually, that is all merely appearance created by the clever use of inlaid wood of different colors. The reality is that the wall is perfectly flat.

BUILDING KNOWLEDGE UPON EXPERIENCE

Just as Descartes raised the astonishing question of whether we can ever tell the difference between wakefulness and sleep, so David Hume asked in all seriousness whether we could be sure that the sun will rise tomorrow. How could there be any question over whether the sun will rise? Hume put the question the other way around, namely, how could you be certain, that is, how do you _know_ that the sun will rise? Common sense tells us that we can expect the sun to rise because it has always risen before. But how can our knowledge of a past event give us any assurance that the same event will occur in the future? We think we have solid knowledge about the future because we build our knowledge on our experience of the past. From the past, we infer the future. We employ what is called the "principle of induction," which is defined as reasoning from a particular instance to a general rule. From our experience of seeing an apple fall, we reason that all bodies fall. But is this knowledge? What more do we know than that we are in the _habit_ of expecting certain events to happen and _until now_ they have happened? We cannot say with certainty that they will happen in the future. If we say we know that they will happen in the future because there is a _uniformity in nature_, we are back where we started because the phrase "uniformity of nature" is exactly what we are trying to prove in the first place when we say that we can be sure that the sun will rise because it has always risen before. Although the "laws of motion" are working today, how can we be sure that they will be working tomorrow?

We can ask the same kind of question about the relation of certain events to each other that we call "cause" and "effect." What more do we know than that so far event _A_ has always been followed by event _B_, that after swallowing aspirin my headache disappears? There is really no reason why _B_ should follow _A_ in the future. But even though we cannot have exact knowledge with certainty about the future, because we never know when the future will be different, we do nevertheless have a _kind_ of knowledge which is called "probable knowledge." Our knowledge, to the extent that it is built on our experience of particular instances or experiments, does not _prove_ that the future will continue to be the same as the past. Nevertheless, the _probability_ that the future will be what we expect it to be makes it possible for us to go about our daily affairs confident that certain causes will be followed by certain effects and that the sun will rise in the morning.

KNOWLEDGE PRIOR TO EXPERIENCE

We have another kind of knowledge which does not require experience to prove that it is true. Moreover, it is true not only with respect to the past, but is always and everywhere true. This knowl-

edge is called "a priori knowledge" because it is prior to or independent of experience. Examples are commonly found in mathematics. We know that two plus two equals four under any and all
circumstances. It may be that at one time we learned to count with
marbles or apples, but we quickly discovered that we could clearly
think of the relations between two and two no matter two of what.
We do not have to assume that we are born with these ideas,
although it is fair to assume that the human mind has a certain
capacity to obey various "laws of thought." As soon as we understand what is meant by "two" and "plus," we are able to move
accurately to "four."

One of the laws of thought is the "law of contradiction," which
states that a thing cannot both be and not be at the same time. We
know, therefore, that bachelors are not married or that a thing cannot be all white and all green at the same time. Merely by the operation of the mind we arrive at conclusions which necessarily must
be true.

Two reasons account for the necessity of the truth of a priori
knowledge. First, in an a priori statement, the subject (bachelor)
already contains the predicate (not married) so that to say that a
bachelor is married would be to commit a contradiction. The consistent use of language guarantees the truth of the a priori statement. Second, a priori statements are true also because the law of
contradiction refers not only to words but to things, so that to say
a bachelor is married is not only an example of an inconsistent use
of language but a contradiction of the actual condition (unmarried)
of a person (bachelor). A priori knowledge is independent of experience only in the sense that once we understand such concepts as
"bachelor" or "two and two," we can by mere thinking see the
truth of a statement. No further observation or experience could
deny the necessary truth of some statements, such as, for example,
that if A is bigger than B and B is bigger than C, then A is bigger
than C.

THE WORLD OF IDEAS

It is fascinating to discover how much of our knowledge is contained in words which do not refer to any particular thing. You
know what I mean when I say "tree" or "triangle" or "man" or

"woman" even before I say "that oak" or "this right triangle" or "John" or "Mary." It may be that after seeing several trees, our mind is able to discover something common in all of them and draw out, or *abstract,* that common element. We came upon a similar way of knowing when we referred to mathematics: after seeing two oranges, two people, or two houses, the mind can grasp the concept of "two" without further reference to two this or two that. When we look at a tree, we *see* an oak but *think* a tree. Similarly, we can speak of qualities such as white without necessarily referring to any white thing. We can think whiteness in the same way that we can think triangularity. More important, when we try to prove something about triangles, we do not think of any particular triangle but rather about what is common, or universally applicable, to all of them.

We can think of such ideas as "beauty" or "justice" without referring to any specific beautiful object or example of justice. Do we have the ideas of beauty and justice before we experience examples of them? How would we ever know whether we are experiencing a beautiful object or that a government acts justly? What impresses us about the world of ideas is its stability, its permanence. Trees change and disappear, but the idea of "tree" continues. Actually, all particular things come and go, but the ideas of "triangularity," "whiteness," "man," "woman," "beauty," and "justice" remain. This contrast between particular things and the world of ideas (or universals) is reflected in the way we know. If we limit our knowledge to particular things, we cannot know as much as when we also focus our thinking on ideas or universals. The question we will want to ask is how these two worlds of knowledge are related to each other.

USING THE WORD "TRUTH"

Our common sense tells us how to use the word "truth" most of the time. When a mother says to her child "tell me the truth," having in mind the disappearance of the cookies, the child knows exactly what is called for. If he took the cookies, the truth is "I took them." If he did not and does not know who did, the truth is "I don't know who took them." Truth can be defined, then, as the proper relation between a statement and a fact. This relation is usually called "correspondence," so that a statement is true if it is based on a corresponding fact. This example of the cookies happens to be an easy one because the statement "I took them" corresponds, that is, "fits," perfectly with the fact that the child took the cookies out of the jar. Complications arise, however, if we ask, for example, if it is true that we see a bent stick in the water. If we use our language carefully, we will discover what is and what is not true in this case. It is true that we see (have an impression of) a bent stick. It is also true that the stick is straight. It is false to say I see a bent stick if I mean that I believe the stick is actually bent. In this case, there are two facts, namely, the impression of bentness and the actual straightness. It happens that we can easily *verify* whether in fact the stick is bent or straight by simply taking the stick out of the water. But not all questions can be settled or verified this easily.

Place yourself back several centuries and imagine how the truth about the sun was discussed. Some people believed it to be true that the sun rises, that is, that the sun moves around the earth. Other scientists thought this could not be true because it did not fit with other knowledge they had about astronomy. For them, the standard of truth was *coherence*, which means that something is true if it is consistent with other valid knowledge. Observations made possible by the invention of the telescope and new mathematical calculations showed that planets, including the earth, revolve around the sun. It appears, then, that the truth is that the sun does not rise in the literal sense.

There is still another theory of truth, namely, the "pragmatic theory," which says that a belief is true if it works. For some people, it works in many practical ways to believe that the sun rises. But is it true?

Summary

We have discovered that in the process of knowing we encounter several problems, namely, that appearance is not always the same as reality; that most of our knowledge is built on experience, but the fact that something has happened in the past does not guarantee that it will also happen in the future; that although objects and events outside us provide most of the raw material of our knowledge, there is nevertheless something in our minds which we bring to these objects to make our knowledge possible; that we need to understand how the world of ideas and the world of things are related to each other; and finally, that there are various ways of defining truth, namely, as the correspondence of a statement with a fact, as the coherence of one piece of knowledge with other valid knowledge, or as a practical idea which works. These are some of the elements of knowledge we will encounter as we consider the thought of some philosophers who sought to answer the question "What can I know?"

SOME PHILOSOPHIES OF KNOWLEDGE

Each of the following philosophers approached the theory of knowledge in a unique way:

(1) *Plato* was especially concerned to make sense out of the confused world of everyday experience. He thought he discovered a world of *ideas* above the world of things. Things, he said, are only a pale copy of ideas. This helped him explain the difference between appearance and reality. Ideas, he said, are more real than things, and for this reason he is called an "idealist."

(2) *Descartes* wondered whether we could ever achieve intellectual certainty. He was bothered by doubt because he thought it is possible to doubt everything we experience or can think of. And so he deliberately pushed his method of doubt in every conceivable direction and to every subject until he discovered something he could not doubt, namely, that he was doubting. Upon the certainty of this knowledge that he was doubting he built a full system of thought using only his rational powers each step of the way; for this reason he is called a "rationalist."

(3) *Hume* disagreed with Descartes and denied that human reason has the power to produce the kind of knowledge Descartes claimed it could. On the contrary, Hume said that we can never know anything more than what we experience with our senses. All our ideas, he said, can be traced back to our impressions of things. Moreover, past knowledge does not guarantee how future events will occur. Because his theory put such severe limits on what we can know, Hume is called a "skeptic."

(4) *Kant* took Hume seriously but also thought that Descartes had something important to say about how we know. Therefore, Kant tried to harmonize the rationalism of Descartes and the skepticism of Hume and in the process developed his own theory of knowledge, which is called "critical idealism."

(5) *William James* was impatient with the endless technical discussions about theories of knowledge. He emphasized the practical aspects of philosophy and said that the way to test a theory or an idea is to try it and see if it makes a difference in life. For this reason, he is called a "pragmatist."

(6) *Analytic philosophers:* These twentieth-century philosophers sought to limit the task of philosophy to the analysis of language in order to distinguish between those propositions which make sense because they can be verified and those which are meaningless because they do not refer to verifiable aspects of our experience. We will refer to Bertrand Russell, Rudolph Carnap, and Ludwig Wittgenstein.

CHAPTER 20

OPINION VERSUS KNOWLEDGE

Plato

Plato (428–348 B.C.) was born in a distinguished family in Athens at a time when culture there was flourishing. Although Plato was aware of the various modes of philosophy circulating in Athens, the most important influence in the formation of his thought was the life and teaching of Socrates (470–399 B.C.). From Socrates he learned that the surest way of going after knowledge is through orderly conversation or dialogue. That is why Plato wrote dialogues, because the dialectic method enabled him to demonstrate how an idea must be constantly subjected to argument and counterargument. Plato wrote about twenty books or dialogues; the first group reflects the influence of Socrates, while the later group shows the development of his new concepts. When he was about forty years old, after writing most of his books, he founded his school, called the Academy of Athens, probably the first university. Aristotle entered this Academy in 367 B.C. at the age of eighteen. The trial and death of Socrates disillusioned Plato about public political life, but he continued to exert great influence through his teaching at the Academy until his death at the age of eighty.

Plato describes how the human mind achieves knowledge and indicates what knowledge consists of, by means of (1) his allegory of the *cave*, (2) his metaphor of the *divided line*, and (3) his doctrine of the *forms*.

The Cave

Plato asks us to imagine some men living in a large cave where from childhood they have been chained by the leg and by the neck so that they cannot move. Because they cannot even turn their heads, they can see only what is in front of them. Behind them is an elevation that rises abruptly from the level where the prisoners are seated. On this elevation there are persons walking back and forth carrying artificial objects, including the figures of animals and human beings made out of wood and stone and various other materials. Behind these walking persons is a fire, and farther back still is the entrance to the cave. The chained prisoners can look only forward against the wall at the end of the cave and can see neither one another or the moving persons nor the fire behind them. All that the prisoners can ever see are the shadows on the wall in front of them, which are projected as persons walking in front of the fire. They never see the objects or the men carrying them, nor are they aware that the shadows are shadows of other things. When they see a shadow and hear a person's voice echo from the wall, they assume that the sound is coming from the shadow, since they are not aware of the existence of anything else. These prisoners, then, recognize as reality only the shadows formed on the wall.

What would happen asks Plato, if one of these prisoners were released from his chains, were forced to stand up, turn around, and walk with eyes lifted up toward the light of the fire? All his movements would be exceedingly painful. Suppose he were forced to look at the objects being carried, the shadows of which he had become accustomed to seeing on the wall. Would he not find these actual objects less congenial to his eyes, and less meaningful, than the shadows? And would not his eyes ache if he looked straight at the light from the fire itself? At this point he would undoubtedly try to escape from his liberator and turn back to the things he could see with clarity, being convinced that the shadows were clearer than the objects he was forced to look at in the firelight.

Plato (*The Bettman Archive*)

Suppose this prisoner could not turn back, but were instead dragged forcibly up the steep and rough passage to the mouth of the cave and released only after he had been brought out into the sunlight. The impact of the radiance of the sun on his eyes would be so painful that he would be unable to see any of the things that he was now told were real. It would take some time before his eyes became accustomed to the world outside the cave. He would first of all recognize some shadows and would feel at home with them. If one were the shadow of a man, he would have seen that shape before as it appeared on the wall of the cave. Next, he would see the reflections of men and things in the water, and this would represent a major advance in his knowledge, for what he once knew only as a solid dark blur would now be seen in more precise detail of line and color. A flower makes a shadow which gives very little, if any, indication of what a flower really looks like, but its image as reflected in the water provides the eyes with a clearer vision of each petal and its various colors. In time, he would see the flower itself. As he lifted his eyes skyward, he would find it easier at first to look at the heavenly bodies at night, looking at the moon and the stars instead of the sun in daytime. Finally, he would look right at the sun in its natural positions in the sky and not at its reflection from or through anything else.

This extraordinary experience would gradually lead this liberated prisoner to conclude that the sun is what makes things visible. It is the sun, too, that accounts for the seasons of the year, and for that reason the sun is the cause of life in the spring. Now he would understand what he and his fellow prisoners saw on the wall, how shadows and reflections differ from things as they really are in the visible world, and that without the sun there would be no visible world.

How would such a person feel about his previous life in the cave? He would recall what he and his fellow prisoners there took to be wisdom, how they had a practice of honoring and commending each other, giving prizes to the one who had the sharpest eye for the passing shadows and the best memory for the order in which they followed each other so that he could make the best guess as to which shadow would come next. Would the released prisoner still think such prizes were worth having, and would he envy the men who received honors in the cave? Instead of envy, he would have only sorrow and pity for them.

If he went back to his former seat in the cave, he would at first have great difficulty, for going suddenly from daylight into the cave would fill his eyes with darkness. He could not, under these circumstances, compete very effectively with the other prisoners in making out the shadows on the wall. While his eyesight was still dim and unsteady, those who had their permanent residence in the darkness could win every round of competition with him. They would at first find this situation very amusing and would taunt him by saying that his sight was perfectly all right before he went up out of the cave and that now he has returned with his sight ruined.

Their conclusion would be that it is not worth trying to go up out of the cave. Indeed, says Plato, "if they could lay hands on the man who was trying to set them free and lead them up, they would kill him."

Most people, this allegory would suggest, dwell in the darkness of the cave. They have oriented their thoughts around the blurred world of shadows. It is the function of *education* to lead men out of the cave into the world of light. Education is not simply a matter of putting knowledge into the soul of a person who does not possess it, any more than vision is putting sight into blind eyes. Knowledge is like vision in that it requires an organ capable of receiving it. Just as the prisoner had to turn his whole body around in order that his eyes could see the light instead of the darkness, so also it is necessary for the entire soul to turn away from the deceptive world of change and appetite that causes a blindness of the soul. Education, then, is a matter of *conversion*, a complete turning around from the world of appearance to the world of reality. "The conversion of the soul," says Plato, "is not to put the power of sight in the soul's eye, which already has it, but to insure that, instead of looking in the wrong direction, it is turned the way it ought to be." But looking in the right direction does not come easily. Even the "noblest natures" do not always want to look that way, and so Plato says that the rulers must "bring compulsion to bear" upon them to ascend upward from darkness to light. Similarly, when those who have been liberated from the cave achieve the highest knowledge, they must not be allowed to remain in the higher world of contemplation, but must be made to come back down into the cave and take part in the life and labors of the prisoners.

Plato said that there are two worlds, the dark world of the cave and the bright world of light. For Plato knowledge was not only possible: it was virtually infallible. What made knowledge infallible was that it was based on what is most *real*. The dramatic contrast between the shadows, reflections, and the actual objects was for Plato the decisive clue to the different degrees to which human beings could be enlightened. Plato saw the counterparts of shadows in all of human life and discourse. Disagreements between men concerning the meaning of justice, for example, were the result of each one's looking at a different aspect of the reality of justice. One person might take justice to mean whatever the rulers in fact command the people to do, on the assumption that justice has to do with rules of behavior laid down by the ruler. Just as a shadow bears some relation to the object of which it is the shadow, so this conception of justice has some measure of truth to it, for justice does have some connection with the ruler. But different rulers command different modes of behavior, and there could be no single coherent concept of justice if men's knowledge of justice were derived from the wide variety of examples of it.

The Sophists were skeptical about the possibility of true knowledge because they were impressed by the variety and constant change in things, and, they argued, since our knowledge comes from our experience, our knowledge will reflect this variety and will therefore be relative to each person. Plato agreed that such knowledge as is based on our sense experiences would be relative and not absolute, but he would not accept the Sophists' notion that *all* knowledge is relative. "The ignorant," writes Plato, "have no single mark before their eyes at which they must aim in all the conduct of their lives. . . . " If all we could know were the shadows, we could never have reliable knowledge, for these shadows would always change in size and shape depending on the, to us, unknown motions of the real objects. Plato was convinced that the human mind is able to discover that "single mark," that "real" object behind all the multitude of shadows, which is to attain true knowledge. There is, Plato believed, a true Idea of Justice, an Idea that can be blurred by rulers and communities. This line of reasoning lay behind his distinction between the world of sense and the world of thought, between the visible world and the intelligible world.

Whereas the allegory of the cave illustrates these distinctions in dramatic terms, Plato's metaphor of the divided line sets forth the stages or levels of knowledge in more systematic form.

The Divided Line

In the process of discovering true knowledge, the mind, says Plato, moves through four stages of development. At each stage, there is a parallel between the kind of object presented to the mind and the kind of thought this object makes possible. These objects and their parallel modes of thought can be diagramed as follows:

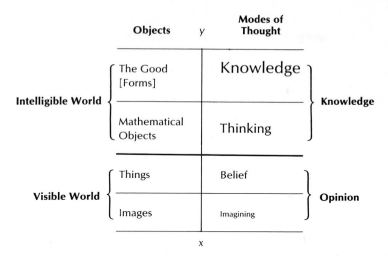

The vertical line from x to y is a continuous one, suggesting that there is some degree of knowledge at every point. But as the line passes through the lowest forms of reality to the highest, there is a parallel progression from the lowest degree of truth to the highest. The line is divided, first of all, into two unequal parts. The upper and larger part represents the intelligible world and the smaller, lower part the visible world. This unequal division symbolizes the lower degree of reality and truth found in the visible world as compared with the greater reality and truth in the intelligible world. Each of these parts is then subdivided in the same proportion as the whole line, producing four parts, each one representing a clearer and more certain mode of thought than the one below. Recalling the allegory of the cave, we can think of this line as beginning in the dark and shadowy world at x and moving up to the bright light at y. Going from x to y represents a continuous process of the mind's enlightenment. The objects presented to the mind at each level are not four different kinds of real objects: rather, they represent four different ways of looking at the same object.

IMAGINING

The most superficial form of mental activity is found at the lowest level of the line. Here the mind confronts images, or the least amount of reality. The word "imagining" could, of course, mean the activity of penetrating beyond the mere appearances of things to their deeper reality. But here Plato means by imagining simply the sense experience of appearances wherein these appearances are taken as true reality. An obvious example is a shadow, which can be mistaken for something real. Actually, the shadow *is* something real; it is a real shadow. But what makes imagining the lowest form of knowing is that at this stage the mind does not know that it *is* a shadow or an image that it has confronted. If a person knew that it was a shadow, he would not be in the state of imagining or illusion. The prisoners in the cave are trapped in the deepest ignorance because they are unaware that they are seeing shadows.

Besides shadows, there are other kinds of images which Plato considered deceptive. These are the images fashioned by the artist and the poet. The artist presents images that are at least two steps removed from true reality. Suppose an artist paints a portrait of Socrates. Socrates represents a specific or concrete version of the Ideal Man. Moreover, the portrait represents only the artist's own view of Socrates. The three levels of reality here are, then, (1) the Idea of Man, (2) the embodiment of this Idea in Socrates, and (3) the image of Socrates as represented on canvas. Plato's criticism of art is that it produces images that, in turn, stimulate illusory ideas in the observer. Again, it is when the image is taken as a perfect version of something real that illusion is produced. For the most part, men know that an artist puts on canvas his own way of seeing a subject. Still, artistic images do shape men's thoughts, and if men restrict their understanding of things to these images with all their distortions and exaggerations, they will certainly lack an understanding of things as they really are.

What concerned Plato most were the images fashioned by the art of using words. Poetry and rhetoric were for him the most serious sources of illusion. Words have the power of creating images before the mind, and the poet and rhetorician have great skill in using words to create such images. Plato was particularly critical of the Sophists, whose influence came from this very skill in the use of words. They could make either side of an argument *seem* as good as the other. In a discussion of justice, for example, the Sophist, or any other artist with words, could create the same distortion that we found in the portrait. Justice as understood in Athens could be taken by a pleader and distorted in favor of a special client. This special pleader's version of justice could be a distortion of the Athenian view; also, the Athenian view might very well be a distortion of the Ideal Justice. If someone heard only the special pleader's version of justice, he would be at least twice removed from the true Idea of Justice. There is no illusion if the special pleader's distortions of Athenian justice are recognized as such. Moreover, it would be possible for some citizens to recognize that Athenian law itself represented some deviations from the true concept of Justice. Everything depends on what the mind has access to as its object. The special pleader does present some degree of truth about Justice but in a very distorted form, just as a shadow gives some evidence of some reality. Imagining, however, implies that a person is not aware that he is observing an image; therefore, imagining amounts to illusion and ignorance.

BELIEF

The next stage after imagining is belief. It may strike one as strange that Plato should use the word "believing" instead of "knowing" to describe the state of mind induced by seeing actual objects. We tend to feel a strong sense of certainty when we observe visible and tangible things. Still, for Plato, seeing constitutes only believing, because visible objects depend on their context for many of their characteristics. There is, then, a degree of certainty that seeing gives us, but this is not absolute certainty. If the water of the Mediterranean looks blue from the shore but turns out to be clear when taken from the sea, one's certainty about its color or composition is at least open to question. That all bodies have weight because we see them fall may seem a certainty, but we now know that this testimony of our vision must also be adjusted to the fact of the weightlessness of bodies in space at certain altitudes. Plato says, therefore, that believing, even if it is based on seeing, is still in the stage of opinion.

The state of mind produced by visible objects is clearly on a level higher than imagining, because it is based on a higher form of reality. But although actual things possess greater reality than their shadows, they do not by themselves give us all the knowledge we want to have about them. Again, justice may be seen in a particular context, but to find justice defined in a different way in another culture does raise the question about the true nature of Justice. Whether it be color, weight, or justice, these properties of things and acts are experienced under particular circumstances. For this reason, our knowledge about them is limited to these particular circumstances. But the mind is unsatisfied with this kind of knowledge, knowing that its certainty could very well be shaken if the circumstances were altered. The scientist and the jurist, therefore, do not want to confine their understanding to these particular cases, but look for principles behind the behavior of things.

THINKING

When a person moves from believing to thinking, he moves from the visible world to the intelligible world, from the realm of opinion to the realm of knowledge. The state of mind that Plato calls "thinking" is particularly characteristic of the scientist. The scientist deals with visible things, but not simply with his vision of them. For him, visible things are symbols of a reality that can be thought but not seen. Plato illustrates this kind of mental activity by referring to the mathematician. The mathematician engages in the act of "abstraction," of drawing out from the visible thing what this thing symbolizes. When a mathematician sees the diagram of a triangle, he thinks about *triangularity* or triangle-in-itself. He distinguishes between the *visible* triangle and the *intelligible* triangle. By using visible symbols, science provides a bridge from the visible to the intelligible world.

Science forces one to think, because the scientist is always searching for laws or principles. Although the scientist may look at a particular object, a triangle or a brain, he goes beyond this particular triangle or brain and thinks about *the* Triangle or *the* Brain. Science requires that we "let go" our senses and rely instead on our intellects. The mind knows that two and two equals four no matter two of what. It knows also that the angles of an equilateral triangle are all equal, regardless of the size of the triangle. Thinking, therefore, represents the power of the mind to abstract from a visible object that property which is the same in all objects in that class even though each such actual object will have other variable properties. We can, in short, think the Idea *Man* whether we observe small, large, dark, light, young, or old persons.

Thinking is characterized not only by its treatment of visible objects as symbols, but also by reasoning from *hypotheses*. By an "hypothesis" Plato meant a truth which is taken as self-evident but which depends on some higher truth. "You know," says Plato, "how students of subjects like geometry and arithmetic begin by postulating odd and even numbers, or the various figures and the three kinds of angle. . . . These data they take as known, and having adopted them as assumptions, they do not feel called upon to give any account of them to themselves or to anyone else but treat them as self-evident." Using hypotheses, or "starting from these assumptions, they go on until they arrive, by a series of consistent steps, at all the conclusions they set out to investigate." For Plato, then, an hypothesis did not mean what it means to us, namely, a temporary truth. Rather, he meant by it a firm truth but one that is related to a larger context. The special sciences and mathematics treat their subjects as if they were independent truths. All Plato wants to say here is that if we could view all things as they really are, we should discover that all things are related or connected. Thinking or reasoning from hypotheses give us knowledge of the truth, but it does bear this limitation, that it isolates some truths from others, thereby leaving the mind still to ask *why* a certain truth is true.

PERFECT INTELLIGENCE

The mind is never satisfied as long as it must still ask for a fuller explanation of things. But to have perfect knowledge would require that the mind should grasp the relation of everything to everything else, that it should see the unity of the whole of reality. Perfect intelligence represents the mind as completely released from sensible objects. At this level, the mind is dealing directly with the *Forms*. The Forms are those intelligible objects, such as Triangle and Man, which have been abstracted from the actual objects. The mind is now dealing with these pure Forms without any interference from even the symbolic character of visible objects. Here, also, the mind no longer uses hypotheses, because they represent limited and isolated truths. This highest level of knowledge is approached to the extent that the mind is able to move beyond the restrictions of hypotheses toward the unity of all Forms. It is by the faculty or power of *dialectic* that the mind moves toward its highest goal, for this is the power of seeing at once the relation of all divisions of knowledge to each other. Perfect intelligence therefore means the *synoptic* view of reality, and this, for Plato, implies the unity of knowledge.

Plato concludes his discussion of the divided line with the summary statement "Now you may take, as corresponding to the four sections, these four states of mind: *intelligence* for the highest, *thinking* for the second, *belief* for the third and for the last *imagining.* These you may arrange as the terms in a proportion, assigning to each a degree of clearness and certainty corresponding to the measure in which their objects possess truth and reality." The highest degree of reality, he argues, was possessed by the Forms, as compared with shadows, reflections, and even visible objects. What he meant by the Forms we must now explore in greater detail.

The Platonic Doctrine of Forms or Ideas

Plato's theory of the Forms or Ideas represents his most significant philosophical contribution. However obscure and unsatisfactory his theory may be to us, it gathers around itself the novel insights that led Plato's philosophy beyond anything that had been thought before him. Basically, the Forms or Ideas are those changeless, eternal, and nonmaterial essences or patterns of which the actual visible objects we see are only poor copies. There is the Form of *the* Triangle, and all the triangles we see are mere copies of that Form. This description of the Forms as nonmaterial realities indicates what was so novel about the Platonic doctrine: Whereas the pre-Socratic philosophers thought of reality as material stuff of some sort, Plato now designated the nonmaterial Ideas or Forms as the true reality. Similarly, whereas the Sophists thought that all knowledge is relative because the material order, which is all they knew, is constantly shifting and changing, Plato argued that knowledge is absolute because the true object of thought is not the material order but the changeless and eternal order of the Ideas or Forms. Although Socrates anticipated this view by holding that there is an absolute Good, which makes possible our judgments of particular goods, Plato went beyond Socrates's ethical concern by adding to the concept of Good a theory of metaphysics, an explanation of the whole structure of reality and the place of morality in it.

The doctrine of Forms represents a serious attempt to explain the nature of existence. We have certain kinds of experiences that raise the question about existence for us. For example, we make judgments about things and behavior, saying about a thing that it is beautiful and about an act that it is good. This suggests that there is somewhere a standard of beauty which *is* different from the things we are judging and that there *is* a standard of good which is somehow separate from the person or his act that we judge. Moreover, visible things change—they come and go, generate and perish. Their existence is brief. Compared with things, Ideas such as Good and Beautiful seem timeless. They have more *being* than things. Plato concluded, therefore, that the real world is not the visible world but rather the intelligible world. The intelligible world is most real, said Plato, because it consists of the eternal Forms.

Knowledge as Recollection

According to Plato, the soul, that is, the human mind, before it is united with the body, is acquainted with the intelligible world or the world of Forms. In this prior existence, the soul has true knowledge. After its union with a human body, a person's mind contains its original knowledge deep in its memory. True knowledge in this world consists of remembering, in reminiscence or recollection. For Plato, then, the human mind is not originally an empty vessel into which knowledge is poured by teaching a person information. On the contrary, what the mind or soul once knew is raised to present awareness by a process of recollection aided by the technique of *dialectic* or the Socratic method. In his dialogue entitled *Meno,* Plato illustrates how Socrates is able to show that even a young uneducated slave boy "knows" some truths of geometry not because somebody taught him that subject but because he naturally knows the relationship of various ideas to each other. This episode is contained in the selection from the *Meno* which follows.

READING

KNOWLEDGE AS RECOLLECTION
Plato

Meno. And how will you enquire, Socrates, into that which you do not know? What will you put forth as the subject of enquiry? And if you find what you want, how will you ever know that this is the thing which you did not know?

Socrates. I know, Meno, what you mean; but just see what a tiresome dispute you are introducing. You argue that a man cannot enquire either about that which he knows, or about that which he does not know; for if he knows, he has no need to enquire; and if not, he cannot for he does not know the very subject about which he is to enquire.

Men. Well, Socrates, and is not the argument sound?

Soc. I think not.

Men. Why not?

Soc. I will tell you why: I have heard from certain wise men and women who spoke of things divine that—

Men. What did they say?

Soc. They spoke of a glorious truth, as I conceive.

Men. What was it? and who were they?

Soc. Some of them were priests and priestesses, who had studied how they might be able to give a reason of their profession: there have been poets also, who spoke of these things by inspiration, like Pindar, and many others who were inspired. And they say—mark, now, and see whether their words are true—they say that the soul of man is immortal, and at one time has an end, which is termed dying, and at another time is born again, but is never destroyed. And the moral is, that a man ought to live always in perfect holiness. *"For in the ninth year Persephone sends the souls of those from whom she has received the penalty of ancient crime back again from beneath into the light of the sun above, and these are they who become noble kings and mighty men and great in wisdom and are called saintly heroes in after ages."* The soul, then, as being immortal, and having been born again many times, and having seen all things that exist, whether in this world or

---

From Plato, *Meno*

in the world below, has knowledge of them all; and it is no wonder that she should be able to call to remembrance all that she ever knew about virtue, and about everything; for as all nature is akin, and the soul has learned all things, there is no difficulty in her eliciting or as men say learning, out of a single recollection all the rest, if a man is strenuous and does not faint; for all enquiry and all learning is but recollection. And therefore we ought not to listen to this sophistical argument about the impossibility of enquiry; for it will make us idle, and is sweet only to the sluggard; but the other saying will make us active and inquisitive. In that confiding, I will gladly enquire with you into the nature of virtue.

Men. Yes, Socrates; but what do you mean by saying that we do not learn, and that what we call learning is only a process of recollection? Can you teach me how this is?

Soc. I told you, Meno, just now that you were a rogue, and now you ask whether I can teach you, when I am saying that there is no teaching, but only recollection; and thus you imagine that you will involve me in a contradiction.

Men. Indeed, Socrates, I protest that I had no such intention. I only asked the question from habit; but if you can prove to me that what you say is true, I wish that you would.

Soc. It will be no easy matter, but I will try to please you to the utmost of my power. Suppose that you call one of your numerous attendants, that I may demonstrate on him.

Men. Certainly. Come hither, boy.

Soc. He is Greek, and speaks Greek, does he not?

Men. Yes, indeed; he was born in the house.

Soc. Attend now to the questions which I ask him, and observe whether he learns of me or only remembers.

Men. I will.

Soc. Tell me, boy, do you know that a figure like this is a square?

Boy. I do.

Soc. And you know that a square figure has these four lines equal?

Boy. Certainly.

Soc. And these lines which I have drawn through the middle of the square are also equal?

Boy. Yes.

Soc. A square may be of any size?

Boy. Certainly.

Soc. And if one side of the figure be of two feet, and the other side be of two feet, how much will the whole be? Let me explain: if in one direction the space was of two feet, and in the other direction of one foot, the whole would be of two feet taken once?

Boy. Yes.

Soc. But since this side is also of two feet, there are twice two feet?

Boy. There are.

Soc. Then the square is of twice two feet?

Boy. Yes.

Soc. And how many are twice two feet? count and tell me.

Boy. Four, Socrates.

Soc. And might there not be another square twice as large as this, and having like this the lines equal?

Boy. Yes.

Soc. And of how many feet will that be?

Boy. Of eight feet.

Soc. And now try and tell me the length of the line which forms the side of that double square: this is two feet—what will that be?

Boy. Clearly, Socrates, it will be double.

Soc. Do you observe, Meno, that I am not teaching the boy anything, but only asking him questions; and now he fancies that he knows how long a line is necessary in order to produce a figure of eight square feet; does he not?

Men. Yes.

Soc. And does he really know?

Men. Certainly not.

Soc. He only guesses that because the square is double, the line is double.

Men. True.

Soc. Observe him while he recalls the steps in regular order. (*To the Boy.*) Tell me, boy, do you assert that a double space comes from a double line? Remember that I am not speaking of an oblong, but of a figure equal every way, and twice the size of this—that is to say of eight feet; and I want to know whether you still say that a double square comes from a double line?

Boy. Yes.

Soc. But does not this line become doubled if we add another such line here?

Boy. Certainly.

Soc. And four such lines will make a space containing eight feet?

Boy. Yes.

Soc. Let us describe such a figure: Would you not say that this is the figure of eight feet?

Boy. Yes.

Soc. And are there not these four divisions in the figure, each of which is equal to the figure of four feet?

Boy. True.

Soc. And is not that four times four?

Boy. Certainly.

Soc. And four times is not double?

Boy. No, indeed.

Soc. But how much?

Boy. Four times as much.

Soc. Therefore the double line, boy, has given a space, not twice, but four times as much.

Boy. True.

Soc. Four times four are sixteen—are they not?

Boy. Yes.

Soc. What line would give you a space of eight feet, as this gives one of sixteen feet;—do you see?

Boy. Yes.

Soc. And the space of four feet is made from this half line?

Boy. Yes.

Soc. Good; and is not a space of eight feet twice the size of this, and half the size of the other?

Boy. Certainly.

Soc. Such a space, then, will be made out of a line greater than this one, and less than that one?

Boy. Yes; I think so.

Soc. Very good; I like to hear you say what you think. And now tell me, is not this a line of two feet and that of four?

Boy. Yes.

Soc. Then the line which forms the side of eight feet ought to be more than this line of two feet, and less than the other of four feet?

Boy. It ought.

Soc. Try and see if you can tell me how much it will be.

Boy. Three feet.

Soc. Then if we add a half to this line of two, that will be the line of three. Here are two and there is one; and on the other side, here are two also and there is one: and that makes the figure of which you speak?

Boy. Yes.

Soc. But if there are three feet this way and three feet that way, the whole space will be three times three feet?

Boy. That is evident.

Soc. And how much are three times three feet?

Boy. Nine.

Soc. And how much is the double of four?

Boy. Eight.

Soc. Then the figure of eight is not made out of a line of three?

Boy. No.

Soc. But from what line?—tell me exactly; and if you would rather not reckon, try and show me the line.

Boy. Indeed, Socrates, I do not know.

Soc. Do you see, Meno, what advances he has made in his power of recollection? He did not know at first, and he does not know now, what is the side of a figure of eight feet: but then he thought that he knew, and answered confidently as if he knew, and had no difficulty; now he has a difficulty, and neither knows nor fancies that he knows.

Men. True.

Soc. Is he not better off in knowing his ignorance?

Men. I think that he is.

Soc. If we have made him doubt, and given him the "torpedo's shock," have we done him any harm?

Men. I think not.

Soc. We have certainly, as would seem assisted him in some degree to the discovery of the truth; and now he will wish to remedy his ignorance, but then he would have been ready to tell all the world again and again that the double space should have a double side.

Men. True.

Soc. But do you suppose that he would ever have enquired into or learned what he fancied that he knew, though he was really ignorant of it, until he had fallen into perplexity under the idea that he did not know, and had desired to know?

Men. I think not, Socrates.

Soc. Then he was the better for the torpedo's touch?

Men. I think so. . . .

Soc. Without any one teaching him he will recover his knowledge for himself, if he is only asked questions?

Men. Yes.

Soc. And this spontaneous recovery of knowledge in him is recollection?

Men. True.

Soc. And this knowledge which he now has must he not either have acquired or always possessed?

Men. Yes.

Soc. But if he always possessed this knowledge he would always have known; or if he has acquired the knowledge he could not have acquired it in this life, unless he has been taught geometry; for he may be made to do the same with all geometry and every other branch of knowledge. Now, has any one ever taught him all this? You must know about him, if, as you say, he was born and bred in your house.

Men. And I am certain that no one ever did teach him.

Soc. And yet he has the knowledge?

Men. The fact, Socrates, is undeniable.

Soc. But if he did not acquire the knowledge in this life, then he must have had and learned it at some other time?

Men. Clearly he must.

Soc. Which must have been the time when he was not a man?

Men. Yes.

Soc. And if there have been always true thoughts in him, both at the time when he was and was not a man, which only need to be awakened into knowledge by putting questions to him, his soul must have always possessed this knowledge, for he always either was or was not a man?

Men. Obviously.

Soc. And if the truth of all things always existed in the soul, then the soul is immortal. Wherefore be of good cheer, and try to recollect what you do not know, or rather what you do not remember.

Men. I feel, somehow, that I like what you are saying.

Soc. And I, Meno, like what I am saying. Some things I have said of which I am not altogether confident. But that we shall be better and braver and less helpless if we think that we ought to enquire, than we should have been if we indulged in the idle fancy that there was no knowing and no use in seeking to know what we do not know;—that is a theme upon which I am ready to fight, in word and deed, to the utmost of my power.

CHAPTER 21

POWER OF REASON

Descartes

Descartes broke with the past by deciding that he would no longer rely on previous philosophers for his ideas. Instead, he set out to build all knowledge on his own rational powers. Nor would he accept an idea as true only because it was expressed by someone with authority. Neither the authority of Aristotle's great reputation nor the authority of the church could suffice to produce the kind of certainty he sought. Descartes was determined to discover the basis of intellectual certainty in his own reason. He therefore gave philosophy a fresh start by using only those truths he could know through his own powers as the foundation for all other knowledge. He was well aware of his unique place in the history of philosophy, for he writes that "although all the truths which I class among my principles have been known from all time and by all men, there has been no one up to the present, who, so far as I know, has adopted them as the principles of philosophy. . . . as the sources from which may be derived a knowledge of all things else in the world. This is why it here remains to me to prove that they are such."

His ideal was to arrive at a system of thought whose various principles were true and were related to each other in such a clear way that the mind could move easily from one true principle to another. But in order to achieve such an organically connected set of truths, Descartes felt that he must make these truths "conform

389

to a rational scheme." With such a scheme he could not only organize present knowledge but could "direct our reason in order to discover those truths of which we are ignorant." His first task therefore was to work out his "rational scheme," his *method.*

Descartes's Method

Descartes's method consists of harnessing the powers of the mind with a special set of rules. He insisted on the *necessity* of method, on systematic and orderly thinking. He was appalled at scholars who sought aimlessly for truth, comparing them to men who, "burning with an unintelligent desire to find treasure continuously roam the streets, seeking to find something that a passerby might have chanced to drop. . . . It is very certain that unregulated inquiries and confused reflections of this kind only confound the natural light and bind our mental powers." Our minds naturally possess two powers, namely, *intuition* and *deduction,* "mental powers by which we are able, entirely without fear of illusion, to arrive at the knowledge of things." But by themselves these powers can lead us astray unless they are carefully regulated. Method consists, therefore, in those rules by which our powers of intuition and deduction are guided in an orderly way.

The Example of Mathematics

Descartes looked to mathematics for the best example of clear and precise thinking. "My method," he writes, "contains everything which gives certainty to the rules of arithmetic." Indeed, Descartes wanted to make all knowledge a "universal mathematics." For he was convinced that mathematical certainty is the result of a special *way of thinking,* and if he could discover this way, he would have a method for discovering true knowledge "of whatever lay within the compass of my powers." Mathematics is not *itself* the method but merely exhibits the method Descartes is searching for; geometry and arithmetic, he says, are only "examples" or "the outer covering" and not "the constituents" of his new method. What is there

Descartes (*New York Public Library Picture Collection*)

about mathematics that led Descartes to find in it the basis of his own method?

In mathematics, Descartes discovered something fundamental about the operation of the human mind. Specifically, he fastened on the mind's ability to apprehend directly and clearly basic truths. He was not so much concerned with explaining the mechanics of the formation of our ideas from experience as he was with affirming the fact that our minds are capable of knowing some ideas with absolute clarity and distinctness. Moreover, mathematical reasoning showed him that we are able to discover what we do not know by progressing in an orderly way from what we do know. If we can discover the mathematical values of certain terms (for example, the degree of an angle) from our knowledge of other terms (for example, the length of lines and degrees of other angles in a triangle), why can we not use this same method of reasoning in other fields as well? Descartes was convinced that we could, for he claimed that his method contained "the primary rudiments of human reason" and that with it he could elicit the "truths in every field whatsoever." To him all the various sciences are merely different ways in which the same powers of reasoning and the same method are used. In each case, the method is the orderly use of intuition and deduction.

Intuition and Deduction

Descartes placed the whole edifice of knowledge on the foundation of intuition and deduction, saying that "these two methods are the most certain routes to knowledge," adding that any other approach should be "rejected as suspect of error and dangerous. . . . " By "intuition," Descartes means an intellectual activity or vision of such clarity that it leaves no doubt in the mind. Whereas the fluctuating testimony of our senses and the imperfect creations of our imaginations leave us confused, intuition provides "the conception which an unclouded and attentive mind gives us so readily and distinctly that we are wholly freed from doubt about that which we understand. . . . " Intuition gives us not only clear notions but also some truths about reality, such as, for example, that *I think*, that *I exist*, and that a *sphere has a single surface*, truths that are basic, simple, and irreducible. Moreover, it is by intuition that we grasp the connection between one truth and another: for example, that two things equal to a thing are equal to each other (if *A B* and *C B*, then *A C*) is made clear to us by intuition.

By "deduction," Descartes means something similar to intuition, describing it as "all necessary inference from facts that are known with certainty." What makes intuition and deduction similar is that both involve truth: by intuition we grasp a simple truth completely and immediately, whereas by deduction we arrive at a truth by a process, a "continuous and uninterrupted action of the mind. . . . " By tying deduction so closely to intuition, Descartes gave a new interpretation of deduction, which up to his time had been identified with a mode of reasoning called the "syllogism." Deduction, as Descartes described it, is different from a syllogism, for whereas a syllogism indicates the relationship of *concepts* to each other, deduction for Descartes indicates the relation of *truths* to each other. It is one thing to move from a fact that is known with certainty to a conclusion that that fact implies, as Descartes indicates we must do by deduction. But it is something different to go from a *premise* to a conclusion as one does in a syllogism. Descartes was aware that one can reason *consistently* from a premise, but he argued that the value of the conclusion would depend on whether the premise was *true* or not. His quarrel with earlier philosophy and theology was that conclusions were drawn logically from premises that were either untrue or else based only on authority. Descartes wanted to rest knowledge on a starting point that had absolute certainty in the individual's own mind. Knowledge requires the use, therefore, of intuition and deduction, where "first principles are given by intuition alone while the remote conclusions . . . are furnished only by deduction." Still, Descartes's *method* does not consist only of intuition and deduction, but also of the rules he formulated for their guidance.

Rules of Method

The chief point of Descartes's rules is to provide a clear and orderly procedure for the operation of the mind. It was his conviction that "method consists entirely in the order and disposition of the objects toward which our mental vision must be directed if we would find out any truth." The mind must begin with a simple and absolutely clear truth and must move step by step without losing clarity and certainty along the way. Descartes spent many years at the task of formulating rules for helping the mind choose appropriate starting points for reasoning and to direct the mind in the ordered process of reasoning. Of the twenty-one rules found in his *Rules for the Direction of the Mind*, the following are among the most important:

Rule III.   When we propose to investigate a subject, "our inquiries should be directed, not to what others have thought, nor to what we ourselves conjecture, but to what we can clearly and perspicuously behold and with certainty deduce...."

Rule IV.   This is a rule requiring that other rules be adhered to strictly, for "if a man observe them accurately, he shall never assume what is false as true, and will never spend his mental efforts to no purpose...."

Rule V.   We shall comply with the method exactly if we "reduce involved and obscure propositions step by step to those that are simpler, and then starting with the intuitive apprehension of all those that are absolutely simple, attempt to ascend to the knowledge of all others by precisely similar steps...."

Rule VIII. "If in the matters to be examined we come to a step in the series of which our understanding is not sufficiently well able to have an intuitive cognition, we must stop short there."

In a similar way, Descartes formulated four precepts in his *Discourse on Method* which he believed were perfectly sufficient, "provided I took the firm and unwavering resolution never in a single instance to fail in observing them."

The *first* was never to accept anything for true which I did not clearly know to be such; . . . to comprise nothing more in my judgment than what was presented to my mind so clearly and distinctly as to exclude all ground of doubt. The *second*, to divide each of the difficulties under examination into as many parts as possible, and as might be necessary for its adequate solution. The *third*, to conduct my thoughts in such order that by commencing with objects the simplest and easiest to know, I might ascend by little and little, and, as it were, step by step, to the knowledge of the more complex. . . . And the *last*, in every case to make enumerations so complete, and reviews so general, that I might be assured that nothing was omitted.

Descartes puts very little emphasis in his method on sense experience and experiment in achieving knowledge. How is it that we know the essential qualities, for example, of a piece of wax, Descartes asks? At one time a piece of wax is hard, has a certain shape, color, size, and fragrance. But when we bring it close to the fire, its fragrance vanishes, its shape and color are lost, and its size increases. What remains in the wax that permits us still to know it is wax? "It cannot," says Descartes "be anything that I observed by means of the senses, since everything in the field of taste, smell, sight, touch, and hearing are changed, and still the same wax nevertheless remains." It is "nothing but my understanding alone which does conceive it ... solely an inspection by the mind," which enables me to know the true qualities of the wax. And, says Descartes, "what I have said here about the wax can be applied to all other things external to me." He relies for the most part on the truths contained in the mind, "deriving them from no other source than certain germs of truth which exist naturally in our souls." Descartes was confident that he could start from the beginning and rethink and rebuild all of philosophy by having recourse solely to his own rational powers and directing them in accordance with his rules. He therefore set out to show that we can have certainty of knowledge not only about mathematical concepts but also about the nature of reality.

Methodic Doubt

Descartes used the method of doubt in order to find an absolutely certain starting point for building up our knowledge. Having set out in his *Rules* that we should never accept anything about which we can entertain any doubt, Descartes now tries to doubt everything, saying that "because I wished to give myself entirely to the search after truth, I thought it was necessary for me ... to reject as absolutely false everything concerning which I could imagine the least ground of doubt. ... " His intention is clear, for he wants to sweep away all his former opinions, "so that they might later on be replaced, either by others which were better, or by the same, when I had made them conform to the uniformity of a rational scheme."

By this method of doubt, Descartes shows how uncertain our knowledge is, even of what seems most obvious to us. What can be clearer than "that I am here, seated by the fire ... holding this paper in my hands. ... " But when I am asleep, I dream that I am sitting by the fire, and this makes me realize that "there are no conclusive indications by which waking life can be distinguished from sleep. ... " Nor can I be sure that *things* exist, for I cannot tell when I am imagining or really knowing, for "I have learned that

[my] senses sometimes mislead me." But surely arithmetic, geometry, or sciences that deal with things must contain some certainty, for "whether I am awake or asleep, two and three together will always make the number five." Here Descartes refers to his long-held belief that there is a God who can do anything: but "how can I be sure that [God] has brought it about that there is no earth, no sky, no extended bodies . . . and that nevertheless I have impressions of these things. . . . And . . . that I am always mistaken when I add two and three. . . . " We cannot be certain that God is supremely good, for "He may be an evil genius not less powerful than deceitful," so that all things I experience "are nothing but illusions and dreams." Descartes is therefore "constrained to confess that there is nothing in what I formerly believed to be true which I cannot somehow doubt."

Reversal of Doubt

At this point Descartes says that "if I am fortunate enough to find a single truth which is certain and indubitable," that will suffice to reverse doubt and establish a philosophy. Like Archimedes, who demanded only an immovable fulcrum to move the earth from its orbit, Descartes searched for his one truth and found it in the very act of doubting.

Cogito and the Self

Although I can doubt that my body exists, or that I am awake, or that I am being deceived, in short that all is illusion or false, one thing remains about which I can have no doubt at all—that *I think.* To doubt is to think, said Descartes, and "it must necessarily be that I who [think am] something; and remarking that this truth, *I think, therefore I am* [*cogito ergo sum*], was so solid and so certain that all the most extravagant suppositions of the skeptics were incapable of upsetting it, I judged that I could receive it without scruple as the first principle of the philosophy that I sought." So clear was the truth of his own existence that again Descartes says, "This conclusion, *I think, therefore I am*, is the first and most certain of all which occur to one who philosophizes in an orderly way." Accordingly, Descartes employed this basic truth for reversing his doubts about the self, things, true ideas, and God.

At first, nothing more is proved by this truth, "I think, therefore I am," than the existence of my thinking self. My doubts still remain about the existence of my own body and about anything else that is other than my thinking. To say *Cogito ergo sum* is to affirm *my* existence: "But what then am I? A thing which thinks. What is a thing which thinks? It is a thing which doubts, understands, affirms, denies, wills, refuses and which also imagines and feels." Throughout, Descartes assumes that because thinking is a fact, there must also be a thinker, "a thing which thinks." This "thing" is not the body, for "I knew that I was a substance the whole nature of which is to think, and that for its existence there is no need of any place, nor does it depend on any material thing." This much then seems absolutely certain, namely, that I, an ego, exist, "for it is certain that no thought can exist apart from a thing which thinks. . . . " But so far the thinker is alone, a Robinson Crusoe, enclosed in his ideas.

Criterion of Truth

To go beyond the certainty of his own existence as a thinking being, Descartes asks again how we know something to be true: "What," he asks, "is required in a proposition for it to be true and certain?" What is there about the proposition *Cogito ergo sum* that makes it certain? "I came to the conclusion that I might assume as a general rule that the things which we conceive very *clearly* and *distinctly* are all true." In this context "clear means "that which is present and apparent to an attentive mind," in the same way that objects are clear to our eyes, and "distinct" refers to "that which is so precise and different from all other objects that it contains within itself nothing but what is clear." The reason, then, that the proposition I think, therefore I am is true is simply that it is clear and distinct to my mind. This is the reason, too, that mathematical propositions are true, for they are so clear and distinct that we cannot help accepting them. But to guarantee the truth of our clear and distinct ideas, Descartes had to prove that God exists and that He is not a deceiver who makes us think that false things are true.

The Existence of God

Descartes cannot use Aquinas's proofs for the existence of God because those proofs are based on the very facts which are still subject to Descartes's doubt, namely, facts about the external world such as *motion* and *cause* among physical things. Instead, Descartes must prove God's existence solely in terms of his rational awareness of his own existence and internal thoughts. He therefore begins his proof by examining the various ideas that pass through his mind.

Two things strike him about these ideas, that they are caused and that according to their content they differ markedly from each other. Ideas are effects, and their causes must be discovered. Some of our ideas seem to be "born with me," some "invented" by me, whereas others "come from without." Our reason tells us that "something cannot be derived from nothing" and also that "the more perfect . . . cannot be a consequence of . . . the less perfect." Our ideas possess different degrees of reality, but "it is manifest by natural light that there must be at least as much reality in the efficient and total cause as in the effect." Some of our ideas, judging by the degree of their reality, could have their origin in myself. But the idea of God contains so much "objective reality" that I wonder whether I could have produced that idea by myself. For "by the name God I understand a substance which is infinite, independent, all-knowing, all-powerful and by which I myself and everything else, if anything else exists, have been created." How can I, a finite substance, produce the idea of an infinite substance? Indeed, how could I know that I am finite unless I could compare myself with the idea of a perfect being? The idea of perfection is so clear and distinct that I am convinced that it could not proceed from my imperfect nature. Even if I were *potentially* perfect, the idea of perfection could not come from that potentiality, for an actual effect must proceed from a being that *actually* exists. For these reasons, Descartes concludes that since ideas have causes, and since the cause must have at least as much reality as the effect, and finally

Classroom, University of Paris, 1600s (*Snark International/Editorial Photocolor Archives*)

since he is finite and imperfect, it must be that the cause of his idea of a perfect and infinite Being comes from outside himself, from a perfect Being who exists, from God. In addition, Descartes concludes that God cannot be a deceiver, "since the light of nature teaches us that fraud and deception necessarily proceed from some defect," which could hardly be attributed to a perfect Being.

In addition to this argument from causation, by which he proved the existence of God, Descartes, following Augustine and Anselm, offered his version of the ontological argument. Whereas in the argument from causation he reasoned that his idea of a perfect Being could not have come from himself because of his own known imperfection, in the ontological argument Descartes sought to demonstrate the existence of God by exploring what the very idea of God implies. He says that if "all which I know clearly and distinctly as pertaining to this object really does belong to it, may I not derive from this an argument demonstrating the existence of God?" How is it possible to move from an analysis of an idea to the certainty that God exists?

Some of our ideas, says Descartes, are so clear and distinct that we immediately perceive what they imply. One cannot, for example, think of a triangle without at once thinking of its lines and angles. Although one cannot think about a triangle without also thinking about its attributes of lines and angles, it does not follow that to think about a triangle implies that it exists. But just as the idea of a triangle implies certain attributes, so also the idea of God implies attributes, specifically the attribute of existence. The idea of God signifies a perfect Being. But the very idea of perfection implies existence. To speak of a nonexistent perfection is to engage in contradiction. One cannot coherently conceive of a Being who is supremely perfect in all respects and at the same time nonexistent. Just as one cannot think the idea of triangle without recognizing its attributes, so also one cannot think the idea God, says Descartes, without recognizing that this idea clearly implies the attribute of existence. Descartes says, "That which we clearly and distinctly understand to belong to the true and immutable nature of anything, its essence or form, can be truly affirmed of that thing. But after we have with sufficient accuracy investigated the nature of God, we clearly and distinctly understand that to exist belongs to His true nature. Therefore we can with truth affirm of God that He exists."

Against this line of reasoning, Descartes's critic Gassendi said that perfection does not imply existence, since existence is not a necessary attribute of perfection. To lack existence, he said, implies no impairment of perfection, only the lack of reality. Kant, as we have seen, went into considerably greater detail in his criticism of these attempts to prove the existence of God.

Existence of Things

From his own existence, Descartes has proved God's existence. Along the way he has also established the criterion of truth and provided thereby the foundation for mathematical thought and for all rational activity. Now Descartes takes another look at the physical world, at his own body and other things, and asks whether he can be certain that they exist. To be a thinking thing does not of itself prove that my body exists, for my thinking self "is entirely and absolutely distinct from my body and can exist without it." How then can I know that my body and other physical things exist?

Descartes answers that we all have the clear and distinct experiences of changing our position and moving about, activities that imply a body, or what he calls "an extended substance." We also receive sense impressions, of sight, sound, and touch, frequently even against our will, and these lead us to believe that they come from bodies other than our own. This overwhelming inclination to believe that these impressions "are conveyed to me by corporeal objects" must come from God; otherwise He could not "be defended from the accusation of deceit if these ideas were produced by causes other than corporeal objects. Hence we must allow that corporeal objects exist." For Descartes, then, knowledge of the self is prior to knowledge of God, and both the self and God are prior to our knowledge of the external world.

Descartes has now reversed all his doubts and has satisfied himself absolutely that the self, things, and God exist. He has concluded that there are thinking things and things that are extended, have dimension.

READING

CERTAINTY AND THE LIMITS OF DOUBT

Descartes

It is now several years since I first became aware how many false opinions I had from my childhood been admitting as true, and how doubtful was everything I have subsequently based on them. Accordingly I have ever since been convinced that if I am to establish anything firm and lasting in the sciences, I must once for all, and by a deliberate effort, rid myself of all

---

From "Meditations" in *Descartes: Philosophical Writings*, trans. Norman Kemp Smith, Modern Library, New York, 1958.

those opinions to which I have hitherto given credence, starting entirely anew, and building from the foundation up. But as this enterprise was evidently one of great magnitude, I waited until I had attained an age so mature that I could no longer expect that I should at any later date be better able to execute my design. This is what has made me delay so long; and I should now be failing in my duty, were I to continue consuming in deliberation such time for action as still remains to me.

Today, then, as I have suitably freed my mind from all cares, and have secured for myself an assured leisure in peaceful solitude, I shall at last apply myself earnestly and freely to the general overthrow of all my former opinions. In so doing, it will not be necessary for me to show that they are one and all false; that is perhaps more than can be done. But since reason has already persuaded me that I ought to withhold belief no less carefully from things not entirely certain and indubitable than from those which appear to me manifestly false, I shall be justified in setting all of them aside, if in each case I can find any ground whatsoever for regarding them as dubitable. Nor in so doing shall I be investigating each belief separately—that, like inquiry into their falsity, would be an endless labor. The withdrawal of foundations involves the downfall of whatever rests on these foundations, and what I shall therefore begin by examining are the principles on which my former beliefs rested.

Whatever, up to the present, I have accepted as possessed of the highest truth and certainty I have learned either from the senses or through the senses. Now these senses I have sometimes found to be deceptive; and it is only prudent never to place complete confidence in that by which we have even once been deceived.

But, it may be said, although the senses sometimes deceive us regarding minute objects, or such as are at a great distance from us, there are yet many other things which, though known by way of sense, are too evident to be doubted; as, for instance, that I am in this place, seated by the fire, attired in a dressing-gown, having this paper in my hands, and other similar seeming certainties. Can I deny that these hands and this body are mine, save perhaps by comparing myself to those who are insane, and whose brains are so disturbed and clouded by dark bilious vapors that they persist in assuring us that they are kings, when in fact they are in extreme poverty; or that they are clothed in gold and purple when they are in fact destitute of any covering; or that their head is made of clay and their body of glass, or that they are pumpkins. They are mad; and I should be no less insane were I to follow examples so extravagant.

None the less I must bear in mind that I am a man, and am therefore in the habit of sleeping, and that what the insane represent to themselves in their waking moments I represent to myself, with other things even less probable, in my dreams. How often, indeed, have I dreamt of myself being in this place, dressed and seated by the fire, whilst all the time I was lying undressed in bed! At the present moment it certainly seems that in looking at this paper I do so with open eyes, that the head which I move is not asleep, that it is deliberately and of set purpose that I extend this hand, and that I am sensing the hand. The things which happen to the sleeper are not so clear nor so distinct as all of these are. I cannot, however, but remind myself that on many occasions I have in sleep been deceived by similar illusions; and on more careful study of them I see that there are no certain marks distinguishing waking from sleep; and I see this so manifestly that, lost in amazement, I am almost persuaded that I am now dreaming.

So disquieting are the doubts in which yesterday's meditation has involved me that it is no longer in my power to forget them. Nor do I yet see how they are to be resolved. It is as if I had all of a sudden fallen into very deep water, and am so disconcerted that I can neither plant my feet securely on the bottom nor maintain myself by swimming on the surface. I shall, however, brace myself for a great effort, entering anew on the path which I was yesterday exploring; that is, I shall proceed by setting aside all that admits even of the very slightest doubt, just as if I had convicted it of being absolutely false; and I shall persist in following this path, until I have come upon something certain, or, failing in that, until at least I know, and know with certainty, that in the world there is nothing certain.

Archimedes, that he might displace the whole earth, required only that there might be some one point, fixed and immovable, to serve in leverage; so likewise I shall be entitled to entertain high hopes if I am fortunate enough to find some one thing that is certain and indubitable.

I am supposing, then, that all the things I see are false; that of all the happenings my memory has ever suggested to me, none has ever so existed; that I have no senses; that body, shape, extension, movement and location are but mental fictions. What is there, then, which can be esteemed true? Perhaps this only, that nothing whatsoever is certain.

But how do I know that there is not something different from all the things I have thus far enumerated and in regard to which there is not the least occasion for doubt? Is there not some God, or other being by whatever name we call Him, who puts these thoughts into my mind? Yet why suppose such a being? May it not be that I am myself capable of being their author? Am I not myself at least a something? But already I have denied that I have a body and senses. This indeed raises awkward questions. But what is it that thereupon follows? Am I so dependent on the body and senses that without them I cannot exist? Having persuaded myself that outside me there is nothing, that there is no heaven, no Earth, that there are no minds, no bodies, am I thereby committed to the view that I also do not exist? By no means. If I am persuading myself of something in so doing I assuredly do exist. But what if, unknown to me, there be some deceiver, very powerful and very cunning, who is constantly employing his ingenuity in deceiving me? Again, as before, without doubt, if he is deceiving me, I exist. Let him deceive me as much as he will, he can never cause me to be nothing so long as I shall be thinking that I am something. And thus, having reflected well, and carefully examined all things, we have finally to conclude that this declaration, *Ego sum, ego existo,* is necessarily true every time I propound it or mentally apprehend it.

But I do not yet know in any adequate manner what I am, I who am certain that I am; and I must be careful not to substitute some other thing in place of myself, and so go astray in this knowledge which I am holding to be the most certain and evident of all that is knowable by me. This is why I shall now meditate anew on what, prior to my venturing on these questionings, I believed myself to be. I shall withdraw those beliefs which can, even in the least degree, be invalidated by the reasons cited, in order that at length, of all my previous beliefs, there may remain only what is certain and indubitable.

What then did I formerly believe myself to be? Undoubtedly I thought myself to be a man. But what is a man? Shall I say a rational animal? No, for then I should have to inquire what is "animal," what "rational"; and thus from the one question I should be drawn on into several others yet more difficult. I have not, at present, the leisure for any such subtle inquiries. Instead, I prefer to meditate on the thoughts which of themselves sprang up in my mind on my applying myself to the consideration of what I am, considerations suggested by my own proper nature. I thought that I possessed a face, hands, arms, and that whole structure to which I was giving the title "body," composed as it is of the limbs discernible in a corpse. In addition, I took notice that I was nourished, that I walked, that I sensed, that I thought, all of which actions I ascribed to the soul. But what the soul might be I did not stop to consider; or if I did, I imaged it as being something extremely rare and subtle, like a wind, a flame or an ether, and as diffused throughout my grosser parts. As to the nature of "body," no doubts whatsoever disturbed me. I had, as I thought, quite distinct knowledge of it; and had I been called upon to explain the manner in which I then conceived it, I should have explained myself somewhat thus: by body I understand whatever can be determined by a certain shape, and comprised in a certain location, whatever so fills a certain space as to exclude from it every other body, whatever can be apprehended by touch, sight, hearing, taste or smell, and whatever can be moved in various ways, not indeed of itself but something foreign to it by which it is touched and impressed. For I nowise conceived the power of self-movement, of sensing or knowing, as pertaining to the nature of body: on the contrary I was somewhat astonished on finding in certain bodies faculties such as these.

But what am I now to say that I am, now that I am supposing that there exists a very powerful, and if I may so speak, malignant being, who employs all his powers and skill in deceiving me? Can I affirm that I possess any one of those things which I have been speaking of as pertaining to the nature of body? On stopping to consider them with closer attention, and on reviewing all of them, I find none of which I can say that it belongs to me; to enumerate them again would be idle and tedious. What then, of those things which I have been attributing not to body, but to the soul? What of nutrition or of walking? If it be that I have no body, it cannot be that I take nourishment or that I walk. Sensing? There can be no sensing in the absence of body; and besides I have seemed during sleep to apprehend things which, as I afterwards noted, had not been sensed. Thinking? Here I find what does belong to me: it alone cannot be separated from me. *I am, I exist.* This is certain. How often? As often as I think. For it might indeed be that if I entirely ceased to think, I should thereupon altogether cease to exist. I am not at present admitting anything which is not necessarily true; and, accurately speaking, I am therefore (taking myself to be) only a thinking thing, that is to say, a mind, an understanding or reason—terms the significance of which has hitherto been unknown to me. I am, then, a real thing, and really existent. What thing? I have said it, a thinking thing. . . .

CHAPTER 22

LIMITS OF KNOWLEDGE

Hume

The only way, says Hume, to solve the problem of disagreements and speculations regarding "abstruse questions" is to "enquire seriously into the nature of human understanding, and show from an exact analysis of its powers and capacity, that it is by no means fitted for such remote and abstruse subjects." Accordingly, Hume carefully analyzed a series of topics that led him to his skeptical conclusion, beginning with an account of the contents of the mind.

Contents of the Mind

Nothing seems more unbounded, says Hume, than man's thought. Although our body is confined to one planet, our mind can roam instantly into the most distant regions of the universe. Nor, it may seem, is the mind bound by the limits of nature or reality, for without difficulty the imagination can conceive the most unnatural and incongruous appearances, such as flying horses and gold mountains. But, although the mind seems to possess this wide freedom, it is, says Hume, "really confined within very narrow limits." In the last

Hume (*New York Public Library Picture Collection*)

analysis, the contents of the mind can all be reduced to the materials given us by the senses and experience, and those materials Hume calls "perceptions." The perceptions of the mind take two forms, which Hume distinguishes as *impressions* and *ideas*.

Impressions and *ideas* make up the total content of the mind. The original stuff of thought is an *impression,* and an *idea* is merely a copy of an impression. The difference between an impression and an idea is only the degree of their vividness. The original perception is an impression, such as when we hear, see, feel, love, hate, desire, or will. These impressions are "lively" and clear when we have them. When we reflect on these impressions, we have ideas of them, and those ideas are less lively versions of the original impressions. To feel pain is an impression, whereas the memory of this sensation is an idea. In every particular, impressions and their corresponding ideas are alike, differing only in their degree of vivacity.

Besides distinguishing between impressions and ideas, Hume argues that without impressions there can be no ideas. For if an idea is simply a copy of an impression, it follows that for every idea there must be a prior impression. Not every idea, however, reflects a corresponding impression, for we have never seen a flying horse or a golden mountain even though we have ideas of them. But Hume explains such ideas as being the product of the minds "faculty of compounding, transposing, or diminishing the materials afforded us by the senses and experience." When we think of a flying horse, our imagination joins two ideas, wings and horse, which we originally acquired as impressions through our senses. If we have any suspicion that a philosophical term is employed without any meaning or idea, we need, says Hume, "but enquire, *from what impression is that supposed idea derived?* And if it be impossible to assign any, this will serve to confirm our suspicion." Hume subjected even the idea of God to this test and concluded that it arises from reflecting on the operations of our own minds "augmenting without limit" the qualities of goodness and wisdom that we experience among human beings. But if all our ideas follow from impressions, how can we explain what we call *thinking,* or the patterns by which ideas group themselves in our minds?

Association of Ideas

It is not by mere chance that our ideas are related to each other. There must be, says Hume, "some bond of union, some associating quality, by which one idea naturally introduces another." Hume calls it "a gentle force, which commonly prevails . . . pointing out to every one those simple ideas, which are most proper to be united in a complex one." It is not a special faculty of the mind that associates one idea with another, for Hume has no impression of the structural equipment of the mind. But by observing the actual patterns of our thinking and analyzing the groupings of our ideas, Hume thought he discovered the explanation of the association of ideas.

His explanation was that whenever there are certain qualities in ideas, these ideas are associated with one another. These qualities are three in number: resemblance, contiguity in time or place, and cause and effect. Hume believed that the connections of all ideas to one another could be explained by these qualities and gave the following examples of how they work: "A picture naturally leads our thoughts to the original [*resemblance*]: the mention of one apartment in the building naturally introduces an enquiry . . . concerning the others [*contiguity*]: and if we think of a wound, we can scarcely forebear reflecting on the pain which follows it [*cause and effect*]." There are no operations of the mind that differ in principle from one of these three examples of the association of ideas. But of these, the notion of cause and effect was considered by Hume to be the central element in knowledge. He took the position that the causal principle is the foundation upon which the validity of all knowledge depends. If there is any flaw in the causal principle, we can have no certainty of knowledge.

Causality

Hume's most original and influential ideas deal with the problem of causality. For Hume, the very idea of causality is suspect, and he approaches the problem by asking the question "What is the origin of the idea of causality?" Since ideas are copies of impressions, Hume asks what impression gives us the idea of causality. His answer is that there is no impression corresponding to this idea. How then does the idea of causality arise in the mind? It must be, says Hume, that the idea of causality arises in the mind when we experience certain relations between objects. When we speak of cause and effect, we mean to say that *A* causes *B*. But what kind of a relation does this indicate between *A* and *B*? Experience furnishes us three relations: first, there is the relation of *contiguity*, for *A* and *B* are always close together; second, there is *priority in time*, for *A*, the "cause," always precedes *B*, the "effect"; and third, there is *constant conjunction*, for we always see *A* followed by *B*. But there is still another relation that the idea of causality suggests to common sense, namely, that between *A* and *B* there is a "necessary connection." But neither contiguity, priority, nor constant conjunction implies "necessary" connection between objects. There is no object, says Hume, that implies the existence of another when we consider objects individually. No amount of observation of oxygen can ever tell us that when mixed with hydrogen it will give us water. We know this only after we have seen the two together: "It is therefore by *experience* only that we can infer the existence of one object from another." While we do have impressions of contiguity, priority, and constant conjunction, we do *not* have any impression of *necessary connections.* Thus causality is not a quality in the objects we observe, but is rather a "habit of association" in the mind produced by the repetition of instances of *A* and *B.*

Insofar as Hume assumed that the causal principle is central to all kinds of knowledge, his attack on this principle undermined the validity of all knowledge. He saw no reason for accepting the principle that *whatever begins to exist must have a cause of existence* as either intuitive or capable of demonstration. In the end, Hume considered thinking or reasoning "as species of sensation," and as such, our thinking cannot extend beyond our immediate experiences.

What Exists External to Us?

Hume's extreme empiricism led him to argue that there is no rational justification for saying that bodies or things have a continued and independent existence external to us. Our ordinary experience suggests that things outside of us do exist. But if we take seriously the notion that our ideas are copies of impressions, the philosophical conclusion must be that all we know are impressions. Impressions are internal subjective states and are not clear proof of an external reality. To be sure, we always act as though there is a real external world of things, and Hume was willing to "take for granted in all our reasonings" that things do exist. But he wanted to inquire into the reason why we think there is an external world.

Our senses do not tell us that things exist independent of us, for how do we know that they continue to exist even when we interrupt our sensation of them? And even when we sense something, we are never given a double view of it whereby we can distinguish the thing from our impression of it; we have only the impression. There is no way for the mind to reach beyond impressions or the ideas they make possible: " . . . let us chase our imagination to the heavens, or to the utmost limits of the universe; we never advance a step beyond our selves, nor can we conceive any kind of existence, but those perceptions which have appeared in that narrow compass. This is the universe of the imagination, nor have we any idea but what is there produced."

Constancy and Coherence

Our belief that things exist external to us, says Hume, is the product of our imagination as it deals with two special characteristics of our impressions. From impressions our imagination becomes aware of both *constancy* and *coherence.* There is a constancy in the arrangement of things when, for example, I look out of my window: there are the mountain, the house, and the trees. If I shut my eyes or turn away and then later look at the same view again, the arrangement is still the same, and it is this constancy in the contents of my impressions that leads my imagination to conclude that the mountain, house, and trees exist whether I think of them or not. Similarly, I put a log on the fire before I leave the room, and when I return it is almost in ashes. But even though a great change has taken place in the fire, I am accustomed to find this kind of change under similar circumstances: "this coherence . . . in their changes is one of the characteristics of external objects. . . . " In the case of the mountain, there is a constancy of our impressions, whereas with respect to the fire our impressions have a coherent relation to the processes of change. For these reasons, the imagination leads us to believe that certain things continue to have an independent existence external to us. But this is a *belief* and not a rational proof, for the assumption that our impressions are connected with things is "without any foundation in reasoning." Hume extends this skeptical line of reasoning beyond objects or things to consider the existence of the *self, substance,* and *God.*

The Self

Hume denied that we have any idea of *self.* This may seem paradoxical, that *I* should say that I do not have an idea of myself, yet
here again Hume wants to test what we mean by a self by asking
"From what impression could this idea be deriv'd?" Is there any
continuous and identical reality which forms our ideas of the self?
Do we have any one impression that is invariably associated with
our idea of *self?* "When I enter most intimately into what I call
myself," says Hume, "I always stumble on some particular perception or other, of heat or cold, love or hatred, pain or pleasure. I
never can catch *myself* at any time without a perception and never
can observe anything but the perception." Hume denies the existence of a continuous self-identity and says about the rest of mankind that "they are nothing but a bundle or collection of different
perceptions." How then do we account for what we think is the
self? It is our power of memory that gives the impression of our
continuous identity. Hume compares the mind to "a kind of theatre
where several perceptions successively make their appearance,"
but adds that "we have not the most distant notion of the place
where these scenes are represented. . . ."

Substance

What led Hume to deny the existence of a continuous self that in
some way retains its identity through time was his thorough denial
of the existence of any form of *substance.* Locke retained the idea
of substance as that *something* which has color or shape, and other
qualities, although he spoke of it as "something we know not
what." Berkeley denied the existence of substance underlying qualities but retained the idea of spiritual substances. Hume denied that
substance in any form exists or has any coherent meaning. If what
is meant by the *self* is some form of substance, Hume argued that
no such substance can be derived from our impressions of sensation. If the idea of substance is conveyed to us by our senses, Hume
asked, " . . . which of them; and after what manner? If it be per-
ceiv'd by the eyes, it must be a colour; if by the ears, a sound; if by

the palate, a taste. . . . We have therefore no idea of substance, distinct from that of a collection of particular qualities. . . . ''

God

It was inevitable that Hume's rigorous premise that ''our ideas reach no further than our experience'' would lead him to raise skeptical questions about the existence of God. Most attempts to demonstrate the existence of God rely on some version of causality. Among these, the argument from design has always made a powerful impact on the mind. Hume is aware of the power of this argument, but he quickly sorts out the elements of the problem, leaving the argument with less than its usual force.

The argument from design begins with the observance of a beautiful order in nature. This order resembles the kind of order the human mind is able to impose on unthinking materials. From this preliminary observation, the mind concludes that unthinking materials do not contain the principle of orderliness within themselves: ''Throw several pieces of steel together, without shape or form; they will never arrange themselves so as to compose a watch. . . . '' Order, it is held, requires activity of a mind, an orderer. Our experience tells us that neither a watch nor a house can come into being without a watchmaker or an architect. From this it is inferred that the natural order bears an analogy to the order fashioned by human effort and that just as the watch requires an ordering cause, so the natural order of the universe requires one. But such an inference, says Hume, ''is uncertain; because the subject lies entirely beyond the reach of human experience.''

If the whole argument from design rests on the proposition *''that the cause or causes of order in the universe probably bear some remote analogy to human intelligence,''* then, says Hume, the argument cannot prove as much as it claims. Hume's criticism of the idea of causality has particular force here. Since we derive the idea of cause from repeated observations of the contiguity, priority, and constant conjunction of two things, how can we assign a cause to the universe when we have never experienced the universe as related to anything we might consider a cause? The use of analogy does not solve the problem, since the analogy between a watch and the universe is not exact. Why not consider the universe the product of a vegetative process instead of a rational designer? And even if the cause of the universe is something like an intelligence, how can moral characteristics be ascribed to such a being? Moreover, if analogies are to be used, which one should be selected? Houses and ships are frequently designed by a group of designers: Should we say there are many gods? Sometimes experimental models are built with no present knowledge of what the finished form will be like: Is the universe a trial model or the final design? By this way of probing, Hume wished to emphasize that the order of the universe is simply an empirical fact and that we cannot infer from it the existence of God. Again, this does not, however, make Hume an atheist. He is simply testing our idea of God the way he had tested our ideas of the self and substance by his rigorous principle of empiricism. He ends, to be sure, as a skeptic, but finally makes the telling point that "to whatever length any one may push his speculative principles of scepticism, he must act and live and converse like other men. . . . It is impossible for him to persevere in total scepticism, or make it appear in his conduct for a few hours."

READING

EMPIRICISM AND THE LIMITS OF KNOWLEDGE

Hume

All the objects of human reason or enquiry may naturally be divided into two kinds, to wit, *Relations of Ideas,* and *Matters of Fact.* Of the first kind are the sciences of Geometry, Algebra, and Arithmetic; and in short, every affirmation which is either intuitively or demonstratively certain. *That the square of the hypotenuse is equal to the square of the two sides,* is a propo-

From David Hume, *An Enquiry concerning Human Understanding,* 1748.

sition which expresses a relation between these figures. *That* three times five is equal to the half of thirty, expresses a relation between these numbers. Propositions of this kind are discoverable by the mere operation of thought, without dependence on what is anywhere existent in the universe. Though there never were a circle or triangle in nature, the truths demonstrated by Euclid would for ever retain their certainty and evidence.

Matters of fact, which are the second objects of human reason, are not ascertained in the same manner; nor is our evidence of their truth, however great, of a like nature with the foregoing. The contrary of every matter of fact is still possible; because it can never imply a contradiction, and is conceived by the mind with the same facility and distinctness, as if ever so conformable to reality. *That the sun will not rise tomorrow* is no less intelligible a proposition, and implies no more contradiction than the affirmation, *that it will rise.* We should in vain, therefore, attempt to demonstrate its falsehood. Were it demonstratively false, it would imply a contradiction, and could never be distinctly conceived by the mind.

It may, therefore, be a subject worthy of curiosity, to enquire what is the nature of that evidence which assures us of any real existence and matter of fact, beyond the present testimony of our senses, or the records of our memory. This part of philosophy, it is observable, has been little cultivated, either by the ancients or moderns; and therefore our doubts and errors, in the prosecution of so important an enquiry, may be the more excusable; while we march through such difficult paths without any guide or direction. They may even prove useful, by exciting curiosity, and destroying that implicit faith and security, which is the bane of all reasoning and free enquiry. The discovery of defects in the common philosophy, if any such there be, will not, I presume, be a discouragement, but rather an incitement, as is usual, to attempt something more full and satisfactory than has yet been proposed to the public.

All reasonings concerning matters of fact seem to be founded on the relation of *Cause and Effect*. By means of that relation alone we can go beyond the evidence of our memory and senses. If you were to ask a man, why he believes any matter of fact, which is absent; for instance, that his friend is in the country, or in France; he would give you a reason; and this reason would be some other fact; as a letter received from him, or the knowledge of his former resolutions and promises. A man finding a watch or any other machine in a desert island, would conclude that there had once been men in that island. All our reasonings concerning fact are of the same nature. And here it is constantly supposed that there is a connexion between the present fact and that which is inferred from it. Were there nothing to bind them together, the inference would be entirely precarious. The hearing of an articulate voice and rational discourse in the dark assures us of the presence of some person: Why? because these are the effects of the human make and fabric, and closely connected with it. If we anatomize

Old Edinburgh (*New York Public Library Picture Collection*)

all the other reasonings of this nature, we shall find that they are founded on the relation of cause and effect, and that this relation is either near or remote, direct or collateral. Heat and light are collateral effects of fire, and the one effect may justly be inferred from the other.

If we would satisfy ourselves, therefore, concerning the nature of that evidence, which assures us of matters of fact, we must enquire how we arrive at the knowledge of cause and effect.

I shall venture to affirm, as a general proposition, which admits of no exception, that the knowledge of this relation is not, in any instance, attained by reasonings *a priori* [that is, prior to experience]; but arises entirely from experience, when we find that any particular objects are constantly conjoined with each other. Let an object be presented to a man of ever so strong natural reason and abilities; if that object be entirely new to him, he will not be able, by the most accurate examination of its sensible qualities, to discover any of its causes or effects. Adam, though his rational faculties be supposed, at the very first, entirely perfect, could not have inferred from the fluidity and transparency of water that it would suffocate him, or from the light and warmth of fire that it would consume him. No object ever discovers, by the qualities which appear to the senses, either the causes which produced it, or the effects which will arise from it; nor can our reason, unassisted by experience, ever draw any inference concerning real existence and matter of fact.

This proposition, *that causes and effects are discoverable, not by reason but by experience,* will readily be admitted with regard to such objects, as we remember to have once been altogether unknown to us; since we must be conscious of the utter inability, which we then lay under, of foretelling what would arise from them. Present two smooth pieces of marble to a man who has no tincture of natural philosophy; he will never discover that they will adhere together in such a manner as to require great force to separate them in a direct line, while they make so small a resistance to a lateral pressure. Such events, as bear little analogy to the common course of nature, are also readily confessed to be known only by experience; nor does any man imagine that the explosion of gunpowder, or the attraction of a loadstone, could ever be discovered by arguments *a priori.* In like manner, when an effect is supposed to depend upon an intricate machinery or secret structure of parts, we make no difficulty in attributing all our knowledge of it to experience. Who will assert that he can give the ultimate reason, why milk or bread is proper nourishment for a man, not for a lion or a tiger?

But the same truth may not appear, at first sight, to have the same evidence with regard to events, which have become familiar to us from our first appearance in the world, which bear a close analogy to the whole course of nature, and which are supposed to depend on the simple qualities of objects, without any secret structure of parts. We are apt to imagine that we could discover these effects by the mere operation of our reason, without experience. We fancy, that were we brought on a sudden into this world, we could at first have inferred that one Billiard-ball would communicate motion to another upon impulse; and that we needed not to have waited for the event, in order to pronounce with certainty concerning it. Such is the influence of custom, that, where it is strongest, it not only covers our natural ignorance, but even conceals itself, and seems not to take place, merely because it is found in the highest degree.

But to convince us that all the laws of nature, and all the operations of bodies without exception, are known only by experience, the following reflections may, perhaps, suffice. Were any object presented to us, and were we required to pronounce concerning the effect, which will result from it, without consulting past observation; after what manner, I beseech you, must the mind proceed in this operation? It must invent or imagine some event, which it ascribes to the object as its effect; and it is plain that this invention must be entirely arbitrary. The mind can never possibly find the effect in the supposed cause, by the most accurate scrutiny and examination. For the effect is totally different from the cause, and consequently can never be discovered in it. Motion in the second Billiard-ball is a quite distinct event from motion in the first; nor is there anything in the one to suggest the smallest hint of the other. A stone or piece of metal raised into the air, and left without any support, immediately falls: but to consider the matter *a priori,* is there anything we discover in this situation which can beget the idea of a downward, rather than an upward, or any other motion, in the stone or metal?

It is certain that the most ignorant and stupid peasants—nay infants, nay even brute beasts—improve by experience, and learn the qualities of natural objects, by observing the effects which result from them. When a child has felt the sensation of pain from touching the flame of a candle, he will be careful not to put his hand near any candle; but will expect a similar effect from a cause which is similar in its sensible qualities and appearance. If you assert, therefore, that the understanding of the child is led into this conclusion by any process of argument or ratiocination, I may justly require you to produce that argument; nor have you any pretence to refuse so equitable a demand. You cannot say that the argument is abstruse, and may possibly escape your enquiry; since you confess that it is obvious to the capacity of a mere infant. If you hesitate, therefore, a moment, or if, after reflection, you produce any intricate or profound argument, you, in a manner, give up the question, and confess that it is not reasoning which engages us to suppose the past resembling the future, and to expect similar effects from causes which are, to appearance, similar. This is the proposition which I intended to enforce in the present section.

CHAPTER 23

━━━━━━

HOW KNOWLEDGE IS POSSIBLE

Kant

Immanuel Kant was impressed by Hume's theory of knowledge. "I openly confess," he said, "that the suggestion of David Hume was the very thing which many years ago first interrupted my dogmatic slumber and gave my investigations in the field of speculative philosophy quite a new direction." But Kant said, "I was far from following [Hume] in the conclusions at which he arrived." Kant rejected Hume's final skepticism. He decided that Hume had not completed the task of explaining how knowledge is acquired. Also, Kant saw some value in Descartes's rationalism. He was fascinated by the way our minds work when thinking about mathematics.

Here, then, Kant faced two extreme theories of knowledge, rationalism on the one hand and empiricism on the other. He realized that both rationalism and empiricism were ignored by the most successful method of thought in his day, namely, the science of physics, especially as formulated by Sir Isaac Newton. Rationalism, because it followed the model of mathematics, seemed to consist merely of relating ideas to one another without making contact with things as they really are. Physics did make this contact successfully. Empiricism as formulated by Hume raised skeptical doubts about *causality*, saying that we cannot be sure a certain effect will always follow a particular cause. Yet physics is built on the reliability of cause and effect. Therefore, Kant set out to discover how the mind works when it is thinking scientifically. In this process he was able to take what he considered important from both rationalism and empiricism to develop his own theory of knowledge, which is known as "critical idealism."

The Way of Critical Philosophy

Kant's *critical* philosophy consists of an analysis of the powers of human reason, by which he meant "a critical inquiry into the faculty of reason with reference to all the knowledge which it may strive to attain independently of all experience." The way of critical philosophy is, therefore, to ask the question "What and how much can understanding and reason know, apart from all experience?" Thus, whereas earlier metaphysicians engaged in disputes about the nature of the supreme being and other subjects that took them beyond the realm of immediate experience, Kant asked the critical question whether the human reason possesses the powers to undertake such inquiries. From this critical point of view Kant thought it foolish for metaphysicians to engage in attempts to construct systems of knowledge even before they had inquired into whether by pure reason alone one can apprehend what is not given to him in experience. Critical philosophy for Kant was therefore not the negation of metaphysics, but rather a preparation for it. If metaphysics has to do with knowledge that is developed by reason alone, that is, prior to experience, or *a priori*, the critical question is how is such a priori knowledge possible.

THE NATURE OF A PRIORI KNOWLEDGE

Kant affirmed that we possess a faculty that is capable of giving us knowledge without an appeal to experience. He agreed with the empiricists that our knowledge begins with experience, but he added that "though our knowledge begins with experience, it does not follow that it all arises out of experience." This was the point that Hume had missed, for Hume had said that all our knowledge

Kant (*New York Public Library Picture Collection*)

consists of a series of impressions, which we derive through our senses. Yet we clearly possess a kind of knowledge that does not come *out of* experience even though it begins *with* experience. Hume was right that we do not, for example, experience or sense *causality*, but Kant rejected his explanation that causality is simply a psychological habit of connecting two events that we call cause and effect. Kant believed that we have knowledge about causality and that we get this knowledge not from sense experience but directly from the faculty of rational judgment and, therefore, a priori.

What, more specifically, is a priori knowledge? Kant replies that "if one desires an example from the sciences, one needs only to look at any proposition in mathematics. If one desires an example from the commonest operations of the understanding, the proposition that every change must have a cause can serve one's purposes." What makes a proposition of mathematics, or the proposition that every change must have a cause, a priori knowledge? It is, says Kant, that this kind of knowledge cannot be derived from experience. Experience cannot show us that *every* change must have a cause, since we have not yet experienced every change. Nor can experience show us that connections between events are *necessary*, for the most experience can tell us is "that a thing is so and so, but not that it cannot be otherwise." Experience, then, cannot give us knowledge about *necessary* connections or about the *universality* of propositions. Yet we do in fact have this kind of knowledge about causality and universality, for these are the notions that characterize mathematics and scientific knowledge. We confidently say that all heavy objects will fall in space or that all instances of five added to seven will equal twelve. That there is such a priori knowledge is clear, but what concerned Kant was how such knowledge can be accounted for. How, in short, can Hume's skepticism be answered?

KANT'S COPERNICAN REVOLUTION

It was clear to Kant that if we assume, as Hume did, that the mind, in forming its concepts, must conform to its objects, there could be no solution to the problem of how knowledge is possible. Hume's theory would work for our ideas of things we have actually experienced. If I ask "How do I know that the chair is brown?" my answer is that I can see it; and if my assertion is challenged, I refer to my experience. When I thus refer to my experience, that settles the question, because we all agree that experience gives us a kind of knowledge that conforms to the nature of things.

But we also have a kind of knowledge which cannot be validated by experience; if I say, for example, that every straight line is the shortest way between two points, I certainly cannot say that I have had experience of every possible straight line. What makes it possible for me to make judgments about events before they even occur, judgments that are universally true and can always be verified? If, as Hume believed, the mind is passive and simply receives its information from the objects, it follows that the mind would have information only about that particular object. But the mind makes judgments about all objects, even those which it has not yet experienced, and in addition, objects do in fact behave in the future according to these judgments we make about them. This scientific knowledge gives us reliable information about the nature of things. But since this knowledge could not be explained on the assumption that the mind conforms to its objects (how could it conform to every straight line, every change?), Kant was forced to try a new hypothesis regarding the relation between the mind and its objects.

Kant's new hypothesis was that it is the objects that conform to the operations of the mind, and not the other way around. He came to this hypothesis with a spirit of experimentation, consciously following the example of Copernicus, who "failing of satisfactory progress in explaining the movements of the heavenly bodies on the supposition that they all revolved round the spectator, . . . tried whether he might not have better success if he made the spectator to revolve and the stars to remain at rest." Seeing an analogy here with his own problem, Kant says that

> hitherto it has been assumed that all our knowledge must conform to objects. But all our attempts to extend our knowledge of objects by establishing something in regard to them *a priori* by means of concepts, have, on this assumption, ended in failure. We must, therefore, make trial whether we may not have more success in the tasks of metaphysics, if we suppose that objects must conform to our knowledge. . . . If intuition must conform to the constitution of the objects, I do not see how we could know anything of the latter *a priori;* but if the object (as object of the senses) must conform to the constitution of our faculty of intuition, I have no difficulty in conceiving such a possibility.

Kant did not mean to say that the mind creates objects, nor did he mean that the mind possesses innate ideas. His Copernican revolution consisted rather in his saying that the mind brings something to the objects it experiences. With Hume, Kant agreed that our knowledge begins with experience, but unlike Hume, Kant saw the mind as an active agent doing something with the objects it experiences. The mind, says Kant, is structured in such a way that it imposes its way of knowing on its objects. By its very nature, the mind actively organizes our experiences. That is, thinking involves not only receiving impressions through our senses but also making judgments about what we experience. Just as a person who wears colored glasses sees everything in that color, so every human being, having the faculty of thought, inevitably thinks about things in accordance with the natural structure of the mind.

The Structure of Rational Thought

Kant says that "there are two sources of human knowledge, which perhaps spring from a common but to us unknown root, namely sensibility and understanding. Through the former objects are *given* to us; through the latter they are *thought.*" Knowledge is, therefore, a cooperative affair between the knower and the thing known. But, although I am able to distinguish the difference between myself as a knower and the thing I know, I can never know that thing as it is in itself, for the moment I know it, I know it as my structured mind permits me to know it. If colored glasses were permanently fixed to my eyes, I should always see things in that color and could never escape the limitations placed on my vision by those glasses. Similarly, my mind always brings certain ways of thinking to things, and this always affects my understanding of them. What, we may ask, does the mind bring to the *given* raw materials of our experience?

THE CATEGORIES OF THOUGHT AND THE FORMS OF INTUITION

The distinctive activity of the mind is to synthesize and to unify our experience. It achieves this synthesis first by imposing on our various experiences in the "sensible manifold" certain forms of intuition: space and time. We inevitably perceive things as being in *space* and *time.* But space and time are not ideas derived from the things we experience, nor are they concepts. Space and time are encountered immediately in intuition and are, at the same time, a priori or, to speak figuratively, lenses through which we always see objects of experience.

   In addition to space and time, which deal particularly with the way we sense things, there are certain categories of thought which deal more specifically with the way the mind unifies or synthesizes our experience. The mind achieves this unifying act by making various kinds of judgments as we engage in the act of interpreting the world of sense. The manifold of experience is judged by us through certain fixed forms or concepts such as *quantity, quality, relation,* and *modality.* When we assert *quantity,* we have in mind one or many. When we make a judgment of *quality,* we make either a positive or negative statement. When we make a judgment of *relation,* we think of cause and effect on the one hand or of the relation of subject and predicate on the other. And when we make a judgment of *modality,* we have in mind that something is either possible or impossible. All these ways of thinking are what constitute the act of synthesis through which the mind strives to make a consistent single world out of the manifold of sense impressions.

THE SELF AND THE UNITY OF EXPERIENCE

What makes it possible for us to have a unified grasp of the world about us? From his analysis of the way our minds work, Kant's answer is that it is the mind that transforms the raw data given to our senses into a coherent and related set of elements. But this leads Kant to say that the unity of our experience must imply a unity of the self, for unless there be a unity between the several operations of the mind, there can be no knowledge of experience. To have such knowledge involves, in various sequences, sensation, imagination, and memory, as well as the powers of intuitive synthesis. Thus it must be the same self that at once senses an object, remembers its characteristics, imposes on it the forms of space and time and the category of cause and effect. All these activities must occur in some single subject; otherwise there could be no knowledge, for if one subject had only sensations, another only memory, and so on, the sensible manifold could never be unified.

Where and what is this single subject that accomplishes this unifying activity? Kant calls it the "transcendental unity of apperception," what we should call the *self.* He uses the term "transcendental" to indicate that we do not experience the self directly even though such a unity, or self, is implied by our actual experience. Thus the idea of this self is a priori as a necessary condition for our experience of having knowledge of a unified world of nature. In the act of unifying all the elements of experience, we are conscious of our own unity, so that our consciousness of a unified world of experience and our own self-consciousness occur simultaneously. Our self-consciousness, however, is affected by the same faculties that affect our perception of external objects. I bring to the knowledge of myself the same apparatus and, therefore, impose on myself as an object of knowledge the same "lenses" through which I see everything. Just as I do not know things as they are apart from the perspective from which I see them, so also I do not know the nature of this "transcendental unity of apperception" except as I am aware of the knowledge I have of the unity of the field of experience. What I am sure of is that a unified self is implied by any knowledge of experience.

PHENOMENAL AND NOUMENAL REALITY

A major impact of Kant's critical philosophy was his insistence that human knowledge is forever limited in its scope. This limitation takes two forms. In the first place, knowledge is limited to the world of experience. Second, our knowledge is limited by the manner in which our faculties of perception and thinking organize the raw data of experience. Kant did not doubt that the world as it appears to us is not the ultimate reality. He distinguished between *phenomenal* reality, or the world as we experience it, and *noumenal* reality, which is purely intelligible, or nonsensual, reality. When we experience a thing, we inevitably perceive it through the "lenses" of our a priori categories of thought. But what is a thing like when it is not being perceived? What is a thing-in-itself (*Ding an sich*)? We can obviously never have an experience of a nonsensuous perception. All objects we know are sensed objects. Still we know that the existence of our world of experience is not produced by the mind. The mind, rather, imposes its ideas on the manifold of experience, which is derived from the world of things-in-themselves. This means that there is a reality external to us that exists independently of us but which we can know only as it appears to us and is organized by us. The concept of a thing-in-itself does not, then, increase our knowledge but reminds us of the limits of our knowledge.

READING

HOW KNOWLEDGE IS POSSIBLE
Kant

I. THE DISTINCTION BETWEEN PURE AND EMPIRICAL KNOWLEDGE

There can be no doubt that all our knowledge begins with experience. For how should our faculty of knowledge be awakened into action did not objects affecting our senses partly of themselves produce representations, partly arouse the activity of our understanding to compare these representations and, by combining or separating them, work up the raw material of the sensible impressions into that knowledge of objects which is entitled experience? In the order of time, therefore, we have no knowledge antecedent to experience, and with experience all our knowledge begins.

But though all our knowledge begins with experience, it does not follow that it all arises out of experience. For it may well be that even our empirical knowledge is made up of what we receive through impressions and of what our own faculty of knowledge (sensible impressions serving merely as the occasion) supplies from itself. If our faculty of knowledge makes any such addition, it may be that we are not in a position to distinguish it from the raw material, until with long practice of attention we have become skilled in separating it.

This, then, is a question which at least calls for closer examination, and does not allow of any off-hand answer:—whether there is any knowledge that is thus independent of experience and even of all impressions of the senses. Such knowledge is entitled *a priori,* and distinguished from the *empirical,* which has its sources *a posteriori,* that is, in experience.

The expression "*a priori*" does not, however, indicate with sufficient precision the full meaning of our question. For it has been customary to say, even of much knowledge that is derived from empirical sources, that we have it or are capable of having it *a priori,* meaning thereby that we do not derive it immediately from experience, but from a universal rule—a rule which is itself, however, borrowed by us from experience. Thus we would say of a man who undermined the foundations of his house, that he might have known *a priori* that it would fall, that is, that he need not have waited

From Immanuel Kant, *Critique of Pure Reason,* trans. Norman Kemp Smith, St. Martin's Press, Inc., Macmillan, London, 1929.

for the experience of its actual falling. But still he could not know this completely *a priori*. For he had first to learn through experience that bodies are heavy, and therefore fall when their supports are withdrawn.

In what follows, therefore, we shall understand by *a priori* knowledge, not knowledge independent of this or that experience, but knowledge absolutely independent of all experience. Opposed to it is empirical knowledge, which is knowledge possible only *a posteriori,* that is, through experience. *A priori* modes of knowledge are entitled pure when there is no admixture of anything empirical. Thus, for instance, the proposition, "every alteration has its cause," while an *a priori* proposition, is not a pure proposition, because alteration is a concept which can be derived from experience.

II. WE ARE IN POSSESSION OF CERTAIN MODES OF A PRIORI KNOWLEDGE, AND EVEN THE COMMON UNDERSTANDING IS NEVER WITHOUT THEM

What we here require is a criterion by which to distinguish with certainty between pure and empirical knowledge. Experience teaches us that a thing is so and so, but not that it cannot be otherwise. First, then, if we have a proposition which in being thought is thought as *necessary,* it is an *a priori* judgment; and if, besides, it is not derived from any proposition except one which also has the validity of a necessary judgment, it is an absolutely *a priori* judgment. Secondly, experience never confers on its judgments true or strict, but only assumed and comparative *universality,* through induction. We can properly only say, therefore, that, so far as we have hitherto observed, there is no exception to this or that rule. If, then, a judgment is thought with strict universality, that is, in such manner that no exception is allowed as possible, it is not derived from experience, but is valid absolutely *a priori.* Empirical universality is only an arbitrary extension of a validity holding in most cases to one which holds in all, for instance, in the proposition, "all bodies are heavy." When, on the other hand, strict universality is essential to a judgment, this indicates a special source of knowledge, namely, a faculty of *a priori* knowledge. Necessity and strict universality are thus sure criteria of *a priori* knowledge, and are inseparable from one another. But since in the employment of these criteria the contingency of judgments is sometimes more easily shown than their empirical limitation, or, as sometimes also happens, their unlimited universality can be more convincingly proved than their necessity, it is advisable to use the two criteria separately, each by itself being infallible.

Now it is easy to show that there actually are in human knowledge judgments which are necessary and in the strictest sense universal, and which are therefore pure *a priori* judgments. If an example from the sciences be desired, we have only to look to any of the propositions of mathematics; if we seek an example from the understanding in its quite ordinary employment, the proposition, "every alteration must have a cause," will serve our purpose. In the latter case, indeed, the very concept of a cause so manifestly contains the concept of a necessity of connection with an effect and of the strict universality of the rule, that the concept would be altogether lost if we attempted to derive it, as Hume has done, from a repeated association of that which happens with that which precedes, and from a custom of connecting representations, a custom originating in this repeated association, and constituting therefore a merely subjective necessity. Even without appealing to such examples, it is possible to show that pure *a priori* principles are indispensable for the possibility of experience, and so to prove their existence *a priori*. For whence could experience derive its certainty, if all the rules, according to which it proceeds, were always themselves empirical, and therefore contingent? Such rules could hardly be regarded as first principles. At present, however, we may be content to have established a pure employment, and to have shown what are the criteria of such an employment.

Such *a priori* origin is manifest in certain concepts, no less than in judgments. If we remove from our empirical concept of a body, one by one, every feature in it which is (merely) empirical, the colour, the hardness or softness, the weight, even the impenetrability, there still remains the space which the body (now entirely vanished) occupied, and this cannot be removed. Again, if we remove from our empirical concept of any object, corporeal or incorporeal, all properties which experience has taught us, we yet cannot take away that property through which the object is thought as substance or as inhering in a substance (although this concept of substance is more determinate than that of an object in general). Owing, therefore, to the necessity with which this concept of substance forces itself upon us, we have no option save to admit that it has its seat in our faculty of *a priori* knowledge. . . .

IV. THE DISTINCTION BETWEEN ANALYTIC AND SYNTHETIC JUDGMENTS

In all judgments in which the relation of a subject to the predicate is thought (I take into consideration affirmative judgments only, the subsequent application to negative judgments being easily made), this relation is possible in two different ways. Either the predicate *B* belongs to the subject *A*, as something which is (covertly) contained in this concept *A*; or *B* lies outside the concept *A*, although it does indeed stand in connection with it. In the one case I entitled the judgment analytic, in the other synthetic. Analytic judgments (affirmative) are therefore those in which the connection of the predicate with the subject is thought through identity; those in which this connection is thought without identity should be entitled synthetic. The former, as adding nothing through the predicate to the concept of the subject, but merely breaking it up into those constituent concepts that have all along been thought in it, although confusedly, can also be entitled explicative. The latter, on the other hand, add to the concept of the subject a predicate which has not been in any wise thought in it, and which no analysis could possibly extract from it; and they may therefore be entitled ampliative. If I say, for instance, "All bodies are extended," this is an analytic judgment. For I do not require to go beyond the concept which I connect with "body" in order to find extension as bound up with it. To meet with this predicate, I have merely to analyse the concept, that is, to become conscious to myself of the manifold which I always think in that concept. The judgment is therefore analytic. But when I say, "All bodies are heavy," the predicate is something quite different from anything that I think in the mere concept of body in general; and the addition of such a predicate therefore yields a synthetic judgment.

Judgments of experience, as such, are one and all synthetic. For it would be absurd to found an analytic judgment on experience. Since, in framing the judgment, I must not go outside my concept, there is no need to appeal to the testimony of experience in its support. That a body is extended is a proposition that holds *a priori* and is not empirical. For, before appealing to experience, I have already in the concept of body all the conditions required for my judgment, I have only to extract from it, in accordance with the principle of contradiction, the required predicate, and in so doing can at the same time become conscious of the necessity of the judgment—and that is what experience could never have taught me. On the other hand, though I do not include in the concept of a body in general the predicate "weight," none the less this concept indicates an object of experience through one of its parts, and I can add to that part other parts of this same experience, as in this way belonging together with the concept. From the start I can apprehend the concept of body analytically through the characters of extension, impenetrability, figure, etc., all of which are thought in the concept. Now, however, looking back on the experience from which I have derived this concept of body, and finding weight to be invariably connected with the above characters, I attach it as a predicate to the concept; and in doing so I attach it synthetically, and am therefore extending my knowledge. The possibility of the synthesis of the predicate "weight" with the concept of "body" thus rests upon experience. While the one concept is not contained in the other, they yet belong to one another, though only contingently, as parts of a whole, namely, of an experience which is itself a synthetic combination of intuitions.

But in *a priori* synthetic judgments this help is entirely lacking. (I do not here have the advantage of looking around in the field of experience.) Upon what, then, am I to rely, when I seek to go beyond the concept A, and to know that another concept B is connected with it? Through what is the synthesis made possible? Let us take the proposition, "Everything which happens has its cause." In the concept of "something which happens," I do indeed think an existence which is preceded by a time, etc., and from this concept analytic judgments may be obtained. But the concept of a "cause" lies entirely outside the other concept, and signifies something different from "that which happens," and is not therefore in any way contained in this latter representation. How come I then to predicate of that which happens something quite different, and to apprehend that the concept of cause, though not contained in it, yet belongs, and indeed necessarily belongs, to it? What is here the unknown = X which gives support to the understanding when it believes that it can discover outside the concept A a predicate B foreign to this concept, which it yet at the same time considers to be connected with it? It cannot be experience, because the suggested principle has connected the second representation with the first, not only with greater universality, but also with the character of necessity, and therefore completely *a priori* and on the basis of mere concepts. Upon such synthetic, that is, ampliative principles, all our *a priori* speculative knowledge must ultimately rest; analytic judgments are very important, and indeed necessary, but only for obtaining that clearness in the concepts which is requisite for such a sure and wide synthesis as will lead to a genuinely new addition to all previous knowledge.

CHAPTER 24

THINKING AND DOING

James

Pragmatism as a Method

William James thought that "the whole function of philosophy ought to be to find out what difference it will make to you and me, at definite instants of our lives, if this world-formula or that world-formula be the true one." His emphasis was on the concrete concerns of life, on facts, on action as it affects and displays power, and on power and action as they affect *my* life *now* and in the determinate future. But pragmatism as such contains no substance or content, no special information about human purpose or destiny. As a philosophy, pragmatism does not have its own creed; it does not offer a world-formula.

"Pragmatism," said James, "is a method only." Still, as a method, pragmatism assumes that human life has a purpose and that rival theories about man and the world would have to be tested against this purpose. There is in fact no single definition of man's purpose; the understanding of human purpose is part of the activity of thinking. Philosophical thinking arises when human beings want to understand things and the setting in which they live; purpose derives its meaning from a sense of being at home in the universe. As a method, pragmatism rejected rationalism chiefly because, said

William James (*Culver Pictures*)

James, it was dogmatic and presumed to give conclusive answers about the world in terms that frequently left the issues of life untouched. By contrast, pragmatism hovered close to life, refusing to close the process of thought prematurely, taking its cue from the proved facts of life, willing to be led to new conceptions of purpose as deeper facets of human emotion and expectations were discovered. Again, as a method, pragmatism did not specify any *particular* results, although it did orient thinking around results, fruits, and consequences. No formulation either in science, theology, or philosophy should be taken as final; all formulations of theory are only approximations. In the last analysis, the meanings of all these theories are to be found not in their internal verbal consistency, but in their capacity to solve problems.

Instead of mere consistency, said James, "you must bring out of each word its practical cash value." Although pragmatism stands

436

for no particular results, as a method in practice its essence is precisely to ensure *results*. When it finds a theory that does not *make* a difference one way or another for practical life, such a theory is abandoned. If, for example, there is a dispute over whether God exists, pragmatism has no preconceived creed to offer, but it does ask whether it makes a difference to believe in God's existence. To raise that question could very well lead one to see the "truth" in the claim of God's existence even though the same person might have rejected a "rational proof" of the existence of God. By asking always what difference an idea makes, James virtually reduced the pragmatic method to the formula "Does it work?" But supporting that formula was the combined methodological apparatus, as James said, of "nominalism—in always appealing to particulars; [of] utilitarianism in emphasizing practical aspects; [of] positivism in its disdain for verbal solutions, useless questions and metaphysical abstractions." It was inevitable that such a method should raise the question whether to say about an idea that "it works" is the same as saying that "it is true."

The Pragmatic Theory of Truth

James made the startling statement that "truth *happens* to an idea." What was so startling about this statement was that the more traditional theories of truth took virtually the opposite view, namely, that truth is a property or quality of an idea. James was rejecting what he called the "copy-view" of truth. This theory assumes that an idea "copies" reality and an idea is therefore true if it copies what is "out there" accurately. Truth is that quality an idea has when it copies accurately. The assumption of the "intellectualists" who hold this theory, said James, is that "truth means essentially an inert static relation. When you've got your true idea of anything, there's an end of the matter. You're in possession; you *know*. . . ." Against this theory, James brought the whole arsenal of his pragmatism. Truth must be the cash value of an idea. What other motive could there be for saying that something is true or not true than to provide workable guides to practical behavior? James would ask

"What concrete difference will its being true make in anyone's actual life?"

By tying truth to life, to action, James rejected the view that truth is a *stagnant* property in ideas. Ideas *become* true; they are *made* true by events. That is why he wanted to say that truth *happens* to ideas. In addition, to say that truth happens to ideas is to make truth a part of experience. Whereas the copy-view of truth assumes that ideas really do copy what is out there, pragmatism says that there rarely is exact copying. Consider, he says, a clock on the wall. We consider it to be a clock not because we have a copy-view of it; we see only its face and hands, but not its internal mechanism, which makes it a clock. Still, our notion of it passes for true, not because our idea of it is an accurate copy, but because we *use* it as a clock and as such it *works*, enabling us to end a lecture "on time" and to catch the train. To be sure, we could check our idea to verify whether it is indeed a clock; but *verifiability* is as good as verification. We do not in fact verify every idea. Indeed, says James, "for one truth-process completed there are a million in our lives that function in this state of nascency." For this reason, truth lives "on a credit system." We do not require in every instance of truth that we should, as it were, see the wheels of the clock. What more would be added to the truth of our idea that that is a clock than we already have in the successful regulation of our behavior?

Ideas become true insofar as they help us to make successful connections between various parts of our experience. Truth is therefore part of the process of experience, of *living*. As part of a process, truth is *made* by the process of successful experience; successful experience *is* the verification process. To say that a truth always is, that it absolutely obtains, would mean that the clock on the wall is a clock whether any one sees it or not. But what James wants to show is that the question about the "truth" of the clock arises only in actual life when we live "as if" that thing on the wall is a clock, and the truth that it is a clock is *made* by our successful behavior. On this theory, says James, there are many *plural* truths, as many truths as there are concrete successful actions. Moreover, James would say that truth is bound up with the personal interests of concrete individuals. By this he meant that truth is not something *capricious*. As bound up with personal interests, the "truth" must lead to successful action; it must *work*. In the long run, a true belief must work beneficially, just as an "untrue" one will work destructively.

If the pragmatist is asked why anyone *ought* to seek the truth. James answers that "our obligation to seek the truth is part of our general obligation to do what pays," just as one ought to seek health because it pays to be healthy. Above all, James thought that the pragmatic theory of truth could render a desperately needed service to philosophy by providing a means for settling disputes. Some disputes cannot be resolved if each party simply affirms that his views are true. James would ask "Which theory fits the facts of real life?" One such dispute, which has exercised philosophers through the ages, is the question of freedom versus determinism.

Role and Status of the Will

William James was convinced that it is not possible to "prove" by any rational mode of argument that the will of man is either free or determined. Apparently equally good arguments could be given for each case. But he was nevertheless convinced that he could put the problem in a new light by applying the pragmatic method, by asking what difference it makes in actual life to accept one or the other side of the dispute. And the dispute was worth undertaking because it implied something momentous about life—either men were driven by external forces or they possessed "freedom" to choose their mode of behavior and therefore possessed the power to shape their lives and, thus, history.

The central issue in this dispute, said James, "relates solely to the existence of possibilities," of things that may, but need not, be. The determinist says that there are no possibilities, that what will be will be: " . . . those parts of the universe already laid down absolutely appoint and decree what the other parts shall be. The future has no ambiguous possibilities in its womb. . . . " However, the indeterminist says that there is a certain amount of "loose play" in the universe, so that the present existence of certain facts and arrangements does not necessarily determine what the future shall be; he says that there are genuine alternatives in the future from which an actual choice can be made. Here, then, are two contradictory points of view. "What divides us into *possibility* men and *antipossibility* men?" asks James. It is, he says, the postulates of rationality. For some men it seems more rational to say that all events are set down from eternity, whereas for others it seems more rational to assume that men can engage in genuine choice. If both these points of view seem equally rational to their respective proponents, how can the dispute be resolved?

This was not for James simply an interesting puzzle. His whole philosophical orientation revolved around this problem of the role and status of the will. With his basic concern about action and choosing those ideas and modes of behavior with the highest cash value, he inevitably saw philosophy in terms of human striving, and this, he was convinced, implied a certain kind of universe. His solution of the problem, therefore, was to ask the simple pragmatic question "What does a deterministic world imply?" If, that is, one says that all events without exception are rigorously determined from the beginning of time so that they could not have happened in any other way, what kind of universe must this be? Using a metaphor, one could only answer that such a universe is like a machine, where each part fits tightly and all the gears are interlocked, so that the slightest motion of one part causes a motion of every other part. There is no loose play in the machine.

"How can such a metaphor be applied to men?" James asks. A man is different from a mechanical part in a machine. What makes a man different is his consciousness. For one thing, a man is capable of a "judgment of regret." But how can one "regret" what could not have been otherwise? The determinist must define the world as a place where what "ought to be" is impossible. Still we are always making judgments not only of regret but of approval and disapproval. Moreover, we seek to persuade others to do or refrain from doing certain actions. In addition, men are punished or rewarded for certain actions. All these forms of judgment imply that a man is constantly facing genuine choices; a "forced" or "determined" act is not a *choice.*

The capacity of choice involves the capacity to recognize alternative influences on one, to hold these alternatives in momentary suspense, and then select one or the other. If one denies such a capacity for choice, the only alternative is the mechanical explanation. But no human beings ever consciously act as if this were a mechanically determined universe. Most of our language and thought processes suggest just the opposite; they suggest that at many points each person in fact faces genuine possibilities, options, real choices.

James did not want to deny the reality of causal relations.

Indeed, his pragmatism rested on the operational formula that *"if we do A, B* will happen." But the word "if" is the clue; we are not forced to do *A,* and therefore *B* will happen only if we decide to choose *A*. James realized that if the determinist charged that his (James's) ideas about free will were determined, and that his assumptions about genuine possibilities were part of the block universe, such charges would indeed bring an end to rational discourse and the problem could no longer be discussed. What would remain, however, would be human beings with hopes, fears, and regrets. In the arena of daily life the assumptions of mechanical determinism would be abandoned, and the pragmatic question would come to the forefront, namely, "What should I do?" or "Which alternative would be better or wiser for me?"

In actual practical life, we see ourselves and others as vulnerable. Men are capable of lying, stealing, and murdering. We judge these to be wrong, not only in retrospect, but wrong because they were not rigorously inevitable when they were done; persons doing these things "could have" done otherwise. James concludes, in this vein, by saying that this problem is finally a "personal" one, that he simply cannot conceive of the universe as a place where murder *must* happen; it is a place where murder *can* happen and *ought not*. In short, for James, the truth about the freedom of the will is decided by the practical consequences of this idea for human behavior.

READING

PRAGMATISM AND THE ENTERPRISE OF KNOWING
James

Some years ago, being with a camping party in the mountains, I returned from a solitary ramble to find every one engaged in a ferocious metaphys-

From William James, "What Pragmatism Means," 1907.

ical dispute. The *corpus* of the dispute was a squirrel—a live squirrel supposed to be clinging to one side of a tree-trunk; while over against the tree's opposite side a human being was imagined to stand. This human witness tries to get sight of the squirrel by moving rapidly round the tree, but no matter how fast he goes, the squirrel moves as fast in the opposite direction, and always keeps the tree between himself and the man, so that never a glimpse of him is caught. The resultant metaphysical problem now is this: *Does the man go round the squirrel or not?* He goes round the tree, sure enough, and the squirrel is on the tree; but does he go round the squirrel? In the unlimited leisure of the wilderness, discussion had been worn threadbare. Every one had taken sides, and was obstinate; and the numbers on both sides were even. Each side, when I appeared, therefore appealed to me to make it a majority. Mindful of the scholastic adage that whenever you meet a contradiction you must make a distinction, I immediately sought and found one, as follows: "Which party is right," I said, "depends on what you *practically mean* by 'going round' the squirrel. If you mean passing from the north of him to the east, then to the south, then to the west, and then to the north of him again, obviously the man does go round him, for he occupies these successive positions. But if on the contrary you mean being first in front of him, then on the right of him, then behind him, then on his left, and finally in front again, it is quite as obvious that the man fails to go round him, for by the compensating movements the squirrel makes, he keeps his belly turned towards the man all the time, and his back turned away. Make the distinction, and there is no occasion for any further dispute. You are both right and both wrong according as you conceive the verb 'to go round' in one practical fashion or the other."

Although one or two of the hotter disputants called my speech a shuffling evasion, saying they wanted no quibbling or scholastic hair-splitting, but meant just plain honest English "round," the majority seemed to think that the distinction had assuaged the dispute.

I tell this trivial anecdote because it is a peculiarly simple example of what I wish now to speak of as *the pragmatic method.* The pragmatic method is primarily a method of settling metaphysical disputes that otherwise might be interminable. Is the world one or many?—fated or free?—material or spiritual?—here are notions either of which may or may not hold good of the world; and disputes over such notions are unending. The pragmatic method in such cases is to try to interpret each notion by tracing its respective practical consequences. What difference would it practically make to any one if this notion rather than that notion were true? If no practical difference whatever can be traced, then the alternatives mean practically the same thing, and all dispute is idle. Whenever a dispute is serious, we ought to be able to show some practical difference that must follow from one side or the other's being right.

A glance at the history of the idea will show you still better what pragmatism means. The term is derived from the same Greek word *pragma*, meaning action, from which our words "practice" and "practical" come. It was first introduced into philosophy by Mr. Charles Peirce in 1878. In an article entitled "How to Make Our Ideas Clear," in the *Popular Science Monthly* for January of that year Mr. Peirce, after pointing out that our beliefs are really rules for action, said that, to develop a thought's meaning, we need only determine what conduct it is fitted to produce: that conduct is for us its sole significance. And the tangible fact at the root of all our thought-distinctions, however subtle, is that there is no one of them so fine as to consist in anything but a possible difference of practice. To attain perfect clearness in our thoughts of an object, then, we need only consider what conceivable effects of a practical kind the object may involve—what sensations we are to expect from it, and what reactions we must prepare. Our conception of these effects, whether immediate or remote, is then for us the whole of our conception of the object, so far as that conception has positive significance at all.

This is the principle of Peirce, the principle of pragmatism. It lay entirely unnoticed by any one for twenty years, until I, in an address before Professor Howison's Philosophical Union at the University of California, brought it forward again and made a special application of it to religion. By that date (1898) the times seemed ripe for its reception. The word "pragmatism" spread, and at present it fairly spots the pages of the philosophic journals. On all hands we find the "pragmatic movement" spoken of, sometimes with respect, sometimes with contumely, seldom with clear understanding. It is evident that the term applies itself conveniently to a number of tendencies that hitherto have lacked a collective name, and that it has "come to stay."

To take in the importance of Peirce's principle, one must get accustomed to applying it to concrete cases. I found a few years ago that Ostwald, the illustrious Leipzig chemist, had been making perfectly distinct use of the principle of pragmatism in his lectures on the philosophy of science, though he had not called it by that name.

"All realities influence our practice," he wrote me, "and that influence is their meaning for us. I am accustomed to put questions to my classes in this way: In what respects would the world be different if this alternative to that were true? If I can find nothing that would become different, then the alternative has no sense."

That is, the rival views mean practically the same thing, and meaning, other than practical, there is for us none. Ostwald in a published lecture gives this example of what he means. Chemists have long wrangled over the inner constitution of certain bodies called "tautomerous." Their properties seemed equally consistent with the notion that an instable hydrogen atom oscillates inside of them, or that they are instable mixtures of two bodies. Controversy raged, but never was decided. "It would never have begun," says Ostwald, "if the combatants had asked themselves what particular experimental fact could have been made different by one or the other view being correct. For it would then have appeared that no difference of fact could possibly ensue; and the quarrel was as unreal as if, theorizing in primitive times about the raising of dough by yeast, one party should have invoked a 'brownie,' while another insisted on an 'elf' as the true cause of the phenomenon."

It is astonishing to see how many philosophical disputes collapse into insignificance the moment you subject them to this simple test of tracing a concrete consequence. There can *be* no difference anywhere that doesn't *make* a difference elsewhere—no difference in abstract truth that doesn't express itself in a difference in concrete fact and in conduct consequent upon that fact, imposed on somebody, somehow, somewhere, and somewhen. The whole function of philosophy ought to be to find out what definite difference it will make to you and me, at definite instants of our life, if this world-formula or that world-formula be the true one.

There is absolutely nothing new in the pragmatic method. Socrates was an adept at it. Aristotle used it methodically. Locke, Berkeley, and Hume made momentous contributions to truth by its means. Shadworth Hodgson keeps insisting that realities are only what they are "known as." But these forerunners of pragmatism used it in fragments: they were preluders only. Not until in our time has it generalized itself, become conscious of a universal mission, pretended to a conquering destiny. I believe in that destiny, and I hope I may end by inspiring you with my belief.

Pragmatism represents a perfectly familiar attitude in philosophy, the empiricist attitude, but it represents it, as it seems to me, both in a more radical and in a less objectionable form than it has ever yet assumed. A pragmatist turns his back resolutely and once for all upon a lot of inveterate habits clear to professional philosophers. He turns away from abstraction and insufficiency, from verbal solutions, from bad *a priori* reasons, from fixed principles, closed systems, and pretended absolutes and origins. He turns towards concreteness and adequacy, towards facts, towards action and towards power. That means the empiricist temper regnant and the rationalist temper sincerely given up. It means the open air and possibilities of nature, as against dogma, artificiality, and the pretence of finality in truth.

At the time it does not stand for any special results. It is a method only. But the general triumph of that method would mean an enormous change in what I called in my last lecture the "temperament" of philosophy. Teachers of the ultra-rationalistic type would be frozen out, much as the courtier type is frozen out in republics, as the ultramontane type of priest is frozen out in protestant lands. Science and metaphysics would come much nearer together, would in fact work absolutely hand in hand.

Metaphysics has usually followed a very primitive kind of quest. You know how men have always hankered after unlawful magic, and you know what a great part in magic *words* have always played. If you have his name, or the formula of incantation that binds him, you can control the spirit, genie, afrite, or whatever the power may be. Solomon knew the names of all the spirits, and having their names, he held them subject to his will. So the universe has always appeared to the natural mind as a kind of enigma, of which the key must be sought in the shape of some illuminating or power-bringing word or name. That word names the universe's *principle*, and to possess it is after a fashion to possess the universe itself. "God," "Matter," "Reason," "the Absolute," "Energy" are so many solving names. You can rest when you have them. You are at the end of your metaphysical quest.

But if you follow the pragmatic method, you cannot look on any such word as closing your quest. You must bring out of each word its practical cash-value, set it at work within the stream of your experience. It appears less as a solution, then, than as a program for more work, and more particularly as an indication of the ways in which existing realities may be *changed*.

Theories thus become instruments, not answers to enigmas, in which we can rest. We don't lie back upon them, we move forward, and, on occasion, make nature over again by their aid. Pragmatism unstiffens all our theories, limbers them up and sets each one at work. Being nothing essentially new, it harmonizes with many ancient philosophic tendencies. It agrees with nominalism, for instance, in always appealing to particulars; with utilitarianism in emphasizing practical aspects; with positivism in its disdain for verbal solutions, useless questions and metaphysical abstractions.

All these, you see, are *anti-intellectualist* tendencies. Against rationalism as a pretension and a method pragmatism is fully armed and militant. But, at the outset, at least, it stands for no particular results. It has no dogmas, and no doctrines save its method. As the young Italian pragmatist Papini has well said, it lies in the midst of our theories, like a corridor in a hotel. Innumerable chambers open out of it. In one you may find a man writing an atheistic volume; in the next some one on his knees praying for faith and strength; in a third a chemist investigating a body's properties. In a fourth a system of idealistic metaphysics is being excogitated; in a fifth the impossibility of metaphysics is being shown. But they all own the corridor, and all must pass through it if they want a practicable way of getting into or out of their respective rooms.

No particular results then, so far, but only an attitude of orientation, is what the pragmatic method means. *The attitude of looking away from first things, principles, "categories," supposed necessities; and of looking towards last things, fruits, consequences, facts.*

So much for the pragmatic method! You may say that I have been praising it rather than explaining it to you, but I shall presently explain it abundantly enough by showing how it works on some familiar problems. Meanwhile the word pragmatism has come to be used in a still wider sense, as meaning also a certain *theory of truth*. I mean to give a whole lecture to the statement of that theory, after first paving the way, so I can be very brief now. But brevity is hard to follow, so I ask for your redoubled attention for a quarter of an hour. If much remains obscure, I hope to make it clear in the later lectures.

One of the most successfully cultivated branches of philosophy in our time is what is called inductive logic, the study of the conditions under which our sciences have evolved. Writers on this subject have begun to show a singular unanimity as to what the laws of nature and elements of fact mean, when formulated by mathematicians, physicists and chemists. When the first mathematical, logical, and natural uniformities, the first laws, were discovered, men were so carried away by the clearness, beauty and simplification that resulted, that they believed themselves to have deciphered authentically the eternal thoughts of the Almighty. His mind also thundered and reverberated in syllogisms. He also thought in conic sections, squares and roots and ratios, and geometrized like Euclid. He made Kepler's laws for the planets to follow; he made velocity increase proportionally to the time in falling bodies; he made the law of the sines for light to obey when refracted; he established the classes, orders, families and genera of plants and animals, and fixed the distances between them. He thought the archetypes of all things, and devised their variations; and when we rediscover any one of these his wondrous institutions, we seize his mind in its very literal intention.

But as the sciences have developed further, the notion has gained ground that most, perhaps all, of our laws are only approximations. The laws themselves, moreover, have grown so numerous that there is no counting them; and so many rival formulations are proposed in all the branches of science that investigators have become accustomed to the notion that no theory is absolutely a transcript of reality, but that any one of them may from some point of view be useful. Their great use is to summarize old facts and to lead to new ones. They are only a manmade language, a conceptual shorthand, as some one calls them, in which we write our reports of nature; and languages, as is well known, tolerate much choice of expression and many dialects.

Thus human arbitrariness had driven divine necessity from scientific logic. If I mention the names of Sigwart, Mach, Ostwald, Pearson, Milhaud, Poincare, Duhem, Ruyssen, those of you who are students will easily identify the tendency I speak of, and will think of additional names.

Riding now on the front of this wave of scientific logic Messrs. Schiller and Dewey appear with their pragmatistic account of what truth everywhere signifies. Everywhere, these teachers say, "truth" in our ideas and beliefs means the same thing that it means in science. It means, they say, nothing but this, *that ideas (which themselves are but parts of our experience) become true just in so far as they help us to get into satisfactory relation with other parts of our experience,* to summarize them and get about among them by conceptual shortcuts instead of following the interminable succession of particular phenomena. Any idea upon which we can rise, so to speak; any idea that will carry us prosperously from any one part of our experience to any other part, linking things satisfactorily, working securely, simplifying, saving labor; is true for just so much, true in so far forth, true *instrumentally.* This is the "instrumental" view of truth taught so successfully at Chicago, the view that truth in our ideas means their power to "work," promulgated so brilliantly at Oxford. . . .

Now pragmatism, devoted though she be to facts, has no such materialistic bias as ordinary empiricism labors under. Moreover, she has no objection whatever to the realizing of abstractions, so long as you get about among particulars with their aid and they actually carry you somewhere. Interested in no conclusions but those which our minds and our experiences work out together, she has no *a priori* prejudices against theology. *If theological ideas prove to have a value for concrete life, they will be true, for pragmatism, in the sense of being good for so much. For how much more they are true, will depend entirely on their relations to the other truths that also have to be acknowledged.* . . .

If there be any life that it is really better we should lead, and if there be any idea which, if believed in, would help us to lead that life, then it would be really *better for us* to believe in that idea, *unless, indeed, belief in it incidentally clashed with other greater vital benefits.* . . .

Pragmatism is willing to take anything, to follow either logic or the senses and to count the humblest and most personal experiences. She will count mystical experiences if they have practical consequences. She will take a God who lives in the very dirt of private fact—if that should seem a likely place to find him.

Her only test of probable truth is what works best in the way of leading us, what fits every part of life best and combines with the collectivity of experiences's demands, nothing being omitted. If theological ideas should do this, if the notion of God, in particular, should prove to do it, how could pragmatism possibly deny God's existence? She could see no meaning in treating as "not true" a notion that was pragmatically so successful. What other kind of truth could there be, for her, than all this agreement with concrete reality?

READING

PRAGMATISM'S CONCEPTION OF TRUTH

James

Truth, as any dictionary will tell you, is a property of certain of our ideas. It means their "agreement," as falsity means their "disagreement," with "reality." Pragmatists and intellectualists both accept this definition as a matter of course. They begin to quarrel only after the question is raised as to what may precisely be meant by the term "agreement," and what by the term "reality," when reality is taken as something for our ideas to agree with.

The popular notion is that a true idea must copy its reality. Like other popular views, this one follows the analogy of the most usual experience. Our true ideas of sensible things do indeed copy them. Shut your eyes and think of yonder clock on the wall, and you get just such a true picture or copy of its dial. But your idea of its "works" (unless you are a clockmaker) is much less of a copy, yet it passes muster, for it in no way clashes with the reality. Even though it should shrink to the mere word "works," that word still serves you truly; and when you speak of the "time-keeping function" of the clock, or its spring's "elasticity," it is hard to see exactly what your ideas can copy.

You perceive that there is a problem here. Where our ideas cannot copy definitely their object, what does agreement with that object mean? Some idealists seem to say that they are true whenever they are what God means that we ought to think about that subject. Others hold the copy-view all through, and speak as if our ideas possessed truth just in proportion as they approach to being copies of the Absolute's eternal way of thinking.

These views, you see, invite pragmatistic discussion. But the great assumption of the intellectualists is that truth means essentially an inert static relation. When you've got your true idea of anything, there's an end of the matter. You're in possession; you *know;* you have fulfilled your thinking destiny. You are where you ought to be mentally; you have obeyed your categorical imperative; and nothing more need follow on that climax of your rational destiny. Epistemologically you are in stable equilibrium.

From William James, "Pragmatism's Conception of Truth," 1907.

Pragmatism, on the other hand, asks its usual question. "Grant an idea or belief to be true, " it says, "what concrete difference will its being true make in any one's actual life? How will the truth be realized? What experiences will be different from those which would obtain if the belief were false? What, in short, is the truth's cash-value in experiential terms?"

The moment pragmatism asks this question, it sees the answer: *True ideas are those that we can assimilate, validate, corroborate and verify. False ideas are those that we cannot.* That is the practical difference it makes to us to have true ideas; that, therefore, is the meaning of truth, for it is all that truth is known as.

This thesis is what I have to defend. The truth of an idea is not a stagnant property inherent in it. Truth *happens* to an idea. It *becomes* true, is *made* true by events. Its verity *is* in fact an event, a process: the process namely of its verifying itself, is veri-*fication*. Its validity is the process of its valid-*ation*.

Take, for instance, yonder object on the wall. You and I consider it to be a "clock," although no one of us has seen the hidden works that make it one. We let our notion pass for true without attempting to verify. If truths mean verification-process essentially, ought we then to call such unverified truths as this abortive? No, for they form the overwhelmingly large number of the truths we live by. Indirect as well as direct verifications pass muster. Where circumstantial evidence is sufficient, we can go without eye-witnessing. Just as we here assume Japan to exist without ever having been there, because it *works* to do so, everything we know conspiring with the belief, and nothing interfering, so we assume that thing to be a clock. We *use* it as a clock, regulating the length of our lecture by it. The verification of the assumption here means its leading to no frustration or contradiction. Verifi*ability* of wheels and weights and pendulum is as good as verification. For one truth-process completed there are a million in our lives that function in this state of nascency. They turn us *towards* direct verification; lead us into the *surroundings* of the objects they envisage; and then, if everything runs on harmoniously, we are so sure that verification is possible that we omit it, and are usually justified by all that happens.

Truth lives, in fact, for the most part on a credit system. Our thoughts and beliefs "pass," so long as nothing challenges them, just as banknotes pass so long as nobody refuses them. But this all points to direct face-to-face verifications somewhere, without which the fabric of truth collapses like a financial system with no cash-basis whatever. You accept my verification of one thing, I yours of another. We trade on each other's truth. But beliefs verified concretely by *somebody* are the posts of the whole superstructure. . . .

Our account of truth is an account of truths in the plural, of processes of leading, realized *in rebus,* and having only this quality in common, that they *pay*. They pay by guiding us into or towards some part of a system that dips at numerous points into sense-percepts, which we may copy mentally or not, but with which at any rate we are now in the kind of commerce vaguely designated as verification. Truth for us is simply a collective name for verification-processes, just as health, wealth, strength, etc., are names for other processes connected with life, and also pursued because it pays to pursue them. Truth is *made,* just as health, wealth, and strength are made, in the course of experience.

CHAPTER 25

WORDS AND THE WORLD

The Analytic Philosophers: Russell, Carnap, and Wittgenstein

The dominant movement of philosophical activity in the contemporary English-speaking world is known as "analytic philosophy." To call it a *movement* rather than a *school* underscores the fact that although analytic philosophy has certain clear distinguishing characteristics, the sources out of which it emerged, the changes it has undergone, and the variety of ways in which it is pursued are many. What unifies all analytic philosophers is their agreement concerning the central task of philosophy. The task of philosophy, they say, is to clarify the meaning of language. In his early work, the *Tractatus Logico-Philosophicus*, Wittgenstein said that "the object of philosophy is the logical clarification of thoughts" so that "the result of philosophy is not a number of philosophical propositions, but to make propositions clear."

To say that the philosopher does not formulate "philosophical propositions" meant for the early analysts that there must be a self-imposed limit on the scope of philosophical activity. Specifically, this meant that, in contrast to the immediately past tradition of nineteenth-century idealism, especially Hegelianism, whose practitioners engaged in constructing complete systems of thought regarding the whole universe, the analysts would now undertake the more modest task of working on individual problems. Not only would these problems be single and manageable, they would all fit into a single class; they would all be problems revolving around the meanings and usages of language. For this reason, it would no longer be the task of the philosopher to investigate the nature of reality, to build complete systems that seek to explain the universe, or to fashion moral, political, and religious philosophies of behavior. Philosophy, in this new key, "is not a doctrine but an activity," and as such, it can produce "no ethical propositions," said Wittgenstein. The philosopher is no longer to consider himself capable of discovering unique forms of information about the world and man. The discovery of facts is the task of the scientist. There are no facts left over for the philosophers after all the sciences have done their work.

The new assumption was that the philosopher can render a genuine service by carefully unpacking complex problems whose origin is found in the imprecise use of language. Scientists themselves, it was felt, had discussed their findings in language that was often misleading and in certain ways ambiguous. That is, scientific language contained ambiguities of logic, not of physical discovery, and the clarification of these logical ambiguities was required. It was assumed, also, that rigorous linguistic analysis could *prevent* the use or abuse of language in ways that would cause us, as A. J. Ayer said, "to draw false inferences, or ask spurious questions, or make nonsensical assumptions." What concerned Ayer was that we often use propositions about nations as though nations were persons, we talk about material things as though we believed in a physical world "beneath" or "behind" visible phenomena, and we use the word "is" in relation to things whose existence we could not possibly want to infer. Philosophy is called on to remove these dangers from our use of language, said Ayer. In a somewhat similar vein, Gilbert Ryle wrote about "Systematically Misleading Expressions," saying that although he would rather allot to philosophy "a sublimer task than the detection of the sources in linguistic idioms of recurrent misconstructions and absurd theories," still, philosophical analysis consists in inquiring about "what it really means to say so and so." In this way, the new philosophy became closely related to the enterprises of science, not as a rival discipline offering propositions of what reality is like but as the proofreader of the scientists' expressions, checking the literature of science for its clarity and logical meaningfulness. It would no longer be the function of the philosopher either to propound vast systems of thought after the manner of Plato, Aristotle, and Hegel or to tell people how they ought to behave. He would instead analyze statements or propositions to discover the causes of ambiguities and the foundations of meaning in language.

What caused this dramatic shift in the enterprise of philosophy? At Cambridge, Bertrand Russell and G. E. Moore had reacted in the early decades of the twentieth century against the system-building of the Hegelian philosophers such as F. H. Bradley, Bernard Bosanquet, and J. E. McTaggart, who had been engaged in ambitious metaphysical speculation. Although Moore did not necessarily want to give up metaphysics, he was especially disturbed by the contrast between metaphysical language and so-called common sense. To him certain statements, such as, for example, McTaggart's famous notion that "time is unreal," seemed "perfectly monstrous." Moore was inspired to analyze language particularly to clarify ordinary language and to make language fit the test of common sense in its meaning. Bertrand Russell, however, was a brilliant mathematician, trained in precise thought, and in comparison with the language of mathematics, metaphysical language seemed to him loose and obscure. He did not want to reject metaphysics any more than Moore did, but he did want to tighten up the language of metaphysics. While Moore set out to analyze common-sense language, Russell tried to analyze "facts" for the purpose of inventing a new language, "logical atomism," which would have the exactness and rigor of mathematics because it would be made to correspond exactly to the "facts." Although neither Moore nor Russell gave up the attempt to understand reality, the way they went about their task emphasized the fact that philosophy is concerned not with discovery but with clarification and, therefore, in a sense, not with truth but with meaning.

Across the channel, a group of mathematicians, scientists, and philosophers formed a group in Vienna in the 1920s, describing themselves as "logical positivists" and known as the "Vienna Circle." Their orientation was rigorously empirical, and they proceeded to reject the whole enterprise of metaphysics. Their ideal for philosophy was the unification of the sciences, hoping thereby to produce a unified system of meaningful and valid knowledge. Among this group were such men as Moritz Schlick, Rudolph Car-

nap, Friedrich Waismann, Herbert Feigl, Otto Neurath, and Kurt
Gödel. A young former student of Bertrand Russell's, Ludwig Wittgenstein, lived nearby, and although he was not a member of the
Circle, he had conversations with its members, and his early book,
Tractatus Logico-Philosophicus (1919), was considered by the
Vienna Circle to express its philosophical point of view with great
accuracy. Not only had Wittgenstein said that "whatever can be
said at all can be said clearly," he concluded his book by saying that
"whereof one cannot speak, thereof one must be silent." This dic-
tum was less harsh than Hume's rigorous conclusion in his *Enquiry*,
where, following the implicit logic of his principles of empiricism,
he wrote:

> When we run over libraries, persuaded of these principles, what
> havoc we must make? If we take in our hand any volume; of divinity
> or school metaphysics, for instance; let us ask, Does it contain any
> abstract reasoning concerning quantity or number? No. Does it con-
> tain any experimental reasoning concerning matter of fact and exis-
> tence? No. Commit it then to the flames: for it can contain nothing
> but sophistry and illusion.

The Vienna Circle philosophers thought of themselves as the
twentieth-century heirs of Hume's empirical tradition. To this tradition they now sought to apply the rigorous apparatus of mathematics and science. If their ideal was to clarify the language of science and the sciences, their first task would have to be the
formulation of a standard for clarity, and this resulted in their
famous *verification principle.* This principle would in time be shown
to suffer from certain defects and require attempts at modification.
These internal difficulties with their central principle as well as
with other aspects of their philosophical concerns, and the scatter-
ing of the members to British and American universities in the
1930s, dissolved the Vienna Circle and gradually led to the decline
of logical positivism.

What followed next in the history of analytic philosophy was
the decisive work of the "new" Wittgenstein. Between his *Tractatus Logico-Philosophicus* (1919) and the posthumous publication of
his famed *Philosophical Investigations* (1953), his thought had
acquired a radically new character, and it is this version of his way
of doing philosophy that has dominated the contemporary philosophical scene in the English-speaking world. The major facets of
analytic philosophy are to be found, then, in Bertrand Russell's *log-*

ical atomism, the Vienna Circle's *logical positivism,* and the later Wittgenstein's *philosophical analysis.*

Logical Atomism

Bertrand Russell's point of departure in philosophy was his admiration for the precision of mathematics. Accordingly, he announced that "the kind of philosophy that I wish to advocate, which I call logical atomism, is one which has forced itself upon me in the course of thinking about the philosophy of mathematics." He wanted to set forth "a certain kind of logical doctrine and on the basis of this a certain kind of metaphysics." Russell thought that since it was possible to construct a logic by which the whole of mathematics could be derived from a small number of logical axioms, as he had already done with A. N. Whitehead in their *Principia Mathematica,* then why could not this logic form the basis of a language that could accurately express everything that could be clearly stated? His assumption was, recalling that in the quotation above he connected "logical atomism" and "a certain kind of metaphysics," that the world would correspond to his specially constructed logical language. The vocabulary of the new logic would, for the most part, correspond to particular objects in the world. To accomplish this task of creating a new language, Russell set out first of all to analyze certain "facts," which he differentiated from "things."

　　"The things in the world," said Russell, "have various properties, and stand in various relations to each other. That they have these properties and relations are *facts.* . . . " Facts constitute for Russell the complexity of the relations of things to each other, and therefore "it is with the analysis of *facts* that one's consideration of the problem of complexity must begin." Russell's basic assumption was that "facts, since they have components, must be in some sense complex, and hence must be susceptible of analysis." The complexity of facts is matched by the complexity of language. For this reason, the aim of analysis is to make sure that every statement represents an adequate picture of the reality, of the facts, of the world.

　　Language, according to Russell, consists of a unique arrangement of words, and the meaningfulness of language is determined by the accuracy with which these words represent facts. Words, in

Bertrand Russell (*United Press International*)

turn, are formulated into propositions. "In a logically perfect language," said Russell, "the words in a proposition would correspond one by one with the components of the corresponding facts." By analysis, certain *simple* words are discovered. These are words that cannot be further analyzed into something more primary and can therefore be understood only by knowing what they symbolize. The word "red," for example, is not capable of further analysis and is therefore understood as a simple *predicate*. Other words, similarly simple, refer to particular things, and as symbols of these things they are *proper names*. Language consists in part, then, of words, which in their simplest form refer to a particular thing and its predicate, as for example a *red rose*. A proposition states a fact.

456

When a fact is of the simplest kind, it is called an "atomic fact." Propositions that state atomic facts are called "atomic propositions." If our language consisted only of such atomic propositions, it would amount only to a series of reports regarding atomic facts. This is what Wittgenstein said in his *Tractatus*, when he wrote that "the world is everything that is the case. . . . What is the case, the fact, is the existence of atomic facts."

It is clear that in our language atomic propositions are put together into more complex propositions. When two or more atomic propositions are linked together with such words as "and" and "or," the result is what Russell calls a "molecular proposition." However, there are no "molecular" *facts*, only atomic facts. For this reason, molecular propositions cannot correspond to molecular facts. How can one test the truth or falsity, then, of molecular propositions? Their truth depends on the truth or falsity of the atomic propositions of which they are made up. Language, on this account, consists of an indefinite number of atomic propositions, whose correspondence with actual facts is settled by empirical methods and techniques. Nothing can be said about the world that is not analyzable down to an atomic proposition, which, in turn, corresponds to an atomic fact. The grammatical independence of each atomic proposition indicates the metaphysical independence of each atomic fact. Again, in an ideal language, words and propositions would correspond to facts. Moreover, it was assumed that after a careful analysis of words and propositions and their corresponding atomic facts, one would arrive at the basic character of language and of the world, and that apart from these facts there would be no residue. Thus the ideal language would express all there is to say about the world. All of reality, on this theory, could be described in statements such as "That is green."

Difficulties developed in the program of logical atomism first of all when Russell and others tried to account for *general* facts. It is one thing to say "That is a white horse," the truth or falsity of which is checked by connecting the *words* "white" and "horse" with the atomic *facts* of this white color and this animal, the horse. It is another thing to say "All horses are white." How would one test the truth or falsity of such a statement? According to logical atomism, one should analyze this statement into its atomic propositions and test *their* truth or falsity. There is no atomic fact corresponding to "all horses . . . ," for this means more than just this horse and that horse, namely, all horses, and this is a *general* fact.

458

KNOWLEDGE

But the whole argument of logical atomism was that only atomic facts exist, and the theory had no way of dealing adequately with so-called general facts unless general facts were accepted as a form of atomic facts. Still, if one were disposed to consider only the particular things recorded by our senses as the basis of our language, as Hume did, singular atomic facts would be the only facts available for human discourse, and language would therefore consist solely of atomic and molecular propositions.

The young Wittgenstein became more and more convinced that philosophy must reject the metaphysical elements in logical atomism. The right method of philosophy would be "to say nothing except what can be said clearly, i.e., the propositions of science. . . ." This became the basic theme of logical positivism.

Logical Positivism

The men who formed the Vienna Circle were by temperament attracted to the methods of science and mathematics. They were disposed to reject metaphysics, as had the earlier positivists, who considered metaphysics as outdated by science. Now they had the additional argument, because of Russell's work in logic and Wittgenstein's powerful formulation of the relation of logic and language in the *Tractatus*, that metaphysics is impossible as shown by the logical and essential character of language. They called themselves "logical positivists," or sometimes "logical empiricists." For the English-speaking world, A. J. Ayer, in his brilliantly lucid and powerfully argued book *Language, Truth and Logic* (1936), did, as he later said with considerable understatement, "something to popularize what may be called the classic position of the Vienna Circle."

This position called for a blanket rejection of metaphysics, and the grounds for this rejection were to be found in the Vienna Circle's famous *verification principle*.

LOGICAL ANALYSIS

Among the foremost members of the Vienna Circle was the eminent positivist Rudolph Carnap. Born in Germany in 1891, he taught in Vienna and Prague from 1926 to 1935. After arriving in the United States in 1936, he taught for many years at the University of Chicago, and from 1954 until his death in 1970 he was associated with the University of California at Los Angeles. "The only proper task of Philosophy," Carnap wrote in his *Philosophy and Logical Syntax*, "is Logical Analysis."

The function of logical analysis, Carnap said, is to analyze all knowledge, all assertions of science and of everyday life, in order to make clear the sense of each such assertion. The purpose of logical analysis is to discover how we can become certain of the truth or falsehood of any proposition. One of the principal tasks of the logical analysis of a given proposition is, therefore, to discover the method of verification of that proposition.

For Carnap, the method of verification of a proposition is either direct or indirect. These two forms of verification are central to scientific method, for in the field of science every proposition, says Carnap, either asserts something about present perceptions or about future perceptions. In both cases, verification is either through direct perception (direct verification) or by the logical connection of already verified propositions (indirect verification). Thus if a scientist were to make an assertion from which no proposition verified by perception could be deduced, it would be no assertion at all. To say, for example, that there is not only a gravitational field but also a *levitational field* cannot be verified. While propositions concerning gravity can be verified by observable effects on bodies, there are no observable effects or laws describing levitation. Assertions about levitation are, says Carnap, no assertions at all because they do not speak about anything. They are nothing but a series of empty words—expressions with no sense.

When logical analysis is applied to metaphysics, Carnap concludes that metaphysical propositions are not verifiable. In Chapter I of his *Philosophy and Logical Syntax*, he says,

> Metaphysical propositions are neither true nor false, because they assert nothing, they contain neither knowledge nor error, they lie completely outside the field of knowledge, of theory, outside the discussion of truth or falsehood. But they are, like laughing, lyrics, and music, expressive. They express not so much temporary feelings as permanent emotional or volitional dispositions. . . . The danger lies in the *deceptive* character of metaphysics; it gives the illusion of knowledge without actually giving any knowledge. This is the reason why we reject it.

Normative ethics and value judgments in general belong, according to Carnap, to the realm of metaphysics. When he applies his method of logical analysis to the propositions of normative ethics, these propositions predictably turn out to be meaningless for him. There can of course be a science of ethics in the form of psychological or sociological or other empirical investigations about the actions of human beings and their effects on other people. But the philosophy of moral values or moral norms does not rest on any facts, since its purpose is to state norms for human action or for making judgments about moral values. The value statement "Killing is evil" has the grammatical form of an assertive proposition. But, says Carnap, "a value statement is nothing else than a command in a misleading grammatical form. It may have effects upon the actions of men, and these effects may be in accordance with our wishes or not; but it is neither true nor false. It does not assert anything and can neither be proved nor disproved."

Carnap was convinced that the propositions of psychology belong to the region of empirical science in just the same way as do the propositions of biology and chemistry. He was aware that many would consider it an offensive presumption to place psychology, "hitherto robed in majesty as the theory of spiritual events," into the domain of the physical sciences. Yet that is what he proceeded to do, saying in his essay on "Psychology and Physical Language" that *"every sentence of psychology may be formulated in physical language."* What he meant by this was that "all sentences of psychology describe physical occurrences, namely, the physical behavior of humans and other animals." This is an extension of the general thesis of physicalism, which Carnap described as holding that "physical language is a universal language, that is, a language into which every sentence may be translated." In effect, Carnap would make psychology an aspect of physics, since all science would become physics and the various domains of science would become parts of unified science. In this manner, propositions in psychology were to be tested by the criterion of verifiability by translating them into physical language. Thus the statement "John is in pain" is translated into a statement describing the observable state S of John's body. This process of translation requires only that there be a scientific law stating that someone is in pain if and only if his bodily condition is in a particular state S. It is then meaningful to say that "John is in pain" and "John's body is in state S" since, while not equivalent, these are interchangeable translations. Only those statements which could be verified or translated into verifiable statements were thought to have meaning. Neither metaphysics, some aspects of psychology, theories of "reality," nor the philosophy of normative values could satisfy the criterion of verifiability and were therefore rejected as meaningless.

THE PRINCIPLE OF VERIFICATION

If the charge against metaphysics was that its language, its propositions or sentences, was *meaningless* or, as Wittgenstein said in the *Tractatus, senseless,* such a charge required the use of some criterion by which to test which sentences did and which did not express a genuine proposition about a matter of fact. Accordingly, the logical positivists formulated the verification principle as the basic criterion for the meaningfulness or the literal significance of a proposition. If a proposition fulfilled the requirements of this criterion, it was considered meaningful, and if a proposition failed to do so, it was considered meaningless.

The *verification principle* consisted of the notion that *the meaning of a statement is the method of its verification.* The assumption behind this principle was that verification must always rest on empirical observation, that is, in sense experience. Any proposition, therefore, that could not be verified by the method of observation would be said to have no meaning. The case of mathematical propositions was treated in a special way, but it was clear that with such a rigorous criterion, metaphysical language could not pass the test of meaningfulness.

The positivists, following the tradition of Hume and Kant, distinguished two types of statements, namely, *analytic* and *synthetic.* Each of these types has a different ground for its meaningfulness. Analytic statements derive their meaningfulness from the definitions of their words or symbols. To say that "all men are mortals" has literal significance because the word "men" is defined in such a way as to include the idea "mortals." In general, in analytic statements the subject already contains or implies the predicate. For the most part, analytic statements do not increase our knowledge, and for this reason they are *tautologies.* Moreover, their meaning does not depend on experience, only on the consistent use of their clearly defined terms. If words with clearly defined terms are used inconsistently, the result is a *contradiction.* A statement, then, that is necessarily true, true because of the meanings of its terms, is a tautology, whereas a statement that is necessarily false is a contradiction. An analytic proposition that is also a tautology is always and in every case necessarily true, because its only test is the meanings of the terms. Thus the truth or falsity of an analytic proposition turns on the logical analysis of meanings. However, *synthetic* propositions are either true or false in each case, and their truth or falsity can be discovered only by reference to some nonlogical or nonlinguistic datum, a fact. Unlike analytic statements, which are *necessarily* either tautologies or contradictions, synthetic statements may be either true or false. Synthetic statements require some sense experience of the object that such a statement refers to in order to advance from its possible to its actual truth.

From this distinction between analytic and synthetic propositions, the positivists formulated their conception of *cognitive meaning* or *literal significance.* Analytic propositions, they said, have a *formal* meaning, since their meaning derives not from facts but from the logical implications of words and ideas, as in mathematics, logic, and the formal sciences. However, synthetic propositions have a factual meaning, because their meaning is based on the empirical observation of the objects referred to in these statements. Synthetic statements are the language of the factual sciences, physics, biology, psychology, and so on. It was at this point that the principle of verification had its decisive application. For now the positivists concluded that there could be only two kinds of statements that could have any meaning at all, namely, *analytic* statements, which are universally and necessarily true because the consistent use of words would never allow them to be anything else, and *synthetic* statements, which are judged as true or false by using the verification principle. Statements that are neither analytic nor synthetic have no cognitive meaning or literal significance; they are simply *emotive.* It takes only brief reflection to realize that into this category of emotive or *noncognitive* language would fall not only metaphysics but also ethics, aesthetics, and religion.

But the verification principle encountered some difficulties. Among these difficulties was, first of all, the serious question of what constituted verification. To answer "sense experience" raised the further question "Whose experience?" The assumption behind the verification principle was that whatever could be said meaningfully would be stated in atomic or elementary statements. Scientific language would be reducible ultimately to *observational state-*

ments. But what is the "fact" that an observation statement reports? Is it a subjective experience about a physical object, or is it a pure picture of that object? The technical problem was whether it is ever possible to translate a person's internal experience into a statement about a physical object, or vice versa. This is the problem of solipsism, the view that the self is the only object of real knowledge and that therefore the experiences of one person cannot be the same as those of another. Each person's experience is different, and all of their experiences are different from the objectively real world. If this is the case, what does the verification principle amount to in the end? Verification statements would mean one thing to one person and something else to others.

In the second place, it was in the very area where this principle was presumed to have its greatest relevance, in the sciences, that its greatest difficulty arose. Scientific knowledge is frequently expressed in the form of universal laws. These "laws" are the basis for scientific *prediction.* But the problem the positivists faced was whether to consider scientific statements meaningful. How can a statement that makes a prediction be verified? Can my present experience, or experiment, tell me anything about the future? Obviously, literal significance or meaning is one thing when we verify the statement "There is a black cow in Smith's barn" and quite another thing when we say, as the scientist does, for example, that when a moving body is not acted on by external forces, its direction will remain constant. The first case is specific and verifiable. The second involves an indefinite number of cases, and any single case in the future can falsify that statement. Since there is no single fact that can verify *now* the future truth of a general scientific statement, such a statement, by a rigorous application of the verification principle, would be meaningless. Moritz Schlick (1882–1936), who became famous as the founder and leader of the Vienna Circle, had said of certain utterances, "If not conclusively verifiable in principle, then not propositions." This would have to apply to scientific as well as other forms of language. For this reason, a compromise in the rigorous application of the principle was proposed, thus giving rise to the distinction between the *strong* and *weak* forms of the verification principle. The weak form said simply that a statement must be at least "verifiable in principle" or *capable* of verification, that is, confirmed in some degree by the observation of something physical.

In the third place, it turned out that the verification principle was not itself verifiable. Critics asked why it should be that the criterion of meaning should be sense experience. The Vienna Circle did not answer this question in any formal way. It may be that for them the verification principle was clearly suggested by the difference between scientific procedures on the one hand and metaphysical speculation on the other. Being oriented chiefly to science, the positivists assumed that only language that referred to physical objects and their interrelationships could have cognitive meaning. Moreover, the techniques of logic as they understood them implied the correspondence between words and facts and between the logical structure of language and the logical relation of facts. The positivists assumed, furthermore, that through *physicalism*, their doctrine that called for the coupling of all statements to physical facts, they could achieve the *unity of science*, and that such a unified knowledge would give sciences a common language and tell us all there is to say.

There was, however, this internal defect in the verification principle, namely, the impossibility of verifying general scientific statements. Gradually, this led not only to a weak form of verification but also to the recognition that statements reflect many forms of experience. For this reason, the initial intensity of positivism was toned down. The blanket rejection of metaphysics and morals was reversed. Instead, analysts began to ask what kind of problem the metaphysicians and moralists were driving at. Ayer described this new temper by saying that "the metaphysician is treated no longer as a criminal but as a patient: there may be good reasons why he says the strange things he does." Ethics, in this view, is no longer nonsense but a discipline whose language is analyzed both for its relation to fact and for its value in pointing to a problem. As it turns out, ethical language is, as R. M. Hare has argued, not *descriptive* but rather *imperative*. C. L. Stevenson has also elaborated the emotive theory of ethics, showing that ethical statements express approval and disapproval and are used particularly for purposes of persuasion. What positivism came ultimately to say about ethics was that it is not possible to derive normative statements, what *ought* to be done, from a description of facts, from what *is*. But even though the analyst still holds that it is not his function as a philosopher to *prescribe* or *exhort* any particular form of behavior, he does accept the task of creatively analyzing moral language for the purpose of clarifying it. That he reserves the right to make value judgements as a *person* underscores the growing recognition that there are modes of human experience besides simply the observation of physical objects and their interrelationships that have meaning and literal significance. Although logical positivism in its classical form dissolved from the weight of its inner difficulties, its impact continues in the analytic movement, which is still concerned overwhelmingly with the usages and analysis of language.

The "New" Wittgenstein

Ludwig Wittgenstein was born in Vienna in 1889. His wealthy family provided a highly creative environment during Ludwig's early years. His father was a successful engineer, and his mother had many artistic interests. Young Wittgenstein studied engineering in Berlin and also became an accomplished musician. He went to England and became acquainted with Bertrand Russell's *Principles of Mathematics* and ultimately became Russell's student at Cambridge University, both as an undergraduate and as an "advanced student." After military service in the First World War, he returned to Vienna, where he completed his first book, *Tractatus Logico-Philosophicus*, which made a strong impression on the Vienna Circle. Earlier, when his father died in 1912, Ludwig inherited a great fortune. When he returned from the war, he took immediate steps to give away all his money. From that time he lived with exceptional frugality. His interest in philosophy was unique, having no precise forerunners. His book, the *Tractatus*, influenced the spread of logical positivism. He eventually rejected and surpassed, as "grave errors," some of the basic ideas of the *Tractatus*, especially the picture-theory of language. His *Philosophical Investigations* became even more influential through its creative impact on the analytic or linguistic movement. In 1937 he succeeded G. E. Moore to the chair of philosophy at Cambridge, where his lectures were "highly unacademic." It is said that he *thought* before his class! One of his colleagues, G. H. von Wright has written "On 29 April 1951 there died at Cambridge, England, one of the most famous and influential philosophers of our time, Ludwig Wittgenstein."

With the appearance of Ludwig Wittgenstein's *Philosophical Investigations* (1953), analytic philosophy adjusted itself to a new

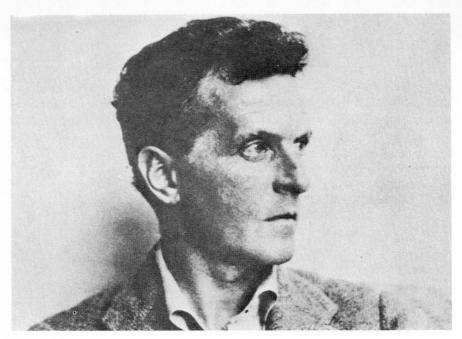

Wittgenstein

point of view. It was still concerned with language, as were logical
atomism and logical positivism. But now the analyst would see the
nature of language in a different light. Wittgenstein, who had provided the most impressive systematic statement of logical atomism
in his *Tractatus Logico-Philosophicus* (1919), had shortly thereafter
repudiated a considerable portion of that book on the grounds that
his theory of language on which it was based was now seen as inadequate. It was inadequate because it assumed that language has
really only one function, namely, to state facts. It was further
assumed that sentences for the most part derive their meanings
from stating facts. More seriously, Wittgenstein had assumed, as did
also Carnap, that the skeleton of all language is a logical one. What
struck him now was the somewhat obvious point that language has
many functions besides simply "picturing" objects. Language
always functions in a *context* and therefore has as many purposes as
there are contexts.

Words, said Wittgenstein, are like "tools in a tool-box; there is
a hammer, pliers, a saw, a screwdriver, a rule, a glue-pot, glue, nails
and screws.—The function of words is as diverse as the functions
of these objects." What made him think earlier that language had
only one function? He had been "held captive" by a "picture" of

language as being the giving of names, as if by Adam, to all things. We are all the victims, he said, of "the bewitchment of our intelligence by means of language." Our incorrect picture of language is "produced by grammatical illusions." To analyze grammar might lead one to discover some logical structure in language. But would that justify the conclusion that all language has essentially the same rules, functions, and meanings? It occurred to Wittgenstein that the assumption that all language states facts and contains a logical skeleton was derived not by observation but by "thought." It was simply assumed that all language, despite certain superficial differences, is alike, the way all games are alike.

Wittgenstein uncovered the flaw in this analogy by taking the case of games and asking "What is common to them all?—Don't say: There *must* be something common, or they would not be called 'games'—but *look and see* whether there is anything common at all.—For if you look at them you will not see something that is common to *all*, but similarities, relationships, and a whole series of them at that. To repeat: don't think, but look." He was apparently saying that logical atomism was the product of thought, of theory, and not of careful observation of the way in fact language operates and is used. Wittgenstein therefore shifted the program of analysis from a preoccupation with logic and the construction of a "perfect" language to a study of the ordinary usages of language. He moved away from what Russell and Carnap were doing and turned now in the direction of G. E. Moore's earlier emphasis on the analysis of ordinary language, testing it by the criterion of "common sense." Wittgenstein was now of the opinion that language does not contain one single pattern alone, that it is as variable as life itself. Indeed, he said that "to imagine a language means to imagine a form of life." For this reason, analysis should consist not of the *definition* of language or its meanings but rather of a careful *description* of its uses: "We must do away with all explanation, and *description alone* must take its place." We must, said Wittgenstein, "stick to the subjects of everyday thinking, and not go astray and imagine that we have to describe extreme subtleties." Confusions arise not when our language is "doing work," but only when it is "like an engine idling."

By recognizing the diversity of the functions of language, Wittgenstein inevitably altered the task of philosophy. For one thing, unlike the positivists, he would not reject the statements of metaphysics outright. Since the new mood was to consider the metaphy-

sician a patient instead of a criminal, the function of philosophy
could now be considered as "therapeutic." Metaphysical language
can indeed create confusion, and the central concern of philosophy
is to deal with problems that baffle and confuse us because of the
lack of clarity. Philosophy is a "battle against the bewitchment of
our intelligence by means of language." Bewitchment causes confusion, and so "a philosophical problem has the form: 'I don't know
my way about.'" Philosophy helps one to find his way, to survey
the scene. "What we do," said Wittgenstein, "is to bring words
back from their metaphysical to their everyday usage." His aim in
philosophy, he said, was "to show the fly the way out of the fly-
bottle." When the fly is out of the bottle, and when words are
brought back from metaphysics to their everyday usage, and when
the person who didn't know his way about now does know the way,
what has happened? Wittgenstein says that philosophy "leaves
everything as it is."

Philosophy does not provide men with new or more information, but adds clarity by a careful description of language. It is as
though one could see all the parts of a jigsaw puzzle but was baffled
by how to put it together; he is actually looking at everything he
needs to solve the problem. Philosophical puzzlement is similar and
can be removed by a careful description of language as we ordinarily use it. What makes us feel trapped as a fly in a bottle is the use
of language in ways other than their ordinary use. Hence "the
results of philosophy are the uncovering of one or another piece of
plain nonsense." By "nonsense" Wittgenstein did not necessarily
mean the language of metaphysics, for, again, he had a basic sympathy for what some metaphysicians were trying to do. If metaphysics displayed resistance or a prejudice that obscures the ordinary usage of words, he agreed that this is "not a *stupid* prejudice."
He saw in the confusions of metaphysics a deep human condition,
saying that "the problems arising through a misinterpretation of
our forms of language have the character of *depth.* They are deep
disquietudes; their roots are as deep in us as the forms of our language and their significance is as great as the importance of our
language."

How, more specifically, does one who doesn't know his way
about find it, or how does the fly escape from the fly-bottle? One
must not expect from Wittgenstein any single systematic answer to
this question. He is too sensitive to the suppleness and variability

of life and language to force on them the straitjacket of a single method. "There is not *a* philosophical method," he says, "though there are indeed methods, like different therapies." Because philosophical problems grow out of language, it is necessary to acquire a basic familiarity with the usages of the language out of which each problem arises. Since there are many kinds of games, there are many sets of rules of the games. Similarly, since there are many languages (that is, the many forms of ordinary language of work, play, worship, science, and so forth), there are many *usages.* Under these circumstances, "the work of the philosopher consists in *assembling reminders* for a particular purpose." In his *Philosophical Investigations,* Wittgenstein "does philosophy" by taking many problems and assembling many reminders of the way language is used as a means of clarifying these problems. But the philosopher, in addition to assembling these uses of language, selects and arranges them in order to get a picture of the landscape. In other words, philosophy does not consist in giving crisp abstract answers to questions. A person who has lost his way wants, rather, a map of the terrain, and this is supplied by the selection and arrangement of concrete examples of the actual use of language in ordinary experience.

But it is not enough to just look at these examples of usage, any more than it is sufficient simply to look at the pieces of the jigsaw puzzle. There must be selection and rearrangement. Then everything is before one that one needs for solving the problem. Still, says Wittgenstein, we frequently "fail to be struck by what, once seen, is *most* striking and most powerful." The most important things are hidden "because of their simplicity and familiarity." But what does it mean to "fail to be struck"? There is no sure method according to Wittgenstein to guarantee that one will "be struck" and thereby find one's way. Apparently the fly can frequently pass the opening of the jar without escaping. In any case, what Wittgenstein sought to do was to shift philosophy's concern from meanings, from the assumption that words carried in them as so much freight "pictures" of objects in the world. Instead, he directed attention, through the assembling, selecting, and arranging of relevant examples, to the actual usages of words. Because most *philosophical* problems were assumed to arise from puzzlements about words, the scrupulous description of their ordinary uses would, it was assumed, eliminate this puzzlement.

Questions for Discussion:
Knowledge

1. Plato's story of the prisoners chained inside the cave is an allegory. State what each element of the allegory represents. Do this for as many elements of the story as you can.

2. Are you satisfied with Descartes's reasons for accepting the truth of the proposition "I think, therefore I am"? Why does Descartes concern himself with this proposition rather than one like "I drink milk shakes, therefore I am"?

3. Do you find it strange that Hume is willing in his philosophical writings to endorse skepticism but is not willing to live the life of a skeptic? Do you think that it would be impossible to live such a life or just very strange and unpleasant?

4. Kant says that while all knowledge begins with experience, it does not follow that all knowledge arises *out of* experience. How does this explanation of knowledge differ from Hume's?

5. Explain how William James's conception of truth differs from the traditional conception. Specifically discuss the difference between James's view that "truth happens to an idea" and the view that an idea is true if it "copies" reality. What are the strengths and weaknesses of James's view?

6. Wittgenstein eventually rejected logical positivism, believing that language does not simply state facts but rather functions in many different ways. What other functions of language can you think of?

Suggested Additional
Readings: Knowledge

Chisholm, Roderick: *Theory of Knowledge*, 2d ed., Prentice-Hall, Englewood Cliffs, N.J., 1977. A contemporary, clear, and comprehensive discussion.

Conford, F. M.: *Plato's Theory of Knowledge*, Bobbs-Merrill, Indianapolis, 1957. Includes two of Plato's important dialogues (*Theatetus* and *Sophist*) and Conford's helpful comments.

Flew, Anthony: *Hume's Philosophy of Belief*, Humanities Press, New York, 1966. Exposition and criticism of Hume's views, particularly in the *Enquiry*.

Frankfurt, Harry: *Demons, Dreamers, and Madmen*, Bobbs-Merrill, Indianapolis, 1970. A careful examination of Descartes's theory of knowledge, particularly in the *Meditations*.

James, William: *Pragmatism: A New Name for Some Old Ways of Thinking*, Harvard, Cambridge, Mass., 1976. A good place to start for further reading of James.

Kemp Smith, Norman: *A Commentary to Kant's "Critique of Pure Reason,"* 2d ed., Humanities Press, New York, 1962. Thorough commentary on Kant's first *Critique*. (See also following entry.)

Korner, S.: *Kant*, Penguin, Baltimore, 1955. A useful introduction to Kant's difficult philosophy.

Mehta, Ved Parkash: *Fly and the Fly-Bottle*, Little, Brown, Boston, 1962. A description of encounters with English philosophers including Russell, Wittgenstein, and Austin.

Schmitt, Richard: "Husserl" and "Phenomenology," in *The Encyclopedia of Philosophy*, ed. Paul Edwards, Macmillan, New York, 1967. A clear exposition of Husserl's difficult philosophy. (*The Encyclopedia of Philosophy* is a very helpful resource on most topics in philosophy.)

Taylor, A. E.: *Plato, The Man and His Work*, Dial, New York, 1936. A standard introduction to Plato.

METAPHYSICS

WHAT IS THERE?

There is an infinite number of atoms and they are invisible on account of their size. The material of the atoms is packed entirely close and can be called what is. . . .

Leucippus (Fifth century B.C.)
from Simplicius, *Commentary on Aristotle*

It seems probable to me that God in the beginning formed matter in solid, massy, hard, impenetrable, moveable particles [atoms] so very hard, as never to wear or break in pieces; no ordinary power being able to divide what God Himself made one. . . .

Sir Isaac Newton
Mathematical Principles (1686)

Modern experimental physics has developed methods of breaking up the nucleus of the atom. . . .

Albert Einstein
Evolution of Physics (1938)

Elementary particles (*Argonne National Laboratory*)

INTRODUCTION

The term "metaphysics" is the title which an ancient editor gave to a collection of Aristotle's essays. Because this book of essays, which Aristotle had called *First Philosophy*, came after his other books covering the biological and physical sciences, the editor labeled it *meta* (the Greek word meaning "after") physics. But *meta* also means "beyond," and so the term "metaphysics" came to refer to the subject matter or reality beyond physical nature or beyond the things we see. Actually, the distinction between science and metaphysics is not always a sharp one. Both science and metaphysics seek knowledge. But metaphysics pursues a kind of knowledge that is not limited to any one particular science. Instead, the metaphysician turns his attention to broad questions which are raised in his mind by our daily experiences. What every metaphysician tries to do is to form a comprehensive view of the whole world and then organize this view into a system of ideas or concepts. Just why anyone would want to engage in constructing such vast systems of thought will become clearer as we consider the major elements of metaphysics.

The Elements of Metaphysics

KNOWLEDGE FOR ITS OWN SAKE

Most of our knowledge has some practical application. The study of ethics helps us lead a good life, religion attempts to provide our lives with meaning, politics enables our communities to flourish, and the sciences help us to control nature and produce things for our health, safety, and survival. But what about metaphysics? There is a deep human urge to understand how we fit into the universe. Indeed, in the first sentence of his *Metaphysics* Aristotle says that "all men by nature desire to know." And we want to know things which do not have immediate practical use, "for even apart from their usefulness, they are loved for themselves."

We enjoy the things we see. The variety of things in nature is a matter of fascination to us. Animals see things too, but their reaction to these things is different from ours. We want not only to sense things, but also to understand everything about them. That is why we pursue a special kind of knowledge, because, as Aristotle says, "we do not regard any of the senses as Wisdom; yet surely these [senses] give the most authoritative knowledge of particulars. But they do not tell us the 'why' of anything—e.g., why fire is hot; they only say *that* it is hot." It could be argued that to discover why something happens and not only that it happens can have practical applications; for example, the discovery of why atoms behave the way they do can lead to harnessing atomic energy. But the motivation to pursue metaphysical knowledge is simply a quest for knowledge for its own sake. This pursuit satisfies man's wonder "in order to know, and not for any utilitarian end," for this knowledge, says Aristotle, "alone exists for its own sake."

WHAT IS THERE?

From the earliest times, philosophers reflected on the question "What is there?" Sometimes they rephrased the question to ask "What is real?" or "What really is?" Their concern was not simply to make a list, an inventory, of all the things in nature. They were puzzled by the fact that things come and go, that they come into being, exist, and then cease to be. But even before asking where things come from and where they go, the question of what anything really is had to be faced. For example, Lucretius describes in his poem *On the Nature of Things* how our senses deceive us when we look on a solid white mass on a distant hill: "Often the fleecy flocks cropping the glad pasture on a hill creep on whither each is called and tempted by the grass bejewelled with fresh dew, and the lambs fed full gambol and butt playfully; yet all this seems blurred to us from afar, and to lie like a white mass on a green hill." What appears to be a white mass from a distance turns out to be a flock of sheep.

Could this also be the case with everything which to our senses appears to be solid? What is a lump of sugar? It can be described as white, hard, and sweet. It may be said that the lump of sugar *is* all these adjectives. But would you have sugar if you put together white, hard, and sweet? These adjectives do not exist as such by themselves. They are adjectives requiring a subject, or, as metaphysicians say, they are secondary qualities requiring a primary quality. *Something* must be white, hard, and sweet. This would mean that secondary qualities do not exist in the same way as primary qualities do. If the sheep were scattered, let's say by a wolf, the solid white mass on the hill would disappear. If the sugar lump were melted, its color and hardness would disappear. In these cases, would the sheep and the sugar disappear or only some of the qualities and adjectives? If, now, we ask "What is there?" or "What really is?" the answer is not all that obvious. Metaphysics focuses finally on the question "What does it mean for something to be?" What, in short, is being? Metaphysics is the study of being and its principles or causes.

ONE AND THE MANY

Another way to address the question "What is there?" is to consider the relationship between the one and the many. We see many human beings, but they all share one thing in common, namely, their *humanness*. There are many trees, but they all share in what we know as *tree*. We have seen in an earlier chapter that Plato thought he solved this problem of the one and the many by saying that the many are temporary and pale copies of the One, which he called "Idea" or "Form." Only the Forms have real being, while the many have a temporary existence. According to this view, there are two worlds, the world of the many, which is the world we move around in, and the world of Ideas and Forms.

Earlier philosophers, in the fifth century B.C., such as Leucippus and Democritus, took quite a different view. They said that the many, by which they meant every conceivable thing in nature, were made of one thing, namely, matter, which they described as small irreducible particles that they called "atoms." In this view, the many are simply a wide variety of combinations or arrangements of the one. Everything in nature is reducible to these constituent particles. So, although there are many things in the world, they are all reducible to one kind of thing, namely, atoms, or matter. This seemed to be too simple an explanation for some, who thought, as Descartes did, that there are at least two basic substances at the heart of reality. Descartes called these two substances "thought" and "extension," or mind and body. His view further complicated matters, for the problem now was how to explain the relationship between mind and body or between soul and body.

Earlier, Aristotle had dealt with this problem in a somewhat different way when he spoke of form and matter. Unlike the first atomists, Aristotle said that we never find matter by itself, nor do we (and here he disagreed with Plato) find form by itself. There can be no form, he said, without matter, nor matter without form. In the Middle Ages, Aquinas took this teaching of Aristotle to mean that when describing man we must account for both body and soul. The soul, said Aquinas, is the form of the body. There cannot be what we call "man" without both body and soul. Body, or matter, is what makes any particular person this specific individual, while the soul is what makes this individual a human being. The one, humanness, is in the many, that is, in each person; in metaphysical terms this means the universal (Man) is in each particular (James and Mary). The conclusion metaphysicians wish to draw from the discussion of the one and the many is that while the many do exist (briefly), only the one (the permanent reality) possesses true being.

CHANGE

One of the earliest concerns of metaphysicians was how to account for change. We experience the fact of change in a wide variety of ways. Things change in quantity, in quality, and in their location. There is also change through generation, that is, being born or coming into being. There is also the change from an acorn to an oak tree, from a child to an adult. These are various forms of change, and each one requires a special explanation. But there was one major form of change that puzzled and still puzzles philosophers, and that is how anything comes to be. One philosopher, Parmenides, held the radical view that there cannot be any change or that what we call change is an illusion. His reasoning was actually very simple. True change, he said, must mean that something that was not at one time later comes into being. But how can something come into being? Only in one of two ways: either from something else or out of nothing. If it comes out of something else, it already existed; if out of nothing, then "nothing" must be treated as though it had some being; otherwise it would be absurd to think that something could come out of nothing, or out of nonbeing. Either way, then, the phrase "comes into being" must mean that what we call change refers to what already exists, in which case there is no real change. While this may be logically clear, it defies common sense.

There is, however, according to Aristotle, a way to account for change. The process of change, he said, expresses the movement from *potentiality* to *actuality*. We say, for example, that a great change takes place when a child grows up and is able to speak and play the piano. At one time the child could not do these things. Aristotle explains this mode of change by saying that the capacity to do these things was in the child as potentiality, just as the capacity to be a parent is potentially in the child. The child comes into being from other beings, from parents. He possesses potentially all the abilities he will eventually fulfill or bring into actuality. Change, for Aristotle, does not mean that something comes into being out of nothing; it simply means that in some way something can at one time be absent (Aristotle calls this "privation") but later come into full being, like the acorn "changing" into an oak. But this movement, or change, from potentiality to actuality requires further explanation. How is this change achieved? How can something which is only potential become actual? This leads us to consider further the causes of being.

THE CAUSES OF BEING

One answer to the question of how things become what they are is to say that they are the product of *chance*. Or one can say, as Sir Isaac Newton did, that God created all the atoms in such a way as to make them function in an orderly manner. Or in a more philosophical vein one can say with Aristotle that the simple example of the creation of a statue can best explain how things come to be. He spoke of four "causes" which we will discuss more fully later. For the present, we will simply list them. First, there has to be the *idea* of something that you want to make; this is the pattern or form of the statue. Second, there must be some *material* out of which to make the statue. Third, there is the *activity* by which the sculptor actually carves out the pattern or form. Fourth, there is the *purpose* or end for which the statue is made. By itself, the marble would never become a statue; without the carving by the sculptor the marble would remain only potentially a statue. Some act is necessary to bring what is potential in the marble into actuality. Whether nature has "purposes" in the broad sense is debated by metaphysicians and scientists. But that some active power or cause is needed to explain motion or change in general seemed obvious to Aristotle, and this led him to his celebrated theory of the Unmoved Mover.

Summary

We have seen that metaphysicians ask some very broad questions about the nature of the world. They do this because the pursuit of this kind of knowledge is desirable for its own sake. Being intelligent beings, they want to know *why* as well as *that* something is. But because appearances received by our senses are at times deceptive, it is not obvious what really exists or what has permanent existence. Is it matter, or mind, or a combination of these? The attempts by Democritus, Plato, and Aristotle to explain the relation between the one and the many provided three different answers to the question "What is there?" namely, matter, Ideas, and some combination of these. What is so obvious to common sense, namely, that things constantly change, is for the metaphysician not so obvious nor all that easy to explain, although the cause of things can be explained either by saying that everything is the product of chance, or that God created and controls all things, or that there are certain basic structures, purposes, and powers in the nature of things. We will now consider some of these elements of metaphysics more fully in the writings of some philosophers.

APPROACHES TO METAPHYSICS

Several approaches to metaphysics represent an interesting sequence of ideas. The philosophers who developed them might even be considered participants in a dialogue. By considering their arguments, we will deal with many of the main themes of metaphysics.

(1) *Lucretius* took the ideas of *Democritus* and Epicurus and composed an impressive poem, *On the Nature of Things,* in which he tries to show in considerable detail that everything consists of matter, of atoms, including mind as well as body.

(2) *Aristotle* takes issue with much of what Democritus had to say; he especially denies the view of Democritus that everything consists of matter and that there is no purpose in the universe.

(3) *Berkeley* developed the bold theory that consciousness and not matter is the basic reality. For something to be, he said, it is necessary for it to be perceived by some conscious being. But what if you are at some time not perceiving the books in your study—do they still exist? Yes, says Berkeley, because God perceives them.

(4) *Spinoza* and *Leibniz* raised the important question whether human beings, as part of nature, possess the freedom to behave the way they wish or whether the mechanical universe determines each person's actions.

(5) *Dialectical materialism* is an interesting approach because it represents a major political philosophy influenced by the writing of Karl Marx. Marx rejected the metaphysical concept of idealism in favor of materialism.

(6) *Bergson* took a fresh look at metaphysics and argued that the wrong answers are given to the question "What is there?" because the wrong method is used to discover what is. The wrong method is the method of *analysis.* What is wrong with the method of analysis is that it distorts the reality being studied, just as analyzing a rose by taking it apart destroys the rose. True reality, he says, is a vibrant, dynamic, continuous *duration* which is grasped not by analysis but by *intuition.*

(7) For *Russell,* the most reliable way to understand what our world is truly like is to consider the evidence science gives us. What is unique about this theory, as the selection from his writings indicates, is his special explanation of just what it is that science, especially physics, tells us about our world and the cosmos.

(8) *Whitehead* asks whether it might not be the case that there is more to nature than what the scientists say about it, that a unique perspective of deep significance might be provided by the poet.

CHAPTER 26

ATOMS AND SPACE

Democritus

Leucippus and Democritus are renowned for their theory that all nature consists of *atoms* and the *void* (space). Although it is difficult to disentangle their individual contributions, it is agreed that Leucippus was the founder of the atomist theory and that Democritus supplied much of the elaboration of it. These two Greek philosophers lived in the fifth century B.C.; the life of Democritus spanned one hundred years (460–360 B.C.). In time, Democritus, because of his great learning, overshadowed Leucippus, to whom, nevertheless, goes the credit for the insight that everything is made of atoms moving in space. But since only some fragments of their writings are available, our selected reading will be taken from a poem written by the Roman philosopher Lucretius (98–55 B.C.) based on the atomic theory of Democritus and his successor Epicurus.

Atoms and the Void

The philosophy of atomism originated, according to Aristotle, as an attempt to overcome the logical consequences of the denial of space by earlier philosophers. Parmenides denied that there could be separate and discrete things because everywhere there was *being*, in which case the total reality would be One. Specifically, he denied the existence of nonbeing or the void, because to say that there *is* the void is to say that there *is something*. It is impossible, he thought, to say that there *is* nothing. Yet, in order to prove that there is motion and change, it is necessary to assume that there is empty space in which things can move. But empty space is nothing; yet to say that it *is* meant for Parmenides that space is part of the total *Is*. By arguing that there is only the One, since there could be no areas of nonbeing between things to give things separate spheres of existing, Parmenides thought he had proved that there could be no motion or change. It was precisely to reject this treatment of space or the void that Leucippus formulated his new theory.

Leucippus affirmed the reality of space and thereby prepared the way for a coherent theory of motion and change. What had complicated Parmenides's concept of space was his thought that whatever exists must be *material*, wherefore space, if it existed, must also be material. Leucippus, however, thought it possible to affirm that space exists without having to say at the same time that it is material. Thus he described space as something like a receptacle that could be empty in some places and full in others. As a receptacle, space, or the void, could be the place where objects move, and Leucippus apparently saw no reason for denying this characteristic of space. Without this concept of space, it would have been impossible for Leucippus and Democritus to develop that part of their philosophy for which they are best known, namely, that all things consist of atoms.

According to Leucippus and Democritus, things consist of an infinite number of particles or units called "atoms." To these atoms both Leucippus and Democritus ascribed the characteristics that Parmenides had ascribed to the One, namely, indestructibility and, therefore, eternity. Whereas Parmenides had said reality consists of a single One, the atomists now said that there are an infinite number of atoms, each one being completely full, containing no empty spaces, therefore being completely hard and indivisible. These atoms exist in space and differ from one another in shape and size, and because of their small size, they are invisible. Since these atoms are eternal, they did not have to be created. Nature consists, therefore, of two things only: namely, *space*, which is a vacuum, and *atoms*. The atoms move about in space, and their motion leads them to form the objects we experience.

Democritus (*New York Public Library Picture Collection*)

The atomists did not think it was necessary to account for the origin of this motion of the atoms in space. The original motion of these atoms, they thought, was similar to the motion of dust particles as they dart off in all directions in a sunbeam even when there is no wind to impel them. Democritus said that there is no absolute "up" or "down," and since he did not ascribe *weight* to atoms, he thought atoms could move in any and all directions. Things as we know them have their origin in the motion of the atoms. Moving in space, the atoms originally were single, individual units, but inevitably they began to collide with each other, and in cases where their shapes were such as to permit them to interlock, they began to form clusters, or what Anaxagoras (500–428 B.C.) called "vortices." In this the atomists resembled the Pythagoreans (ca. 525–500 B.C.), who had said that all things are numbers. Things, like numbers, are made up of combinable units, and things, for the atomists, were simply combinations of various kinds of atoms. Mathematical figures and physical figures were, therefore, thought to be similar.

In the beginning, then, there were atoms in space. Each atom is like the Parmenidean One, but although they are indestructible, they are in constant motion. The stuff about which some earlier philosophers (Thales, Anaximenes, Heraclitus, and Empedocles) spoke—namely, water, air, fire, and earth—the atomists described as different clusters of changeless atoms, the product of the movement of originally single atoms. The four elements were not the primeval "roots" of all other things but were themselves the product of the absolutely original stuff, the atoms.

The atomists produced a mechanical conception of the nature of things. For them, everything was the product of the collision of atoms moving in space. Their theory had no place in it for the element of *purpose* or *design*, and their materialistic reduction of all reality to atoms left no place, and in their minds no need, for a creator or designer. They saw no need to account either for the origin of the atoms or for the original motion impelling the atoms, since the question of origins could always be asked, even about God. For them, to ascribe eternal existence to the material atoms seemed as satisfactory as any other solution.

So formidable was this atomistic theory that although it went into a decline after Aristotle and during the Middle Ages, it was revived and provided science with its working model for centuries to come. Sir Isaac Newton (1642–1727) still thought in atomistic terms when he wrote his famous *Principia*, in which, having deduced the motion of the planets, the comets, the moon, and the sea, he wrote in 1686:

> I wish we could devise the rest of the phenomena of Nature by the same kind of reasoning from mechanical principles, for I am induced by many reasons to suspect that they may all depend upon certain forces by which the particles of bodies, by some causes hitherto unknown, are either mutually impelled towards one another and cohere in regular figures, or are repelled and recede from one another.

This theory of bodies in motion as the explanation of nature held sway until the quantum theory and Einstein gave the twentieth century a new conception of matter, denying the attribute of indestructibility to the atoms.

Democritus was concerned with two other philosophical problems besides describing the structure of nature: namely, the problem of knowledge and the problem of human conduct. Being a thorough materialist, Democritus held that *thought* can be explained in the same way that any other phenomenon can, namely, as the movement of atoms. He distinguished between two different kinds of perception, one of the senses and one of the understanding, both of these being physical processes. When the eye sees something, this something is an "effluence" or the shedding of atoms by the object, forming an "image." These atomic images of things enter the eyes (and other organs of sense) and make an impact on the soul, which is itself made up of atoms. Whereas Protagoras said that our senses are all equally reliable, that everything we sense really is what we sense it to be, Democritus disagreed, saying that "there are two forms of knowledge, the trueborn and the bastard. To the bastard belong all these: sight, hearing, smell, taste, touch. The trueborn is quite apart from these."

What distinguishes these two modes of thought is that whereas "trueborn" knowledge depends only on the object, "bastard" knowledge is affected by the particular conditions of the body of the person involved. This is why two persons can agree that what they have tasted is an apple (trueborn) and still disagree about the taste (bastard knowledge), one saying the apple is sweet and the other saying it is bitter, so that, concludes Democritus, "by the senses we know in truth nothing sure, but only something that changes according to the disposition of the body and of the things that enter into it or resist it." Still Democritus had to say that both sensation and thought are the same type of mechanical process.

When Democritus came to the other problem, however, the problem of ethics, he appears to have departed from his mechanical view of things. For one thing, if all reality is mechanically interlocked, there would hardly be any point in giving advice on how to behave, since each person's movements would be determined by the movement of other things, and conduct would not be within a person's control. Despite this technical contradiction in his philosophy, Democritus developed a very lofty set of rules for human behavior, urging moderation in all things along with the cultivation of culture as the surest way of achieving the most desirable goal of life, namely, cheerfulness.

READING

ATOMS MOVING IN SPACE
Lucretius

All nature . . . is built of these two things: for there are bodies and the void. . . .

Since we have found existing a twofold nature of two things far differing, the nature of body and of space, in which all things take place, it must needs be that each exists alone by itself and unmixed. For wherever space lies empty, which we call the void, body is not there; moreover, wherever body has its station, there is by no means empty void. Therefore the first bodies are solid and free from void. Moreover, since there is void in things created, solid matter must needs stand all round, nor can anything by true reasoning be shown to hide void in its body and hold it within, except you grant that what keeps it in is solid. Now it can be nothing but a union of matter, which could keep in the void in things. Matter then, which exists with solid body, can be everlasting, when all else is dissolved. Next, if there were nothing which was empty and void, the whole would be solid; unless on the other hand there were bodies determined, to fill all the places that they held, the whole universe would be but empty void space. Body, then, we may be sure, is marked off from void turn and turn about, since there is neither a world utterly full nor yet quite empty. There are therefore bodies determined, such as can mark off void space from what is full. These cannot be broken up when hit by blows from without, nor again can they be pierced to the heart and undone, nor by any other way can they be assailed and made to totter; all of which I have above shown to you but a little while before. For it is clear that nothing could be crushed in without void, or broken or cleft in twain by cutting, nor admit moisture nor likewise spreading cold or piercing flame, whereby all things are brought to their end. And the more each thing keeps void within it, the more is it assailed within by these things and begins to totter. Therefore, if the first bodies are solid and free from void, as I have shown, they must be everlasting. Moreover, if matter had not been everlasting, ere this all things had wholly passed away to nothing, and all that we see had been born again from nothing. But since I have

From *Lucretius De Rerum Natura*, ed. and trans. Cyril Bailey, Clarendon Press, 1947. By permission of the Oxford University Press.

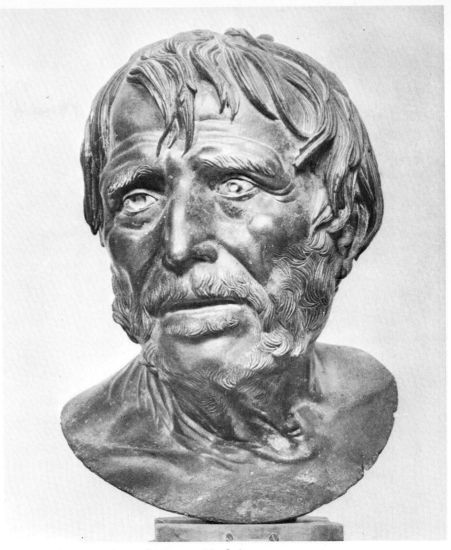

Lucretius (*Roman National Museum, Naples*)

shown above that nothing can be created from nothing, the first-beginnings must needs be of immortal body, into which at their last day all things can be dissolved, that there may be matter enough for renewing things. Therefore the first-beginnings are of solid singleness, nor in any other way can they be preserved so through the ages from infinite time now gone and renew things. . . .

Or, again, things which seem to us hard and compact, these, it must needs be, are made of particles more hooked one to another, and are held together close-fastened at their roots, as it were by branching particles. First

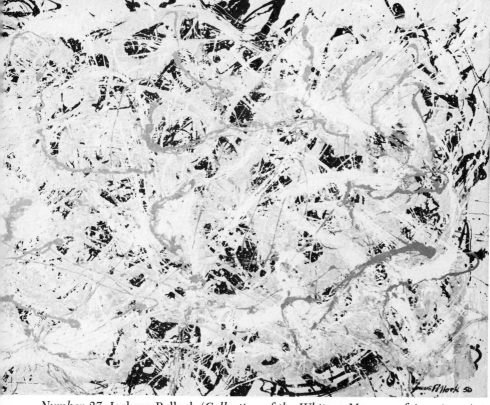

Number 27, Jackson Pollock (*Collection of the Whitney Museum of American Art, New York*)

of all in this class diamond stones stand in the forefront of the fight, well used to despise all blows, and stubborn flints and the strength of hard iron, and brass sockets, which scream loud as they struggle against the bolts. Those things indeed must be made of particles more round and smooth, which are liquid with a fluid body: for indeed a handful of poppy-seed moves easily just as a draught of water; for the several round particles are not checked one by the other, and when struck, it will roll downhill just like water. Lastly, all things which you perceive flying asunder in an instant, like smoke, clouds and flames, it must needs be that even if they are not made entirely of smooth and round particles, yet they are not hampered by particles closely linked, so that they can prick the body, and pass into rocks, and yet not cling one to another: so that you can easily learn that, whatever things we see allayed by the senses, are of elements not closely linked but pointed. But because you see that some things which are fluid, are also bitter, as is the brine of the sea, it should be no wonder. . . . For because it is fluid, it is of smooth and round particles, and many rugged painful bodies are mingled in it; and yet it must needs be that they are not hooked and held together: you must know that they are nevertheless spherical, though rugged, so that they can roll on together and hurt the senses. And that you may the more think that rough are mingled with smooth first-beginnings, from which is made the bitter body of the sea-god, there is a way of sundering them and seeing how, apart from the rest, the fresh water, when it trickles many a time through the earth, flows into a trench and loses its harshness; for it leaves behind up above the first-beginnings of its sickly saltness, since the rough particles can more easily stick in the earth. . . .

Come now, I will unfold by what movement the creative bodies of matter beget diverse things, and break up those that are begotten, by what force they are constrained to do this, and what velocity is appointed them for moving through the mighty void: do you remember to give your mind to my words. For in very truth matter does not cleave close-packed to itself, since we see each thing grow less, and we perceive all things flow away, as it were, in the long lapse of time, as age withdraws them from our sight: and yet the sum of all is seen to remain undiminished, inasmuch as all bodies that depart from anything lessen that from which they pass away, and bless with increase that to which they have come; they constrain the former to grow old and the latter again to flourish, and yet they abide not with it. Thus the sum of things is ever being replenished, and mortals live one and all by give and take. Some races wax and others wane, and in a short space the tribes of living things are changed, and like runners hand on the torch of life.

If you think that the first-beginnings of things can stay still, and by staying still beget new movements in things, you stray very far away from the true reasoning. For since they wander through the void, it must needs be that all the first-beginnings of things move on either by their own weight or sometimes by the blow of another. For when as they move, again and again, they have met and clashed together, it comes to pass that they leap asunder at once this way and that; for indeed it is not strange, since they are most hard with solid heavy bodies, and nothing bars them from behind. And the more you perceive all the bodies of matter tossing about, bring it to mind that there is no lowest point in the whole universe, nor have the first-bodies any place where they may come to rest, since space is without bound or limit, and I have shown in many words, and it has been proved by true reasoning that it spreads out immeasurable towards every quarter everywhere. And since that is certain, no rest, we may be sure, is allowed to the first-bodies moving through the deep void, but rather plied with unceasing, diverse motion, some when they have dashed together leap back at great intervals apart, others too are thrust but a short way from the blow. And all those which are driven together in more close-packed union and leap back but a little space apart, entangled by their own close-locking shapes, these make the strong roots of rock and the brute bulk of iron and all other things of their kind. Of the rest which wander through the great void, a few leap far apart, and recoil afar with great spaces between; these supply for us thin air and the bright light of the sun. Many, moreover, wander on through the great void, which have been cast back from the unions of things, nor have they anywhere else availed to be taken into them and link their movements. And of this truth, as I have said, a likeness and image is ever passing presently before our eyes. For look closely, whenever rays are let in and pour the sun's light through the dark places in houses: for you will see many tiny bodies mingle in many ways all through the empty space in many ways all through the empty space right in the light of the rays, and as though in some everlasting strife wage war and battle, struggling troop against troop, nor ever crying a halt, harried with constant meetings and partings; so that you may guess from this what it means that the first-beginnings of things are for ever tossing in the great void. . . .

. . . Since the first-beginnings are so far beneath the ken of our senses, and so much smaller than the things which our eyes first begin to be unable to descry, yet now that I may assure you of this too, learn in a few words how fine in texture are the beginnings of all things. First of all there are living things sometimes so small that a third part of them could by no means be seen. Of what kind must we think any one of their entrails to be? What of the round ball of their heart or eye? what of their members? what of their limbs? how small are they? still more, what of the several first-beginnings whereof their soul and the nature of their mind must needs be formed? do you not see how fine and how tiny they are? . . .

Now it is left to explain in what manner the other senses perceive each their own object—a path by no means stony to tread.

First of all, every kind of sound and voice is heard, when they have found their way into the ears and struck upon the sense with their body. For that voice too and sound are bodily you must grant, since they can strike on the senses. Moreover, the voice often scrapes the throat and shouting makes the windpipe over-rough as it issues forth; since, indeed, the first-beginnings of voices have risen up in too great a throng through the narrow passage, and begun to pass forth: and then, in truth, the door to the mouth too is scraped when the throat is choked. There is no doubt then that voices and words are composed of bodily elements, so that they can hurt. And likewise it does not escape you how much body is taken away and drawn off from men's very sinews and strength by speech continued without pause from the glimmer of rising dawn to the shades of dark night, above all if it is poured out with loud shouting. And so the voice must needs be corporeal, since one who speaks much loses a part from his body. Now roughness of voice comes from roughness in its first-beginnings, and likewise smoothness is begotten of their smoothness. . . .

Come now, I will tell in what manner the impact of smell touches the nostrils. First there must needs be many things whence the varying stream of scents flows and rolls on, and we must think that it is always streaming off and being cast and scattered everywhere abroad; but one smell is better fitted to some living things, another to others, on account of the unlike shapes of the elements. And so through the breezes bees are drawn on however far by the scent of honey, and vultures by corpses. Then the strength of dogs sent on before leads on the hunters whithersoever the cloven hoof of the wild beasts has turned its steps, and the white goose, saviour of the citadel of Romulus' sons, scents far ahead the smell of man. So diverse scents assigned to diverse creatures lead on each to its own food, and constrain them to recoil from noisome poison, and in that way are preserved the races of wild beasts.

This very smell then, whenever it stirs the nostrils, may in one case be thrown farther than in another. But yet no smell at all is carried as far as sound, as voice, I forbear to say as the bodies which strike the pupil of the eyes and stir the sight. For it strays abroad and comes but slowly, and dies away too soon, its frail nature scattered little by little among the breezes of air. . . .

But by what means that gathering together of matter established earth and sky and the depths of ocean, and the courses of sun and moon, I will set forth in order. For in very truth not by design did the first-beginnings of things place themselves each in order with foreseeing mind, nor indeed did they make a compact what movements each should start; but because many first-beginnings of things in many ways, driven on by blows from time everlasting until now, and moved by their own weight, have been wont to be borne on, and to unite in every way and essay everything that they might create, meeting one with another, therefore it comes to pass that scattered abroad through a great age, as they try meetings and motions of every kind, at last those come together, which, suddenly cast together, become often the beginnings of great things, of earth, sea, and sky, and the race of living things. . . .

CHAPTER 27

CAUSES OF BEING

Aristotle

Aristotle's answer to the question "What is there?" represents an interesting contrast to his predecessors. The earliest philosophers said that what "really is" is matter. While they defined matter in various ways, Democritus offered the most influential version of this theory with his notion of atoms moving in space. Plato, Aristotle's teacher, argued that Ideas, or Forms, are the true reality. In Book I of his *Metaphysics* Aristotle traces the development of the various conceptions of matter and of Plato's Forms and concludes that although these earlier theories had some plausible insights, they were, nevertheless, inadequate. They were inadequate primarily because they did not offer a full enough explanation of the process of *change.* In particular, Aristotle felt that they had overlooked the causes of motion, that is, how things come into being and why they behave the way they do. By "motion" Aristotle meant change, and change, he thought, must be explained in terms of "causes" or "becauses." Aristotle concluded that it is not enough to say that all things consist of matter and possess form; what needs to be added, he said, is how things in nature become what they are and for what purpose they strive.

Knowledge for Its Own Sake

In his work entitled *Metaphysics* (a term that indicates the position of this work among his other writings, namely, *beyond*, or coming after, *Physics*) Aristotle develops what he called the science of "first philosophy." Throughout his *Metaphysics*, he is concerned with a type of knowledge that he thought could be rightly called "wisdom." He begins this work with the statement "All men by nature desire to know." This innate desire, says Aristotle, is not only a desire to know in order to do or make something. In addition to these pragmatic motives, there is in man a desire to know certain kinds of things simply for the sake of knowing. An indication of this, says Aristotle, is "the delight we take in our senses; for even apart from their usefulness they are loved for themselves" inasmuch as our seeing "makes us know and brings to light many differences between things."

There are different levels of knowledge. Some men know only what they experience through their senses, as, for example, when they know that fire is hot. But, says Aristotle, we do not regard what we know through the senses as wisdom. To be sure, our most authoritative knowledge of particular things is acquired through our senses. Still, this kind of knowledge tells us only the "that" of anything and not the "why"; it tells us, for example, *that* fire is hot but not *why*. Similarly, in medicine, some men know only *that* medicines heal certain illnesses. This knowledge, based on specific experiences, is, according to Aristotle, on a lower level than the knowledge of the medical scientist who knows not only *that* a medicine will heal but knows also the reason *why*. In the various crafts, the master craftsmen "know in a truer sense and are wiser than the manual workers, because they know the *causes* of the things that are done."

Wisdom is therefore more than that kind of knowledge obtained from sensing objects and their qualities. It is even more than knowledge acquired from repeated experiences of the same kinds of things. Wisdom is similar to the knowledge possessed by the scientist who begins by looking at something, then repeats these sense experiences, and finally goes beyond sense experience by thinking about the causes of the objects of his experiences. There are as many sciences as there are definable areas of investigation, and Aristotle deals with many of them, including physics,

Aristotle (*Culver Pictures*)

ethics, politics, and aesthetics. In each case, the respective science is concerned with discovering the causes or reasons or principles underlying the activity of its special subject matter; thus, for example, in physics one asks what causes material bodies to move, in ethics what causes the good life, in politics what causes the good state, and in aesthetics what causes a good poem. Sciences differ not only in their subject matter but also in their relation to one another. Some sciences depend on others, such as when the physicist must rely on the science of mathematics. In the hierarchy of sciences, Aristotle says that "the science which knows to what end each thing must be done is the most authoritative of the sciences, and more authoritative than any ancillary science." In addition to the specific sciences, then, there is another science, first philosophy, or what we now call "metaphysics," which goes beyond the subject matter of the other sciences and is concerned with "first principles and causes." These "first principles and causes" are the true foundation of *wisdom*, for they give us knowledge not of any particular object or activity, but rather knowledge of true reality.

Metaphysics deals with knowledge at the highest level of abstraction. This knowledge is abstract because it is about what is universal instead of what is particular. Every science has its own level of abstraction inasmuch as it deals with the first principles and causes of its subject matter, such as when the physicist talks about the principles of motion in general as distinguished from describing the motion of this planet or that pendulum. Wisdom has to do, then, with the abstract levels of knowledge and not with the levels of visible things, for, as Aristotle says, "sense-perception is common to all, and therefore easy and no mark of Wisdom." True wisdom, first philosophy, or metaphysics is the most abstract and also the most exact of all the sciences because it tries to discover the truly first principles from which even the first principles of the various sciences are derived. True knowledge is therefore found in what is most knowable, and, says Aristotle, "the first principles and the causes are most knowable . . . and from these, all other things come to be known . . . " We are led, then, to consider more specifically the subject matter of metaphysics.

The Problem of Metaphysics Defined

The various sciences seek to find the first principles and causes of specific kinds of things, such as material bodies, the human body, the state, a poem, and so on. Unlike these sciences, which ask "What is such-and-such a thing like and why?" metaphysics asks a far more general question, a question that each science must ultimately take into account, namely, "What does it mean to be anything whatsoever?" What, in short, does it mean *to be?* It was precisely this question that concerned Aristotle in his *Metaphysics*, making metaphysics for him "the science of any existent, as existent." The problem of metaphysics as he saw it was therefore the study of being and its "principles" and "causes."

Aristotle's metaphysics was to a considerable extent an outgrowth of his views on logic and his interest in biology. From the viewpoint of his logic, "to be" meant for him to be something that could be accurately defined and that could therefore become the subject of discourse. From the point of view of his interest in biology, he was disposed to think of "to be" as something implicated in a dynamic process. "To be," as Aristotle saw the matter, always meant to be *something*. Hence all existence is individual and has a determinate nature. All the categories Aristotle dealt with in his logical works, categories (or predicates) such as *quality, relation, posture, place*, and so on, presuppose some subject to which these predicates can apply. This subject to which all the categories apply Aristotle called "substance" (*ousia*). To be, then, is to be a particular kind of substance. Also, "to be" means to be a substance as the product of a dynamic process. In this way, metaphysics is concerned with *being* (that is, existing substances) and its *causes* (that is, the processes by which substances come into being).

Substance as the Primary Essence of Things

A major clue to what is meant by substance is discovered, Aristotle thought, in the way we know a thing. Having in mind again the categories or predicates, he says that we know a thing better when we know *what it is* than when we know the color, size, or posture it has. The mind separates a thing from all its qualities and focuses on what a thing really is, on its *essential nature*. We recognize that all *men* are men in spite of their different sizes, colors, or ages. *Some-*

thing about each concretely different man makes him a man in spite of the unique characteristics that make him this particular man. At this point, Aristotle would readily agree that these special characteristics (categories, predicates) also exist, have some kind of being. But the being of these characteristics is not the central object of metaphysical inquiry.

The central concern of metaphysics is the study of substance, the essential nature of a thing. In this view, substance means "that which is not asserted of a subject but of which everything else is asserted." Substance is what we know as basic about something, *after* which we can say other things about *it*. Whenever we define something, we get at its essence *before* we can say anything about it, such as when we speak of a large table or a healthy man. Here table and man are understood in their "essence," in what makes them a table or a man, before they are understood as large or healthy. To be sure, we can know only specific and determinate things, actual individual tables and men. At the same time, the essence, or substance, of a table or a man has its existence separate from its categories or its qualities. This does not mean that a substance is ever in fact found existing separately from its qualities. Still, if we can know the essence of a thing, "tableness" let us say, as "separable" from these particular qualities, round, small, and brown, there must be some universal essence that is found wherever one sees a table, and this essence or substance must be independent of its particular qualities inasmuch as the essence is the same even though in the case of each actual table the qualities are different.

What Aristotle seems to be saying is that a thing is more than the sum of its particular qualities. There is something "beneath" (*sub stance*) all the qualities; thus any specific thing is a combination of qualities, on the one hand, and a substratum to which the qualities apply, on the other. With these distinctions in mind, Aristotle was led, as was Plato before him, to consider just how this essence, or universal, was related to the particular thing. What, in short, makes a substance a substance; is it *matter* as a substratum or is it *form?*

Matter and Form

Although Aristotle distinguished between matter and form, he nevertheless said that we never find matter without form or form without matter in nature. Everything that exists is some concrete individual thing, and every *thing* is a unity of matter and form. Substance, therefore, is a composite of form and matter.

Plato, it will be recalled, argued that Ideas or Forms, such as Man or Table, have a separate existence. Similarly, he treated *space* as the material substratum or the stuff out of which individual things were made. For Plato, then, this primary stuff of space was molded by the eternally existing Forms into individual shapes. This was Plato's way of explaining how there could be many individual things that all have one and the same, that is, universal, nature or essence while still being individual. This universal, Plato said, is the Form, which exists eternally and is separate from any particular thing and is found in each thing only because the thing (this table) *participates* in the Form (tableness, or Ideal Table).

Aristotle rejected Plato's explanation of the universal Forms, rejecting specifically the notion that the Forms existed separately from individual things. Of course, Aristotle did agree that there are universals, that universals such as Man and Table are more than merely subjective notions. Indeed, Aristotle recognized that without the theory of universals, there could be no scientific knowledge, for then there would be no way of saying something about all members of a particular class. What makes scientific knowledge effective is that it discovers classes of objects (for example, a certain form of human disease), so that whenever an individual falls into this class, other facts can be assumed also to be relevant. These classes, then, are not merely mental fictions but do in fact have objective reality. But, said Aristotle, their reality is to be found nowhere else than in the individual things themselves. What purpose, he asked, could be served by assuming that the universal Forms existed separately? If anything, this would complicate matters, inasmuch as everything, that is, not only individual things but also their relationships, would have to be reduplicated in the world of Forms.

Moreover, Aristotle was not convinced that Plato's theory of Forms could help us know things any better, saying that "they help in no wise towards the knowledge of other things. . . . " Since presumably the Forms are motionless, Aristotle concluded that they could not help us understand things as we know them, which are full of motion, nor could they, being immaterial, explain objects of which we have sense impressions. Again, how could the immaterial Forms be related to any particular thing? That things *participate* in the Forms was not a satisfactory explanation for Aristotle, leading him to conclude that "to say that they are patterns and that other things share in them, is to use empty words and poetical metaphors."

When we use the words "matter" and "form" to describe any specific thing, we seem to have in mind the distinction between what something is made of and what it is made into. This, again, disposes our minds to assume that what things are made of, matter, exists in some primary and unformed state until it is made into a thing. But again Aristotle argues that we shall not find anywhere such a thing as "primary matter," that is, matter without form. Consider the sculptor who is about to make a statue of Venus out of marble. He will never find marble without some form; it will always be this marble or that, a square piece or an irregular one, but he will always work with a piece in which form and matter are already combined. That he will give it a different form is another question. The question here is "How does one thing become another thing?" What, in short, is the nature of *change?*

The Process of Change: The Four Causes

In the world around us we see things constantly changing. Change is one of the basic facts of our experience. For Aristotle, the word "change" means many things, including motion, growth, decay, generation, and corruption. Some of these changes are *natural,* whereas others are the products of *human art.* Things are always taking on new form; new life is born and statues are made. Because change always involves taking on new form, several questions can be asked concerning the process of change. Of anything, says Aristotle, we can ask four questions, namely, (1) What is it? (2) What is it made of? (3) By what is it made? and (4) For what end is it made? The responses to these four questions represent Aristotle's four *causes.* Although the word "cause" refers in modern use primarily to an event prior to an effect, for Aristotle it meant an explanation. His four causes represent therefore a broad pattern or framework for the total explanation of anything or everything. Taking an object of art, for example, four causes might be (1) a statue (2) of marble (3) by a sculptor (4) for a decoration. Distinguished from objects produced by human art, there are those things which are produced *by nature.* Although nature does not, according to Aristotle, have "purposes" in the sense of "the reason for," it does always and everywhere have "ends" in the sense of having built-in ways of behaving. For this reason, seeds sprout and roots go down (not up!) and plants grow and in this process of change move toward their "end," that is, their distinctive function or way of being. In nature, then, change will involve these same four elements. Aristotle's *four causes* are therefore (1) the *formal* cause, which determines what a thing is, (2) the *material* cause, or that out of which it is made, (3) the *efficient* cause, by what a thing is made, and (4) the *final* cause, the "end" for which it is made.

Aristotle looked at life through the eyes of a biologist. For him, nature is *life.* All things are in motion, in the process of becoming and dying away. The process of reproduction was for him a clear example of the power inherent in all living things to initiate change and to reproduce their kind. Summarizing his causes, Aristotle said that "all things that come to be come to be by some agency and from something, and come to be something." From this biological viewpoint, Aristotle was able to elaborate his notion that form and matter never exist separately. In nature, generation of new life involves, according to Aristotle, first of all an individual who already possesses the specific form which the offspring will have (the male parent); there must then be the matter capable of being the vehicle for this form (this matter being contributed by the female parent); from this comes a new individual with the same specific form. In this example, Aristotle indicates that change does not involve bringing together formless matter with matterless form. On the contrary, change occurs always in and to something that is already a combination of form and matter and that is on its way to becoming something new or different.

Potentiality and Actuality

All things, said Aristotle, are involved in processes of change. Each thing possesses a power to become what its form has set as its end. There is in all things a dynamic power of striving toward their "end." Some of this striving is toward external objects, such as when a man builds a house. But there is also the striving to achieve ends that pertain to one's internal nature, such as when a man fulfills his nature as a man by the act of thinking. This self-contained end of anything Aristotle called its "entelechy."

That things have ends led Aristotle to consider the distinction between *potentiality* and *actuality*. This distinction is used by Aristotle to explain the processes of change and development. If the *end* of an acorn is to be a tree, in some way the acorn is only potentially a tree but not actually so at this time. A fundamental mode of change, then, is the change from potentiality to actuality. But the chief significance of this distinction is that Aristotle argues for the priority of actuality over potentiality. That is, although something actual emerges from the potential, there could be no movement from potential to actual if there were not first of all something actual. A boy is potentially a man, but before there could be a boy with that potentiality there had to be prior to him an actual man.

Since all things in nature are similar to the relation of a boy to a man or an acorn to a tree, Aristotle was led to see in nature different levels of being. If everything were involved in change, in generation and corruption, everything would partake of potentiality. But, as we have seen, for there to be something potential, there must already be something actual. To explain the existence of the world of potential things, Aristotle thought it was necessary to assume the existence of some actuality at a level above potential or perishing things. He was led to the notion of a Being that is pure actuality, without any potentiality, at the highest level of being. Since change is a kind of motion, Aristotle saw the visible world as one composed of things in motion. But motion, a mode of change, involves potentiality. Things are potentially in motion but must be moved by something that is actually in motion. Again, to explain motion ultimately led Aristotle to speak of the "Unmoved Mover."

The Unmoved Mover

For Aristotle, the Unmoved Mover did not mean the same thing as a *first* mover, as though motion could be traced back to a *time* when motion began. Nor was the Unmoved Mover considered by him a *creator* in the sense of later theology. From his previous distinction between potentiality and actuality, Aristotle concluded that the only way to explain how motion or change can occur is to assume that something actual is *logically* prior to whatever is potential. The fact of change must imply the existence of something actual, something *purely* actual without any mixture of potentiality. This Mover is not, according to Aristotle, an *efficient* cause in the sense of exerting a power or force, or as expressing a *will.* Such acts would imply potentiality, such as when one says that God "willed" to create the world. This would mean that *before* God created the world, he was potentially capable or intended to create it.

Aristotle did not think of the Unmoved Mover as a Being that *thinks* or prescribes *purposes* for the world. In a sense, the Unmoved Mover does not know anything precisely because it is not a kind of being as much as it is a way of explaining the fact of motion. All nature is full of striving toward fulfilling all its particular entelechies. Each thing is aiming at perfecting its possibilities and its *end*, aiming, that is, at becoming the perfect tree, the perfectly good man, and so on. The aggregate of all these strivings constitutes the large-scale processes of the world order so that it can be said that all reality is in the process of change, moving from its potentialities and possibilities to the ultimate perfection of these potentialities. To explain this comprehensive or general motion, to make it intelligible, Aristotle referred to the Unmoved Mover as the "reason for" or the "principle of" motion. For this reason, the Unmoved Mover stood for him as the actual and, because there is here no potentiality, the *eternal* principle of motion. Since this explanation of motion implies an eternal activity, then, there was never a "time" when there was not a world of things in process. For this reason, too, Aristotle denied that there was a "creation" in time.

Although there are passages in Aristotle that have a distinctly religious and theistic flavor, the dominant mood of his thought on this matter is less religious than it is scientific. Still, to speak of an Unmoved Mover involved Aristotle in certain metaphorical language. In explaining how an Unmoved Mover can "cause" motion, he compared it to a beloved who "moves" the lover just by being the object of love, by the power of attraction and not by force. In a more technical way, Aristotle considered the Unmoved Mover as the *form* and the world as the substance. From the point of view of his four causes, Aristotle considered the Mover as the *final* cause, in the way that the form of man is in the boy, directing the motion

of his change toward a final, that is, fixed or appropriate, natural
end. By being a final cause, the Unmoved Mover thereby, in relation to the world, becomes also *efficient* cause, through the power
of attraction, by being desired and loved, by inspiring the striving
toward natural ends, a process that goes on eternally.

What in Aristotle's thought was the unconscious principle of
motion and immanent form of the world, the Unmoved Mover,
became, especially at the hands of Aquinas in the thirteenth century, the philosophical description of the God of Christianity. Aristotle's Unmoved Mover could be said to be pure understanding,
pure *nous*, and since it must think the best, it "thinks itself . . . and
its thinking is a thinking of thinking . . . throughout all eternity."
Such a "God" is not the religious God who becomes involved in the
affairs of man. Aristotle's "God" is immanent in the world, making
the world an intelligible order.

READING

CAUSES AND PURPOSE IN NATURE

Aristotle

WISDOM THE KNOWLEDGE OF CAUSES

All men by their very nature feel the urge to know. That is clear from the
pleasure we take in our senses, for their own sake, irrespective of their utility. Above all, we value sight; disregarding its practical uses, we prefer it, I
believe, to every other sense, even when we have no material end in view.
Why? Because sight is the principal source of knowledge and reveals many
differences between one object and another.

Animals are endowed with sense-perception, from which some of
them derive memory; others do not, and are therefore less intelligent and
less able to learn than the former. Some animals, though possessed of mem-

---

From *Aristotle's Metaphysics*, trans. and ed. John Warrington. Intro. by Sir David Ross,
Everyman's Library, E. P. Dutton & Co., Inc., New York, 1956.

ory, are unable to hear sounds and therefore cannot be taught; these creatures, which include bees and suchlike, are said to have instinct.

Brute beasts live by sense-impression and memory with but a small share in connected experience, whereas the human race lives by art and science. Man derives experience through memory: his several acts of memory give rise to a single effect which we call experience. The latter is easily confused with art and science, which are, however, its results; for as Polus rightly says: "Experience produced science, inexperience chance." You have art where from many notions of experience there proceeds one universal judgment applying in all similar cases. Thus, the judgment that a certain remedy was good for Callias, Socrates, and various other persons suffering from a particular disease is a matter of experience; but the judgment that such and such a remedy is good for all men of similar constitution (e.g., phlegmatic or bilious) suffering from such and such a disease (a burning fever, for instance) belongs to science.

From a practical point of view, certainly, there is little to choose between art and experience: an experienced man, in fact, is more successful than one who has theory alone. Knowledge and proficiency, however, are thought to belong more properly to art than to experience, and artists are considered wiser than those who are limited to experience. This suggests that Wisdom is always proportionate to the degree of knowledge; for an artist knows the cause of a thing, while the other does not. He who has only experience knows that a thing *is* so, but not *why* it is so, whereas an artist knows the why and wherefore. This is why a master craftsman in any trade is more highly esteemed, is considered to know more, and therefore to be wiser than an artisan, because he understands the reason for what is done. He is said to be wiser, not indeed for what he can do, but on account of his theoretical knowledge. The artisan's work may be compared in one sense with the unconscious activity of certain inanimate agents like fire, excepting that the latter operate according to their nature whereas the artisan does so by habit.

Generally speaking, the proof of a man's knowledge or ignorance is his ability or inability to teach; and we therefore hold that knowledge consists in art rather than in experience, for the artist is capable of transmitting his knowledge to others, whereas the man of simple experience cannot.

Wisdom, again, is not to be identified with sense-perception which, though it is our primary source of knowledge, can never tell us *why* anything is so (e.g., why fire is hot), but only that it *is* so. In the early stages of civilization a pioneer in any field which required the exercise of something more than sense-perception was probably admired by his fellow men not so much because his discovery was useful as because he appeared a wise man and superior to themselves. It is also probable that, as the horizons of knowledge were gradually enlarged, exponents of the fine arts were invariably considered wiser than those of the useful arts, whose knowledge was directed to mere utility; and it was only when these two kinds of art had been established that there arose others which aimed neither at utility nor at sensible satisfaction. These theoretical arts, moreover, were evolved in places where men had plenty of free time: mathematics, for example, originated in Egypt, where a priestly caste enjoyed the necessary leisure.

The difference between art, science, and kindred mental activities has already been explained in the *Ethics*. My present point is that all agree that what we ordinarily call Wisdom is concerned with first causes or principles. Hence, as I said earlier, we consider an experienced man wiser than one who has only sensation, an artist than a merely experienced man, a master-craftsman than an artisan, and the speculative sciences as more learned than the productive. Thus it is clear that Wisdom is the knowledge of certain principles and causes.

PHYSICS
Aristotle

THE FOUR CAUSES (OR "BECAUSES")

We have next to consider in how many senses "because" may answer the question "why." For we aim at understanding, and since we never reckon that we understand a thing till we can give an account of its "how and why," it is clear that we must look into the "how and why" of things coming into existence and passing out of it, or more generally into the essential constituents of physical change, in order to trace back any object of our study to the principles so ascertained.

Well then, (1) the existence of *material* for the generating process to start from (whether specifically or generically considered) is one of the essential factors we are looking for. Such is the bronze for the statue, or the silver for the phial. (Material *aitia*.) Then, naturally, (2) the thing in question cannot be there unless the material has actually received the *form* or characteristics of the type, conformity to which brings it within the definition of the thing we say it is, whether specifically or generically. Thus the interval between two notes is not an octave unless the notes are in the ratio of 2 to 1; nor do they stand at a musical interval at all unless they conform to one or other of the recognized ratios. (Formal *aitia*.) Then again, (3) there must

From Aristotle, *The Physics*, trans. by Philip P. Wicksteed and Francis M. Cornford, Vol. I, Loeb Classical Library, Harvard Press.

be something to initiate the process of the change or its cessation when the process is completed, such as the act of a voluntary agent (of the smith, for instance), or the father who begets a child; or more generally the prime, conscious or unconscious, *agent* that produces the effect and starts the material on its way to the product, changing it from what it was to what it is to be. (Efficient *aitia*.) And lastly, (4) there is the *end* or purpose, for the sake of which the process is initiated, as when a man takes exercise for the sake of his health. "Why does he take exercise?" we ask. And the answer "Because he thinks it good for his health" satisfies us. (Final *aitia*.) Then there are all the intermediary agents, which are set in motion by the prime agent and make for the goal, as means to the end. Such are the reduction of superfluous flesh and purgation, or drugs and surgical instruments, as means to health. For both actions and tools may be means, or *"media,"* through which the efficient cause reaches the end aimed at.

This is a rough classification of the causal determinants (*aitiai*) of things; but it often happens that, when we specify them, we find a number of them coalescing as joint factors in the production of a single effect, and that not merely incidentally; for it is *qua* statue that the statue depends for its existence alike on the bronze and on the statuary. The two, however, do not stand on the same footing, for one is required as the material and the other as initiating the change.

Also, it can be said of certain things indifferently that either of them is the cause or the effect of the other. Thus we may say that a man is in fine condition "because" he has been in training, or that he has been in training "because" of the good condition he expected as the result. But one is the cause as aim (final *aitia*) and the other as initiating the process (efficient *aitia*).

Again, the same cause is often alleged for precisely opposite effects. For if its presence causes one thing, we lay the opposite to its account if it is absent. Thus, if the pilot's presence would have brought the ship safe to harbour, we say that he caused its wreck by his absence.

But in all cases the essential and causal determinants we have enumerated fall into four main classes. For letters are the causes of syllables, and the material is the cause of manufactured articles, and fire and the like are causes of physical bodies, and the parts are causes of the whole, and the premises are causes of the conclusion, in the sense of that out of which these respectively are made; but of these things some are causes in the sense of the *substratum* (e.g., the parts stand in this relation to the whole), others in the sense of the essence—the whole or the synthesis or the form. And again, the fertilizing sperm, or the physician, or briefly the voluntary or involuntary *agent* sets going or arrests the transformation or movement. And finally, there is the goal or *end* in view, which animates all the other determinant factors as the best they can attain to; for the attainment of that "for the sake of which" anything exists or is done is its final and best possible achievement (though of course "best" in this connexion means no more than "taken to be the best").

PURPOSE AS "FINAL CAUSE" IN NATURE

We must now consider why Nature is to be ranked among causes that are final, that is to say purposeful; and further we must consider what is meant by "necessity" when we are speaking of Nature. For thinkers are forever referring things to necessity as a cause, and explaining that, since hot and cold and so forth are what they are, this or that exists or comes into being "of necessity"; for even if one or another of them alleges some other cause, such as "Sympathy and Antipathy" or "Mind," he straight away drops it again, after a mere acknowledgement.

So here the question rises whether we have any reason to regard Nature as making for any goal at all, or as seeking any one thing as preferable to any other. Why not say, it is asked, that Nature acts as Zeus drops the rain, not to make the corn grow, but of necessity (for the rising vapour must needs be condensed into water by the cold, and must then descend, and incidentally, when this happens, the corn grows), just as, when a man loses his corn on the threshing-floor, it did not rain on purpose to destroy the crop, but the result was merely incidental to the raining? So why should it not be the same with natural organs like the teeth? Why should it not be a coincidence that the front teeth come up with an edge, suited to dividing the food, and the back ones flat and good for grinding it, without there being any design in the matter? And so with all other organs that seem to embody a purpose. In cases where a coincidence brought about such a combination as might have been arranged on purpose, creatures, it is urged, having been suitably formed by the operation of chance, survived; otherwise they perished, and still perish, as Empedocles says of his "man-faced oxen."

Such and suchlike are the arguments which may be urged in raising this problem; but it is impossible that this should really be the way of it. For all these phenomena and all natural things are either constant or normal, and this is contrary to the very meaning of luck or chance. No one assigns it to chance or to a remarkable coincidence if there is abundant rain in the winter, though he would if there were in the dog-days; and the other way about, if there were parching heat. Accordingly, if the only choice is to assign these occurrences either to coincidence or to purpose, and if in these cases chance coincidence is out of the question, then it must be purpose. But, as our opponents themselves would admit, these occurrences are all natural. There is purpose, then, in what is, and in what happens, in Nature.

Further, in any operation of human art, where there is an end to be achieved, the earlier and successive stages of the operation are performed for the purpose of realizing that end. Now, when a thing is produced by Nature, the earlier stages in every case lead up to the final development in the same way as in the operation of art, and *vice versa,* provided that no impediment balks the process. The operation is directed by a purpose; we may, therefore, infer that the natural process was guided by a purpose to the end that is realized. Thus, if a house were a natural product, the process would pass through the same stages that it in fact passes through when it is produced by art; and if natural products could also be produced by art, they would move along the same line that the natural process actually takes. We may therefore say that the earlier stages are for the purpose of leading to the later. Indeed, as a general proposition, the arts either, on the basis of Nature, carry things further than Nature can, or they imitate Nature. If, then, artificial processes are purposeful, so are natural processes too; for the relation of antecedent to consequent is identical in art and in Nature.

This principle comes out most clearly when we consider the other animals. For their doings are not the outcome of art (design) or of previous research or deliberation; so that some raise the question whether the works of spiders and ants and so on should be attributed to intelligence or to some similar faculty. And then, descending step by step, we find that plants too produce organs subservient to their perfect development—leaves, for instance, to shelter the fruit. Hence, if it is by nature and also for a purpose that the swallow makes her nest and the spider his web, and that plants make leaves for the sake of the fruit and strike down (and not up) with their roots in order to get their nourishment, it is clear that causality of the kind we have described is at work in things that come about or exist in the course of Nature.

Also, since the term "nature" is applied both to material and to form, and since it is the latter that constitutes the goal, and all else is for the sake of that goal, it follows that the form is the final cause.

Now there are failures even in the arts (for writers make mistakes in writing and physicians administer the wrong dose); so that analogous failures in Nature may evidently be anticipated as possible. Thus, if in art there are cases in which the correct procedure serves a purpose, and attempts that fail are aimed at a purpose but miss it, we may take it to be the same in Nature, and monstrosities will be like failures of purpose in Nature. So if, in the primal combinations, such "ox-creatures" as could not reach an equilibrium and goal should appear, it would be by the miscarriage of some principle, as monstrous births are actually produced now by abortive developments of sperm. Besides, the sperm must precede the formation of the animal, and Empedocles' "primal all-generative" is no other than such sperm.

In plants, too, though they are less elaborately articulated, there are manifest indications of purpose. Are we to suppose, then, that as there were "ox-creatures man-faced" so also there were "vine-growths olive-bearing"? Incongruous as such a thing seems, it ought to follow if we accept the principle in the case of animals. Moreover, it ought still to be a matter of chance what comes up when you sow this seed or that.

In general, the theory does away with the whole order of Nature, and indeed with Nature's self. For natural things are exactly those which do move continuously, in virtue of a principle inherent in themselves, towards a determined goal; and the final development which results from any one such principle is not identical for any two species, nor yet is it any random result; but in each, there is always a tendency towards an identical result, if nothing interferes with the process. A desirable result and the means to it may also be produced by chance, as for instance we say it was "by luck" that the stranger came and ransomed the prisoner before he left, where the ransoming is done as if the man had come for that purpose, though in fact he did not. In this case the desirable result is incidental; for, as we have explained, chance is an incidental cause. But when the desirable result is effected invariably or normally, it is not an incidental or chance occurrence; and in the course of Nature the result always is achieved either invariably or normally, if nothing hinders. It is absurd to suppose that there is no purpose because in Nature we can never detect the moving power in the act of deliberation. Art, in fact, does not deliberate either, and if the shipbuilding art were incorporate in the timber, it would proceed by nature in the same way in which it now proceeds by art. If purpose, then, is inherent in art, so is it in Nature also. The best illustration is the case of a man being his own physician, for Nature is like that—agent and patient at once.

That Nature is a cause, then, and a goal-directed cause, is above dispute.

CHAPTER 28

MODES AND MONADS

Spinoza and Leibniz

Baruch Spinoza was born in Amsterdam in 1632 in a family of Portuguese Jews who had fled from persecution in Spain. He was trained in the study of the Old Testament and the Talmud and was familiar with the writings of the Jewish philosopher Maimonides. Having been forced to leave Amsterdam, he eventually went, in 1663, to The Hague, where he carried on his literary career, of which his *Ethics* is the crowning work. In 1677 he died of consumption at the age of forty-five.

Spinoza's Method

In common with Descartes, Spinoza thought that we can achieve exact knowledge of reality by following the method of geometry. Descartes had worked out the basic form of this method for philosophy, starting with clear and distinct first principles and attempting from these to deduce the whole content of knowledge. What Spi-

Spinoza

noza added to Descartes's method was a highly systematic arrangement of principles and axioms. Whereas Descartes's method was
simple, Spinoza almost set out literally to write a geometry of philosophy, that is, a complete set of axioms or theorems (about 250
altogether) that would explain the whole system of reality the way
geometry explains the relations and movement of things. In geometry, conclusions are demonstrated, and Spinoza believed that our
theory of the nature of reality could also be demonstrated. He
believed that our rational powers are capable of forming ideas that
reflect the true nature of things: "Every definition or clear and distinct idea," says Spinoza, "is true." It must follow, therefore, that
a complete and systematic arrangement of true ideas will give us a

true picture of reality, for "the order and connection of ideas is the same as the order and connection of things."

The order of things also provides the pattern for the order in which the philosopher should arrange his subjects. It is of utmost importance to observe this order carefully if we are to understand the various aspects of nature accurately. If, for example, we say that things depend for their nature on God, we must first know all that we can about God before we can understand things. For this reason, Spinoza could find little value in Francis Bacon's method, which consisted of enumerating observations of visible events and drawing conclusions from these observations. Nor would he use Aquinas's method of accounting for the existence of God by first of all analyzing the nature of our ordinary experience with things and persons. At this point, too, Spinoza rejects Descartes's approach, for Descartes started with a clear and distinct idea of his *own* existence and from the formula "I think, therefore I am" proceeded to deduce the other parts of his philosophy. Because in the true nature of things God is prior to everything else, Spinoza believed that philosophy must formulate ideas about God first so that these ideas could appropriately affect the conclusions we draw about such matters as man's nature, his way of behaving, and the relation of his mind and body. And because Spinoza had such novel things to say about God, it was inevitable that he would say novel things also about human nature. Spinoza, therefore, begins his philosophy with the problem of the nature and existence of God.

God

Spinoza offered a strikingly unique conception of God, in which he identified God with the whole cosmos. His famous formula was *Deus sive Natura*, "God or Nature," as if to say that these two words are interchangeable. Although this pantheism could be found in such Biblical descriptions of God as He "in whom we live and move and have our being," Spinoza stripped the idea of God of earlier meanings by emphasizing not the *relation* between God and man but a basic *unity* between them: "Whatever is," he said, "is in God, and nothing can exist or be conceived without God." The clue to Spinoza's unique conception of God is found in his definition: "God

I understand to be a being absolutely infinite, that is, a substance consisting of infinite attributes, each of which expresses eternal and infinite essence."

God and the World: The Modes

Spinoza does not contrast God and the world as if they were as different and distinct as cause and effect, as though God were the immaterial cause and the world the material effect. He has already established that there is only one substance and that the word "God" is interchangeable with "Nature."

Modes and Necessity

Since the world consists of the modes of God's attributes, everything in the world acts in accordance with necessity; that is, everything is determined. For the modes in which thought and extension take form in the world are determined by God's substance, or, as Spinoza says, these modes represent "everything which follows from the necessity of the nature of God." Spinoza gives us a picture of a tight universe where every event unfolds in the only possible way in which it can occur, for "in the nature of things nothing contingent is granted, but all things are determined by the necessity of divine nature for existing and working in a certain way." In a special way God is free, not that He could have created a different kind of world, but that though He had to create just what He did, He was not forced to do this by some external cause, only by His own nature. However, man is not even that free, for he is determined to exist and behave according to God's substance, of whose attributes man is a mode. All modes of God's attributes are fixed from eternity, for "things could not have been produced by God in any other manner or order than that in which they were produced." All the things we experience "are nothing else than modifications of the attributes of God [Nature], or modes by which attributes are expressed in a certain and determined manner." Thus everything is intimately connected, the infinite substance providing a continuity through all things, particular things being simply modes or modifications of the attributes of substance, or Nature, or God.

No Final Cause

Because everything is eternally as it must be, and because particular events are simply finite modifications of substance, there is no direction toward which things are moving, no *end*, no *purpose*, no *final* cause. From our human vantage point, men try to explain events as either fulfilling or frustrating some purpose of history. Ideas of purpose, says Spinoza, are derived from our tendency to act with an end in view. From this habit we tend to look at the universe as though it too had some goal. But this is a wrong way of looking at the universe and indeed at our own behavior. For neither the universe nor human beings are pursuing purposes; they are only doing what they must. This "truth might have lain hidden from the human race through all eternity, had not mathematics, which does not deal with final causes but with the essences of things, offered to men another standard of truth." And the truth is that all events are a continuous and necessary set of modifications of the eternal substance, which simply *is*. Thus Spinoza reduced the biological to the mathematical.

The Levels of Knowledge

But how can Spinoza claim to know the ultimate nature of reality? He distinguishes between three levels of knowledge and describes how we can move from the lowest to the highest. We begin with the things most familiar to us, and, says Spinoza, "the more we understand individual things the more we understand God." By refining our knowledge of things, we can move from (1) *imagination*, to (2) *reason*, and finally to (3) *intuition*.

At the level of *imagination,* our ideas are derived from sensation, as when we see another person. Here our ideas are very concrete and specific, and the mind is passive. Although our ideas on this level are specific, they are vague and inadequate, for we know things only as they affect our senses—I know that I *see* a person, but as yet I do not know simply by looking at him what his essential nature is. I can form a general idea, such as *man,* by seeing several men, and the ideas I form from experience are useful for daily life, but they do not give me true knowledge.

The second level of knowledge goes beyond imagination to *reason.* This is scientific knowledge. All men can participate in this kind of knowledge because it is made possible by man's sharing in the attributes of substance, in God's thought and extension. There is in man what is in all things, and since one of these common properties is mind, man's mind shares in the mind that orders things. At this level man's mind can rise above immediate and particular things and deal with abstract ideas, as he does in mathematics and physics. At this level, knowledge is *adequate* and *true.* If we ask Spinoza how we know that these ideas of reason and science are true, he replies in effect that truth validates itself, for "he who has a true idea knows at the same time that he has a true idea, nor can he doubt concerning the truth of the thing."

The third and highest level of knowledge is *intuition.* Through intuition we can grasp the whole system of nature. At this level we can understand the particular things we encountered on the first level in a new way, for at that first level we saw other bodies in a disconnected way, and now we see them as part of the whole scheme. This kind of knowing "proceeds from an adequate idea of the formal essence of certain attributes of God to the adequate knowledge of the essence of things." When we reach this level we become more and more conscious of God and hence "more perfect and blessed," for through this vision we grasp the whole system of Nature and see our place in it, giving us an intellectual fascination with the full order of Nature, of God.

Mind and Body

Descartes also struggled with the difficult problem of explaining how the mind interacts with the body. This was for him virtually insolvable because he assumed that mind and body represent two distinct substances. For Spinoza, however, this was no problem at all because he viewed mind and body as attributes of a single substance. There is only one order of Nature, to which both the body and mind belong. Man is a single mode. It is only because we are able to consider man as a mode of extension that we speak of his body, and as a mode of thought that we speak of his mind. There can be no separation of mind and body because they are aspects of the same thing. For every body there is a corresponding idea, and, in general, Spinoza says that the mind is the idea of the body, which is his way of describing the relationship of the mind to the body. The structure within which the mind and body operate is the same. Thus man is a finite version of God, for he is a mode of God's attributes of thought and extension.

Determinism: Is the Will Free?

The central feature of Spinoza's account of human behavior is that he treats man as an integral part of Nature. When Spinoza says that he looks on "human actions and desires exactly as if I were dealing with lines, planes and bodies," his point is that human behavior can be explained just as precisely in terms of causes, effects, and mathematics as any other natural phenomenon. Although men think they are *free* and are able to make *choices*, they are victims of an illusion, for it is only human ignorance that permits us to think we possess freedom of the will. Men like to think that in some special way they stand outside the rigorous forces of cause and effect, that though their wills can cause actions, their wills are themselves not affected by prior causes. But Spinoza argued for the unity of all Nature, with man as an intrinsic part of it. Spinoza therefore develops a naturalistic ethics whereby all human actions, both mental and physical, are said to be determined by prior causes.

If all our desires and actions are determined by external forces, how can there be any occasion for morality? Here Spinoza resembles the Stoics, who also argued that all events are determined. The Stoics called for resignation and acquiescence to the drift of events, saying that though we cannot control events, we can control our attitudes. In a similar way, Spinoza tells us that through our knowledge of God we can arrive at "the highest possible mental acquiescence." Morality, therefore, consists of improving our knowledge by moving from the level of confused and inadequate ideas up to the third level of intuition, where we have clear and distinct ideas of the perfect and eternal arrangement of all things in God. Only knowledge can lead us to happiness, for only through knowledge can we be liberated from the bondage of our passions. We are enslaved by passions when our desires are attached to perishable things and when we do not fully understand our emotions. The more we understand our emotions, the less excessive will be our appetites and desires. And "the mind has greater power over the emotions and is less subject thereto, in so far as it understands all things as necessary."

We must study not only our emotions but the whole order of Nature, for it is only from the perspective of eternity that we can really understand our own particular lives, for then we see all events through the idea of God as cause. Spiritual unhealthiness, says Spinoza, can always be traced to our "excessive love for something which is subject to many variations and which we can never be masters of." But we possess by nature the desire for and the capacity for higher degrees of perfection, and we achieve levels of perfection through our intellectual powers. Passions enslave us only when we lack knowledge. But "from this kind of knowledge necessarily arises the intellectual love of God. From this kind of knowledge arises pleasure accompanied by the idea of God as cause, that is, the love of God; not in so far as we imagine Him as present, but in so far as we understand Him to be eternal; this is what I call the intellectual love of God." This love of God is of course not the love of a divine person but is more akin to the mental pleasure we have when we understand a mathematical formula or a scientific operation. That the way to morality described here is "exceedingly hard" Spinoza was willing to admit, adding that "all things excellent are as difficult as they are rare." What made ethics difficult for Spinoza was his metaphysics, for if all things and actions are "necessary," how can one imagine, much less respond to, any alternative standard of behavior?

Leibniz

Gottfried Wilhelm von Leibniz was born at Leipzig in 1646 and entered the university there at the age of fifteen. At Leipzig he studied philosophy, going next to Jena to study mathematics and then to Altdorf, where he completed the course in jurisprudence and received the doctorate in law at the age of twenty-one. With extraordinary vigor he lived actively in the two worlds of action and thought. He was the author of several significant works, including *New Essays on Human Understanding,* in which he examines systematically Locke's *Essay; Essays in Theodicy,* which deals with the problem of evil; *Discourse on Metaphysics;* the *New System of Nature and the Interaction of Substances;* and the *Monadology.* He was in the service of the House of Hanover, but when George I became King of England, Leibniz was not invited to go with him, possibly because of his fierce quarrel with Sir Isaac Newton, whom he accused of plagiarizing his discovery of the calculus. His public influence declined, and in 1716, neglected and unnoticed, he died at the age of seventy.

Substance

Leibniz was dissatisfied with the way Descartes and Spinoza had described the nature of substance, because he felt they had distorted our understanding of human nature, freedom, and the nature of God. To say, as Descartes did, that there are two independent substances, thought and extension, was to produce the impossible dilemma of trying to explain how those two substances could interact as body and mind either in man or in God. Spinoza had tried to solve the dilemma by saying that there is only one substance with two knowable attributes, thought and extension. But to reduce all reality to a single substance was to lose the distinction between the various elements in nature. To be sure, Spinoza spoke of the world as consisting of many *modes*, in which the attributes of thought and extension appear. Still, Spinoza's view of the world was a pantheism in which God was everything and everything was part of everything else. To Leibniz, this conception of substance was inadequate because it blurred the distinctions between God, man, and nature each of which Leibniz wanted to keep separate. Paradoxically, Leibniz accepted Spinoza's single-substance theory and his mechanical model of the universe but presented such a unique theory of this one substance that he was able to speak of the individuality of persons, the transcendence of God, and the reality of purpose and freedom in the universe.

Leibniz

Extension versus Force

Leibniz challenged the fundamental assumption on which both
Descartes and Spinoza had built their theory of substance, namely,
that *extension* implies actual size and shape. Descartes assumed that
"extension" refers to a material substance that is extended in space
and is not divisible into something more primary. Spinoza, too, considered extension as an irreducible material attribute of God or
Nature. Leibniz disagreed. Observing that the bodies or things we
see with our senses are divisible into smaller parts, why can we not

520

assume that all things are compounds or aggregates? "There must be," he said, "simple substances, since there are compound substances, for the compound is only a collection or *aggregatum* of simple substances."

There is nothing new in saying that things must be made of simple substances, for, as we have seen, Democritus and Epicurus had argued centuries before that all things consist of small atoms. But Leibniz rejected this notion of atoms, because Democritus had described these atoms as extended bodies, as irreducible bits of matter. Such a particle of matter would have to be considered lifeless or inert and would have to get its motion from something outside itself. Rejecting the idea of matter as primary, Leibniz argued that the truly simple substances are the "monads," and these are "the true atoms of nature . . . the elements of things." The monads differ from atoms in that atoms were viewed as extended bodies, whereas Leibniz described the monad as being *force* or *energy*. Leibniz therefore said that matter is not the primary ingredient of things, but that monads with their element of force constitute the essential substance of things.

Monads

Leibniz wanted to emphasize that substance must contain life or a dynamic force. Whereas Democritus's material atom would have to be acted on from outside itself in order to move or become a part of a large cluster, Leibniz said that simple substance, the monad, is "capable of action." He added that "*compound* substance is the collection of *monads. Monas* is a Greek word which signifies unity, or that which is one. . . . Simple substances, lives, souls, spirits are unities. Consequently all nature is full of life."

Monads are unextended; they have no shape or size. A monad is a point, not a mathematical or a physical point, but a metaphysically existent point. Each monad is independent of other monads, and monads do not have any causal relation to each other. It is difficult to imagine a *point* that has no shape or size, yet Leibniz wanted to say just this in order to differentiate the monad from a material atom. Actually, his thinking here resembles the twentieth-century notion that physical particles are reducible to energy or that particles are a special form of energy. Essentially, Leibniz was saying that monads are logically prior to any corporeal forms. True substances, then, are monads, and these Leibniz also calls "souls" to emphasize their nonmaterial nature. Each monad is different from the others, and each possesses its own principle of action, its own force, and, says Leibniz, "there is a certain sufficiency which makes them the source of their internal actions and, so to speak, incorporeal automata." Monads are not only independent and different. They also contain the source of their activity within themselves. Moreover, in order to emphasize that the rest of the universe does not affect their behavior, Leibniz says that the monads are *windowless*. But there must be some relation between all the monads which make up the universe, some explanation for their orderly actions. This explanation Leibniz finds in his idea of a *preestablished harmony*.

Preestablished Harmony

Each monad behaves in accordance with its own created purpose. These *windowless* monads, each following its own purpose, form a unity or the ordered universe. Even though each is isolated from the other, their separate purposes form a large-scale harmony. It is as though several clocks all struck the same hour because they keep perfect time. Leibniz compares all these monads to "several different bands of musicians and choirs, playing their parts separately, and so placed that they do not see or even hear one another . . . nevertheless [they] keep perfectly together, by each following their own notes, in such a way that he who hears them all finds in them a harmony that is wonderful, and much more surprising than if there had been any connection between them." Each monad, then, is a separate world, but all the activities of each monad occur in harmony with the activities of the others. In this way it can be said that each monad mirrors the whole universe (but from a unique perspective), in the sense that if anything "were taken away or supposed different, all things in the world would have been different" from what they are like at present. Such a harmony as this could not be the product of an accidental assortment of monads but must be, said Leibniz, the result of God's activity, whereby this harmony is preestablished.

Evil and the Best of All Possible Worlds

The harmony of the world led Leibniz to argue not only that God had preestablished it, but also that in doing this God has created the best of all possible worlds. Whether this is the best or even a good world is open to question because of the disorder and evil in it. Leibniz was aware of this fact but considered it compatible with the notion of a benevolent Creator. In his perfect knowledge, God could consider all the possible kinds of worlds he could create, but his choice must be in accord with the moral requirement that the world should contain the greatest possible amount of good. Such a world would not be without imperfection. On the contrary, the world of creation consists of limited and imperfect things, "for God could not give the creature all without making it God; therefore there must needs be . . . limitations also of every kind." The source of evil is not God but rather the very nature of things God creates, for since these things are finite or limited, they are imperfect. Evil, then, is not something substantial but merely the absence of perfection. Evil for Leibniz is privation. This is why Leibniz could say that "God wills *antecedently* the good and *consequently* the best," since the most that God can do, in spite of his goodness, is to create the best possible world. As a final consideration, Leibniz agrees that we cannot rightly appraise evil if we consider only the particular evil thing or event. Some things that in themselves appear to be evil turn out to be the prerequisites for good, such as when "sweet things become insipid if we eat nothing else; sharp, tart and even bitter things must be combined with them, so as to stimulate the taste." Again, events in our lives, taken by themselves, lose their true perspective. Leibniz asks,

> If you look at a very beautiful picture, having covered up the whole of it except a very small part, what will it present to your sight, however thoroughly you examine it . . . but a confused mass of colors, laid on without selection and without art? Yet if you remove the covering, and look at the whole picture from the right point of view, you

will find that what appeared to have been carelessly daubed on the canvas was really done by the painter with very great art.

Freedom

How can there be any freedom in the determined world Leibniz portrays, where God preestablishes an orderly arrangement by infusing specific purposes into the several monads? Each monad is involved in developing its built-in purpose, and "every present state of a simple substance is naturally a consequence of its preceding state, in such a way that its present is big with its future." Each person, whose identity centers around a dominant monad, his soul, must represent in this mechanical view an unfolding of a life that has been set from the beginning. Yet, since the basic nature of this person is thought, his development through life consists in overcoming confused thoughts and arriving at true ideas, which lie in all of us in the murky form of potentiality seeking to become actual. When our potentialities become actual, we see things as they really are, and this, says Leibniz, is what it means to be free. For him freedom does not mean volition, the power of choice, but rather self-development, so that although one is determined to act in specific ways, it is his own internal nature that determines his acts and not outside forces. Freedom in this sense means the ability to become what one is destined to be without obstructions, and it also means a quality of existence whereby one's knowledge has passed from confusion to clarity. The free man is one who knows why he does what he does. It was along these lines that Leibniz thought he had succeeded in reconciling his deterministic view of nature with freedom.

Whether Leibniz succeeded in reconciling his world of monads with the notion of freedom is certainly questionable. Although he does at one point speak of freedom in terms of "choice in our will" and say that "free and voluntary mean the same thing," still his dominant emphasis appears to be on determinism, on the notion of a mechanical-like universe, a spiritual machine. Actually, Leibniz does not use the mechanical model in describing the universe, for if he did, he would have to say that the various parts of the universe act on each other the way parts of a clock affect the movements of each other. In a sense, Leibniz's explanation is even more rigorously deterministic than the mechanical model suggests, for his monads are all independent of each other, are not affected by each other, but behave in accordance with their original purpose, which they received from the beginning through God's creation. This kind of determinism is more rigorous because it does not depend on the vagaries of external causation, but on the given and permanently fixed internal nature of each monad.

CHAPTER 29

MIND, THE TRUE REALITY

Berkeley

George Berkeley was born in Ireland in 1685. At the age of fifteen he entered Trinity College, where he studied mathematics, logic, language, and philosophy. After taking his B.A. degree, he became a clergyman in the Church of England, rising to Bishop in 1734. He became famous as an author; his books include *Essays toward a New Theory of Vision* (1709), *A Treatise concerning Principles of Human Knowledge* (1710), and *Three Dialogues between Hylas and Philonous.* He traveled in France, Italy, and America, where he hoped to create a college (one of the colleges at Yale is named after him). He influenced American philosophy through his frequent associations with Jonathan Edwards. From America he returned to Ireland, where he was Bishop of Cloyne until age sixty-eight, when he retired to Oxford; he died there a year later in 1753. He is buried in Christ Church Chapel in Oxford.

George Berkeley was a member of that group known today as the "British Empiricists," who also included Locke and Hume. John Locke had developed a theory of knowledge which Berkeley

Berkeley (right) (*Yale University Art Gallery Gift of Isaac Lothrop of Plymouth, Massachusetts*)

accepted, namely, that all our knowledge depends on our sense experience. This was a radical change from earlier theories as developed, for example, by such rationalists as Descartes, Leibniz, and Spinoza. As compared with the more grandiose ideas of the rationalists, Locke's theory of knowledge seemed to agree with the ordinary experience of common sense. Berkeley was influenced by John Locke's new theories. But it is ironic that Locke's common-sense approach to philosophy should have influenced Berkeley to formulate a philosophical position that at first seems so much at odds with common sense. Berkeley became the object of severe criticism and ridicule for denying what seemed most obvious to anyone. Berkeley had set out to deny the existence of matter. Dr. Samuel Johnson must have expressed the reaction of many when he kicked a large stone and said about Berkeley, "I refute him thus."

Berkeley's startling and provocative formula was that "to be is to be perceived," *esse est percipi.* Clearly this would mean that if something were not perceived, it would not exist. Berkeley was perfectly aware of the potential nonsense involved in this formula, for he says, "Let it not be said that I take away Existence. I only declare the meaning of the word so far as I comprehend it." Still, to say that the existence of something depends on its being perceived does raise for us the question whether it exists when it is not being perceived. For Berkeley the whole problem turned on how we interpret or understand the word "exists": "The table I write on I say exists; that is, I see and feel it: and if I were out of my study I should say it existed; meaning thereby that if I were in my study I might perceive it, or that some other spirit actually does perceive it." Here Berkeley is saying that the word "exists" has no other meaning than the one contained in his formula, for we can know no instance where the term "exists" is used without at the same time assuming that a mind is perceiving something. To those who argued that material things have some kind of *absolute* existence without any relation to their being perceived, Berkeley replied, "That is to me unintelligible." To be sure, he said, "the horse is in the stable, the books in the study as before, even if I am not there. But since we know of no instance of anything's existing without being perceived, the table, horse, and books *exist* even when I do not perceive them because someone does perceive them."

How did Berkeley come upon this novel view? In his *New Theory of Vision* he argued that all our knowledge depends on actual vision and other sensory experiences. In particular, Berkeley argued that we never sense *space* or *magnitude;* we only have different visions or perceptions of things when we see them from different perspectives. Nor do we *see* distance; the distance of objects is *suggested* by our experience. All that we ever see is the qualities of an object that our faculty of vision is capable of sensing. We do not see the *closeness* of an object; we only have a different vision of it when we move toward or away from it. The more Berkeley considered the workings of his own mind and wondered how his ideas were related to objects outside of his mind, the more certain he was that he could never discover any object independent of his ideas. "When we do our utmost to conceive the existence of external bodies," he said, "we are all the while contemplating our own ideas." Nothing seems easier for us than to imagine trees in a park or books in a closet without anyone's looking at them. But what is all this, says Berkeley, except "framing in your mind certain ideas-which you call *books* and *trees* . . . But do not *you* yourself perceive or think of them all the while?" It is impossible, he concluded, ever to think of *anything* except as related to a mind. We never experience something that exists outside of us and separate from us as our ideas of "close" and "far" might suggest. There is nothing *out there* of which we do not have some perception.

It was Locke's philosophy that had raised doubts in Berkeley's mind about the independent existence of things, about the reality of matter. Locke had failed to push his own theory of knowledge to conclusions that to Berkeley seemed inevitable. When Locke spoke of substance as "something we know not what," he was only a short step from saying that it was nothing, which Berkeley did say. Locke's treatment of the relation between ideas and things assumes there is a real difference between primary and secondary qualities, between an object's size and shape on the one hand and its color, taste, and smell on the other. He assumed that whereas color exists only as an idea in the mind, size has to do with an object's *substance,* that reality that exists "behind" or "under" such secondary qualities as color and is therefore independent of a mind, is inert matter.

Berkeley, however, argued that size, shape, and motion, "abstracted from all other qualities, are inconceivable." What, for example, is a cherry? It is soft, red, round, sweet, and fragrant. All these qualities are ideas in the mind that the cherry has the power to produce through the senses, so that the softness is felt, the color is seen, the roundness is either felt or seen, the sweetness is tasted, and the fragrance is smelled. Again, the very existence of all these qualities consists in their being perceived. And, apart from these qualities, there is no sensed reality—in short, nothing else. The cherry, then, consists of all the qualities we perceive; the cherry (and all things) represents a complex of sensations. To say that besides the qualities perceived by the senses there are more primary qualities, such as shape and size, is to assume, says Berkeley, that primary and secondary qualities can be divided. It is impossible, he said, even to conceive of shape or size as independent of perception and therefore independent of secondary qualities. Is it possible, he asks, to separate primary and secondary qualities "even in thought?" He adds, "I might as easily divide a thing from itself. . . . In truth, the object and the sensation are the same thing, and cannot therefore be abstracted from each other." A thing *is,* therefore, the sum of its perceived qualities, and it is for this reason that Berkeley argued that to be is to be perceived. Since substance, or matter, is never perceived or sensed, it cannot be said to exist. If substance does not exist and if only sensed qualities are real, then only thinking or, as Berkeley says, *spiritual* beings exist.

Besides leading Locke's empirical philosophy to what he thought were obvious conclusions, Berkeley was also contending with a complex of problems, to which he referred in his *Principles of Human Knowledge* as " . . . *the chief causes of error and difficulty in the Sciences, with the grounds of Scepticism, Atheism and Irreligion, . . . inquired into.*" It was the notion of *matter* that caused all the difficulties, for if an inert material substance is admitted as really existing, where is there any place for spiritual or immaterial substances in such a universe? Also, would not scientific knowledge, based on general ideas drawn from the behavior of things, give us a complete philosophy without requiring the idea of God, leading to "the monstrous systems of atheists?" This is not to say that Berkeley arbitrarily denounced the idea of matter because of these theological consequences, but that he had additional reasons for pressing his views, which, he was convinced, were intrinsically right.

Matter, a Meaningless Term

Locke had said that substance, or matter, supports or acts as a *substrate* to the qualities we sense. In Berkeley's *First Dialogue between Hylas and Philonous*, Hylas expresses Locke's view: " . . . I find it necessary to suppose a material *substratum*, without which [qualities] cannot be conceived to exist." Philonous replies that the word "substratum" has no clear meaning for him and that he would want to "know any sense, literal or not literal, that you understand in it." But Hylas admits that he cannot assign any definite meaning to the term "substratum," saying "I declare I know not what to say." From this the conclusion is drawn that "The *absolute* existence of unthinking things [matter] are words without meaning." This is not to say that sensible things do not possess reality, but only that sensible things exist only insofar as they are perceived. This of course implies that only ideas exist, but Berkeley adds that "I hope that to call a thing 'idea' makes it no less real." Aware that his idealism can be ridiculed, Berkeley writes: "What therefore becomes of the sun, moon, and stars? What must we think of houses, rivers, mountains, trees, stones; nay even of our own bodies? Are all these so many chimeras and illusions of fancy?" By his principles, he says, "we are not deprived of any one thing in nature. Whatever we see, feel, hear, or any wise conceive or understand, remains as secure as ever, and is as real as ever. There is a *rerum natura*, and the distinction between realities and chimeras retains its full force." If this is the case, why say that only *ideas*, instead of *things*, exist? In order, says Berkeley, to eliminate the useless concept of matter: "I do not argue against the existence of any one thing that we can apprehend, either by sense or reflexion. . . . The only thing whose existence we deny, is that which philosophers call matter or corporeal substance. And in doing of this, there is no damage done to the rest of mankind, who, I dare say, will never miss it."

Science and Abstract Ideas

Since it was the science of his day, particularly physics, that relied so heavily on the notion of matter, Berkeley had to come to terms with its assumptions and methods. Science had assumed that we can, and must, distinguish between appearance and reality. The sea appears blue but is really not. Berkeley challenged the scientist to show whether there is any other reality than the sensible world. In this analysis Berkeley was pursuing the principle of empiricism and was trying to refine it. Physicists, he said, were obscuring science by including metaphysics in their theories: They used such words as "force," "attraction," "gravity" and thought they referred to some real physical entity. Even to speak of minute particles whose motions cause the quality of color is to engage in a rational and not empirical analysis. What disturbed Berkeley most was that scientists used general or abstract terms as though these terms accurately referred to real entities, particularly to an underlying material substance in nature. Nowhere, Berkeley argues, do we ever come upon such a substance, for substance is an abstract idea. Only sensed qualities really exist, and the notion of substance is a misleading inference drawn from observed qualities: "As several of these [qualities] are observed to accompany each other, they come to be marked by one name, and so to be reputed as one *thing*. Thus, for example, a certain colour, taste, smell, figure, and consistence having been observed to go together, are accounted one distinct thing, signified by the name apple; other collections of ideas constitute a stone, a tree, a book and the like sensible things." Similarly, when scientists observe the operations of things, they use such abstract terms as "force" or "gravity" as though these were things or had some real existence in things. But "force" is simply a word describing our sensation of the behavior of things and gives us no more knowledge than our senses and reflections give us.

Berkeley did not mean to destroy science any more than he wanted to deny the existence of the "nature of things." What he did want to do was to clarify what scientific language was all about. Terms such as "force," "gravity," and "causality" refer to nothing more than clusters of ideas which our minds derive from sensation. We experience that heat melts wax, but all we know from this experience is that what we call "melting wax" is always accompanied by what we call "heat." We have no knowledge of any single thing for which the word "cause" stands. Indeed, the only knowledge we have is of particular experiences. But even though we do not have firsthand knowledge of the causes of all things, we do know the order of things. We experience order, that *A* is followed by *B*, even though we have no experience of *why* this occurs. Science gives us a description of physical behavior, and many mechanical principles can be accurately formulated from our observations that are useful for purposes of prediction. Thus Berkeley would leave science intact, but he would clarify its language so that nobody would think that science was giving us more knowledge than we can derive from the sensible world. And the sensible world shows us neither substance nor causality.

God and the Existence of Things

Since Berkeley did not deny the existence of things or their order in nature, it was necessary for him to explain how things external to our minds exist even when *we* don't perceive them and how they achieve their order. Thus, elaborating his general thesis that to be is to be perceived, Berkeley says that "when I deny sensible things an existence out of the mind, I do not mean my mind in particular, but all minds. Now it is plain they have an existence exterior to my mind, since I find them by experience to be independent of it. There is therefore some other mind wherein they exist, during the intervals between the time of my perceiving them." And because all human minds are intermittently diverted from things, "there is an *omnipresent eternal Mind,* which knows and comprehends all things, and exhibits them to our view in such a manner and according to such rules as he himself hath ordained, and are by us termed the *Laws of Nature."* The existence of things therefore depends on the existence of God, and God is the cause of the orderliness of things in nature.

Again, Berkeley did not want to deny, for example, that even if I left the room, the candle would still be there, and that when I returned after an interval of time, it would have burned down. But this meant for Berkeley only that experience has a certain regularity that makes it possible for us to predict what our future experiences will be. To say that candles burn even when *I* am not in the room still does not prove that material substance exists independently from a mind. It seemed a matter of common sense to Berkeley to say that we can know about the candle only because we actually experience a perception of it. In a similar way, we know that we exist because we have an awareness of our mental operations.

If, then, I try to describe or interpret reality in terms of my experience, I come first to the conclusion that there are other persons like myself who have minds. From this it can be assumed that since I have ideas, other persons likewise have ideas. Apart from my finite mind and the finite minds of others, there is a greater mind analogous to mine, and this is God's mind. God's ideas constitute the regular order of nature. The ideas that exist in men's minds are God's ideas, which He communicates to men so that the objects or things that we perceive in daily experience are caused not by *matter* or *substance,* but by God. It is God, too, who coordinates all experiences of finite minds, ensuring regularity and dependability in experience, which, in turn, enables us to think in terms of the "laws of nature." Thus the orderly arrangement of ideas in God's mind is communicated to the finite minds or spirits of human beings, allowance being made for the differences in competence between the Divine and finite minds. The ultimate reality, then, is spiritual, God, and not material, and the continued existence of objects when *we* are not perceiving them is explained by God's continuous perception of them.

To say, as Berkeley does, that men's ideas come from God implies a special interpretation of causation. Again, Berkeley did not deny that we have an insight into causation; he insisted only that our sense data do not disclose to us a unique causal power. We do not, for example, when considering how and why water freezes, discover any power in cold that forces water to become solid. We do, however, understand causal connections through our mental operations. We are, for example, aware of our volition: we can will to move our arm, or, what is more important here, we can produce imaginary ideas in our minds. Our power to produce such ideas suggests that perceived ideas are also caused by a mental power. But whereas imaginary ideas are produced by finite minds, perceived ideas are created and caused to be in us by an infinite mind.

Berkeley was confident that through his treatment of the formula *esse est percipi* he had effectively undermined the position of philosophical materialism and religious skepticism. Locke's empiricism inevitably implied skepticism insofar as he insisted that knowledge is based on sense experience and that substance, or the reality behind appearances, could never be known. Whether Berkeley's arguments for the reality of God and spiritual beings successfully refuted materialism and skepticism remains a question, for his arguments contained some of the flaws he held against the materialists. His influence was nevertheless significant, but it was his empiricism and not his idealism that had lasting influence. Building on Locke's empiricism, Berkeley made the decisive point that the human mind reasons only and always about particular sense experiences, that abstract ideas refer to no equivalent reality. Hume, who carried empiricism to its fullest expression, spoke of Berkeley as "a great philosopher [who] has disputed the received opinion in this particular, and has asserted that all general ideas are nothing but particular ones. . . . I look upon this to be one of the greatest and most valuable discoveries that has been made of late years in the republic of letters."

READING

NO SUCH THING AS MATTER
Berkeley

Hylas. You were represented in last night's conversation, as one who maintained the most extravagant opinion that ever entered into the mind of man, to wit, that there is no such thing as *material substance* in the world.

Philonous. That there is no such thing as what Philosophers call *material substance,* I am seriously persuaded: but, if I were made to see anything absurd or sceptical in this, I should then have the same reason to renounce this that I imagine I have now to reject the contrary opinion.

Hylas. What! can anything be more fantastical, more repugnant to common sense, or a more manifest piece of Scepticism, than to believe there is no such thing as *matter?*

Philonous. Softly, good Hylas. What if it should prove, that you, who hold there is, are, by virtue of that opinion, a greater sceptic, and maintain more paradoxes and repugnances to common sense, than I who believe no such thing?

Hylas. You may as soon persuade me, the part is greater than the whole, as that, in order to avoid absurdity and Scepticism, I should ever be obliged to give up my opinion in this point.

Philonous. Well then, are you content to admit that opinion for true, which, upon examination, shall appear most agreeable to common sense, and remote from Scepticism?

Hylas. With all my heart. Since you are for raising disputes about the plainest things in nature, I am content for once to hear what you have to say. . . .

Philonous. Make me to understand the differences between what is immediately perceived, and a sensation.

Hylas. The sensation I take to be an act of the mind perceiving; besides which, there is something perceived; and this I call the *object.* For example, there is red and yellow on that tulip. But then the act of perceiving those colours is in me only, and not in the tulip.

From George Berkeley, *Three Dialogues between Hylas and Philonous,* First Dialogue, 1713.

Philonous. What tulip do you speak of? Is it that which you see?

Hylas. The same.

Philonous. And what do you see beside colour, figure, and extension?

Hylas. I acknowledge, Philonous, that, upon a fair observation of what passes in my mind, I can discover nothing else but that I am a thinking being, affected with variety of sensations; neither is it possible to conceive how a sensation should exist in an unperceiving substance. But then, on the other hand, when I look on sensible things in a different view, considering them as so many modes and qualities, I find it necessary to suppose a material substratum, without which they cannot be conceived to exist.

Philonous. Material substratum call you it? Pray, by which of your senses came you acquainted with that being?

Hylas. It is not itself sensible; its modes and qualities only being perceived by the senses.

Philonous. I presume then it was by reflection and reason you obtained the idea of it?

Hylas. I do not pretend to any proper positive idea of it. However, I conclude it exists, because qualities cannot be conceived to exist without a support.

Philonous. It seems then you have only a relative notion of it, or that you conceive it not otherwise than by conceiving the relation it bears to sensible qualities?

Hylas. Right.

Philonous. Be pleased therefore to let me know wherein that relation consists.

Hylas. Is it not sufficiently expressed in the term *substratum* or *substance?*

Philonous. If so, the word *substratum* should import that it is spread under the sensible qualities or accidents?

Philonous. How say you, Hylas, can you see a thing which is at the same time unseen?

Hylas. No, that were a contradiction.

Philonous. Is it not as great a contradiction to talk of *conceiving* a thing which is unconceived?

Hylas. It is.

Philonous. The tree or house therefore which you think of is *conceived* by you?

Hylas. How should it be otherwise?

Philonous. And what is conceived is surely in the mind?

Hylas. Without question, that which is conceived is in the mind.

Philonous. How then came you to say, you conceived a house or tree existing independent and out of all minds whatsoever?

Hylas. That was I own an oversight; but stay, let me consider what led me into it.—It is a pleasant mistake enough. As I was thinking of a tree in a solitary place where no one was present to see it, methought that was to conceive a tree as existing unperceived or unthought of—not considering that I myself conceived it all the while. But now I plainly see that all I can do is to frame ideas in my own mind. I may indeed conceive in my own thoughts the idea of a tree, or a house, or a mountain, but that is all. And this is far from proving that I can conceive them *existing out of the minds of all Spirits*.

Philonous. You acknowledge then that you cannot possibly conceive how any one corporeal sensible thing should exist otherwise than in a mind?

Hylas. I do.

Philonous. And yet you will earnestly contend for the truth of that which you cannot so much as conceive?

Hylas. I profess I know not what to think; but still there are some scruples remain with me. Is it not certain I *see* things at a distance? Do we not perceive the stars and moon, for example, to be a great way off? Is not this, I say, manifest to the senses?

Philonous. Do you not in a dream too perceive those or the like objects?

Hylas. I do.

Philonous. And have they not then the same appearance of being distant?

Hylas. They have.

Philonous. But you do not thence conclude the apparitions in a dream to be without the mind?

Hylas. By no means.

Philonous. You ought not therefore to conclude that sensible objects are without the mind, from their appearance or manner wherein they are perceived.

Hylas. I acknowledge it. But doth not my sense deceive me in those cases?

Philonous. By no means. The idea or thing which you immediately perceive, neither sense nor reason informs you that it actually exists without the mind. By sense you only know that you are affected with such certain sensations of light and colours, &c. And these you will not say are without the mind.

Hylas. True: but, beside all that, do you not think the sight suggests something of *outness* or *distance*?

Philonous. Upon approaching a distant object, do the visible size and figure change perpetually, or do they appear the same at all distances?

Hylas. They are in a continual change.

Philonous. Sight therefore doth not suggest or any way inform you that the visible object you immediately perceive exists at a distance or will be perceived when you advance farther onward; there being a continued series of visible objects succeeding each other during the whole time of your approach.

Hylas. It doth not; but still I know, upon seeing an object, what object I shall perceive after having passed over a certain distance: no matter whether it be exactly the same or no: there is still something of distance suggested in the case.

Philonous. Good Hylas, do but reflect a little on the point, and then tell me whether there be any more in it than this:—From the ideas you actually perceive by sight, you have by experience learned to collect what other ideas you will (according to the standing order of nature) be affected with, after such a certain succession of time and motion.

Hylas. Upon the whole, I take it to be nothing else.

Philonous. Now, is it not plain that if we suppose a man born blind was on a sudden made to see, he could at first have no experience of what may be suggested by sight?

Hylas. It is.

Philonous. He would not then, according to you, have any notion of distance annexed to the things he saw; but would take them for a new set of sensations existing only in his mind?

Hylas. It is undeniable.

Philonous. But, to make it still more plain: is not *distance* a line turned endwise to the eye?

Hylas. It is.

Philonous. And can a line so situated be perceived by sight?

Hylas. It cannot.

Philonous. Doth it not therefore follow that distance is not properly and immediately perceived by sight?

Hylas. It should seem so.

Philonous. Again, is it your opinion that colours are at a distance?

Hylas. It must be acknowledged they are only in the mind.

Philonous. But do not colours appear to the eye as coexisting in the same place with extension and figures?

Hylas. They do.

Philonous. How can you then conclude from sight that figures exist without, when you acknowledge colours do not; the sensible appearance being the very same with regard to both?

Hylas. I know not what to answer.

Philonous. But, allowing that distance was truly and immediately perceived by the mind, yet it would not thence follow it existed out of the mind. For, whatever is immediately perceived is an idea: and can any idea *exist* out of the mind?

Hylas. To suppose that were absurd: but, inform me, Philonous, can we perceive or know nothing beside our ideas?

Philonous. As for the rational deducing of causes from effects, that is beside our inquiry. And, by the senses you can best tell whether you perceive anything which is not immediately perceived. And I ask you, whether the things immediately perceived are other than your own sensations or ideas? You have indeed more than once, in the course of this conversation, declared yourself on those points; but you seem, by this last question, to have departed from what you then thought.

Hylas. To speak the truth, Philonous, I think there are two kinds of objects—the one perceived immediately, which are likewise called *ideas;* the other are real things or external objects, perceived by the mediation of ideas, which are their images and representations. Now, I own ideas to not exist without the mind; but the latter sort of objects do. I am sorry I did not think of this distinction sooner; it would probably have cut short your discourse.

Philonous. Are those external objects perceived by sense, or by some other faculty?

Hylas. They are perceived by sense.

Philonous. How! is there anything perceived by sense which is not immediately perceived?

Hylas. Yes, Philonous, in some sort there is. For example, when I look on a picture or statue of Julius Caesar, I may be said after a manner to perceive him (though not immediately) by my senses.

Philonous. It seems then you will have our ideas, which alone are immediately perceived to be pictures of external things, and that these also are perceived by sense, inasmuch as they have a conformity or resemblance to our ideas?

Hylas. That is my meaning.

Philonous. And, in the same way that Julius Caesar, in himself invisible, is nevertheless perceived by sight; real things, in themselves imperceptible, are perceived by sense.

Hylas. In the very same.

Philonous. Tell me, Hylas, when you behold the picture of Julius Caesar, do you see with your eyes any more than some colours and figures, with a certain symmetry and composition of the whole?

Hylas. Nothing else.

Philonous. And would not a man who had never known anything of Julius Caesar see as much?

Hylas. He would.

Philonous. Consequently he hath his sight, and the use of it, in as perfect a degree as you?

Hylas. I agree with you.

Philonous. Whence comes it then that your thoughts are directed to the Roman emperor, and his are not? This cannot proceed from the sensations or ideas of sense by you then perceived; since you acknowledge you have no advantage over him in that respect. It should seem therefore to proceed from reason and memory: should it not?

Hylas. It should.

Philonous. Consequently, it will not follow from that instance that anything is perceived by sense which is not immediately perceived. Though I grant we may, in one acceptation, be said to perceive sensible things mediately by sense—that is, when, from a frequently perceived connexion, the immediate perception of ideas by one sense suggest to the mind others, perhaps belonging to another sense, which we wont to be connected with them. For instance, when I hear a coach drive along the streets, immediately I perceive only the sound; but, from the experience I have had that such a sound is connected with a coach, I am said to hear the coach. It is nevertheless evident that, in truth and strictness, nothing can be *heard* but *sound;* and the coach is not then properly perceived by sense, but suggested from experience. So likewise when we are said to see a red-hot bar of iron; the solidity and heat of the iron are not the objects of sight, but suggested to the imagination by the colour and figure which are properly perceived by that sense. In short, those things alone are actually and strictly perceived by any sense, which would have been perceived in case that same sense had then been first conferred on us. As for other things, it is plain they are only suggested to the mind by experience, grounded on former perceptions. But, to return to your comparison of Caesar's picture, it is plain, if you keep to that, you must hold the real things or archetypes of our ideas are not perceived by sense, but by some internal faculty of the soul, as reason or memory. I would therefore fain know what arguments you can draw from reason for the existence of what you call *real things* or *material objects.* Or, whether you remember to have seen them formerly as they are in themselves; or, if you have heard or read of any one that did.

Hylas. I see, Philonous, you are disposed to raillery; but that will never convince me.

Philonous. My aim is only to learn from you the way to come at the knowledge of *material beings.* Whatever we perceive is perceived immediately or mediately: by sense; or by reason and reflection. But, as you have excluded sense, pray show me what reason you have to believe their existence; or what *medium* you can possibly make use of to prove it, either to mine or your own understanding.

Hylas. To deal ingenuously, Philonous, now I consider the point, I do not find I can give you any good reason for it. But, thus much seems pretty plain, that it is at least possible such things may really exist. And, as long as there is no absurdity in supposing them, I am resolved to believe as I did, till you bring good reasons to the contrary.

*Philonous.*What! is it come to this, that you only believe the existence of material objects, and that your belief is founded barely on the possibility of its being true? Then you will have me bring reasons against it: though another would think it reasonable the proof should lie on him who holds the affirmative. And, after all, this very point which you are now resolved to maintain, without any reason, is in effect what you have more than once during this discourse seen good reason to give up. But, to pass over all this;

if I understand you rightly, you say our ideas do not exist without the mind; but that they are copies, images, or representatives, of certain originals that do?

Hylas. You take me right.

Philonous. They are then like external things?

Hylas. They are.

Philonous. Have those things a stable and permanent nature, independent of our senses; or are they in a perpetual change, upon our producing any motions in our bodies, suspending, exerting, or altering, our faculties or organs of sense?

Hylas. Real things, it is plain, have a fixed and real nature, which remains the same notwithstanding any change in our sense, or in the posture and motion of our bodies; which indeed may affect the ideas in our minds, but it were absurd to think they had the same effect on things existing without the mind.

Philonous. How then is it possible that things perpetually fleeting and variable as our ideas should be copies or images of anything fixed and constant? Or, in other words, since all sensible qualities, as size, figure, colour, &c., that is, our ideas, are continually changing upon every alteration in the distance, medium, or instruments of sensation; how can any determinate material objects be properly represented or painted forth by several distinct things, each of which is so different from and unlike the rest? Or, if you say it resembles some one only of our ideas, how shall we be able to distinguish the true copy from all the false ones?

Hylas. I profess, Philonous, I am at a loss. I know not what to say to this.

Philonous. But neither is this all. Which are material objects in themselves—perceptible or imperceptible?

Hylas. Properly and immediately nothing can be perceived but ideas. All material things, therefore, are in themselves insensible, and to be perceived only by our ideas.

Philonous. Ideas then are sensible, and their archetypes or originals insensible?

Hylas. Right.

Philonous. But how can that which is sensible be like that which is insensible? Can a real thing, in itself *invisible,* be like a *colour;* or a real thing, which is not *audible,* be like a *sound?* In a word, can anything be like a sensation or idea, but another sensation or idea?

Hylas. I must own, I think not.

Philonous. Is it possible there should be any doubt on the point? Do you not perfectly know your own ideas?

Hylas. I know them perfectly; since what I do not perceive or know can be no part of my idea.

Philonous. Consider, therefore, and examine them, and then tell me if there be anything in them which can exist without the mind? or if you can conceive anything like them existing without the mind?

Hylas. Upon inquiry, I find it is impossible for me to conceive or understand how anything but an idea can be like an idea. And it is most evident that *no idea can exist without the mind.*

Philonous. You are therefore, by our principles, forced to deny the reality of sensible things; since you made it to consist in an absolute existence exterior to the mind. That is to say, you are a downright sceptic. So I have gained my point, which was to show your principles led to Scepticism.

Hylas. For the present I am, if not entirely convinced, at least silenced.

CHAPTER 30

DIALECTICAL MATERIALISM

Marx

Karl Marx once said that "the philosophers have only *interpreted* the world differently: the point is, however, to *change* it." That Karl Marx helped to change the modern world is one of the striking facts of our time. Throughout Marx's intellectual development, the subject of metaphysics played a significant role. At the University of Berlin, he encountered the philosophy of Hegel. At the University of Jena, Marx wrote a doctoral dissertation at the age of twenty-three entitled "On the Difference between the Democritean and Epicurean Philosophies of Nature." In the end, Marx rejected the idealism of Hegel in favor of his own new conception of *materialism,* to which he added a version of the dynamic element of Hegel's *dialectic.*

When Karl Marx was at the University of Berlin, the dominant intellectual influence was the philosophy of Hegel, and accordingly, Marx was for the time being deeply impressed by Hegel's idealism and his dynamic view of history. He became a member of a group of young radical Hegelians who saw in Hegel's approach to philosophy the key to a new understanding of man, the world, and history. Hegel had centered his thought around the notion of *Spirit* or *Mind.*

To Hegel, Absolute Spirit or Mind is God. God is the whole of reality. God is identical with all of Nature, and therefore God is found also in the configurations of culture and civilization. History consists in the gradual self-realization of God in the sequence of time. What makes Nature knowable is that its essence is Mind, and what produces history is the continuous struggle of Mind or Spirit or Idea to realize itself in perfect form. Thus God and the world are one. The basic reality is therefore Spirit or Mind. For this reason, Hegel had concluded that the rational basis of reality, the Idea, is in a continuous process of unfolding from lower to higher degrees of perfection, and this is the process we know as history. History is a dialectic process moving in a triadic pattern from *thesis* to *antithesis* and finally to *synthesis.*

Whether Marx ever accepted Hegel's idealism in all its fullness is not certain, but what did strike him with force was Hegel's method of identifying God and Nature. Hegel had said that "Spirit [God] is alone reality. It is the inner being of the world, that which essentially is and is *per se.*" Whatever there is, and whatever there is to know, exists as the world of Nature; besides the world and its history there is nothing. This rejection of the older theology, which had separated God and the world, is what struck Marx as being novel and significant.

Although Hegel had not intended his views to destroy the foundations of religion, the radical young band of Hegelians at the University of Berlin undertook a "higher criticism" of the Gospels. David Strauss wrote a critical *Life of Jesus* in which he argued that much of Jesus's teaching was a purely mythical invention, particularly those portions which referred to another world. Bruno Bauer went even further by denying the historical existence of Jesus. Using the Hegelian method of identifying God and the world, these radical writers shattered the literal interpretation of the language of the Gospels and considered its only value to lie in its pictorial power, not in its truth. The inevitable drift of Hegelianism was to identify God with man, since man, among all things in Nature, embodies the element of Spirit or Mind in a unique way. It was then only another step, which Hegel had not taken, but which the young radicals, among them Marx, did take, to the position of philosophical theism.

What began to take shape in Marx's mind from his exposure to Hegelianism was (1) the notion that there is only one reality and that this can be discovered as the embodiment of rationality in the world, (2) the recognition that history is a process of development and change from less to more perfect forms in all of reality, including physical nature, social and political life, and human thought, and (3) the assumption that the thoughts and behavior of men at any given time and place are caused by the operation in them of an identical spirit or mind, the spirit of the particular time or epoch. Although these were the general themes which Hegelianism seemed to be engendering in Marx's mind, other influences moved into his thought, causing him to reject portions of Hegel's philosophy and to reinterpret these three themes of Hegelianism accordingly. In particular, the appearance of Ludwig Feuerbach's writings, shortly after Marx had finished his doctoral dissertation, had a decisive effect on the young radical Hegelians and especially on Marx.

Marx now acknowledged that Feuerbach was the pivotal figure in philosophy. Most important of all, Feuerbach had shifted from God to man the focal point of historic development. That is, whereas Hegelian thought said that it was Spirit or Idea that was progressively realizing itself in history, Feuerbach said that it is really man who is struggling to realize himself. Man, and not God, was in some way alienated from himself, and history has to do with man's struggle to overcome his self-alienation. Clearly, if this was in fact the condition of man, Marx thought, the world should be changed in order to facilitate man's self-realization. This is what led Marx to say that hitherto "the philosophers have only *interpreted* the world differently: the point is, however, to *change* it." Marx had grounded his thought in two major insights, Hegel's dialectical view of history and Feuerbach's emphasis on the primacy of the material order. Now he was ready to embark on a program of forging these ideas into a full-scale instrument of social analysis and, most important of all, to undertake a vigorous and practical program of action.

The political party which grew out of Marx's philosophy is devoted to a program of action. Nevertheless, discussions about metaphysics play an important role in the party's literature. This materialistic conception of nature provides a strong basis for action. The following selected reading indicates that Marxism does not reject metaphysics but rather replaces idealism with a metaphysics of materialism.

READING

MATERIALISM AND THE CAUSE OF CHANGE

Marxism

Dialectical materialism is the world outlook of the Marxist-Leninist party. It is called dialectical materialism because its approach to the phenomena of nature, its method of studying and apprehending them, is *dialectical,* while its interpretation of the phenomena of nature, its conception of these phenomena, its theory, is *materialistic.*

Historical materialism is the extension of the principles of dialectical materialism to the study of social life, an application of the principles of dialectical materialism to the phenomena of the life of society, to the study of society and of its history.

When describing their dialectical method, Marx and Engels usually refer to Hegel as the philosopher who formulated the main features of dialectics. This, however, does not mean that the dialectics of Marx and Engels is identical with the dialectics of Hegel. As a matter of fact, Marx and Engels took from the Hegelian dialectics only its "rational kernel," casting aside its idealistic shell, and developed it further so as to lend it a modern scientific form.

"My dialectic method," says Marx, "is not only different from the Hegelian, but is its direct opposite. To Hegel, the life-process of the human brain, i.e., the process of thinking, which under the name of 'the Idea,' he even transforms into an independent subject, is the demiurgos of the real world, and the real world is only the external, phenomenal form of 'the Idea.' With me, on the contrary, the ideal is nothing else than the material world reflected by the human mind, and translated into forms of thought" (Karl Marx, *Capital,* Vol. 1, p. 19, Foreign Languages Publishing House, Moscow, 1961). . . .

Dialectics comes from the Greek *dialego,* to discourse, to debate. In ancient times dialectics was the art of arriving at the truth by disclosing the contradictions in the argument of an opponent and overcoming these contradictions. There were philosophers in ancient times who believed that the

From "Dialectical and Historical Materialism," in *History of the Communist Party of the Soviet Union,* Commission of the Central Committee of the C.P.S.U., Moscow, 1939.

disclosure of contradictions in thought and the clash of opposite opinions was the best method of arriving at the truth. This dialectical method of thought, later extended to the phenomena of nature, developed into the dialectical method of apprehending nature, which regards the phenomena of nature as being in constant movement and undergoing constant change, and the development of nature as the result of the development of the contradictions in nature, as the result of the interaction of opposed forces in nature.

In its essence, dialectics is the direct opposite of metaphysics.

1) The principal features of the Marxist *dialectical method* are as follows:

a) Contrary to metaphysics, dialectics does not regard nature as an accidental agglomeration of things, of phenomena, unconnected with, isolated from, and independent of, each other, but as a connected and integral whole, in which things, phenomena are organically connected with, dependent on, and determined by, each other. . . .

b) Contrary to metaphysics, dialectics holds that nature is not a state of rest and immobility, stagnation and immutability, but a state of continuous movement and change, of continuous renewal and development, where something is always arising and developing, and something always disintegrating and dying away. . . .

The dialectical method regards as important primarily not that which at the given moment seems to be durable and yet is already beginning to die away, but that which is arising and developing, even though at the given moment it may appear to be not durable, for the dialectical method considers invincible only that which is arising and developing. . . .

c) Contrary to metaphysics, dialectics does not regard the process of development as a simple process of growth, where quantitative changes do not lead to qualitative changes, but as a development which passes from insignificant and imperceptible quantitative changes to open, fundamental changes, to qualitative changes; a development in which the qualitative changes occur not gradually, but rapidly and abruptly, taking the form of a leap from one state to another; they occur not accidentally but as the natural result of an accumulation of imperceptible and gradual quantitative changes. . . .

Describing dialectical development as a transition from quantitative changes to qualitative changes, Engels says:

"In physics . . . every change is a passing of quantity into quality, as a result of a quantitative change of some form of movement either inherent in a body or imparted to it. For example, the temperature of water has at first no effect on its liquid state; but as the temperature of liquid water rises or falls, a moment arrives when this state of cohesion changes and the water is converted in one case into steam and in the other into ice" (*Dialectics of Nature*). . . .

d) Contrary to metaphysics, dialectics holds that internal contradictions are inherent in all things and phenomena of nature, for they all have their negative and positive sides, a past and a future, something dying away and something developing; and that the struggle between these opposites, the struggle between the old and the new, between that which is dying away and that which is being born, between that which is disappearing and that which is developing, constitutes the internal content of the process of development, the internal content of the transformation of quantitative changes into qualitative changes.

The dialectical method therefore holds that the process of development from the lower to the higher takes place not as a harmonious unfolding of phenomena, but as a disclosure of the contradictions inherent in things and phenomena, as a "struggle" of opposite tendencies which operate on the basis of these contradictions.

"In its proper meaning," Lenin says, "dialectics is the study of the contradiction *within the very essence of things*" (Lenin, *Philosophical Notebooks,* Russ. ed., p. 263). . . .

As to Marxist philosophical materialism, it is fundamentally the direct opposite of philosophical idealism.

2) The principal features of Marxist philosophical *materialism* are as follows:

a) Contrary to idealism, which regards the world as the embodiment of an "absolute idea," a "universal spirit," "consciousness," Marx's philosophical materialism holds that the world is by its very nature *material,* that the multifold phenomena of the world constitute different forms of matter in motion, that interconnection and interdependence of phenomena, as established by the dialectical method, are a law of the development of moving matter, and that the world develops in accordance with the laws of movement of matter and stands in no need of a "universal spirit." . . .

b) Contrary to idealism, which asserts that only our mind really exists, and that the material world, being, nature, exists only in our mind, in our sensations, ideas and perceptions, the Marxist materialist philosophy holds that matter, nature, being, is an objective reality existing outside and independent of our mind; that matter is primary, since it is the source of sensations, ideas, mind, and that mind is secondary, derivative, since it is a reflection of matter, a reflection of being; that thought is a product of matter which in its development has reached a high degree of perfection, namely, of the brain, and the brain is the organ of thought; and that therefore one cannot separate thought from matter without committing a grave error. Engels says:

"The question of the relation of thinking to being, the relation of spirit to nature is the paramount question of the whole of philosophy. . . . The answers which the philosophers gave to this question split them into two great camps. Those who asserted the primacy of spirit to nature . . . comprised the camp of *idealism*. The others, who regarded nature as primary, belong to the various schools of materialism" (Karl Marx, *Selected Works,* Eng. ed., Vol. I, pp. 430–431).

And further:

"The material, sensuously perceptible world to which we ourselves belong is the only reality. . . . Our consciousness and thinking, however supra-sensuous they may seem, are the product of a material, bodily organ, the brain. Matter is not a product of mind, but mind itself is merely the highest product of matter" (*Ibid.,* p. 435). . . .

c) Contrary to idealism, which denies the possibility of knowing the world and its laws, which does not believe in the authenticity of our knowledge, does not recognize objective truth, and holds that the world is full of "things-in-themselves" that can never be known to science, Marxist philosophical materialism holds that the world and its laws are fully knowable, that our knowledge of the laws of nature, tested by experiment and practice, is authentic knowledge having the validity of objective truth, and that there are no things in the world which are unknowable, but only things which are still not known, but which will be disclosed and made known by the efforts of science and practice.

CHAPTER 31

NATURE, SCIENCE, AND POETRY

Bergson, Russell, and Whitehead

Henri Bergson was born in Paris in 1859 of a Polish father and English mother. His brilliance was recognized early, and he was made professor of philosophy at Angers Lycée at the age of twenty-two. By 1900 he was Distinguished Professor of Modern Philosophy at the College de France. His writings earned him a worldwide reputation for their lucidity and style. Among his books are *An Introduction to Metaphysics* (1903), *Creative Evolution* (1907), and *Two Sources of Morality and Religion* (1932). His brilliant lectures attracted people from many countries to hear him in Paris, where he lived until his death in 1941 at the age of eighty-two.

Analysis versus Intuition

At the center of Bergson's philosophy is his conviction that there are "two profoundly different ways of knowing a thing." The first way, he says, "implies that we move around the object," and the

553

Bergson (*New York Public Library Picture Collection*)

second, that "we enter into it." Knowledge derived in the first way depends on the vantage point from which we observe an object, and therefore this mode of knowledge will be different for each observer and on that account *relative*. Moreover, knowledge derived by observation is expressed in symbols, where the symbol used can refer not only to this specific object but also to any and all similar objects. The second kind of knowledge, however, is *absolute*, says Bergson, because in this case, by "entering" the object we overcome the limitations of any particular perspective and grasp the object as it really is.

554

Bergson illustrates these two modes of knowing with several examples. First, there is the example of the movement of an object in space. My observation of this object, he says, will vary with the point of view, moving or stationary, from which I observe it. When I try to describe this motion, my expression of it will vary with the points of reference to which I relate it. Both in observing and describing the moving object, I am placed outside of it. In describing the object's motion, I think of a line that is divided into units and express this through the symbol of a graph with a series of points through which the object is thought to move. By contrast to this attempt to plot and chart movement in terms of discrete units of space, there is, says Bergson, the true movement, a continuous flow, where there are in reality no points being crossed.

Suppose, says Bergson, that you were inside the object as it moved. You would then know the object as it really is and moves and not only as translated into the symbolic language of points and units of distances, for "what I experience will depend neither on the point of view I may take up in regard to the object, since I am inside the object itself, nor on the symbols by which I may translate the motion, since I have rejected all translations in order to possess the original." Instead of trying to grasp the movement from where I stand, from my static position, I must try to grasp the object's motion from where *it* is, from within, since the motion is in the object itself.

When a person raises his arm, he has a simple and single perception of the movement he has created; he has an "absolute" knowledge of this movement. But, says Bergson, for me,

> watching it from the outside, your arm passes through one point, then through another, and between these points there will be still other points. . . . Viewed from the inside, then, an absolute is a simple thing; but looked at from the outside, that is to say, relatively to other things, it becomes, in relation to these signs which express it, the gold coin for which we never seem able to finish giving small change.

The case is the same when we take a character in a novel. The author takes great pains to describe his traits and to make him engage in action and dialogue. But, says Bergson, "all this can never be equivalent to the simple and indivisible feeling which I should experience if I were able for an instant to identify myself with the person of the hero himself." The reason why descriptive traits do not help me know this particular hero is that such traits are merely symbols, "which can make him known to me only by so many comparisons with persons or things I know already." Such symbols take me outside of him, and "they give me only what he has in common with others and not what belong to him alone." It is not possible, says Bergson, to perceive what constitutes a person's "essence" from without, because by definition his essence is internal and therefore cannot be expressed by symbols. Description and analysis require the use of symbols, but symbols are always "imperfect in comparison with the object of which a view has been taken, or which the symbols seek to express." Not all the photographs of Paris, taken from every conceivable point of view, and not even motion pictures, would ever be equivalent to the real Paris in which we live and move. Not all the translations of a poem could render the inner meaning of the original. In every example, there is the original, which we can know absolutely only by entering into it, compared with the "translation" or copy, which we know only relatively depending on our vantage point and the symbols we use for expression.

What, more precisely, does it mean to "go around" an object and to "enter into it?" To go around an object is what Bergson means by that special activity of the intellect that he calls "analysis." By contrast, to enter into an object is what is implied by his use of the term "intuition." By intuition, Bergson means "the kind of *intellectual sympathy* by which one places oneself within an object in order to coincide with what is unique in it and consequently inexpressible." The basic contrast between science and metaphysics turns on the difference between analysis and intuition.

Bergson contended that in the end scientific reasoning, insofar as it is based on analysis, falsifies the nature of whatever object it analyzes. This follows, he said, from the fact that "analysis . . . is the operation which reduces the object to elements already known, that is, to elements common both to it and other objects." Therefore, "to analyze . . . is to express a thing as a function of something other than itself." To analyze a rose is to take it apart and discover its constituents. From such an analysis we do in fact derive knowledge of the rose, but in such a state of analysis, the rose is no longer the living thing it was in the garden. Similarly, the science of medicine discovers much knowledge of human anatomy by dissecting a body.

In every case, says Bergson, the analytic intellect learns, iron-ically, by destroying the object's essence. Its essence is its dynamic, thriving, pulsing, living, continuing existence—its *duration.* Anal-ysis, however, interrupts this essential duration; it *stops* life and movement; it separates into several independent and static parts what in true life is a unified, organic, and dynamic reality.

The language of analytic science tends, moreover, to exagger-ate even further this static and disjointed conception of things through its use of symbols. Each new object is described by science by using as many symbols as there are ways of looking at a thing. The content of each such perception is, says Bergson, *abstracted,* that is, drawn or lifted out from the object. Thus the intellect forms a series of concepts about a thing, "cutting out of reality according to the lines that must be followed in order to act conveniently upon it." Since we think in terms of our language, that is, in terms of single concepts, we tend to analyze things into as many concepts as there are ways of looking at, moving around, an object. This is, says Bergson, the ordinary function of scientific analysis, namely, to work with symbols. Even the sciences concerned with life "confine themselves to the visible form of living beings, their organs and ana-tomical elements. They make comparisons between these forms, they reduce the more complex to the more simple; in short, they study the workings of life in what is, so to speak, only its visual symbol."

There seems to be, says Bergson, a "symmetry, concord and agreement" between our intellect and matter, as though our intel-lects were made to analyze and utilize matter. Indeed, he says, "our intelligence is the prolongation of our senses"; even before there was either science or philosophy, "the role of intelligence was already that of manufacturing instruments and guiding the action of our body on surrounding bodies." If, then, the intellect has been made to utilize matter, "its structure has no doubt been modelled upon that of matter." But it is precisely for this reason that the intellect has a limited function; its very structure and function fit it for analysis, for separating what is unified into its parts. Even when it comes to the study of the most concrete reality, namely, the *self,* the intellect, proceeding analytically, is never capable of discover-ing the true self. As all other sciences, psychology analyzes the self into separate "states," such as sensations, feelings, and ideas, which it studies separately. To study the self by studying separately the various psychical states is, says Bergson, like trying to know Paris by studying various sketches, all of which are labeled "Paris." The psychologists claim to find the "ego" in the various psychical states, not realizing that "this diversity of states has itself only been obtained . . . by transporting oneself outside the ego altogether. . . . " And "however much they place the states side by side, multiplying points of contact and exploring the intervals, the ego always escapes them. . . . "

But there is another way, says Bergson, of knowing the self, and that is by intuition. As he says, "there is one reality, at least, which we all seize from within, by intuition and not by simple analysis. It is our own personality through time—our self which endures." Like Descartes, Bergson founded his philosophy on the immediate knowledge of the self. But whereas Descartes built a system of rationalism on his self-knowledge, Bergson set forth the method of intuition, which was in sharp contrast to rationalism. Intuition, Bergson argued, is a kind of intellectual sympathy. It enables one's consciousness to become identified with an object; intuition "signifies . . . immediate consciousness, a vision which is scarcely distinguishable from the object seen, a knowledge which is contact or even coincidence." Most important of all, says Bergson, "to think intuitively is to think in duration." This is the difference between analytic and intuitive thought. Analysis begins with the static and reconstructs movement as best it can. By contrast, "intuition starts from movement, posits it, or rather perceives it as reality itself, and sees in immobility only an abstract movement, a snapshot taken by our mind. . . . " Ordinarily, analytic thought pictures the new as a new arrangement of what already exists; although nothing is ever lost, neither is anything ever created. But "intuition, bound up to a duration which is growth, perceives in it an uninterrupted continuity of unforeseeable novelty; it sees, it knows that the mind draws from itself more than it has, that spirituality consists in just that, and that reality, impregnated with spirit, is creation." Intuition, then, discovers that the self, our life, is a *duration*, a continuous flux.

The inner life of the self is compared by Bergson to a continual rolling up, "like that of a thread on a ball, for our past follows us, it swells incessantly with the present that it picks up on its way; and consciousness means memory." An even better way of thinking about the self, he says, is to imagine an infinitely small elastic body, which is gradually drawn out in such a manner that from that original body comes a constantly lengthening line. While even this image is not satisfactory to him, Bergson does see in it an analogy to human personality in that the drawing out of the elastic body is a continuous action representing the duration of the ego, the pure mobility of the self. But whatever images are used to describe it, "the inner life is all this at once: variety of qualities, continuity of progress, and unity of direction. It cannot be represented by images." And again: "No image can replace the intuition of duration."

Bergson centered his attention on the process in all things that he called "duration." His criticism of classical schools of philosophy was that they failed to take duration, or becoming, seriously. For the most part, philosophers such as Plato, Descartes, and Kant sought to interpret the world through fixed structures of thought. This was particularly the case with Plato, whose notion of the Forms provides us with a static structure of reality. Even the empiricists, in spite of their preoccupation with experience, analyzed experience into static components, as in the case of Hume, who described knowledge in terms of individual "impressions." Neither the rationalists nor the empiricists, Bergson charged, took the matter of mobility, development, becoming, and duration seriously. Just how this metaphysical notion of duration could be employed in scientific knowledge Bergson did not make entirely clear. But he was certain that to "think in duration" is to have a true grasp of reality. Such thought also gives us a more accurate notion of *time,* real, continuous time, as compared with the "spatialized" time created by the intellect.

Only when we think of time and motion in such "spatialized" terms do we encounter the celebrated paradoxes of Zeno (b. ca. 489 B.C.). Zeno said that a flying arrow really does not move, because at each instant the arrow occupies a single point in space, which would mean that at each instant the arrow is at rest; otherwise it would not occupy a given space at a given instant of time. Zeno's argument would be unassailable, says Bergson, if his assumption about space and time were correct. But he argues that Zeno was in error in assuming that there are real positions in space and discrete units of time: These so-called positions are, says Bergson, merely *suppositions* of the intellect, and the units of time are only the artificial segments into which the analytic intellect slices what in reality is a continuous flow. What Zeno's paradoxes show us is that it is impossible to construct mobility out of static positions or true time out of instants. Although the intellect is capable of comprehending static segments, it is incapable of grasping movement or duration. Only intuition can grasp duration. And reality is duration. Reality, says Bergson, does not consist of *things*, but only of "things in the making, not self-maintaining *states*, but only changing states. . . ." Rest is only apparent, for all reality "is tendency, if we agree to mean by tendency an incipient change of direction."

"Elan Vital"

Is not the doctrine of evolution an example of how science can successfully understand duration and becoming? After examining the major conceptions of evolution, Bergson concludes that none of these scientific theories is adequate, and therefore he offers a theory of his own. The particular inadequacy he found in the other theories was their inability to give a convincing account of how the transition is made through the gap that separates one level (animal) from a higher level (human). Charles Darwin (1809–1882) referred to variations among members of a species, but he did not explain how such variations in a species could occur; he inferred that either slowly or suddenly a change occurs, presumably in some part of the organism. This overlooks the functional unity of an organism, which requires that any variation in one part must be accompanied by variations throughout the whole organism. Darwin did not explain how this can occur, leaving unanswered the question of how there can be a continuity of function despite successive changes of form. Another theory attributed evolution to the special "effort" employed by certain organisms, causing them to develop capacities favorable to survival. But can such acquired characteristics be transmitted from one generation to the next? Bergson insisted that although "effort" had some promising implications, it was too haphazard a notion to explain the overall process of development.

Evolution, said Bergson, is best explained in terms of a vital impulse, the *élan vital*, which drives all organisms toward constantly more complicated and higher modes of organization. The élan vital is the essential interior element of all living beings—and is the creative power that moves in unbroken continuity through all things. Since the intellect can grasp only static things, it is not capable of grasping the élan vital, since this is the essence of duration, of movement, and "all change, all movement, [is] . . . absolutely indivisible." Knowing, for Bergson, is a secondary activity; more basic and therefore primary is living. Intuition and consciousness, not analytic intellect, grasp this primary life and discover it to be a continuous and undivided process of which all things are expressions and not parts. All things are motivated by this élan vital; the élan vital is the fundamental reality. We discover it first through the immediate awareness of our own continuous self: We discover that we *endure.*

Here finally is where intuition must challenge intellect, for intellect by its natural function transforms, and thereby falsifies, movement into static states. The truth that intuition discovers about reality is that it is continuous, that it cannot be reduced to parts, and that the creative process caused by the élan vital is irreversible. "To get a notion of this irreducibility and irreversibility," says Bergson, "we must do violence to the mind, go counter to the natural bent of the intellect. But that is just the function of philosophy."

Whereas the intellect would describe evolution as a single steady line moving upward through measurable levels, intuition suggests divergent tendencies at work. The vital impulse, says Bergson, moved in three discernible directions, producing vegetative beings, anthropoids, and vertebrates, including finally man. Distinguishing intellect and intuition, he says that the emergence of intellect and matter occurred together, and these were intended to work together: "our intellect, in the narrow sense of the word, is intended to secure the perfect fitting of our body to its environment, to represent the relations of external things among themselves—in short, to think matter." Moreover, "matter is weighted with geometry." But neither matter nor geometrical figures represent ultimate reality. The élan vital must itself resemble consciousness, from whence emerges life and all its creative possibilities. Evolution is creative precisely because the future is open—there is no preordained "final" goal; duration constantly endures, producing always genuinely novel events like an artist who never knows precisely what he will create until he has created his work. Bergson finally refers to the creative effort of the élan vital as being "of God, if it is not God himself."

Russell

Bertrand Russell was born in England in 1872 and died in 1970 at the age of ninety-eight. He was left an orphan at age three and was raised by his grandmother, who arranged to have him educated at home by tutors and governesses. At age eighteen he became an undergraduate at Trinity College at Cambridge University, where he earned a first-class degree with distinction. He became an attaché at the British embassy in Paris, was later a lecturer at Trinity College, and ultimately became a world-renowned figure famous for his brilliant books, his unconventional moral and political views, and his difficulties with all institutional authorities. Among his writings is the book *Principia Mathematica,* which he coauthored with Alfred North Whitehead in 1910–1913. His book *Introduction to Mathematical Philosophy* was written in prison. Although he suffered for his views on conscientious objection, pacifism, agnosticism, and marriage and morals, he received many honors for his vast literary achievements, including the Order of Merit in 1949 and the Nobel Prize in 1950.

READING

UNDERSTANDING THE COSMOS

Russell

The view to which I have been gradually led is one which has been almost universally misunderstood and which, for this reason, I will try to state as simply and clearly as I possibly can. I am, for the present, only endeavouring to state the view, not to give the reasons which have led me to it. I will,

From Bertrand Russell, *My Philosophical Development,* chap. 2, "My Present View of the World," George Allen & Unwin Ltd, London, 1959.

however, say this much by way of preface: it is a view which results from a synthesis of four different sciences—namely, physics, physiology, psychology and mathematical logic. Mathematical logic is used in creating structures having assigned properties out of elements that have much less mathematical smoothness. I reverse the process which has been common in philosophy since Kant. It has been common among philosophers to begin with how we know and proceed afterwards to what we know. I think this a mistake. Because knowing how we know is one small department of knowing what we know. I think it a mistake for another reason: it tends to give to knowing a cosmic importance which it by no means deserves, and thus prepares the philosophical student for the belief that mind has some kind of supremacy over the non-mental universe, or even that the non-mental universe is nothing but a nightmare dreamt by mind in its un-philosophical moments. This point of view is completely remote from my imaginative picture of the cosmos. I accept without qualification the view that results from astronomy and geology, from which it would appear that there is no evidence of anything mental except in a tiny fragment of space-time, and that the great processes of nebular and stellar evolution proceed according to laws in which mind plays no part.

If this initial bias is accepted, it is obviously to theoretical physics that we must first look for an understanding of the major processes in the history of the universe. Unfortunately, theoretical physics no longer speaks with that splendid dogmatic clarity that it enjoyed in the seventeenth century. Newton works with four fundamental concepts: space, time, matter and force. All four have been swept into limbo by modern physicists. Space and time, for Newton, were solid, independent things. They have been replaced by space-time, which is not substantial but only a system of relations. Matter has had to be replaced by series of events. Force, which was the first of the Newtonian concepts to be abandoned, has been replaced by energy; and energy turns out to be indistinguishable from the pale ghost which is all that remains of matter. Cause, which was the philosophical form of what physicists called force, has also become decrepit. I will not admit that it is dead, but it has nothing like the vigour of its earlier days.

For all these reasons, what modern physics has to say is somewhat confused. Nevertheless, we are bound to believe it on pain of death. If there were any community which rejected the doctrines of modern physics, physicists employed by a hostile government would have no difficulty in exterminating it. The modern physicist, therefore, enjoys powers far exceeding those of the Inquisition in its palmiest days, and it certainly behoves us to treat his pronouncements with due awe. For my part, I have no doubt that, although progressive changes are to be expected in physics, the present doctrines are likely to be nearer to the truth than any rival doctrines now before the world. Science is at no moment quite right, but it is seldom quite wrong, and has, as a rule, a better chance of being right than the theories of the unscientific. It is, therefore, rational to accept it hypothetically.

It is not always realized how exceedingly abstract is the information that theoretical physics has to give. It lays down certain fundamental equations which enable it to deal with the logical structure of events, while leaving it completely unknown what is the intrinsic character of the events when they happen to us. Nothing whatever in theoretical physics enables us to say anything about the intrinsic character of events elsewhere. They may be just like the events that happen to us, or they may be totally different in strictly unimaginable ways. All that physics gives us is certain equations giving abstract properties of their changes. But as to what it is that changes, and what it changes from and to—as to this, physics is silent.

The next step is an approximation to perception, but without passing beyond the realm of physics. A photographic plate exposed to a portion of the night sky takes photographs of separate stars. Given similar photographic plates and atmospheric conditions, different photographs of the same portion of the sky will be closely similar. There must, therefore, be some influence (I am using the vaguest word that I can think of) proceeding from the various stars to the various photographic plates. Physicists used to think that this influence consisted of waves, but now they think that it consists of little bundles of energy called photons. They know how fast a photon travels and in what manner it will, on occasion, deviate from a rectilinear path. When it hits a photographic plate, it is transformed into energy of a different kind. Since each separate star gets itself photographed, and since it can be photographed anywhere on a clear night where there is an unimpeded view of the sky, there must be something happening, at each place where it can be photographed, that is specially connected with it. It follows that the atmosphere at night contains everywhere as many separable events as there are stars that can be photographed there, and each of these separable events must have some kind of individual history connecting it with the star from which it has come. All this follows from the consideration of different photographic plates exposed to the same night sky.

Or let us take another illustration. Let us imagine a rich cynic, disgusted by the philistinism of theatregoers, deciding to have a play performed, not before live people, but before a collection of cine-cameras. The cine-cameras—supposing them all of equal excellence—will produce closely similar records, differing according to the laws of perspective and according to their distance from the stage. This again shows, like the photographic plate, that at each cine-camera a complex of events is occurring at each moment which is closely related to the complex of events occurring on the stage. There is here the same need as before of separable influences proceeding from diverse sources. If, at a given moment, one actor shouts, "Die, Varlet!" while another exclaims, "Help! Murder!" both will be recorded, and therefore something connected with both must be happening at each cine-camera.

To take yet another illustration: suppose that a speech is recorded simultaneously by a number of gramophones, the gramophone records do not in any obvious way resemble the original speech, and yet, by a suitable mechanism, they can be made to reproduce something exceedingly like it. They must, therefore, have something in common with the speech. But what they have in common can only be expressed in rather abstract language concerning structure. Broadcasting affords an even better illustration of the same process. What intervenes between an orator and a man listening to him on the radio is not, on the face of it, at all similar either to what the orator says or to what the listener hears. Here, again, we have a causal chain in which the beginning resembles the end, but the intermediate terms, so far as intrinsic qualities are concerned, appear to be of quite a different kind. What is preserved throughout the causal chain, in this case as in that of the gramophone record, is a certain constancy of structure.

These various processes all belong purely to physics. We do not suppose that the cine-cameras have minds, and we should not suppose so even if, by a little ingenuity on the part of their maker, those in the stalls were made to sneer at the moments when those in the pit applauded. What these physical analogies to perception show is that in most places at most times, if not in all places at all times, a vast assemblage of overlapping events is taking place, and that many of these events, at a given place and time, are connected by causal chains with an original event which, by a sort of prolific heredity, has produced offspring more or less similar to itself in a vast number of different places.

What sort of picture of the universe do these considerations invite us to construct? I think the answer must proceed by stages differing as to the degree of analysis that has been effected. For present purposes I shall content myself by treating as fundamental the notion of "event." I conceive each event as occupying a finite amount of space-time and as overlapping with innumerable other events which occupy partially, but not wholly, the same region of space-time. The mathematician who wishes to operate with point-instants can construct them by means of mathematical logic out of assemblages of overlapping events, but that is only for his technical purposes, which, for the moment, we may ignore. The events occurring in any given small region of space-time are not unconnected with events occurring elsewhere. On the contrary, if a photographic plate can photograph a certain star, that is because an event is happening at the photographic plate which is connected by what we may call heredity with the star in question. The photographic plate, in turn, if it is photographed, is the origin of a fresh progeny. In mathematical physics, which is only interested in exceedingly abstract aspects of the matters with which it deals, these various processes appear as paths by which energy travels. It is because mathematical physics is so abstract that its world seems so different from that of our daily life. But the difference is more apparent than real. Suppose you study population statistics, the people who make up the items are deprived of almost all the characteristics of real people before they are recorded in the census. But in this case, because the process of abstraction has not proceeded very far, we do not find it very difficult to undo it in imagination. But in the case of mathematical physics, the journey back from the abstract to the concrete is long and arduous, and, out of sheer weariness, we are tempted to rest by the way and endow some semi-abstraction with a concrete reality which it cannot justly claim. . . .

We have seen that, for purely physical reasons, events in many different places and times can often be collected into families proceeding from an original progenitor as the light from a star proceeds from it in all directions. The successive generations in a single branch of such a family have varying degrees of resemblance to each other according to circumstances. The events which constitute the journey of the light from a star to our atmosphere change slowly and little. That is why it is possible to regard them as the voyage of single entities called photons, which may be thought of as persisting. But when the light reaches our atmosphere, a series of continually odder and odder things begins to happen to it. It may be stopped or transformed by mist or cloud. It may hit a sheet of water and be reflected or refracted. It may hit a photographic plate and become a black dot of interest to an astronomer. Finally, it may happen to hit a human eye. When this occurs, the results are very complicated. There are a set of events between the eye and the brain which are studied by the physiologist and which have as little resemblance to the photons in the outer world as radio waves have to the orator's speech. At last the disturbance in the nerves, which has been traced by the physiologist, reaches the appropriate region in the brain; and then, at last, the man whose brain it is sees the star. People are puzzled because the seeing of the star seems so different from the processes that the physiologist discovered in the optic nerve, and yet it is clear that without these processes the man would not see the star. And so there is supposed to be a gulf between mind and matter, and a mystery which it is held in some degree impious to try to dissipate. I believe, for my part, that there is no greater mystery than there is in the transformation by the radio of electro-magnetic waves into sounds. I think the mystery is produced by a wrong conception of the physical world and by a Manichaean fear of degrading the mental world to the level of the supposedly inferior world of matter.

The world of which we have been speaking hitherto is entirely an inferred world. We do not perceive the sort of entitites that physics talks of, and, if it is of such entities that the physical world is composed, then we do not see the eye or the optic nerve, for the eye and the optic nerve, equally, if the physicist is to be believed, consist of the odd hypothetical entities with which the theoretical physicist tries to make us familiar. These entities, however, since they owe their credibility to inference, are only defined to the degree that is necessary to make them fulfil their inferential purpose. It is not necessary to suppose that electrons, protons, neutrons, mesons, photons, and the rest have that sort of simple reality that belongs to immediate objects of experience. They have, at best, the sort of reality that belongs to "London." "London" is a convenient word, but every *fact* which is stated by using this word could be stated, though more cumbrously, without using it. There is, however, a difference, and an important one, between London and the electrons: we can see the various parts of which London is composed, and, indeed, the parts are more immediately known to us than the whole. In the case of the electron, we do not perceive it and we do not perceive anything that we know to be a constituent of it. We know it only as a hypothetical entity fulfilling certain theoretical purposes. So far as theoretical physics is concerned, anything that fulfils these purposes can be taken to *be* the electron. It may be simple or complex; and, if complex, it may be built out of any components that allow the resultant structure to have the requisite properties. All this applies not only to the inanimate world but, equally, to the eyes and other sense organs, the nerves, and the brain.

But our world is not wholly a matter of inference. There are things that we know without asking the opinion of men of science. If you are too hot or too cold, you can be perfectly aware of this fact without asking the physicist what heat and cold consist of. When you see other people's faces you have an experience which is completely indubitable, but which does not consist of seeing the things which theoretical physicists speak of. You see other people's eyes and you believe that they see yours. Your own eyes as visual objects belong to the inferred part of the world, though the inference is rendered fairly indubitable by mirrors, photographs and the testimony of your friends. The inference to your own eyes as visual objects is essentially of the same sort as the physicist's inference to electrons, etc.; and, if you are going to deny validity to the physicist's inferences, you ought also to deny that you know you have visible eyes—which is absurd, as Euclid would say.

We may give the name "data" to all the things of which we are aware without inference. They include all our observed sensations—visual, auditory, tactile, etc. Common sense sees reason to attribute many of our sensations to causes outside our own bodies. It does not believe that the room in which it is sitting ceases to exist when it shuts its eyes or goes to sleep. It does not believe that its wife and children are mere figments of its imagination. In all this we may agree with common sense; but where it goes wrong is in supposing that inanimate objects resemble, in their intrinsic qualities, the perceptions which they cause. To believe this is as groundless as it would be to suppose that a gramophone record resembles the music that it causes. It is not, however, the *difference* between the physical world and the world of data that I chiefly wish to emphasize. On the contrary, it is the possibility of much closer resemblances than physics at first sight suggests that I consider it important to bring to light.

I think perhaps I can best make my own views clear by comparing them

with those of Leibniz. Leibniz thought that the universe consisted of monads, each of which was a little mind and each of which mirrored the universe. They did this mirroring with varying degrees of inexactness. The best
monads had the least confusion in their picture of the universe. Misled by
the Aristotelian subject-predicate logic, Leibniz held that monads do not
interact, and that the fact of their continuing to mirror the same universe is
to be explained by a preestablished harmony. This part of his doctrine is
totally unacceptable. It is only through the causal action of the outer world
upon us that we reflect the world in so far as we do reflect it. But there are
other aspects of his doctrine which are more in agreement with the theory
that I wish to advocate. One of the most important of these is as to space.
There are for Leibniz (though he was never quite clear on this point) two
kinds of space. There is the space in the private world of each monad,
which is the space that the monad can come to know by analysing and
arranging data without assuming anything beyond data. But there is also
another kind of space. The monads, Leibniz tells us, reflect the world each
from its own point of view, the differences of points of view being analogous to differences of perspective. The arrangement of the whole assemblage of points of view gives us another kind of space different from that in
the private world of each monad. In this public space, each monad occupies a point or, at any rate, a very small region. Although in its private world
there is a private space which from its private point of view is immense, the
whole of this immensity shrinks into a tiny pin-point when the monad is
placed among other monads. We may call the space in each monad's world
of data "private" space, and the space consisting of the diverse points of
view of diverse monads "physical" space. In so far as monads correctly mirror the world, the geometrical properties of private space will be analogous
to those of physical space.

Most of this can be applied with little change to exemplify the theory
that I wish to advocate. There is space in the world of my perceptions and
there is space in physics. The whole of the space in my perceptions, for me
as for Leibniz, occupies only a tiny region in physical space. There is, however, an important difference between my theory and that of Leibniz, which
has to do with a different conception of causality and with consequences
of the theory of relativity. I think that space-time order in the physical world
is bound up with causation, and this, in turn, with the irreversibility of physical processes. In classical physics, everything was reversible. If you were
to start every bit of matter moving backwards with the same velocity as
before, the whole history of the universe would unroll itself backwards.
Modern physics, starting from the Second Law of Thermodynamics, has
abandoned this view not only in thermodynamics but also elsewhere.
Radioactive atoms disintegrate and do not put themselves together again.
Speaking generally, processes in the physical world all have a certain direction which makes a distinction between cause and effect that was absent in

classical dynamics. I think that the space-time order of the physical world involves this directed causality. It is on this ground that I maintain an opinion which all other philosophers find shocking: namely, that people's thoughts are in their heads. The light from a star travels over intervening space and causes a disturbance in the optic nerve ending in an occurrence in the brain. What I maintain is that the occurrence in the brain *is* a visual sensation. I maintain, in fact, that the brain consists of thoughts—using "thought" in its widest sense, as it is used by Descartes. To this people will reply "Nonsense! I can see a brain through a microscope, and I can see that it does not consist of thoughts but of matter just as tables and chairs do." This is a sheer mistake. What you see when you look at a brain through a microscope is part of your private world. It is the effect in you of a long causal process starting from the brain that you say you are looking at. The brain that you say you are looking at is, no doubt, part of the physical world; but this is not the brain which is a datum in your experience. *That* brain is a remote effect of the physical brain. And, if the location of events in physical space-time is to be effected, as I maintain, by causal relations, then your percept, which comes after events in the eye and optic nerve leading into the brain, must be located in your brain. I may illustrate how I differ from most philosophers by quoting the title of an article by Mr. H. Hudson in *Mind* of April 1956. His article is entitled, "Why we cannot witness or observe what goes on 'in our heads'." What I maintain is that we *can* witness or observe what goes on in our heads, and that we cannot witness or observe anything else at all.

We can approach the same result by another route. When we were considering the photographic plate which photographs a portion of the starry heavens, we saw that this involves a great multiplicity of occurrences at the photographic plate: namely, at the very least, one for each object that it can photograph. I infer that, in every small region of space-time, there is an immense multiplicity of overlapping events each connected by a causal line to an origin at some earlier time—though, usually, at a very slightly earlier time. A sensitive instrument, such as a photographic plate, placed anywhere, may be said in a sense to "perceive" the various objects from which these causal lines emanate. We do not use the word "perceive" unless the instrument in question is a living brain, but that is because those regions which are inhabited by living brains have certain peculiar relations among the events occurring there. The most important of these is memory. Wherever these peculiar relations exist, we say that there is a percipient. We may define a "mind" as a collection of events connected with each other by memory-chains backwards and forwards. We know about one such collection of events—namely, that constituting ourself—more intimately and directly than we know about anything else in the world. In regard to what happens to ourself, we know not only abstract logical structure, but also qualities—by which I mean what characterizes sounds as opposed to colours, or red as opposed to green. This is the sort of thing that we cannot know where the physical world is concerned.

There are three key points in the above theory. The first is that the entities that occur in mathematical physics are not part of the stuff of the world, but are constructions composed of events and taken as units for the convenience of the mathematician. The second is that the whole of what we perceive without inference belongs to our private world. In this respect, I agree with Berkeley. The starry heaven that we know in visual sensation is inside us. The external starry heaven that we believe in is inferred. The third point is that the causal lines which enable us to be aware of a diversity of objects, though there are some such lines everywhere, are apt to peter out like rivers in the sand. That is why we do not at all times perceive everything.

I do not pretend that the above theory can be proved. What I contend is that, like the theories of physics, it cannot be disproved, and gives an answer to many problems which older theorists have found puzzling. I do not think that any prudent person will claim more than this for any theory.

Whitehead

Alfred North Whitehead was born in England in 1861 and died in Cambridge, Massachusetts in 1947. He was educated at Trinity College at Cambridge University, where he later taught mathematics. Later, he served as dean of science at University College, University of London. In 1924 he became professor of philosophy at Harvard University. His books covered a wide range of intellectual interests, including *The Concept of Nature* (1920), *Religion in the Making* (1926), *The Function of Reason* (1929). His first book, *Principia Mathematica* (1910–1913), was a collaborative effort with Bertrand Russell. At Harvard, Whitehead produced two additional major works, *Process and Reality* (1929) and *Science and the Modern World* (1925), from which the following excerpt is selected.

READING

NATURE BEYOND THE GRASP
OF SCIENCE
Whitehead

We quickly find that the Western peoples exhibit on a colossal scale a peculiarity which is popularly supposed to be more especially characteristic of the Chinese. Surprise is often expressed that a Chinaman can be of two religions, a Confucian for some occasions and a Buddhist for other occasions. Whether this is true of China I do not know; nor do I know whether, if true, these two attitudes are really inconsistent. But there can be no doubt that an analogous fact is true of the West, and that the two attitudes involved are inconsistent. A scientific realism, based on mechanism, is conjoined with an unwavering belief in the world of men and of the higher animals as being composed of self-determining organisms. This radical inconsistency at the basis of modern thought accounts for much that is half-hearted and wavering in our civilisation. It would be going too far to say that it distracts thought. It enfeebles it, by reason of the inconsistency lurking in the background. After all, the men of the Middle Ages were in pursuit of an excellency of which we have nearly forgotten the existence. They set before themselves the idea of the attainment of a harmony of the understanding. We are content with superficial orderings from diverse arbitrary starting points. For instance, the enterprises produced by the individualistic energy of the European peoples presuppose physical actions directed to final causes. But the science which is employed in their development is based on a philosophy which asserts that physical causation is supreme, and which disjoins the physical cause from the final end. It is not popular to dwell on the absolute contradiction here involved. It is the fact, however you gloze it over with phrases. Of course, we find in the eighteenth century Paley's famous argument, that mechanism presupposes a God who is the author of nature. But even before Paley put the argument into its final form, Hume had written the retort, that the God whom you will find will be the sort of God who makes that mechanism. In other words, that mechanism can, at most, presuppose a mechanic, and not merely a mechanic but *its*

---

mechanic. The only way of mitigating mechanism is by the discovery that it is not mechanism.

When we leave apologetic theology, and come to ordinary literature, we find, as we might expect, that the scientific outlook is in general simply ignored. So far as the mass of literature is concerned, science might never have been heard of. Until recently nearly all writers have been soaked in classical and renaissance literature. For the most part, neither philosophy nor science interested them, and their minds were trained to ignore them.

There are exceptions to this sweeping statement; and, even if we confine ourselves to English literature, they concern some of the greatest names; also the indirect influence of science has been considerable.

A side light on this distracting inconsistency in modern thought is obtained by examining some of those great serious poems in English literature, whose general scale gives them a didactic character. The relevant poems are Milton's *Paradise Lost,* Pope's *Essay on Man,* Wordsworth's *Excursion,* Tennyson's *In Memoriam.* Milton, though he is writing after the Restoration, voices the theological aspect of the earlier portion of his century, untouched by the influence of the scientific materialism. Pope's poem represents the effect on popular thought of the intervening sixty years which includes the first period of assured triumph for the scientific movement. Wordsworth in his whole being expresses a conscious reaction against the mentality of the eighteenth century. This mentality means nothing else than the acceptance of the scientific ideas at their full face value. Wordsworth was not bothered by any intellectual antagonism. What moved him was a moral repulsion. He felt that something had been left out, and that what had been left out comprised everything that was most important. Tennyson is the mouthpiece of the attempts of the waning romantic movement in the second quarter of the nineteenth century to come to terms with science. By this time the two elements in modern thought had disclosed their fundamental divergence by their jarring interpretations of the course of nature and the life of man. Tennyson stands in this poem as the perfect example of the distraction which I have already mentioned. There are opposing visions of the world, and both of them command his assent by appeals to ultimate intuitions from which there seems no escape. Tennyson goes to the heart of the difficulty. It is the problem of mechanism which appalls him,

> *"The stars," she whispers, "blindly run on."*

This line states starkly the whole philosophic problem implicit in the poem. Each molecule blindly runs. The human body is a collection of molecules. Therefore, the human body blindly runs, and therefore there can be no individual responsibility for the actions of the body. If you once accept that the molecule is definitely determined to be what it is, independently of any determination by reason of the total organism of the body, and if you further admit that the blind run is settled by the general mechanical laws, there can be no escape from this conclusion. But mental experiences are derivative from the actions of the body, including of course its internal behaviour. Accordingly, the sole function of the mind is to have at least some of its experiences settled for it, and to add such others as may be open to it independently of the body's motions, internal and external.

There are then two possible theories as to the mind. You can either deny that it can supply for itself any experiences other than those provided for it by the body, or you can admit them.

If you refuse to admit the additional experiences, then all individual responsibility is swept away. If you do admit them, then a human being may be responsible for the state of his mind though he has no responsibility for the actions of his body. The enfeeblement of thought in the modern world is illustrated by the way in which this plain issue is avoided in Tennyson's poem. There is something kept in the background, a skeleton in the cupboard. He touches on almost every religious and scientific problem, but carefully avoids more than a passing allusion to this one.

This very problem was in full debate at the date of the poem. John Stuart Mill was maintaining his doctrine of determinism. In this doctrine volitions are determined by motives, and motives are expressible in terms of antecedent conditions including states of mind as well as states of the body.

It is obvious that this doctrine affords no escape from the dilemma presented by a thoroughgoing mechanism. For if the volition affects the state of the body, then the molecules in the body do not blindly run. If the volition does not affect the state of the body, the mind is still left in its uncomfortable position.

Mill's doctrine is generally accepted, especially among scientists, as though in some way it allowed you to accept the extreme doctrine of materialistic mechanism, and yet mitigated its unbelievable consequences. It does nothing of the sort. Either the bodily molecules blindly run, or they do not. If they do blindly run, the mental states are irrelevant in discussing the bodily actions. . . .

The doctrine which I am maintaining is that the whole concept of materialism only applies to very abstract entities, the products of logical discernment. The concrete enduring entities are organisms, so that the plan of the *whole* influences the very characters of the various subordinate organisms which enter into it. In the case of an animal, the mental states enter into the plan of the total organism and thus modify the plans of the successive subordinate organisms until the ultimate smallest organisms, such as electrons, are reached. Thus an electron within a living body is different from an electron outside it, by reason of the plan of the body. The electron blindly runs either within or without the body; but it runs within the body in accordance with its character within the body; that is to say, in accordance with the general plan of the body, and this plan includes the mental state. But the principle of modification is perfectly general throughout nature, and represents no property peculiar to living bodies. . . .

The discrepancy between the materialistic mechanism of science and the moral intuitions, which are presupposed in the concrete affairs of life, only gradually assumed its true importance as the centuries advanced. . . .

The literary romantic movement at the beginning of the nineteenth century, just as much as Berkeley's philosophical idealistic movement a hundred years earlier, refused to be confined within the materialistic concepts of the orthodox scientific theory. . . .

It is, however, impossible to proceed until we have settled whether this refashioning of ideas is to be carried out on an objectivist basis or on a subjectivist basis. By a subjectivist basis I mean the belief that the nature of our immediate experience is the outcome of the perceptive peculiarities of the subject enjoying the experience. In other words, I mean that for this theory what is perceived is not a partial vision of a complex of things generally independent of that act of cognition; but that it merely is the expression of the individual peculiarities of the cognitive act. Accordingly what is common to the multiplicity of cognitive acts is the ratiocination connected with them. Thus, though there is a common world of thought associated with our sense-perceptions, there is no common world to think about. What we do think about is a common conceptual world applying indifferently to our individual experiences which are strictly personal to ourselves. Such a conceptual world will ultimately find its complete expression in the equations of applied mathematics. This is the extreme subjectivist position. There is of course the half-way house of those who believe that our perceptual experience does tell us of a common objective world; but that the things perceived are merely the outcome for us of this world, and are not *in themselves* elements in the common world itself.

Also there is the objectivist position. This creed is that the actual elements perceived by our senses are *in themselves* the elements of a common world; and that this world is a complex of things, including indeed our acts of cognition, but transcending them. According to this point of view the things experienced are to be distinguished from our knowledge of them. So far as there is dependence, the *things* pave the way for the *cognition,* rather than *vice versa.* But the point is that the actual things experienced enter into a common world which transcends knowledge, though it includes knowledge. The intermediate subjectivists would hold that the things experienced only indirectly enter into the common world by reason of their dependence on the subject who is cognising. The objectivist holds that the things experienced and the cognisant subject enter into the common world on equal terms. . . .

Some people express themselves as though bodies, brains, and nerves were the only real things in an entirely imaginary world. In other words, they treat bodies on objective principles, and the rest of the world on subjectivist principles. This will not do; especially, when we remember that it is the experimenter's perception of another person's body which is in question as evidence.

But we have to admit that the body is the organism whose states regulate our cognisance of the world. The unity of the perceptual field therefore must be a unity of bodily experience. In being aware of the bodily experience, we must thereby be aware of aspects of the whole spatio-temporal world as mirrored within the bodily life. . . . My theory involves the entire abandonment of the notion that simple location is the primary way in which things are involved in space-time. In a certain sense, everything is everywhere at all times. For every location involves an aspect of itself in every other location. Thus every spatio-temporal standpoint mirrors the world.

If you try to imagine this doctrine in terms of our conventional views of space and time, which presuppose simple location, it is a great paradox. But if you think of it in terms of our naïve experience, it is a mere transcript of the obvious facts. You are in a certain place perceiving things. Your perception takes place where you are, and is entirely dependent on how your body is functioning. But this functioning of the body in one place, exhibits for your cognisance an aspect of the distance environment, fading away into the general knowledge that there are things beyond. If this cognisance conveys knowledge of a transcendent world, it must be because the event which is the bodily life unifies in itself aspects of the universe.

This is a doctrine extremely consonant with the vivid expression of personal experience which we find in the nature-poetry of imaginative writers such as Wordsworth or Shelley. The brooding, immediate presences of things are an obsession to Wordsworth. What the theory does do is to edge cognitive mentality away from being the necessary sub-stratum of the unity of experience. That unity is now placed in the unity of an event. Accompanying this unity, there may or there may not be cognition.

At this point we come back to the great question which was posed before us by our examination of the evidence afforded by the poetic insight of Wordsworth and Shelley. This single question has expanded into a group of questions. What are enduring things, as distinguished from the eternal objects, such as colour and shape? How are they possible? What is their status and meaning in the universe? It comes to this: What is the status of the enduring stability of the order of nature? There is the summary answer, which refers nature to some greater reality standing behind it. This reality occurs in the history of thought under many names, The Absolute, Brahma, The Order of Heaven, God. The delineation of final metaphysical truth is no part of this lecture. My point is that any summary conclusion jumping from our conviction of the existence of such an order of nature to the easy assumption that there is an ultimate reality which, in some unexplained way, is to be appealed to for the removal of perplexity, constitutes the great refusal of rationality to assert its rights. We have to search whether nature does not in its very being show itself as self-explanatory. By this I mean, that the sheer statement, of what things are, may contain elements explanatory of why things are. Such elements may be expected to refer to depths beyond anything which we can grasp with a clear apprehension. In a sense, all explanation must end in an ultimate arbitrariness. My demand is, that the ultimate arbitrariness of matter of fact from which our formulation starts should disclose the same general principles of reality, which we dimly discern as stretching away into regions beyond our explicit powers of discernment. Nature exhibits itself as exemplifying a philosophy of the evolution of organisms subject to determinate conditions. Examples of such conditions are the dimensions of space, the laws of nature, the determinate enduring entities, such as atoms and electrons, which exemplify these laws. But the very nature of these entities, the very nature of their spatiality and temporality, should exhibit the arbitrariness of these conditions as the outcome of a wider evolution beyond nature itself, and within which nature is but a limited mode.

One all-pervasive fact, inherent in the very character of what is real, is the transition of things, the passage one to another. This passage is not a mere linear procession of discrete entities. However we fix a determinate entity, there is always a narrower determination of something which is presupposed in our first choice. Also there is always a wider determination into which our first choice fades by transition beyond itself. The general aspect of nature is that of evolutionary expansiveness. These units, which I call events, are the emergence into actuality of something. How are we to characterise the something which thus emerges? The name "*event*," given to such a unity, draws attention to the inherent transitoriness, combined with the actual unity. But this abstract word cannot be sufficient to characterise what the fact of the reality of an event is in itself. A moment's thought shows us that no one idea can in itself be sufficient. For every idea which finds its significance in each event must represent something which contributes to what realisation is in itself. Thus no one word can be adequate. But conversely, nothing must be left out. Remembering the poetic rendering of our concrete experience, we see at once that the element of value, of being valuable, of having value, of being an end in itself, of being something which is for its own sake, must not be omitted in any account of an event as the most concrete actual something. "Value" is the word I use for the intrinsic reality of an event. Value is an element which permeates through and through the poetic view of nature. We have only to transfer to the very texture of realisation in itself that value which we recognise so readily in terms of human life.

Questions for Discussion: Metaphysics

1. The universe described by the atomists is one of pure chance. Would it matter to you if this metaphysical claim made by the atomists were correct?

2. All the philosophers we have studied so far in this section have offered some account of substance. Why does Berkeley reject this concept?

3. What does it mean to say that a social system or movement must be evaluated not from the standpoint of "eternal justice," but from the standpoint of the conditions that gave rise to it? Is this a plausible claim?

4. Is freedom of the will or ethics possible in the world described by Spinoza and Leibniz?

5. Bergson refers to a rose to distinguish two ways of knowing it, namely, by intuition and by analysis. Can we know another person in these two different ways? Which way of knowing tells us the "true" nature of the rose or the person?

6. According to Whitehead, what do some poets know about nature, human nature, that the scientist apparently does not know or recognize?

Suggested Additional Readings: Metaphysics

Bergson, Henri: *An Introduction to Metaphysics*, Bobbs-Merrill, Indianapolis, 1955. A lively, concise work.

————: *Time and Free Will*, Humanities Press, New York, 1971. An animated discussion of these metaphysical issues.

Borges, Jorge Luis: *Labyrinths: Selected Stories and Other Writings*, New Directions Press, New York, 1969. Intriguing fiction inspired by reflection on metaphysics.

The Empiricists, Doubleday Anchor Books, Garden City, N.Y., 1960. Includes Berkeley's major works along with those of his predecessor, John Locke, against whom many of Berkeley's arguments are directed.

Lathan, Ronald E.: *On the Nature of the Universe*, Penguin, Baltimore, 1951. An excellent prose translation of Lucretius's *De Rerum Natura.*

Lovejoy, Arthur O.: *The Great Chain of Being*, Harvard, Cambridge, Mass., 1936. An exciting history of metaphysics.

Pirsig, Robert: *Zen and the Art of Motorcycle Maintenance*, Bantam, New York, 1976. An engaging novel and yet a serious inquiry into issues raised by seventeenth and eighteenth century metaphysicians.

The Rationalists, Doubleday Anchor Books, Garden City, N.Y., 1960. Contains the important works of Spinoza and Leibniz.

Stevens, Wallace: "A Collect of Philosophy," in *Opus Posthumous*, Knopf, New York, 1957. A major poet examines metaphysical thinking.

Taylor, Richard: *Metaphysics*, 2d ed., Prentice-Hall, Englewood Cliffs, N.J., 1974. A useful general introduction to metaphysics.

KEY CONCEPTS

GLOSSARY

KEY CONCEPTS

Appearance: How something presents itself to our senses as compared with its true reality. The oar appears bent in the water, but it really is not bent.

Aesthetics: The branch of philosophy concerned with the analysis of concepts such as beauty or beautiful as standards for judging works of art.

Autonomy: Independence from external authority; in Kant, freedom of the will to make its own law or rule of conduct in contrast to heteronomy (being subject to someone else's rules).

Categorical Imperative: According to Kant, the absolute moral law understood as a duty by any rational creature, to be compared with hypothetical imperatives, which permit exceptions.

Cause: A cause is something that has the power to produce a change, motion, or action in another thing; this change (effect) can be explained in terms of the behavior of the cause.

Change: The alteration of anything, the rearrangement of something's parts, the coming into being of something that did not exist before, and the decline and dissolution of something.

Cognition: In the broadest sense, knowledge, or, the act of knowing.

Cognitive Meaning: A statement has cognitive meaning if (a) it asserts something that is true simply because the words used necessarily and always require the statement to be true (as in mathematics) or (b) it asserts something that can be judged as true or false by verifying it in experience.

Deduction: A process of reasoning by which the mind relates the truth of a proposition to another proposition by inferring that the truth of the second proposition is involved in and therefore derived from the first proposition (*see* **Induction**).

Determinism: The theory that every fact or event in the universe is determined or caused by previous facts or events: human behavior and the events of history follow strict laws of causation or necessary connection. Accordingly, in this view, human beings do not possess freedom of the will or the power to originate independent or genuine choices.

Dialectic: A process of reasoning based on the analysis of opposing propositions. Socrates used the dialectic method of teaching by distinguishing between opinion and knowledge. Hegel and Marx developed dialectical conceptions of history in which for Hegel opposing ideas were the key while for Marx history is explained as the conflict of material forces.

Dogmatism: The act of making a positive assertion without demonstration by either rational argument or experience.

Dualism: A theory which holds that there are two independent and irreducible substances, such as mind and body, the intelligible world of ideas and the visible world of things, and the forces of good and evil.

Empiricism: The theory which says that experience is the source of all knowledge, thereby denying that human beings possess inborn knowledge or that they can derive knowledge through the exercise of reason alone.

Epistemology: The branch of philosophy which studies the nature, origin, scope, and validity of knowledge.

Essence: The chief characteristic, quality, or necessary function which makes a thing what it uniquely is.

Ethics: (1) a set of rules for human behavior; (2) a study of judgments of value, of good and evil, right and wrong, desirable and undesirable; and (3) theories of obligation or duty or why we "ought" to behave in certain ways. (Greek, *ethicos*; Latin, *moralis*)

Existentialism: A mode of philosophy which focuses on the existing individual person; instead of searching for truth in distant universal concepts, existentialism is concerned with the authentic concerns of concrete existing individuals as they face choices and decisions in daily life.

Idealism: The view that mind is the ultimate reality in the world.

Idealism is, accordingly, opposed to materialism which views material things as the basic reality from which mind emerges and to which mind is reducible.

Induction: Proceeding from the observation of some particular facts to a generalization (or conclusion) concerning all such facts (*see* **Deduction**).

Instrumentalism: John Dewey's theory of how thought functions by emphasizing the practical function of thought in determining future consequences; thought is therefore viewed as instrumental in producing consequences.

Intuition: Direct and immediate knowledge, or the immediate apprehension by the self of itself, of the truth of certain propositions, of the external world, and of values, without the prior need for the ability to define a term, to justify a conclusion, or to build upon inferences.

Logical Positivism: The view that statements are meaningful only if they can be verified either directly or indirectly in experience. Logical positivism seeks to analyze all claims to knowledge, all assertions of science and everyday life; only those assertions have meaning which are verified by empirical facts or are connected logically with such facts and are therefore verifiable.

Man: (*As used throughout this book*) A human being, or the human creature regarded abstractly and without regard to gender; hence, the human race or humanity.

Materialism: The view that matter constitutes the basis of all that exists in the universe. Hence combinations of matter and material forces account for every aspect of reality, including the nature of thought, the process of historical and economic events, and the standard of values based on sensuous bodily pleasures and the abundance of things; the notion of the primacy of spirit or mind and rational purpose in nature is rejected.

Metaphysics: The branch of philosophy concerned with the question of the ultimate nature of reality. Unlike the sciences which focus on various aspects of nature, metaphysics goes beyond particular things to enquire about more general questions such as what lies beyond nature, how things come into being, what it means for something to be, and whether there is a realm of being which is not subject to change and which is therefore the basis of certainty in knowledge.

Perception: The discovery, by the senses, of knowledge about the world; the apprehension of everyday objects, for example, trees, through sense impressions.

Pluralism: The view that there are more than one (Monism) or two (Dualism) ultimate and separate substances making up the world.

Positivism: John Stuart Mill defined positivism as follows: "We [positivists] have no knowledge of anything but Phenomena, and our knowledge of phenomena is relative, not absolute. We know not the essence, not the real mode of production, of any fact, but only its relations to other facts in the way of succession or of similitude. These relations are constant; that is, always the same in the same circumstances."

Pragmatism: According to William James, pragmatism is a method of solving various types of problems, such as "Does God exist?" or "Is man's will free?" by looking at the practical consequences of accepting this or that answer. James says, "The pragmatic method tries to interpret each notion (or theory) by tracing its respective practical consequences. . . . If no practical difference whatever can be traced . . . they mean practically the same thing" and that ends the argument. As a theory of *truth*, James says that an idea is true if it works in daily life.

Rationalism: The philosophical view that emphasizes the ability of human reason to grasp fundamental truths about the world without the aid of sense impressions.

Relativism: The view that there is no absolute knowledge, that truth is different for each individual, social group, or historic period and is therefore relative to the circumstances of the knowing subject.

Scholasticism: Refers to the method of learning in the medieval cathedral schools where a combination of philosophy and theology was taught by emphasizing logical or deductive form, and basing thinking and its conclusions upon the sayings or writings of key figures of the past whose tradition was viewed as authoritative.

Skepticism: Some skeptics doubt that any knowledge achieved so far is absolute and therefore continue to seek after more refined and reliable versions of truth; other skeptics doubt whether it is ever possible to attain perfect certainty of knowledge.

Solipsism: The theory that the self alone (*solus*, "alone"; *ipse*, "self") is the source of all knowledge of existence, a view that sometimes leads to the conclusion that the self is the only reality.

Substance: A separate and distinct thing; that which underlies phenomena; the essence of a thing.

Teleology: *Telos* is the Greek word for "purpose," hence teleology is the study of purpose in human nature and in the events of history; in ethical theory (teleological ethics) an action is considered good if it is conducive to fulfilling the purposes of human nature.

Utilitarianism: In this view, an action is considered good or right if its consequence is the greatest happiness (pleasure) of the greatest number. In that case, the action is *useful* (utilitarian) in producing as much or more good than any alternative behavior.

Verification: Demonstrating or proving something to be true either by means of evidence or by formal rules of reasoning.

INDEX

Thales 624–546 B.C.
Pythagoras active ca. 525–500 B.C.
Anaxagoras 500–428 B.C.
Protagoras ca. 490–421 B.C.
Leucippus ca. 490–430 B.C.
Empedocles ca. 490–430 B.C.
Zeno b. ca. 489 B.C.
Socrates ca. 470–399 B.C.
Democritus ca. 460–360 B.C.
Plato ca. 428–ca. 348 B.C.
Aristotle 384–322 B.C.
Pyrrho ca. 361–ca. 270 B.C.
Epicurus 341–271 B.C.
Lucretius ca. 96–55 B.C.
Epictetus ca. 60–117
Sextus Empiricus ca. 200
Saint Augustine 354–430
Saint Anselm 1033–1109
Saint Bonaventura 1221–1274
Saint Thomas Aquinas 1225–1274
Michel de Montaigne 1533–1592
Galileo 1564–1642
Thomas Hobbes 1588–1679
René Descartes 1596–1650
Blaise Pascal 1623–1662
Baruch Spinoza 1632–1677
John Locke 1632–1704
Sir Isaac Newton 1642–1727
Gottfried Leibniz 1646–1716
George Berkeley 1685–1753